CHRISTIANITY & LEISURE

Issues for the Twenty-first Century

CHRISTIANITY & LEISURE

Issues for the Twenty-first Century

VOLUME II

Edited by: Paul Heintzman and Glen Van Andel

Dordt College Press

Cover by Rob Haan
Layout by Carla Goslinga

Copyright © 2017 by Dordt College Press

Unless noted otherwise, all quotations from Scripture are taken from The Holy Bible, New International Version® NIV®. Copyright © 1973, 1978, 1984, 2011 by Biblica, Inc.™ Used by permission. All rights reserved worldwide.

Scripture taken from THE MESSAGE. Copyright © by Eugene Peterson, 1993, 1994, 1995. Used by permission of NavPress Publishing Group.

Fragmentary portions of this book may be freely used by those who are interested in sharing the authors' insights and observations, so long as the material is not pirated for monetary gain and so long as proper credit is visibly given to the publisher and the author. Others, and those who wish to use larger sections of text, must seek written permission from the publisher.

Printed in the United States of America.

Dordt College Press   www.dordt.edu/DCPcatalog
498 Fourth Avenue NE
Sioux Center, Iowa 51250
ISBN: 978-1-940567-19-8

The Library of Congress Cataloging-in-Publication Data is on file with the Library of Congress, Washington, D.C.
Library of Congress Control Number: 2017962171

TABLE OF CONTENTS

Preface i
Contributors iii

Section 1: LEISURE THEORY AND HISTORY

Section Introduction: Paul Heintzman 1

1. The Wonder of Leisure 5
   Margaret Hothem

2. From Sabbath to Weekend: Religious Advocacy for a Weekly Day of Recreation 15
   Karl E. Johnson

3. Holistic Leisure: A Paradigm for Leisure in Christian Perspective 35
   Paul Heintzman

4. Leisure and Spirituality: An Engaged and Responsible Pursuit of Freedom in Work, Play, and Worship 56
   Douglas Joblin

5. Quality of Life in a Christian Community: A Conceptual Investigation of Flow Experiences and HPERD Responsibilities .. 82
   Marcia Jean Carter

Section 2: LEISURE RESEARCH

Section Introduction: Paul Heintzman 91

6. A Social Psychological Investigation of the Relationship between Christianity and Contemporary Meanings of Leisure: An Australian Perspective 96
   John Schulz and Christopher Auld

7. The Meaning of Leisure for Older Persons 121
   Lois Hoitenga Roelofs

8. Multicultural Perspectives on Leisure 137
   Margaret Hothem

9. Source of Beliefs as a Constraint to Participation in Select Leisure Activities: A Congregational Analysis 150
   Steven N. Waller

10. Spiritual Development of Participants in a College Wilderness Program: A Case Study 180
    Valerie J. Gin

11. The Role of Leisure in the Spirituality of New Paradigm Christians 195
    Jennifer Livengood

12. The Monastery as a Restorative Environment 222
    Pierre Ouellette, Rachel Kaplan, and Stephen Kaplan

13. Leisure Studies and Spirituality: A Christian Critique 249
    Paul Heintzman

Section 3: ETHICAL AND APPLIED ISSUES

Section Introduction: Paul Heintzman 265

14. Leisure, Ethics, and the Golden Rule 267
    Paul Heintzman

15. Redeeming Play: A Christian Perspective 285
    Glen Van Andel

16. Can Play Build Character? 305
    Arthur Holmes

17. Toward a Theology of Risk 311
    Bud Williams

18. Seeking the Common Good: Challenges and Opportunities for Recreation Programmers 331
    Don DeGraaf

Section 4: THERAPEUTIC RECREATION

Section Introduction: Glen Van Andel 353

19. A Christian Perspective on Therapeutic Recreation 355
    Cathy O'Keefe

20. Christian Spirituality and Therapeutic Recreation 363
    Glen Van Andel and Paul Heintzman

21. Ethical Principles in Services to Persons with Disabilities 382
    Joseph D. Teaff

22. Reconceptualizing Health for Christians with
    Chronic Illness and Disabilities 394
    Youngkhill Lee and Bryan P. McCormick

23. Leisure-Spiritual Coping:
    A Model for Therapeutic Recreation and Leisure Services 407
    Paul Heintzman

Section 5: WELLNESS, SPIRITUALITY, AND HEALTH

Section Introduction: Glen Van Andel 437

24. Holistic Leisure and Spiritual Health: A Model 440
    Paul Heintzman

25. The Flow Experience: An Integration of Spiritual and Leisure
    Well-Being 463
    Marcia Jean Carter

26. Canoeing and Spirituality Journeying by Canoe: The Relationship
    between the Canoe and Spirituality 475
    Thomas Peace

27. Love-Centered Wellness 485
    Robert D. Weathers

28. Purpose, Commitment, and Then What: A Consideration of Stress
    and Burnout for Christian Coaches and Teachers 493
    Ted Comden

29. Spirituality and Wellness 506
    John Byl

Preface

In 1989, a number of academics and practitioners met at Calvin College in Grand Rapids, Michigan, to discuss theoretical and practical concepts and ideas related to Christianity and leisure. With the success of the original event, conferences were organized in successive years. This conference eventually led to the formation of the Christian Society for Kinesiology and Leisure Studies (CSKLS) in 2004 and the annual CSKLS conference, which has now been hosted by many colleges and universities across North America (see Appendix).

In 1994, a book titled *Christianity and Leisure: Issues in a Pluralistic Society* (Heintzman, Van Andel, & Visker, 1994/2006) was published that contained some of the papers from the first four conferences. It was our hope that the book would begin to fill the void in the body of knowledge regarding Christianity and leisure. The response to this book was positive. It became a valuable resource for Christian professionals in this area and was adopted as a primary or secondary textbook in courses at a variety of institutions. Subsequently it was revised and republished in 2006.

As the conference expanded more into the area of sports and wellness, a second book titled *Physical education, sports, and wellness: Looking to God as we look at ourselves* (Byl & Visker, 1999) was published that included papers from conferences held between 1994 and 1998. It was the hope that this second book would expand the body of knowledge available to Christian professionals working in sport, physical education, wellness, and related areas.

The current book includes papers related to Christianity and leisure that were presented at the conferences held between 1994 and 2010. As these papers were presented in the decades before and after the year 2000, we have titled this book: *Christianity and Leisure: Issues for the 21st Century*. Compared to the previous two books, many of the papers in this book have already been published in peer reviewed academic journals (see the copyright permissions for a list of these papers), which demonstrates the value of these papers to the larger recreation leisure studies field.

Since 2010, CSKLS has been publishing the peer-reviewed *Journal of the Christian Society for Kinesiology and Leisure Studies*. It is expected that in the future papers presented at the annual CSKLS conference will be published in this or other peer-reviewed journals rather than in a book format.

We are grateful to the authors who contributed to this book. Their biographies may be found at the beginning of the book. Our hope is that the thoughts, ideas, and concepts presented in this book will be used, debated, and discussed by professors, students, and practitioners as they continue to wrestle with the challenge of thinking and acting Christianly in relation to recreation and leisure.

Paul Heintzman
Glen Van Andel

References

Byl, J., & Visker, T. (1999). *Physical education, sports, and wellness: Looking to God as we look at ourselves.* Sioux Center: Dordt College Press.

Heintzman, P., Van Andel, G., & Visker, T. (Eds.). (1994/rev. ed. 2006). *Christianity and leisure: Issues in a pluralistic society.* Sioux Center: Dordt College Press.

Contributors

CHRISTOPHER AULD is the Deputy Vice Chancellor, International College of Management, Sydney, Australia. Previously he worked at Griffith University including terms as Dean (International), Griffith Business School; Head, Department of Tourism, Sport and Hotel Management; and Head, School of Leisure Studies. He has also been Associate Professor, Institute of Human Performance, the University of Hong Kong and Visiting Professor, University of Technology Sydney. Prior to his academic career, Chris worked in policy and program development roles with the Federal Department of Sport, Recreation and Tourism in Australia. In 2010 he was elected as a Senior Fellow and Founding Member of the World Leisure Academy.

JOHN BYL received his Ph.D. from State University of New York at Buffalo and is professor emeritus of Physical Education at Redeemer University College. Dr. Byl is a noted author and co-author of numerous articles and over 30 books including the popular college text, *Christian Paths to Health and Wellness*. His research interests lie in the nature of tournament organization; wellness; and the history of sports, particularly Canadian women's experience before 1950. John has received several prestigious awards for his service to numerous nonprofit organizations that promote physical education, sport, play and recreation.

MARCIA JEAN CARTER received her Re.D. from Indiana University and served as Assistant Dean in the College of Education and Human Services and Professor in the Department of Recreation, Park and Tourism Administration, Western Illinois University. Dr. Carter helped to develop the National Council for Therapeutic Recreation Certification and was its first Chair. She has co-authored several textbooks including *Therapeutic Recreation a Practical Approach; Effective Management in Therapeutic Recreation Service; and Recreation Therapy with Individuals Living in the Community: An Inclusive Approach*. Marcia has also served as an editor or reviewer for several professional journals and received numerous professional awards for her service.

TED COMDEN received his Ph.D. from Michigan State University and is Professor and Chair Emeritus of the Department of Health and Exercise Science at Spring Arbor University. Over his thirty-nine-year career in higher education that included time at Biola University, Ted also coached track and field, which prompted his concern about over-commitment and burnout for Christians who were highly committed to their roles as teacher-coaches. Other areas of study and research included curriculum development, exercise physiology, and personal wellness from a Christian perspective.

DON DEGRAAF received his Ph.D. from the University of Oregon and is professor of Kinesiology and Director of Off-Campus Programs at Calvin College. He has served as a former U.S. Peace Corps Volunteer in the Philippines and has also worked in Korea, Hong Kong, and the Netherlands, which has contributed to his passion for international education and global engagement. His teaching has focused on experiential education, nonprofit management, youth development and leisure and life satisfaction. He has written numerous articles and co-authored ten textbooks including the recent *There and Back: Living and Learning Abroad*. This book encourages students who are preparing for off-campus study programs to think deeply about the challenges they will encounter; to document their growth; and to explore, affirm and expand their faith.

VALERIE J. GIN received her Ed.D. from Boston University and is Professor and Co-Chair of the Department of Kinesiology at Gordon College. Val is a two-time recipient of the prestigious Gordon College Distinguished Faculty Award. She has published numerous articles and book chapters and co-authored two books: *Focus on Sport in Ministry* (2004) and *When Girls Became Lions* (2015). Val is the founding co-chair of the Sport and Christianity Group, which wrote the "Declaration on Sport and Christian Life," and the co-editor of the *Journal of Christian Society of Kinesiology and Leisure Studies*. Val enjoys spending her summers training international sport leaders in Africa and Asia.

PAUL HEINTZMAN, Associate Professor of Leisure Studies at the University of Ottawa, holds a Ph.D. in Recreation and Leisure Studies (Waterloo) and a Masters of Christian Studies degree (Regent, Vancouver). His teaching focuses on leisure concepts, parks as well as recreation and the environment. He authored *Leisure and Spirituality: Biblical, Historical and Contemporary Perspectives* (2015), edited a special issue of *Leisure/Loisir* on leisure and spirituality (2009), and co-edited *Christianity and Leisure: Issues in a Pluralistic Society* (1994/2006). Paul has received the Society of Park and Recreation Educators' Innovation of Teaching

Award (2003) and CSKLS Literary Award (2007, 2016).

ARTHUR HOLMES (1924–2011) received his PhD from Northwestern University and was Professor of Philosophy at Wheaton College, Illinois (1951–1994). He is remembered for his contribution to Christian higher education in the United States not only by teaching and building the philosophy department at Wheaton, but also by writing influential books and articles about the philosophy of Christian education as well as articles on Christianity and play, participating in the creation of the Society of Christian Philosophers, and encouraging his students to go on for graduate study and become academic leaders in their own rights.

MARGARET HOTHEM received her Ed.D. from Boston University in Leisure Studies. She is Professor Emeritus of Recreation and Leisure Studies at Gordon College where she initiated the Department of Recreation and Leisure Studies. Peggy's research interest focuses on the spiritual aspect of leisure in Christian faith communities. During her teaching tenure, Peggy received the Distinguished Service award from the Christian Society for Kinesiology, Leisure, and Sport Studies; as well as the Massachusetts Recreation and Park Association Humanitarian Award. Since her retirement in 2013, Peggy has given lectures on the Sabbath and leisure during mission trips to India and Bolivia. She currently serves on the national board of the Lord's Day Alliance.

DOUGLAS JOBLIN retired from Huntington federated in Laurentian University in Sudbury in 2006. He was President-Principal and Associate Professor in Religious Studies and Gerontology at that time. He arrived in Sudbury in 1974, after spending four years in Smooth Rock Falls as ordained minister of that community's United Church of Canada, and one year traveling around the world with his wife Sylvia. They have three children, all married and living in Sudbury, and four grandchildren. Doug taught many different courses: *Religion and the New Generation, God Play and Games, The Christian Faith and Interpersonal Communication, Religion and Childhood, The Human Prospect, Religion and Passages, Aging in a Multicultural Society,* and *Men and Aging.*

KARL E. JOHNSON, Executive Director of Chesterton House, a Center for Christian Studies at Cornell University in Ithaca, New York, received his bachelor's, master's, and doctoral degrees from Cornell University. Karl previously served as the Dan Tillemans Director of the Cornell Team and Leadership Center, a division of Cornell Outdoor Education. Karl was recognized as a 1999 Academy of Leisure Sciences Future Scholar and has received several writing awards, including the 2014 Literary Award of the Christian Society of Kinesiology and Leisure Studies. His interests include human relations with the natural landscape, from wilderness to urban environs.

RACHEL KAPLAN, Professor Emerita, University of Michigan, was previously the Samuel T. Dana Professor of Environment and Behavior in the School of Natural Resources and Environment and Professor of Psychology. With Avik Basu she is co-editor of *Fostering Reasonableness: Supportive Environments for Bringing out Our Best* (with Avik Basu) and co-author of *The Experience of Nature: A Psychological Perspective* (with Stephen Kaplan) and *With People in Mind: Design and Management of Everyday Nature* (with Stephen Kaplan and Robert L. Ryan). She has written widely on the role the environment plays in helping people become more reasonable, effective, and psychologically healthy.

STEPHEN KAPLAN is Professor Emeritus of Psychology and of Computer Science and Engineering at the University of Michigan, where he taught for 50 years. His influential work on Attention Restoration Theory and the Reasonable Person Model, conceptual clarity, commitment to application, and fundamental contributions to the development of environmental psychology are widely recognized. His many publications are frequently cited and his work has spawned far-reaching research programs. With Rachel Kaplan he has co-authored a number of books, including *Humanscape: Environments for People* and *Cognition* and *Environment: Functioning in an Uncertain World*.

YOUNGKHILL LEE received his Ph.D. from the University of Oregon and is currently a professor of Therapeutic Recreation in the Kinesiology Department at Calvin College. He has co-authored several books and published nearly 100 articles on topics of rehabilitation, recreation therapy, leisure, and aging. Youngkhill is also an Associate Editor for the Therapeutic Recreation Journal, and The Open Rehabilitation Journal. His research interests include posttraumatic growth, everyday life of people with physical disabilities, and Christian faith of people with disabilities.

JENNIFER LIVENGOOD, throughout her career in higher education and instructional design, has designed, developed, evaluated, and revised face-to-face, online, blended, and hybrid courses while working as a professor at Chicago State University, the University of Nevada, Las Vegas (UNLV) and as an instructional designer in the higher education and for-profit sectors. Jennifer is currently an instructional technologist for the Harvard University Kennedy School of Government and is providing support for the Bloomberg Harvard City Leadership Initiative. Jennifer earned her Ph.D. and M.S.W. from University of Illinois at Urbana-Champaign and her B.A. in Psychology from Southern Illinois University at Carbondale.

BRYAN P. MCCORMICK received his Ph.D. from Clemson University and is currently a Professor of Recreation, Park and Tourism Studies at Indiana University. Bryan has served as a member of the Public Health-World Health Organization for the American Therapeutic Recreation Association, Associate Editor of the *Journal of Leisure Research*, and is the co-author of *Conceptual Foundations for Therapeutic Recreation*. Dr. McCormick's research has focused on the social and community functioning of individuals with severe mental illness cross culturally.

CATHY O'KEEFE received her M.Ed. In Therapeutic Recreation from the University of South Alabama and devoted her career at the University of South Alabama to teaching and service, emphasizing a collaborative and transdisciplinary focus to the social issues of our day. Cathy and her husband, Dennis, have been affiliated with L'Arche, an international federation of communities serving people with intellectual disabilities for over forty years. She writes and speaks on topics related to leisure and spirituality, grief and loss, and life review. Though rooted in the Christian tradition, her research interests lie in a global spiritual approach to compassion, happiness, and quality of life.

PIERRE OUELLETTE is a retired professor from the School of Kinesiology and Leisure at Moncton University, located in the Canadian province of New Brunswick. His research interests were in the areas of leisure, gerontology and spirituality. More specifically, his recent work examined the relationship between Benedictine spirituality and contemplative leisure. During his career, he also studied the leisure behavior of older people participating in a wide array of recreation activities including membership in senior clubs. He holds advanced degrees both in leisure studies (New York University) and theology (Laval University).

THOMAS PEACE is an assistant professor of Canadian history at Huron University College. His research focuses on schooling, education, and settler colonialism in late eighteenth- and early nineteenth-century in northeastern North America. Along with Kathryn Labelle, he is the editor of *From Huronia to Wendakes: Adversity, Migrations, and Resilience, 1650–1900*. He is also a contributor to and editor at ActiveHistory.ca, where he writes broadly on the state of the historian's craft in Canada.

LOIS HOITENGA ROELOFS received her M.S. in Psychiatric Nursing and Ph.D. in Nursing Science from the University of Illinois at Chicago. Her research focus on aging and leisure in both her master's and doctoral work stemmed from experiences with older persons living with depression due to the losses in their lives. She is currently a professor emeritus of Nursing at Trinity Christian College. Her interest in leisure and aging continues as she blogs on her own life at loisroelofs.com. She is also the author of a career memoir, *Caring Lessons: A Nursing Professor's Journey of Faith and Self* (Deep River Books, 2010).

JOHN SCHULZ (Ph.D.) is Principal Teaching Fellow in the School of Education, University of Southampton, England. John is Director of the Digital Media Studio and is currently developing an online M.Sc. program and a MOOC in Mathematics-Education. John also contributes to the doctoral and masters programs. Prior to Southampton, John worked at the University of Edinburgh where he lectured in Sport and Recreation. John is originally from Australia where he studied at Griffith University. Before his academic career, John was on the Board of Directors for Scripture Union in Australia and was involved in the training of camp leaders.

JOSEPH D. TEAFF received his Ed.D. in Leisure Education from Columbia University and was Professor of Therapeutic Recreation in the Department of Recreation at Southern Illinois University for twenty years until his retirement. Joe published numerous articles on therapeutic recreation and a popular textbook entitled, *Leisure Services with the Elderly*. His scholarly interests were in the areas of leisure and aging, therapeutic recreation management, travel and tourism, and the philosophy of leisure. Dr. Teaff passed away in 2016.

GLEN VAN ANDEL received his Re.D. from Indiana University and was Professor of Recreation at Calvin College until his retirement in 2008. He co-authored an introductory textbook in therapeutic recreation entitled *Therapeutic Recreation: A Practical Approach* and has presented numerous papers at professional conferences and published several articles in professional journals. Glen was a founding member of the Christian Society for Kinesiology, Leisure, and Sport Studies and his scholarly interests lie in the areas of therapeutic recreation, philosophy of leisure, and Christian perspectives on play and leisure.

STEVEN N. WALLER received his Ph.D. from Michigan State University and his D.Min. from the United Theological Seminary. He is currently a professor in the recreation and sport management program,

Department of Kinesiology, Recreation, & Sport Studies at the University of Tennessee-Knoxville and is the Co-Director of the UTKs Center for the Study of Sport and Religion. Steve has authored numerous publications including his most recent book, *Leisure and Fellowship in the Life of the Black Church: Theology and Praxis*. His research interests include: religious/spiritual constraints to leisure/sport participation; structural barriers to career advancement for minorities and women in recreation and sport organizations; institutional evil; and professional issues in sports chaplaincy.

ROBERT D. WEATHERS received his Ed.D. from Brigham Young University and spent 32 of his forty-two-year career in higher education at Seattle Pacific University. While his primary responsibilities were in Exercise Science, the course that he taught most frequently throughout his career was Wellness. Frequently this course was taught in conjunction with extended backpacking, sea kayaking, and whitewater kayaking expeditions as he believes that such experiences provide an optimal laboratory for studying interactions among the different aspects of who we are.

BUD WILLIAMS received his Ed.D. from Northern Illinois University and has spent most of his career with the Department of Applied Health Science at Wheaton College teaching courses on motor development and motor learning. Bud enjoys applying his course materials through a variety of skilled motor activities with family, friends, and students and yearly skis several 51km marathons as one of the many skilled physical activities that interface with his academic interests related to fitness over the lifespan. He also maintains an active role in promoting Christian thinking by contributing papers on wellness, sport ethics, and risk taking.

Section One

LEISURE THEORY

At least seven concepts of leisure exist within the leisure studies field: (1) the classical state of being view, (2) leisure as activity, (3) leisure as free time, (4) leisure as a function of social class, (5) the psychological experience view known as a state of mind, (6) feminist perspectives, and (7) the holistic view (Heintzman, 2013). Christian reflections on the last five views have been rare, as throughout Christian history two understandings of leisure have been dominant. One tradition has been that of a Christianized classical understanding of leisure adapted from the Greek notion of *schole*. Augustine, Aquinas, medieval monastic writers, as well as modern (e.g., Pieper, 1952) and contemporary (e.g., Doohan, 1990) Roman Catholic writers reflect this understanding of leisure. This view is probably best represented by Pieper's (1952) well known statement that

> Leisure, it must be clearly understood, is a mental and spiritual attitude – it is not simply the result of external factors, it is not the inevitable result of spare time, a holiday, a week-end or a vacation. It is, in the first place, an attitude of mind, a condition of the soul. (pp. 40–41)

In the first chapter of this book, Peggy Hothem defines leisure according to the classical state of being view and draws extensively upon Pieper's understanding of leisure to explore the wonder of leisure. Hothem explains how the wonder of leisure is rooted in divine worship and involves the celebration of life through the attitudes of calmness, contemplation, and wholeness.

Although Christian versions of classical leisure such as expressed by Pieper (1952) continue to this day in the Roman Catholic Church, with the Reformation and the development of Protestant theology there was a move away from classical understandings of leisure to activity understandings. Leisure as activity may be defined as "non-work activity in which people engage during their free time – apart from obligations of work, family and society" (Murphy, 1974, p. 4). Closely related to the activity view is leisure as free time, since time free from work is necessary to engage in leisure activity. In Chapter 2, Karl Johnson argues that English and American Puritan Sabbatarians lobbied for designated days of recreation in order to preserve a Sabbath free from work and recreation, and later, nineteenth-century American Protestant Sabbatarians were strong supporters of the Saturday half-holiday movement. Together these Sabbatarians contributed to securing a weekly Saturday free from work which translated into fewer work hours, fewer work days, and the modern weekend. Thus Sabbatarians were visionary innovators of modern leisure time.

Like most Christian writings on leisure, Volume 1 of *Christianity and Leisure* (Heintzman, Van Andel, & Visker, 2006) focused on traditional concepts of leisure such as the classical, activity, and time views and did not reference concepts prevalent in the leisure studies literature over the last few decades. However, one chapter in Volume 1 introduced a Christian perspective on the holistic understanding of leisure. Dahl (2006) wrote:

> Work and leisure are not distinct; they lie on a continuum. . . . Leisure is being able to combine work, worship, and recreation in a free and loving, holistic way which integrates these three elements as much as possible. Although a person goes to different places to perform different functions, leisure lies in integrating these three aspects in order to experience wholeness in one's life, family, and community. (p. 95)

In this second volume of conference papers, two chapters develop a holistic understanding of leisure. In Chapter 3, Heintzman advocates a holistic concept primarily because this concept can encompass the variety and richness of the biblical material relevant to leisure, but also because it offers the opportunity to combine the two historical Christian traditions of leisure – the classical state of being view of Roman Catholicism and the activity view prevalent in Protestantism. An examination of biblical materials reveals that leisure encompasses two dimensions: a quantitative and a qualitative, with one relating to human doing and the other to human being.

Partly building upon Dahl's (2006) holistic understanding of leisure as "worcreation" presented in the first volume of Christianity and leisure, in Chapter 4 Doug Joblin examines models of leisure from historical and contemporary perspectives, and then proposes a holistic model of leisure as an engaged and responsible pursuit of an attitude of freedom in work, play, and worship. Joblin believes that a holistic model of leisure might inspire a renaissance of leisure in a way that helps center people's spirituality.

There has been very little Christian reflection on the social psychological concept of leisure as a state of mind or even connections made between Christianity and this understanding of leisure that dominated leisure studies in the 1980s and 1990s and is still prevalent today. One of the few connections between Christianity and this psychological state-of-mind view was made by Isabella Csikszentmihalyi (1988), who used the flow theory to explain why the Jesuit order was so successful during the 1500s and 1600s. In Chapter 5, Marcia Carter uses the flow state (intensely absorbing experiences where the challenge of an activity matches the skill level of the individual so that the person loses track of both time and awareness of self) to investigate the relationship between both individual and community wellbeing and quality of life. As characteristics of flow experiences are found in both spirituality and leisure, Carter describes how Christians can generate experiences that lead to both holistic wellbeing and spiritual freedom in their personal and community relationships.

Paul Heintzman

References

Csikszentmihalyi, I.S. (1988). Flow in historical context: The case of the Jesuits. In M. Csikszentmihalyi & I.S. Csikszentmihalyi (Eds.), Optimal experience: Psychological studies of flow in consciousness (pp. 232–48). Cambridge: Cambridge University Press.

Dahl, G. (2006). Whatever happened to the leisure revolution? In P. Heintzman, G.E. Van Andel, & T.L. Visker (Eds.), Christianity and leisure: Issues in a pluralistic society (Rev. ed., pp. 85–97). Sioux Center: Dordt College Press.

Doohan, L. (1990). *Leisure: A spiritual need.* Notre Dame, IN: Ave Maria Press.

Heintzman, P., Van Andel, G.E., & Visker, T.L. (Eds.). (2006). *Christianity and leisure: Issues in a pluralistic society* (Rev. ed.). Sioux Center: Dordt College Press.

Murphy, J. F. (1974). *Concepts of leisure: Philosophical implications.* Englewood Cliffs, NJ: Prentice Hall.

Pieper, J. (1952). *Leisure: The basis of culture.* New York: Pantheon Books (1963, Random House).

Chapter 1

THE WONDER OF LEISURE

Margaret Hothem

Several years ago, when my son Joel was in pre-school Junior Church, the curriculum of that little worship service was based on actively engaging the children with the Bible stories. After the story was read, the children were prompted to ask "I wonder" questions. One by one, the children would ask such questions as,

I wonder how the blind man felt when he could see for the first time?

I wonder how Jesus felt when he was going to the cross?

I wonder if Jesus liked to play like other children?

Joel and I continued this "I wonder. . ." game many times as we would drive in the car and he would try to stump me with his "I wonder…" questions:

I wonder why the grass is green?

I wonder if the horses are cold?

I wonder how the birds know how to find their nests?

I wonder if Jesus liked ice cream?

Those precious moments in the car would pass all too quickly, and then I would find myself in the college classroom with students who appeared to have lost their sense of wonder. As those students had progressed through the educational system and learned the answers to many of their childhood questions, a horrible thing happened. They became satisfied with those answers and thereby ceased to wonder. Rachel Carson (1956) described this occurrence:

> A child's world is fresh and new and beautiful, full of wonder and excitement. It is our misfortune that for most of us that clear-eyed vision, that true instinct for what is beautiful and awe-inspiring, is dimmed and even lost before we reach adulthood. (p. 42)

Revised version of paper presented at the 1998 conference.

What happens between childhood wonder and adult information-satisfaction? The all-too-frequent students (as well as many faculty) are so accustomed to surfing the net and skimming the surface, that we have either not experienced the joy of wonder, or are too busy with our cliché culture to dive for the treasures of wisdom that can be found in the times of wonder. Wonder cannot be experienced without reflection. The psalmist David wrote, "When I consider your heavens, the work of your fingers, the moon and the stars, which you have set in place, what is mankind that you are mindful of them?" (Ps. 8:3–4). Even Solomon (Prov. 6:6) suggests that a good use of time is to go to the ant and "consider its ways and be wise!" In order for us to marvel and wonder about God and his creation, we must think about the things that we already know to be true: **This is our Father's world and he does speak to those who take the time to listen** . . . and that is the wonder of leisure: "Be still, and know that I am God" (Ps. 46:10).

"**Be still** and know that I am God" – is this a state of being that is even possible in our academic culture today? I am proposing that being still and allowing the full presence of God to envelop us is the wonder of leisure, which is received as a gift from our Father. Listening to God, however, requires time to meditate, pray, and think about those truths of who our Father is, the grace that he bestows on his children, and the marvel of his creation. Paul wrote to the Philippians (4:8) ". . . whatever is true, whatever is noble, whatever is right, whatever is pure, whatever is lovely, whatever is admirable – if anything is excellent or praiseworthy – **think about such things**" [bold added]. When Paul penned these words, he was not on a cruise vacation, nor was he admiring the sunset on a mountaintop peak experience. He was in a dark, rat-infested, depressing prison, being tormented and persecuted – suffering under the effects of sin, but hopeful in that which he knew to be true. It was indeed a wonder that he wrote,

> . . . for I have learned to be content in whatever the circumstances. I know what it is to be in need, and I know what it is to have plenty. I have learned the secret of being content in any and every situation, whether well fed or hungry, whether living in plenty or in want. I can do all this through him who gives me strength. (Phil. 4:11–13)

That Paul could even write this is a testimony of his willingness to receive life as a gift because he knew his Savior.

Wonder is a special gift given to us by our heavenly Father, but it is up to us to be willing to receive it. The *American Heritage Dictionary of the English Language* (n.d.) defines wonder as "the emotion aroused by something awe-inspiring, astounding, or marvelous." Anyone who is exposed to it cannot shake off the effects. The experience of wonder is something that will change the way we look at life. There is insight and wisdom for living that comes from the wonder of leisure, but this form of leisure is at a premium. For those who have not reflected on the various meanings of leisure in our society, I am not defining leisure as free time or as recreational-diversionary activities, but I call us back to the classical meaning of leisure that is rooted not only in Greek philosophy, but in a Christian worldview.

In his book *Leisure: The Basis of Culture* (1952), Joseph Pieper poignantly defines leisure:

> Leisure, it must be clearly understood, is a mental and spiritual attitude – it is not simply the result of external factors, it is not the inevitable result of spare time, a holiday, a weekend or a vacation. It is, in the first place, an attitude of mind, a condition of the soul. . . . Leisure implies (in the first place) an attitude of non-activity, of inward calm, of silence; it means not being "busy," but letting things happen. . . . For leisure is a receptive attitude of mind, a contemplative attitude, and it is not only the occasion but also the capacity for steeping oneself in the whole of creation.
>
> Furthermore, there is also a certain serenity in leisure. That serenity springs precisely from our inability to understand, from our recognition of the mysterious nature of the universe; it springs from the courage of deep confidence, so that we are content to let things take their course. . . . (pp. 40–41)

Leisure is more than free time or recreational activities. It's a quality of living rooted in freedom. This is not a self-serving freedom that declares one's right to happiness and pleasure. Rather it is a freedom to let go of *our* agendas, *our* compulsions, *our* need to prove ourselves through work and activity.

In many ways, it takes courage to be leisured. In an article titled "The Courage to Be Leisured," Wilson (1981) described a receptive quality to leisure that is a rare occurrence in most people's lives.

> Leisure is identified as a process rather than a state; a vigorous involvement rather than enervated withdrawal; a willing surrender of the whole self to experience. . . . [Leisure] is a bold willingness to experiment and to let things happen without a brittle adherence to specified means and ends. . . . One might even argue that a talent for entering into leisure processes is an important feature of the best-integrated, most highly cultivated individual personalities. (p. 285)

The courage that Wilson described is the courage to "let go." It demands that "the individual be strong enough to fight down the demons of work-shunning guilt, of comfortable routine, of the closely defended self. If you will, leisure calls for the strength to be weak and the self-control to be abandoned" (Wilson, p. 300).

Leisure then is a willingness to let things happen without a compelling adherence to specific means and ends, except for the glorification and enjoyment of God. It has a gratuitous quality and is more involved with the process than the product. Realizing God's divine purpose, leisure is an opportunity for one's freedom of expression. One's response to God as creator is expressed in the willingness to surrender the whole self to the experience.

In a similar way, Robert Lee (1964), in his book *Religion and Leisure*, wrote:

> Leisure is the growing time of the human spirit. Leisure provides the occasion for learning and freedom, for growth and expression, for rest and restoration, for rediscovering life in its entirety. Leisure is a part of man's ultimate concern. It is a crucial part of the very search for meaning in life. . . . Increasingly it is in our leisure that either the meaningfulness or the pointlessness of life will be revealed. (p. 33)

What does my leisure tell me about the meaningfulness of my life? What does your leisure tell you about your life? I passionately believe that when we allow ourselves to receive the gift of the wonder of leisure, we can begin to answer the basic questions of life that so many of us avoid asking:

Who am I?
Why did God create me?
What is the purpose of life?
What do I live for?
What gives my life meaning?
Why do I work? Study? Play? Have relationships?
Who is God?
How can I glorify and enjoy God, even in the midst of confusion, disappointment, suffering and pain?

These are just some of the *wonder* questions that can be pondered in those times of leisure if we have the courage to be receptive. In so doing, we experience the grace that God desires to bestow on us. Again, the Psalmist David wrote, "Surely everyone goes around like a mere phantom; in vain they rush about, heaping up wealth without knowing whose it will finally be. But now, Lord, what do I look for? My hope is in you" (Ps. 39:6–7). When we *look* to find our hope in God, this is not a quick scan, but a savoring of the delectable taste of knowing in whom we hope.

Is the wonder of leisure possible during times of stress, confusion, anxiety, disappointment, and even crisis? Is it an illusion that is theoretically presented by leisure philosophers who comfortably sit in their soft-cushioned chairs and describe a utopian culture that is free from the taint of sin? As Christian leisure scholars, we are called to closely examine our theology of leisure and the integration of our faith with our discipline. What is the importance of teaching our students the value of exercise, proper nutrition, recreation skill development, sport, and healthy living, when underneath the facade of their existence, students are longing to be known, to have a purpose, and to find answers to those basic questions of life? Our academic discipline is very important in our liberal arts colleges, but we must know why we are doing what we are doing!

How and why do we study leisure in a world that is hungry, hurting, and desperately in need of hearing the gospel of Jesus? For several years at the beginning of a senior course on the philosophy of leisure, I would always ask my students that question. This question was particularly heartfelt to me last year as I prepared for the course. I was experiencing excruciating pain due to an unwanted, litigated divorce in which I daily met persecution and uncertainty of the future. How could I espouse the virtues of leisure when my personal world was falling apart, and I felt very emotionally unsafe? Could I experience leisure as the state of being which Pieper expressed so articulately, the philosophy that was a foundation in my teaching of leisure for many years?

As I opened the first day of that course with the question, "How do we even talk about leisure when our lives have been ravaged in different ways by the result of sin?" I was absolutely amazed at the words, the confidence, and even the passion that the Lord gave me. More boldly than ever, I proclaimed that the gift of leisure is a wonder that can only be experienced because of the **grace** of our Lord, if we are willing to receive it. The wonder of leisure can and does come only as we allow ourselves to be totally surrendered to the lordship of Christ and obedience to his Word. Leisure is not a luxury item, nor does it need a utilitarian purpose. When leisure is experienced as a gift of grace, God graciously gives us hope and healing. Life's difficulties do not disappear, but for some glorious moments, our attention is focused on the love of Christ and the hope of redemption through his sacrifice.

On one particular day, the oppression of divorce was so great upon me that I could function only by God's grace. I went for my daily leisure walk in which I poured out my heart to the Lord. It was a cold, gray

March day, and as I turned the corner onto my street, the sun suddenly broke through the clouds. It was as if I was seeing a glimpse of the glory of the Lord. My broken heart broke into praise as I realized the love of Jesus. That was a moment of leisure's wonder which I only could receive. It was not planned nor manipulated. In my weakness, the Lord gave me the courage to let go and to be receptive to the wonder of leisure.

Leisure as just free time and diversionary recreational activities are not God's promises as the rights of believers, but the leisure that is rooted in rest and divine worship is truly a wonder. And so, during that term, I encouraged my students to dig even deeper with me into the purposes of studying leisure. As together we shared common fears, anxieties, and questions, we also shared our hopes and insights on God's truth. In a serendipitous way, most of those students experienced the wonder of leisure as we questioned, reflected, prayed, studied, and shared our lives.

It is obvious that many of our students experience an academic drought in their liberal arts experiences. They are thirsty for an educational opportunity that will stir the "wonder" fire within them, but diversionary activities and the crunch of information overload are too enticing, and hence, they leave our institutions without experiencing the wonder and marvel of God's creation and their own purpose for being.

In an article entitled "Education as Play and the Fall into Serious Work," Hyers (1983) stated:

> Education . . . is born out of play. It is the result of the capacities of the human mind to go beyond sheer biological rhythms and physiological necessities: to play with existence. Most, if not all, human culture is a super addition to the basic physical requirements of survival and preservation of the species. And education is the learning, elaboration, and re-creation of this human culture. (pp. 58–59)

Hyers' thesis is that institutions, and the expectations of students, have turned a liberal arts education into a training ground for work. Education in fact becomes work itself, and the possible scintillating play of learning turns into boredom.

> The excitement of a new discovery becomes the ho-hum of yawning acquaintance, thoughtful reflection is reduced to note-taking, imagination is limited to imagining what the next exam will be like, and the sense of wonder shrivels to wondering whether one will pass the course or not. (Hyers, p. 59)

At the very heart of a Christian liberal arts education should be a thirst for knowledge, joy of learning, marvel at God and his creation, love of wisdom, and a spirit of wonder. Those of us who have studied leisure theories know that the word *leisure* is rooted in the Greek word *schole* (education), and the Latin word *licere* (to be free). A leisure education does not imply a form of entertainment and random activities and experiences, but rather the cultivation of inquisitiveness, fascination, and wonder of who we are, and who is the God that created us for his glory and his enjoyment. As leisure educators, we can establish classroom environments that encourage students to reflect on these questions, but only if we are willing to reflect on them ourselves. We have a unique opportunity to provide classrooms in which the wonder of leisure can be experienced. We can give students the time within our classes to reflect and be vulnerable with who they are, why God created them, and what the purpose of their lives is.

Pieper (1952) presents a justification that leisure is the preserver of freedom, of education, and of culture. Is this a concept of leisure that is relevant to contemporary Christian students in our liberal arts colleges? How do our students perceive leisure and its relationship to education and their faith? It has been my experience that when students read Pieper, they have mixed reviews. Typically, a couple of students readily embrace the magnitude of intellectual and spiritual wisdom in Pieper's philosophy. It even gives them a sense of pride and significance in their study of leisure. They start seeing the connection, and indeed the integration, of their liberal arts studies with their faith and their chosen discipline. They experience the jewels of leisure's delight with vigor, awe, and wonder.

Unfortunately, many students need to be prodded to understand a concept of leisure that goes beyond free time and recreational activities. They have known nothing else but a superficial satisfaction with the tedious routines of life, interspersed with moments of diversion. In many ways, they have lost the ability to enjoy leisure. Pieper (1952) predicts this when he states. "For one can only be bored if the spiritual power to be leisurely has been lost" (p. 59). When I challenge my students to consider that it takes spiritual power to enjoy leisure, they initially are puzzled by the concept.

Why does it take spiritual power to enjoy leisure? This is a good "I wonder" question! In my class, we explore the effect of the utilitarian and rational philosophies on our understanding of leisure, and ask: Does that take spiritual power? We also closely examine the contemplative meaning of leisure as stated by Pieper (1952), which more obviously requires spiritual power if one is to experience leisure through worship of the divine.

Typically, a student will ask if Pieper's (1952) concept of leisure is only possible with the academic elite, and is it really possible for the average student to appreciate the contemplative meaning of leisure. After all, Pieper's philosophy of leisure was greatly influenced by the writings of Plato and Aristotle. In Aristotle's *Nichomachean Ethics*, Aristotle embraced leisure as happiness or an end in itself. How does one attain happiness? According to Aristotle, it is through virtue, or excellence of the soul. Virtue is pleasant because it is honorable and good. Therefore, virtue is the source of true pleasure or leisure. How does one get virtue? Aristotle stated that knowledge and the wisdom of contemplative leisure leads to moral action. Therefore, Aristotle prescribed that the good life is attained through the pursuit of wisdom, the pleasure of contemplative leisure, and results in virtuous living.

Aristotle's idealism was based on the assumption that humans are basically rational beings, and thus the rational person will choose wisely, and therefore experience happiness. But the word *happiness* obviously is difficult to define and has different meanings for different people. Parducci (1995), in researching the physiological experience of happiness in his book *Happiness, Pleasure, and Judgment*, explained Aristotle's concept of happiness as being prescriptive. That is, its purpose is to dispose people to behave in certain ways. For example, "happiness is doing what is right" or "happiness is being kind to others" (p. 10). But contrast the humanism of Aristotle with the happiness found in Scripture. For example, Psalm 32:1–2 reads, "Blessed [happy] is the one whose transgressions are forgiven, whose sins are covered. Blessed is the one whose sin the LORD does not count against them and in whose spirit is no deceit." This is grace. It is not earned or deserved. The awareness and acceptance of grace is truly a wonder as we experience the leisure to reflect on it.

Pieper (1952), a Roman Catholic theologian, does not just reiterate the humanism of the ancient Greek philosophers, but integrates theology in his description of divine worship and rest:

> To rest from work means that time is reserved for divine worship. . . . Separated from the sphere of divine worship, of the cult of the divine, and from the power it radiates, leisure is as impossible as a celebration of a feast. Cut off from the worship of the divine, leisure becomes laziness and work inhuman. (pp. 57, 59)

Therefore, the celebration of divine worship is an essential part of a full human existence. This spiritual description of leisure has been a generic philosophical quality of leisure that has significantly impacted leisure theorists for many years.

Even as a young leisure scholar in the early 1980s, I was enthralled when I first read Pieper's (1952) book. The idea that leisure is rooted in divine worship and involves the celebration of life through the attitudes of calmness, contemplation, and wholeness had not previously been a part of my understanding of leisure. But it made sense to me that leisure provided the time and the state of being in which I not only could glorify the Lord, **but** enjoy him. It prompted me to conduct my doctoral dissertation on the *Integration of Christian Faith and Leisure* (Hothem, 1983). I was intrigued with the question of whether evangelical theologians described and experienced the type of leisure proposed by Pieper. However, I was disappointed to find that the theologians I interviewed had given very little consideration to the phenomenon of leisure, and the theological concept described by Pieper was rarely experienced.

In this research project (Hothem, 1983), it was obvious that work had spiritual meaning to the theologians who were interviewed, and leisure was primarily seen as rest, reward, change, relief, or recuperation. Clearly, leisure and work were viewed dualistically, and leisure functioned in a utilitarian role to work. Leisure as a state of being was generally not a recognized concept to these theologians. The outcome of that research led me to question whether the spiritual dynamic of leisure is too idealistic for most people's experiences. If evangelical theologians, who would be expected to have considered the influence of their faith on all aspects of their life, did not describe the spiritual qualities of leisure, then who would?

And yet, over the years, I have tenaciously held on to this spiritual concept of leisure, believed it, taught it, and attempted to live it. I could support and articulate the theology of leisure with Scripture, and I had experienced its holistic qualities. However, it was through the test of my own personal crisis that I not only appreciated the holistic meaning of leisure, but realized that when I received the gift of leisure from the Lord, there were healing qualities. This was another amazing wonder!

Through my own experience of walking in a deep valley, and yet experiencing God's grace to carry me through, I am even more convinced that the wonder of leisure as described by Pieper (1952) is very real. It is real not just because of the rest that is found in leisure, nor the existential feelings of divine worship. The wonder of leisure is God's grace that allows us to sing the doxology as found in Romans 11:33–34, 36:

> Oh, the depth of the riches of the wisdom and knowledge of God!
> How unsearchable his judgments,
> and his paths beyond tracing out!
> "Who has known the mind of the Lord?
> Or who has been his counselor? . . ."

For from him and through him and to him are all things.
To him be the glory forever! Amen.

References

Carson, R. (1956). *The sense of wonder*. New York: Harper & Row.

Hothem, M. (1983). *The integration of Christian faith and leisure: A qualitative study*. (Unpublished Ed.D. dissertation). Boston University. Boston, MA.

Hyers, C. (1983). Education as play and the fall into serious work. *Education Digest*, 49(6), 58–60.

Lee, R. (1964). *Religion and leisure in America*. New York: Abingdon Press.

Parducci, A. (1995). *Happiness, pleasure, and judgment*. Mahwah, NJ: Lawrence Erlbaum Associates.

Pieper, J. (1952). *Leisure: The basis of culture* (A. Dru, Trans.) New York: Pantheon Books (1963, Random House).

Wilson, R. (1981). The courage to be leisured. *Social Forces*, 60, 282–303.

Wonder (n.d.). In *American Heritage Dictionary of the English Language*, (5th ed.). Retrieved on January 18, 2012, from: http://www.thefreedictionary.com/wonder

Chapter 2

FROM SABBATH TO WEEKEND: RELIGIOUS ADVOCACY FOR A WEEKLY DAY OF RECREATION

Karl E. Johnson

The modern weekend is a relatively recent innovation, brought about largely by impersonal forces such as industrialization and the emergence of a large middle class. But it was also brought about by a coalition of labor leaders and religious reformers. The earliest advocates for a weekly day of recreation were in fact Sabbatarians – those who believed civil law should reflect the fourth commandment's injunction to "keep the Sabbath holy."

In contrast to abolitionists and suffragists, who are remembered as successful and progressive, Sabbatarians are often remembered as failures and as enemies of religious liberty. To be sure, there are some good reasons for such judgment. When Jewish, Catholic, and Lutheran immigrants arrived in America with diverse Sabbath practices in the nineteenth century, for example, many Protestant Sabbatarians supported Sabbath laws as a symbolic means of asserting that America was a Christian nation. Moreover, in the long run, Sabbatarians largely failed in their goal to secure quiet Sundays free from both labor and recreation. Sunday or "blue laws" may remain on the books, but they are largely ignored and regarded as relics of an earlier era.

Still, the judgment that Sabbatarians were on the wrong side of history is too simple. At the beginning of the twenty-first century, a spate of articles, books, and organizations are turning to Sabbath-keeping as an antidote to the frantic and harried pace of modern life. Not only religious but also secular authors and organizations are appropriating the concept of Sabbath as a resource for resistance to time poverty. Take Back

---

Revised version of paper presented at the 1998 conference.

Your Time, an organization that advocates for more time off for American workers, has partnered with religious organizations toward this end; Balance4Success has a campaign entitled Taking Back Sunday; and atheist author Sam Harris has stated that "We may even want, for perfectly rational reasons, to say we want a Sabbath in this country" (Meacham, 2007, p. 58). Simply put, rumors of Sabbatarianism's death have been greatly exaggerated.

Judging Sabbatarianism a singular failure is also ironic because the movement actually succeeded at least in some respects. "In their effort to realize their vision of a day set apart from the world," writes McCrossen (1999), "Sabbatarians lost the battles but won the war: the state does not treat Sunday like the other days of the week. More importantly, neither do the American people" (p. 151). Sabbatarians were also successful with respect to an accomplishment for which they are seldom credited: establishing a weekly day of recreation. The weekend, which has become one of the most central and enduring features of modernity, arrived first in England and America – two nations with the strongest Sabbatarian traditions. The question arises: Is this a coincidence?

This paper argues that the weekend arrived first in England and America largely because of Sabbatarian advocacy. The topic is treated in three sections. First, Puritan Sabbatarians, especially in England but also in America, advocated for designated days of recreation as a means of preserving a religious Sabbath free from labor and recreation. Second, shifting the focus to America, nineteenth-century Sabbatarians were the earliest and most vocal supporters of the Saturday half-holiday movement. Third, Jewish Sabbatarians took the lead in advocating for the five-day week in the early twentieth century. Sabbatarians were thus in part innovators who helped usher in a distinctively modern ecology of time.

English Puritans and Days of Recreation

We speak of leisure quantitatively – as a thing that can be measured – but perhaps the most significant difference between premodern and modern leisure is the qualitative transformation that made it measurable. In medieval England, as with premodern societies more generally, the boundary between labor and leisure was more fluid than fixed (Thomas, 1964; Thompson, 1967). Moreover, labor was seasonal and irregular. Seedtime and harvest were punctuated by many ales, wakes, fairs, saints' days, and festival seasons such as the twelve days of Christmas and pre-Lenten carnival. Since the industrial revolution, by contrast, leisure has tended to be periodic and regular, taking place primarily on weekends.

This transformation of leisure began as part of a larger transformation of society that had two primary sources, both associated with Puritans – the Reformation and the dissolution of traditional society (Hall, 1989). The emerging system of merchant capitalism began the process of decoupling labor from the rhythms of seedtime and harvest, and gave artisans and laborers more incentive to work longer hours than had peasants for whom compensation was not as closely tied to time. By the early to mid-seventeenth century, historians thus identify an "industrious sort of people" (Hill, 1967, pp. 124–144) and "an industrious revolution" (De Vries, 2008) – a trend toward longer labor and less leisure that preceded the industrial revolution. This newfound work ethic and "spirit of capitalism," in Weber's famous phrase, found ideological justification in the Reformation doctrine of vocation, which effectively refashioned work from a necessary evil to a source of moral virtue.

The historical implications of the work ethic for recreation and leisure are complicated and contested. While much popular literature depicts Puritans as opposed to most forms of recreation and leisure, many historians (Daniels, 1995; Struna, 1977; Wagner, 1979) suggest that the Puritans were fairly typical Elizabethans in their enjoyment of singing, dancing, hunting, fishing, wrestling, bowling, and even drinking and sex. The confusion is largely a category error. With respect to both belief and behavior, Puritans affirmed and enjoyed what they called "lawful recreations," or those activities they judged refreshing rather than dissipating. For reasons of both doctrine and discipline, however, they vehemently denounced and prohibited "play" in the sense of unruly festivals that entailed rituals of inversion (Hall, 1989, pp. 166–212). Doctrinally, Puritans opposed saints' days and the liturgical calendar for their Roman and pagan associations, as well as for the suggestion that some days are more holy than others. With respect to discipline, Puritans were also concerned about the rowdiness and licentiousness associated with church-ales, maypoles, Morris dances, Christmas wassailing, and pre-Lenten carnival (Burke, 1978, pp. 208–209). Protestant reformers thus pursued a program of calendrical reform. Whatever the causal relationship between Protestantism and the spirit of capitalism, Puritans and the industrious sort of people both had an interest in cleansing or "de-festivalizing" (Cressy, 1989, p. xii) the medieval calendar and replacing the old, irregular patterns of labor and leisure with a more regular pattern of work and rest.

Central to this project of calendrical reform was the Sabbath. To late sixteenth century writers such as Philip Stubbs (1583), Richard Greenham (1592), and Nicholas Bownd (1606), the Sabbath was a holy day, not a holiday.[1] In their view, keeping the Sabbath holy entailed ceasing not only from labor but also from physical recreation because, as Bownd said, "we cannot have the present delight in the use of [honest recreations and lawful delights], and yet at the same time be occupied in the hearing of the word, and such other parts of God's holy worship and service as he requireth of us upon the Sabbath-day" (Cox, 1865, p. 150). Although at the beginning of the seventeenth century such Sabbatarian views can be found among Anglicans as well as Puritans, and in fact the distinction between Anglican and Puritan was not yet as firm as it would soon become, the view that recreation refreshes the body and rest refreshes the soul increasingly came to be associated with Puritanism. Sunday, in this view, is the day of the soul; because "recreation belongs not to rest but to labour," recreation's proper time is the "secular" days of the week (E.E. as quoted in White, 1635, p. 234). Although this statement is commonly attributed to Francis White, the Anglican Bishop of Ely, often with the implication that Anglican and Puritan views regarding Sunday recreation were relatively continuous into the seventeenth century (e.g., McCrossen, 2000; Struna, 1996), White is actually quoting a writer whom he is criticizing. To White (1635), one of the main purposes of the Sabbath was always "to refresh and recreate people after toile and hard labour" (White, p. 237, see also Cox, 1865, pp. 166–73). That White's book was commissioned by King Charles, dedicated to Archbishop William Laud, and subtitled "A Defense of the Orthodoxal Doctrine of the Church of England against Sabbatarian novelty," suggests that by the early seventeenth century, Anglican and Puritan views on Sunday recreation were distinct. In short, the view that recreation "belongs not to rest" had become a Puritan distinctive.

But if recreation was not allowed on Sunday, when was it possible? None other than King James I asked this very question of those who would restrict Sunday recreation. When, in 1617, the magistrates of Lancashire County outlawed all Sunday recreation, James responded with a declaration affirming "the Anglican position" that recreation belonged properly to holy days, including Sundays. Acknowledging the emerging challenge of finding time for recreation, James wrote in *The Book of Sports*, "For when shall the common people have leave to exercise, if not upon the Sundays and holy days, seeing they must apply their labour and win their living in all working days?" (as quoted in Whitaker, 1933, p. 93).

---

[1] For more accessible excerpts of these works, see Cox, 1865, pp. 140–141, 145–151.

The conflict over Sunday recreation was thus political as well as theological. Because Sunday recreation competed with worship, Puritans seeking to reform the culture and the Church of England had a vested interest in Sunday as a day of rest, understood narrowly as worship and "the hearing of the word." The church and crown, by contrast, because they sought to win the allegiance of the people and ward off any seditious assemblies (Hill, 1967, pp. 196–197), had a vested interest in Sunday as a day of recreation. Simply put, Sabbatarianism became more controversial in the years leading up to the English Civil War because it signified nonconformity.

Puritans were not deaf to the concern regarding time for recreation. In order to maintain and promote strict adherence to Sunday as a day of rest and worship, they advocated for designated days of recreation. Twenty years prior to the *Book of Sports* controversy, for example, Bownd wrote:

> We do exhort them that be in government to give some time to their children and servants, for their honest recreation, upon other days, that they be not driven to take it upon this, seeing they can no more want it altogether than their ordinary food. And as we have seen that they are bound to give them some time to work for themselves, unless they will, by their over-much straitness, compel them to it upon the day of rest; so must they spare also some few hours for their refreshing now and then; seeing they can no more want the one than the other. (Cox, 1865, p. 150)

Similar views were advocated by William Perkins (Birley, 1993, p. 80) and, most notably, by the Puritan-led Long Parliament. In 1647, after burning the *Book of Sports*, Parliament passed an ordinance on June 8 that abolished all holy days and festivals other than the weekly Sabbath, including Christmas, Easter, and Whitsuntide. The same ordinance established "That all scholars, apprentices, and other servants" were to have "such convenient reasonable recreation and relaxation from their constant and ordinary labours on every second Tuesday in the month throughout the year, as formerly they have used to have on such aforesaid festivals, commonly called Holy Days" (Ordinances of the Puritan Parliament as quoted in Whitaker, 1933, pp. 156–157). An additional ordinance passed on June 28, 1647, established that shops were to close and masters not to detain apprentices or servants "on the said day of recreation, ... unless market-days, fair-days, or other extraordinary occasion" (Ordinances of the Puritan Parliament as quoted in Cox, 1865, p. 235).[2] This idea of designated days of recreation clearly traveled to New

---

2   There are different versions of the texts in circulation. For excerpts and discussions see (Cox, 1865, p. 235; Hill, 1967, pp. 164, 197–198; Scholes, 1934, pp. 110–111; Solberg, 1977, p. 158; Wagner, 1979, pp. 149–150; Whitaker, 1933, pp. 156–157).

England, where Rhode Island passed a similar ordinance in 1654, and there is some evidence of Tuesday recreation in Massachusetts (Struna, 1996, p. 87).

Tuesday as a day of recreation does not appear to have been practiced widely in either England or New England. Nevertheless, the significance of the Puritan doctrine of the Sabbath for recreation is not merely in what it negated, but also in what it affirmed. Puritans advocated a pattern of recreation that was not only lawful and moderate, but also secular and regular. In this sense, modern leisure, in both its regularity and brevity, looks less like a departure from Puritan ideals than a fulfillment of them. Oliver Cromwell, who retired to Hampton Court from Saturday to Monday instead of taking the long summer vacations preferred by his predecessors, is thus said to have invented "that modified form of enjoyment to which hard-worked citizens have, in our day, given the name of the 'week-end'" (Gardiner, 1901, p. 288).

Nineteenth-Century Sabbatarians and the Saturday Half-Holiday in America

Although Sabbath-keeping enjoyed a kind of taken-for-granted status in seventeenth century New England, Sabbatarianism became a particularly intense political movement – what Chamlee (1968) called "the Sabbath crusade" – in the nineteenth century. When the Post Office Act of 1810 effectively opened post offices on Sundays, for example, Sabbatarians throughout the United States sent hundreds of petitions to Congress to protest (Fuller, 2003; John, 1995; Kramnick & Moore, 1996; McCrossen, 2000; Rohrer, 1987). This fervor was in part a function of the disestablishment of church and state. Given their negative associations with the Church of England, most evangelical and other Protestant Christians welcomed disestablishment, at least at the federal level. They did not, however, abandon their ideal of America as a Christian nation, but rather pursued the goal through more voluntary means (Handy, 1971). And the Sabbath, in the words of Lyman Beecher (1835), was "Heaven's consecrated instrumentality for the efficacious administration of the government of mind in a happy social state" (p. 40). In the absence of an established church, practices such as Sabbath-keeping bore the burden of preserving America as a Christian nation.

A second reason for the politicization of the Sabbath is related to industry (McCrossen, 2000). During the half century starting in 1840, the United States became the most modern and industrialized nation in the world. As factories went up in northeastern cities, factory owners and workers tussled over work habits, time regularity, and even workers' behavior after hours. Immigrants and native-born American workers from more rural environs arrived at factories with "premodern" work habits including drinking, gambling, singing, storytelling, reading the newspaper, coming and going without permission, and playing games of various sorts (Gutman, 1976). Owners, by contrast, employed the clock, the whistle, the work ethic, and piece-rate work as means of bringing regularity to worker behavior. Worker resistance found expression through tardiness, absenteeism, turnover, and the founding of labor unions. Over time, owners and workers struck a compromise: owners received the regularity they wanted, while workers secured shorter hours.

A byproduct of this industrializing process was the separation of leisure from work with respect to both time and space. As urban density made open space scarce and displaced forms of recreation familiar to those who had arrived from farms and shipyards, workers and their children took their games and festivals to the only public space they had – the streets. They also took to the saloons, theaters, and dime museums provided by leisure entrepreneurs, such as P.T. Barnum, who catered to the new demand for "going out" and who created new entertainment districts such as Coney Island and Times Square. Other groups responded differently to this crisis of leisure space. Members of the middle class largely responded by *separating* themselves into private clubs, taking excursions to resorts, and renovating their homes to include parlors with sofas and pianos. Methodists responded by *imitating* these resorts, creating alternative religious resorts such as the Chautauqua Institution, Ocean Grove, and Asbury Park, while the evangelical YMCA movement provided urban youth with pools and gymnasiums as alternative places to play. Yet another creative response to the crisis of leisure space was the parks movement. Unitarians (Bellows, 1857; Hale, 1900; Sawyer, 1847) in particular believed that the path to improving and uplifting immigrants and workers lay in *integrating* them with "the moral and religious part of the community" (Sawyer, 1847, p. 247) in public spaces such as Central Park. Although much of what has been written about the parks movement highlights the role of reformers, park advocacy came also from workers demanding more and better places to play (Hardy, 1982; Rosenzweig, 1979).

If the separation of leisure from work resulted in new, designated recreation spaces, so too with time (McCrossen, 2000). The byproduct of weekdays becoming pure workdays was that the demand for recreation among workers became concentrated on Sunday. Although theologically liberal Christians including Unitarians and many members of mainline churches increasingly accepted Lyceum lectures, the opening of museums, and other cultural opportunities as consistent with Sabbath ideals, they also generally opposed boisterous and especially commercialized recreation on Sunday. Indeed, not only clergy and religious moralists but many who cared about respectability and decorum desired to maintain the quiet standards of "the Puritan Sabbath." Just as reformer initiative and worker discontent combined to generate the idea of parks as a designated leisure space, so too they combined to generate the idea of Saturday afternoon as a designated leisure time.

The Saturday half-holiday movement got its start in England, where as early as 1845, *Evangelical Magazine* joined the Early Closing Association (founded in 1842) in advocating for early closing on Saturday (Whitaker, 1973, p. 50). To be sure, the idea of a Saturday half-holiday was not entirely new in the nineteenth century. At least one English source from the eighteenth century (Bourne, 1725) finds "a great Deference paid to *Saturday afternoon*" (p. 116), which the author attributes to Sabbath observance laws predating the Reformation. (More specifically, he attributes this deference to laws dating to 958 in England and 1203 in Scotland, when the Sabbath was understood to begin on Saturday at "noontide" – i.e., three o'clock in the afternoon). Nevertheless, the long hours required of industrial laborers forced the issue. The issue was also forced by "St. Monday," a tradition of absenteeism on the part of some workers attributed to a combination of worker resistance to the regulation of time and the particular problem of Sunday drinking that carried over into Monday (Reid, 1976, 1996). Due to its transgressive nature, this early and unofficial version of the two-day weekend posed a cultural problem. The Saturday half-holiday, by providing a designated and approved time for lawful recreation and Sabbath preparation, presented a solution that appealed to employers and Sabbatarians alike.

Although the Saturday half-holiday movement did not gain much traction in the United States until the mid-1880s, Sabbatarians advocated for it decades earlier. A "more holy observance of the Sabbath will follow," wrote Unitarian minister Frederick Sawyer (1847), if evening labor is abolished and Saturday afternoon is established "as a *quasi* holiday period, when neither clerks, apprentices, journeymen, nor any other class of persons, are expected to be at their business posts" (pp. 318–319). Sawyer was sympathetic to clerks and apprentices who recreated on Sunday, but proposed Saturday as a solution to the Sunday problem:

> [A]s much as I prize the institution of the Sabbath, and believe in the wisdom of observing it as a day sacred to rest, as well as to holy devotion, I should be more astonished, if, under such circumstances, those over-tasked clerks and apprentices should fail to desecrate it. No! If a holy observance of the Sabbath is to be brought about, we must begin at the root of the evil, and give all classes time, during secular hours, for recreation and amusement, so that, when the Sabbath comes, it shall find us prepared, both in body and in mind, to welcome it as a delightful season of rest, both from the toils of business, and the excitements of amusements. (pp. 319–320)

The following year, Justin Edwards (1848), temperance crusader and secretary of the American and Foreign Sabbath Union, also endorsed the idea of a Saturday half-holiday. Before the movement really gained any momentum, the New York Sabbath Committee (1881) was also on record in its favor:

> The importance of healthful recreation, and the free opening of museums, art galleries, etc., for the working classes, no one can deny. But this end is reached by the Saturday half-holiday, and by the shorter hours of daily labor, becoming so common in this country; while Sunday is saved to the higher uses and enjoyments of home and the worship of God. (p. 17)

Likewise, Sabbatarian activist Wilbur Crafts (1894) favored early closing on Saturday in order to provide "time for recreation outside the Sabbath" (p. 419).

From the earliest days of the movement in England, women especially were believed to benefit from more time for Sabbath preparation. In America, the Young Ladies Christian Association ("A Saturday Half-Holiday," 1874) advocated for half-holidays as early as 1874. Later, perhaps in part because women were believed to suffer disproportionately from "neurasthenia," a disorder of the central nervous system caused by the new fast-paced but physically sedentary work environment, the federal government's standards for the Employment of Women (Juvenile Protective Association of Chicago, 1918) stated that "The Saturday half-holiday should be considered an absolute essential for women under all conditions" (p. 3).

In 1887, 40 years after Sawyer first proposed a half-holiday, and exactly 240 years after the Puritan-led English Parliament first proposed designated days of recreation, New York State passed a law recognizing every Saturday afternoon as a legal holiday (Laws of the State of New York, 1887). Under pressure from unhappy financiers and employers, the state senate, which had previously approved the bill unanimously, sent the governor a bill less than a year later proposing to repeal the legislation, and to limit the half-holiday to summers only. Labor unions protested, calling the Saturday half-holiday "the greatest boon ever bestowed on workingmen" (Stevens, 1912, p. 524). Governor David Hill also protested. Strictly speaking, he pointed out the law affected only banks and public offices. "There is otherwise no compulsion anywhere. The law may be regarded as simply declaratory of the public desire that the people should observe the day, but it provides no penalties for its violation" (*Public papers of David B. Hill, governor, 1888,* 2008, p. 67). In defending the legislation, Hill also invoked the argument from Sabbath observance:

> Recreation is desirable as well as rest and religious worship. If Sunday is the only day upon which recreation is possible to a large portion of our population, it will of necessity be used by them for that purpose. Our American Sunday will be better observed by setting apart the whole or a portion of every Saturday for the recreation and amusement which is now being crowded into Sunday. (p. 67)

The first Saturday holiday legislation in America was thus grounded in part on "civil Sabbatarianism," the view that Sabbath observance was a public good and not merely a matter of private religiosity.

Although the New York law was "declaratory of public desire" rather than compulsory, the public desire was great indeed. Support for the Saturday half-holiday was widespread, and included Catholics as well as Protestants, and liberals as well as conservatives. The practice spread throughout the state and the country, and in 1892 Congress passed a similar half-holiday law pertaining to the District of Columbia ("An Act Making Saturday a half holiday"). The earliest and most vocal advocates of the movement, however, had been those opposed to Sunday recreation. From Sawyer to Edwards, and from the Young Ladies Christian Association to the New York Sabbath Committee, nineteenth-century Sabbatarians' advocacy for the Saturday half-holiday was not a reluctant accommodation to modernity but an innovation born out of the old, Puritan distinction between rest and recreation. As one historian (Whitaker, 1973) wrote of the British context, "advocates of the claims of Sunday as a day apart were in the forefront of the movement for greater opportunities for recreation on the week-day" (p. 44).

The Five-Day Week, 1900–1940

As a result of agitation by organized labor, combined with the growing conviction among Progressive reformers and enlightened business leaders that shorter hours would continue facilitating increased productivity, working hours continued to decrease between 1900 and 1920. Although data on average working hours are "treacherous abstractions that disguise enormous differences between regions and industries" (Rodgers, 1978, p. 106), the data suggest that between 1905 and 1920 nonagricultural work decreased from 57.2 to 50.6 hours. In manufacturing, during the same period, the workweek decreased from 54.5 hours to 48.1 hours. The first two decades of the twentieth century were thus the "most productive period of shorter hours agitation in United States history" (Roediger & Foner, 1989, p. 177).

The five-day week and two-day weekend were thus in part byproducts of shorter hours. Labor leaders, however, were generally indifferent to how those hours were organized, and in any case were not the earliest advocates of the five-day week. As with the half-holiday, advocacy for the five-and-two rhythm was grounded on a distinction between rest and recreation, and promoted primarily by those with religious interests. This time, however, the impetus came from Jews rather than Christians.

The movement for the five-day week picked up in the 1920s in New York City, especially in the garment industry. The Amalgamated Clothing Workers of America resolved to pursue the five-day week in 1920, and unions began calling strikes between 1920 and 1927 (Hunnicutt, 1988, p. 71). This was not a coincidence. At the time, one in three city residents, and an even higher percentage of garment industry workers, was Jewish. Indeed, the earliest champion of the five-day week was Rabbi Bernard Drachman, president of the Orthodox Jewish Sabbath Alliance.

Drachman advocated for the five-day week as early as 1910, no less than sixteen years before the American Federation of Labor (AFL) took up the cause (Hunnicutt, 1979). His rationale was simple. When it came to Sabbath-keeping, Jews in America faced a dilemma. They desired to observe the Sabbath on Saturday but lived in a nation with deeply Protestant rhythms and laws. Although some Reform Jews adopted Sunday as their Sabbath for practical reasons, Orthodox Jews did not. The problem was not just that Orthodox Jews sought Saturday off from work, but they also sought the freedom to open their shops and return to work on Sunday – an approach that ran into strong resistance from Protestants. Drachman articulated the five-day week as a way through this impasse. Realizing the "practical difficulties" of extending different communities of faith the liberty to rest and worship on different days of the week, Drachman (1915/1979) said:

> I wish to put before you a proposal, based upon a practical consideration of the question. . . : the proposal of a weekly Holy day and Holiday, that is to say that there should be two days of rest weekly. This solution of the problem would, I believe, cope with all the difficulties, which are so keenly felt by all those interested in the question of Sabbath observance. (p. 223)

Although his proposal for two full days off from work was innovative, Drachman's distinction between holy day and holiday was essentially the same as that made by Protestant Sabbatarians before him.

By the 1920s, supporters of the five-day week included organized labor; Orthodox, Reform, and Conservative rabbis; Seventh Day Adventists, who also wished to worship on Saturday; Catholics, who had less attachment to the work ethic than most Protestants, as well as stronger sympathies for ethnic immigrants and the working class; and even a few business leaders, most notably Henry Ford. Curiously, Protestant Sabbatarians – those who led the charge for the Saturday half-holiday – seemed ambivalent. The New York Sabbath Committee (1915), though it published Drachman's (1915) proposal for the five-day week both in its bulletin and as an offprint, prefaced the article with three questions:

> First, since neither the Divine law nor human necessity requires more than one weekly rest day, would not two be resisted as excessive? second, since it is difficult to protect one, how could we hope to protect two? third, what kind of a Sabbath would either have, while the other enjoyed a hilarious holiday? (p. 8)

Other explanations for Protestant ambivalence to the five-day week are also possible. Sabbatarianism was on the decline in the early twentieth century, in part because it was a victim of its own success. In the nineteenth century, Sabbatarians forged successful alliances with workers because they shared a common interest in abolishing Sunday work. Although Sabbatarians' interest in Sunday as *Sabbath rest* was narrower than labor's interest in Sunday as *rest and recreation*, political expediency united them in the cause of the civil Sabbath. Opposition to Sunday labor, however, increased the possible uses of Sunday leisure, and once Sunday leisure largely was secured, the interests of workers and reformers diverged. Taking Chicago as an example, whereas the Chicago Sabbatarian Association had partnered with labor unions in the 1880s to oppose Sunday trains, the Association alienated workers by opposing Sunday opening of the Columbian Exposition in 1893, which featured the world's first Ferris wheel among other amusements (McCrossen, 2000; Mirola, 1999). In response to the argument that one person's Sunday amusement meant another's Sunday labor, the AFL and Knights of Labor responded that Sunday labor was not itself a problem, so long as all workers received at least one day off per week. Simply put, workers who once supported blue laws now opposed them. By the 1920s, Protestant Sabbatarians were almost certainly ambivalent about the five-day week in part because the movement's most vocal advocates – Jews, Adventists, and organized labor – tended also to be the most vocal critics of blue laws.

Arguably, Sabbatarians were victims of their own success in a deeper sense as well. Not only did Sabbatarian opposition to Sunday labor open the door to Sunday leisure, but the commercial amusement revolution in turn sanctioned pleasure seeking, which most Sabbatarians despised even more than Sunday labor. For most of the nineteenth century, Sabbatarianism thrived in part because it fit with the Victorian ethos: it "symbolized the injunctions to duty and self-discipline, the obligations of careful, watchful control of self and time that were at the heart of the Protestant Reformation" (Rodgers, 1978, p. 107). By the end of the century, however, the gospel of work competed with the "gospel of play" (p. 108), the "gospel of recreation" (Spencer, 1883) the "gospel of relaxation" (James, 1899) and the "gospel of consumption" (Hunnicutt, 1988). As scarcity gave way to abundance, economist Simon Patten (1907–1968) argued in his bestseller that self-discipline and self-denial must give way to an economy based upon consumption and the pursuit of pleasure. Cultural historians describe this transformation of sensibilities as a transition not only from production to consumption, but also from providence to progress (Lasch, 1991), character to personality (Susman, 1979), and salvation to self-realization (Lears, 1983). Whereas the older idea of providence suggested "moral wisdom lay in the limitation rather than in the multiplication of needs and desires," Lasch (1991) wrote, "The modern conception of progress depends on a positive assessment of the proliferation of wants" (p. 45). Needless to say, such cultural developments were anathema to religious moralists for whom work and productivity remained the core of the moral life.

As Sabbatarians ambivalent about the five-day week appear to have sensed, the gospel of consumption posed a threat to the Victorian values they espoused. Take, for example, the role of Ford Motor Company, which gave the five-day week a tremendous boost by transitioning workers to a five-day schedule in 1926. Ostensibly, the new policy was a boon to Sabbath observance. "The five-day week," said Ford ("Ford Adjusting Pay to Five-Day Week," 1926):

> provides the opportunity for physical recreation on the sixth day and leaves the seventh day free for moral and religious observation. It helps restore

the Sabbath to its former high place. . . . The five-day week by giving people the sixth day for physical recreation and the seventh for religious observance will go far toward bringing Christianity nearer to the people. (p. 24)

In contrast to most Sabbatarians, however, Ford had little fear of the new leisure or of affluence. Whereas to Drachman and other leading Jewish Sabbatarians, the weekly holiday was for *culture*, to Ford it was for *consumption*. "This is not philanthropy," a company spokesperson said of the new policy ("Ford Raises Pay of Men to Meet the 5-Day Week," 1926). "It is simply good business. More leisure gives more people more time to spend on automobiles, and the more leisure there is to spend in riding the more cars will be needed in which to ride" (p. 1). Whereas Drachman's ideal of a weekly holiday for culture attempted to reinforce Sabbatarian sensibilities regarding self-denial and self-improvement, Ford's ethic of consumption competed with them. And in practice, the democratization of motorcar excursions meant that Sunday excursions increasingly competed with Sunday worship. Ford may have been the first person to refer to Saturday and Sunday as a "two day holiday" (as quoted in Crowther, 1926, n.p.), a formulation that would have been anathema to Christian and Jewish Sabbatarians alike.

Through the 1920s, the fate of the five-day movement remained uncertain. The trend toward shorter hours slowed, and resistance to the idea among industrialists remained. As late as 1929, less than 3 percent of workers in manufacturing enjoyed the five-day week (National Industrial Conference Board, 1929). In the 1930s, however, the Depression and the New Deal accomplished what the religious-labor coalition alone could not. Up against overproduction and unemployment, industrialists increasingly saw the logic of, or at least lost the ability to resist, a shorter workweek. When the Fair Labor and Standards Act (FLSA) capped the workweek for those involved in interstate commerce at 40 hours beginning in 1940, the act was largely symbolic. Not only did the act not apply to most workers, but given that average weekly hours had already fallen to below 35 (Hunnicutt, 1988, p. 1), the act was largely ratifying a change that had already come to pass. Nevertheless, the legislation gave significant symbolic sanction to the 40-hour week and, indirectly, to the five-day week. Despite its limited scope, we might say that the FLSA, like the Saturday half-holiday law, was "declaratory of public desire." Indeed, scholars and pundits already had begun pondering the "problem of leisure" (Keynes, 1963; Lippmann, 1930).

Conclusion

Conventional wisdom suggests that Sabbatarians failed in their goal to secure a quiet and noncommercial Sunday for rest and worship. Moreover, many histories of recreation in America unfold according to a narrative by which workers and immigrants gradually secured the right to recreate from middle class Protestant reformers who attempted to restrict worker choices and exercise "social control" over workers' free time.[3] In one influential account, America learned to play precisely by outgrowing the old "puritanic prejudice" against play, a process that rendered Sabbatarianism "inevitably foredoomed" (Dulles, 1965, pp. 101, 208).

To be sure, workers and Protestant Sabbatarians often clashed over Sunday. When it came to Saturday, however, there was much more consensus. In fact, though organized labor led the movement for shorter hours in both the nineteenth and twentieth centuries, clergy and lay religious leaders led the movement for clustering hours off on Saturday. Following the Puritans, who were the earliest advocates of designated days of recreation, nineteenth-century Protestant Sabbatarians and twentieth-century Jewish Sabbatarians were the earliest advocates of the Saturday half- and full-holiday, respectively. Simply put, it took the interests of religion to translate shorter hours into fewer days (Roediger & Foner, 1989, p. 237). That Sabbatarians led the way to successfully securing a weekly holiday, resulting in what we now know as the modern weekend, challenges received notions regarding the relationship of recreation and religion, as well as our usual juxtaposition of religious reformers as either reactionary or progressive, theocratic or socialist.

In maintaining a distinction between rest and recreation, Sabbatarians became visionary innovators of modern leisure time. What they did not envision, however, is the extent to which their advocacy of a weekly holiday would defeat their primary purpose of protecting a weekly holy day. In opening up time that leisure entrepreneurs filled with commercial entertainments, Sabbatarians unwittingly contributed to commercialization and even consumerism – the proliferation of wants that they so abhorred. Daniel Rodgers (1978) argued that the work ethic, by contributing to industrialization, which in turn devoured middle-class assumptions about the moral preeminence of work, contained the seeds of its own destruction. So too with Sabbatarianism; Saturday as a weekly holi-

---

3   The critical literature on the social control thesis is substantial (Banner, 1973; Jones, 1977; Kohl, 1985; Muraskin, 1976). Most cultural historians now take cultural transmission to be a two-way process rather than a "trickle-down" process.

day "destabilized" Sunday as a designated day of rest (McCrossen, 2000, p. 150). That Sabbatarianism as an organized movement finally fizzled at the same time the weekend arrived further suggests that Sabbatarians were victims of their own success.

Although Sabbatarians could not have foreseen that a weekly holiday would cannibalize the weekly holy day they treasured, the recent resurgence of interest in the Sabbath suggests that they may have been on to something in their distinction between rest and recreation. At issue in the debate is nothing less than the nature of freedom. To Sabbatarians, the freedom to recreate noisily on any day of the week results in less, not more, of other cultural goods, such as the ability to rest, worship, and enjoy quiet contemplation. In this view, constraints enable freedom. Judith Shulevitz ("Bring Back the Sabbath," 2003), a Jewish writer with progressive sensibilities, agrees with the Puritans on this matter. To Shulevitz, the Sabbath stands athwart the treadmill of producing and consuming, including most of our recreational and leisure activities, which fail "to reproduce the benefits of the Sabbath." Observing that even our weekends are hectic and therefore stressful, another secular Jew (Kaiser, 2010) asks, "Does society need a mandatory time-out?" And in yet another lament over the ways in which active and commercial recreation often mitigate against true leisure, Rybczynski (1991) provocatively asks: "have we become enslaved by the weekend?" (p. 17). If recent trends are any indication, Sabbatarians may yet serve as a resource for those concerned with consumer capitalism's colonization of time and the discontents of ceaseless striving.

References

An Act Making Saturday a Half Holiday for Banking and Trust Company Purposes in the District of Columbia, 52nd Cong., 2nd Sess. United States Statutes at Large (1892).

Banner, L.W. (1973). Religious benevolence as social control: A critique of an interpretation. *Journal of American History, 60*, 23–41.

Beecher, L. (1835). *A plea for the West.* Cincinnati, OH: Truman & Smith.

Bellows, H.W. (1857). *The relation of public amusements to public morality: Especially of the theatre to the highest interests of humanity.* New York: C.S. Francis.

Birley, D. (1993). *Sport and the making of Britain.* Manchester, UK: Manchester University Press.

Bourne, H. (1725). *Antiquitates vulgares; or, the antiquities of the common people.* Newcastle, UK: J. White.

Bownd, N. (1606). *The true doctrine of the Sabbath*. London: Felix Kingston.

Burke, P. (1978). *Popular culture in early modern Europe*. New York: Harper & Row.

Chamlee, R.Z., Jr. (1968). The Sabbath crusade: 1810–1920. (Unpublished doctoral dissertation). George Washington University, Washington, DC.

Cox, R. (1865). *The literature of the Sabbath question*. Edinburgh, UK: Neill.

Crafts, W.F. (1894). *The Sabbath for man* (7th ed.). Baltimore, MD: Authors' Union.

Cressy, D. (1989). *Bonfires and bells: National memory and the Protestant calendar in Elizabethan and Stuart England*. London: Weidenfeld & Nicolson.

Crowther, S. (1926, October). Henry Ford: Why I favor five days' work with six days' pay. *World's Work*, 613–616. Retrieved on November 16, 2015 from: https://en.wikisource.org/wiki/HENRY_FORD:_Why_I_Favor_Five_Days%27_Work_With_Six_Days%27_Pay .

Daniels, B.C. (1995). *Puritans at play: Leisure and recreation in colonial America*. New York: St. Martin's Press.

De Vries, J. (2008). *The industrious revolution: Consumer behavior and the household economy, 1650 to the present*. Cambridge: Cambridge University Press.

Drachman, B. (1915). A weekly holy day and holiday. *The Bulletin of the New York Sabbath Committee* 2(2), 8–10.

Drachman, B. (1915/1979). The Jewish Sabbath question. An Appendix (pp. 216–225) in B.J. Hunnicutt. (1979). The Jewish Sabbath movement in the early twentieth century. *American Jewish History* 69(2), 196–225.

Dulles, F.R. (1965). *A history of recreation: America learns to play* (2nd ed.). Englewood Cliffs, NJ: Prentice-Hall.

Edwards, J. (1848). *The proper mode of keeping the Sabbath: Being the fourth number of the Sabbath manual*. New York: American Tract Society.

Ford adjusting pay to five-day week. (1926, November 14). *New York Times*.

Ford raises pay of men to meet the 5-day week. (1926, November 15). *The Washington Post*.

Fuller, W.E. (2003). *Morality and the mail in nineteenth-century America*. Urbana, IL: University of Illinois Press.

Gardiner, S.R. (1901). *Oliver Cromwell*. London: Longmans, Green.

Greenham, R. (1592). *A treatise of the Sabbath*. London: n.p.

Gutman, H.G. (1976). *Work, culture, and society in industrializing America: Essays in American working-class and social history*. New York: Knopf.

Hale, E.E. (1900). Public amusement for poor and rich. *The works of Edward Everett Hale* (pp. 321–354). Boston: Little, Brown.

Hall, D.D. (1989). *Worlds of wonder, days of judgment*. New York: Alfred A. Knopf.

Handy, R.T. (1971). *A Christian America: Protestant hopes and historical realities*. New York: Oxford University Press.

Hardy, S. (1982). *How Boston played: Sport, recreation, and community, 1865–*

1915. Boston: Northeastern University Press.
Hill, C. (1967). *Society and Puritanism in pre-revolutionary England* (2nd ed.). New York: Schocken.
Hunnicutt, B.K. (1979). The Jewish Sabbath movement in the early twentieth century. *American Jewish History* 69(2), 196–225.
Hunnicutt, B.K. (1988). *Work without end: Abandoning shorter hours for the right to work*. Philadelphia, PA: Temple University Press.
James, W. (1899, April). The gospel of relaxation. *Scribner's* 25.
John, R.R. (1995). *Spreading the news: The American postal system from Franklin to Morse*. Cambridge, MA: Harvard University Press.
Jones, G.S. (1977). Class expression versus social control? A critique of recent trends in the social history of 'leisure'. *History Workshop* 4, 163–170.
Juvenile Protective Association of Chicago. (1918). *The Saturday half-holiday*. Chicago: Author. Retrieved on January 25, 2010 from http://galenet.galegroup.com/
Kaiser, M. (2010, March 30). The case for the Sabbath, even if you're not religious. *The Atlantic*, Retrieved on January 25, 2010 from http://www.theatlantic.com/culture/archive/2010/03/the-case-for-the-Sabbath-even-if-youre-not-religious/38187/
Keynes, J.M. (1963). Economic possibilities for our grandchildren. *Essays in persuasion* (pp. 358–373). New York: Norton.
Kohl, L.F. (1985). The concept of social control and the history of Jacksonian America. *Journal of the Early Republic* 5(1), 21–34.
Kramnick, I., & Moore, R.L. (1996). *The godless constitution: The case against religious correctness*. New York: Norton.
Lasch, C. (1991). *The true and only heaven: Progress and its critics*. New York: Norton.
Laws of the State of New York, 1887 (1887). Albany, NY: Banks & Brothers.
Lears, T.J.J. (1983). From salvation to self-realization: Advertising and the therapeutic roots of the consumer culture, 1880–1930. In R. W. Fox, & T. J. J. Lears (Eds.), *The culture of consumption: Critical essays in American history, 1880–1980* (pp. 1–38). New York: Pantheon.
Lippmann, W. (1930, April). Free time and extra money. *Woman's Home Companion* 57, 31–32.
McCrossen, A. (1999). "Sabbatarianism in nineteenth-century America". In D. K. Adams, & C. A. van Minnen (Eds.), *Religious and secular reform in America* (pp. 133–158). New York: New York University Press.
McCrossen, A. (2000). *Holy day, holiday: The American Sunday*. Ithaca, NY: Cornell University Press.
Meacham, J. (2007, April 9). God debate: Sam Harris vs. Rick Warren. *Newsweek* 149(15), 58–63.
Mirola, W.A. (1999). Shorter hours and the Protestant Sabbath: Religious framing and movement alliances in late-nineteenth-century Chicago. *Social Science History* 23(3), 395–433.

Muraskin, W.A. (1976). The social control theory in American history: A critique. *Journal of Social History* 9(4), 559–569.

National Industrial Conference Board. (1929). *The five-day week in manufacturing industries.* New York: Author.

New York Sabbath Committee. (1881). *Sunday in the United States.* New York: Author.

New York Sabbath Committee. (1915). Preface to "A weekly holy day and holiday." *The Bulletin of the New York Sabbath Committee* 2(2), 8.

Patten, S. (1907/1968). *The new basis of civilization.* Cambridge, MA: Harvard University Press.

Public papers of David B. Hill, governor, 1888 (2008). Albany, NY: BiblioBazaar.

Reid, D.A. (1976). The decline of Saint Monday, 1766–1876. *Past and Present* 71(1), 76–101.

Reid, D.A. (1996). Weddings, weekdays, work and leisure in urban England 1791–1911: The decline of Saint Monday revisited. *Past and Present* 153(1), 135–163.

Rodgers, D.T. (1978). *The work ethic in industrial America, 1850–1920.* Chicago: University of Chicago Press.

Roediger, D.R., & Foner, P. S. (1989). *Our own time: A history of American labor and the working day.* New York: Greenwood Press.

Rohrer, J.R. (1987). Sunday mails and the church-state theme in Jacksonian America. *Journal of the Early Republic* 7(1), 53–74.

Rosenzweig, R. (1979). Middle–class parks and working–class play: The struggle over recreational space in Worcester, Massachusetts, 1870–1910. *Radical History Review* 21, 31-48.

Rybczynski, W. (1991). *Waiting for the weekend.* New York: Penguin Books.

A Saturday half–holiday. (1874, August 11). *New York Times.*

Sawyer, F.W. (1847). *A plea for amusements.* New York: D. Appleton.

Scholes, P.A. (1934). *The Puritans and music in England and New England: A contribution to the cultural history of two nations.* London: Oxford University Press.

Shulevitz, J. (2003, March 24). Bring back the Sabbath. *New York Times Magazine,* Retrieved on January 25, 2012 from http://www.nytimes.com/2003/03/02/magazine/bring-back-the-Sabbath.html

Solberg, W.U. (1977). *Redeem the time: The Puritan Sabbath in early America.* Cambridge, MA: Harvard University Press.

Spencer, H. (1883). The gospel of recreation. *The Popular Science Monthly* 22, 354–359.

Stevens, G.A. (1912). Public holidays for working people. In New York State Department of Labor, Bureau of Labor Statistics (Ed.), *New York Typographical Union no. 6: Study of a modern trade union and its predecessors* (pp. 522–526). Albany, NY: J.B. Lyon.

Struna, N.L. (1977). Puritans and sport: The irretrievable tide of change. *Journal of Sport History* 4(1), 1–21.

Struna, N.L. (1996). *People of prowess: Sport, leisure, and labor in early Anglo-America.* Urbana, IL: University of Illinois Press.

Stubbs, P. (1583). *The anatomie of abuses.* London: Richard Jones.

Susman, W.I. (1979). 'Personality' and the twentieth century culture. In J. Higham, & P. K. Conkin (Eds.), *New directions in American intellectual history* (pp. 212–226). Baltimore, MD: Johns Hopkins University Press.

Thomas, K. (1964). Work and leisure in pre-industrial society. *Past and Present* 29(1), 50–66.

Thompson, E.P. (1967). Time, work-discipline, and industrial capitalism. *Past and Present* 38(1), 56–97.

Wagner, H. (1979). Puritan attitudes towards recreation in early seventeenth-century New England: With particular consideration of physical recreation. (Unpublished doctoral dissertation). University of Saarlandes, Saarbrücken, Germany.

Whitaker, W.B. (1933). *Sunday in Tudor and Stuart times.* London: Houghton.

Whitaker, W.B. (1973). *Victorian and Edwardian shopworkers: The struggle to obtain better conditions and a half-holiday.* Totowa, NJ: Rowman & Littlefield.

White, F. (1635). *A treatise of the Sabbath-day.* London: Richard Badger.

Chapter 3

HOLISTIC LEISURE: A PARADIGM FOR LEISURE IN CHRISTIAN PERSPECTIVE

Paul Heintzman

> Imagine... the bewilderment a naive researcher suffers when discovering that leisure may be free time, freedom, an activity, a state of mind, or a license of some sort. Grasping the meaning of leisure is sufficiently frustrating that our innocent colleague might prudently move onto a seemingly simpler concept.... (Sylvester, 1990, p. 292)

Much time is spent in leisure sciences and leisure studies trying to define leisure. Theorists puzzle over the meaning of leisure, but no single conceptualization emerges for it or for the related terms of recreation and play. Definitions of leisure abound. Traditional definitions of leisure include: (1) leisure as free time, (2) leisure as a function of social class, (3) leisure as anti-utilitarian activity, (4) leisure as nonwork activity, (5) the classical view of leisure as a condition of mind or state of being, and (6) the holistic view of leisure (Murphy, 1974). Within this context, the search for meaning becomes a daunting task.

In this paper, I will develop, through a three-stage process, a Christian conceptualization of leisure arising from a synthesis of biblical, historical, and contemporary sources. First, six traditional concepts of leisure will be critiqued from a Christian perspective based on biblical material. Second, I will argue that the biblical idea of a rhythm in life supports the view of leisure as nonwork time or activity that refreshes and restores, which has been the dominant view of leisure within Protestantism. Meanwhile, the concept of rest, reflective of the quality of life offered in Jesus Christ, provides support for what has historically been called the classical state of being view of leisure that originated in Greek society but was adapted by Augustine, Aquinas, and medieval monastics. Third, I will argue that the classical and Protestant views of leisure are not

---

Revised version of paper presented at the 1994 conference.

mutually exclusive but together provide a comprehensive, holistic view of leisure. Finally, this holistic view of leisure will be related to patterns of work in contemporary society.

A Critique of the Concepts of Leisure

The Free Time Concept of Leisure

The discretionary or free time approach to conceptualizing leisure simply reduces leisure to a quantity of time. To conceive of leisure as free time is both limiting and confusing. While leisure is associated with freedom, freedom cannot be broken up into blocks of time. Gordon Dahl (1972) noted that "Free time is an alien and spurious notion to any Christian who reflects theologically upon the details and dynamics of his life" (p. 61). All of a Christian's time is free, since life is a free gift, given by God and intended to be freely accepted by the people of God. Therefore, we cannot earn free time, for all of our time is freely given apart from any work on our part. At the same time, none of our time is free, for it all comes under the lordship of Christ, whether we are working or engaged in recreation. Free time implies that when a person is not working or otherwise obligated, one may do whatever one desires. But a Christian is not free to do anything one desires during nonwork hours, for all of one's time is to be offered to God. In his discussion of Christian freedom, Luther characterized the Christian as always living simultaneously in total freedom and total responsibility (Dahl, 1972). A person cannot break up one's life into distinct periods, some of which are regarded as free and others that are not. Therefore, for the Christian, the notion of free time is not very helpful.

At least three problems arise from the attempt to define leisure as free time. First, the equation of leisure with free time is at the same time too broad and too narrow. It is too broad if it refers to all the time except for that time in which we are engaged in paid employment. Much of the time we spend away from our jobs is still devoted to work-related activities such as household maintenance. Yet the notion of free time is too narrow if it implies that leisure is only the residual time left over after one has fulfilled all the obligations that contemporary life demands of a person. If this concept is brought to its logical conclusion, there would be almost no leisure. For if one completed all the expected role responsibilities of every area of one's life, the residual time would be minimal. Many people today are so busy that they simply discover they have no such thing as free time.

The second problem of defining leisure entirely in terms of time is that it does not give any normative guidance for leisure. While the notion of free time is helpful in presenting sociological data on the uses of time, it implies nothing about the moral direction of leisure. The concept of free time runs counter to responsible involvement in our interdependent society. Free time assumes that a person's work is one's only real responsibility and implies that when a person is not working, one can spend one's time doing anything one desires to do. However, this is neither realistic nor desirable in our increasingly complex and interdependent society. Sociologist Bennett Berger (1963) maintained that sociology "has taught us that no time is free of normative constraints . . ." (p. 29); while freedom and non-obligation are associated with leisure, discretionary time cannot be removed from the context of responsibility to God for our use of time. All time and activities are to be brought under God's sovereignty.

Third, to conceptualize leisure entirely in terms of time misses so much of the qualitative dimension of leisure – the spiritual attitude of rest, joy, freedom, and the rejoicing in God and the gift of his creation inculcated by the Sabbath, along with the quality of life characterized by rest, peace, abundant life, and freedom available to us in Jesus Christ as described in Scripture (Heintzman, 2006). Not everything one does in one's discretionary time can be claimed to be leisure. Nevertheless, discretionary time or quantitative leisure may be used to develop and nurture the qualitative dimension of leisure. Nelvin Vos (1979) wrote:

> Free time is only potentially a time of experiencing leisure. Rather than emphasizing time itself, we should focus on the person. Leisure depends not only on available time, but also on the person's freedom to experience all time *qualitatively* rather than *quantitatively*. Leisure is not a matter so much of time, free or otherwise, but rather is a quality of living, a way of looking at life. (pp. 14–15)

The time remaining after work and other obligations can be called discretionary time, but not leisure. Discretionary time may be used in a variety of ways: it may remain as empty idleness; be filled with unproductive activities or the consumption of material goods; or spent in the cultivation and nurture of the qualitative dimension of leisure. Therefore free time is only potential leisure.

In summary, free time is an element of leisure, but leisure should not be limited to segments of time. Yet freedom from work and other obligations is definitely an essential dimension of leisure. At one level, the Sabbath suggests that we need periods of time each week that are free from both work and all other work-related activities (Heintzman,

2006). Exodus 34:21a reads "Six days you shall labor, but on the seventh day you shall rest." Both the Mosaic legislation and the prophets stressed that no work is to be done on the Sabbath. So the Sabbath inculcated that Israel's life, in addition to work, also possessed the element of free time. At this level the Sabbath was a quantity of time in which no work was performed. Likewise, leisure, in a quantitative sense, is a period of time in which no work is performed. Yet the Sabbath was more than a quantity of time in which no work was to be performed. The Old Testament taught that the Sabbath was to be observed not only by a cessation from work but by a rest that was of the nature of worship. So while there is the necessity to have periods of time free from work and work-related activities in our lives this is not the totality of leisure.

Leisure as a Function of Social Class

In *The Theory of the Leisure Class,* Thorstein Veblen (1912) illustrated how the wealthy ruling classes, throughout history, have been identified by their possession and use of leisure. Veblen was critical of the idle rich who exploited and lived on the toil of others while totally engaging themselves in a life of conspicuous consumption. From his analysis arose the conceptualization of a leisure class.

While the notion of a leisure class may be useful in a descriptive analysis of the sociological structure of a society, it cannot be normative in any Christian understanding of leisure. The implication of the humanitarian motive for the observance of the Sabbath in Exodus 23:12 (cf. Deut. 5:14), which teaches that the domestic slave and alien are also to rest on the Sabbath, is that all members of society are entitled to a break from work, and therefore leisure in at least a quantitative sense. The biblical view does not lend support to the social structuring of society such as in the Greece of Aristotle's day, when slaves made it possible for a few to have a life of leisure, nor does it support a leisure class who live a life of conspicuous consumption at the expense of the working class as is described by Veblen (1912).

With the diffusion of culture, the spread of wealth, the greater influence of the mass media, greater mobility, and a reduction of working hours, there has been a democratization of the leisure class in modern society. Leisure, as associated with the concept of a leisure class, has become accessible to all. "Unfortunately," observed Leonard Doohan (1981), "for many, the increase in non-working hours has led to a fruitless mimicking of a previous leisured class" (p. 162). This mimicking is often driven by the desire to "keep up with the Joneses."

A wide variety of entertainments, sports, weekend excursions, prepackaged holidays, and vacations are available to most North Americans for consumption. These pursuits often necessitate consumer goods – recreational vehicles, cottages, specialty clothes, DVD players, etc. For many, leisure does not go beyond this consumption of nonwork related possessions and entertainments. This pursuit of leisure through the consumption of material goods, which is very prevalent in our society, confuses the real meaning and true satisfaction of leisure with the purchasing of consumer goods. People who fill their free time with consumption activities do not understand or truly experience leisure.

The pursuit of leisure through the consumption of material goods in today's society is not that different than the acquisition of material possessions described in the second chapter of Ecclesiastes. The writer amassed houses, vineyards, gardens, parks, fruit trees, reservoirs, slaves, herds, flocks, silver, gold, treasures, singers, and a harem. Yet, the writer concluded in 2:11: ". . . when I surveyed all that my hands had done and what I had toiled to achieve, everything was meaningless, a chasing after the wind; nothing was gained under the sun." It is the same today, as nothing is gained by an accumulation of consumption goods. Leisure, if defined in terms of conspicuous consumption, does not lead to any ultimate satisfaction or meaning in life.

The Anti-Utilitarian Concept of Leisure

The anti-utilitarian concept of leisure is characterized by "doing your own thing," creative self-development and self-expression, self-actualization, and the enjoyment of the natural existences and pleasures of life. One positive feature of this concept of leisure – often characteristic of the counterculture – is that it bestows intrinsic value on leisure instead of making it subservient to work. It rejects the idea that every activity has to be utilitarian or work-oriented. It emphasizes our "being" over our "doing" in its belief that each person is free and unique, and that one's worth is not determined by one's role in the economic system of production and consumption. Thus it reacts against the activity orientation of the traditional work ethic.

From a Christian perspective, a positive aspect of the "doing your own thing" ethic is, as Dahl (1972) wrote, "its clear affirmation of personal dignity and freedom in the face of all the depersonalizing forces of contemporary culture – including aspects of bureaucracy, technology, and mass-media" (p. 80). Another positive aspect of this concept of leisure is its emphasis on the enjoyment of the natural existences and pleasures of life. The book of Ecclesiastes teaches that we are to enjoy all the gifts of God's good creation (2:24–26, 3:12–13, 3:22, 5:17–19, 7:14, 8:15, 9:7–9, 11:9–12:1). However, Christians have far too often ignored the gifts of this life in their overemphasis upon the other worldly dimensions of salvation.

However, there are at least three problems with the anti-utilitarian concept of leisure as it is generally conceived and practiced. First, in practice, due to humanity's sinful nature, the enjoyment of the natural existences and pleasures of life often turns into a hedonistic pleasure-seeking, a gratification of fleshly desires. Ecclesiastes 4 teaches that pleasure seeking, both simple and sophisticated, shares in the meaninglessness of all earthly phenomena experienced within the earthly horizon unless there is recognition of the divine. Qoheleth concludes: "I said to myself, 'Come now, I will test you with pleasure to find out what is good.' But that also proved to be meaningless" (Eccles. 2:1). As Michael Eaton (1983) pointed out, it is not the morality of pleasure-seeking that is under consideration here, but rather, the secular person is shown the failure of a hedonistic and narcissistic lifestyle on its own premises. Instead, Ecclesiastes teaches that life is to be enjoyed as a gift from God.

The second problem is the morality, or lack thereof, associated with anti-utilitarian leisure. In today's society, many of the values and morals of the Christian faith have been rejected in favor of much more pragmatic and relativistic ones. Francis Bregha (1980) described the result of this trend as follows:

> More and more people are occupying their leisure with a bewildering variety of acts and deeds that leave their trace on their neighbours and communities. The leisure of one becomes sometimes offensive to another one – morally as well as otherwise. To preach the sanctity of self-fulfillment in an increasingly interdependent society does not solve anything, to hide behind the jargon of "enabling everyone to reach his/her full potential" leads us nowhere. . . . After all, my self-actualization could be your de-actualization, my self-fulfillment achieved at the cost of your emptiness. To view leisure as morally neutral or even as "good per se" denotes a naiveté that should have died out with Rousseau. (p. 30)

Therefore not only is "doing your own thing" not ultimately satisfying, but there is the possibility that it will harm one's fellow citizens.

Third, the self-discovery and self-development that is characteristic of this concept of leisure is usually carried out from a humanistic orientation that is not open to the divine. A humanistic approach to life is not enough to guarantee the fruits of leisure. "Rather the integral human development that results must naturally include the religious" dimension, or an openness to the divine (Doohan, 1981, p. 164). It is true that in the last few decades there has been an increasing openness to the religious element, especially among counterculture and new consciousness and new age groups, through the influence of Eastern traditions that encourage people to lose themselves in the all-pervading cosmic Being. Meditation according to the Eastern tradition – the long slow route to self-awareness – has become popular. There is some good in this, for there is a tendency in our society to be so busy in activity and doing that one is not in touch with oneself. However, it is not sufficient to get in touch with the deep inner self, for the inner self is itself the root of the problem. Only a radical change in one's innermost being, a change that only Jesus Christ can bring about, brings hope of a radical transformation of life.

True self-development occurs when a person is brought into relationship with Christ and is able to fully become the person one was created and intended to be. Dahl (1972) wrote:

> Leisure means freedom, but not . . . the kind of sweaty freedom that comes from the defiance of social mores, nor the teary freedom that accompanies abandoned commitments and broken relationships. Leisure is rather that sense of freedom which is realized when a person experiences more fully his uniqueness and worth as an individual and his acceptance and relationship as part of the world around him. A person finds leisure when he discovers who he is, what he can do with his life, and what an abundance of happy circumstances and relationships in which his life is cast. A Christian experiences leisure when he comes into full awareness of the freedom he has in Christ, . . . the freedom to be and become the new man after Christ's own splendid example. (pp. 70–71)

True leisure, in the sense of the possibility to fulfill one's potential and uniqueness, is only ultimately possible if one comes to Christ.

Leisure as Nonwork Activity

The activity concept views leisure as nonwork behavior or activity in which people engage during their free time. This activity quite often has a utilitarian purpose such as relaxation, entertainment, and personal development, and is frequently seen as being subservient to work either as a reward for past work or as an activity that refreshes one to go back to work.

This activity concept of leisure is closely associated with the idea of a rhythm to life. However, the opportunity to engage in leisure activities has traditionally been organized around work, the dominant and primary element in the rhythm. Thus the opportunity to engage in leisure activities is not only scheduled around work but is subservient to work and often serves work.

This concept of leisure has been the predominant one amongst Protestants and especially the Puritans. The Puritan ethic was the program of an active life. Work was the dominant activity in life. Yet the Puritans recognized the need for recreation in their lives, although it often had to be utilitarian: "anything that gave refreshment to the body or spirit" (Dennison, 1983, p. 80). "Seasonable merriment" was used to describe the recreation that was appropriate and that contributed to the main goal in life – devotion to a sovereign God through work. Since work was the dominant reality in life, the other dimensions in life were not seen as separate. Rather, "Puritanism was rooted in a view of life as a unified whole under the sovereignty of God" (Lee, 1964, p. 70). In this unified whole, there were periods of work and periods of seasonable merriment. In some respects, this rhythm to life in Puritanism reflects the biblical rhythm to life; periods of work interspersed with periods of nonwork on the Sabbath and during annual agricultural festivals.

Yet there are serious problems with the activity concept of leisure. Dahl (1972) pointed out that most people in today's society approach leisure with the residual traces of the Puritan and rationalist tradition. Not only is work made the center of their lives, but it is also the reference point for all other aspects of life. This tradition emphasizes that all time must be used to do something. We must be constantly active, on the go, busy. We are culturally conditioned that to be busy is a sign of a righteous or virtuous state. A Western person is characterized as a doer, being in perpetual motion, and always asking "What shall I do?" so that doing the right thing is more important than "being the right person." Spence (1973) wrote "'Do, Do, Do,' is our motto. 'Rush, Rush, Rush' – we revolve in a 'Rat Race.' Holy is the man who keeps busy." If leisure is restricted to activity as is suggested by this concept, then "how deadly exhaustive and surely meaningless it would soon become" (pp. 38–39). Robert Banks (1983) has enumerated the effects of this constant activity: the threat to physical and psychological health; the decline in social life, including the weakening of interpersonal relationships; the decline in political life; the erosion of thought and leisure; and the undermining of religious sensitivity and the subversion of spiritual life.

Another problem of this notion of leisure is that when leisure is subservient to work, it has no intrinsic value. If work is the center of life, then leisure cannot be truly appreciated; any form of non-activity is considered as idleness and suspect unless it can be justified in terms of work. There is no time for the enjoyment of the created world or much appreciation for contemplation unless its purpose is to purify the mind for more dedicated and disciplined work. Recreational activities reflect a work-orientation in that they usually are "designed to develop physical and mental skills that would be useful in work" (Dahl, 1972, p. 64).

A third problem is that when leisure is reduced to activity, the pursuit of leisure may become a continual quest for entertainment and amusement, for something to fill one's time. While entertainment may be beneficial, enjoyable, and refreshing, to narrow leisure to the pursuit of entertainment ignores a great deal of the qualitative dimension of leisure as suggested by the biblical material of Sabbath and rest. The idea that leisure is primarily activity used to fill or kill time contributes to disillusionment and despair, for it neglects the "being" dimension of our lives. "When our leisure," wrote Bernard Hahn (1985) "involves nothing but seeking entertainment, we soon forget who we are and why we are here" (p. 15). The appeal to creation theology in the Exodus account of the Sabbath commandment suggests that the Sabbath is a time set aside for humans to reflect on God and his purpose, a time to recognize that life is a gift from God and not just the result of human work. Therefore, to fill up our time with constant activity, amusement, and entertainment is to deny God. Leisure is not merely constructive activity, entertainment, or distraction.

The Classical View of Leisure

The classical view of leisure emerged in ancient Greece. *Schole*, which meant "leisure," was a state of being that implied freedom or the absence of the necessity of being occupied.

A crucial question for Christians to ask is: If we accept the classical conception of leisure, are we accepting Greek categories of thinking instead of biblical ones? In his book *The Christian at Play*, Robert Johnston (1983), although acknowledging that the theological task involves the consideration of traditional sources, quickly dismissed the classical Greek model of play [leisure] – and also the Protestant model – after only a brief one-page discussion of it, in favor of' the "Hebraic" model. Similarly, Leland Ryken (1987), in his book *Work and Leisure in Christian Perspective*, devoted only one page to the description of the Greek ideal of leisure, which he believes "remains a standard for excellence in leisure" (p. 78). But we cannot dismiss the classical view of leisure so quickly, for at least three reasons. First, as Joseph Pieper (1952) has pointed out, "the Christian and Western conception of the contemplative life is closely linked to the Aristotelian notion of leisure" (p. 21). Second, the concept of leisure originated in Greek society. If we want to do justice to the semantic background of leisure we cannot simply ignore the classical concept. While we may disagree with its content, we can take it, like John took the Greek work *logos* in the first chapter of his Gospel, or Paul took the statue to the unknown God in Acts 17, and fill it with Christian content. Indeed, this is what those of the medieval monastic period did (Leclerq, 1982). Third, Joseph Owens (1981) has illustrated how Aristotle's conception of leisure "does not offer us any detailed blueprint. It requires us to do our own thinking" (p. 723). The contemplative and intellectual life envisaged by Aristotle was left open for application and development down through the centuries. It has and can be embodied in different ways by different people such as Augustine's "contemplative life" (*otium*) that was a reflection and meditation upon God and God's truth; the *vita contemplative* of Aquinas that was centered in the beatific vision of God and oriented to the eternal (Owens); and the monastic life of leisure that anticipated eternal rest, as expressed in terms such as *otium* (leisure), *quies* (quiet), *vacatio* (freedom), and *sabbatum* (rest) (Leclerq, 1982). Unfortunately, many contemporary leisure scholars turn to Aristotle for guidance in their thinking about leisure; however, they completely ignore how the classical concept of leisure has been adapted by Christians throughout the centuries.

At this point it is helpful to discuss *Leisure: The Basis of Culture*, the work of the Catholic philosopher Joseph Pieper (1952), who not only sought to revive the classical concept of leisure in the last century but centered it in divine worship. Owens (1981) commented that Aristotle's concept is open to being developed in this direction. Pieper considers leisure to be the primary basis of any culture in the past, present, or future. For Pieper, culture is dependent on leisure for its very existence, and leisure in turn is only possible if it has a strong and vital link with divine worship:

> The soul of leisure, it can be said, lies in "celebration." Celebration is the point at which the three elements of leisure come to a focus: relaxation, effortlessness, and the superiority of "active leisure" to all functions. But if celebration is the core of leisure, then leisure can only be made possible and justifiable on the same basis as the celebration of a festival. *That basis is divine.* (p. 56)

Leisure implies celebration, and celebration is rooted in divine worship; worship is therefore considered to be the wellspring of leisure. I concur with Pieper. Our leisure must be God-centered and God-directed in order to guarantee the fruits of leisure. We can infer from the Sabbath as a sign of the covenant between God and humans as seen in Exodus 31:16 and 17 that leisure finds its deepest meaning and fullest potential within the context of a relationship to God (Heintzman, 2006).

Separated from divine worship leisure, according to Pieper (1952), becomes idleness and laziness:

> Idleness, so far from being synonymous with leisure, is more nearly the inner prerequisite which renders leisure impossible: it might be described as the utter absence of leisure, or the very opposite of leisure. Idleness and the incapacity for leisure correspond with one another. Leisure is the contrary of the both. (p. 40)

Pieper (1952) goes on to define leisure:

> Leisure, it must be clearly understood, is a mental and spiritual attitude – it is not simply the result of external factors, it is not the inevitable result of spare time, a holiday, a week-end or a vacation. It is, in the first place, an attitude of mind, a condition of the soul. (p. 40)

Although Pieper does not provide a biblical background to his concept of leisure, the mental and spiritual attitude of which he speaks is not all that different from a qualitative dimension of leisure developed from the biblical account: the spiritual attitude of rest, joy, freedom, and the rejoicing in God inculcated by the Sabbath, along with the quality of life characterized by rest, peace, abundant life, and freedom available to us in Jesus Christ (Heintzman, 2006).

Pieper (1952) continued:

> Leisure is a form of silence, of that silence which is the prerequisite of the apprehension of reality. . . . For leisure is a receptive attitude of mind, a contemplative attitude, and it is not only the occasion but also the capacity for steeping oneself in the world of creation. (p. 41)

This steeping of oneself in the world of creation is similar to the idea expressed by the appeal to creation theology as a motivation for Sabbath observance in Exodus 20. The Sabbath inculcates an attitude of rejoicing and celebrating the gifts of God's good creation. Similarly, in Ecclesiastes Qoheleth teaches the enjoyment of creation, God's gift to humanity. Likewise, leisure is that rejoicing and celebrating in, and enjoyment of, creation.

Thus leisure is characterized by a receptive and contemplative approach to life along with a celebrating and enjoying of creation that receives its vitality from divine worship, from a relationship with the God who has made himself known to us in Jesus Christ. Leisure, in this spiritual sense, not only provides inner direction, purpose, and meaning in life, but is also the basis of culture.

The major problem with the classical view of leisure is the tendency to emphasize human being at the expense of human doing. In this view of leisure, as Johnston (1983) noted, "Contemplation, not activity, becomes our goal; the monastery, not the workbench, the place" (p. 130). In Greek society, leisure (*schole*) was idealized and work (*aschole*) was disdained. In medieval monastic culture the monastic life of spiritual works was usually set above the active life. Pieper (1952) also seemed to idealize leisure above work: "Leisure [is] utterly contrary to the ideal of 'worker' in each of its three aspects . . . as activity, as toil, as a social function" (p. 40). The creational ordinance of work is minimized. Yet the Bible suggests that both work and rest are basic to the created nature of humanity. Even those writing from outside the biblical perspective, such as Thomas Goodale (1980), believe that humans are intended to be workers:

> We live in a world of work and we have no reason to think we should not. We are workers and have no reason to think we should not be, not because Calvin walks in the land but because the world's work (dare we say God's work?) remains to be done. Surely there is no end to the worthwhile work that must be done. (pp. 42–43)

The Holistic Concept of Leisure

The traditional concepts of leisure may be placed into one of two categories. The quantitative category includes the free time, social class function and activity definitions of leisure. The second category, a qualitative one, views leisure as a state of being, and includes both the classical and anti-utilitarian views of leisure. The former category includes behavioral and temporal definitions while the latter category includes attitudinal and existential definitions. The holistic concept of leisure encompasses both categories of definitions (Murphy, 1974).

A holistic approach unites the two previously opposed traditions of leisure: leisure as an end or as a means, as being or as doing, as a qualitative concept or as a quantitative concept. In the classical tradition, leisure is defined as a spiritual and mental attitude, as a style of life and a state of being that was first expressed by Aristotle and other Greek aristocrats, adapted in the medieval monastic practice of *otium* and more recently advocated by Pieper. The strength of the classical view of leisure is its emphasis on humans' being, on the qualitative dimension of leisure. However, as we have seen, this view often minimizes the creational ordinance of work.

In contrast to the classical interpretation, the second tradition of post-Hellenic Christianity and the Protestant ethic emphasizes work and views "leisure as therapy, rest, relaxation, social control, recreation for subsequent productive effort – and generally, therefore, as instrumental in character" (Kaplan, 1974, pp. 230–231). In this Protestant ethic of serving God through constant work and the forgoing of pleasures, leisure is viewed as a recreative and restorative activity that is of secondary significance to the development and spreading of culture. This "Protestant" view of leisure, influenced by Calvinist theology, contributed to the separation of work and leisure, since work was valued as the most important aspect of life while leisure, defined in terms of free time, was relegated to secondary importance.

The strengths of the Protestant view are its recognition of the creational ordinance of work along with the recognition of a rhythm to life – the alternation of periods of work and nonwork or quantitative leisure – that reflects the biblical pattern to life. However, the free time and activity concepts of leisure that the Protestant view incorporates are essentially quantitative approaches to the conceptualization of leisure, and as such, leisure has no intrinsic value. The activity concept maintains that perpetual doing is much more important than our being, the qualitative dimension to leisure. But doing is not the primary element in any satisfactory conceptualization of leisure. The time element is definitely necessary, but not sufficient to develop a complete explanation of leisure. The "freedom from" (i.e., time free from work and other obligations as is suggested by the humanitarian motivation of the Sabbath) along with the "freedom for" (i.e., free for activity) are necessary, but these freedoms in and of themselves cannot be equated with leisure. Leisure consists of more than simply quantitative components.

The holistic tendency unites these two historical traditions – leisure as an end and leisure as a means of relaxation and refreshment, the emphasis on being and on doing, the qualitative dimension and the quantitative dimension. In this blend, the weaknesses of each tradition are counterbalanced by the strengths of the other tradition.

The holistic concept of leisure is advocated here not primarily because it offers the opportunity to combine the two historical traditions, although this is a good reason, but because the holistic concept of leisure is able to encompass the variety and richness of the biblical material relevant to leisure. An examination of biblical materials revealed that leisure encompasses two dimensions: a quantitative and a qualitative, one relating to our doing, and the other to our being (Heintzman, 2006). First, the Sabbath teaches a rhythm to life: six days of work and one of nonwork (quantitative leisure). Second, the qualitative dimension is seen in the spiritual attitude of rest, joy, freedom, and celebration in both God and his creation, inculcated by the Sabbath and that culminates in the rest, peace, abundant life and freedom available in Jesus Christ. The holistic concept of leisure is advocated here because it has the capacity to encompass both the quantitative and qualitative dimensions of leisure as inferred from Scripture.

The Relationship of Work and Leisure

A Christian philosophy of leisure cannot be arrived at in isolation from the other dimensions of life. Both work and rest are basic to the created nature of humanity. Furthermore, work flows from our being, from our life in Christ.

How do we relate our biblical understanding of work to the contemporary perceptions of the relationship of work and leisure? Kunjo Odaka (1966) has classified workers according to five types of living related to work and leisure. These five perceptions of the relationship between work and leisure were defined as follows:

1. Work-oriented-unilateral – "work is man's duty. I wish to devote myself wholly to my work without any thought of leisure."
2. Leisure-oriented-unilateral – "Work is no more than a means for living. The enjoyment of leisure is what makes human life worth living."
3. Identity – "There is no distinction between work and leisure. I therefore have no need of being liberated from work in order that I may enjoy leisure."
4. Split – "Work is work and leisure is leisure. Modern man gets his work done smartly, and enjoys his leisure moderately."
5. Integrated – "Work makes leisure pleasurable, and leisure gives new energy to work. I wish to work with all my might, and to enjoy leisure." (Odaka as quoted in Parker, 1983, pp. 81–82)

In his book *The Christian at Play*, Johnston (1983) adapted Odaka's classification for articulating a Christian approach to work and play. He advocates that Christians ought to accept an "integrated" relationship of work and play. Using these same five possible lifestyles as a framework, I will discuss the relationship of work and leisure. Based on the understandings of leisure and work that I have developed from the biblical and historical sources, I will argue that the "identity" approach is the most appropriate response. Let us critique each of the five possible relationships individually.

Work-oriented-unilateral

In the work-oriented-unilateral lifestyle, work is the supreme value in life, while leisure is subservient. This work-oriented-unilateral approach to life is characteristic of the Protestant and secular work ethics. In the religious and secular world, views that have dominated Western society since the Reformation, humans have been regarded as *homo faber*, humans as workers, and one's main function has been to work at one's particular place in society. The saying "one does not work to live; one lives to work," is a good description of this approach to life. The problem with the emphasis on humans as *homo faber* is that the value of leisure is minimized. Margaret Mead (1958) observed that: "Within traditional American culture there runs a persistent belief that all leisure must be earned by work and good works. And second, while it is enjoyed, it must be seen in a context of future work and good works" (pp. 10–12). When work becomes one's only focus, it blinds one to the other dimensions of a person's created nature. Scripture suggests that work and rest are basic to the nature of humans. Although humans are workers, that is not the whole truth about humanity's nature and destiny since humans were created to glorify and enjoy God forever.

Furthermore, for Christians, work is never the central determinant of our worth. Pierre Berton (1968) has written: "Work seems to be the one thoroughly acceptable way that a man can demonstrate his worth to himself and his peers" (p. 17). Yet as James Houston (1981) wrote, "The glorification of work and its rewards both distort the human psyche as well as obscure the true meaning of work. For the essence of 'man lies not in what he does, but in who he is'" (p. 41). Therefore we cannot accept the work-oriented-unilateral approach to the relationship of work and leisure, for it exalts humans as *homo faber* to the detriment of the other dimensions of humans' created nature.

Leisure-oriented-unilateral

In the leisure-oriented-unilateral approach to the relationship between work and leisure, the experiencing of leisure is the primary value in life. This approach can be seen in classical Greek culture where leisure was idealized and work despised; in some expressions of the medieval monastic culture where the contemplative life was emphasized at the expense of the active life; and in some expressions of the more recent anti-utilitarian concept of leisure wherein hedonistic and narcissistic pursuits are valued above responsible participation in society. In both the classical and monastic cultures the notion of *homo faber*, humans as workers was minimized in favor of the contemplative life. In the anti-utilitarian view of leisure, the idea of *homo faber*, humans as workers, is rejected in favor of *homo ludens*, humans as players. In all three cases, a human's "being" is emphasized above a human's "doing." The creational intention of humans as workers is minimized. But to emphasize leisure at the expense of work is contrary to our nature, as Jacques Ellul (1964), among others, noted:

> To assert that the individual expresses his personality and cultivates himself in the course of his leisure is to accept the suppression of half of the human personality. History compels the judgement that it is in work that human beings develop and affirm their personality. When the human being is no longer responsible for his work and no longer figures in it, he feels spiritually outraged. The annihilation of work and its compensation with leisure resolves the conflicts by referring them to a subhuman plane. To gamble that leisure will enable man to live is to cut him off completely from part of life. (pp. 399–400)

The biblical account teaches us that work is something that makes us fully human; therefore the leisure-oriented-unilateral approach to life, with its narrowing of work to a means for living, is not acceptable to the Christian.

Split

The split" approach to life views work and leisure as two separate categories. In this approach, the human is both a worker, *homo faber*, and a player, *homo ludens*, but there is a clear distinction between the two roles in life. In earlier societies, which reflected *Gemeinschaft*, there was no clear distinction between work and leisure;, rather this distinction came about historically through a variety of influences that included: (1) the fixed times in monastic culture for manual labor and for spiritual activities; (2) the Reformers' confusion of vocation, work, and job, where the Christian's calling (1 Cor. 7:20) tended to be narrowed to the work associated with a specific position in society (Marshall, 1980), that contributed to work being defined as time devoted to a job; and (3) the glorification of work that accompanied industrialism, through which work came to be the most significant aspect of life, while leisure was relegated to free time. The divorcing of work and leisure is characteristic of the average worker today, who often despairs of finding satisfaction in or through one's job, but believes work is a necessity in life in order to earn an income to provide for the good life.

Johnston (1983) noted that "a biblical notion of Christian vocation will have nothing to do with such compartmentalization and secularization" (p. 132). Rather than separating work and leisure, we are to "do all to the glory of God." In my critique of the free time concept of leisure, I suggested that all of life is freely given by God, and therefore we cannot divide life into distinct segments of work and leisure. Furthermore, Ecclesiastes teaches that all of life, including work, is to be enjoyed. It is not suggested that work is to be compartmentalized from the other elements of life that are to be enjoyed. Therefore I conclude that the split approach to life is not appropriate for the Christian.

Integrated

In the integrated approach to life, "work makes leisure pleasurable and leisure gives new energy to work. I wish to work with all my might, and to enjoy leisure" (Odaka, 1983, p. 82). Johnston (1983) advocated that this is the style of life God intended for us: "Christians are created and called to consecrate both their work and their play" (p. 134). However, Johnston proceeded, "play is God's appointment, his gift to humankind which is meant to relativize and refresh our endeavors putting them in their God-intended perspective" (p. 134). Although throughout his book Johnston wrote about play as non-purposeful activity and that it has intrinsic value in itself, he now portrays play as a means "to relativize and refresh one's endeavors" (p. 134). In this view, humans are still both humans the workers, *homo faber*, and humans the players, *homo ludens*; however, the worker serves the player and the player serves the worker.

Identity

The identity approach to life, in which work and leisure are merged, is more consistent with the holistic concept of leisure advocated above. The holistic perspective suggests that one's life is not fragmented into a number of spheres such as work, leisure, family and religion, but that all aspects of life are considered as part of the whole. In the holistic view of life, work and leisure are inextricably related and fused. This does not mean that work and leisure, especially when leisure is considered as a spiritual attitude and a condition of being, can be equated with each other, but rather that they can be experienced at the same time, unlike the work-oriented-unilateral, leisure-oriented-unilateral, split, and integrated approaches to life that all make a clear temporal distinction between work and leisure.

The holistic, or Odaka's identity, approach to life, in which there is a fusion of work and leisure, is a more helpful approach than the traditional approaches that place work and leisure in an antithesis. From a Christian perspective, the ultimate meaning in life is found neither in work nor leisure. As Arthur Holmes (1983) wrote:

> In the final analysis, a human being is neither *homo faber* nor *homo ludens*. A person at the heart of his being is *homo religiosis*, his life to be lived in responsible relationship to God, and it is worship that is his most distinctive activity, not work and not play. (p. 228)

And as Pieper (1952) has shown, worship is the wellspring of leisure. Leisure originates in a right relationship with God. Thus leisure is primarily seen in a qualitative sense, as a spiritual attitude and as a condition of being.

When leisure is considered as a spiritual attitude and a condition of being, then work and leisure may occur simultaneously. In fact our leisure, as a condition of our being, is reflective of the quality of life we have in Christ, and from this life in Christ flows our work, our activity, our doing. "Leisure is both the source and climax of genuine work" wrote Banks (1983, p. 194). Work is an expression in the form of service to God and humanity, of thanksgiving and gratitude to Christ, one's divine master. Thus James Houston (1981) could write:

> True leisure then is the expression that we give to the Lordship of Jesus Christ . . . the constant recognition that our identity does not lie in our work roles, that our identity is only in Jesus Christ, and that the stronger our identity grows in Christ, the less neurotic our activities will become and the freer we shall be from the enslavement of work. . . . Our vocation will then look less and less like a job to do, and more and more a source of rejoicing in gratitude of what we are privileged to do to the glory of God. (pp. 45–47)

But how, in our daily lives, do we resolve the tension between "being" and "doing," rest and work? Scripture teaches that both rest and work are basic to the created nature of humanity. To resolve such a tension, William Still (n.d.) advocated "simultaneous rest and work":

> Therefore we must learn to act properly, with a due balance of rest and work, which we may say is to work *from* a position and attitude of rest . . . as Christians we ought to live with a restful ease, even in busyness and in energetic activity, which not only ought to enable us to get through our work, but to do so more efficiently and therefore also more enjoyably. (pp. 39–42)

So our work is to flow from a quality of life, a spiritual attitude characterized by rest in God. Still (n.d.) also mentioned that we are to have a "due balance of rest and work." This brings us to the second dimension of leisure: the quantitative dimension and the idea of rhythm to life. So far we have been emphasizing the qualitative dimension – leisure as a condition of our being.

While most of the biblical material related to leisure supports a qualitative definition of leisure, the Bible also supports a quantitative dimension to leisure (Heintzman, 2006). The Sabbath teaches a rhythm to life – six days of work and one of nonwork. The implication is that the Sabbath suggests some rhythm or cycle of work and leisure (in a quantitative sense) is necessary for wellbeing and wholeness. Thus, in addition to leisure as a spiritual attitude that undergirds all of life, "periods are necessary when leisure is lived more intensely" (Doohan, 1990, p. 36). Doohan (1981) wrote:

> We have a leisurely approach to life which must be nourished by times of intensified leisure. The latter will include, among other things, play, friendship, sharing, an absence of oppression in favor of a happy and cheerful affirmation of oneself, a feeling of at-homeness in the world, and a capacity to steep oneself in the beauty of the universe. It will demand a form of silence and inward calm leading to a receptive attitude of mind above all; it will be a varied celebration of life – men's and women's looking upon creation and seeing that it is good. (pp. 165–166)

In conclusion, a Christian holistic conceptualization of leisure has two dimensions: a qualitative and a quantitative. The qualitative dimension is the spiritual attitude and condition of being that reflects the quality of life available in Jesus Christ. This qualitative dimension of leisure is not limited to a certain time period; thus it may be experienced simultaneously with work, and in fact work may be conceived of as an expression of this attitude. The quantitative dimension of leisure consists of certain times and activities, ranging from silent contemplation to an active celebration and rejoicing in the gifts of creation, in which an intensification of leisure is experienced. Thus all of our life should be characterized by a spiritual attitude of leisure, but at the same time, our life should exhibit a rhythm of periods of work and periods of intensified leisure.

References

Banks, R. (1983). *The tyranny of time: When 24 hours is not enough.* Downers Grove, IL: InterVarsity.

Berger, B.M. (1963). The sociology of leisure: Some suggestions. In E. Smigel (Ed.), *Work and leisure.* New Haven, CT: College & University Press.

Bregha, F. (1980). Leisure and freedom re-examined. In T.L. Goodale & P.A. Witt (Eds.), *Recreation and leisure: Issues in an era of change* (pp. 30–37). State College, PA: Venture.

Dahl, G. (1972). *Work, play and worship in a leisure-oriented society.* Minneapolis: Augsburg.

Dennison, J.T. Jr. (1983). *The market day of the soul: The Puritan doctrine of the Sabbath in England 1532–1760.* Lanham, MD: University Press of America.

Doohan L. (1981). The spiritual value of leisure. *Spirituality Today* 31(2), 157–167.

Doohan, L. (1990). *Leisure: A spiritual need.* Notre Dame, IN: Ave Maria Press.

Eaton, M. (1983). *Ecclesiastes.* Downers Grove, IL: InterVarsity.

Ellul, J. (1964). *The technological society.* (Trans. J. Wilkinson). New York: Random House.

Goodale, T.L. (1980). If leisure is to matter. In T.L. Goodale & P.A. Witt (Eds.), *Recreation and leisure: Issues in an era of change* (pp. 38–49). State College, PA: Venture.

Hahn, B.J. (1985, June 3). Approaching leisure redemptively: Leisure misunderstood. *Christian Renewal* 3(19), 6–7, 15.

Heintzman, P. (2006). Implications for leisure from a review of the biblical concepts of Sabbath and rest: In P. Heintzman, G.E. Van Andel & T.L. Visker (Eds.), *Christianity and leisure: Issues in a pluralistic society* (Rev. ed., pp. 14–31). Sioux Center: Dordt College Press.

Holmes, A. (1977). *All truth is God's truth.* Grand Rapids: Eerdmans.

Houston, J. (1981). The theology of work. In *Looking at lifestyles professional priorities: A Christian Perspective.* Proceedings from the Conference for Physicians and Dentists, Banff, AB, May 2–8, 1981. Vancouver, BC: Christian Medical and Dental Society of Canada.

Johnston, R.K. (1983). *The Christian at play.* Grand Rapids: Eerdmans.

Kaplan M. (1974). New concepts of leisure today. In J. Murphy, *Concepts of leisure: Philosophical implications* (pp. 229–236). Englewood Cliffs, NJ: Prentice Hall.

Leclerq, J. (1982). *The love of learning and the desire for God: A study of monastic culture.* New York: Fordham University.

Lee, R. (1964). *Religion and leisure in America: A study in four dimensions.* New York: Abingdon Press.

Marshall, P. (1980). Vocation, work and jobs. In P. Marshall, E. Vanderkloet, P. Nijkamp, S. Griffioen, & H. Antonides (Eds.), *Labour of love: Essays on work* (pp. 1–19). Toronto: Wedge.

Mead, M. (1958). The pattern of leisure in contemporary American culture. In E. Larrabee & R. Meyersohn (Eds.), *Mass leisure*. Glencoe, IL: Free Press.

Murphy, J. (1974). *Concepts of leisure: Philosophical implications*. Englewood Cliffs, NJ: Prentice Hall.

Owens, J. (1981, December). Aristotle on leisure. *Canadian Journal of Philosophy* 16, 713–724.

Parker, S. (1983). *Leisure and Work*. London: George Allen & Unwin.

Pieper. J. (1952). *Leisure: The basis of culture* (A. Dru, Trans.). New York: Pantheon Books (1963, Random House).

Ryken, L. (1987). *Work and leisure in Christian perspective*. Portland, OR: Multnomah.

Spence, D. (1973). *Towards a theology of leisure with special reference to creativity*. Ottawa, ON: Canadian Parks & Recreation Association.

Still, W. (1985). *Rhythms of rest and work* (3rd ed.). Aberdeen, Scotland: Gilcomston South Church, 1985.

Sylvester, C. (1990). Interpretation and leisure science: A hermeneutical example of past and present oracles. *Journal of Leisure Research* 22(4), 290–295.

Veblen, T. (1912). *The theory of the leisure class*. New York: Vanguard Press.

Vos, N. (1979). To take life leisurely. *Reformed Journal* 29(5), 14–16.

Chapter 4
LEISURE AND SPIRITUALITY: AN ENGAGED AND RESPONSIBLE PURSUIT OF FREEDOM IN WORK, PLAY, AND WORSHIP

Douglas Joblin

Leisure is essentially spiritual. . . . When people experience leisure, their spirits soar and their humanity finds larger expression. (Dahl, 1972, pp. 72–73)

In the November 10, 1999, *Globe and Mail,* editorial cartoonist Brian Gable pictured a young child tucked in bed reading a good night story book. The book's title was *20th Century Fairy Tales: 'The Leisure Society.'* Sitting beside the young child was his middle-aged female caregiver, slouched and sprawled out in a chair, sound asleep, cell phone and notes resting on her outstretched lap. The cartoon was a response to a Statistics Canada report released the day before that indicated Canadians were working harder and enjoying themselves, less. In an article in *The National Post* of May 14, 2001, Noah Richler declared that one of the great failed promises of the latter half of the twentieth century was that people would have to continue to work as hard as they currently do; it was meant to be a leisure society. Honoré (2004), in *In Praise of Slow,* stated that "the leisure revolution remains the stuff of fantasy. Work still rules our lives. . ." (p. 218). More than a decade earlier, Schor (1991) had already written about the decline of leisure in *The Overworked American.* She declared then that this decline was unexpected.

Whatever happened to leisure? It emerged in the 1960s and 1970s as a revolutionary new way of living that would sweep across the Western world and put the job, and the industrial revolution that had set the job at the very center or core of people's lives, in a much more appropriate place. Leisure was to be the baby-boomers' radically new model for living. Why has leisure seemingly become relegated to the world of fairy tales,

---
Revised version of paper presented at 2007 conference.

failed promises, the stuff of fantasy, having experienced a most unexpected decline especially in North America? There are three basic reasons. The first is the continuing dominance of work at jobs and home. The second is that no one model of leisure has emerged to provide some kind of clarity of its meaning so that people can commit to it as a way of life. Rybczynski (1991), in *Waiting for the Weekend* noted that "leisure is the most misunderstood word in our vocabulary" (p. 224). Andrews (2006) suggested leisure still seeks clarity. In *Slow Is Beautiful*, she declared that "as I've studied the concept in the past several months, I've been overwhelmed with what leisure really means and how the term has been a wicket of controversy over the years" (pp. 140–141). Third, leisure not only seems to elude clarity but also often lacks any connection to people's spirituality. Such a connection would provide a holistic model of leisure and hopefully inspire a renaissance of leisure as an exciting and vibrant paradigm that helps center their spirituality. As Dahl (1972) declared: "when people experience leisure, their spirits soar and their humanity finds larger expression" (p. 73).

It is not my intention to examine in much detail reasons for the continuing dominance of work in the world and its impact on people. They have been and continue to be most significant. Schor's (1991) studies, for instance, revealed that the unexpected increase in working hours in the later part of the twentieth century affected the great majority of North Americans and created a "profound structural crisis of time. . . . Stress is on the rise, partly owing to the 'balancing act' of reconciling the demands of work and family life" (p. 5). She explained that "child neglect, marital stress, sleep deprivation and stress-related illnesses all have other causes. But the growth of work has exacerbated each of these social problems" (p. 13). Work's demands and impacts continue unabated. More recently Schor (2003) stated that "Americans are now working even more than they did when *The Overworked American* was published" (p. 7). "Recent trends in working hours are almost astonishing" (p. 10), she noted. In his edited book *Take Back Your Time*, De Graff (2003) observed "how American vacations have become an endangered species . . . and that 'mandatory' overtime demands" (p. 2) are steadily increasing. Nazareth (2007), in *The Leisure Economy*, explained that "the boom years of the 1990s have been accompanied by a boom in technology [e.g., cell phones, Blackberries, laptop computers] that has meant workers can work wherever they are – in their offices, in their homes or on the road . . . [exacerbating] patterns of overwork and job stress. . ." (p. 37). Bibby's (2006) surveys of Canadians in *The Boomer Factor* revealed that all these concerns continue to be problematic. "It's not just our imaginations," he observed. "The time demands on us [are] greater than ever . . . [and] can lead to a serious erosion of our own lives and those of the people closest to us. Being overextended can wring the joy out of life" (pp. 86–87). Other consequences of the ongoing dominance of work will blend into this paper. However, my basic intention is to explain how various models of leisure persist, hence making it a most confusing and often misunderstood word, and then propose a holistic model of leisure that would form a core component of people's spirituality so that people can commit to its vibrant and exciting way of living.

How am I defining spirituality? Spirituality is about the path that people follow in life and the experience of an inner presence of the divine or sacred as they follow this path. The path consists of sets of belief, standards of behavior, and rituals that are bridges to the divine or sacred. Eck (2003), in *Encountering God,* suggested that spirituality has these outer dimensions. Then, she declared, it is the art and discipline of people becoming alert, awakened, and paying attention to the way these dimensions connect with their own inner spirit and finding themselves, as Thomas Merton wrote to her in a letter, "engulfed in such happiness that it cannot be explained" (p. 150). This inner presence of happiness is important to clarify. Most writings about happiness distinguish between emotional and spiritual happiness. Emotional happiness comes and goes; a spiritual happiness is a persistent sense of wellbeing about life. Myers (1992), in *The Pursuit of Happiness*, explained:

> well-being outlasts yesterday's moment of elation, today's buoyant mood and tomorrow's hard time; it is an ongoing perception that this time of one's life, or even life as a whole, is fulfilling, meaningful, and pleasant. It is what some people experience as joy – not an ephemeral euphoria, but a deep and abiding sense that, despite all the day's woes, all is, or will be, well. Even when the surface waters churn, the deep currents run sure. (p. 24)

It is this kind of spiritual happiness that, as Vanier (2001) noted in *Made for Happiness*, the Greek philosophers, Jewish people, and Jesus in the Beatitudes sought to understand and explain. It is also what people most desire. "Happiness," he declared, "whatever else people may say, is the great concern of our life. . . . To be happy, to know happiness, is the great desire of every man and woman" (p. ix).

My quest therefore is to propose a model of leisure that shapes and directs people's paths through life because it nurtures and sustains an inner presence of the divine or sacred as an experience of a persistent happiness and wellbeing. That will not happen unless leisure is understood in a holistic and spiritual context. Otherwise it will continue to be so misunderstood, or simply reduced to a segment of time or activities, that it has little or no meaning for people. Leisure, if linked clearly to spirituality, can transform not only people's lives but also whole societies. In fact, Goodale and Godbey (1995), in *The Evolution of Leisure,* suggested that "in the evolution of leisure, we see the ultimate measure of human progress. Ultimately it will assert itself. Leisure will assert itself because it is where human change, however unwittingly, is leading us" (p. xiii).

Leisure and Freedom

What prompted the emergence of leisure in the later part of twentieth century as a model for life's purpose and ultimate measure of human progress? There were four basic social factors: the emergence of the job, the growth of free time, increasing affluence, and the democratization of all three. The job was becoming the means for adult men and women and teenagers to provide for their needs and desires. Free time from full-time jobs was increasing daily, weekly, annually, and over their lifetimes. Some people began working six, not eight, hours a day (at my university, for instance, the working day has been six and a-half hours minus two 20-minute breaks since the early 1970s), and five, not the biblical six, days a week, hence becoming a weekend people and hoping to become a long weekend people; vacation time was increasing; and retirement could happen at age 55 or earlier, not 65. Affluence from jobs was also increasing as family and personal incomes were steadily rising. People therefore had more disposable income for more products, and if people did not have the money for what they needed or wanted, credit was becoming readily available and encouraged. "Buy now, pay later" was a modern day saying and practice as people and governments borrowed money freely. A new freedom for a playful and luxurious lifestyle was emerging in the Western world.

The growth in jobs, free time, and affluence was being democratized in the sense that almost everyone in North America was able to enjoy these new freedoms. Most, if not all, societies have had wealthy upper leisure classes of people with time and money to spend and do as they pleased. By the 1980s, however, as Florida (2004) explained in *The Rise of the Creative Class,* ordinary working people could purchase the amenities of life that only the rich, written about at the turn of the twentieth century by Thorstein Veblen in his famous theory of the wealthy "leisure class," could afford (pp. 169–170). These social factors were prompting all kinds of new personal freedoms: freedom from having to work long hours, freedom from having to live at a basic level of existence, freedom from having family and groups such as religious groups determining people's choices of lifestyle, freedom to make their own choices, freedom to have an increasing selection of choices to make. The word *freedom* was another popular modern-day word and value that helps explain the emergence of leisure as a term to describe these revolutionary changes that were happening because of its Greek, Latin, and French association with freedom. The new generation of baby boomers had the freedom, time, and affluence to be at leisure. But what was leisure? How was leisure being defined? There was much confusion and misunderstanding about its meaning. As leisure became the subject of academic disciplines throughout the West, three basic models emerged, each defining leisure from its own unique perspective of freedom.

One was the model of free time, but with many, hence confusing, variations. Schor (1991), for instance, defined leisure as free time from total working hours of "paid employment and household labor" (p. 13). Rybczynski (1991) said leisure was a matter of *Waiting for the Weekend*, so reduced leisure to the weekend. Fox (1994), in *The Reinvention of Work*, limited his understanding of leisure even further, to one day of the week, namely "the *Shabbat* or *Sabbath*, a day of rest" (p. 169). It was a day to rest from work so people could worship by giving thanks and praise for creation in "a cosmological awakening to the original blessing in [their] lives" (p. 270). Csikszentmihalyi (1997), in *Finding Flow*, stated that "time left over from productive and maintenance necessities is free time, or 'leisure' . . ." (p. 12). Andrews (2006) began her definition of leisure as "time away from work. That should be obvious," she declared (p. 143).

Another model presents leisure as play, as activities free from work. For instance, Kelly (1982), in *Leisure*, noted that when people are asked to define leisure, most respond in terms of particular kinds of activities such as sports, concerts, trips, visiting friends, and family (p. 4). Gini (2003), in *The Importance of Being Lazy*, declared that "we are marked, molded, identified and known to ourselves and others by what we do for a living (work) and how we play (leisure)" (pp. 41–42). Ramsay (2005), in *Reclaiming Leisure*, also defined leisure as activities separate from work. "*Leisure activities*," he observed, "which, since they stand outside our work and daily pressures, will be opportunities for *play* and *reflection*. . ." (p. 42). Stebbins (2007), in *Serious Leisure*, defined it as "uncoerced activity engaged in during free time, which people want to do. . ." (p. 4). His model seems to embrace free activity, free time, and experience.

I am part of the third "free" experience model and am inviting people to appreciate the advantages of this perspective and commit themselves to it as their model of leisure. A first ingredient of leisure emerges from its classical understanding as an attitude or state of being that people can experience not only in an immediate moment or activity, but also in all of time and all of life's activities. As Pieper (1952) declared in *Leisure: The Basis of Culture*:

> Leisure is a mental and spiritual attitude – it is not simply the result of external facts; it is not the inevitable result of spare time, a holiday, a weekend or a vacation. It is, in the first place, an attitude of mind, a condition of the soul . . . an attitude of contemplative "celebration". . . . (pp. 40, 42)

Dahl (1972) stated that leisure was a spiritual experience of enduring freedom. He was critical of conventional notions of leisure that often equated leisure "with free time, meaning, in most cases, time which is free from work" (p. 61). He noted, in fact, that "many people experience their greatest freedom when they are working . . ." (p. 61).

Kelly (1982) also pointed out that leisure needed to be understood from an experiential perspective. He was critical of popular notions of leisure as "free" activities. It was important to discover what the activities people named as their leisure or play had in common, which he suggested was an anticipation of satisfaction. He explained:

> the common element is not place, nor is it the nature of the activity, the companions, the time of day or of the week, or even the kind of satisfaction that is gained. The only common element seems to be that each occasion has been chosen with some sense of satisfaction anticipated. None had to be done. None were sheer duty. (p. 4)

Searle and Brayley (1993), in *Leisure Services in Canada*, distinguished carefully between these three models of leisure, but were quite evasive when asked to prescribe any one model. They concluded that it was not particularly useful to provide a simple answer to such a complex question. They did agree, however, that leisure was "essentially a subjective experience . . . characterized by freedom to choose, intrinsic motivation and the enjoyment derived from the experience . . ." (p. 37). Doohan's (1990) model of leisure also begins as "an attitude to life that includes rest and creative self-development, but it also touches the very personal inner spirit of each individual, and it must be discovered as such" (p. 31).

What is at the heart of this experience, attitude, or state of being that touches people's inner spirit? Iso-Ahola (1999) suggested that "it seems indisputable that a sense of freedom – autonomy – is the central defining characteristic of leisure" (p. 36). De Grazia (1964), in *Of Time, Work, and*

Leisure, described it as an experience of a "freedom from the necessity of being occupied" (p. 12). There is, in other words, an absence of obligation, coercion, and having to be occupied, hence a presence of choice, personal control, and wanting to be occupied. His model, like Pieper's (1952), Dahl's (1972), and Doohan's (1990), focused on the classical state of being free that is an ongoing, deep, and abiding way to approach life. Other writers refer more to a free state of mind which results from specific moments or situations. Csikszentmihalyi (1997), for instance, described leisure as an experience of *flow* (p. 29). *Flow* happens when people become so totally absorbed in an activity that their involvement seems effortless and time flies. Cooper (1998), in *Playing in the Zone,* noted that athletes call *flow* "being in *the zone* . . . with its rich ambiguity and layers of meaning . . ." (p. 21). Pavelka (2000), in *It's Not About Time!* explained that leisure emerges out of moments of positive self-expression, thus enabling people to experience freedom, choice, arousal, flow, and being in the zone (pp. 49–57). Andrews (2006) declared that "the real meaning of leisure has to do with a near-mystical experience where time stops and you feel connected to life, expanded by life, transformed by life" (p. 140). It is important to distinguish carefully between these two perspectives of leisure; however, I would maintain that experiences described as flow or being in the zone could also be used by people to name an ongoing and abiding orientation to life and be not only a state of mind in one particular moment, but also a state of being pervading all of life. Myers' (1992) chapter titled "'Flow' in Work and Play" (p. 127) is an indication of such a possibility. People, in other words, are experiencing freedom from necessity in whatever they are doing; their spirits soar; there is a happiness that often cannot be explained.

Why posit that the experiential, spiritual model is more appropriate than understanding leisure as time and/or activities free from work? One is that time and activities are not always liberating, hence enjoyable, experiences for people. Myers (1992) cited studies by Csikszentmihalyi, for instance, where he was struck by "the relative poverty of experience in free time . . ." (p. 136). As de Grazia (1964) warned:

> Leisure and free time live in two different worlds. . . . Anybody can have free time. Not everybody can have leisure. . . . Free time refers to a special way of calculating a special kind of time. Leisure refers to a state of being, a condition of man [*sic*], which few desire and fewer achieve. (p. 5)

A similar concern is expressed with an understanding of leisure as play. The activity itself does not determine whether or not it is a liberating, hence joyful, experience, but what happens to people in the activity.

Another concern, as already noted, is the separation of leisure and work as though people could never experience freedom in their work, hence include it as part of leisure. Work, in fact, is often understood as opposite to leisure. For many it is. Stebbins (2007) cited statistics stating that "one in five Canadians dread going to work and three of five consider their jobs significantly disagreeable obligations" (p. 59). I want to embrace work as part of leisure.

Finally, what about worship? Dahl (1972) posited that people's daily lives revolve around work, play, and worship. Many studies of leisure seem to address life from a holistic perspective but often make little if any reference to worship and the sacred beliefs, natural spaces, buildings, times, communities, prayer, meditation, contemplation, rituals, Sabbaths, sweat lodges, vision quests, retreats, rites of passage, pilgrimages, and festivals that are part of this aspect of life. Pavelka (2000), for instance, wanted people to know they could be at leisure in their play and work but only made any significant reference to worship when he described the Buddhist concept of mindfulness as a way to understand how individuals could experience leisure when snowboarding (p. 57). Florida (2004) noted that the new creative class of people was seeking to transform work, leisure, community, and everyday life by moving to integrated eco-systems or habitats "where all forms of creativity – artistic and cultural, technological and economic – can take root and flourish" (p. 218). Nazareth (2007), in a similar vein, suggested that to rebrand communities for the new leisure economy, there needed to be good "theatre, festivals, fireworks or outdoor recreation activities" (p. 238). Neither Florida nor Nazareth makes any mention of worship, religion, and/or spirituality, yet these are often the most important aspects of life for people. It seems that worship can be a most neglected area in literature and studies about leisure. I want to embrace worship as part of leisure, too.

So my quest to define leisure begins by understanding leisure as an attitude or state of being marked by freedom and all its rich layers and ambiguities of meaning. It embraces all of life: work, play, and worship. Equally important is that leisure is being engaged and responsible in these activities. Succinctly stated, then, leisure is an engaged and responsible pursuit of freedom in work, play, and worship. Leisure is spiritual because it is a holistic model that shapes and directs the paths that people can follow as they journey through life. It alerts and awakens them to life's purpose. It is also spiritual, because it can connect people to a presence of the divine or sacred as it engulfs them in happiness.

Leisure and Engagement

Leisure needs to be understood as a physical, mental, emotional, spiritual, social, and/or cultural engagement in life because it is in being engaged and not passive that freeing, mystical, and life-enhancing experiences worthy of the name leisure can happen. Dahl (1972), for instance, warned about the common perception of leisure as a passive way of being involved in life.

> Some people conceive of leisure as a primarily passive experience and expect to realize it by merely switching to the right channel, or finding the right hobby, or perhaps simply waiting for something (or someone) to come along and turn them on. . . . Their quest for leisure then becomes a search for entertainment – and it often ends in mere time-filling (or time-killing) distractions. (p. 68)

Leisure, for Dahl, meant much more than being entertained. People needed to be "actively engaged – with one another and their times – and their engagement needs to be a meaningful one, not merely one that fills (or kills) time" (p. 68). Why is it so important for people to be actively engaged with others and their times?

Here, Myers' (1992) research is instructive. He noted that some people think that being introverted and withdrawn will nurture less stress and more serenity and peace than being actively engaged with others. "Rather," he explained, "in study after study, extroverts – sociable, outgoing people – report greater happiness and satisfaction with life" (p. 120). He cited studies by Csikszentmihalyi who reported that people were "unhappiest when they are alone and nothing needs doing: For people in our studies who live by themselves and do not attend church, Sunday mornings are the lowest part of the week, because with no demands on attention, they are unable to decide what to do. . . . For many, the lack of structure of those hours is devastating" (p. 137). What a contrast to Fox's (1994) model of leisure as a time for people to give praise and thanks for all of creation on the Sabbath!

Myers (1992) continued as he challenged people who passively engage in life to become more physically, mentally, and socially active in order to experience happiness.

> The problem seems to be our culture's reliance on television and other forms of passive leisure and on our inability to structure our free time in ways that would enhance our well-being. Well-being resides not in mindless passivity but in mindful challenge. So, off your duffs, couch [and now also mouse and thumb] potatoes. Pick up your camera. Tune up that

instrument. Sharpen those woodworking tools. Get out those quilting needles. Inflate the family basketball. Pull down a good book. Oil the fishing reel. It's time to head out to the garden store. To invite friends over for tea. To pull down a Scrabble game. To write a letter. To go for a drive. Rather than vegetating in self-focused idleness, lose yourself in the flow of active work and play. You may be surprised what happens. (pp. 137–138)

Pieper (1952) also expressed great concern about passive idleness but with a unique understanding of its meaning. He noted that idleness, which in the old sense of the word meant a deep-seated lack of calm, rendered "leisure impossible: it might be described as the utter absence of leisure, or the very opposite of leisure" (p. 40).

Iso-Ahola (1997) warned against people becoming passive and escape-oriented rather than active and seeker-oriented "either by maintaining a sedentary lifestyle and/or by resorting to such health-damaging behaviors as drug use. Active leisure lifestyle, on the other hand," as research has proven, he continued, "promotes health because participation in various leisure activities is geared towards seeking intrinsic rewards through use of one's cognitive, physical and social skills" (p. 135).

Ramsay (2005) also expressed great concern about people's passivity. He sought to reclaim a very mindful and spiritual understanding of leisure. He distinguished between consumerist and reflective leisure. Consumerist leisure is an addiction to consuming and possessing what industries have produced. He noted further that consumerism

> rejects eternal realities and spiritual truths. With no God, cosmic answers or first principles there is nothing worthy of contemplation; leisure, then, quietly drops the contemplative ideals and dedicates itself not to other reflective experiences that divert us from our daily burdens, but instead to securing interesting and enjoyable experiences that are within our price range or, preferably, just above it. . . . Its nice face embraces increased freedom of choices. . . . Its nasty face expresses acquisitiveness, possessiveness, what the ancient Greeks called *pleonexia*: the desire for more than one's appropriate share. (pp. 37–38)

Reflective leisure, he explained, is a "thoughtful, quiet reflection on our circumstances and our fates which puts us in charge, reminds us of what is good about modern life, how blessed modernity is, and prepares us to carry on" (p. 43). It helps to "transform our lives and prepare us for spectacular, transcendent visions of happiness" (p. 42). He expanded on activities such as recreation, reading, travel, music, sports, and the arts, which were leisure when they enabled people to realize Aristotle's contemplative ideal that "consisted in beholding with wonder the basic truths and the principles that explain all things" (p. 43).

Andrews (2006) also posited the importance of understanding leisure as a physical, mental, spiritual, and social engagement in life. She asked people what they thought were leisure activities: "reading, sitting in the sun, gardening, studying, walking, writing a poem, having a coffee at a café, shopping, watching television" (p. 141). She noted that shopping and watching television "are our primary non-working activities, but," she continued, "I'm not including them in my definition of leisure. The rest of the list belongs" (p. 141). Leisure, she stated, means "avoiding commercialism" and "prepackaged entertainment" (p. 144) because it is a more reflective way of being that opens people to life, the universe, and "a commitment to grow in wisdom" (p. 142).

Leisure therefore prescribes an engagement in life because it nurtures and sustains experiences of happiness. Kleiber (2000), however, warned about the way leisure studies have focused too much on high-intensity activity with its "concentrated effort, competence, and commitment" as sources of happiness and not enough on "relaxation and receptivity" (p. 82). He called for a return to Pieper's (1952) model of leisure that embraces a dialectic tension of times to pause for reflection and times to engage in intense festive affirmations of the goodness of life. Such balance between resting and being busy, as Heintzman's (2000) research indicated, is "viewed as being conducive to spiritual well-being, and well-being in general" (p. 60).

Honoré (2004) has also warned about the dangers of high intensity engagement. He explained that people today are so busy working in their jobs and at home that they are stressed out because they have too much to do and not enough time to do it all. Even when they do have free time, he observed, they "rush to fill up every spare moment with activity. An empty slot in the diary is more often a source of panic than pleasure" (p. 218). His quest was *In Praise of Slow,* so that people could better savor their activities and not rush them. He pleaded for people to join the slow movement, to start working less hard, to take more time with their eating and drinking, relationships, sex, raising children, exercising, healing, and meditation. He argued for slower hobbies such as "gardening, reading, painting, making crafts [because] all of these satisfy the growing nostalgia for a time when the cult of speed was less potent, when doing one thing well, and taking real pleasure from it, was more important than doing everything faster" (p. 218). Andrews (2006) has joined Honoré in encouraging people to remember that *Slow Is Beautiful.* "The Slow Life," she declared, "is about joy, leisure and community" (p. 8). People, in other words, need to take more time to savor what they are doing so their spirits have time to soar and their humanity can find larger expression.

Leisure and Balance

Balance has become another current key word to describe a holistic lifestyle. One expression of balance, similar to what Heintzman's research indicated, as noted above, is embracing what Cox (1977) in *Turning East* described as "the *via activa* and the *via contemplativa*" (p. 68) into one's life. Another is a balance or appropriate integration of life's basic activities. When people are asked to explain what is meant by a balanced expression of activity, their responses are often very Freudian. I suggest Freudian, because as Terr (1999) wrote in *Beyond Love and Work*, most will reflect what Sigmund Freud observed in his 1930 *Civilization and Its Discontents*: "love and work (*Lieben und Arbeiten*) [are] the two occupations that principally enable us to endure the pressures common to all civilizations" (p. 12). Terr does not agree. She asked: "But where, I often wonder, is play in all of this?" (p. 12). And I would add, but where is worship in all of this, too?

Dahl (1972), as noted earlier, has outlined most succinctly what is meant by a holistic understanding of life's activities. He stated that people's lives revolve around their work, play, and worship. The quest is for people to understand the roles that these activities should have and how they can be "creatively integrated into their lifestyle" (p. 12). Work refers to those activities that have some degree of necessity attached to them such as the duties people must engage in to meet their own and other's basic survival and health needs, making a living, jobs, managing a family and home, and providing direction for community groups and municipal, provincial/state, and national governments. Play refers to those activities beyond necessity that do not have to be done to ensure people's survival. People could live without them, yet they freely choose to create and engage in them because of the delight they bring to life. Where would humankind be, for instance, without music, dance, art, sculpture, theatre, movies, puppetry, architecture, toys, pets, fashion, jewelry, humor, stories, games, friendships, intimate relationships, playful sex, family, hobbies, parks, travel, and sports? Gini (2003), as noted earlier, described how people are molded, identified, and known to themselves and others by their work and play, but how are they also molded, identified, and known by their worship? As noted earlier, worship embraces an incredible variety of activities; for many it is the center of their lives and the reference point for all other activities. I maintain, however, that work and play are as important as worship, and that all need to be appropriately integrated into people's lives as part of a holistic model of leisure.

The quest for balance and appropriate integration may seem the simplest to explain, but the most difficult to realize. Dahl (1972), for instance, warned at the very beginning of the leisure revolution that this difficulty emerged from people's tendency "to worship their work, to work at their play, and to play at their worship" (p. 12). What does he capture in this succinct insight? First, the worship of work has been and continues to be a problem for many people, not only because of the increasing demands of work at jobs, often because people have no choice but to overwork in order to survive, but also because of people's commitment to their jobs and/or work at home and the work-a-holism that can develop from such devotion. Bibby (2006) cited studies by "pollsters Darrel Bricker and John Wright in their book *What Canadians Think* [who] caution us to remember that, for most people, work takes priority over everything. . ." (p. 115). Workplaces love the loyalty of the workaholic, but as Oates (1971) observed in *Confessions of a Workaholic*, "those who adopt a workaholic way of life let all other values go – family, friendships, spiritual associations, everything" (p. 13).

Second, people work at their play in that their play often mimics the structured and stressful dynamics of work or is done only if there is some benefit for their work. Often they have too little time for play, but perhaps of greater concern, they have no interest in play. However, as Tiger's (1992) *In Pursuit of Pleasure* warned, "All work and no play will not only make Johnny [and Jill] dull [people] but stupid ones" (p. 7). Stebbins (2004) expressed great concern about the impact of the baby boomers' worship of work as they begin retirement. "The prevailing work ethic has painted all leisure in inferior tones. Pity those unhappy retirees who saw their work as everything and now see their "forced" leisure as basically a badge of their own uselessness" (p. 121). Sheehy (1995), in *New Passages,* stated that this generation would actually need "permission to play" (p. 357). Terr (1999) declared that adults needed to move beyond love and work to play, because "when people are playing, there is a sense of good-humored, spirited, even sparkling, pleasure" (pp. 29–30). As Flocker (2004), in *The Hedonism Handbook,* proclaimed, "pleasure is good. Eden was fun. Excess may be bad, but self-deprivation is just stupid" (pp. 16–17).

Finally, Dahl (1972) expressed concern that people's worship had become quite meaningless. It was more "some sort of game [they] play each week" rather than "a total life response to God . . ." (p. 19). Cox (1969), in *The Feast of Fools,* maintained that people were not so much playing at their worship as they had become so immersed in the materialistic world that they no longer engaged in worship. He observed that

> [people] have paid a frightful price for the present opulence of Western industrial society. . . . While gaining the whole world, [they have] been losing [their own] souls. [They] have purchased prosperity at the cost of a staggering impoverishment of the vital elements of [their] lives. These elements are *festivity* – the capacity for genuine revelry and joyous celebration, and *fantasy* – the faculty for envisioning radically alternate life situations. (p. 7)

Dahl (2006) declared that a solution to this problem of balance and integration was to understand leisure as "worcreation which is . . . being able to combine work, worship and recreation in a free and loving, holistic way . . . in order to experience wholeness in one's life, family, and community" (p. 90). Balance, in other words, is people seeking creative and liberating experiences in all of life's activities. It is embracing the "abundance of happy circumstances and relationships in which life is cast" (Dahl, 1972, p. 70).

Leisure and Responsibility

The responsible ingredient of leisure has been implied since the very beginning of this paper. Leisure is about enhancing the quality of life and its goodness. This assumption undergirds the thinking of most who write about leisure as well. They posit that leisure is not simply doing as one pleases. Those who understand leisure only as a freedom to choose need to be reminded of the concern explained by Rojek (1999) in a chapter intriguingly titled "Deviant Leisure: The Dark Side of Free-Time Activity." People could conclude that leisure means anything goes, that people have a freedom to be irresponsible, destructive, and evil if they so choose. When people take time to think about leisure, however, they recognize that leisure is about the enhancement of life and so requires that people be responsible and thus moral in their choices. Morality gives order to life and affects people's choices as it enables them to make distinctions between good and evil, right and wrong, and appropriate and inappropriate actions and behavior. People, either consciously or often quite subconsciously, follow certain principles, guidelines, directives, traditions, customs, ideals, codes, laws, and/or moral sentiments in their pursuit of creative courses of action for their lives rather than destructive paths.

For Aitken (1976), the root problem that leisure poses for people is a moral one, because people have a freedom to make their own choices about how they will live life. He raised two critical concerns with regard to people's freedom of choice. First, he posited that "part of the moral problem is a preoccupation with triviality" (p. 5). Since people lacked a clear understanding of leisure, Aitken, like Dahl (1972), Myers (1992), Ramsay (2005), and Andrews (2006), was concerned that they would choose unedifying pastimes. Rojek (1999) and Iso-Ahola (1999) might add concern regarding choices made for more destructive activities such as deviant, criminal, and/or health damaging pastimes. People therefore need to be more aware and make more conscious choices about how they engage in life. Second, Aitken worried that people would forfeit their right of choice and simply drift from one pursuit to another. They would not manage their time well and experience boredom and apathy. As a result, Lee (1964) warned, people would face an "erosion of meaning, a great emptiness that haunts them as they drift" (p. 21). To realize the promise of leisure, Aitken maintained that what was required was a fundamental reassertion of human values based on an ethics of responsibility.

Aitken (1976) posited that people's essential vocation in life was a call to be responsible. He described how Niebuhr (1963) in *The Responsible Self* suggested that "responsibility best defines the nature of people's moral experience" (Aitken, p. 238). He contrasted an ethics of responsibility with both teleological ethics, which names goals or ends people ought to pursue, and deontological ethics, which names duties or obligations which people ought to obey. For Niebuhr, the key to responsibility was the element of response to people's life situations. People do not live in private isolation but in communities of persons; hence their morality needs to be shaped by concrete claims and actions made on their lives by others and not simply abstract ends or goals, duties or obligations. Teleology asks what the good or ideal is; deontology asks what the right or law is. The ethics of responsibility asks what is going on and then determines what the fitting or appropriate actions are. It is a broader concept of moral experience, Aitken argued, because it stresses that life is lived within a community of persons and contains the assumption that people are free and self-determining. The ethics of responsibility, therefore, calls people to assess each situation and make their own decision about what they ought to do in light of their interpretation of what is good and right and so fitting and appropriate.

Aitken maintained that personal maturity and public service for others and the whole of creation were the bases of a responsible ethics and so were to shape and direct people's growth and development, management of time, and choice of activities. The virtues and ego strengths that are named to mark personal maturity and standards of behavior are the most significant aspects of people's spirituality. Erik Erikson, as noted by Fowler (1984) in *Becoming Adult, Becoming Christian,* has assumed something of the role of guru for his studies that assessed "the development of the kinds of strengths that are essential for moral and nonmoral virtue" (p. 21). He posited that there were eight basic stages or phases of growth and development through the life journey. Each stage was marked with a particular challenge that resulted in the development of ego strengths or weaknesses. People's caregivers were responsible for providing an appropriate context within which these ego strengths could develop in their childhood years. People in their adult years then needed to continue to deal with the challenges in each stage and seek to nurture the appropriate ego strengths in themselves, building on the previous strengths. Capps (1987), in *Deadly Sins and Saving Virtues,* develops these dynamics of growth and development in a unique way, in that he links the list of eight deadly sins (there was an earlier list of eight that were reduced to what are commonly known today as the traditional seven deadly sins) to each of Erikson's eight stages, positing that the deadly sins can be overcome through the cultivation of each of the eight ego strengths or virtues. There are various lists of virtues. Aristotle's four cardinal virtues were justice, prudence, temperance, and fortitude. Paul's three theological virtues were faith, hope, and love (1 Cor. 13:13). Noddings (2003), in *Caring, a Feminine Approach to Ethics and Moral Education,* adds another dimension to basic virtues that influence people's moral choices. For her, goodness was nurtured and sustained by sentiment, feeling, and care. She noted that in moral discussions, "the mother's voice has been silent. Human caring and the memory of caring and being cared for, which I shall argue form the foundation of ethical response, have not received attention except as outcomes of ethical behavior" (p. 1).

I find Erikson's list (cited by Fowler, 1984) more but not fully comprehensive, so prefer it, especially in light of the way Capps (1987) links each of the challenges of the eight stages to a deadly sin, and then links each of the stages to the Beatitudes attributed to Jesus (Matt. 5: 3–12, Luke 6: 20–23) (See Table 1). For example, in infancy, the challenge is trust versus mistrust; the saving virtue is hope, the deadly sin is gluttony, and the corresponding beatitude is those who are pure in heart. I think it essential to add a ninth stage to Erikson's eight stages for the sake of frail and dependent people. Blessed or happy are those, as Jesus is said to have proclaimed in the Beatitudes, whose lives are full of hope, will, purpose, competence, fidelity, love, care, and wisdom. As Schuller (1987) said in *The Be (Happy) Attitudes*, "each contains the spiritual motivation to alter a human being's attitude . . . they are eight positive attitudes that will transform any life" (p. 16).

Leisure as a responsible engagement in life, therefore, addresses the negative connotation that leisure is simply a selfish, private, more introverted pursuit of fun, amusement, deviant, and/or health-damaging activities. It also addresses the issue of leisure as an escape from making decisions about life and so drifting aimlessly through life. Leisure thrives when people are making choices that enhance the goodness of their own and others' lives. Goodness is realized in people's care for themselves, which seeks the development of their full potential by nurturing their own maturity and wholeness; living life with abandon; and celebration in their work, play, and worship. Goodness is also realized in affirming leisure as a right for all and engaging in actions that promote care and justice for others in public service and for the whole of creation. Leisure requires this very complex ingredient of responsibility and the virtues, principles, and sentiments that inform people's assessing of situations and deciding on appropriate responses.

Table 1

Life Stages and Corresponding Challenges, Virtues, Sins, and Beatitudes

Life Stage	Challenge	Saving Virtue	Deadly Sin	Beatitude
Infancy	Trust vs mistrust	Hope	Gluttony	The pure in heart
Early childhood	Autonomy vs. shame and doubt	Will	Anger	The meek
Mid-childhood	Initiative vs. guilt	Purpose	Greed	Those who hunger and thirst for righteousness
Late childhood	Industry vs. inferiority	Competence	Envy	The poor in spirit
Adolescence	Indentity vs. identity confusion	Fidelity	Pride	Those persecuted for righteousness' sake
Young adulthood	Intimacy vs. isolation	Love	Lust	The peacemakers
Mid-adulthood	Generativity vs. stagnation	Care	Apathy	The merciful
Senior adulthood	Integrity vs. despair	Wisdom	Melancholy	Those who mourn
Frail and dependent people	Being vs. doing	Joy	Apathy and melancholy	The pure in heart

Note. Adapted from D. Capps (1988).

Leisure and Happiness

Leisure links itself to people's spirituality by positing that their path in life is to seek to be free, engaged, and responsible in their work, play, and worship. Leisure links itself to people's spirituality secondly by declaring that this path nurtures and sustains what people most desire: a persistent happiness and wellbeing, an inner presence, stated from a spiritual perspective, of the divine or sacred. Many people have difficulty experiencing such happiness. As Bibby's (2006) surveys revealed, "30% of Canadians feel they ***should be getting more out of life,*** while close to 25% find themselves troubled about ***the purpose of life*** itself" (p. 115). Andrews (2006) expressed concern regarding these difficulties with experiencing happiness. She declared:

> it's imperative that we understand happiness because the pursuit of happiness is being used to seduce people into the corporate consumer lifestyle that is destroying our planet and putting us at war. Understanding happiness is important because if we are going to be able to get people to change, we must show them alternative ways of living that truly make them happy and do not destroy life. (p. 15)

Many studies of happiness abound. I think that with the decline of leisure as a model for living, happiness has emerged to take its place. Like leisure, however, it too needs clarity about what nurtures and sustains it. I believe that leisure will engulf people in happiness. What I do to assess my position as I am reading treatises on who is happy and why, is ask what they say about people being free, engaged, and responsible in their work, play, and worship. I look to determine if these dynamics could form a basis for their insights into sources of happiness. I want to put leisure to the test, so to speak, but need to limit my focus, and therefore will examine briefly what David Myers' (1992) research in *The Pursuit of Happiness* says about who is happy and why.

First, what does Myers' (1992) research suggest about leisure as a state of being marked by freedom, that is, a presence of choice, control and wanting to be occupied, and an absence of coercion, obligation, and having to be occupied? He noted that those who have a basic sense of control over their lives report positive feelings of wellbeing. Those who have little or no control, or freedom of choice, report very negative feelings. "In concentration camps, in prisons, even in factories, colleges and well-meaning nursing homes, people who have little control experience lowered morale, more stress, and more health problems" (p. 114). He continued, "people thrive best under conditions of democracy and personal freedom" (p. 115). As Bibby (2006) noted, what Canadian adults and teenagers have said in surveys over the last twenty years is that number one on their value list and what most makes them happy is "freedom" (p. 112). He stated that "what Canadians are saying is this: 'when we grow up and as we grow old, we want to have sufficient personal freedom so we can think and act in ways that suit us'" (p. 129).

Second, what does Myers' (1992) research suggest about the relationship between being engaged and happiness? As has already been cited, engaged, not passive, involvement leads to happiness. Passivity leads to escapism, boredom, listlessness, and apathy. Happiness emerges out of people being physically, emotionally, thoughtfully, spiritually, socially, and culturally engaged. Honoré (2004) and Andrews (2006), as already noted, affirmed the need for slow activity. I would reiterate Kleiber's (2000) quest for a restoration of "relaxation and receptivity" (p. 82). As Myers observed, sleep and solitude are essential parts of people's daily activities. Myers hesitated with advice regarding such moments of stillness, particularly sleep, because he did not want to sound like "a parental voice from the past, but it's true," he declared. "A good sleep predisposes a good mood. In experiments, subjects deprived of sleep often feel a general malaise, especially during their sleepiest times" (p. 138). He continued on to note that

> the experiences of great philosophers, scientists, artists and religious visionaries confirm the creative power of solitude. Being freed from distractions may trigger vivid fantasies and deep insights. . . . Daily quiet time affirms the value of rest, not as an otherworldly end, but as a spiritual recharging for living actively. (p. 140)

Third, what does Myers' (1992) research suggest about the importance of balancing life's basic activities of work, play, and worship? He did not specifically address such a question, but one can find that trilogy affirmed. What I found intriguing about his chapter on "'Flow' in work and play," in addition to his insights into how people could experience *flow* in their work and play, was that this chapter concluded with an affirmation of the importance of rest, sleep, and solitude as noted above. Happy are those, in other words, who punctuate their work and play with worship activities such as prayer, meditation, contemplation, vision quests, and spiritual retreats. Myers cited Thomas Merton, who declared that "it is in silence, and not in commotion, in solitude and not in crowds, that God best likes to reveal himself" (p. 140). It would have been most appropriate, perhaps, to have titled that chapter "'Flow' in work, play, and worship."

Myers (1992) expanded on worship in his concluding chapter, where he cited research that indicated how people's faith and active involvement in community enhance happiness. "Survey after survey across North America and Europe," he observed, "reveal that religious people more often than nonreligious people report feeling happy and satisfied with life" (p. 183). He warned that faith is not a guarantee of a bliss that is immune from suffering and stress. He advised people that religions making such guarantees can be debilitating because they are founded on promises of social protection from setbacks and tragedy. Such faith systems are bound to lead to disillusionment, because all people are vulnerable to such difficulties. A wholesome faith, on the contrary, recognizes that people will encounter suffering, failures, and disappointments, and provides resources such as rituals and ceremonies so that people can see themselves through such trials and tribulations without losing their faith and happiness. These resources also include an engaged involvement in a caring community within which people are constantly seeking a sense of meaning and purpose in life. He noted that beliefs within such faith communities need to include humility rather than arrogance with regard to people's hopes, dreams, and abilities; self-acceptance rather than rejection of self; willingness to serve others; and a wholesome perspective of the life journey that includes dying and death. Happy are those who take the leap into such engaged faith communities. As Myers affirmed:

> the tools of empirical science cannot prove any faith true or false, nor has anyone as yet used them to show that one faith produces more joy than another. Fortunately, those who wish to become people of faith needn't await such proof before risking a leap across the crevasse of uncertainty.... Mindful of our capacity for error, we can retain humility and openness while betting our lives on a worthy hope, a hope that nurtures peace and love and justice, and joy. (p. 204)

Fourth, what does Myers' (1992) research suggest about an ethics of responsibility and happiness? Two basic points have been made about responsibility thus far. The first is that the ethics of responsibility is a more appropriate basis for moral action because people, rather than simply following the goals and ideals of teleological ethics or obeying the rules and laws of deontological ethics, must assess astutely the situation and decide for themselves what to do. Personal control, as has already been noted, is a very important source of happiness. Second, the virtues or ego strengths of a personal maturity that take people into public service to care for the rights of others and all of creation were cited as bases for assessing ways of being responsible.

Myers (1992) was encouraging people to take personal control over their lives and assess carefully, first, what research suggested about mistaken myths for realizing happiness, then what research suggested about authentic sources of happiness. His purpose was to inform so that people could make their own choices about appropriate and inappropriate ways and means of pursuing happiness. As for public service and care, he expressed great concern regarding the individualism of today and the seeming unwillingness of people to care for others. Myers suggested that happiness actually "makes people less self-focused and more altruistic. . . . Doing good makes us feel good. Altruism enhances our self-esteem" (p. 195). Leisure, in other words, can emerge by reading in between the lines of Myers' research as a source of happiness. Happy are those, his research could declare, who are engaged and responsible in their pursuit of freedom in their work, play, and worship.

A Renaissance of Leisure

Leisure has become such a misunderstood word that it has disappeared from the public lexicon as a possible model that directs and shapes the path people follow in life. People are not certain whether it refers to some segment of time or activities separate and apart from work, or some long-lost ideal of the generation of baby boomers not worth seeking to reclaim. The ongoing dominance of work and the way this industrial type of work developed in the Western world is breaking into every other nation in the world, meaning that the same kinds of debilitating dynamics that have been described earlier will happen there as well. So let me pause and fantasize, and as Cox (1969) would say, engage in "envisioning radically alternative life situations" (p. 7). What would happen if governments, political parties, public health units, businesses, universities, colleges, schools, and religious communities examined carefully what they were doing to ensure that people were free to be engaged and responsible in their work, play, and worship? Are they actually doing leisure without actually giving it this name? What would happen if parents asked the same question about how they were raising their children? What would happen if individuals asked this question of themselves and their lifestyles? If leisure is to experience a renaissance today, it may have to begin from the grassroots, but if so, it needs to be clearly explained; it needs to be linked to spirituality so that it provides a holistic path that embraces not just a segment of time or activities but all of time and all of our human activities. And how do we understand the experience of a persistent sense of happiness and wellbeing as divine or sacred? Perhaps people just need to do leisure, and test out such a lifestyle to see if it really does nurture and sustain a mystical and transcendent happiness that sometimes cannot be explained.

Myers (1992) stated that people need to recognize that, while invisible social forces greatly impact on them, "it is also true that we have the power to affect our own destinies for we are the creators as well as the creatures of our social worlds. We may be products of our past, but we are also architects of our future" (p. 122). Fox (2002), in *Creativity*, concurred. He proclaimed, "I do not see any way out of humankind's multiple dilemmas except the one route that got us here in the first place: our powerful creativity" (p. 9). People have the creative power, in other words, to nurture and sustain leisure in their own lives and the societies in which they live.

How to go about making changes in our lives is one of the greatest challenges people can face. Our creativity may be the best of human virtues; it can also be the most dangerous. As Fox (2002) warned, people "can choose not to develop their creativity . . . or turn it over to others and to institutions . . . or use it for demonic purposes" (p. 231). Do we simply give in to the ongoing dominance of work at our jobs and in our homes to the exclusion of play and worship? Do we succumb to the passive and/or irresponsible lifestyles that those invisible and visible social forces of our culture often portray for us and seduce us into believing that that is just the way it is and nothing can be done to change it? Do we drift along, letting others address personal, local, and global dilemmas? Or do we join Fox (2002) and "opt for the 'good deeds that glorify'? We must," (p. 231) he declared. Myers might suggest that people try "acting [their] way into a new way of thinking" (p. 121) by doing leisure. He argued that when people are seeking to enhance their self-esteem, personal control, optimism, and/or extroversion, for instance, "a potent strategy is to get up and start doing that very thing. Don't worry that you do not feel like it. Fake it. Pretend self-esteem. Feign optimism. Simulate outgoingness" (p. 124). It may seem phony at first, he suggested, but the new roles, behavior, and accompanying attitudes suddenly begin to fall into place. He might suggest that people participate in engaged and responsible work, play, and worship. See if experiences of a freedom from necessity and happiness happen. See if there is an incredible, mystical, and energizing experience that could be understood as divine or sacred that emerges within one's own inner spirit and starts to pervade all of life. Transformation may take much time but be so well worth it.

Leisure can be one of the most hopeful promises for the future. As de Grazia (1964) noted, work can ennoble us; leisure can help perfect us (p. 416). Goodale and Godbey's (1995) proclamation is worth repeating: "leisure will assert itself because it is where human change, however unwittingly, is leading us" (p. xiii). I am seeking a renaissance of leisure by presenting a holistic model that will give better clarity to its meaning so people can commit to it both as a path to follow and as their life's purpose. Moreover, I am inviting people to include this path as part of their spirituality, because I believe it will connect them with the divine or sacred as a remarkably mysterious experience that ranges from an overall satisfaction, contentment, and being at peace with life to moments when we are engulfed in such happiness that it cannot be explained. Eck (2003) proclaimed that "just being awake, alert and attentive is no easy matter. I think it is the greatest spiritual challenge we face. Finally, I think it is the only one" (p. 145). My hope is that the spirituality of leisure can once again awaken and alert people to be attentive to an engaged and responsible pursuit of freedom so they are fully and joyously alive in their work, play, and worship.

References

Aitken, B. (1976). *Vocation and leisure*. (Unpublished doctoral dissertation). University of Strasbourg, France.
Andrews, C. (2006). *Slow is beautiful*. Gabriola Island, BC: New Society.
Bibby, R. (2006). *The boomer factor*. Toronto: Bastian.
Capps, D. (1987). *Deadly sins and saving virtues*. Philadelphia, PA: Fortress.
Cooper, A. (1998). *Playing in the zone*. Boston: Shambhala.
Cox, H. (1969). *The feast of fools*. Cambridge, MA: Harvard University Press.
Cox, H. (1977). *Turning east*. New York: Simon & Schuster.
Csikszentmihalyi, M. (1997). *Finding flow: The psychology of engagement with everyday life*. New York: Basic.
Dahl, G. (1972). *Work, play and worship*. Minneapolis: Augsburg.
Dahl, G. (2006). Whatever happened to the leisure revolution? In P. Heintzman, G.E. Van Andel, & T.L. Visker (Eds.), *Christianity and leisure: Issues in a pluralistic society* (Rev. ed., pp. 85–97). Sioux Center: Dordt College Press.
De Graff, J. (2003). *Take back your time*. San Francisco: Berrett-Koehler.
de Grazia, S. (1964). *Of time, work and leisure*. New York: Doubleday.
Doohan, L. (1990). *Leisure: A spiritual need*. Notre Dame, IN: Ave Maria.
Eck, D. (2003). *Encountering God*. Boston: Beacon.
Flocker, M. (2004). *The hedonism handbook*. Cambridge, MA: Da Capo.
Florida, R. (2004). *The rise of the creative class*. New York: Basic Books.
Fox, M. (1994). *The reinvention of work*. San Francisco: Harper.

Fox, M. (2002). *Creativity.* New York: Tarcher/Putnam.
Fowler, J. (1984). *Becoming adult, becoming Christian.* San Francisco: Harper & Row.
Gable, B. (1999, November 10). *The Globe and Mail,* p. A11.
Gini, A. (2003). *The importance of being lazy.* New York: Routledge.
Goodale, T., & Godbey, G. (1988). *The evolution of leisure.* State College, PA: Venture.
Heintzman, P. (2000). Leisure and spiritual well-being relationships: A qualitative study. *Society and Leisure* 23(1), 41–69.
Honoré, C. (2004). *In praise of slow.* Toronto: Random House.
Iso-Ahola, S.E. (1997). A psychological analysis of leisure and health. In J.T. Haworth (Ed.), *Work, leisure and well-being* (pp. 131–144). New York: Routledge.
Iso-Ahola, S.E. (1999). Motivational foundations of leisure. In E.L. Jackson & T.L. Burton (Eds.), *Leisure studies: Prospects for the twenty-first century* (pp. 35–49). State College, PA: Venture.
Kelly, J. (1982). *Leisure.* Englewood Cliffs, NJ: Prentice-Hall.
Kleiber, D.A. (2000). The neglect of relaxation. *Journal of Leisure Research* 32(1), 82–86.
Lee, R. (1964). *Religion and leisure in America.* Nashville, TN: Abington.
Myers, D. (1992). *The pursuit of happiness.* New York: Avon.
Nazareth, L. (2007). *The economics of leisure.* Mississauga, ON: John Wiley & Sons.
Niebuhr, H.R. (1963). *The responsible self.* New York: Harper & Row.
Noddings, N. (2003). *Caring, a feminine approach to ethics and moral education* (2nd ed.). Berkeley, CA: University of California.
Oates, W. (1971). *Confessions of a workaholic.* Nashville, TN: Abington.
Pavelka, J. (2000). *It's not about time!* Carp, ON: Creative Bound.
Pieper, J. (1952). *Leisure: The basis of culture* (A. Dru, Trans.). New York: Pantheon Books (1963, Random House).
Ramsay, H. (2005). *Reclaiming leisure.* New York: Palgrave Macmillan.
Richler, N. (2001, May 14). Working too hard. *The National Post,* pp. A1, A3.
Rojek, C. (1999). Deviant leisure: The dark side of free-time activity. In E.L. Jackson & T.L. Burton (Eds.), *Leisure studies: Prospects for the twenty-first century* (pp. 81–94). State College, PA: Venture.
Rybczynski, W. (1991). *Waiting for the weekend.* New York: Viking.
Schuller, R.H. (1987). *The be (happy) attitudes.* New York: Bantam.
Sheehy, G. (1995). *New passages.* New York: Ballantine Books.
Schor, J. (1991). *The overworked American.* New York: Basic Books.
Schor, J. (2003). The (even more) overworked American. In J. de Graff (Ed.), *Take back your time: Fighting overwork and time poverty in America* (pp. 6–11). San Francisco: Berrett-Koehler.
Searle, M.S., & Brayley, R.E. (1993). *Leisure services in Canada: An introduction.* State College, PA: Venture.

Stebbins, R.A. (2004). *Between work and leisure*. New Brunswick, NJ: Transaction.
Stebbins, R.A. (2007). *Serious leisure*. New Brunswick, NJ: Transaction.
Terr, L. (1999). *Beyond love and work*. New York: Simon & Schuster.
Tiger, L. (1992). *The pursuit of pleasure*. New York: Simon & Schuster.
Vanier, J. (2001). *Made for happiness*. Toronto: Anansi.

Chapter 5
QUALITY OF LIFE IN A CHRISTIAN COMMUNITY: A CONCEPTUAL INVESTIGATION OF FLOW EXPERIENCES AND HPERD RESPONSIBILITIES

Marcia Jean Carter

We all strive for happiness and satisfaction. As Christians, we realize meaning comes from the enjoyment of God forever. Quality of life is the phrase used to describe experiences that lead to attainment of life-satisfaction. Holistic wellbeing is the integrative feature of quality of life. Without spiritual wellness, each of the other wellness dimensions becomes imbalanced and meaningless. Spiritual wellness is a means to, and an end result of, quality of life.

As described by Csikszentmihalyi (1990) a flow experience brings us closer to accomplishing what we would like to do before we die, and how close we come to attaining this goal becomes the measure for the quality of our lives. Freedom, choice, harmony, and transformation are characteristics and outcomes of flow experiences. These are also appropriate descriptors of play, leisure, and spirituality. Individual and community identity are found in play, leisure, and spirituality. As Christians, we have the responsibility to balance personal dimensions of wellbeing while also promoting community harmony and connectedness.

The intent of this paper is to explore the Christian's role in personal and community quality of life experiences. The flow theory offers a paradigm to investigate the relationship between individual and community wellbeing and the quality of life. Characteristics of flow experiences are embodied in play, leisure, and spirituality. Outcomes of flow experiences include happiness, satisfaction, and quality of life. The Christian creates

Revised version of paper presented at the 1996 conference.

experiences that result in spiritual freedom and holistic wellbeing in their personal and community relationships.

Quality of Life

Quality of life is the phrase coined to describe the happiness that results from an inner harmony or peace. Experiences that contribute to quality of life are those that result in feelings of mastery, competence, and control. Without the support of faith, the joy of living is not realized. Csikszentmihalyi (1990), the theorist who defined the qualities and outcomes of flow experiences, believes that quality of life is not improved by the acquisition of material goods but rather by the happiness that is derived through direct control of present moment experiences. The control of consciousness enables mastery of the present and determines the quality of life. Consciousness is not only cognitive awareness but also commitment of emotions and will. Genuinely happy people enjoy what they are doing, are satisfied with their lives, do not regret the past, and look to the future with confidence. These persons enjoy each moment, live in the present, and "have a way of making those around them also a bit more happy" (Csikszentmihalyi, 1990, p. 10). The flow theorist introduces an approach to living that suggests a relationship between quality of life and faith. The connection comes with the integration of cognition, emotion, and the will to control our present moments and instill happiness in others.

Quality of life is associated with experiences that promote optimal wellbeing or holistic wellbeing. A number of interpretations are given to the wellness concept. Most describe wellness as an effort to stay healthy and achieve our highest potential. The term is an umbrella term that denotes several activities undertaken to help individuals change their behaviors in order to improve health, quality of life, and total wellbeing. Holistic wellness models organize these activities into behavioral categories having intellectual, physical, emotional, and social dimensions. Spirituality is introduced as either an integrative dimension or an element similar to each of the other four behavioral dimensions. Optimum wellness exists when each dimension is balanced and fully developed. However, Chandler, Holden, and Kolander (1992) believe that high-level wellness is achieved only when the spiritual element is developed within each of the behavioral areas. Outward behavioral changes (e.g., balancing work and leisure) are a cue that personal changes are occurring, yet without accompanying spiritual growth, maintenance of positive behavioral change becomes difficult. The authors believe spiritual growth, along with behavioral change, "will more likely lead to transformation of the self with its accompanying opportunity to achieve higher level wellness" (Chandler et al., 1992, p. 17).

The concept of holistic wellbeing or high level wellness moves beyond a consideration of behaviors necessary to maintain functional wellbeing to an investigation of the values that constitute our life plan. Sylvester (1989) believes the quality of reflective thinking that human beings have allows them to direct their own lives. This quality allows us to exercise choices over our life course that lead to happiness, which he defines as "the harmonious arrangement of quality of life values exercised . . . over the life course" (Sylvester, 1989, p. 13). Happiness is an ethical state that includes all the best virtues "such as love, play, sport, health, laughter, knowledge, friendship, reflection, spirituality, civic involvement, and aesthetic expression and appreciation" (Sylvester, 1989, p. 13). Without adequate levels of health, happiness is difficult to pursue. Sylvester (1989) links leisure to health and happiness by postulating "leisure is the freedom to pursue quality of life values" (p. 15). Leisure pursuits are intrinsically motivated behaviors through which our values are expressed and the quality of our lives is enhanced.

Iso-Ahola (1980) also supported the relationship between leisure and quality of life behaviors. In his study of the relationship of leisure satisfaction to life satisfaction, Iso-Ahola (1980) noted the association of an optimum level of arousal (level of interest) and incongruity (motivational behaviors that cause people to seek out more complexity or novelty during interactions) with perceived quality of life and leisure satisfaction. Iso-Ahola (1980) theorized that when active recreation introduces novelty and familiarity, stability and change, and variety and similarity, life and leisure satisfaction are at their highest because leisure behavior is optimally arousing or incongruous. From his review of the research literature, he concluded that optimally arousing leisure is conducive to psychological wellbeing.

The good life is achieved by taking charge or control. Through reflective experiences, we turn inward to self and make choices that balance behavioral dimensions of change so growth occurs through spiritual development. Quality of life implies engaging in experiences that are worthy of our desire and effort (Sylvester, 1989). The total person acts in a positive, proactive, personal manner to achieve oneness or shalom.

Quality of life is therefore descriptive of a process and outcomes that are value laden. It is not only what we do during our life course but how we do it. The quality of each moment determines the satisfaction we have with ourselves, others, and our relationship with God.

Play and Leisure

Play and leisure are integrative life course experiences that embody values inherent in the quality of life concept. Johnston (1983) noted in the preface to his book *The Christian at Play* that "the person at play is expressing his or her God-given nature" (p. vii). He further stated, "play is a comprehensive human experience . . . [that] affords at least a momentary integration of life" (Johnston, 1983, p. vii). According to Dahl (1972), leisure possesses some of the qualities found within play: "Leisure is . . . a sense of freedom which is realized when a person experiences more fully both his uniqueness and worth as an individual and his acceptance and relationship as part of the world around him" (p. 70). Like Johnston, Dahl (1972) recognized spirituality in leisure: "A Christian experiences leisure when he comes into full awareness of the freedom he has in Christ" (pp. 70–71). Integration, freedom, self-identity, and community are virtues found in play and leisure experiences. Each definition also identifies the fundamental essence of spiritual expression in the process and outcome of living fully forever.

Characteristics and outcomes of play and leisure describe spirituality and vice versa; the essence of spirituality is found in the experiences of play and leisure. Johnston (1983) summarized the characteristics of play when he stated:

> The player is called into play by a potential co-player and/or play object, and while at play, treats other players and/or "playthings" as personal, creating with them a community that can be characterized by "I-Thou" . . . relationships. (p. 34)

Play is an autotelic experience. People engage in play for its own sake without the expectation of a future benefit or reward. Johnston (1983) organized the consequences of being at play into five outcomes:

1) A continuing sense of delight or joy;
2) Affirmation of a united self;
3) Creation of common bonds with the world;
4) Outward movement of one's spirit toward the sacred; and
5) Transcendence of workaday world toward freedom.

The intrinsic value of play restores life's fundamental sacredness. Play is universal and fundamental. Play occurs throughout life and brings to life personal and communal identity grounded on holism and spiritual wellbeing.

Leisure means freedom. Leisure involves the whole person. The freedom represented by leisure allows and enables holistic wellbeing. Like play, leisure experiences are characterized by, and have outcomes found in, quality wellbeing and spirituality. Dahl (1972) suggested the contemporary meaning of leisure has three characteristics:

1) Leisure is essentially spiritual, because the freedom it creates re-opens us so we transcend the economic and social world and partake of eternity;
2) Leisure is a quality or style of life, because it allows us to discover the presence of living for each moment in our daily being; and
3) Leisure is a synthesizing factor, because it brings harmony and integration and allows us to transform from inside out.

Leisure is an attitude and a means to achieve fulfillment and satisfaction. It is a central life force that brings balance into one's life. During leisure experiences, we view life holistically and from the inside out. Leisure offers the opportunity to move toward personal and communal harmony. In a leisure experience, we perceive ourselves to be competent. This offers the opportunity for self-improvement and reflection. As we look inward, we gain feelings of confidence and believe we are free to shape the present moment and enter relevant and meaningful relationships: I-thou commitments. The outcome of leisure is the enjoyment of life, knowing who we are, and sharing with others the gifts of freedom and wellbeing.

Play and leisure experiences have characteristics found in quality of life. Outcomes of play and leisure are autotelic yet conducive to life satisfaction and happiness. Play and leisure, like any other experiences, are not good in the absolute sense but rather because in and of themselves they have the potential to make life more intense, meaningful, and sacred. Each promotes flow experiences that enable balance, spiritual growth, and holism.

Flow Theory – Optimal Experiences

The theory of optimal experience based on the concept of flow presents a paradigm we may use to organize and plan personal and community experiences to improve our quality of life and empower others to do the same. The theory presented by Csikszentmihalyi (1990) depicts the dynamic and emergent nature of becoming whole. Flow makes the present enjoyable and builds self-confidence so holistic change and growth result in commitments to one another and contributions to humankind (Csikszentmihalyi, 1990). The characteristics of a flow state are embodied in play, leisure, and spirituality. Likewise, outcomes of flow are found during play, leisure, and spirituality. Thus, a meaningful Christian life is characterized by inner congruence and balance, which enables personal strength and serenity and community harmony and unity.

Quality of life is enhanced, as enjoyment is built into daily activities. Enjoyment is characterized by novelty, creativity, accomplishment, change, and forward movement toward complexity (Csikszentmihalyi, 1990). Enjoyment is found in how we live rather than what experiences we have. Through reflection, we discover the qualities within experiences that are likely to promote enjoyment or the attainment of a flow state.

Specific activities facilitate the flow state (Csikszentmihalyi, 1990). Flow results when the opportunities for challenge in an experience are commensurate with the participant's skill levels (e.g., cognitive, emotional, physical and social). Without a perceived balance between skills and challenges, we enter negative states of either boredom or anxiety. We tend not to enjoy an activity for any length of time unless its complexity increases. Motivation to continue the activity remains high as participants discover new challenges with skill enhancement. The enjoyment we receive from an experience is, therefore, not necessarily a direct outcome of our actual skill level but our perceptions and feelings of the skills we think we have within the social context of the experience. A flow state is self-transforming because it results in self-growth. The growth of self leads to integrative behavioral changes and development of I-thou relationships. The state of flow brings a sense of discovery, creative use of self, movement toward higher levels of performance, and growth in consciousness.

Living in a Christian Community

Our spirituality is at the core of the self and mediates interactions in the larger community. Quality of life is multidimensional and involves the management of physical, mental, emotional, and social behaviors and change to attain holistic wellbeing. Behavioral change occurs in a social community of work, love, life, and leisure. Spirituality is the core that balances each dimension of personal growth and promotes community stewardship.

The Christian has a moral responsibility to promote community wellbeing. Play and leisure activities that enrich our lives occur initially within the family, then in the community. A Christian facilitates family and community growth through play and leisure experiences that foster empowerment. Labonte (1996) described empowerment as a process that encourages supportive relationships resulting in community connectedness. As shown in Figure 1, community quality of life has dimensions similar to the behavioral areas of individual wellbeing. To achieve holistic wellbeing, balance and unity among the dimensions are essential. Christians encourage play and leisure activities that promote the physical health necessary to maintain meaningful experiences and social interactions. A common vision brings harmony to I-thou relationships. Christians foster experiences and relationships that promote perceptions of unity, control, growth, and change. Through social relationships and meaningful experiences, holistic wellbeing is achieved.

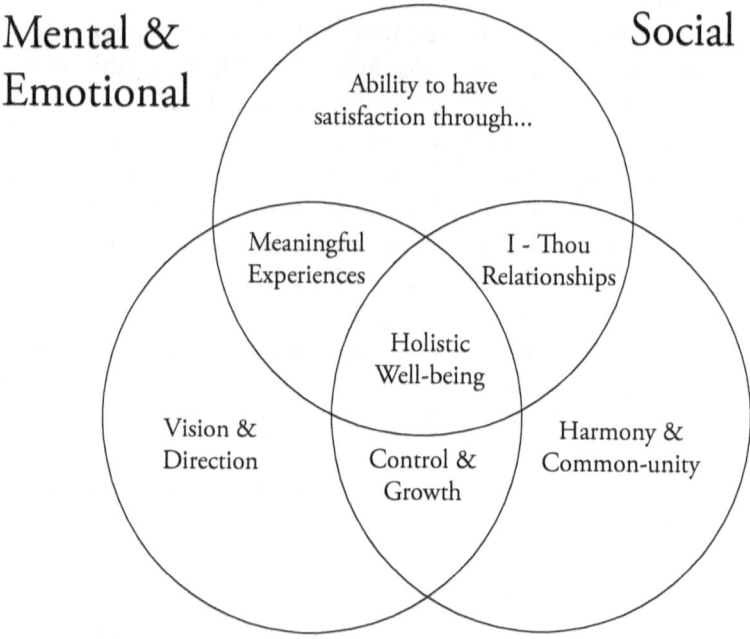

Figure 1: Christian stewardship promotes holistic community quality of life.

Christians encourage others to develop appropriate skills so they have the strength and serenity to face daily challenges. Social experiences are the conduit to transformational relationships. Members gain the control and direction needed to balance behavioral change and growth while harmony and common-unity are nurtured throughout the community. Christians at play and leisure are creating opportunities for reflective experiences that bring satisfaction. Play and leisure with family and community create opportunities for self-growth and community empowerment. Holistic well-being is achieved as spirituality facilitates integration and growth within each individual and through I-thou relationships found in community interactions.

References

Chandler, C.K., Holden, J.M., & Kolander, C.A. (1992). Counseling for spiritual wellness: Theory and practice. *Journal of Counseling & Development* 71, 168–175.

Csikszentmihalyi, M. (1990). *Flow: The psychology of optimal experience.* New York: HarperCollins.

Dahl, G. (1972). *Work, play, and worship in a leisure-oriented society.* Minneapolis: Augsburg.

Iso-Ahola, S.E. (1980). *The social psychology of leisure and recreation.* Dubuque, IA: Brown.

Johnston, R.K. (1983). *The Christian at play.* Grand Rapids: Eerdmans.

Labonte, R. (1996). Community empowerment and leisure. *Leisurability* 23(1), 4–20.

Sylvester, C. (1989). Quality assurance and quality of life: Accounting for the good and healthy life. *Therapeutic Recreation Journal* 23(2), 7–22.

SECTION TWO

LEISURE RESEARCH

Although Christians throughout history have reflected upon leisure and how it is to be understood from a Christian perspective, there has been little empirical research on how Christians actually define and practice leisure. Only a small amount of empirical research exists on the leisure of a variety of Christian groups: Amish (Anderson & Autry, 2011); Old Order Mennonites and Amish (Wenger, 2003); evangelical theologians (Hothem, 1983); Assemblies of God (Livengood, 2004); Brethren (Collins, 1993); and the Black Church (Waller, 2009, 2010). A related body of empirical research, comprised mainly of doctoral dissertations, exists on church recreation (e.g., Wesner, 1995). Consistent with this pattern of little empirical research on the leisure of Christians, only one chapter in the first volume of *Christianity and Leisure* (Heintzman, Van Andel, & Visker, 2006) was an empirical study (Keller, Naylor & Stirling, 2006); however, this study was on sports, not leisure. In contrast, the largest section of this second volume of *Leisure and Spirituality* is by far this section on leisure research, which consists of seven empirical studies and one chapter that critiques empirical research on leisure and spirituality.

The first three chapters in this section examine leisure meanings for a variety of populations. In Chapter 6, John Schulz and Christopher Auld used questionnaires to conduct a social psychological investigation of the contemporary meanings of leisure held by Australian Christians. However, they found little evidence to suggest that leisure meanings were strongly linked to religion. They speculate that while there are theological and biblical books and articles on leisure, these writings often do not reach the wider population. While Schulz and Auld's chapter involves a quantitative study of a large population, the next two chapters involve qualitative studies of very specific populations. The meaning of leisure for older persons living in retirement homes is explored by Lois Hoitenga Roelofs in Chapter 7. For these persons, leisure tended to be viewed positively and be considered as nonwork time characterized by relaxation, choice, and enjoyment. In Chapter 8, Margaret Hothem reports a research study that explored the leisure meanings, functions, and constraints as expressed by international students at a Christian liberal arts college. For many of these students, leisure was nonwork time or activity.

Leisure constraints have received increasing attention in recent decades (e.g., Jackson, 2005). In her study of international students (Chapter 8), Hothem found that these students' leisure was constrained by their cultural values that were different than the culture they were living in, lack of time, and lack of resources (e.g., transportation, money). The next chapter, Chapter 9, has a very specific focus upon leisure constraints. In a study that utilizes participatory action research methodology, Steven Waller investigates whether religious doctrine and personal beliefs are a constraint to participation in leisure activities for congregants at a Baptist church in southern Ohio. Findings suggested that not only do religious belief systems influence leisure choices and behaviors, but that structural, interpersonal, and intrapersonal leisure constraints all exist within the congregation.

One area related to Christianity and leisure where there is considerably more empirical research is that which focuses on the outcomes of Christian wilderness, outdoor education, and outdoor adventure programs (e.g., Anderson-Hanley, 1996; Bobilya, Akey, & Mitchell, 2011; Griffin, 2003; Griffin & Leduc, 2009; Heintzman, 2007; LeDuc, 2002). In Chapter 10, Valerie Gin adds to this research focus with a study of the spiritual development of participants in a college wilderness program, specifically Gordon College's La Vida program. As with previous studies, such as Heintzman's (2007) study, many factors including program components, program principles, and the group itself contributed to spiritual outcomes.

In the last two decades, there has been a proliferation of research on leisure and spirituality. Much of the early research (e.g., McAvoy & Stringer, 1992) focused on outdoor and wilderness experiences such as Gin's research in Chapter 10. However, now there is an extensive body of empirical literature on leisure and spirituality in all leisure settings and not just outdoor settings (Heintzman, 2016a, 2016b). However, with only a few exceptions (Berkers, 2012; Kraus, 2010), very little of this research has focused on Christians and Christian spirituality. Another exception is Livengood's (2009) study of the role of leisure in the spirituality of New Paradigm Christians which has been republished as Chapter 11 in this book. Livengood discovered that solitary leisure activities, leisure with others, and leisure in a natural environment created by God were important to spiritual outcomes for New Paradigm Christians.

An activity that Christians have traditionally associated with spiritual growth and development is that of retreats. In Chapter 12, Pierre Ouellette, Rachel Kaplan, and Stephen Kaplan investigate the motivations, activities, and effects of an individual retreat in a Benedictine monastery. The authors conclude that the monastery is a restorative environment consistent with attention restoration theory.

The final chapter in this section is not an empirical study but a critique of the empirical studies on leisure and spirituality that have proliferated over the last two decades. In Chapter 13, Paul Heintzman identifies and explains six areas of concern within the current study of leisure and spirituality. For example, the history of Christian spirituality has much to contribute to the present study of the relationship between leisure and spirituality, yet this tradition is largely ignored in contemporary discussion of the topic. Nevertheless, as Heintzman (2011) has pointed out elsewhere, some present-day findings on leisure and spirituality merely confirm what has been known throughout the history of Christian spirituality.

Paul Heintzman

References

Anderson, S.C., & Autry, C.E. (2011). Research note: Leisure behaviour of the Amish. *World Leisure Journal* 53(1), 57–66.

Anderson-Hanley, C. (1996). Spiritual well-being, spiritual growth and Outward Bound-type programs: A comparative study. Paper presented at the annual meeting of the Christian Association for Psychological Studies, April. St Louis, MO.

Berkers, V. (2012). *Religion, spirituality and leisure: A relational approach. The experience of religion and spirituality of Dutch New Christians and New Spirituals during leisure activities* (Unpublished master's thesis). Utrecht University, Netherlands.

Bobilya, A.J., Akey, L., & Mitchell, D., Jr. (2011). Outcomes of a spiritually focused wilderness orientation program. *Journal of Experiential Education* 33(4), 301–322.

Collins, C.W. (1993). Leisure and Christianity: The case of the Brethren. In A.J. Veal, P. Jonson, & G. Cushman (Eds.), *Leisure and tourism: Social and environmental change: Papers from the World Leisure and Recreation Association Congress, Sydney, Australia, July 16–19, 1991* (pp. 290–297). Sydney: Centre for Leisure and Tourism Studies, University of Technology; Sharbot Lake, ON: World Leisure and Recreation Association.

Daniel, B. (2007). The life significance of a spiritually oriented, Outward Bound-type wilderness expedition. *Journal of Experiential Education* 29(3), 386–389.

Griffin, J. (2003). The effects of an adventure-based program with an explicit spiritual component on the spiritual growth of adolescents. *Journal of Experiential Education* 25(3), 351.

Griffin, J., & LeDuc, J. (2009). Out of the fish tank: The impact of adventure programs as a catalyst for spiritual growth. *Leisure/Loisir* 33(1), 197–215.

Heintzman, P. (2007). Rowing, sailing, reading, discussing, praying: The spiritual and lifestyle impact of an experientially based, graduate, environmental education course. Paper presented at the Trails to Sustainability Conference, Kananaskis, Alberta, Canada.

Heintzman, P. (2011). "There is nothing new under the sun": A weaving of social scientific research findings on leisure and spirituality with wisdom from Christian classics of spirituality. In *An evolving tapestry: Weaving together threads of leisure*. 12th Canadian Congress on Leisure Research, May, 2011 (pp. 148–152). St. Catharines, ON: Department of Recreation and Leisure Studies, Brock University.

Heintzman, P. (2016a). Religion, spirituality and leisure. In G. Walker, D. Scott, & M. Stodolska (Eds.), *Leisure matters: The state and future of leisure studies* (pp. 67–75). State College, PA: Venture.

Heintzman, P. (2016b). Spirituality and the outdoors. In B. Humberstone, H. Prince, & K. Henderson (Eds.), *Routledge international handbook of outdoor studies* (pp. 388–397). New York: Routledge.

Heintzman, P., Van Andel, G.E., & Visker, T.L. (Eds.). (2006). *Christianity and leisure: Issues in a pluralistic society* (Rev. ed.). Sioux Center: Dordt College Press.

Hothem, M. (1983). *The integration of Christian faith and leisure: A qualitative study*. (Unpublished Ed.D. Dissertation). Boston University, MA.

Jackson, E.L. (Ed.). (2005). *Constraints to Leisure*. State College, PA: Venture.

Keller, K.A., Naylor, G.H., & Stirling, D.R. (2006). Competition in church sport leagues. In P. Heintzman, G.E. Van Andel, & T.L. Visker (Eds.), *Christianity and leisure: Issues in a pluralistic society* (Rev. ed., pp. 220–226). Sioux Center: Dordt College Press.

Kraus, R. (2010). They danced in the Bible: Identity integration among Christian women who belly dance. *Sociology of Religion* 71(4), 457–482.

LeDuc, J. (2002). *The relationship between adventure-based programs and spiritual development in high school adolescents at a Christian camp* (Unpublished master's thesis). University of California, Chico.

Livengood, J. (2004). Religion and leisure: An examination of the Assemblies of God Church. In W.T. Borrie & D. Kerstetter (Comps.), Abstracts of the 2004 Leisure Research Symposium (p. 23). Ashburn, VA: National Recreation and Park Association.

Livengood, J. (2009). The role of leisure in the spirituality of new paradigm

Christians. *Leisure/Loisir* 33(1), 389–417.

Stringer, L.A., & McAvoy, L.H. (1992). The need for something different: Spirituality and the wilderness adventure. *The Journal of Experiential Education* 15(1), 13–21.

Waller, S.N. (2009). Doctrinal beliefs as a determinant of sin associated with select leisure activities. *Journal of Unconventional Parks, Tourism & Recreation Research* 2(1), 7–18.

Waller, S.N. (2010). Leisure in the life of the 21st century Black Church: Re-thinking the gift. *Journal of the Christian Society for Kinesiology and Leisure Studies* 1(1), 33–47.

Wenger, L. (2003). *Unser satt leit: Our sort of people. Health understandings in the Old Order Mennonite and Amish community.* (Unpublished Master's thesis). University of Waterloo, ON.

Chapter 6
A Social Psychological Investigation of the Relationship between Christianity and Contemporary Meanings of Leisure: An Australian Perspective

John Schulz and Christopher Auld

Throughout history, religion in the form of individual beliefs, social institutions, and specific church doctrines has consistently provided commentary, boundaries, and alternatives to leisure. Few people would deny the historical connection between leisure and religion, especially given the apparent dominant influence of Christian principles and practices on western conceptions of leisure. Although the historical relationship has been clearly documented (deLisle, 2003; Lee, 1964), the connection in contemporary times is less clear. Despite the substantial amount of research into both leisure and religion, few studies have focused on their interrelationships or similarities.

There are many occasions when leisure and religion deal with essentially similar elements of life. Both leisure and religion often involve issues of self-actualization and finding meaning in life (Kelly & Freysinger, 2000). Lee (1964) argued that religion has had a major positive influence "on the historical development of leisure through the observances of holidays and festivals" (p. 127). There is also a growing use of sport and leisure pursuits by Christian churches to further their aims. For instance, the Promise Keepers and other Christian groups in the USA have adopted sport as a mechanism for reducing their separation and exclusion from society (Randels & Beal, 2002; Jarvie, 2006). Furthermore, there is increasing evidence to suggest that, for some people, religion is considered a form of leisure. For example, Dune (2000) noted that "involvement

---

Revised and expanded version of paper presented by John Schulz at the 2000 conference.

with the church is . . . one option among many in which people might engage in their leisure time" (p. 27).

There are also times when modern perceptions of leisure and Christianity appear to be quite distinct and are often incompatible practices. For example, the Protestant churches on the Isle of Lewis, in Scotland, recently prevented surfing competitions from occurring on a Sunday as the events were disturbing the island residents' observance of the Sabbath (Jarvie, 2006). For many people, leisure revolves around freedom, enjoyment, and intrinsic motivation, while religion often appears to be the antithesis of these ideals – controlling, solemnizing, and presenting life in very utilitarian terms. While this may be a somewhat negative understanding, this perception suggests a conflict between the underlying values that "stress the serious against the pleasurable, the functional against the intrinsic and the ascetic against the expressive" (Kelly, 1990, p. 65).

This paper explores these apparent similarities and contradictions by adopting a social psychological perspective. In particular, the research investigates the relationship between the meanings an individual associates with leisure and their religious experiences and practices. Three specific research questions are examined:

> RQ1 To what extent is an individual's meaning of leisure associated with their religious beliefs?
>
> RQ2 To what extent is an individual's meaning of leisure associated with the feeling and affective dimension of religion?
>
> RQ3 To what extent is an individual's meaning of leisure associated with their religious behavior?

For the purposes of this study, the religious experiences under study are restricted to those expressions associated with Christianity. In Australia, despite a decline in the 1970s and 1980s, affiliation to Christianity has remained high and moderately constant (Bouma, 2006). Approximately 70 percent of the population in Australia identify with the Christian religion and non-Christian religions account for less than 5 percent of the population (Australian Bureau of Statistics, 2003). Furthermore, other research (see Francis & Kaldor, 2002) indicates that church attendance (20 percent attend at least monthly, and a further 20 percent attend from two to eleven times a year) and personal prayer (20 percent pray daily, 12 percent pray weekly, and 21 percent pray occasionally) are still considered relevant practices in Australia. There is also evidence to suggest (Bouma & Lennon, 2003) that the overall amount of religious activity is comparable to that of sport, which suggests that religion is not a trivial concern to Australians. Therefore, Christianity appears to have great potential to influence contemporary meanings of leisure in Australia.

One contentious theme in the study of religion is the term "spirituality" and the view that spiritually is something different or separable from religion (see Bouma, 2006; Zinnbauer et al., 1997). This problem is particularly noticeable in sociological treatments of religion. For example, Bouma (2000) stated, "the 'term' religion is now used to primarily refer to social organizations such as churches, synagogues, mosques, temples" and spirituality refers to "experiences of and ways of relating to that which is 'more,' 'beyond' and 'greater than' the ordinary" (p. 388). Psychologists and social psychologists of religion disagree with this view by suggesting that all religious faiths and religious experiences have a spiritual component that has associated cognitive, affective, and behavioral responses (Loewenthal, 2000). This psychological approach does not treat spirituality as a new alternative to institutionalized religion but rather as one of the many elements of the religious experience. The research reported in this paper has adopted this latter perspective.

Literature Review

The meaning of leisure has been the focus of substantial academic interest and attempts to capture the essence of leisure can be traced through several distinct orientations, each associated with a characteristic definition of leisure (Samdahl, 1991). For instance, early definitions were influenced by Greek, Roman, and Latin philosophies (see Dare, Welton & Coe, 1998); in the 1960s and 1970s leisure was defined in relation to work (Wilenski, 1960), specific times (de Grazia, 1964), or activities (Dumazadier, 1967); and more contemporary approaches focused on psychological attributes and the subjective dimensions of leisure (see Neulinger & Breit, 1969; Shaw, 1985). While these approaches have all provided important insights into possible meanings of leisure, they contain several limitations. Generally, each orientation viewed leisure from a specific perspective and excluded (or at least did not overtly address) the possibility that individuals may have viewed leisure from an alternative perspective. Furthermore, each orientation did not consider that individuals may have had more than one meaning associated with leisure. A final problem is that each approach suggested that the meaning of leisure was a static entity that was independent of psychological and cultural changes, and of the participants' context.

Subsequent researchers have attempted to overcome these problems by examining leisure from a variety of alternative methodological perspectives. For example, Kelly (1996), Rojek (1995), and others argued that life has become compartmentalized. Individuals participate in numerous communities: a work community, a family community, a religious community, and/or a leisure community. Each community is independent and the experiences in one community, apart from competing for time, rarely influence the others. Rojek argued that people see leisure as a chance for distraction rather than serious engagement, depthless rather than immersed experiences, and hunger for novelty and fast leisure. He believed that people look for short experiences with low commitment and high excitement. This can be seen through the proliferation of leisure activities such as packaged tours, internet chat rooms, and extreme sports.

In contrast to Kelly (1996) and Rojek (1995), Hultsman (1995) suggested that leisure was "a lived experience." He argued leisure was "a way of being," which was not tied to events, activities, or concepts of freedom. For him, life is taken as a whole and is seamless and not segmented. The various aspects of life (play, education, work, social, and family relations) blend and are not compartmentalized. In this perspective, leisure is integrated into the daily actions and experiences of the individual, and therefore reflects an individual's circumstance.

Another researcher (Watkins, 2000) believed that the meanings that an individual associated with leisure could not be separated from the individual's context and circumstances; consequently he explored the range of possible meanings for leisure from a phenomenographic perspective (see Marton, 1986). Watkins and Bond (2007) argued that individuals hold multiple meanings of leisure rather than one meaning and that these meanings could be described qualitatively along several dimensions (context, intention, action, emotion, and outcome). They reported four broad categories that described the ways individuals experience the meaning of leisure: leisure as simply passing time and preventing boredom, leisure as a chance to exercise choice and display competence, leisure as an escape from the stresses and concerns of life, and leisure as an opportunity to achieve fulfillment in life and find happiness.

A question raised by these latter perspectives is the nature of the conditions that would influence the adoption or acceptance of particular meanings and behaviors associated with leisure. Traditionally, in the social sciences, work, family, and religion are commonly thought to shape the meanings that people attribute to aspects of their lives and consequently leisure (Gillespie, Leffler, & Lerner, 2002). The influence of the first two, work and family, have been well explored (e.g., Currie, 2004; Harrington, 2006; Lewis, 2003); however, the influence of religion has received substantially less attention.

Recent events, such as the conflict in the Middle East; the bombings in New York, London, Madrid, and Bali; and the continuing threat of the Al-Qaeda have suggested that religion is still a powerful influence upon human thought and behavior (Fontana, 2003) and therefore has the potential to affect leisure. One way this influence has occurred, in western societies like Australia and the United States, is through the public policy-making processes (Bouma, 2006). The Christian church has been one of the most powerful lobby groups and has constantly influenced government discussion concerning appropriate uses of leisure spaces and leisure provision. For example, in Australia, most mainstream Christian denominations have been outspoken on issues such as Sunday trading, gambling, prostitution, and recreational drug use. Similarly, politicians who espouse Christian beliefs and principles have used their position to exert control or censorship over various forms of entertainment such as the internet, films, and television (see Marr, 1999).

Furthermore, in Australia, religious groups are some of the largest providers of recreational programs (Bouma, 2006) such as playgroups, camping programs, youth groups, children's clubs, and activities for families and older adults. Churches and religious organizations also provide social services for the community in the form of educational facilities, hospitals, nursing homes, aged care facilities, and respite for the disabled and their families. Many of these social services include the provision of leisure programs. However, the rationale for the provision of these services is blurred. For instance, leisure can be seen simultaneously as a way of providing for the needs of membership, as an avenue for helping the community, and/or as a means of expanding membership (see, for example, Vawser, 1992).

The third way that religious groups may influence the meaning and behaviors associated with leisure is through particular teaching and theological perspectives. Heintzman (2006) argued that the biblical concepts of Sabbath and "rest" have important implications for the understanding of leisure. For example, he suggested that the work and nonwork cycle described in the Old Testament "is necessary for well-being and wholeness" (p. 25). Rest, on the other hand, has a stronger meaning and is associated with personal peace. These two concepts provide both quantitative (nonwork) and qualitative (peace) understandings for leisure. Alternative perspectives on the relationship between theological concepts and the understanding of leisure can be seen in the writings of Pieper (1952), a Roman Catholic theologian, and Ryken (2006), an Evangelical Protestant.

From a social psychological perspective, religion also has a significant effect on an individual's attitudes and behavior (McIntosh, 1995). Religion affects what individuals perceive and how they understand what they perceive. For some people, religion even helps them interpret a situation beyond the available information by providing cues to filling missing pieces of what is perceived, and consequently religion can affect how some people respond. Religion has been demonstrated to influence, for example, voluntarism (Evans & Kelley, 2004); altruism (Eckert & Lester, 1997); life satisfaction (Lewis, Joseph, & Noble, 1996); and sexual behavior (Petersen & Donnenwerth, 1997).

Empirical research has focused on this aspect of the religion/– leisure relationship in a variety of ways. Some researchers have examined the extent to which the wider population holds particular religious attitudes and behaviors concerning leisure. For instance, Lenski (1963) focused on the daily activities (including leisure) of individuals in the United States of America. He divided leisure activities into forms of self-indulgence (shopping, relaxing, visiting friends, etc.) and productive or constructive activities (social service work, sewing, gardening, studying, etc.). Respondents were asked to select the type of activities in which they participated. Lenski found that the content of a person's belief influenced their choice of leisure. For example, Protestant women were more likely to participate in "productive activities" and Catholic women were more likely to participate in "self-indulgent activities." He further concluded that unlike the Protestant belief, the Catholic belief system does not seem to exert its influence strongly into other aspects of life (including leisure). Interestingly, the names of the two leisure categories used by Lenski (self-indulgent and constructive or productive) are value laden themselves and reflect a somewhat work-oriented perspective.

When Bouma and Dixon (1986) replicated Lenski's study in Australia, they operationalized leisure as participation in specific activities, namely attendance at cinemas and sporting events. However, because they observed no differences in leisure behavior between those people claiming some religious affiliation and those people that did not, the leisure elements were dropped from further discussion. They stated, "if there is no difference among Australians, there is no point in asking whether there is a religious impact" (p. 27). However, this result was more likely a limitation of their limited operationalization of leisure, which defined leisure purely in terms of pre-selected activities. Furthermore, while two individuals could participate in the same leisure activity, the motivation for participation may be associated with a variety of different beliefs and attitudes.

A second group of studies examined the relationship between religion and leisure in very specific contexts or with particular faiths or denominations. For example, Bundt (1981) examined the Jewish tradition, and argued that worshipping God was a leisure experience, and therefore she sought to determine whether Jewish teachings continued to influence its followers' views and behaviors in various aspects of life, especially leisure. Her findings indicated that, for practicing Jews, leisure is based on adherence to the structured weekly calendar rather than on the individual's perception of the need to rest or some psychological state. Therefore, the Sabbath was the Jewish expression of leisure, and that leisure was an important element in the celebration practices of the Sabbath.

In contrast, Hothem (1983) focused on evangelical Christians. Ten subjects were interviewed at length concerning their perception of leisure, the relationship of their work and leisure, their perception of freedom in their leisure experiences, and the priority of leisure. She concluded that the perception of leisure was shaped as much by internal influences such as personal attitudes, beliefs, motives, and emotions, as by external influences of social structure, social groups, and role requirements. However, other research suggested these attitudes appear related to a theological perspective. Collins (1993) examined the leisure perceptions of individuals from an Open Brethren community in New Zealand. While his findings differed from Hothem, as he found support for a relationship between individuals' religious beliefs and their understanding of leisure, Collins further suggested that many people might not be consciously aware of the interconnections between leisure and religion. He also argued that there was an apparent contrast between the articulation of writers who approached leisure from a Christian orientation (see Dahl, 1972; Johnston, 1983, 2006; or Pieper, 1952) and the attitudes and behavior of Christians toward leisure.

One of the more recent studies (Freeman, Palmer, & Baker, 2006) explored the meanings of leisure for women who belong to the Church of Jesus Christ of Latter-Day Saints (LDS) and were stay-at-home mothers. They argued that the beliefs of the women in the study provided a foundation for their world view, which created a framework for the evaluation of their choices about life and leisure. This framework was informed by a complex system of behavioral guidelines and sense of meaning. Unlike many of the mainstream studies of women's leisure, the LDS women in this study felt that the role of full-time, stay-at-home mothers was valued by their husbands, their church, and the immediate church community. Consequently, these women happily associated leisure with family responsibilities such as parenting. This research highlighted the importance of understanding contextual elements, such as a person's religious beliefs and practices, in examining people's understanding of leisure.

A third approach has been to treat leisure as a factor that contributes toward wellbeing, and in particular spiritual aspects of wellbeing. Because of spirituality's similarity to psychological definitions of religion, the findings of these studies are discussed here. Ragheb (1993), in a study of leisure and perceived wellness, conceptualized wellness to have five components: physical, mental, emotional, social, and spiritual. He found that both leisure participation and leisure satisfaction were found to be positively associated with spiritual wellness. Heintzman's (1999; see also Heintzman & Mannell, 2003) research involved three studies, each examining an aspect of the relationship between leisure and spiritual wellbeing. The first study involved a secondary analysis of data from a park camper survey, which examined the extent that introspection/spirituality enhanced the park experience. The study found that natural settings were likely to be associated with introspection/spirituality and added to the satisfaction of the experience. The second study involved in-depth interviews with eight people who had expressed an interest in spirituality. All the participants associated their leisure experiences with their spiritual wellbeing. From the results of the first two studies, a spiritual wellbeing instrument was developed and then administered to 248 people. In summary, the findings suggested that aspects of leisure style, namely activity, time, motivation, and setting, had the potential to enhance or detract from spiritual wellbeing. The results of these studies (Heintzman, 1999; Ragheb, 1993) suggested that leisure has the potential to be a significant contributor to spiritual wellbeing.

Another way that the religious experience and meaning of leisure relationship has been examined is to treat religious involvement as a leisure experience. Several social commentators have noted that individuals treat their religious involvement in the same manner that others look toward gyms for fitness and clubs for sport. Carson (2000) observed that the religious environment has become a "religious supermarket" in which individuals shop around searching for the faith of their choice and the organization that can provide the best for their religious needs.

This attitude is also noticeable through the proliferation of spirituality workshops, self-help courses, and associated publications (Metcalf, 2001; Thomas, 2000).

Following this argument, Neitz and Spickard (1990) argued that a religious worship service sometimes functioned as a "flow" experience (see Csikszentmihalyi, 1975) similar to that experienced by rock climbers. They suggested that the parallel of overcoming the everyday self is clear, as many traditions see cultivating a "no-self" attitude and developing charity or selflessness as a religious goal. Neitz and Spickard also argued that a parallel existed to the challenge and mastery aspects within the flow state. Religious followers use words like "discipline" and "seeking perfection," implying that they seek something like mastery. Sometimes "mastering" their religion involves letting go of "this-world" concerns (also see Pieper, 1952). They also argued that religious practices combined routine with uncertainty, thus producing a challenging state "beyond boredom and anxiety." Rituals offer enough drama to avoid boredom, but not so much as to arouse uneasiness.

Although the literature has suggested that, in the past, religion, through institutions and individual beliefs, has had a substantial influence on the meaning and, consequently, the expressions and manifestations of leisure, what is less clear is religion's role in shaping the meaning of leisure in contemporary society. There is little empirical support in either direction. Furthermore, in some instances, religion might be viewed as a form of leisure. The study outlined in the next section examines potential relationships between an individual's religious experience and behaviors and the meanings of leisure in contemporary western society.

Method

The study population consisted of residents of Brisbane, the capital city of the state of Queensland in Australia. Brisbane was decided upon for two reasons. Firstly, Brisbane is a moderately large urban city (population: 1.6 million) with a relatively heterogeneous population, thus providing the potential for a diverse range of responses. Secondly, the residents of Brisbane were a convenient and accessible population for the researchers. A systematic random sampling technique (Babbie, 2001) was used to select participants that represented the wider Brisbane population. Three suburbs were randomly chosen from each of the four city council regions, and a starting point within each of the 12 chosen suburbs was selected by using a random number table to generate map grid references. Collectors then provided the residents of every third dwelling with a self-administered questionnaire. The collector then arranged a time to return and collect the completed questionnaire. A variety of collection times and days ensured a more diverse range of respondents. Furthermore, collectors ensured a balance of male and female responses using quotas.

After coding and entering, the data were screened according to procedures recommended by Tabachnick and Fidell (2006), which addressed issues such as the normality of distributions and the identification of univariate outliers. Following these processes, the data were checked for the assumptions of homogeneity of the variance-covariance matrices and multicollinearity that were required for analyses of variance. None of these assumptions was violated. A total of 475 completed questionnaires were collected and the respondents consisted of 275 females (58.5 percent) and 197 males (41.5 percent). The mean age of the respondents was 42.4 years, the median age was 40, and the respondents ranged in age from 15 to 91.

Leisure Meaning

The meaning of leisure was measured using the Leisure Meaning Inventory (Schulz & Watkins, 2007). This inventory is a 23-item psychometric scale measuring the four categories of leisure meaning identified by Watkins and Bond (2007), namely: Leisure as Passing Time, Leisure as Exercising Choice, Leisure as Escaping Pressure, and Leisure as Achieving Fulfilment. Each of these categories was measured by a series of items using a five-point Likert scale ranging from 1 (strongly disagree) to 5 (strongly agree). Table 1 provides an overview of each of the categories and their particular dimensions. One of the strengths of Watkins and Bond's research was that each of these categories and dimensions were grounded in the language and meanings of the participants, thereby facilitating higher levels of face and content validity. Furthermore, the LMI was piloted amongst several nonstudent samples to provide further evidence of the validity of the categories and questions for a wider population. During these stages, the overall internal reliability of the LMI was reported at .81, and the internal reliability of each of the categories ranged from .66 to .74 (Schulz & Watkins, 2007). In the present study, the internal reliability of the categories ranged from .64 to .74 and the overall scale was .82.

Table 1

The Leisure Meaning Categories and Aspects of Their Dimensions

			Dimension			
Category	Context	Intention	Time	Act	Emotion	Outcome
Passing Time	Spare Time	To fill time	Left over	Sedentary	Physical-relaxation fun	Self entertainment
Exercising Choice	Obligations	To gain control	Free time	Autonomy	Enjoyment emotional-relaxation	Self determination
Escaping Pressure	Pressures	To get away	Time out	Disengage	Mental-relaxation pleasure	Self maintenance
Achieving Fulfilment	Opportunities	To be content	Timeless	Reflection	Happiness	Self actualization

Note. Adapted from Watkins and Bond (2007).

Religion

Most researchers (see Glock, 1962; Loewenthal, 2000) suggest that there are three main elements or dimensions to religion: the belief (or cognitive) dimension, the feeling (or affective) dimension, and a behavioral dimension. Each of these dimensions has the potential to influence a person's understanding of leisure, and therefore they became the framework for the operationalization of religion in this study. The belief dimension is related to specific faiths or belief systems and therefore needed to be operationalized from the dominant perspective of the sample population – in this case Christianity. For this study, beliefs were operationalized by using the Batson, Schoenrade, and Ventis (1993) Orthodoxy Scale, one of the more widely used psychometric tests of orthodox beliefs. This scale consisted of 10 items and involved a five-point Likert scale response format ranging from 1 (strongly disagree) to 5 (strongly agree). In addition to this, each participant was asked to indicate denominational affiliation, which was then categorized into the most commonly used theological groupings for religious research in Australia (see Bouma, 2006). These were: Anglican; Catholic; Protestant (Baptists, Presbyterians, Wesleyan Methodists, Assemblies of God, and Salvation Army); Uniting (even though the Uniting Church is Protestant, it is commonly grouped separately due to its membership size); other Christian; no religious affiliation; and non-Christian faiths. The other-Christian category included those people who had responded as "Christian" or indicated that they were affiliated with one of the smaller denominations or churches such as Seventh Day Adventist, Jehovah Witness, and the Church of Jesus Christ of Latter Day Saints (Mormon). The non-Christian grouping consisted of religious groups such as Judaism, Hinduism, and Buddhism. Whilst the diversity of religious groups in the non-Christian category was large, there were insufficient numbers in any of the groups to enable any meaningful statistical analysis.

The feeling dimension was explored using the Intrinsic Religiosity, Extrinsic Religiosity, and Quest Scales developed by Batson et al. (1993). Each of these scales involve a five-point Likert scale response format ranging from 1 (strongly disagree) to 5 (strongly agree). The reliability of the Intrinsic Religiosity, Extrinsic Religiosity, and Quest scales has been well documented. In a review of their psychometric properties, Burris (1999) reported that the internal reliabilities of these scales ranged from the high .70s to the mid .80s and Extrinsic Religiosity was usually in the high .70s. Likewise, Burris reported the Quest scale's reliability to range from .75 to .81 and test-retest reliability to range from .71 to .78. The

Cronbach Alpha reliabilities for Intrinsic Religiosity, Extrinsic Religiosity, and Quest in this study were .92, .82, and .85 respectively.

The behavioral dimension was operationalized by asking participants to indicate the frequency of their prayer and their attendance at church or place of worship. These responses were recorded into "regularly" (pray–at least weekly; attendance–at least monthly), "occasionally," and "never" categories.

Demographic Variables

Research has indicated that religious experiences and behaviors vary with age (Argyle & Beit-Hallahmi, 1975; Bouma & Dixon, 1986). For instance, older people attend church far more often than younger people (Argyle & Beit-Hallahmi). Likewise, females are usually more religious than males are (Argyle & Beit-Hallahmi). Therefore, the exploration of the relationship between leisure and religion may be confounded by the influence of age and gender and, consequently, a selection of sociodemographic questions was included. These questions also enabled an examination of the representativeness of the sample.

Statistical Techniques

Mean scores and standard deviations were calculated for each of the major variables, followed by Cronbach Alphas to determine the internal reliability of the scales. The GLM function of SPSS Version 14 was then used to perform a series of multivariate analyses of covariance to address each of the research areas. If significant differences were observed, post hoc analyses using Bonferroni were undertaken. Significance was set at the 0.05 level.

Results

Each of the leisure categories was measured on a five-point scale and the mean represents the extent of agreement with the particular category. The mean score for Leisure as Passing Time was 2.46; Leisure as Exercising Choice was 3.79; Leisure as Escaping Pressure was 3.72; and Leisure as Achieving Fulfilment was 3.13. Similarly, the majority of the dimensions of religion were measured on a five-point scale and the mean represents the extent of agreement with the particular element. Orthodox beliefs were 3.39; intrinsic religiosity was 2.79; extrinsic religiosity was 2.50; and quest was 2.86. The religious behavioral measures indicated that 62.1 percent of the respondents attended a church or a place of worship at least several times a year, and 68.9 percent indicated they prayed regularly. The statistical properties of these variables are provided in Table 2.

Table 2

Statistical Properties of the LMI categories, Age, Orthodox Beliefs, Intrinsic Religiosity, Extrinsic Religiosity, and Quest

	mean	s.d.	Alpha
Leisure as Passing Time	2.46	0.85	0.74
Leisure as Exercising Choice	3.79	0.84	0.66
Leasure as Escaping Pressure	3.72	0.79	0.74
Leisure as Achieving Fulfilment	3.13	0.82	0.64
Orthodox Belief	3.39	1.31	0.97
Intrinsic Religiosity	2.79	1.11	0.92
Extrinsic Religiosity	2.50	0.83	0.82
Quest	2.86	1.02	0.85

RQ1 to what extent is an individual's meaning of leisure associated with their religious beliefs?

A three-way multivariate analysis of covariance was undertaken to determine the influence of orthodox beliefs on leisure meaning. The four leisure meanings were entered as dependent variables, with orthodox beliefs entered as an independent variable with three levels (high, medium, and low). Adjustment was made for two covariants: age and gender. Both gender (Wilks' Lambda = 0.962; F = 4.238; df = 4; p = 0.002) and age (Wilks' Lambda = 0.966; F = 3.774; df = 4; p = 0.005) were related to the four leisure meanings, and after adjustment was made for these covariants, the multivariate test suggested that orthodox belief did not significantly affect the leisure meanings (Wilks' Lambda = 0.973; F = 1.453; df = 8; p = 0.171).

A six-way multivariate analysis of covariance was undertaken to distinguish the influence of religious affiliation on leisure meaning. The four leisure meanings were entered as dependent variables, with religious affiliation as an independent variable. Age and gender were entered as covariants. Age (Wilks' Lambda = 0.967; F = 3.744; df = 4; p = 0.005) and gender (Wilks' Lambda = 0.956; F = 4.973; df = 4; p = 0.001) were both related to the leisure meanings, and after adjustment was made for these two variables, the results of the multivariate test indicated that religious affiliation was significantly associated with leisure meanings (Wilks' Lambda = 0.904; F = 1.854; df = 24; p = 0.007).

The univariate analysis indicated that there were differences between religious affiliation in how the respondents viewed both Leisure as Passing Time (F = 2.395; df = 6; p = 0.027) and Leisure as Achieving Fulfillment (F = 2.153; df = 6; p = 0.046). Two post hoc analyses using Bonferroni were undertaken. The first indicated that Anglicans (M = 2.28) were less likely to consider leisure as passing time than those people who indicated they had no religious affiliation (M = 2.67). The second post hoc test indicated that the Protestant denominations (M = 3.44) were more likely to consider leisure as an opportunity to achieve fulfilment than individuals who indicated that they had no religious affiliation (M = 2.99) (see Table 3).

Table 3

A Comparison of the Mean Scores, of Leisure as Passing Time and Leisure as Achieving Fulfilment, for Each Religious Affiliation category

Religious Affiliation	Percent of Sample	Leisure as Passing Time	Leisure as Achieving Fulfilment
Anglican	16.6	2.38[a]	3.09
Other Christian	10.7	2.35	3.17
Uniting Church	6.7	2.37	3.17
Protestant	10.3	2.40	3.44[b]
Roman Catholic	21.5	2.46	3.22
No religious affiliation	30.5	2.67[a]	2.99[b]
Non-Christian[c]	3.6		

(F - 2.395; df = 6; p = 0.027)   (F = 2.153; df = 6; p = 0.046).

[a]Anglicans reported significantly lower scores on the Leisure as Passing-Time category than those people with no religious affiliation
[b]Nonconformists reported significantly higher scores on the Leisure as Achieving Fulfilment category than those people with no religious affiliation.
[c]This category's members were from too diverse religious groups to provide meaningful information for analysis.

RQ2 to what extent is an individual's meaning of leisure associated with the feeling and affective dimension of religion?

A 3x3x3 multivariate analysis of covariance was used to identify the influence of intrinsic religiosity, extrinsic religiosity, and quest on leisure meaning. The four leisure meanings were entered as dependent variables with intrinsic religiosity (high, medium, and low), extrinsic religiosity (high, medium, and low), and quest (high, medium, and low) as independent variables with age and gender entered as covariants. The influence of gender was significant (Wilks' Lambda = 0.966; $F = 3.512$; $df = 4$; $p = 0.008$); however, age was not (Wilks' Lambda = 0.989; $F = 1.073$; $df = 4$; $p = 0.369$). The multivariate test indicated that only extrinsic religiosity (Wilks' Lambda = 0.941; $F = 3.078$; $df = 8$; $p = 0.002$) was significantly related to leisure meanings, and no interactions were observed.

After the influence of gender was removed, the univariate analyses indicated that extrinsic religiosity affected both Leisure as Escaping Pressure ($F = 9.275$; $df = 2$; $p < 0.000$) and Leisure as Achieving Fulfillment ($F = 3.926$; $df = 2$; $p = 0.020$). A Bonferroni post hoc analysis was undertaken for these two dependent variables. Individuals with high extrinsic religiosity ($M = 4.20$) were more likely to consider leisure as escaping pressure than those individuals with medium ($M = 3.73$) or low ($M = 3.59$) extrinsic religiosity. Furthermore, individuals with high extrinsic religiosity ($M = 3.52$) were more likely to consider leisure as an opportunity to achieve fulfilment than those people with medium ($M = 3.15$) or low ($M = 3.09$) extrinsic religiosity (see Table 4).

Table 4

A Comparison of the Mean Scores, of Leisure as Escaping Pressure and Leisure as Achieving Fulfilment, for Varying Levels of Extrinsic Religiosity

Extrinsic Religiosity	Leisure as Escaping Pressure	Leisure as Achieving Fulfilment
Low	3.59[a]	3.09[a]
Medium	3.73[a]	3.15[a]
High	4.20	3.52
	(F - 9.275; $df = 2$; $p < 0.000$)	(F = 3.926; $df = 2$; $p = 0.020$).

[a]Significantly different to High Extrinsic Religiosity at the 0.05 level (Bonferroni post hoc analysis)

RQ3 to what extent is an individual's meaning of leisure associated with their religious behavior?

A 3x3 multivariate analysis of covariance was used to identify the influence of frequency of attendance and prayer on leisure meaning. The four leisure meanings were entered as dependent variables with attendance and prayer as independent variables with age and gender entered as covariants. The results of the multivariate test suggested that after the effect of the relationship of the covariants was removed (age–Wilks' Lambda = 0.969; $F = 3.366$; $df = 4$; $p = 0.010$; gender–Wilks' Lambda = 0.954; $F = 4.997$; $df = 4$; $p = 0.001$), the effect of both attendance (Wilks' Lambda = 0.966; $F = 1.789$; $df = 8$; $p = 0.076$) and prayer (Wilks' Lambda = 0.985; $F = 0.801$; $df = 8$; $p = 0.602$) were not significant. There was also no significant interaction between these variables (Wilks' Lambda = 0.971; $F = 0.781$; $df = 16$; $p = 0.708$).

Discussion

The results of the analysis suggested that the people in the sample drawn from Australian society still maintain a predominantly Christian religious belief system. The participants in the study did not discount the existence of God; there were varying levels of participation in prayer and church attendance, and different aspects of religion were still considered relevant to their day-to-day lives. However, there was limited evidence to suggest that religion influenced the meanings that individuals in society associated with leisure. In this study, agreement with the orthodox beliefs of Christianity did not affect the meanings individuals associated with leisure, although affiliation with particular Christian denominations did. Additionally, those individuals with an extrinsic religious outlook appeared to associate leisure with escaping pressure and/or as an opportunity to achieve fulfillment, more so than other groups.

The Effect of Affiliation

Two Christian denominational groupings were identified as having a significant effect on the meanings individuals within the groupings associated with leisure. The Anglicans in this study were the least likely to view leisure as passing time, and the Protestant denominations were more likely to view leisure as an opportunity to achieve fulfillment. It is possible that these findings are linked to the theological orientations and teachings of these religious groups. For instance, the Anglican Church has a complex understanding of leisure. This is in part due to a reaction to the theologically conservative Protestant teachings of the seventeenth century. In this period, the head of the Church of England proclaimed Sunday as a day dedicated to worshipping God and participating in recreational activities. In particular, he decreed in the *Book of Sports* that, "dancing, archery, harlequinades, theatrical displays and similar recreations belong to the true Sunday observance" (quoted in Lee, 1966, p. 259). The implications of this was that people who attended the Church of England associated Sunday with both worshipping God and engaging in recreational pursuits. These attitudes towards the current procedures for the observance of Sunday and the use of recreation were transported to Australia. The Anglican Church still retains many of the conservative teachings from its roots (Blombery, 1996).

Similarly, the teaching in many Protestant churches may make their members more likely to associate leisure with opportunities to achieve fulfillment than those with no religious affiliation. In the current study, the Protestant category was comprised of denominations such as Baptists, Presbyterians, Wesleyan Methodists, Assemblies of God, and The Salvation Army. These churches have a reputation for being slightly stricter and having more control or influence over their membership than other denominations (Burke & Hughes, 1996; Hughes, 1996). One of the processes often advocated by these denominations is sanctification, which involves a moral and spiritual transformation that encourages the believer to become perfect or "Christ-like." It is possible that the process of sanctification advocated by some denominations and Christian groups could be equated with self-actualization and fulfillment (Tamney & Johnson, 1989) and consequently be associated with certain meanings of leisure.

The Effect of Extrinsic Religiosity

In this study, having a strong extrinsic religious outlook also influenced participants' understanding of leisure. Those individuals who scored high in extrinsic religiosity viewed leisure as a way of escaping pressure more strongly than those with low to moderate levels of extrinsic religiosity. Similar findings were identified with this group's association of leisure with achieving fulfilment. Allport and Ross's (1967) research indicated that people with a strong extrinsic religiosity often view their religion in utilitarian ways and thereby "use" their religion for social or personal benefit. This utilitarian approach may therefore spill over to leisure, and consequently leisure could be used to achieve religious aims. For example, the role of leisure may be perceived as something that repairs or renews people so that they can fulfil their religious duties. Similarly, people with a strong extrinsic outlook may use leisure to provide the sanctification or self-actualizing experiences required by their religion. It is worth noting that extrinsic religiosity has been demonstrated to be strongly prevalent in nonconformist churches (Donahue, 1985; Genia, 1996).

This finding highlighted one of the often-perceived commonalties between leisure and religion. Religion is concerned with questions of perfection, ultimate purposes, and meaning, and leisure can be concerned with similar issues – self-actualization: becoming perfect or who you are meant to be (Godbey, 1999). Leisure also provides opportunities for religious-like experiences. For example, wilderness retreats are often undertaken by people to enhance their religiosity (Heintzman, 1999) and a significant proportion of tourist activity, especially in Europe and the Middle East, revolves around people visiting sacred sites or undertaking "pilgrimages" to religious locations for religious purposes (see Eade, 1992; Ouellette, Kaplan, & Kaplan, 2005; Vukonic, 1996). There is also additional evidence to suggest that leisure can facilitate religious and spiritual experiences. For example, Collins (1993) concluded, "Leisure has the potential to free the mind of the individual in a way that facilitates more receptivity to the spiritual realm" (p. 295).

Despite these effects, religion for the most part was largely unassociated with the individual categories of leisure meaning. This finding may provide support for some of the current theories concerning religion in contemporary society. As Berger (1999) argued, people have not given up on religion, but rather the range of phenomena influenced by religion has dwindled. This is similar to Bouma and Dixon's (1986) earlier conclusions, which suggested that, "When one takes a close look at one's life the opportunity for decision-making, in which specifically religious beliefs will have any impact, is rather rare" (p. 179). They argued that people only draw on their religion when they believe that their religion is relevant to the issue at hand. Doohan (1990) made similar observations and argued that this separation was primarily the result of the scant attention that the Christian church has paid to the understanding of leisure, and this neglect has "contributed in no small measure to our incomplete theology of other aspects of Christian living" (p. 13).

However, there may be equally plausible interpretations of the findings that tend to suggest less support for some current perspectives of religion in contemporary society. For example, it could be that religious individuals may allow their religion to influence their understanding of leisure, and yet the understanding of leisure could be different from one person to another so that there are no significant relationships between religion and what leisure means.

Second, it is possible that individuals see a strong relationship between their individual religious experiences and the meanings they associate with leisure; however, the categories of leisure used in this study may not have adequately reflected their view of leisure. A range of other Christian perspectives on leisure exists, including the classical state of being view (Pieper, 1952; Doohan, 1990); an activity perspective (Ryken, 2006); a balance between work and play (Johnston, 1983); a holistic view (Heintzman, 2006); and an emphasis on free time (Neville, 2004). It appears that none of these meanings is addressed adequately by the LMI and the research design.

Implication, Limitations, and Future Research

The main implication for religious organizations (and in particular Christian organizations) is that it is uncertain whether people see a connection between their religion and their understanding of leisure. The absence of significant relationships between religion and leisure is not a problem per se; however, if societal standards are at odds with the standards desired by religious organizations, then religious organizations may not have prior claim on their members' leisure attitudes or behaviors. Furthermore, when people are confronted with new or ambiguous leisure experiences, then they are unlikely to draw on their religion for interpretation unless they have received teaching on the topic. There are numerous theological and biblical treatments of leisure in Christian magazines and newspapers; however, these writings do not always reach the wider population. For the church and other religious groups to remain relevant for their members, religious organizations should be providing guidance on everyday issues such as leisure.

As with any study, this research was limited by the operationalization of the major variables and subsequently the range of questions asked of the participants. The Christian tradition was chosen as a focus for this research because of its relative predominance in Australia. This approach clearly limits the range of applicability of the measures and, as a result, the generalizability of the conclusions drawn from the research. The influence of non-Christian religion with leisure was not examined. Furthermore, many of the instruments used in this study were developed to detect religious and spiritual life in the American context, which may not be sufficiently sensitive to detect Australian forms of this phenomenon

(Bouma, 2006). Similarly, leisure was operationalized using particular understandings of leisure, which may have obscured other aspects of the relationship between leisure and religion.

While there are factors that limit the generalizability of the study, there are also clear indicators of issues requiring further investigation. One of the implications of this study echoes Godbey's (1999) concerns about the leisure industry. Godbey believed that there would be an upturn in the number of people seeking religious experiences through their leisure. However, he had doubts concerning the ability of the leisure industry to provide or combine religious or spiritual aspects with leisure experiences, since few, if any, training programs in the leisure industry include aspects of the religious experience or spirituality in the curriculum. The present study discovered that a relationship exists between aspects of religion and leisure experiences that are associated with achieving fulfillment. Furthermore, for some individuals, participation in leisure activities such as wilderness experiences may serve to provide religious benefits. These findings provide opportunities for leisure providers to incorporate aspects of religion in the various leisure programs that they offer. What form these aspects take, however, would be dependent on the elements of the clients' religious experience and practices and therefore would require further investigation. However, as Godbey stated, leisure providers are not currently in the position to capitalize on the religious elements of leisure.

The conclusions and limitations of this study provide a basis to make several recommendations about directions for future research. Firstly, since this research indicates that far from the underlying conflict between leisure and religion as suggested by Kelly (1990) there is apparently little connection between these two significant components of people's lives. Consequently, the findings raise an important question about what factors are associated with the meaning of leisure in the contemporary world. Secondly, this study was set in a country that appears to espouse predominately Christian values and practices; it would be interesting and useful to undertake similar research in countries that embrace nonwestern religious heritages. Thirdly, there is increasing evidence to suggest that the effect of affiliation has shifted from the denominational level to the congregation, and consequently future research could focus on particular congregations possibly utilizing case study style designs. Finally, since there is evidence to suggest expressions of religion are becoming more personal and individualistic, future researchers may find qualitative methodologies to be a more fruitful avenue of research for this topic.

References

Allport, G., & Ross, J. (1967). Personal religious orientation and prejudice. *Journal of Personality and Social Psychology* 5, 432–443.

Argyle, M., & Beit-Hallahmi, B. (1975). *The social psychology of religion*. Boston: Routledge & K. Paul.

Australian Bureau of Statistics. (2003). *2003 census data*. Canberra, Australia: Australian Government Printing Office.

Batson, D., Schoenrade, P., & Ventis, W. (1993). *Religion and the individual: A social psychological perspective*. Oxford: Oxford University Press.

Babbie, E. (2001). *The practice of social research* (9th ed.). Belmont, CA: Wadsworth.

Berger, P. (1999). The desecularization of the world: A global overview. In P. Berger (Ed.), *The Desecularization of the World*. Grand Rapids: Eerdmans.

Bouma, G. (2000). Religion and spirituality. In R. Jureidini & M. Poole (Eds.), *Sociology: Australian connections* (2nd ed.). Sydney, Australia: Allen & Unwin.

Bouma, G. (2006). *Australian soul: Religion and spirituality in the twenty-first century*. Melbourne, Australia: Cambridge University Press.

Bouma, G., & Dixon, B. (1986). *The religious factor in Australian life*. Melbourne, Australia: MARC Publishing.

Bouma, G., & Lennon, D. (2003). Estimating the extent of religious and spiritual activity in Australia using time-budget data. *Journal for the Scientific Study of Religion* 42(1) 107–112.

Blombery, T. (1996). *The Anglicans in Australia*. Melbourne, Australia: Christian Research Association.

Bundt, B.A.K. (1981). *Leisure and religion: A contemporary Jewish Sabbath paradigm*. Unpublished doctoral dissertation, University of Minnesota, Minneapolis.

Burke, D., & Hughes, P. (1996). *The Presbyterians in Australia*. Melbourne, Australia: Christian Research Association.

Burris, C. (1999). Religious orientation scale. In P. Hill & R. Hood (Eds.), *Measures of religiosity*. Birmingham, AL: Religious Education Press.

Carson, V. (2000, December 23). The spiritual supermarket. *The Australian*, p. 18.

Collins, C.W. (1993). Leisure and Christianity: The case of the Brethren. In A.J. Veal, P. Jonson, & G. Cushman (Eds.), *Leisure and tourism: Social and environmental change: Papers from the World Leisure and Recreation Association Congress, Sydney, Australia, July 16–19, 1991* (pp. 290–297). Sydney: Centre for Leisure and Tourism Studies, University of Technology, Sydney. Sharbot Lake, ON: World Leisure and Recreation Association.

Csikszentmihalyi, M. (1975). *Beyond boredom and anxiety*. San Francisco: Jossey-Bass.

Currie, J. (2004). Motherhood, stress and the exercise experience: Freedom or constraint? *Leisure Studies* 23(3), 225–242.

Dahl, G. (1972). *Work, play, and worship in a leisure-oriented society*. Minneapolis: Augsburg.
Dare, B., Welton, G., & Coe, W. (1998). *Leisure in western thought* (2nd ed.) Dubuque, IA: Kendall Hunt.
de Grazia, S. (1964). *Of time, work and leisure*. New York: Doubleday.
deLisle, L. (2003). Keys to the Kingdom or Devil's playground? The impact of institutionalized religion on the perception and use of leisure. *Annals of Leisure Research* 6(2), 83–102.
Donahue, M. (1985). Intrinsic and extrinsic religiousness: Review and metaanalysis. *Journal of Personality and Social Psychology* 48(2), 400–419.
Doohan, L. (1990). *Leisure: A spiritual need*. Notre Dame, IN: Ave Maria Press.
Dumazadier, J. (1967). *Toward a society of leisure*. New York: Free Press.
Dune, J. (2000). *McDonaldization of the church*. London: Darton, Longman, & Todd.
Eade, J. (1992). Pilgrimage and tourism at Lourdes, France. *Annals of Tourism Research* 19, 18–23.
Eckert, R., & Lester, D. (1997). Altruism and religiosity. *Psychological Reports* 81, 562.
Evans, M., & Kelley, J. (2004). *Australian economy and society: Religion, morality and public policy in international perspective 1984–2002*. Sydney: Federation Press.
Fontana, D. (2003). *Psychology, religion, and spirituality*. London: British Psychological Society.
Francis, L., & Kaldor, P. (2002). The relationship between psychological well-being and Christian faith and practice in an Australian population sample. *Journal for the Scientific Study of Religion* 41(1), 179–184.
Freeman, P., Palmer, A., & Baker, B. (2006). Perspectives on leisure of LDS women who are stay-at-home mothers. *Leisure Sciences* 28, 203–221.
Genia, V. (1996). I, E, Quest and fundamentalism as predictors of psychological and spiritual well-being. *Journal for the Scientific Study of Religion* 35(1), 56–64.
Gillespie, D., Leffler, A., & Lerner, E. (2002). If it weren't for my hobby, I'd have a life: Dog sports, serious leisure, and boundary negotiations. *Leisure Studies* 21, 285–304.
Glock, C. (1962). On the study of religious commitment. Review of recent research bearing on religious character formation. Supplement to *Religious Education, 42*, 98–110.
Godbey, G. (1999). *Leisure in your life: An exploration*. State College, PA: Venture.
Harrington, M. (2006). Sport and leisure as contexts for fathering in Australian families. *Leisure Studies, 25*(2), 165–183.
Heintzman, P. (2006). Implications for leisure from a review of the biblical concepts of Sabbath and rest: In P. Heintzman, G.E. Van Andel & T.L. Visker (Eds.), *Christianity and leisure: Issues in a pluralistic society* (Rev. ed.,

pp. 14–31). Sioux Center: Dordt College Press.

Heintzman, P. (1999). *Leisure and spiritual well-being: A social scientific exploration.* (Unpublished doctoral dissertation). University of Waterloo, ON.

Heintzman, P., & Mannell, R. (2003). Spiritual functions of leisure and spiritual well-being: Coping with time pressure. *Leisure Sciences, 25,* 207–230.

Hothem, M.A. (1983). *The integration of Christian faith and leisure: A qualitative study.* (Unpublished doctoral dissertation). Boston University, MA.

Hughes, P. (1996). *The Pentecostals in Australia.* Melbourne, Australia: Christian Research Association.

Hultsman, J. (1995). Spelling leisure. *Leisure Studies* 14, 87–101.

Jarvie, G. (2006). *Sport, culture, and society: An introduction.* London: Routledge.

Johnston, R. (1983). *The Christian at play.* Grand Rapids: Eerdmans.

Johnston, R. (2006). Work and play: A Biblical perspective. In P. Heintzman, G.E. Van Andel, & T.L. Visker (Eds.), *Christianity and leisure: Issues in a pluralistic society.* (Rev. ed., pp. 3–13). Sioux Center: Dordt College Press.

Kelly, J. (1990). *Leisure* (2nd ed.). Englewood Cliffs, NJ: George Allen & Unwin.

Kelly, J. (1996). *Weber revisited: Leisure, values and religion.* Paper presented at the World Leisure and Recreation Association 4th World Congress, Cardiff, Wales.

Kelly, J., & Freysinger, V. (2000). *21st century leisure: Current issues.* Needham Heights, MA: Allyn & Bacon.

Lee, F. (1966). *The covenantal Sabbath.* London: The Lord's Day Observance Society.

Lee, R. (1964). *Religion and leisure in America: A study in four dimensions.* New York: Abingdon Press.

Lenski, G.E. (1963). *The religious factor: A sociological study of religion's impact on politics, economics, and family life* (Rev. ed.). New York: Doubleday.

Lewis, S. (2003). The integration of paid work and the rest of life. Is postindustrial work the new leisure? *Leisure Studies* 22(4), 343–345.

Lewis, C., Joseph, S., & Noble, K. (1996). Is religiosity associated with life satisfaction? *Psychological Reports* 79(2), 429–431.

Loewenthal, K. (2000). *The psychology of religion: A short introduction.* Oxford: One World.

Marr, D. (1999). *The high price of heaven.* St. Leonards, NSW: Allen & Unwin.

Marton, F. (1986). Phenomenography: A research approach to investigating different understandings of reality. *Journal of Thought* 21(3), 28–49.

McIntosh, D. (1995). Religion as schema, with implications for the relation between religion and coping. *Journal for the Scientific Study of Religion* 5(1), 1–16.

Metcalf, F. (2001, November 3). Life: Shelf life. *Courier Mail,* p. 14.

Neitz, M., & Spickard, J. (1990). Steps toward a sociology of religious experience: The theories of Mihaly Csikszentmihalyi and Alfred Schutz. *Sociological Analysis* 51(1), 25–33.

Neulinger, J., & Breit, M. (1969). Attitude dimensions of leisure. *Journal of Leisure Research* 1(3), 255–261.

Neville, G. (2004) *Free time: Towards a theology of leisure.* Birmingham, UK: University of Birmingham Press.

Ouellette, P., Kaplan, R., & Kaplan, S. (2005). The monastery as a restorative environment. *Journal of Environmental Psychology* 25(2), 178–188.

Petersen, L., & Donnenwerth, G. (1997). Secularisation and the influence of religion on beliefs about premarital sex. *Social Forces* 75(3), 1071–1089.

Pieper, J. (1952). *Leisure: The basis of culture* (A. Dru, Trans.). New York: Pantheon Books (1963, Random House).

Randels, G., & Beal, B. (2002). What makes a man? Religion, sport, and negotiating masculine identity in the Promise Keepers. In T. Magdalinski & T. Chandler (Eds.), *With God on their side: Sport in the service of religion* (pp. 160–177). London: Routledge.

Ragheb, M. (1993). Leisure and perceived wellness: A field investigation. *Leisure Sciences* 15(1), 13–24.

Rojek, C. (1995). *Decentring leisure: Rethinking leisure theory.* London: Sage.

Ryken, L. (2006). The Puritan ethic and Christian leisure for today. In P. Heintzman, G.E. Van Andel, & T. Visker (Eds.), *Christianity and leisure: Issues in a pluralistic society.* (Rev. ed., 32–49). Sioux Center: Dordt College Press.

Samdahl, D. (1991). Issues in the measurement of leisure: A comparison of theoretical and connotative meanings. *Leisure Sciences* 13, 33–49.

Schulz, J., & Watkins, W. (2007). The development of the leisure meanings inventory. *Journal of Leisure Research* 39, 477–497.

Shaw, S. (1985). The meaning of leisure in everyday life. *Leisure Sciences* 7, 1–24.

Tabachnick, B., & Fidell, L. (2006). *Using multivariate statistics* (5th ed.). Northridge, CA: Harper Collins.

Tamney, J., & Johnson, S. (1989). Fundamentalism and self actualization. *Review of Religious Research* 30(3), 276–286.

Thomas, M. (2000, April 22). Future of faith. *Courier Mail,* p. 25.

Vawser, N. (1992). Leisure time – a way of appropriate evangelism. *Australian Ministry* 4, 24.

Vukonic, B. (1996). *Tourism and Religion* (S. Matešić, Trans.). Tarrytown, NY: Elsevier.

Watkins, M. (2000). Ways of learning about leisure meanings. *Leisure Sciences* 22, 93–107.

Watkins, M., & Bond, C. (2007). Ways of experiencing leisure meanings. *Leisure Sciences* 29, 287–307.

Wilenski, H. (1960). Work, careers, and social integration. *International Social Science Journal* 12(4), 543–560.

Zinnbauer, B., Pargament, K., Cole, B., Rye, M., Belavich, T., Hipp, K. et al. (1997). Religion and spirituality: Unfuzzying the fuzzy. *Journal for the Scientific Study of Religion* 36(4), 549–56.

Chapter 7
THE MEANING OF LEISURE FOR OLDER PERSONS

Lois Hoitenga Roelofs

Because of decreasing fertility and mortality, the proportion of older persons has been increasing in developing countries (Grigsby, 1991). Consequently, projections indicate that Americans 65 and older, who comprised 12 percent of the total population in 1985, will comprise 19.5 percent in 2025 (United States Bureau of the Census, 1987).

These population projections are generating special interest in the role of leisure in older person's lives (Carp, 1990; Cutler & Hendricks, 1990; Howe, 1987; Neulinger, 1981). As a result of fewer work and family commitments, older persons have more leisure. However, exactly how leisure contributes to their lives remains unclear (Kelly, Steinkamp, & Kelly, 1986).

Leisure and older persons have been studied in other disciplines since the passage of the Social Security Act in 1935 (MacNeil, 1988). But only in recent years has this topic attracted the attention of nurse researchers (Chin-Sang & Allen, 1991; Johnson, McSweeney, & Webster, 1989). This attention is appropriate, since more and more nurses will be caring for older persons. Leisure may well turn out to be a key concern in gerontological nursing practice.

Statement of the Problem

This study addressed the question: What is the meaning of leisure for older persons? Typically, investigators have studied leisure participation but not the meaning of leisure. Leisure participation studies have focused on time, costs, barriers, activities, and frequencies (Beard & Ragheb, 1980; Gunter, 1987; Howe, 1987; Shaw, 1985). Kelly (1982)

Revised version of paper presented at the 1996 conference.

claimed that although participation data do contribute to the meaning of leisure, the meaning is crucial in itself. He defined "meaning" as the "definition of activity by a participant" (p. 23), explaining that "leisure is not in the time or the action, but in the actor" (p. 22). Hence, the meaning of leisure is viewed not as a quantity, but as a quality, or as the subjective experience of the actor.

The meaning of leisure for older persons is also important, because many older persons eventually assume a "roleless role" (Miller, 1968, p. 374). Neulinger (1981) posited that the role-less role occurs from various separations that influence older persons' lives. Some separations include loss of work from retirement; loss of spouse from death or divorce; loss of active parental role from launching of children; and, finally, loss of familiar environments from moves, perhaps necessitated by loss of health, to institutional settings.

Finally, the meaning of the concept of leisure has become important to nursing since 1980, when the North American Nursing Diagnosis Association (NANDA) accepted its first leisure-related diagnosis for clinical testing, diversional activity deficit (Kim & Moritz, 1982). In 1988, the eighth NANDA conference defined this diagnosis as "the state in which an individual experiences decreased stimulation from or interest or engagement in recreational or leisure activities" (Carroll-Johnson, 1989, p. 544). Because NANDA is using the concepts of leisure, recreation, and diversion interchangeably, concept development studies are needed to determine if these concepts are synonymous in meaning.

In summary, the meaning of leisure for older persons is important because it varies for each person, influences the eventual role-less role of old age, and is a new concept in the nursing diagnosis literature. Therefore, the purpose of this study was to conceptualize the meaning of leisure for older persons. Specific research questions were: (a) How do older persons define leisure? and (b) What is the meaning of leisure activity for older persons?

Method

The study of the meaning of leisure for older persons was conducted using Schwartz-Barcott and Kim's (1986) hybrid model of concept development. The hybrid model identifies, analyzes, and refines concepts in the beginning stage of theory development. The model is labeled hybrid because it sequentially meshes theoretical, fieldwork, and analytical phases. This paper focuses on the fieldwork phase. Grounded theory (Chenitz & Swanson, 1986; Glaser, 1978; Glaser & Strauss, 1967; Strauss & Corbin, 1990) guided the fieldwork phase of the hybrid model. Rooted in symbolic interaction theory (Blumer, 1969; Mead, 1934), this method emphasizes that meaning guides behavior.

Setting and Sample

The site chosen for the study was a not-for-profit 326-bed retirement home in the suburban U.S. Midwest. The home was governed by a board elected by an association representing a church denomination and was licensed by the state as a sheltered care facility. Research entry was negotiated into this site by a personal interview with the home's administrator. The sample of this study consisted of 40 residents in this home. Subjects were selected by theoretical sampling. This method of simultaneous data collection, coding, and analysis enabled "sampling on the basis of concepts that have proven theoretical relevance to the evolving theory" (Strauss & Corbin, 1990, p. 176). To generate as many concepts as possible, participants were selected from subgroups according to age, gender, and state of health. Subjects were invited individually to participate in the study. Generally, the investigator knocked on a resident's door several days ahead of time, introduced herself if necessary, and explained the study.

Data Collection and Data Analysis

Data collection consisted of participant observation and intensive interviewing (Lofland & Lofland, 1984) during the summer of 1990. During the first two weeks of the data collection period, participant observation was conducted on 10 days for a total of 32 hours. The schedule included such things as eating in the communal dining room, braving the territoriality of the coffee shop, participating in a monthly birthday party, and roasting on a bus trip in 100-degree weather to an outdoor Temple Lippizan horse show. All participant observation experiences were recorded in field notes.

After this period of participant observation, 40 intensive interviews were conducted using an investigator-designed interview guide. If the resident agreed to participate in the study, an appointment was scheduled for a two-hour time period. The average length of the taped interview was 70 minutes. The remainder of the two hours was spent discussing demographic data and touring the room to see and hear about memorabilia. The taped interview data generated over 1,350 pages of transcription; the average length of a transcription was 34 pages.

Data analysis was simultaneous with data collection and involved the use of constant comparison method (Stern, 1980; Wilson, 1977), analytic memoing (Glaser & Strauss, 1967), process memoing (Lincoln & Guba, 1985), and matrix development (Miles & Huberman, 1984, 1994). Trustworthiness of the data (Lincoln & Guba, 1985; Sandelowski, 1986) was enhanced by integrating several strategies into the research design. For example, personal process memoing helped avoid the bias of "going native," and maintaining an audit trail provided documentation of all research activities.

Results

Sample Characteristics

All subjects in this study sample were Caucasian, Protestant, and of Dutch ethnicity. Dutch persons were studied because the author wished to expand previous research with this population (Roelofs, 1981) and because ethnic leisure studies are rare. Also, ethnicity influences how persons define their situations, including leisure. In his study of the history of Dutch Americans, Bratt (1984) described this conservative subculture as follows: "If there is one thing these people have insisted on, it is that religion includes all of life, that it stands as the source and judge of all other human activity" (p. ix). Thus, it is reasonable to expect that religious beliefs also would permeate their meaning of leisure.

The mean age of the sample was 81 years (SD = 7.4 years); the median age was 83. Ages varied from 66 through 94. The majority of the sample was over 75 (n = 30, 75 percent), female (n = 26, 65 percent), widowed (n = 31, 77.5, educated through the seventh or eighth grade (n = 25, 62.5 percent), and a resident in the home for four years or less (n = 26, 65 percent).

Conceptual Framework

The conceptual framework inductively derived from this study is the model of authoring leisure. In this model, the term "authoring" refers to an active process of creating leisure experiences, while the term "leisure" refers to nonwork activities. "Authoring leisure" emerged as the core category and is defined as a dynamic process in which older persons actively initiate leisure activities of their choice.

Strauss and Corbin's (1990) paradigm of grounded theory directed the development of the model of authoring leisure. The paradigm consists of six linear phases: (a) causal condition, (b) phenomenon, (c) context, (d) intervening condition, (e) action and interaction strategies, and (f) consequences.

Causal condition: Retirement. The causal condition of the phenomenon of leisure was retirement. The sample consisted of older persons who were retired from their usual occupations or work roles. An 80-year-old female reflected on the meaning of leisure for her in retirement:

> [Leisure time] is such a wonderful time . . . when you've cooked and baked and cleaned for over 66 years. . . . Sometimes I think, "Lord, do I deserve this? I have such an easy life now. Do I really deserve this, that you're so good to me?" . . . [I have] so much to be thankful for.

The phenomenon: Leisure. The second phase of the model called the phenomenon, or central event, was leisure. For most of the subjects, retirement was the first time that they encountered much leisure. An 82-year-old woman recalled her early socialization to work:

> You thought every minute had to count, do something. And I think that that really influenced me. You know, never waste your time. Never sit with your hands folded. If we couldn't find something to do, [my parents] found something to do for us.

The context: Retirement home. The phenomenon of leisure was experienced in the context of a retirement home. A few subjects moved into the home because they wanted to, but most moved in because they felt they needed to. One 83-year-old man summarized:

> It will be ten years ago that [my wife and I] moved in, and we came here because of my health. . . . I don't think anybody is here because they chose to come here. It's a wonderful place to be though. I just, ah, am reconciled to the fact that I'm going to be here until they carry me out.

Intervening conditions: Definition of leisure. The third phase of the model, intervening conditions, was addressed by the first research question: How do older persons define leisure?

Leisure was viewed positively by most subjects. Their responses conveyed an independent spirit of doing what they wanted to do, when they wanted to do it, and for only as long as they wanted. Subjects' definitions of leisure yielded four themes. A theme was considered as such if expressed by at least 20 subjects (50 percent of sample). The four themes that emerged from the data are: (a) nonwork time, (b) relaxation, (c) choice, and (d) enjoyment.

Nonwork time. The first theme, nonwork time, consisted of free time left over after work, home, church, and community obligations were completed. One man defined it this way:

> Ah, leisure to me, means, ah, outside of work – daily work. The time you have to spare. Not necessarily, I don't mean that we shouldn't do anything in that time. There's always something we should do in our leisure time, if possible. (15)

Relaxation. The second theme, relaxation, encompassed a variety of restful responses such as relaxing, unwinding, taking it easy, and having no cares. One woman explained:

> [Leisure] means relax. Of course, as you get older, then it means more like you have no cares or worries, see. You just do what you like to do, and you take your leisure time about doing it. (18)

Choice. The third theme, choice, entailed not only choosing leisure activities, but also the time and duration of choosing the time and duration of participating in those activities. One woman said:

> Leisure means to me to be able to do something that I want to do, you know, without being pressured. And, ah, without it having to be something I have to do. Or I can do it anytime I want to without pressure. (39)

Enjoyment. The fourth and final theme, enjoyment, encompassed a variety of joyful responses such as fun, pleasure, enjoyment, happiness, and satisfaction. For one woman, having fun helped balance her life:

> Leisure means a time of enjoyment and a time of rest away from your daily activities . . . at the end of the day, it's just really nice to have a little time of leisure, because all work and no play makes Jack a pretty dull boy. (13)

Based on these four themes, leisure may be defined as nonwork time that may be spent in a relaxing and enjoyable way.

Action and interaction strategies: The meaning of leisure activity. The fourth phase of the model, action and interaction strategies, was addressed in this study by the second research question: What is the meaning of leisure activity to older persons? The meanings participants ascribed to their favorite leisure activities reflected the strategies they used to author leisure.

Subjects were asked to choose their favorite leisure activities. Their choices were grouped into six categories. A category was developed if similar activities were expressed by a minimum of 10 subjects (25 percent of sample). The six categories and examples of corresponding activities are: (a) crafts/handwork (making various items, sewing, knitting, crocheting, and embroidering); (b) games (playing physically passive games like card and board games; playing physically active games such as pool, dartball, volleyball, and shuffleboard); (c) media (watching television, listening to the radio or tape cassettes); (d) reading (reading books, magazines, and newspapers); (e) service (fixing things, running errands, visiting others, writing letters); and (f) word puzzles (working on crossword and word search puzzles).

The subjects' meaning of leisure activities was embedded in strategies they used in the process of authoring leisure. Authoring leisure, as the core category, encompassed six strategies. Strategies were included in the analysis if expressed by a minimum of 10 (25 percent of sample). The six strategies were: (a) educating, (b) continuing, (c) contributing, (d) competing, (e) edifying, and (f) engaging.

Educating. The first strategy of authoring leisure, educating, involved both thinking and learning. One woman felt that working on word search puzzles kept her mind busy:

> Well, in the first place, I think that [working on puzzles] keeps you alert. It keeps your mind going, because you have to find words, and sometimes you don't recall the spelling of them, and that way it keeps you on top with your spelling – your mental capacity is richer. (7)

One man explained that he liked to read so he could discuss world events:

> The only way you can learn anything is by reading. . . . [I want to learn] so you can carry on an intelligent conversation with someone else. (11)

Continuing. The second strategy of authoring leisure, continuing, was reflected primarily in statements that explained how subjects chose their leisure activities as favorites because they had always liked them or had always done them. One man told why he enjoyed watching a ball game:

> I enjoy the game. I always enjoyed the game when I was young. I played, ah, we wouldn't have any teams or anything like that; we just played together. (9)

Although one woman's interest in reading began in childhood, she added a later reason:

> I always loved to read. . . . I can remember as a little kid getting books

from the library and reading. Ah, in fact, the first gift that my husband gave me when I was going with him was a Grace Livingston Hill book. (39)

Contributing. The third strategy, contributing, involved service activities such as helping other people, being a friend to others, and donating time or talent to worthy causes. One man talked of why he liked working with tools:

I like to help people with, ah, odd jobs. . . . I enjoy working with tools. . . . I get a lot of satisfaction out of doing it, because I feel like I'm – I want to help somebody. (9)

When asked what made her choose helping in the Activity Department as a favorite activity, one woman responded:

Well, I feel like I'm doing something for them. . . . [Cutting stamps has] come up in the last years . . . and they are sent to a certain place, and they get money for them, and the money goes for purchasing Bibles. . . . It goes to a good purpose. (4)

Competing. The fourth strategy, competing, involved both winning and competing. One woman reported that she liked to win at playing cards:

Everyone likes to win, so you use your noodle a little bit. (14)

One man reported pleasure from playing pool, whether he won or not:

I like good competition. Yah, I'm playing [pool] with an individual that's pretty much on the same level as me, and it works out great. (34)

Edifying. The fifth strategy, edifying, involved feeding one's soul and gaining inner satisfaction. One woman explained why she liked watching pastors on television:

I feel I'm strengthened by [religious TV programs] spiritually. . . . It gives you encouragement to be faithful in what you believe. . . . (7)

One man described why he liked to visit those who were homebound:

Well, ah, if I go and visit somebody, I first go here and pray that the Lord will be with me and help me know what to say and that it may all be to the honor and glory of his name . . . if it goes satisfactory, then I come back . . . and thank the Lord. (29)

The sixth and final strategy of authoring leisure, engaging, was used primarily in sedentary activities that required active, rather than passive, engagement, in activities chosen to pass the time. For one woman, working on word search puzzles kept her actively engaged:

[I like to work on puzzles because it is] just the idea of getting it done up. Look for them, you know? . . . Relax and find them. They pass the time. (32)

Another woman crocheted simple stitches so she could watch TV at the same time:

[Crocheting is my very favorite] because it fits in very well. . . . I can sit there and watch television if I want to, and I can crochet at the same time. I don't get something that has a lot of counting, and it's a great pastime. (36)

Consequence: Leisure satisfaction. The fifth and final phase of the model is the consequence phase. Authoring strategies used by these subjects led to the consequence of leisure satisfaction. The following definition of leisure satisfaction was derived from this study:

Leisure satisfaction is the sense of contentment that older persons experience as a result of authoring leisure. The process of authoring leisure enables older persons to meet their individual needs by using the strategies of: (a) educating, (b) continuing, (c) contributing, (d) competing, (e) edifying, and (f) engaging.

In summary, the results suggested the causal condition of retirement led to the phenomenon of leisure within the context of the retirement home. How participants defined leisure – nonwork time characterized by relaxation, choice, and enjoyment – was an intervening condition that influenced the phenomenon of leisure. Furthermore, the meanings ascribed to their favorite leisure activities reflected the strategies of educating, continuing, contributing, competing, edifying, and engaging. Finally, these strategies led to leisure satisfaction. This conceptual framework is illustrated in Figure 1.

Figure 1. The model of authoring leisure.

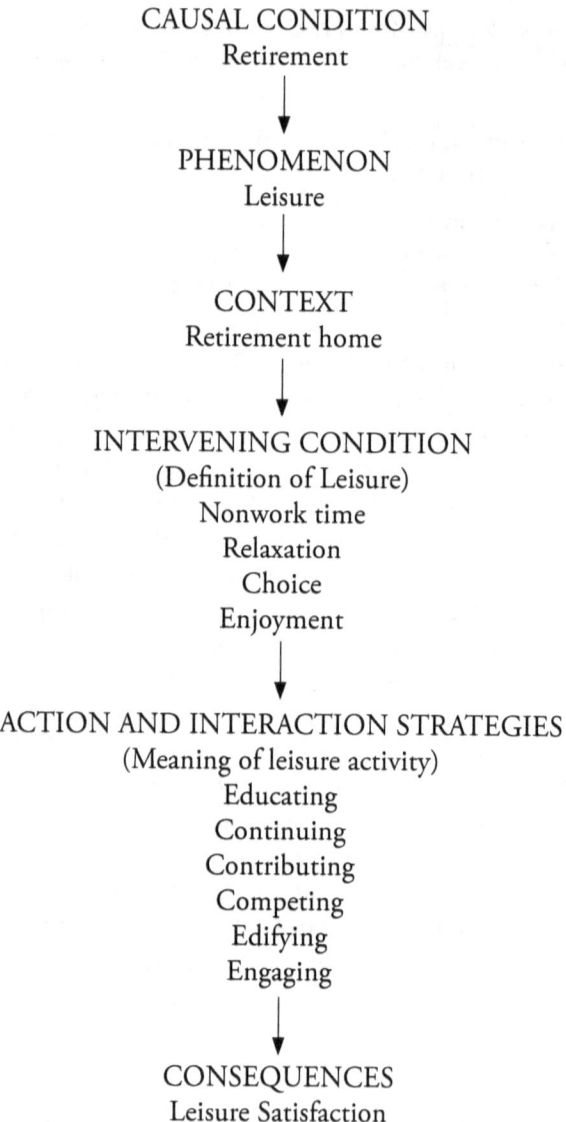

Discussion

The findings from the empirical phase of the present study support the importance of the concept of leisure for older persons. With respect to the nursing diagnosis of diversional activity deficit, the findings address some of its etiological factors (Carpenito, 1989). For example, situational factors such as retirement were supported as the causal condition of the phenomenon of leisure in the model of authoring leisure. In addition, maturational factors such as sensory and motor deficits were addressed, as older persons described adaptations in leisure participation due to these deficits. For example, one woman told of needing special glasses to read. Another woman said that due to declining vision, she listened to her radio or tapes, rather than read. Furthermore, one man explained that, because he was no longer physically able to play pool, he watched others play instead. Even though several subjects referred to having sensory and motor deficits, most were still able to meet their individual needs and achieve leisure satisfaction.

The findings also confirmed the importance of leisure for older persons by addressing the need identified in the nursing diagnosis literature to examine the developmental stage in relationship to diversional activity deficit (Kim, McFarland, & McLane, 1984). Empirical validation of how older persons defined leisure and the meaning of leisure activity helped to establish the existence and importance of the concept of leisure to this population. For example, the data revealed that retirement resulted in older persons having more leisure time than at earlier times in their lives and, indeed, more than they could recall their parents ever had. Subsequently, upon moving into the retirement home, leisure time increased because of having fewer household duties. In fact, several noted that leisure "is all we have here."

Additionally, the findings confirmed the importance of leisure satisfaction as the consequence of authoring leisure and is supported by numerous leisure satisfaction studies that found a positive effect of leisure participation on leisure satisfaction (Foret, 1986; Ragheb & Griffith, 1982), of leisure satisfaction on psychological wellbeing (Mancini, 1978), of leisure satisfaction on life satisfaction (Foret, 1986; Ragheb & Griffith, 1982; Russell, 1987; Sneegas, 1986), and of both leisure participation and leisure satisfaction on anxiety levels (Kaufman, 1988).

Suggestions for Future Research

Several suggestions are obvious for research. First, the study should be replicated with older persons of different ethnic groups. For example, the question could be asked if these active, satisfied, older Dutch persons are representative of others in their age cohort or if they are unique.

Second, similar concept development studies should be conducted on the concepts of diversion and recreation. Resulting definitions of these concepts should be compared to the definition of leisure. This would help determine if the interchangeable use of the three concepts is appropriate in the NANDA nursing diagnosis of diversional activity deficit.

Third, the study should be replicated to further develop the model of authoring leisure. For instance, the linear phases and the relationships among the linear phases could be strengthened.

Fourth, this research leads to a proposal for a new nursing diagnosis: impaired ability to author leisure. This diagnosis is defined as the state in which an individual experiences a limitation of ability to actively initiate activities of her/his choice that provide relaxation and/or enjoyment during nonwork time. This definition derives from two sources of data: first the subjects' definitions of leisure as: (a) nonwork time, (b) relaxation, (c) choice, and (d) enjoyment; and second, the definition of the core category of authoring leisure as a dynamic process in which older persons actively initiate leisure activities of their choice. Further research should be done on the diagnosis to identify and validate etiologies, defining characteristics, and nursing interventions.

Implications for Practice

First, the findings of the present study suggest that health care professionals work together to promote leisure satisfaction for older persons. The participant observation part of this study enabled the nurse investigator to spend time with the activity department staff and discover that the nurse's knowledge of medical problems, nursing care needs, and medications sometimes affected the residents' leisure participation. Conversely, the nurse found that some subjects shared health-related information with only the activity therapist because of a perceived threat of the nurse's ability to influence transfer to a higher level of care. A team approach of sharing information would optimize the facilitation of leisure satisfaction and improved quality of life for residents.

Second, health promotion (Pender, 1987) is a major goal for all health professionals. Caldwell and Smith (1988) posit that the role of leisure in relationship to health is often overlooked. Therefore, health professionals should be aware of how they can include leisure planning in their care. Their leisure planning should encompass a person's total lifestyle, including not only physical activities, but also activities that would promote the social, emotional, intellectual, and spiritual dimensions of health, thereby achieving leisure satisfaction.

Third, health professionals should be aware that the meaning of leisure for older persons guides their leisure behavior. This is consistent with grounded theory, founded upon symbolic interaction theory (Blumer, 1969; Mead, 1934) that directed the fieldwork phase of this study. Symbolic interaction theory holds that meaning guides behavior. In other words, the meaning of leisure for older persons influences how they author leisure. For example, one participant described how his religious beliefs about leisure influence his personal authoring of leisure:

> I am the author of that time, you might as well say. I don't know how to express it really. But I am not under somebody . . . you are free from work . . . you are your own boss. . . . We are Christians. And we know that if it comes down to it, there is not time really for yourself. It's God's time. And, I might sound awfully, ah, religious, and I like a little fun and so, too, but I was brought up that way that whatever you do, do everything to the honor and glory of God. And I try to do that. And I think that includes a little joke once in a while, too.

In summary, all health professionals, in their role of health promotion, should be made aware that they must assess the ability of older persons to author their leisure experiences, either alone or with others, and assist them to achieve optimal leisure satisfaction, using authoring strategies such as: (a) educating, (b) continuing, (c) contributing, (d) competing, (e) edifying, and (f) engaging.

Acknowledgement: The author acknowledges the mentorship of Kathleen A. Knafl, PhD, for an extended period of research on leisure.

References

Beard, J.G., & Ragheb, M.G. (1980). Measuring leisure satisfaction. *Journal of Leisure Research* 12, 20–33.

Blumer, H. (1969). *Symbolic interactionism: Perspective and method.* Englewood Cliffs, NJ: Prentice-Hall.

Bratt. J.D. (1984). *Dutch Calvinism in modern American: A history of a conservative subculture.* Grand Rapids: Eerdmans.

Caldwell, L.L., & Smith, E.A. (1988, March/April). Leisure: An overlooked component of health promotion. *Canadian Journal of Public Health* 79, 44–48.

Carp, F.M. (1990). Leisure activities of retired persons in the United States: Comparisons with retired persons in the People's Republic of China. *International Journal of Aging and Human Development* 31(1), 45–55.

Carpenito, L.J. (1989). *Nursing diagnosis: Application to clinical practice* (3rd ed.). Philadelphia, PA: Lippincott.

Carroll-Johnson, R.M. (Ed.), *Classification of nursing diagnoses: Proceedings of the eighth conference.* Philadelphia, PA: Lippincott.

Chenitz, W.C., & Swanson, J.M. (1986). *From practice to grounded theory: Qualitative research in nursing.* Menlo Park, CA: Addison-Wesley.

Chin-Sang, V., & Allen, K.R. (1991). Leisure and the older black woman. *Journal of Gerontological Nursing* 12(1), 30–34.

Cutler, S.J., & Hendricks, J. (1990). Leisure and time use across the life course. In R.H. Binstock & L.K. George (Eds.), *Handbook of aging and the social sciences* (3rd ed.) (pp. 169–185). San Diego, CA: Academic Press.

Foret, C.M. (1986). *Life satisfaction, leisure satisfaction, and leisure participation among young-old and old-old adults with rural and urban residence* (Doctoral dissertation). Available from ProQuest Dissertations and Theses Global database. (UMI No. 8608486).

Howe, C.Z. (1987). Selected social gerontological theories and older adult involvement: A review of the literature. *The Journal of Applied Gerontology* 6, 448–463.

Glaser, B.G. (1978). *Theoretical sensitivity.* Mill Valley, CA: Sociology Press.

Glaser, B.G., & Strauss, A.L. (1967). *The discovery of grounded theory: Strategies for qualitative research.* Chicago: Aldine.

Grigsby, J.S. (1991). Paths for future population aging. *Gerontologist* 31, 195–203.

Gunter, B.G. (1987). The leisure experience: Selected properties. *Journal of Leisure Research* 19, 115–130.

Johnson, S.W., McSweeney, M., & Webster, R.E. (1989). Leisure: How to promote inpatient motivation after discharge. *Journal of Psychosocial Nursing* 27(9), 29–31.

Kaufman, J.E. (1988). Leisure and anxiety: A study of retirees. *Activities, Adaptation & Aging* 11(1), 1–9.

Kelly, J.R. (1982). *Leisure*. Englewood Cliffs, NJ: Prentice-Hall.

Kelly, J.R., Steinkamp, M.W., & Kelly, J.R. (1986). Later life leisure: How they play in Peoria. *Gerontologist* 26, 531–537.

Kim, M.J., & Moritz, D.A. (Eds.). (1982). *Classification of nursing diagnoses: Proceedings of the third and fourth national conferences*. New York: McGraw-Hill.

Kim, M.J., McFarland, G.K., & McLane, A.M. (Eds.). (1984). *Classification of nursing diagnoses: Proceedings of the fifth national conference*. St. Louis, MO: Mosby.

Lincoln, Y.S., & Guba, E.G. (1985). *Naturalistic inquiry*. Beverly Hills, CA: Sage.

Lofland, J., & Lofland, L.H. (1984). *Analyzing social settings* (2nd ed.). Belmont, CA: Wadsworth.

MacNeil, R.D. (1988). Leisure programs and services for older adults: Past, present and future research. *Therapeutic Recreation Journal* 22, 24–35.

Mancini, J.A. (1978). Leisure satisfaction and psychologic well-being in old age: Effects of health and income. *Journal of the American Geriatrics Society* 26, 550–552.

Mead, G.H. (1934). *Mind, self, and society*. Chicago: University of Chicago.

Miles, M. B., & Huberman, A.H. (1984). *Qualitative data analysis: A sourcebook of new methods*. Beverly Hills, CA: Sage.

Miller, S.J. (1968). The social dilemma of the aging leisure participant. In B.L. Neugarten (Ed.), *Middle age and aging: A reader in social psychology* (pp. 366–374). Chicago: University of Chicago.

Neulinger, J. (1981). *To leisure: An introduction*. Boston: Allyn & Bacon.

Pender, N.J. (1987). *Health promotion in nursing practice* (2nd ed.). Norwalk, CT: Appelton & Lange.

Ragheb, M.G., & Griffith, C.A. (1982). The contribution of leisure participation and leisure satisfaction to life satisfaction of older persons. *Journal of Leisure Research* 14, 295–306.

Roelofs, L. (1981). *Leisure preferences of the institutionalized elderly*. (Unpublished master's thesis). University of Illinois at the Medical Center, Chicago.

Roelofs, L.H. (1999). The meaning of leisure. *Journal of Gerontological Nursing* 25(10), 32–39.

Russell, R.V. (1987). The importance of recreation satisfaction and activity participation to the life satisfaction of age-segregated retirees. *Journal of Leisure Research* 19, 273–283.

Sandelowski, M. (1986). The problem of rigor in qualitative research. *Advances in Nursing Science* 8(3), 27–37.

Schwartz-Barcott, D., & Kim, H.S. (1986). A hybrid model for concept development. In P. Chinn (Ed.), *Nursing research methodology: Issues and implementation* (pp. 91–101). Rockville, MD: Aspen.

Shaw, S.M. (1985). The meaning of leisure in everyday life. *Leisure Sciences* 7, 1–24.

Sneegas, J.J. (1986). Components of life satisfaction in middle age and later life adults: Perceived social competence, leisure participation, and leisure satisfaction. *Journal of Leisure Research* 18, 248–258.

Stern, P.N. (1980). Grounded theory methodology: Its uses and processes. *Image* 12, 20–23.

Strauss, A., & Corbin, J. (1990). *Basics of qualitative research: Grounded theory procedures and techniques.* Newbury Park, CA: Sage.

United States Bureau of the Census. (1987). International Population Reports, Series P-95, No. 78, *An aging world.* Washington, DC: United States Government Printing Office.

Wilson, H.S. (1977). Limiting intrusion – Social control of outsiders in a healing community. *Nursing Research* 26, 103–110.

Chapter 8

MULTICULTURAL PERSPECTIVES ON LEISURE

Margaret Hothem

For most college students, the meaning and role of leisure is frequently taken for granted. When prodded with questions concerning the characteristics of leisure, they begin to understand that leisure is a complex phenomenon. It has multiple meanings and a wide spectrum of motivations, satisfactions, activities, and environments that make the phenomenon multidimensional *and* inherently ambiguous. The determination of one's perception of leisure is based upon intrinsic perceived satisfactions of leisure as well as external social, cultural, and environmental factors.

To help clarify one's own values about what role leisure can play in one's life, various psychological models have been presented (Crandall, 1979; Csikszentmihalyi, 1975; Neulinger, 1981a). Most contemporary researchers agree that the elements of perceived freedom and intrinsic satisfaction are important criteria in realizing leisure (Beard & Ragheb, 1980). Several researchers in the field of leisure are also interested in the psychological dimensions of self-concept functions (Ingham, 1987; Lee & Halberg, 1989) and identify formation (Kelly, 1983; Samdahl & Kleiber, 1989).

Whereas psychological models reveal the diversity of the experiences, the significance of the activity, and the context for leisure meanings, leisure also is a social space that is learned and shaped by various sociological and cultural factors. Sociologists and social-psychologists of leisure (Iso-Ahola, 1979; Kaplan, 1960; Kelly, 1990) see leisure as a learned behavior. Although styles vary, it is one's culture – the learned and transmitted elements of life – which greatly influence leisure's social context

---

Revised version of paper presented at the 1995 conference.

(Kelly, 1987). This ethnicity of leisure does not deny psychological meanings; rather, it presents the understanding of leisure from a pluralistic perspective.

Understanding the importance of leisure in one's life is to explore the various psychological and socio-cultural factors that influence this complex phenomenon. Personal factors such as age, gender, personality, life goals, motivations, and satisfactions are dynamically interwoven with cultural distinctives of race, religion, socio-economic factors, education, geography, political influence, time perspective, and cultural traditions.

The need for a study on multicultural differences as expressed by international college students became apparent to me in an introductory college class that I teach called "Leisure and Human Behavior." The purpose of the course is to challenge students to think through the psychological and sociological factors that influence one's perceptions and expressions. When we discussed the various meanings of leisure, I observed that international students would frequently respond differently than American-born students. Leisure typically was described by international students as an important aspect of life quality characterized by informal, unstructured social experiences, rather than an activity or escape. These students also implied that their perception of leisure affected their academic work, socialization, and transition into the college community.

In the class, the American-born students seemed to appreciate what they could learn from the leisure-lifestyle values of the international students. Hence, interactive pluralism on multicultural differences was occurring within the classroom environment, and education was enhanced as students were learning to appreciate cultural differences that previously were taken for granted. Based on these classroom experiences, I set out to explore more directly some of the psycho-socio-cultural differences in leisure meanings by researching related literature and by interviewing international students at Gordon College.

Why do we need to study multi-cultural perspectives on leisure on the college campus? This study assumes that for many international students, the transition into the American campus life is not an easy one. Frequently there are language difficulties, different study habits, feelings of alienation, loneliness from family separation, environmental changes, and other transition difficulties. Most institutions that warmly welcome international students attempt to meet many of these transition difficulties through various academic and student development programs.

Over the past few years, the Coalition of Christian Colleges and Universities has encouraged its member institutions to enhance diversity, which promotes pluralism and enriches the college campus. This initiative is imperative if we are to equip students for participation in the modern world. Strategies to meet this contemporary goal have included increased minority and international student and faculty recruitment, curriculum evaluation, and student activities that spotlight cultural diversity (Lee & Rice, 1991). Although these attempts have merit, in many ways they are still tokens of multicultural understanding, and the enrichment process has only just begun.

There is a need for all sectors of the Christian college campus to provide a climate that embraces cultural diversity and is sensitive to interactive pluralism. Not only is there a need to appreciate each other's cultural experiences and heritage, but there is a need to be mutually enriched by multiculturalism. Interactive pluralism requires not only "knowing about," but understanding, appreciating, and *learning from each other.*

Whereas some attention has now been given to the curricular aspect of our campuses, we must also analyze its social structure. The social ethos of a college is determined by the voluntary social interactions of the college's constituencies (Allen, 1991). "Ultimately, it is the informal dimension of an institution's social structure which discourages minority participation and encourages attrition" (Allen, 1991, p. 147).

The quality of leisure as a major contributing factor to campus life satisfaction is not consciously considered by most colleges. Leisure is usually viewed as superfluous to the education process. As an example, it is taken for granted that the international student will easily assimilate into the campus's extra-curricular recreational programs. This is not necessarily true. Considering one's leisure needs is not as simple as merely providing recreational activities. Leisure is realized by understanding the meanings *and* the expectations that people bring to those activities. These meanings and expectations are greatly influenced by both psychological and socio-cultural factors.

Purpose of the Study

The focus of this study was to explore international students' perceptions of leisure. There is limited research on college students' perceptions of leisure (Caldwell, Smith, & Weissinger, 1992) as well as limited research on multicultural differences (Hutchinson, 1988; Kraus, 1994).

The primary objective of this research was to explore the characteristics, meaning and functions, expectations, and role of leisure as expressed by international students at a Christian liberal arts college. Other objectives that directed the study were: (1) to identify the concepts individuals use to define their perceptions of leisure; (2) to determine whether international students share the same perceptions of leisure as North American students and, if not, to identify these perceptual differences; (3) to examine commonalities and differences among different individuals' concepts of leisure, free time, and work; (4) to investigate the determinants of leisure satisfactions and overall life satisfaction; and (5) to examine differences in leisure constraints.

Method

Study participants were selected through a convenience sampling technique. All 32 registered international students at Gordon College were invited to participate in the study. The students were informed of the study's purpose and the time commitment that would be expected of them. They were also assured that their responses would remain anonymous. Of the 32 potential international students, 15 agreed to participate in the study.

The method chosen for this study was the intensive interview. Hour-long interviews were tape recorded and then transcribed verbatim. The interviews were held in conversation style with open-ended probing questions. The students were first given a few common meanings of leisure, such as leisure as free time, leisure as freely chosen activities, leisure as a state of being, and leisure as an experience that is defined by the characteristics of perceived freedom and intrinsic motivation. Students were then asked to describe in their own words what leisure meant to them. If they had difficulty in articulating a definition or experience that was similar to leisure meanings as found in leisure literature, prompting questions were given to them.

The researcher was aware that data obtained using the intensive interviewing technique is difficult to analyze compared to quantitative data, but the overall purpose of the research was to be explorative. From the transcribed interviews, themes began to surface, and descriptions and sample responses were categorized under these themes. Again, the purpose of the research was not to be deductive in its nature, but rather inductive by listening to the stories of the interviewees.

The participants were from the countries of Ethiopia (2), Kenya, France, Bulgaria, Argentina, Indonesia, Sri Lanka, Palestine, China (2), Cambodia, Swaziland, Korea, and Zambia. Obviously this global approach to an understanding of leisure makes generalizations impossible, because each student spoke about leisure from his or her unique psychological and socio-cultural perspective. This research, however, was not meant to be conclusive, but rather to initiate a discussion on (1) the meaning of leisure as determined by cultural presuppositions; (2) the role and function of leisure; (3) constraints to leisure; and (4) leisure satisfaction as a contributing factor to quality of campus life.

Results

The Meaning of Leisure

Undertaking any research project of leisure entails first a confrontation with the "What is leisure?" question. The pluralism and abstraction of the term *leisure* makes an investigation into its meaning challenging, particularly when crossing language and cultural differences. Simplified definitions of leisure consider the phenomenon as free time, freely chosen activity, as a state of being, or as an experience that is defined by the characteristics of perceived freedom and intrinsic motivation. Although the researcher personally considered the definition of leisure to be a subjective state characterized by perceived freedom and the ability to act in relatively self-determined ways, the interviewees were invited to freely describe their own interpretation of leisure. It was discovered early in the process of interviewing that the researcher's definition of leisure was not readily grasped by many of the interviewees, and therefore expressions of fun and enjoyable experiences were commonly used to open the dialogue.

Leisure as social interaction. The most common idea of leisure as expressed by almost all the international students was that leisure is a social space. For most of the students, their cultural meaning of leisure was centered on their familial relationships. Time and activity with family and close friends was very important to them. An Ethiopian student described a typical day in her home: "My mom would be cooking in the house, and in our culture, when people come in you make coffee and invite your neighbors. To make coffee, you have to grind the coffee and make everything. It's like a ceremony."

This need for close social interaction as a critical characteristic within the leisure context is also an important criterion in determining leisure satisfaction in college. Another student from Zambia expressed his desire for this type of leisure at college:

> Since I came to the United States, I want to sit and talk. That is leisure for me, just sitting and just chatting with people in a group. But here everyone is busy; they say, "No, no time to sit. It's not you, just no time."

Particularly, socializing around meals is an important leisure experience. A few of the students mentioned their frustration with the lack of leisureliness of the meal times at college. "American students are too rushed and don't know how to enjoy their meals," stated a French student.

When the students experienced the social aspect of leisure, they described leisure as a relaxed, enjoyable expectation that is an integral part of their lives. A Palestinian student commented:

> With my friends and I, we have a good time sitting down and talking about different things in our lives. We'll talk about politics, philosophy, girls, and things like that. We all have good things to say about it, we just sit down and talk. That is fun. That is leisure.

Holistic concept of leisure. A holistic concept of leisure beyond the social space was described by a few of the students. Characteristics by which they identified leisure included a feeling of freedom, the enjoyment of life, and fun activities. A Kenyan student perhaps expressed best a holistic perspective on leisure:

> In my culture, time is not urgent. We can play with our time, even when working. We can talk to friends on the way and everything is at a moderate pace. Time is not our master. You can control it; it does not control you as it does here. . . . Quality leisure time helps you to grow internally, spiritually, morally.

Leisure as nonwork time or activity. Although there were some elements that would suggest a more holistic perspective of leisure, many of the students perceived leisure in a dualistic role to study and work. Leisure becomes a purposeful activity or period of time that serves a function. Leisure, as influenced by study and work, has the function of change, compensation, and reward, and time for relaxation and restoration. In reviewing these descriptions of leisure, the international students revealed more similarities than differences with American-born students, as leisure was primarily viewed as free time, i.e. time free from the necessity of study and work. "If I had to define it [leisure], it would be a time where I can get my worries off my mind and not have to think about work or school," commented a student from Argentina. When asked his definition of leisure, a Korean student responded: "I see it as activity and free time. . . . Doing what I like. When I am tired and when I want to be alone. If I have the time, I would define that as being leisure."

This free time concept of leisure also held frustrations for many of the students who did not perceive much free time in their schedules. A Cambodian student frequently referred to leisure as illusive free time:

I think that I need a little free time to sit down, listen to music, and relax from studies. . . . Americans seem to always have free time. They like to have free time, but it is because they are all done with their work. They are all done with their work so they have free time; they go to play sports. They play whatever. For me, it is hard to find free time because I struggle with the language. . . . I would like to change the time for me. I would change it to have more free time to relax and have fun.

The Argentinean student acknowledged his need for free time: "I've always lived a busy life. Free time is something I don't have a lot of. It [leisure] is important, but I have very little time to have it so I tend to value it a lot."

Functions of Leisure

Change. For leisure to be experienced, an important criterion was the aspect of change: change of pace, change of location, change of activity. A Sri Lankan student was very adamant about the necessity of change in order to experience leisure: "If you are going to have leisure, it's got to be totally unplanned, totally unexpected, no time limits, just there by itself." He went on to describe his perception of the strict structure of the college campus, and then again emphasized the importance of change: "I want to be totally out of that place [study environment] and have a different surrounding. . . . If you are going to really enjoy leisure, you've got to go somewhere else, do something different." Even if the activity is not a preferred choice, change of environment is important. An Ethiopian student described this need for change: "There are times when I go just for the sake of going out, and maybe I don't like it because it's something I'm not interested in, but it is important to have leisure."

Reward. Leisure as free time was frequently viewed as time to enjoy chosen activities, but it also had a function of compensation for study. It was seen as a reward. A Chinese student described her experience of leisure in this way: "I think leisure is what you can do during your free time after your studies are done . . . [hesitates and then laughs] but I never get my studies done. . . . I think leisure for me is everything except for study and except for homework. It's my reward." In a similar expression, a French student stated: "Work is very important. You work hard and then you get your leisure."

Restoration, recuperation, and relaxation. The primary function of leisure as expressed by the majority of interviewed students was that of restoration, recuperation, and relaxation. "If I do not have leisure things, I am stressed and can't study. If I don't have a chance to do leisure things, my brain gets stuck. If I don't relax, I think that's going to affect my study," stated an Indonesian student. The necessity of leisure as recuperation was important to the Palestinian student:

> I think taking that time is not just a good thing, but an essential thing. You can only go so far and then you break down. You have to fill up the gas in your engine again. . . . I can't live without recreation. You know, you can only take so much; then you need that recreational thing.

When asked how the experience of leisure has affected her education, a Chinese student recognized the importance of balance in her life:

> For me, I think like the saying "Play hard, and live hard." So I believe if you can play you can study. You can work. If you can't play, you can't work. I mean we should put those two things together. We should combine those together instead of just doing one thing. Like, I think we just can't simply play. You know we have to do our work, but we just can't simply do our work without play either.

In summary, there were many functions of leisure as expressed by these international students. There was an aspect of holism which was expressed in familial and social intimacies; however, these students were very aware of the utilitarian role of leisure. The functional characteristics of leisure, such as "change from study and work," "reward for study and work," and "restoration and relaxation that contribute toward work" were frequently described by these students. Study was the most important aspect of these students' lives, and leisure was justified for its significant contribution to that cause.

Constraints to Leisure

The perceived constraints to leisure that were expressed by the international students related to the meaning that they gave to leisure. Leisure is part of the social structure and is therefore not really free, but constrained by the norms, values, and resources of society (Kelly, 1992). Leisure that is meaningful is often activity that is shared with a social group, and the constraints that inhibit leisure are frequently of social origin. For these international students, leisure is not just activity for the sake of activity, but rather, informal social interaction, which is important to the leisure context.

Different cultural values. For those students who perceived leisure holistically in a social space, there were constraints when friends did not share the same value of leisure. When international students were accustomed to experiencing leisure in terms of family and intimate social relationships, leisure can be inhibited on the college campus. Leisure was realized when students perceived themselves free to express their identities in a social context. However, the different cultural values toward free time usage and resources frequently contributed to this constraint and resulted in feelings of loneliness and isolation. An Ethiopian student lamented, "summer, fall, winter, all the time, everyone is busy and that is frustrating for me because then we are never going to get time to just relax and spend time talking and being together. It is very lonely." Another Ethiopian student had similar thoughts:

> People are really tied up in this country. At home, no one plans what they are going to do tomorrow. I could call up my friend and do crazy things that we didn't plan, and go somewhere. Whereas here you have to plan things and be put on somebody's calendar. . . . Everything is so fast and I can't do things with friends like I would normally do because friendship is not really real to me here. It's different, the idea of fun for me and for American students. We don't have fun in the same way. So it makes it hard to plan leisure with an American friend because of the many differences.

Lack of time. Students who described leisure in a functional role to serve work and study perceived external constraints from a lack of time and a lack of resources, such as transportation and money. Many international students come from cultures that do not have limitations on leisure experiences based on time boundaries. The ebb and flow of life to which they are accustomed, conflicts with the strict time schedules of North American campus life. Cultural perspectives on time that are different than American time values can also constrain leisure. When asked to compare American perspectives on time with that of his home country, the student from Zambia replied: "It is much different, we do not hurry. Here, everyone is always busy going somewhere. It is important to be on time here. In my country, it is important just to arrive."

When leisure was expressed as free time and viewed in a functional role in relation to work and study, students were frequently frustrated with the lack of leisure. The Palestinian student commented on his frustration: "I take my education very seriously and there is so much work, that I rarely take time for leisure. I try to make time for it because I know it helps me study better, but I feel guilty if I take time off." A student from Bulgaria viewed leisure as free time that he didn't experience: "I almost forget what it is to have free time. It is hard to find such time. . . . I wouldn't say at college I have a good experience with leisure just because I don't have any." If leisure, therefore, is viewed as free time that is rarely experienced, this constraint influences the international student's perception of college life.

Lack of resources (transportation, money). Another external constraint to leisure was a perceived lack of resources, such as transportation and money. As mentioned earlier, the characteristic of change was very important to the international students' concept of leisure. This change is frequently mentioned in terms of place, that is, leisure was enhanced when the student could have a change from the work-study environment. When leisure involved transportation and money, it was constrained if the campus was somewhat isolated or not close to public transportation.

Lack of transportation was frequently mentioned by the interviewed students. "Over here, I need a car to do everything. In France, we had public transportation and we were a lot more free to go wherever we wanted without having to depend on other people's cars," stated the student from France. A student from China lamented:

> It's that there is not much to do here. And the school is kind of far away from other places. If you want to go out and eat or something, there is no way we can go. It is hard for the international students.

The student from Indonesia suggested that even the freedom of leisure has changed somewhat for her due to the lack of transportation:

> It's [leisure] kind of different here, but in my home we never worry about anything. We don't worry about who is going to bring me there because in my country we have public transportation. Whenever I want to go somewhere, I don't have the freedom to go.

Besides a lack of transportation as a major constraint to the experience of leisure, a lack of money was also an inhibiting factor for some international students. The student from Argentina stated, "I need a change to have leisure, but I don't have much time because I have to work, and I don't have money to go anywhere. Everything costs so much money, so I just stay on campus."

In summary, the constraints of leisure were basically described as a difference in perspective regarding the social aspect of leisure. International students can easily feel lonely, not only due to separation from home, but because of cultural values that place family and social intimacies in a central role to life. Students express a discontent with their quality of life when the freedom to express this need of intimacy is inhibited due to the busyness of friends, strict time schedules, and lack of transportation and money. This discontent, in turn, can affect their academic efforts and general satisfaction with campus life.

Discussion

Are these international students satisfied with their experiences of leisure and the way those experiences influence perceived campus quality of life? Satisfaction with leisure reflects self-efficacy: that is, a confidence in one's self to produce and regulate events (Samdahl, 1992). Self-efficacy is related to intrinsic motivation and interest that is expressed through leisure. If a campus is interested in promoting self-efficacy and satisfaction with campus life, then an understanding of leisure meanings, experiences, and values can influence these goals. For many international students, the greatest satisfaction came through intimate social interaction and availability of leisure resources.

The college campus needs to consider the role of leisure in the overall transition and satisfaction of the international students. There are both similarities and differences in expressions of leisure held by American and international students. The influence of unique cultural values upon study, work, time, and their relationships needs to be understood. Purposeful leisure awareness and leisure counseling can be an effective means to help international students become aware of how their culture differs from American culture.

Leisure counseling can help international students explore what leisure means to them from their own unique cultural experiences. Strategies can be suggested to help the student integrate his/her experience of leisure into a typical day on campus. The student should also be encouraged to reflect on any differences in time perceptions and, if necessary, use time diaries that include a study schedule and a leisure component. Leisure counseling can also help a student consider the meaning of leisure beyond the component of free time, which easily becomes illusive on the college campus.

International students can be assisted in the cultural transition through encouraging their involvement in leisure "subcultures" (hobby groups, activity interests, etc.). As a student identifies some of his/her previous leisure experiences and activities, information can be given to them concerning how, where, and with whom they can continue some of their interests.

An idea that surfaced through the interviews is a "Friendship Club," a pool of American students who are interested in befriending an international student. A leisure inventory survey could be conducted of these American students as well as the international students, and then students could be matched according to their leisure interests. The American student could encourage, include, and assist his/her international friend in enjoying these leisure interests, and consequently a friendship might develop. It is not just the activity that is important, but the social meaning of the activity that is the desired outcome.

Because leisure is so closely associated with family and intimate social relationships, the campus can recruit faculty, staff, and even community families to "adopt" an international student. A host family can invite their student into their home for meals; include them in family events; and orient the student to American customs, values, and expressions. This strategy not only has the potential of meeting the need for familial and social relationships, but can provide a change of place and pace that many of the international students see as an important characteristic of leisure.

The entire campus community not only can become sensitized to the transitional needs of the international students, but can also encourage interactional pluralism. Classrooms and resident halls can purposefully engage the international students in discussions that allow North Americans to learn about these cultural customs, values, and social interactions that are integrally entwined with leisure, work, and time perceptions. There is much we can learn concerning quality of life issues from international students, including the importance of lifestyle balance, social relationships, traditions, and cultural heritage. A better understanding of the multicultural perspectives of leisure can be a positive force on our college campuses in supporting our international students and contributing to constructive relationships between international and American students.

References

Allen, H.L. (1991). Racial minorities and evangelical colleges: Thoughts and reflections of a minority social scientist. In D.J. Lee, A.L. Nieves, & H.L. Allen (Eds.), *Ethnic minorities and evangelical Christian colleges* (pp. 145–158). Lanham, MD: University Press of America.

Beard, J.B., & Ragheb, M. (1980). Measuring leisure satisfaction. *Journal of Leisure Research* 12(1), 12–33.

Caldwell, L., Smith, E.A., & Weissinger, E. (1992). The relationship of leisure activities and perceived health of college students. *Society and Leisure* 15(2), 545–556.

Csikzentmihalyi, M. (1975). *Beyond boredom and anxiety*. San Francisco: Jossey-Bass.

Hutchison, R. (1988). A critique of race, ethnicity, and social class in recent leisure-recreation research. *Journal of Leisure Research* 20, 10–30.

Ingham, R. (1987). Psychological contributions to the study of leisure: Part two. *Leisure Studies* 6(1), 1–14.

Iso-Ahola, S.E. (1980). *Social psychological perspectives on leisure and recreation.* Springfield, IL: Charles C. Thomas.

Kaplan, M. (1960). *Leisure in America: A social inquiry.* New York: Macmillan.

Kelly, J.R. (1983). *Leisure identities and interactions.* London: Allen & Unwin.

Kelly, J.R. (1987). *Freedom to be: A new sociology of leisure.* New York: Macmillan.

Kelly, J.R. (1990). *Leisure* (2nd ed.). Englewood Cliffs, NJ: Prentice-Hall.

Kelly, J.R. (1992). *Sociology of leisure.* State College, PA: Venture.

Kelly, J.R. (1994). *Leisure in a changing America.* New York: Macmillan.

Lee, Y., & Halberg, K.J. (1989). An exploratory study of the relationship between shyness and perceptions of freedom in leisure. *Leisure Sciences* 11, 217–227.

Lee, D.J., & Rice, R.R. (1991). Ethnic identity and multiculturalism: Concepts, history, research, and policy. In D.J. Lee, A.J. Nieves, & H.L. Allen (Eds.), *Ethnic-minorities and evangelical Christian colleges* (pp. 65–143). Lanham, MD: University Press of America.

Neulinger, J. (1981a). *The psychology of leisure* (2nd ed.). Springfield, IL: Charles C. Thomas.

Samdahl, D., & Kleiber, D. (1989). Self-awareness and leisure experience. *Leisure Sciences* 11, 1–10.

Samdahl, D. (1992). Leisure in our lives: Exploring the common leisure occasion. *Journal of Leisure Research* 24, 19–32.

Chapter 9

SOURCE OF BELIEFS AS A CONSTRAINT TO PARTICIPATION IN SELECT LEISURE ACTIVITIES: A CONGREGATIONAL ANALYSIS

Steven N. Waller

Thinking about how our religious upbringing and subsequent religious convictions influence our leisure attitudes, behaviors and choices are not something people typically consider. The manner in which we integrate our faith into our daily living has everything to do with our choices related to participation in generally accepted leisure pursuits such as gambling, social drinking, and attending movies. The value conflicts associated with religion and leisure have been well documented over the course of modern history. In Christianity, history reveals an appreciation and advocacy for leisure, as well as instances in which leisure is negatively portrayed. For example, early and medieval Christians had a positive view of the classical understanding of leisure. The early church fathers advocated for *otium sanctum*, or holy leisure. They encouraged a sense of balance in life; an ability to be at peace through the activities of the day, every day; an ability to pace oneself (Foster, 1978). Great medieval thinkers such as Thomas Aquinas were proponents of the contemplative life – *vita contemplative* – as opposed to the active life – *vita activa* (Jalbert, 2009). Renowned Trappist monk Thomas Merton also encouraged sacred leisure as a part of the contemplative life (Merton & Shannon, 2004). In summary, in Christianity there is an ongoing appreciation for leisure as an important facet of Christian living (Doohan, 1990).

Conversely, when leisure is understood as an activity, history has revealed how some leisure activities have been viewed both positively and

---

Revised version of paper presented at the 2007 conference.

negatively. For example, positively, Reformer John Calvin wrote:

> Ivory and gold, and riches of all kinds, are certainly blessings of Divine Providence; not only permitted, but expressly designed for the use of men; nor are we anywhere prohibited to laugh, or to be satiated with food, or to annex new possessions to those already enjoyed by ourselves or by our ancestors, or to be delighted with musical harmony, or to drink wine. (p. 72)

However, at various points in history, the religious community began to oppose some leisure pursuits such as attending the theater, secular music and art, dance, gambling, and Sunday sports spectatorship (de Grazia, 1964; Kelly, 1982; Kraus, 1990, 1994; McCrossen, 2000), although an unenthusiastic view of one or more leisure pursuits does not necessarily reflect a negative view of leisure. The impetus of these prohibitions was to promote the idea of "purity of conduct." The principal tools the church used to restrict leisure choices and influence the moral behavior of parishioners was religious doctrine and tradition. Invariably, these restrictive ideas related to leisure permeated some denominations within Protestant Christianity. As a result, prohibitive statements regarding dancing, gambling, secular music, and card playing were infused into the congregational culture and doctrinal statements of churches aligned with Protestant, Christian denominations (Holland, 2002). Notwithstanding the renewed attention given to religious freedom in making leisure choices, "some people's religious beliefs intentionally and fully shape their recreation choices, while others express beliefs that unintentionally and partially shape their recreation choices" (Byl, 2006, p. 210).

As efforts are made to chronicle the relationship between religion and leisure over time, the discourse must be approached with caution. For every misgiving that may be pointed out about leisure and its interface with religion, there are far more virtuous aspects that can be illustrated (Ryken, 2002; Neville, 2004). Moreover, Johnson (2009) noted, "Our attitude toward recreation and our attitude toward history . . . should be much the same. On the one hand, we should value them not only for their usefulness but also for their own sake" (p. 51).

A case study utilizing a local congregation is an appropriate point of departure to begin exploring the relationship between religious beliefs, religious tradition, church doctrine, and leisure. The present study replicates a previous study published in the *Journal of Unconventional Parks, Tourism and Recreation Research* (Waller, 2009). Case studies are valuable as a method because they allow the researcher to explore a program, activity, process, or other unit of analysis in detail (Creswell, 2003). This case study, utilizing action research (AR) methodology, examines how religious doctrine and personal beliefs influence attitudes about eleven leisure activities among congregants within a mid-size Baptist church. The study also seeks to determine if congregational change and transformation can result from sharing the findings of the study. This case study is significant because it examines the interface between religion and leisure at a micro level and reveals how religious socialization and subsequent personal and corporate beliefs influence leisure attitudes and behaviors. Leisure constraints theory (Crawford, Jackson, & Godbey, 1991) provides the theoretical foundation for the study and a framework for examining the possible barriers to leisure participation that may be tied to religious beliefs.

Literature Review

Religious beliefs have profound implications for daily living. These beliefs influence the way religion is practiced across faith traditions (Fontana, 2003). The ideals and beliefs of religion define, to some extent, the relation of humans to a supreme being and delineate those human qualities and behaviors that are worthy and those that are sinful. All these beliefs will shape the leisure values and behavior of religious people. Organized religion influences what forms of leisure pastimes are acceptable (Abinate, Robb, & Smith, 1995).

Congregational Influences on Leisure Attitudes and Behaviors

Religious socialization typically begins in the home and then is undertaken at the congregational level. At both points the individual begins to learn and internalize attitudes, values, and behaviors within the context of a religious system of beliefs and practices. Furthermore, religious socialization as a process is a lifetime endeavor (Neugarten, 1977). To the extent that individuals are involved in a church or religious belief system and exposed to doctrine, a socializing influence occurs (Brown & Gary, 1990). The process of interacting with others as well as exposure to religious scriptures, rituals, and fellowship activities influences the formation of values, attitudes, and behaviors that may affect individuals not only in a church setting, but also in various endeavors in the wider community.

Congregations are essential to the religious health of the United States and are central to the religious wellbeing of more than half of Americans (Ammerman, 2005). Examining the religious and spiritual dynamics of congregations also helps researchers to better understand: (1) the manner in which religious socialization, indoctrination, and assimilation impact the lives of people that participate in mainstream, organized religion; (2) how to facilitate the changing of attitudes, behaviors, and beliefs within congregations; and (3) how the dynamics of congregational life influence individuals that belong to them and the communities in which they are present (Dudley & Ammerman, 2002).

In many Protestant congregations, pastors are the primary agents for religious socialization. The pastor generates resources used for religious socialization utilizing the Christian Bible, doctrine, and other denominational resources (Oswalt, 1987). Russell (2005) noted that "most religious organizations are concerned with human goodness and thus often teach doctrines that promote healthful expressions of leisure" (p. 74). Exposure and adherence to messages of religious elites (clergy) is thought to result in changes in the attitudes of believers who find religious messages credible, due to the connection of specific messages with a generally accepted theological basis (Jelen & Chandler, 1996). Oswalt (1987) and Randolph (1970) argued that the manner in which pastors embrace leisure in their lives will play a role in shaping the attitudes of congregants about leisure. Moreover, Randolph surmised that leisure plays an important role in worship, makes the church relevant, and creates a fun or "swinging" environment (p. 16).

The institutionalization of beliefs based on the conveyance of religious doctrine through religious socialization shapes beliefs about nonreligious activities. Moreover, shared beliefs are an important facet of living in community with other Christians, particularly within congregations. Overall, tension remains between espoused Christian beliefs about the sanctity of certain types of leisure pursuits, the secularization of Sunday, and personal choices to participate in leisure pastimes that collide with congregational beliefs. Leisure activities such as gambling (Diaz, 2000) and dancing (Lawless, 1983) are construed as sinful and immoral, which is the reason some religions forbid or strongly advise against it. Congregants are frequently socialized to believe that dancing will lead to immoral "sins of the flesh" due to the possibilities of eroticism. Gambling in some instances is assigned the same immoral status as dancing. This may be a function of the doctrinal and tradition-based beliefs about the sinful nature of the activity. An awareness and avoidance of sin is part of the ethos of organized Christian religion at the denominational and congregational levels. Perceptions about sin associated with a leisure pursuit can be transmitted within the culture of religious institutions for extended periods of time.

Leisure Constraints

Research pertaining to leisure constraints has grown steadily over the past several years, representing a coherent body of literature that has evolved and changed with new and emerging understandings. Leisure constraints has become a distinctive subfield of leisure studies (Jackson, 2005). Leisure constraints were originally conceptualized as a mechanism for better understanding barriers to activity participation. Jackson (1988) articulated this focus, suggesting that "constraints per se are best viewed as a subset of reasons for not engaging in a particular behavior" (p. 211). Over the last decade, the study of leisure constraints has heightened understanding of the broader influences that shape people's everyday leisure behaviors. On the whole, leisure constraints research seeks to "investigate factors that are assumed by researchers and/or perceived or experienced by the individuals to limit the formation of leisure preferences and/or prohibit participation and enjoyment in leisure" (Jackson, 2000, p. 62). In 1987, Crawford and Godbey developed a hierarchical model of leisure constraints, which was later refined by Crawford, Jackson, and Godbey (1991). The model identified a three-fold typology of constraints to leisure: intrapersonal, interpersonal, and structural constraints. Intrapersonal constraints involve psychological conditions that are internal to the individual such as personality factors, attitudes, or more temporary psychological conditions such as mood. Interpersonal constraints are those that arise out of interaction with others such as family members, friends, coworkers, and neighbors. Structural constraints include such factors as the lack of opportunities or the cost of activities that result from external conditions in the environment. Each type of constraint is relevant to the study of religion and leisure. Constraints to leisure typically do not exist in a social vacuum, but are immersed in the political, ideological, religious, and power structures surrounding people's lives (Livengood & Stodolska, 2004).

Since the advent of leisure constraints research, the majority of studies have focused on variables such as gender, race and ethnicity, socio-economic status, culture, and geographic location as major constraints to leisure participation (Jackson, 2005). Until recently, spirituality and religious beliefs have been left out of the study of constraints.

Christian Attitudes to Leisure

The available scholarly and professional literature reveals that research related to Christian spirituality/religion and its relationship to leisure began with a small group of researchers but continues to grow

(Heintzman, 1987, 2006a, 2006b; Livengood, 2006; Van Andel & Heintzman, 1996). The mass of research generated by leisure studies scholars that examines leisure attitudes within Christian denominations and congregations is growing (e.g., Livengood, 2006; Schulz & Auld, 2009; Trunfio, 1991). This corpus of scholarship provides useful insights into the intersection of leisure and religion from the vantage points of the individual and congregation. Other researchers in parallel disciplines such as congregational studies and religious education have also begun to explore the value of leisure in a variety of contexts (Ammerman, 2005; Moran 1979; Schnase, 2007).

A series of non-empirical essays helps to provide additional insights into Christian attitudes about leisure. Stolz (2009), in his essay, noted that Christian churches as voluntary associations are bound to their religious mission, and their congregations play an important role in providing spiritual, educational, and leisure services that are beneficial to their members.

Wimberly (2002), in the book *Aging, Spirituality, and Religion: A Handbook, Volume 2,* suggested that local churches play a role in providing leisure activities for aging adults by providing leisure opportunities that are readily available, accessible, and include safe facilities. Finally, Reeves (1980), in her essay that critiqued the relationship between leisure and religious values as expressed by clergy, noted that social leisure is important to the life of local Christian churches. Reeves contended that clergy play a major role in interpreting the value of leisure in congregational settings. Given that norms change relative to time and place, the question of what is moral recreational activity may be a decisive force in pluralistic communities. Thus, there is a need to develop religious prescriptions for leisure. The points brought forth in the work of Stolz, Wimberly, and Reeves illustrate the importance of the positive aspects of leisure in the life of the individual and the congregation.

Additionally, there are empirical studies that explore Christian attitudes about leisure in congregational life that inform thinking on the subject. For example, Ammerman (2005) conducted a study of Protestant and Catholic congregations in ten states in the United States. Between 1997 and 1999, more than 700 face-to-face interviews were conducted with church leaders and parishioners on a range of topics related to congregational life (e.g., doctrinal issues, fellowship, leisure, and outreach). Based on the data collected, Ammerman concluded that what people experience in congregations may shape their families and leisure in many ways. The range of positive, "healthy" leisure pursuits participated in by congregations and their individual members is wide. Moreover, Ammerman noted that mainline Protestant congregations are very likely to organize leisure activities for their members and their local communities in light of their interest in community development and activism (p. 65). In essence, at the congregational level, leisure is valuable spiritual and community capital for the individual and congregation.

Lawless (1983), in her study of Pentecostalism, noted several observations about this strand of Christianity and its encounter with leisure. In-depth interviews were conducted with eight adherents of Pentecostalism about their religious practices. One salient observation about Pentecostals that Lawless noted was "the blanket refusal of Pentecostals to participate in modern American amusements and entertainments" (p. 41). The rejection included participation in leisure pursuits such as movies, ball games, card playing, liquor drinking, dancing, and television viewing. Lawless (1983) further noted that Pentecostals "use their own rejection of the ways of the world as a comment on the sad lives of the people 'in the world' and as a means of enhancing their own sense of group identity at the same time" (p. 89). The findings presented by Lawless must be interpreted with caution for multiple reasons. First, there is a lack of clarity about the methods used in the study. Second, despite the interesting nature of some of the findings, they do not represent the position of all Pentecostal congregations about the identified leisure activities. The inherent value of this study is that the observations presented by the researcher illustrated the power of religious beliefs as both a positive and a potential negative constraint to leisure. As indicated in the study, religious beliefs may help the adherent refrain from indulgence in potentially harmful activities or exercise restraint if there is a choice to participate in an activity such as gambling. On the other hand, the possible negative influence may come about as a result of the leisure being portrayed negatively and then internalized as a part of the religious socialization of the individual and congregation.

Tamney (2005) explored how two conservative, Protestant congregations infused teachings about "sinful" leisure pursuits – drinking alcohol, gambling, social dancing, movies, and television shows produced by nonbelievers – into congregational life. One church was Pentecostal and the other Free Will Baptist. The pastors of these congregations were asked to rate the importance and frequency of religious teachings on a four-point scale: 1) it is a major teaching of the congregation; 2) it is one of the teachings of the congregation; 3) it is mentioned once in a while; and 4) or it is never mentioned. Both pastors placed little emphasis on giving up movies or television programming produced by nonbelievers. The pastor of the Free Will Baptist church indicated that doctrinal teachings on abstaining from drinking, gambling, and social dancing were major teachings of the congregation. This study serves as an example of how religious doctrine may influence perceptions about leisure activities at the congregational level within the two respective denominations. The caution that emanates from this study is that the results are not fully representative of the doctrinal positions of all Pentecostal and Free Will Baptist congregations, as only two pastors participated in this study.

Similarly, Livengood (2006) examined perceived barriers to leisure among members of new paradigm churches in Illinois. Semi-structured interviews were conducted with seventeen congregation members. Four key themes evolved from interviews with congregants: (1) personal spirituality was not considered a constraint to leisure participation; (2) some interviewees did see their faith as an impediment in previous stages of their life; (3) other interviewees noted their Christian faith was a constraint on their leisure pursuits; and (4) some participants indicated they did not participate in leisure pursuits that were considered unchristian. Among interviewees, references were made to the struggle with interpreting appropriateness of leisure activities based on their faith, legalism espoused when active with previous congregations, and attempts by older and more spiritually mature persons to negotiate perceived barriers. This study is important because it directs attention to the transition of thought regarding religious beliefs, leisure, and the ethos of a congregation. The findings illustrate that greater emphasis is being placed on spirituality and faith convictions as opposed to doctrine and religious tradition that is sometimes couched in congregational dynamics.

Overall, this sampling of non-empirical essays and data-driven studies points to the role that religion plays in shaping leisure behaviors. Even though the present review of literature is not exhaustive, the essays and studies included illustrate the positive and negative aspects of religion as a constraint to leisure choices and behaviors. Religious practices that may be perceived as constraints to leisure such as honoring and keeping the Sabbath, stewardship of our time and bodies, and the abstaining from the consumption of alcohol are helpful to the constructive and godly use of our leisure when explained and practiced in the proper context. In addition to the religious constraints to leisure that may be grounded in doctrine or tradition, social norms also constrain leisure choices and behaviors when it comes to activities such as gambling, consumption of pornography, vandalism, and substance abuse, all of which are engaged in during leisure time (Russell, 2005). In essence, religious constraints that may be perceived as controlling and negative to some may indeed be a safeguard to participation in leisure pursuits that may be physically, psychologically, spiritually, or relationally harmful.

The works cited in the previous paragraphs help to illustrate that leisure can be positive, even though some activities may have a negative stigma attached to them by religious institutions and society as a whole. Inevitably, how Christians assign value to leisure begins with a sound biblical, theological, and moral/ethical framework coupled with an understanding of societal norms for the appropriate use of leisure. Often what is missing amidst the encouragement to consume and enjoy leisure in both religious and secular environments is the conversation about, and instruction in, the ethical and moral use of leisure. Invariably, one's leisure choices and behaviors should not do harm to one's self or to others (Heintzman, 2015) nor demean the gift of leisure (Waller, 2010) as a given by God. Trunfio (1991), commenting on the ethics of leisure, stated, "When leisure is perceived as a virtue, there are moral guidelines which guide that experience. A Christian commitment to excellence in leisure results in the fulfillment of God's divine purpose with self as well as others" (p. 158).

Based on the available scholarship (non-empirical and empirical), there is a need to further examine the interface between religion and leisure at the micro level of a congregation and heighten our understanding of how religious socialization and subsequent personal and corporate beliefs influence leisure attitudes and behaviors. The purpose of this case study, utilizing action research (AR) methodology, is to examine how religious doctrine and personal beliefs influence attitudes about eleven leisure activities among congregants within a mid-size Baptist church. Additionally, the present study seeks to ascertain whether congregational change and transformation can result from sharing the findings of the study.

An Overview of Action Research

Action research (AR) is a reflective process of progressive problem solving led by individuals working with others in teams or as part of a community of practice to improve the way they address issues and solve problems. In the present study, the congregation serves as the community of practice. Greenwood and Levin (1998) define AR as "social research that is carried out by a team encompassing a researcher and members of a community seeking to improve their situation" (p. 4). AR is commonly used in educational environments, but over time has proven useful in alternative settings such as congregations (Dokecki, Newbrough, & O'Gorman, 2001; Keys & Frank, 1987). Action research methodology has seldom been used in leisure research as evidenced by the limited number of published articles in journals such as the *Journal of Leisure Research, Leisure Studies,* or *Leisure Sciences* (Floyd, Bacarro, & Thompson, 2008). Pedlar (1995) explored the interdependence between community members and communitarian principles of social organization using action research. Action research has the potential to respond to many challenges that influence the quality of life within communities. Pedlar concluded that, "Through action research, people's everyday life experiences can be considerably enhanced. Action research offers a vehicle to foster change through the rejuvenation of community and the realization that exists in leisure and recreation" (p. 138). Moreover, Pedlar recommended that the academic community should recognize the importance of AR and "embrace it as a bona fide scholarly endeavor" (p. 138).

One strand of AR that is more engaging than others is participatory action research (PAR). PAR is a collaborative method by which researchers and those they study enter into a partnership to identify the best way to study a problem and make sure that the results of the research make a difference to those who were studied. Participants are major stakeholders in the research process and become vested in the outcomes of the study. In the present study, PAR was utilized by means of involving context associates (CAs) – members of the church being studied who voluntarily assisted with the research project. The eight CAs helped to identify the key facets of the history of the church, the tradition of the congregation, and the members' disposition toward key leisure pursuits that were tagged as sinful over the history of the church. The CAs also provided assistance with survey collection. There was also a concern over the negative value assigned to leisure activities such as dancing, gambling, and the perceived individual and corporate tension that negative appropriation created. Finally, interest in the study resulted from a desire to better understand how leisure attitudes might influence personal and congregational leisure choices.

The Research Context

The Congregation

The congregation in this study is located in a city in southern Ohio. The pseudonym "ABC Church" is used to protect the identity of the congregation. The church is 78 years old, has had three pastors in its history, and is affiliated with the National Baptist Convention, USA. According to church records, there were 450 adult members aligned with the congregation at the time of the study, with 120 being labeled as "active disciples" – those who attended at least one weekly Bible study, participated in at least one of 30 ministries, and monetarily contributed to the church on a regular basis. The church is a confessing congregation in that it regularly recites key doctrinal statements such as the *Church Covenant* and the *Baptist Articles of Faith* on a scheduled basis. A high percentage of congregants are second- or third-generation members.

The traditional and conservative theological underpinnings of the church are frequently the determinants of leisure choices and behaviors. Based on doctrinal beliefs, the congregational theology is such that leisure activities that lie in tension with perceived or actual biblical teachings are labeled as sinful. Sin and avoidance of intentional and/or unintentional sin is a major Christian education theme. For example, in their weekly church bulletin, sin is addressed within the context of the theological concept of salvation. The following statement illustrates the previous point:

> . . . 1) God loves you and wants to bless your life; 2) your sin separates you from God's blessings; 3) Jesus' death satisfies your sin debt; and 4) you must accept Jesus as your personal Savior by Faith. God will bless you, if you obey (1 Cor. 2:9), and punish you (see Heb. 12.6), if you don't. (ABC Church, 2007)

Additionally, congregants are regularly encouraged to avoid all "appearances of evil" based on their understanding of 1 Thessalonians 5:22 in which the Apostle Paul wrote, "Reject every kind of evil." This admonishment carries over into their leisure choices. Within the congregation, activities such as games of chance; playing cards and/or bingo for money; consumption of alcohol; dancing; watching television shows containing sex, violence, or abuse language (curse words); attending "R" rated movies; and listening to secular music (interpreted by the congregation as music with morally questionable lyrics) are all considered to be sinful and congregants have historically been persuaded to refrain from participation.

Congregational Theologies

To effectively examine the nuances associated with religious life in mainstream religious organizations, empirical research of congregations is necessary (Welch, 1989). The congregation is a finite and irreducible unit of religious socialization in American culture (Jelen & Chandler, 1996). Congregations have both official and unofficial ideas about what constitutes sin and how to operate within the world (Ammerman, Jackson, Dudley, & McKinney, 1998). These theologies are primarily developed by scripture, creeds, prayers, doctrinal teachings, sermons, and an assortment of catechistic materials. Congregational theologies are either *explicit* or *implicit*. *Explicit theology* refers to the official doctrinal position of the congregation. The Bible, *Church Covenant*, *Baptist Beliefs* (Mullins, 1925), and *Baptist Articles of Faith* serve as primary source material for the ABC church's explicit theology. The *Church Covenant* is corporately recited on the first Sunday of each month and the *Articles of Faith* are taught corporately bi-monthly. *Implicit theology* is defined as the genuine but fragmented theologies members of the congregation believe.

For example, Article Fifteen, entitled *Of the Christian Sabbath*, directly addresses two key topics, the Christian Sabbath and sinful types of recreation:

> We believe that the first day of the week is the Lord's Day, or Christian Sabbath; and is to be kept sacred to religious purposes, by abstaining from all secular labor and sinful recreations; by the devout observance of all the means of grace, both private and public; and by preparation for the rest that remains for the people of God. (Jordan, 1997, p. 30)

Two points of tension lie in this article: 1) the mandate relating to the Christian Sabbath; and 2) the term "sinful recreations." First, does this mandate apply only to Sunday, or should it be complied with each day? Traditionally, the interpretation of this article and associated doctrine pertaining to Sabbath observance limits participation in recreation pursuits on Sunday. Second, what is meant by the term "sinful recreation"?

An understanding of implicit theology is important because it demonstrates how the beliefs of individual members differ from beliefs of the congregation. In the context, the trappings of the implicit theology of the congregation were gauged when CAs were asked to give examples of activities that the congregation has historically spoken out against. One CA noted,

> I was raised to believe [that], as a Christian, drinking liquor, playing cards, and dancing was sin . . . the devil's work.

A second CA offered the following statement,

> I didn't realize that Christians weren't supposed to dance until I was in high school. By that time, I'd been going to every school dance that had been held since 7th grade. When I asked what was sinful about dancing, I was told that it caused "lust" and brought on sinful thoughts.

These comments illustrate that some forms of recreation are not viewed positively by the congregation.

Methods

Research Questions

Pursuant to the examination of the context, the theoretical framework, and the review of literature, the following action research questions were developed to guide the present study:
1. Do doctrinal beliefs within the congregation influence individual beliefs about the perceived sinful nature of eleven leisure activities identified by congregants?
2. Will the congregation be open to change and transformation as a result of sharing the results of the present study?
3. Will new Christian education and ministry initiatives be developed as a result of the congregation's experience with the action research project?

Questionnaire Construction

A three-part, written questionnaire was developed in consultation with CAs. The first section requested demographic data from the sample. The second section sought to explore the level of agreement among the sample about church doctrinal issues that may influence leisure choices and behaviors. The final section was developed to query respondents' beliefs about eleven leisure activities congregants deemed sinful. The group of perceived sinful leisure activities was established based on the conveyance of congregational history by CAs, other members, comments from pastoral sermons, and doctrinal beliefs as expressed in the *Church Covenant* and the *Baptist Articles of Faith* (Jordan, 1997). Leisure activities included: drinking beverages that contain alcohol; playing cards; playing bingo for money; gambling; watching "R" rated movies; dancing; watching television shows that included nudity and inappropriate language (curse words); failure to exercise; attending a sporting event on Sunday; listening to secular music; and attending a comedy show at a comedy club. For each activity, respondents were asked to indicate whether they believed the activity was sinful by answering yes or no. Finally, each respondent was asked to indicate whether the primary source of their belief about the eleven leisure activities was scripture (the Bible), church doctrine (*Baptist Articles of Faith, Baptist Church Covenant, Baptist Beliefs*), or a personal belief. In this study the term "personal belief" was defined as a belief that is not grounded in either scripture or church doctrine.

Sample Selection and Data Collection

A purposive sample of 100 congregants was drawn from members that attended the Sunday school program. The CAs sought out volunteers to complete the questionnaire. Despite the limitations of nonprobability sampling, purposive sampling was useful in light of the specific nature of the study (congregational case study), time restrictions, and costs (Riddick & Russell, 1999). Data were collected over a two-week period. One hundred surveys were distributed to congregants prior to the Sunday school period and collected immediately afterward. No identifiable markers were placed on the questionnaire to protect the identities of the respondents. Upon collection of the questionnaires by the CAs, they were placed in a box in the administrative office of the church and then collected by the researcher. A total of 89 completed surveys were returned for a response rate of 89 percent. Descriptive statistics, including frequencies and percentages, were used to analyze the demographic characteristics of the sample. Pearson's chi-square was used to examine research questions. Additionally, Cramer's V (V) was used to measure the strength of association between variables.

Results

Sample Profile

Respondents consisted of 54 females (60.7 percent) and 35 males (39.3 percent). The highest percentage (42.6 percent) were in the 51+ age category and the majority of congregants participating in the study were married (77.5 percent). Nearly 50 percent (49.4 percent) of respondents earned masters' degrees and reported earnings of $50,000+ annually (47.2 percent). The majority of the sample (42.7 percent) indicated they were employed in professional occupations. The mean length of membership in the congregation was 12.3 years ($SD = 6.23$), and 60.7 percent of the respondents held membership for ten years or more. Table 1 provides the demographic details for the sample.

Table 1

Demographic Profile of the Sample

	Frequency	Percent
Sex		
Female	54	60.7
Male	35	39.3
Age category		
21-30	4	4.5
31-40	15	16.9
41-50	26	29.2
51+	44	49.4
Marital status		
Married	69	77.5
Single	20	22.5
Highest degree earned		
High school diploma	10	11.2
Associates	17	19.1
Bachelors	18	20.2
Masters	44	49.4
Income level		
$20,000-$29,999	8	9.0
$30,000-$39,999	11	12.4
$40,000-$49,999	28	31.5
> $50,000	42	47.2
Occupational category		
Student	17	17
Technical/trade	15	15
Small business ownder	19	19
Professional	39	39
Lengh of membership in congregation		
< 10 years	35	35
> 10 years	54	54

Testing the Congregational Culture

As a part of the survey study, participants were asked whether: (1) their religious beliefs guided their choices of leisure pastimes; and (2) they believed participation in some of the identified leisure activities would lead to sinful behaviors based on their understanding of the congregation's major doctrinal statements – the Bible, the *Church Covenant* and the *Articles of Faith*. Approximately 70 percent (69.7 percent) of the sample indicated that their religious beliefs guided their choices in leisure activities while the remaining 30 percent (30.3 percent) suggested otherwise. On the question of whether some types of leisure activities can lead to sinful behavior based on their understanding of doctrinal statements, the majority of the sample (60.7 percent) indicated no.

To determine whether there was consensus among the sample about the two questions posed, consensus analysis was conducted. This technique provides a methodology for discovering patterns of agreement and disagreement concerning a domain of knowledge among individuals within a specified social setting (Caulkins & Hyatt, 1999). The test revealed 15 negative competencies and strong eigenvalues (1st = 114.00, 2nd = 0.00, ratio of largest to next = 100.00). The large eigen ratio indicated a good fit to the consensus model; however, the presence of negative competence scores indicated a lack of total consensus within the sample (Borgatti, Everett, & Freeman, 1999). In other words, within the sample, respondents were in agreement that their religious beliefs serve as a moral compass for their leisure choices, but did not necessarily agree that participation in this battery of leisure activities will lead to sinful acts.

Source of Belief about the Leisure Activity

When the study participants were asked about the source of their belief (scripture, church doctrine, or a personal belief) about the perceived sin associated with the leisure activities identified by the congregation, the category "personal" belief was cited most often. Table 2 provides a summary by activity and source. Surprisingly, only a very small percentage of the respondents named the Bible as their primary source of belief, with the exception of "failure to exercise" (41.6 percent). In this instance, the major source of belief was "personal" (48.3 percent) and only exceeded the Bible as the primary source of belief by a small percentage (6.7 percent). This fact may be attributed to the respondent's understanding of the body as the temple where the Spirit of God dwells (1 Cor. 6:19). Finally, the leisure activity that respondents associated the most with "church doctrine" was dancing (25.8 percent). This level of response may be assigned to the church tradition that encouraged congregants to avoid the potential for lustful behaviors as a function of the physical closeness and type of dancing done in modern society.

Table 2

Summary of the Source of Belief about the Sinful Nature of Leisure Activities

Leisure Activity	Bible	Church Doctrine	Personal Belief
Dancing	23(25.8%)	52(58.4%)	
Drinking beverages that contain alcohol	13(14.6%)	6(6.7%)	70(78.7%)
Gambling	17(19.1%)	8(9.0%)	64(71.9%)
Playing bingo for money	4(4.5%)	4(4.5%)	81(91.0%)
Playing cards	15(16.9%)	8(9.0%)	66(74.2%)
Watching "R" rated movies	8(9.0%)	6(6.7%)	75(84.3%)
Watching television with nudity and inappropriate language	10(11.2%)	13(14.6%)	66(74.2%)
Failure to exercise	37(41.6%)	9(10.1%)	43(48.3%)
Attending a sporting event on Sunday	20(22.5%)	13(14.6%)	56(62.9%)
Attending a comedy show at a comedy club	4(4.5%)	7(7.9%)	78(87.6%)
Listening to secular music with morally questionable lyrics	7(7.9%)	8(9.0%)	74(83.15%)

Perceived Sinfulness of Leisure Pastimes

The research question addressed the association between the perceived sinfulness of select leisure pursuits named by congregants and the source of the respondent's belief (scripture, doctrinal/church teaching, or personal). Table 3 provides a summary of the results of statistical testing. The results of chi-square tests revealed no significant association between drinking beverages that contain alcohol, gambling, playing bingo for money, playing cards, watching "R" rated movies, failure to exercise, or attending sporting events on Sunday as leisure activities and the source of belief. However, significant, moderate-to-strong associations were found for the following leisure pursuits: dancing $[X^2 (2, N = 89) = 6.40, p < .04, V = .27]$; watching television that included nudity and inappropriate language $[X^2 (2, N = 89) = 8.78, p < .01, V = .31]$; attending a comedy show at a comedy club [X^2 (2, N = 89) = 14.80, $p < .001$, V = .41]; and listening to secular (nonchurch) music [X^2 (2, N = 89) = 11.56, $p < .001$, V = .36].

Table 3

Summary of Statistical Testing: Leisure Activity-Source of Belief

Perceived Sinful Leisure Activity	X^2	df	p-value	V
Dancing	6.40	2	.04*	.27
Drinking beverages that contain alcohol	1.20	2	.59	.12
Gambling	5.01	2	.08	.24
Playing bingo for money	1.47	2	.48	.13
Playing cards	1.16	2	.56	.11
Watching "R" rated movies	2.51	2	.47	.15
Watching television with nudity and inappropriate language	8.78	2	.01**	.31
Failure to exercise	5.37	2	.07	.25
Attending a sporting event on Sunday	.63	2	.73	.09
Attending a comedy show at a comedy club	14.80	2	.001***	.41
Listening to secular music with morally questionable lyrics	11.56	2	.001***	.36

* $p < .05$ ** $< .01$ *** $p < .001$

In summary, where a significant association was found between the perceived sinfulness of a leisure activity and the source of belief, respondents varied in their beliefs. The majority believed that dancing and watching television programming containing nudity and inappropriate language were sinful but attending a comedy show at a comedy club and listening to secular music were not. For those leisure activities where a significant association was found between the belief and source of belief, the latter appeared to be predominately personal, followed by scripture and church doctrine.

Lessons Learned

One critical element embedded in the AR methodology is assessing the tangible lessons learned and subsequent actions that resulted from participating in the study. McNiff et al. (2003) argued that "learnings" (tacit and explicit knowledge generated from the study) and transformation aid in validating the research results (pp. 132–136). Based on the implementation of this AR study and the results, the congregation experienced multiple lessons learned. First, the AR methodology was useful within a congregational setting. Engaging congregational members as CAs helped with creating interest in the study as well as helping the researcher to give context to the results within the socio-cultural-historical backdrop of the congregation. For example, after consulting field notes from the study, one CA noted that "what people put down on paper isn't necessarily what they practice in their private lives." Second, religious doctrine and tradition are significant influences in the corporate life of the congregation under study. For some, leisure choices were guided and constrained by the source of belief (Bible, church doctrine, or personal belief). It must also be noted that within the sample, the responses of some study participants may have been driven by all three sources concurrently. Third, the feedback obtained from the CAs that assisted with the study suggested there was a need for open dialogue at the congregational level to help reframe personal and corporate beliefs about leisure. Finally, after the study, the CAs expressed to the pastor the need to understand the biblical and theological basis of leisure to avoid assigning a "sin" value to leisure activities that, if done with proper restraint, may not be sinful at all. For example, what does God say, through the Bible, about gambling (playing cards and going to casinos) and consumption of beverages containing alcohol in a social setting?

Transformative Actions

Pursuant to some of the lessons learned from the study, the congregation began to take steps to change individual and corporate perceptions about leisure. For example, based on the results of the study and feedback from the CAs, a request was made to the pastor of the church to have pastoral teachings (corporate teachings led by the pastor) and teaching notes about Christian leisure and fun, and their relationship to spiritual growth. Within this context, teaching notes are short essays on select topics that are used to inform and serve as a tool in spiritual growth, personal development, and theological transformation. Within six months of the completion of the study, the CAs, under the supervision of the pastor, began to develop and implement teaching notes and specialty classes as a part of their Christian education effort. In retrospect, this action may have been done to help the congregation further understand the positive, redeeming qualities of leisure and focus less on the perceived sin associated with certain types of leisure activities.

Additionally, the pastor of the church preached a series of sermons related to healthy lifestyles and the abundant life for the Christian. In addition to the thirty ministries that the congregation was implementing at the time of the study, two new ministries were added: Healthy Living, and Recreation and Fellowship. Moreover, the church incorporated additional leisure activities into all major church-sponsored retreats and the annual church picnic. Finally, the congregation constructed a new Family Life Center that contained spaces for recreation programming and for the Christian education, health, and recreation/fellowship endeavors. Sharing the results of the study with the congregation served to affirm the need for the facility as a place to promote the positive utilization of leisure in the life of the church.

Discussion

The purpose of this action research case study was three-fold: 1) to determine whether an association existed between beliefs about eleven leisure activities perceived to be sinful and the source of the belief – scripture, church doctrine, or personal beliefs; 2) to determine if congregational change and transformation results from sharing the findings of the study; and 3) to ascertain whether new Christian education and ministry initiatives would be developed as a result of the congregation's experience with the action research project. Leisure constraints theory served as the theoretical framework for the study.

Source of Belief about Select Leisure Activities

The results of the study indicate that structural (religious doctrine), interpersonal (congregational ethos), and intrapersonal (personal beliefs about leisure activities) constraints exist within this congregation. The data generated from this study also support the fact that religious belief systems influence leisure choices and behaviors (Reysen, 2006) and that shared religious beliefs ultimately become engrained in congregational culture (Ammerman et al., 1998). The results of this study are consistent with the work of Wilson, Keyton, Johnson, Geiger, and Clark (1993) who, after studying a comparable United Methodist congregation, concluded, "the social praxis of local churches are such that its core beliefs are produced and reproduced. Members know the philosophy and can communicate the philosophy, even when there are areas of disagreement" (p. 285).

The findings also revealed that religious tradition and conservative theology still exist within some Protestant congregations and have some level of influence in shaping leisure attitudes and behaviors among practicing Christians (Shamir, 1988). The fact that in this study there was no significant relationship found between the perceived sin associated with seven of the designated leisure activities and the source of belief of the respondents may also suggest that people in the sample are giving less weight to the power of religious tradition and are scrutinizing congregational theologies about leisure more carefully. Invariably, the study participants may have considered the fact that there is a wide range of leisure activities that may be construed as nonbeneficial but their perceived stigma has little to do with the enjoyment of leisure.

Religious socialization, inclusive of the transmission of beliefs over the duration of congregational membership, may have played a significant role in individual and congregational beliefs about the perceived sinful nature of the select leisure activities. In light of the fact that the congregation under study is a confessing church (the regular recitation of church doctrinal beliefs) and is frequently admonished in print and orally to avoid the appearance of sin, inevitably religious beliefs will influence leisure attitudes and choices. This observation is akin to a similar finding reported by Schulz and Auld (2009) who investigated the relationship between Christianity and contemporary meanings of leisure among churches in Australia. When reporting the effects of religious affiliation on leisure meanings, the researchers concluded that theological orientations and teachings of religious groups may influence meanings assigned to leisure (p. 137). Furthermore, in the same study, Schulz and Auld, after examining how extrinsic religiosity influenced participant's understanding of leisure, concluded that ". . . religious individuals may allow their religion to influence their understanding of leisure and yet the understanding of leisure could be different from one person to another so that there is no significant relationships between religion and leisure meanings" (p. 139). In the present study, it is possible that there were varying personal definitions of the term "sinful recreations" as it appears in the *Articles of Faith*. Subsequently, the manner in which participants gave meaning to this key term may have influenced their perception of sin associated with the designated leisure activities.

The results of the study also illustrate that reinforcement of beliefs generates congregational loyalty and commitment. As previously noted, the congregation is a confessing church and thus key doctrinal statements are taught and recited regularly. Shamir (1988) argued that internalized individual and corporate beliefs regarding leisure impact commitment to religious organizations. Furthermore, Mohler (2005) and Tamney (2005) contend that strictness in beliefs and practices lead to heightened commitment on the part of members and are a hallmark of growth for conservative, Christian congregations such as the one examined in this case study.

The results of this case study also illustrate the efficacy of individual beliefs in contrast to alignment with scripture or church doctrine. Many of the prohibitions against leisure pursuits such as dancing, gambling, going to night clubs, and listening to secular music still exist within Protestant churches, including Baptists (Holland, 2002). The ability to marshal one's personal and spiritual resources to maneuver through the actual or perceived constraints becomes essential to enhancing the quality of life of the individual and congregation. Across all eleven leisure activities in the group, the most frequently cited source of belief was "personal." The magnitude of this response may be partially explained by the possible convergence of scripture, church doctrine, and experience that formed the personal belief of the respondents. Inherently, congregants are very much aware of the scriptural and doctrinal basis for the belief about the perceived sinful nature of the leisure activity, but ultimately the truths associated with the belief rests with the individual (Hoge & Polk, 1980). The previous statement is illustrated in the study when participants were asked whether some types of leisure activities can lead to sinful behavior based on their understanding of doctrinal statements and the majority of the sample (60.7 percent) indicated no. Furthermore, this may explain why no significant association was found between seven of eleven leisure activities when the source of belief was considered.

The shared implicit and explicit theologies of the congregation in this study did not supplant personal beliefs. Consensus analysis revealed that the congregation in the current study agreed corporately on the matters relating to sin and leisure, but ultimately, the moral compass of the individual prevailed. Likewise, Tamney (2005) concluded, after interviewing members of a conservative congregation, that ". . . the pastor and church may not want the membership to do such things as drink, smoke, gamble, but they cannot make people do things" (p. 296). The practical truth is that personal belief systems invariably clash with institutional and group belief systems. The leadership of a congregation is now forced to reconsider the role of doctrine and religious tradition in both guiding and constraining the congregation and its membership.

Lessons Learned

First, the congregation studied was well suited for the AR methodology. There was no resistance to implementing the study; the CAs were engaging and the congregation was open to hearing and utilizing the results of the study in ways that were meaningful to them. The manner in which the congregation embraced the AR methodology is similar to the findings reported in other congregational studies (Dokecki et al., 2001; Martin, 2000, 2001). Second, church doctrine and religious tradition are important to stabilizing congregations, but they can also be sources of tension and potential discord. Within this congregation, beliefs related to Article Fifteen ("Of the Christian Sabbath") including the "sinful recreations" section, are a point of tension. At the core of the problem may be how the study participants and other congregants interpret the term "sinful recreations." Undergirding the problem may be an implied negative association with Sunday leisure pursuits. Even though a level of disagreement with the implied and/or explicit theologies of congregations is inevitable (Ammerman et al., 1998; Dudley & Ammerman, 2002), some of the tension can be mitigated through leisure education and praxis. The congregation's consent to be an active part of this AR represented a step toward resolution of conflicting definitions, theologies, and general tension related to leisure. Martin (2001) noted similar congregational conflicts as a part of an action research project implemented at a Baptist church in Canada. Several of the sources of tension for the congregation surrounded ministry efforts and the need to change. Furthermore, Anderson (1990) suggested that a tension many churches feel is remaining true to their theological beliefs, while working diligently to be flexible in the strategies by which they share and practice those beliefs.

In this study, one of the learnings that occurred for the CAs and congregation was the need to have further discourse about the findings and clarification about the biblical and theological aspects of leisure and leisure choices. The desire to enter into a dialogue with the pastor and later expand the dialogue to include the congregation is consistent with the ongoing conversation tenet of action research (Ammerman et al., 1998; Dudley & Ammerman, 2002; Greenwood & Levin, 1998). Overall, the learnings experienced by the CAs and the congregation in this study were consistent with similar learnings reported as a result of utilizing AR.

Transformative Actions

Change and transformation are eminent in AR (McNiff et al., 2003). Martin (2001) argued that "action research works well in a congregational setting by being deliberately transformative. Change is an essential component of action research and should be an essential component of congregational life" (p. 264). The transformative actions reported in this study are an important part of the AR project, but they were not the primary focus of the study. The reported development of teaching notes by the pastor and other biblical and theological lessons related to leisure topics were simply byproducts of the research. These actions may reflect the need for further spiritual growth within this congregation. The transformative actions reported in this study are consistent with the acts of change reported in other congregational studies (Dokecki et al., 2001; Martin 2001; Wallis, 1993).

Limitations

There were some key limitations to this research endeavor. First, the sample was small and the unit of analysis was one Baptist congregation. The study of multiple, less traditional, congregations within the same denomination may have produced different results. Second, the activities contained in the group of perceived sinful leisure pursuits, while supported by the literature, is by no means comprehensive. Subsequently, there may be other leisure pastimes that are equally frowned upon by this congregation. The activities listed were generated by congregation members and CAs who may have been biased based on their own religious socialization and tenure within the congregation. Third, despite the brief descriptors that were given for the terms "scripture," "church doctrine," and "personal belief" when respondents were asked to indicate the source of their belief about the eleven leisure activities, it is possible that some of the respondents may have interpreted the term "personal belief" to mean a belief that is not necessarily grounded in scripture and/or church doctrine. Thus, the data generated had to be interpreted with additional caution. Finally, the results can only be generalized to comparable, homogenous congregations.

Recommendations for Future Research

Additional research is needed to further explore the relationships between religious beliefs, especially intra- and inter-denominational doctrine, and "taboo" leisure pursuits. Replicating the study utilizing multiple congregations within the same denomination and utilizing congregations across multiple strands of the same denomination would yield useful data in helping to further understand the relationship between Christian religious doctrine, tradition, and leisure attitudes and behaviors. Second, scripture and biblical principles must be aligned with queries made about the perceived sin associated with some leisure activities to allow for proper framing and context. This will add additional clarity to the "personal beliefs" category, which will benefit the researcher and potential respondents. Third, there is a need to hone in on the process of religious socialization over the lifespan and how it influences leisure attitudes and choices. A well-done qualitative study will provide fresh insights into how religious oriented constraints to leisure develop within an individual.

Fourth, there are two additional theoretical frameworks that may be helpful in examining the relationship between religious beliefs and leisure behavior and choices. The deprivation theory (Glock & Stark, 1965) suggests that people deprive themselves of pleasurable and enjoyable activities in order to sustain their religious beliefs (religiosity). The doctrinal beliefs theory (Hoge & Carroll, 1978; Hoge & Polk, 1980) examines the process of religious socialization and the internalization of religious beliefs. As people join congregations, they are exposed to both the socializing mechanisms within the church and also exposed regularly to church doctrine. Subsequently, doctrine becomes internalized and then is used as a moral framework for decision making. Both theories will prove useful in examining the relationship between religious beliefs and how leisure choices are made.

Finally, given the powerful influences of religious socialization and personal relationships within the community of faith (Cornwall, 1987), an examination of the key strategies congregants employ to move beyond religious beliefs, especially those that may be inaccurate or false, could be explored. Constraints negotiation has evolved into a growing area of research (Hubbard & Mannell, 2001; Loucks-Atkinson & Mannell, 2007) and is invaluable in the quest to understand how people transcend the barriers to leisure. The negotiation of constraints to leisure participation is complex, and the process becomes increasing complicated when religious beliefs and doctrine are intertwined.

Conclusion

Congregations, just as individuals, have unique personalities, and they manifest particular corporate cultures. This unique identity is shaped by factors such as history, social location, structure, membership size, and beliefs. Practices of a congregation have a history. They establish a tradition, because congregants relate together in valued activities that are repeated over time and that create and sustain human community.

The enjoyment of leisure is an important facet of our personal and congregational lives. Our attitudes, behaviors, and choices related to leisure are shaped by the manner in which we are religiously socialized. The Christian belief system, inclusive of scripture, covenants, and doctrinal statements, influence how adherents consume leisure. The present case study provides a foundation for future congregation-based research pertaining to religion and leisure. The growing body of research that examines the relationship between religion, spirituality and leisure will help inform future scholarship. With the constant evolution of leisure constraints research, there is a need for more specificity. For example, little attention has been given to the examination of both positive and negative religious/spiritual constraints to leisure. An examination of the religious and spiritual factors that liberate and constrain individual and corporate leisure behaviors would be invaluable to our current and future understanding of leisure behavior.

References

ABC Church. (2007). Salvation and active membership. *Context Weekly Church Bulletin.*

Abinate, M.D., Robb, J., & Smith, K. (1995). *God saw that it was good: Work and leisure in Christian life.* Seattle, WA: Ministry Center for Catholic Community.

Ammerman, N. (2005). *Pillars of faith: American congregations and their partners.* Berkeley, CA: University of California Press.

Ammerman, N.T., Jackson, C.W., Dudley, C.S., & McKinney, W. (1998). *Studying congregations.* Nashville, TN: Abingdon Press.

Anderson, L. (1990). *Dying for change: An arresting look at the new realities confronting churches and para-church ministries.* Minneapolis: Bethany House.

Borgatti, S.P., Everett, M.G., & Freeman, L.C. (1999). *UCINET 5.0 Version 1.00.* Natick, MA: Analytic Technologies.

Brown, D.R., & Gary, L.E. (1990). Religious socialization and educational attainment among African Americans: An empirical assessment. *The Journal of Negro Education* 60(1), 411–426.

Byl, J. (2006). Faith-based recreation. In Human Kinetics (Ed.), *Introduction to recreation and leisure* (pp. 208–216). Champaign, IL: Human Kinetics.

Calvin, J. (1813). *Institutes of the Christian Religion* (J. Allan, Trans.). London: J. Walker.

Caulkins, D., & Hyatt, S.B. (1999). Using consensus analysis to measure cultural diversity in organizations and social movements. *Field Methods* 11(1), 5–26.

Cornwall, M. (1987). The social basis of religion: A study of factors influencing religious belief and commitment. *Review of Religious Research* 29(1), 54–55.

Crawford, D.W., & Godbey, G. (1987). Reconceptualizing barriers to family leisure. *Leisure Sciences* 9, 119–127.

Crawford, D.W., Jackson E.L., & Godbey, G. (1991). A hierarchical model of leisure constraints. *Leisure Sciences* 13, 309–320.

Creswell, J.W. (2003). *Research design: Qualitative, quantitative, and mixed methods approaches* (2nd ed.). Thousand Oaks, CA: Sage.

de Grazia, S. (1964). *Of time, work and leisure.* New York: Doubleday.

Diaz, J. D. (2000). Religion and gambling in sin-city: A statistical analysis of the relationship between religion and gambling patterns in Las Vegas residents. *The Social Science Journal* 37(3), 453–458.

Dokecki, P., Newbrough, J., & O'Gorman, R. (2001). Toward a community-oriented action research framework for spirituality: Community psychological and theological perspectives. *Journal of Community Psychology* 29(5), 497–518.

Doohan, L. (1990). *Leisure: A spiritual need.* Notre Dame, IN: Ave Maria Press.

Dudley, C.S., & Ammerman, N.T. (2002). *Congregations in transition: A guide for analyzing, assessing, and adapting in changing communities.* San Francisco: Jossey-Bass.

Floyd, M.F., Bacarro, J.N., & Thompson, T.D. (2008). Research on race and ethnicity in leisure studies: A review of five major journals. *Journal of Leisure Research* 40(1), 1–22.

Fontana, D. (2003). *Psychology, religion, and spirituality.* Malden, MA: BPS Blackwell.

Foster, R. (1978). *Celebration of discipline.* New York: Harper & Row.

Glock, C.Y., & Stark, R. (1965). *Religion and society in tension.* Chicago: Rand McNally.

Greenwood, D.J., & Levin, M. (1998). *Introduction to action research: Social research for social change.* Thousand Oaks, CA: Sage.

Heintzman, P. (1987). The relevance of Christianity's biblical and historical heritage for a philosophy of leisure in contemporary society. In C.Z. Howe & K.A. Henderson (Eds.), *Abstracts of proceedings of the 10th anniversary Leisure Research Symposium* (p. 9). NRPA Congress for Recreation and Parks, September 17–21, 1987, New Orleans, LA.

Heintzman, P. (2006a). Implications for leisure from a review of the biblical concepts of Sabbath and rest. In P. Heintzman, G.E. Van Andel, & T.L. Visker (Eds.), *Christianity and leisure: Issues in a pluralistic society* (Rev. ed., pp. 14–31). Sioux Center: Dordt College Press.

Heintzman, P. (2006b). Listening for a leisure remix in ancient Israel and early Christianity. *Leisure Sciences* 28, 431–435.

Heintzman, P. (2015). *Leisure and spirituality: Biblical, historical, and contemporary perspectives.* Grand Rapids: Baker Academic.

Hoge, R., & Carroll, J.W. (1978). Determinants of commitment and participation in suburban Protestant churches. *Journal for the Scientific Study of Religion* 17(2), 107–127.

Hoge, R. & Polk, D.T. (1980). A test of theories of Protestant church participation and commitment. *Review of Religious Research* 21(3), 315–329.

Holland, J.W. (2002). *Black recreation: A historical perspective.* Chicago: Burnham.

Hubbard, J., & Mannell, R.C. (2001). Testing competing models of the leisure constraint negotiation process in a corporate employee recreation setting. *Leisure Sciences* 23(3), 145–163.

Jackson, E.L. (1988). Leisure constraints: A survey of past research. *Leisure Sciences* 10, 203–215.

Jackson, E.L. (2000). Will research on leisure constraints still be relevant in the twenty-first century? *Journal of Leisure Research* 32(1), 62–68.

Jackson, E.L. (2005). *Constraints to leisure.* State College, PA: Venture.

Jalbert, J.E. (2009). Leisure and liberal education: A plea for usefulness. *Philosophical Studies in Education* 40, 223–233.

Jelen, T.G., & Chandler, M.A. (1996). Patterns of religious socialization: Communalism, associationalism and the politics of lifestyle. *Review of Religious Research* 38(2), 142–158.

Johnson, K.E. (2009). Problematizing Puritan play. *Leisure/Loisir* 33(1), 33–54.

Jordan, L.G. (1997). *The Baptist standard church directory and busy pastor's guide.* Nashville, TN: Sunday School Publishing Board/National Baptist Convention.

Kelly, J.R. (1982). *Leisure.* Englewood Cliffs, NJ: Prentice-Hall.

Keys, C., & Frank, S. (1987). Community psychology and the study of organizations: A reciprocal relationship. *American Journal of Community Psychology* 15(3), 239–251.

Kraus, R. (1990). *Recreation and leisure in modern society* (4th ed.). San Francisco: HarperCollins.

Kraus, R. (1994). *Leisure in a changing America: Multicultural perspectives.* New York: McMillan.

Lawless, E.J. (1983). Brothers and sisters: Pentecostals as a religious folk group. *Western Folklore* 42(2), 85–104.

Livengood, J.S. (2006). Perceptions of leisure constraints by members of new paradigm churches. Retrieved October 10, 2007, from http://www.diversitylab.uiuc.edu/ abstract_lrs2006_livengood.html

Livengood, J., & Stodolska, M. (2004). The effects of discrimination and constraints negotiation on leisure behavior of American Muslims in the post-September 11 America. *Journal of Leisure Research* 36, 183–208.

Loucks-Atkinson, A., & Mannell, R.C. (2007). Role of self-efficacy in the constraints negotiation process. The case of individuals with fibromyalgia syndrome. *Leisure Sciences* 29, 19–36.

Martin, B. (2000). Living education: Action research as a practical approach to congregational education. *Religious Education* 95(2), 151–166.

Martin, B. (2001). Transforming a local church congregation through action research. *Educational Action Research* 9(2), 261–278.

McCrossen, A. (2000). *Holy day, holiday: The American Sunday*. Ithaca, NY: Cornell University Press.

McNiff, J., Lomax, P., & Whitehead, J. (2003). *You and your action research project* (2nd ed.). New York: RoutledgeFarmer.

Merton, T., & Shannon, W. (2004). *The inner experience: Notes on contemplation*: San Francisco: HarperCollins.

Mohler, R.A. (2005). Why are conservative churches growing? Retrieved December 7, 2007, from http://www.albertmohler.com/commentary_print.php?cadate=2005-05-19.

Moran, G. (1979). Articles on work, leisure, and religious education. *Religious Education: The Official Journal of the Religious Education Association* 74(2), 159–170.

Mullins, E.Y. (1925). *Baptist beliefs*. Valley Forge, PA: Judson Press.

Neugarten, B.L. (1977). Personality and aging. In J.E. Birren & K.W. Schaie (Eds.), *Handbook of psychology of aging* (pp. 626–649). New York: Van Nostrand Reinhold.

Neville, G. (2004). *Free time: Towards a theology of leisure*. Birmingham, UK: University of Birmingham Press.

Oswalt, J. (1987). *The leisure crisis: A biblical perspective for guilt-free living*. Wheaton, IL: Victor Books.

Pedlar, A. (1995). Relevance and action research in leisure studies. *Leisure Sciences* 17(2), 133–140.

Randolph, D.J. (1970). *The swinging church: Christian mission on leisure revolution*. Nashville, TN: Tidings.

Rearick, M., & Feldman, A. (1999). Orientations, purposes and reflection: A framework for understanding action research. *Teaching and Teacher Education* 15(4), 333–350.

Reeves, J.B. (1980). The leisure problem and the role of clergy. *Pastoral Psychology* 29(2), 123–133.

Reysen, S. (2006). Secular versus religious fans: Are they different? An empirical examination. *Journal of Religion and Popular Culture* 12(1), 1. Retrieved October 9, 2006, from http://www.usask.ca/relst/jrpc/art12-secularvsreligious-print.html

Riddick, C.C., & Russell, R.V. (1999). *Evaluative research in recreation, park, and sport settings: Searching for useful information*. Champaign, IL: Sagamore.

Russell, R.V. (2005). *Pastimes: The context of contemporary leisure* (3rd ed.). Champaign, IL: Sagamore.

Ryken, L. (2002). *Work and leisure in Christian perspective*. Eugene, OR: Wipf & Stock.

Shamir, B. (1988). Commitment to leisure. *Sociological Perspectives* 31(2), 238–258.

Schnase, R. (2007). *Five practices of fruitful congregations.* Nashville, TN: Abingdon Press.

Schulz, J., & Auld, C. (2009). A social psychological investigation of the relationship between Christianity and contemporary meanings of leisure: An Australian perspective. *Leisure/Loisir* 33(1), 121–146.

Stolz, J. (2009). A silent battle. Churches and their secular competitors. Retrieved August 31, 2010, from http://www.unil.ch/webdav/site/ors/shared/WP_07-2007.pdf

Tamney, J.B. (2005). Does strictness explain the appeal of working-class conservative Protestant congregations? *Sociology of Religion* 66(3), 283–302.

Trunfio, M. (1991). A theological perspective on the ethics of leisure. In G.S. Fain (Ed.), *Leisure and ethics: Reflections on the philosophy of leisure* (pp. 156–160). Reston, VA: American Association for Leisure and Recreation.

Van Andel, G., & Heintzman, P. (1996). Christian spirituality and therapeutic recreation. In C. Sylvester (Ed.), *Philosophy of therapeutic recreation: Ideas and issues* (Vol. II), (pp. 71–85). Arlington, VA: National Recreation and Park Association.

Waller, S.N. (2009). Doctrinal beliefs as a determinant of sin associated with select leisure activities. *Journal of Unconventional Parks, Tourism, & Recreation Research* 2(1), 7–18.

Waller, S.N. (2010). Leisure in the life of the 21st century Black Church: Rethinking the gift. *Journal of the Christian Society for Kinesiology and Leisure Studies* 1(1), 33–47.

Wallis, J.L. (1993). Modeling churches as collective action groups, *International Journal of Social Economics* 17(1), 59–72.

Welch, M.R. (1989). Surveying denominations and congregations: An introduction. *Review of Religious Research* 31(2), 113–114.

Wilson, G.L., Keyton, J., Johnson, G.D., Geiger, C., & Clark, J.C. (1993). Church growth through member identification and commitment: A congregational case study. *Review of Religious Research* 34(3), pp. 259–272.

Wimberly, A. (2002). Congregational care in the lives of Black older adults. In M.A. Kimble, S.H. McFadden, & M. Park (Eds.), *Aging, spirituality, and religion: A handbook* (vol. 2, pp. 101–120). Minneapolis: Augsburg.

Chapter 10

SPIRITUAL DEVELOPMENT OF PARTICIPANTS IN A COLLEGE WILDERNESS PROGRAM: A CASE STUDY

Valerie J. Gin

Both outdoor educators and Christian colleges have been interested in the education of the whole person – mind, body, and spirit. While there has been much research on the benefits of wilderness experiences, there is little known about the effects of wilderness experiences on spiritual development (Anderson-Hanley, 1996; Burton, 1981; Ewert & Heywood, 1991; Gass, 1993). "If spiritual experiences are to be a purposeful element of adventure programs, then there is a need to know more about spirituality in general, and specifically about spiritual experiences in the context of wilderness adventure activities" (Stringer & McAvoy, 1992, p.13). There has also been a call for research that specifically addresses the relationship between program characteristics and outcomes by investigating the nature of an individual's experience (Burton, 1981; Hattie, Marsh, Neill, & Richards, 1997; Anderson-Hanley, 1996).

This study analyzed a 12-day college wilderness program, La Vida, through direct observation of the participants' experience as well as the dialogue and writing of the participants themselves. The study sought to discover if there is a relationship between La Vida's spiritual development goals and the participants' experience.

Literature Review

The Outward Bound movement began in Germany in the 1920s with Kurt Hahn, the headmaster of Salem School, a private preparatory

---

Revised version of paper presented at the 1999 conference.

boarding school. The foundation of Hahn's philosophy was to create an educational environment where "healthy passions, the craving for adventure, joy of exploration, zest for building, devotion to a skill demanding patience and care, love of music, painting, or writing would flourish" (Miner, 1990, p. 60). Outward Bound has since become an international organization that offers a myriad of adventure-oriented and experiential activities (Anderson-Hanley, 1996; Burton, 1981; Shore, 1977). Because the Outward Bound framework has been utilized by other organizations, the term "Outward Bound-type program" (OBTP) was coined.

An OBTP usually consists of a 10- to 23-day program for groups of eight to twelve participants. The basic curriculum entails a training phase, expedition phase, solo phase, final expedition usually without the leaders, and concluding phase (Anderson-Hanley, 1996; Burton, 1981). OBTPs promote the exploring of one's beliefs, values, and both intra- and interpersonal roles by providing the experience of group problem-solving initiatives, challenging one's limits, and group discussions.

Little research exists that has evaluated spiritual development in Outward Bound-type programs (Anderson-Hanley, 1997; Fox, 1997; Stringer & McAvoy, 1992). Stringer and McAvoy (1992) investigated the wilderness environment and wilderness adventure programs in an effort to see if they were "conducive to spiritual development" (p. 13). The study utilized Lincoln and Guba's (1985) paradigm of naturalistic inquiry: pre-trip questionnaires, field observations, post-trip interviews, and analyses of participants' journals. The researchers studied two groups: an eight-day canoe trip that consisted of people with and without disabilities, and a group of college students that participated in a ten-day backpack trip as part of a wilderness leadership class. Study results showed that the two major contributing factors to spirituality during the expedition for participants on both trips were the sharing of experiences, thoughts, and opinions with others on the trip, and being in the wilderness. Other positive factors included the physical challenges and activities, camaraderie of group members, confronting and dealing with personal questions, having a predisposition toward spiritual reflection, prompting by other participants and leaders, time off, and the structural components and organization of the trip itself. Inhibiting factors included not having enough time to process, not having enough time alone, not participating in the trip for a spiritual experience, and having too large of a group. The term "'spirituality' was used in the broadest sense to include both religious and non-religious connotations" (Stringer & McAvoy, p. 13, 1992). A month after the trip, the participants were able to remember and talk about how the experience had an impact on their lives.

The spiritual development of college students was the focus of a comparative outcome study by Anderson-Hanley (1996) of the effects of two OBTP interventions and a wait-listed/control condition. Spiritual wellbeing (Ellison, 1983) and a subjective spiritual growth rating were utilized. The results of a repeated measures pre-test, post-test, and follow-up MANOVA revealed no significant time by intervention condition interaction. The hypothesis of improved spiritual wellbeing as a result of participating in the OBTP was not supported. It was proposed that ceiling effects in the Spiritual Well-Being Scale might have restricted the ability to detect changes in the scores. However, in the subjective spiritual growth rating, a one-way ANOVA revealed a significant effect for the intervention conditions on the post-test. Both the expedition and adventure classes reported significantly more spiritual growth than the wait-list/control condition.

Fox (1997) studied six women who took part in a spiritual wilderness experience in Croajingolong National Park in Victoria, Australia. The participants in the study identified three factors that contributed to their positive spiritual experience: a structured time of solitude, being in nature, and the safe environment of a women-only group. Solitude was viewed by the participants as a time of personal reflection to learn about oneself, to overcome fears, and to work through everyday concerns in a safe environment. Journal writing was cited as a helpful tool during the solo time. The ability to escape from everyday routines and stress, in addition to relaxing in a place of natural wonder and fresh air, added to the sense of spirituality for the women in the study. The women reported that they felt safe, nurtured, and more relaxed as a result of being with just women during their wilderness experience. It was thought that being in a women-only group enabled the participants to step out of traditional gender roles and explore what it means to be a woman and to experience powerful connections with other women.

La Vida Program

As indicated by the above literature review, there are only a small number of research studies that have investigated the impact of a college wilderness program upon spiritual development. An examination of the La Vida program provides the opportunity to augment recent research on the relationship between wilderness program participation and spiritual development.

La Vida is a twelve-day wilderness backpacking expedition that is part of the core curriculum requirement at Gordon College, a private Christian liberal arts college in Wenham, Massachusetts. The mission statement of the college states, "Gordon College strives to graduate men and women distinguished by intellectual maturity and Christian character, committed to a lifestyle of servanthood and prepared for leadership roles in their home, workplaces, churches and communities worldwide" (Gordon College 2000–2001, p. 6). La Vida became a core requirement after students testified about "what a tremendous spiritual impact the expedition had on their lives" (Obenschain & Wilder, 1984, p. 1).

La Vida's mission is "to provide a supportive, experiential learning environment which encourages participants to explore the meaning of their relationship with Jesus Christ" (Obenschain & Wilder, 1993, p. 1). The La Vida curriculum states that to achieve this goal, "participants engage in adventure activities that challenge them spiritually, mentally, and physically, thereby initiating the process of self-discovery and character development within the context of Christian community" (Obenschain & Wilder, 1993, p. 1). La Vida activities are followed by group discussions and times of reflection to help students reflect on "critical issues such as personal commitment, servanthood, leadership and the integration of God's Word into one's daily life" (p. 2). This integration methodology is termed an "explicit approach" model, where stated goals and program structure are explicitly designed to promote spiritual growth and development (Anderson-Hanley, 1997; Tan, 1996).

La Vida leaders, like most adventure educators, have a strong sense of mission. Whether or not La Vida fulfills its own mission statement and program goals has not been explored beyond short open-ended evaluation forms, final papers, and anecdotal student testimonies. Thus the research questions that guided this research study were as follows: Is there a relationship between La Vida's spiritual development goals and the participants' experience? What are the contributing factors that play a role in participants' spiritual development?

Methodology

This study evaluated the La Vida program through direct observation of the participants' experience, through the dialogue and writing of the participants themselves, and through quantitative measures of spirituality. The investigator went on the expedition as a participant and recorded observations and formative data.

The subjects for this study were ten Gordon College students who participated in the twelve-day La Vida expedition. The group was randomly chosen to be a part of the study, and each student signed informed consent forms for participation. Students were informed that the investigator was trying to "find out as much about La Vida as possible."

Interviews were used "to gather descriptive data in the subjects' own words so that the researcher could develop insights on how subjects interpret their experience" (Bogden & Bicklen, 1992, p. 96). Pre-trip and post-trip interviews of each participant were tape-recorded. Throughout the expedition, participants recorded their experiences through taped conversations, taped informal interviews, and taped individual reactions to obtain the participant's perspective during the natural flow of a particular experience or activity. Data also included personal journals, final papers, a group journal, and a written evaluation. All recorded data were transcribed and coded. Comparative analyses were utilized between all data sources to ascertain an accurate description of the student's experiences. Comparing and contrasting similarities and differences between verbal and written data sources established an authentic account of the participants' experiences.

The Spiritual Well-Being Scale (Ellison, 1983) and the Spiritual Maturity Index (Ellison, 1996) were also used to assess the spiritual objectives of La Vida participants. The Spiritual Well-Being Scale is a twenty-item instrument, with two subscales, that was used to measure the spiritual dimension of the students. The ten-item religious wellbeing subscale contains items that refer to God and assess the transcendental dimension of spirituality (Ellison, 1983). The ten-item existential wellbeing subscale measures a person's relationship to the surrounding world and their sense of life satisfaction and life purpose (Ellison, 1983). Each test item is on a six-point Likert scale. The Spiritual Well-Being Scale showed test-retest reliability above .85 in samples after one, four, and ten weeks (Ellison, 1983).

The Spiritual Maturity Index (SMI) is a thirty-item test on a six-point Likert scale. The SMI was designed to complement the Spiritual Well-Being Scale. The SMI measures spiritual maturity as a continuous developmental process. In a study of its reliability, the SMI had a Cronbach Alpha of .865 and a standardized item alpha of .878, which indicates that it has fairly high internal consistency and reliability. However, known group differences did not show strong support for the SMI's construct validity (Ellison, 1996).

Results

The results of this investigation are organized according to the spiritual development goals of the La Vida program (Obenschain & Wilder, 1984, 1993):

- To provide a supportive experiential learning environment that encourages participants to explore the meaning of their relationship with Jesus Christ;
- The participants engage in adventure activities that will challenge them spiritually, mentally, and physically, initiating the process of self-discovery and character development within the context of Christian community;
- To provide experiences for participants to learn the meaning of commitment to God and others.

Samples of unedited data, representative of data collected (Gin, 1998), are presented in this section of the paper. The data sources are cited as follows: the investigator's field notes and observations (FN), group conversations (GC), the participants' individual journal entries (J), group journal entries (GJ), exit interviews (EI), evaluation forms (EF), and final papers (FP). Hypothetical names were given to each of the participants to protect their anonymity.

Exploring the Meaning of a Relationship with Jesus Christ

The data strongly supported the goal of providing a supportive experiential learning environment that encouraged participants to explore the meaning of their relationship with Jesus Christ. La Vida principles that were introduced and implemented throughout the expedition played a key role in setting the framework for the supportive learning environment. The La Vida principles presented are: 1) be here now, 2) challenge by choice, and 3) commitment move.

The first full day the group was in the Adirondack Mountains, the head Sherpa told the group about the "be here now" principle. She explained that to "be here now" is to be 100 percent involved in the moment and not to be thinking about or worried about what lies ahead.

> If you find that someone in the group is daydreaming or not 100 percent here, we would encourage you to say, 'be here now' as a gentle reminder to each other. We want you to get the most of your experience so we will just tell you what you need to know as you need to know it. (GC)

The framework, "challenge by choice," was established as an introduction to the ropes course activity during the second day of La Vida. The head Sherpa introduced the principle of "challenge by choice" to the group:

We are going to leave it up to you as much as possible to say that it's your choice what to participate in and how much to participate in. You're not going to be pressured or coerced into doing activities. That's something that I hope will free everybody up to feel a sense of relaxation and a sense of feeling like they can go forward and try their limits and press your strengths and see what you can do. We will encourage you to test your limits and try things. (GC)

Throughout the trip, the Sherpa asked the group members to verbalize their goals, feelings, questions, and concerns. Either before or after each of the group initiatives, a prayer was offered, a passage of Scripture was read encouraging students to explore the meaning of their relationship with Christ during that particular activity, and a challenge was given to the group.

On the morning of the rock climb, the head Sherpa introduced the idea of a commitment move. All the La Vida brochures and t-shirts have a statement that reads, "La Vida . . . a commitment move." The leader told the students to be strong and courageous and lean on the Lord to support them as they climbed. She explained that there will be tough spots that will be hard to get around, or by, during their climb. A commitment move is when you go for something that is a little beyond your reach and you are not sure if you can do it or not. Participants were instructed that if they were to go for it, they were to yell "commitment move" so their team could encourage them and also let their belayer know they were making a commitment to go for a difficult move (GC).

Reflecting on the idea of a commitment move on day four, Kim wrote in the group journal, "We talked this morning about commitment moves: times when one is unsure they will be able to finish what they are attempting. It's a time to ask for support and acknowledge our need. It's a situation with many parallels to our spiritual walk" (GJ).

La Vida provided many structured group activities that created the supportive experiential learning environment, which encouraged participants to explore their relationship with Jesus Christ. Each of the following group activities provided data to affirm this objective in the participants' experience: 1) writing the covenant, 2) climbing the wall initiative, 3) the rock climb, 4) climbing Mount Marcy, 5) finals, and 6) solo.

The participants themselves revealed through their conversations and journal writing that they were indeed exploring their relationship with Jesus Christ. Ben wrote after the ropes course, "God is going to teach me many things on this trip and I just pray that I can have an open heart and mind" (J). Kim commented in her journal after the rock climb:

> Challenge by choice. What a great concept. All the positives with none of the negatives. God, I'm sorry that so often I take the reins and run. I feel so comfortable at shaping my life without you and am so immersed in the illusion of my own control than in the past when I lived a God dependent life. I have also been thinking of the upcoming commitment moves in my life and how so often I make commitments only to myself. . . . I do know that I want to live a committed Christian life. (J)

It was comfortable and natural for conversations to revolve around Scripture and application to spiritual principles. Not only did students speak of Scripture in application to their own lives, but they also encouraged each other with Scripture and practical application. During several of the hikes, the participants were quoting Scripture verses to each other and singing praise songs.

Challenges Initiating Self-Discovery and Character Development

Participants were challenged spiritually, mentally, and physically as they engaged in adventure activities that La Vida provided. Spiritually, the group was challenged as a result of the direct application of Scripture that preceded or followed the activity itself. After the wall, which is a group initiative challenging students to overcome a 15' barrier, the Sherpa talked about each of the individuals in the group being part of the body of Christ as described in 1 Corinthians 12. It was pointed out that,

> different parts of the body played significant roles to achieve the success of getting everyone over the wall. The group was encouraged to think about how in life, the body of Christ needs to help each other out. The group was reminded throughout the trip to consider what kinds of things in their lives are like "the wall." (FN)

The Sherpa did an excellent job of providing appropriate Scripture, facilitating discussions, and encouraging application of those biblical principles.

Through self-discovery, students were challenging themselves throughout the expedition. Nate challenged himself to be humble in a journal entry on day six,

> God is humbling us through this journey, to see how pure our hearts are when the going gets tough. Every little thing we do, God is testing our hearts. This experience uncovers all the layers of our hearts – like an onion, sort of. Hopefully I will be humble enough to learn my shortcomings that are uncovered as I go through this journey. Lord I ask for your guidance and blessings in doing so. (J)

The challenges of the expedition brought out many character traits that the participants wanted to change in themselves. In his journal, Ken addressed a desire to be more loving. He wrote,

> How do you, Ken, understand the balance between excellence and grace? In other words, what does it mean to ask excellence in all things of myself and yet fully comprehend the meaning of failure in my strides. . . . I feel I can, only if the Lord grants me strength to show my brothers and sisters my unconditional love for them. O Lord how I desire this ability! Will you help me? Thank you. Love me unconditionally that I may demonstratively advocate this in all I do. I need to be a godly steward of mouth, word and most importantly heart. God I love you with all I have. (J)

The group was challenged mentally by solving group initiatives and other problem-solving activities, such as crossing rivers and reading maps. Other mental challenges included the group covenant edict not to complain, bringing up the rear of the group, persevering, "being here now," not knowing what time it was, and what the purpose of La Vida is. When Dan was asked in his exit interview what challenged him the most, he replied, "I was challenged to be here now. I get caught up in my fears about the future, and I realize how I missed out on things because I was doing that" (EI).

Each of the participants talked about, wrote about, and experienced the physical challenges of the twelve-day experience. The strenuousness of the hikes proved to be one of the greatest challenges for the participants. The group was able to endure and persevere through snow-covered trails and wet, slippery descents. The hikes were key factors in the experience because they physically challenged the group beyond what they thought they could endure. Besides the physical challenges, the hikes also promoted social, emotional, and spiritual challenges as well. Challenges helped Rose with her spiritual development as illustrated by her comment in a group discussion:

> Deuteronomy 8:2 is really sticking out to me because I'm really starting to see what comes out of me when I'm being tested. It's good, because it makes me realize more and more that God is really good to us and he's really faithful and consistent in his love, especially because we're not. I praise him for that. (GC)

On the first full day of hiking, the group had hoped to reach its destination by lunch. When lunch time arrived and the group was only halfway to its goal, the participants were irritable, and negative attitudes emerged. Ben stated to the group, "I was frustrated about the pace, because I felt that we were going and then stopping. I like to just go continuously and then break" (GC). Erin challenged Ben's commitment to the group:

> If we are going to do this as a team, and if that means that we have to stop and go a lot, even if that's uncomfortable and frustrating, we just have to live with that. So we just need to deal with our frustrations, because our goal is to get through this together. (GC)

Alliances formed between team members based on their gripes and complaints. Though there was a mini-upsurge of attitude on day five when the group successfully climbed Mount Marcy, the highest peak in New York State, the lengthy, treacherous hike down brought morale down as well. During a heated group conversation after a long hike, Pete explained his emotional state:

> The only thing I know that I need to be is a follower of God and I don't feel like I have to try to do anything. God knows what he's doing and he's got my life under his control. So I think that right now it's good that we're all tired. It's good that we're discouraged, it's good that we're irritated because people are realizing that you can struggle and you can continue to still love God and God still loves you even though you are completely exhausted to the point of being pissed off at other people. (GC)

Confronted with the physical, spiritual, emotional, and social challenges, all the participants wrote reflections in their journals about issues such as personal commitment, servanthood, leadership, and integration of God's Word into their daily lives.

Commitment to God and Others

Through the Spiritual Maturity Index scores, as well as the participants' writing and behavior, the data clearly revealed that La Vida helped participants deepen their commitment to God and others. The SMI (Ellison, 1996) provides both a mature and an immature score. It was found through the t-tests that there was a significant increase in the mature scores (pre-test $M = 35.70$, post-test, $M = 90.10$) and no difference in the immature scores (pre-test $M = 53.90$, post-test $M = 55.50$) of the participants. These results show a significant statistical increase in the spiritual maturity of the participants during the La Vida expedition.

The Spiritual Well-Being Scale (Ellison, 1983) measured two aspects of spiritual wellbeing: existential wellbeing, which is the horizontal dimension that involves wellbeing in relation to the world around us; and religious wellbeing, which is the vertical dimension involving wellbeing in relationship to God. A t-test revealed that there was no significant difference between the means of the overall spiritual wellbeing pre-test ($M = 107.30$) and post-test ($M = 105.10$), for the religious wellbeing pre-test ($M = 53.7$) and post-test ($M = 51.5$) and the existential wellbeing pre-test ($M = 53.60$)

and post-test (M = 53.60). Thus there were no statistical differences in the spiritual wellbeing of the participants from pre-test to post-test.

The group covenant played a key role in teaching the participants about commitment. On the evening of the sixth day, the group engaged in a lively discussion about personal commitment to the group covenant. Rose summarized the situation in the group journal:

> We talked last night and the Sherpas encouraged us to make this kind of "commitment move" and we were so successful at confronting issues. I think we were afraid of offending people and were therefore willing to ignore confrontation and deal for the remaining time with each other and all our accumulated bitterness. I know I was. But we did it [commitment move] and we did it in love. I only pray that we will continue to look to Christ first and draw our strength from Him and not from our flawed vindictiveness and sin. (GJ)

The participants learned that commitment had to be more than words. Cari wrote in her final paper what she had learned about commitment to her group:

> Groups have always been a mystery to me. Although I do not really shy away from them, I don't attempt to be a real part of them either. The intensity, domination, gossip, and exclusiveness that usually comes with groups has always made me suspicious and hesitant. And although I've always listened and believed teachings about loving one another as brothers and sisters in Christ, I couldn't imagine how that could work. . . . On La Vida, living with 10 people under such intense circumstances, the question arose again immediately. The temptation to withdraw into my own world and slide along was almost irresistible. My hope in the group experience . . . was practically shattered as soon as I saw the strong personalities and cliques within our group. I was ready to give up hope, but one of my friends wasn't. She really cared what happened and since she was going to risk caring, I thought I could, too. By confrontations and apologies, we dug through problems and personalities and it worked. . . . We feel like a team now. It doesn't feel fake, finally it feels real . . . there is a way that we can all be brothers and sisters in Christ. . . . Never has the Body of Christ made as much sense as it does now. (FP)

Not only did the group experience play a major role in helping participants learn about commitment, but the solo experience did as well. Kim wrote her thoughts about commitment in her journal during her solo:

> What I do know is that I want to live a committed Christian life. Complacency sucks. . . . Like the assistant Sherpa says I cannot guarantee that I will be serving the Lord in 10 years but I can serve Him now. Being here now. (J)

There was strong evidence in the conversations and writings of the students that they learned the meaning of commitment to God and to others throughout their La Vida experience.

Discussion

Data revealed that there was a strong relationship between La Vida's spiritual goals and the participants' experience. The Spiritual Maturity Index revealed that there was a significant difference between the t-test results of the pre-trip and post-trip mean scores. Statistical differences in the participants' scores on the SMI indicated that La Vida did help participants mature as Christians.

The La Vida evaluation form that each participant filled out asked the question, "Has your relationship with Christ grown or been challenged?" Nine of the ten participants responded that their relationship with Christ had grown. The lone uncertain response indicated the possibility of growth. Pete stated, "I have certainly been challenged in my relationship with Christ but I won't know until I process all of this, how much I have actually grown in my relationship with Him" (EF). All ten participants concurred that their relationship with Christ was challenged.

The Spiritual Well-Being Scale scores of the La Vida students revealed that there was no significance between the pre- and post-tests. This study mirrored Anderson-Hanley's (1996) results that concluded there was no statistical significance in spiritual wellbeing as a result of the OBTP in her study. The initial pre-test scores were high in the pre-test and seemed to suggest the same ceiling effect that was found in the Anderson-Hanley study.

The results of the study concluded that there is a strong relationship between La Vida's spiritual development goals and the participants' experiences. But what are the specific factors in the La Vida program that influenced and challenged spiritual development in the participants?

Many factors enabled La Vida to achieve its goals in the participants' experience. Major contributing factors cited by the participants as having an impact on their spiritual development were: the La Vida program elements – ropes course, rock climb; La Vida principles – be here now, challenge by choice, and commitment move; hikes – pace of, difficulty of; solo; group covenant; and the use of Scripture. Another key factor was the group itself: sharing with others, living with others, interpersonal conflicts, encouraging each other, and challenging each other. The group dynamics and group process definitely played a significant role that helped build a strong relationship between La Vida's goals and the participants' experience.

The La Vida program was designed to bring the participants through a growth process, and the goals were intended to be progressive. La Vida elements were interrelated and interdependent. It was evident in the investigator's field notes that the group development process, the La Vida principle of commitment move, and the group covenant were the predominant influences that affected spiritual development in the participants' experience.

Group Development Process

The group development process that unfolded in the participants' experience became a vital means that affected change in the individuals and was an end in itself (Ewert & Heyward, 1991). This phenomenon of the group process was one of the major factors that allowed many of La Vida's goals to be achieved. The experience of the process eventually produced a product that was positive and constructive in reaching La Vida's overall goals. The social challenges proved to be one of the most powerful factors for the participants' achievement of the goals. The group members not only went through a group discovery process but a self-discovery process as well. This concurs with Stringer and McAvoy's (1992) results that sharing with group members and group camaraderie were factors that contributed to spiritual development.

La Vida's Principle of Commitment Move

As the physical challenges of backpacking became more difficult each day, the group experienced fragmentation and became subject to frustrations that caused major discomforts. The physical risks of the trust fall, group initiatives, ropes course, and rock climb were easier for the group to make than the social and emotional risks that came later in the expedition. The challenge of making a commitment move as evidenced on the rock climb was much easier than to take a risk and make a commitment move with the group. When group members made the commitment to invest not just physically, but spiritually, emotionally, and socially into the group, the students realized the value of group cooperation and personal commitment, and they learned much about themselves.

Group Covenant

Learning occurred not merely through the completion of La Vida elements and tasks but through the whole process. La Vida was successful because the accomplishments of the elements did not outweigh the physical, emotional, social, and spiritual growth that was achieved in the participants' experience. This was particularly evident in the group's struggle with the covenant. The new covenant that was rewritten near the end of the expedition was not that different than the original covenant, but the process of thinking and rethinking it, wording it, living up to it, and being held accountable to it enabled the participants to grow, to be challenged, and to take ownership for it. It was not the covenant itself that needed to change, but the participants themselves.

The participants not only learned to deal with immediate needs and concerns, but showed profound insights in their reflections on how to apply what they learned to their future situations. If life applications are indeed made, this wilderness experience will have a positive impact on their lives in the future.

Further Study

Recommendations for further study include case studies of OBTPs to give further insight into the relationship of spiritual development and wilderness experiences. More research is also needed in the group development process. A follow-up study with the participants of this study group would reveal if growth and changes made on La Vida were sustained.

References

Anderson-Hanley, C.M. (1996). Spiritual well-being, spiritual growth and Outward Bound-type programs: A comparative outcome study. Paper presented at the annual meeting of the Christian Association for Psychological Studies, St. Louis, MO.

Anderson-Hanley, C.M. (1997). Adventure programming and spirituality: Integration models, methods, and research. *Journal of Experiential Education* 20(2), 102–108.

Bogden, R.C., & Bicklen, S.K. (1992). *Qualitative research for education.* Boston: Allyn & Bacon.

Burton, L.M. (1981). *A critical analysis and review of the research on Outward Bound and related programs* (Doctoral dissertation). Available from ProQuest Dissertations and Theses Global database. (UMI No. 303181743).

Ellison, C.W. (1983). Spiritual well-being: Conceptualization and measurement. *Journal of Psychology and Theology* 11, 330–340.

Ellison, C.W. (1996). *Spiritual maturity index.* Unpublished paper made available by author.

Ewert, A., & Heywood, J. (1991). Group development in the natural environment: Expectations, outcomes and techniques. *Environment and*

Behavior 23, 592–615.

Fox, R.J. (1997). Women, nature and spirituality: A qualitative study exploring women's wilderness experience. In D. Rowe & P. Brown (Eds.), *Proceedings, ANZALS conference 1997* (pp. 59–64). Newcastle, NSW: Australian and New Zealand Association for Leisure Studies, and the Department of Leisure and Tourism Studies, University of Newcastle.

Gass, M.A. (1993). *Adventure therapy: Therapeutic applications of adventure programming.* Dubuque, IA: Kendall/Hunt.

Gin, V.J. (1998). *Evaluation of a wilderness program for college students* (Doctoral dissertation). Retrieved from ProQuest Dissertations and Theses Global database. (UMI No. 304416972).

Gordon College (2000–2001). Catalog. Wenham, MA: Author.

Hattie, J.H., Marsh, H.W., Neill, J.T., & Richards, G.E. (1997). Adventure education and Outward Bound: Out of class experiences that make a lasting difference. *Review of Educational Research 63*(1), 43–87.

Lincoln, Y.S., & Guba, E.G. (1985). *Naturalistic inquiry.* Beverly Hills, CA: Sage.

Miner, J.L. (1990). The creation of Outward Bound. In J.C. Miles & S. Priest (Eds.), *Adventure education.* State College, PA: Venture.

Obenschain, R., & Wilder, E. (1984). *La Vida…a commitment move.* [Brochure]. Wenham, MA: Gordon College.

Obenschain, R., & Wilder, E. (1993). The *La Vida expedition Sherpa training manual.* (Unpublished manuscript). Wenham, MA: Gordon College.

Shore, A. (1977). *Outward bound: A reference volume.* New York: Topp Litho.

Stringer, L.A., & McAvoy, L.H. (1992). The need for something different: Spirituality and wilderness adventure. *Journal of Experiential Education 15*(1), 13–20.

Tan, S.Y. (1996). Religion in clinical practice: Implicit and explicit integration. In E. Shafranske (Ed.), *Religion and the clinical practice of psychology* (pp. 365–387). Washington, DC: American Psychological Association.

Chapter 11
THE ROLE OF LEISURE IN THE SPIRITUALITY OF NEW PARADIGM CHRISTIANS

Jennifer Livengood

Religion is a fundamental part of life for many people (Spilka & McIntosh, 1997). According to the Baylor Religion Survey (Baylor University, 2005), about 80 percent of Americans believed in God, or a higher power. Grim and Masci (2008) suggested a diversity of beliefs among adults residing in the United States, with approximately 50 percent identifying themselves as Christians. Numerous beliefs and practices exist amongst Christian adherents. According to the Pew Forum on Religion and Public Life (2008), 26.3 percent of the U.S. adult population were evangelical Protestants, 18.1 percent are mainline Protestants, 6.9 percent are members of historically Black churches, and 23.9 percent are Catholic.

It is reasonable to assume that religion affects numerous aspects of people's lives, including leisure and recreation. For example, religious doctrines may dictate what leisure or recreation activities are acceptable or unacceptable to the followers. Additionally, recreation or fellowship with one's congregation may be emphasized over activities with people outside of the religious group. Leisure can also be utilized as outreach to the surrounding community. Furthermore, leisure and recreation provided by faith-based organizations increase the recreational opportunities for everyone within a community, including individuals not associated with the religious organization. Additionally, churches form partnerships with secular organizations to provide much needed services for children, teens, families, and senior adults (Emard, 1990; Henderson et al., 2001; Livengood & Place, 2007; Wesner, 1995).

New paradigm churches (also known as seeker churches) are a recent development within Christianity that integrates elements of present-day culture in church functioning (Anderson, 1992; Miller, 1997;

Revised version of paper presented at the 2006 conference.

Sargeant, 2000). Although new paradigm churches span different denominations, they have a contemporary way of conducting services. The format of their services is very current and includes, but is not limited to, contemporary music, casual dress, and technical presentation formats such as video or PowerPoint (Sargeant, 2000). Additionally, worship services are geared toward each participant's spiritual experience. Moreover, evangelistic goals of new paradigm churches involve relational messages and outreach, which are customized to the culture and personality of the members (Anderson, 1992). A major facet of new paradigm is the focus on catering to the needs of contemporary people, especially those who are not current members of the church. Comfort of all participants, especially newcomers, is essential within new paradigm churches. Specifically, practical methodologies for introducing first-time visitors allow for easy access to information regarding worship services and church-related programs, such as recreation (Anderson, 1992).

Although several studies have examined the relationship of leisure and spirituality (Fox, 1997; Frederickson & Anderson, 1999; Heintzman, 2000, 2002b, 2007; Stringer & McAvoy, 1992; Sweatman & Heintzman, 2004), few have examined the relationship between religious-based spirituality and leisure. While Huizinga (1955), Johnston (1983), Kelly (1987), and Pieper (1998) have suggested that leisure is a significant part of the lives of Christians and that it could lead toward a deeper relationship with God, empirical investigations have not been conducted to verify their views. Additionally, existing examinations of the relationship between leisure and religion have largely relied on historical accounts (Conner, 1992; Goodale & Godbey, 1988; Kelly, 1990; Wesner, 1995) and were written prior to recent developments in Christianity such as new paradigm churches. Leisure and recreation are becoming increasingly important parts of the church repertoire, and thus a thorough analysis of the place of leisure in the life of Christians could significantly contribute to the leisure studies literature.

Similarly, with some exceptions (e.g., Miller, 1997; Sargeant, 2000), issues related to new paradigm churches have largely been neglected in the religious studies literature. One of the reasons for this scarcity of research is the fact that new paradigm churches are not usually part of any major denominational structure (Miller, 1997). By focusing on the new paradigm or seeker churches, the religious studies literature could be expanded in two main ways. First, as Miller (1997) and Sargeant (2000) suggested, the new paradigm or seeker churches are a major cultural development in Protestant Christianity that deserves attention. Second, new paradigm churches have made leisure and recreation a major part of their offering. Thus, by focusing on these contemporary churches, the religious studies literature could be expanded to include information on leisure and recreation experienced by its members.

The membership of new paradigm churches has been rapidly increasing in recent years. Churches that identify with new paradigm Christianity extend across numerous denominations, which creates major difficulties in calculating the total number of members within this present-day Christian movement. Additionally, many religious data sources are limited to traditional denominational classifications and do not account for new paradigm churches (Miller, 1998). Moreover, Miller suggests that new paradigm Christianity is creating a unique form of Christianity that does not conform to current denominational classification structures. One way of determining an accurate number of new paradigm Christians is to analyze specific churches that meet the definition of a new paradigm church. For example, Saddleback Valley Community Church in California experienced an increase of 9,000 members over the span of 15 years (Sargeant, 2000), while Willow Creek Church in South Barrington, Illinois, which began meeting in a movie theater, currently has four weekend services, which average about 18,000 attendees in total (Kellstedt & Green, 2003). The increase in attendance of new paradigm churches is important to note in light of the decline in membership in traditional mainline churches (Miller, 1997). Miller argued that Christian churches have to reinvent their format in order to speak to a modern society and to attract Christians and non-Christians to a more faithful life. It has also been suggested that what makes new paradigm churches attractive to a broad population are the recreational opportunities provided as part of the church's repertoire (Miller, 1997; Sargeant, 2000).

Available anecdotal evidence suggests that recreational and social programming constitutes a major part of this modern interpretation of Christianity. For example, ABC News (2001) reported that Mariners Church in the Los Angeles area provides many leisure and recreational attractions such as an artificial lake, food court, coffee house, rock-climbing wall, and jumbo video screens. Besides recreational facilities, many new paradigm churches also offer social programming such as small groups, poetry workshops, singles groups, music lessons, and creative writing workshops. According to Sargeant (2000), new paradigm churches that have a large congregation also employ numerous professionals and volunteers, including recreational and event planning staff, to manage their programs and services.

Examination of the leisure behavior of new paradigm church members could provide important information for recreation and leisure scholars. For instance, an empirical study on the leisure experiences of new paradigm Christians in relation to spirituality could expand findings of previous inquiries on leisure and spirituality. The purpose of this study was to improve our understanding of the role of recreation and leisure within two new paradigm churches – Vineyard and Tapestry – and in the lives of their members. The objective of this study was to examine how the leisure experiences of new paradigm Christians are related to their spirituality. The research questions of this study were: (1) do new paradigm Christians consider leisure activities to be spiritually meaningful, and (2) how is leisure related to their spirituality?

Literature Review

Philosophical and Theological Arguments for Leisure

From a philosophical standpoint, it has been argued that leisure is essential to human life and spirituality. For example, Josef Pieper (1998) claimed that leisure is the basic foundation for the cultural life of humans: "Culture depends for its very existence on leisure, and leisure, in its turn, is not possible unless it has a durable and consequently living link with the *cultus*, with divine worship" (p. xiv). Pieper suggested that there is a difference between the concepts of leisure and work and maintained that work should be considered as toil, whereas leisure can be seen as contemplative (thought-provoking) or as a celebration. He claimed that leisure is primarily concerned with finding the essence of life and of what it means to be human in God's world, as well as to understand one's culture. Leisure aids in defining culture by adding freedom, education, and humanity or, specifically, a holistic view of life, which cannot be obtained from work alone. Specifically, leisure is a mental and spiritual attitude through which a person can attain oneness with a spiritual reality. Moreover, leisure has the qualities of quietness or inward calm, and it cannot be diminished to the utilitarian purpose of preparing one for work.

As explained by Pieper (1998), leisure can be seen to be philosophically consistent with the Christian lifestyle. More recently, research by Miller (1997) and Sargeant (2000) suggested that leisure is an important part of the broader operations of the new paradigm church. However, it is also important to note that, historically, such a positive relationship between leisure and religion has not always been congruent with church doctrines and practices.

Leisure and Recreation as Being in Conflict with Christian Ideals

Leisure has not always been viewed as a positive force by Christian leaders and scholars, as the historical connections between Christianity and leisure have often been conflictual in nature. For example, it is often thought that Puritans viewed leisure as a destructive force, which had potential to disrupt one's relationship with God. Time was seen as a precious gift from God that should not be wasted on leisure pursuits (Cross, 1990). Certain leisure activities such as drinking or gambling were specifically banned by the Puritan community. Such rules were most strictly enforced on the Sabbath. Drinking became the subject of further scrutiny after the Second Great Awakening, when the Temperance Movement was established (Ahlstrom, 1972). It is important to note that Puritans were not entirely opposed to leisure. For example, the Puritan ethic also included a positive holistic view of leisure (Ryken, 2002). Ryken (2002) noted that leisure, in moderation, was viewed as desirable within the Puritan Christian lifestyle, and that recreation within Puritan communities had the purpose of renewing and uplifting participants.

Brightbill (1965) also suggested that leisure time constitutes a challenge for Christian institutions because it allows for idleness, which can be an open forum for unchristian activities and degradation of one's religious character. Despite these negatives, Brightbill claimed that free time can be occupied with positive Christian activities. Ryken (2002) argued that many Christians face a challenge of how to live in a world of secular leisure that is inconsistent with their religious values. Moreover, some Christians have neglected their own leisure in an effort to fully focus on evangelistic aspects of Christianity. Ryken further commented that if one is to live a Christian lifestyle, then it is necessary to understand how to pursue leisure that fits within the teachings of Christianity.

Positive Relationship between Christian Spirituality and Leisure

Contrary to literature that suggests that leisure is in conflict with religion and spirituality, some scholars have argued that a positive relationship between leisure and religion/spirituality, may exist. Brightbill (1965) reported that there are many similarities between religion, spirituality, and leisure. All three are voluntary pursuits that help to increase the quality of life. All of these activities also share common elements such as fairness, hope, enjoyment, purposefulness, and worthwhile feelings (Brightbill, 1965). The state of mind one experiences during leisure can also be a pathway to a religious encounter (Kelly, 1987). Johnson (1932) suggested that a reciprocal relationship may exist between attending church and leisure experience. Specifically, Christianity can inspire leisure pursuits, and leisure can affect Christian thought and practice. According to Lehman (1974), leisure activities can also provide certain benefits to Christians, such as helping them understand their vocation and life, as well as learning what is consistent or inconsistent with their faith. Teaff (2006) suggested that "Christian spirituality thrives best in a leisure atmosphere where time and space are allotted for 'being' as well as 'doing'" (p. 115).

Some authors have also claimed that Christianity advocates a balanced life that includes leisure (Brightbill, 1965; Dahl, 1972; Ernce, 1987; Ryken, 2002). According to these authors, working too much and neglecting leisure and recreation is not encouraged by the Christian faith. Leisure, which is considered a gift from God, is viewed as having an important positive effect on people. Ryken (2002) suggested that leisure helps to add balance to life and facilitates psychological, physical, and spiritual wellbeing. The Christian life should be filled with rich and satisfying experiences that include leisure. Lee (1964, as quoted in Ryken, 2002) specifically commented:

> A Christian understanding of time beckons us to accept all time as God's gift, including our leisure: to live our life in terms of the quality of its events; to be willing to commit ourselves to act during leisure; and to open ourselves to the joy of living leisure in the creative love of God and man. (p. 213)

Ernce (1987) reported that Southern Baptist Christians believe that each person's life encompasses spiritual, physical, mental, and emotional domains. The optimal situation is when all of these aspects of life are fulfilled.

Furthermore, according to Ryken (2002), worship and leisure have common elements, such as time away from work, taking people away from the routine of life, and providing a spiritual dimension, which can make the meaning of life more clear. Norden (1965) also argued that the Christian tradition advocates a balanced lifestyle that includes leisure. According to Norden, society has the potential to distort the meaning of leisure, and it is a Christian's responsibility to understand the importance of leisure and to communicate it to other people. Leisure should not be seen solely as a time away from work, but rather as a gift from God that Christians are to enjoy.

Another suggested benefit of leisure and recreation within a church setting is the social interaction that can accompany such pursuits (Ryken, 2002). Through leisure experiences within the church, families as well as individuals can make social connections (Kelly, 1987). Norden (1965) also suggested that social relationships can be viewed as leisure within the Christian lifestyle. Socializing with family and time spent with others in prayer, scripture reading, singing songs, or praising God are recognized as particularly beneficial ways of spending free time. Visiting friends and neighbours, another area Norden identified as leisure, allows for developing engaging relationships, which can help people gain direction in life.

Leisure Studies Scholarship on the Leisure and Spirituality Relationship

To provide a foundation for understanding the relationship between leisure and spirituality among new paradigm Christians, it is paramount to examine the scholarship related to this topic. Leisure can have different and complex meanings. One of these meanings has been described as spiritual (Godbey, 1989). Leisure has also been considered a form of spiritual experience (Kelly, 1987; Godbey, 1989; McDonald & Schreyer, 1991) which goes beyond the traditional ways of thinking about leisure as only a combination of mental and physical states (Heintzman & Van Andel, 1995). Some authors have also argued that the states of consciousness that one enters into during leisure, such as calm, ecstasy, or altered perception, are similar to the consciousness that one has when spiritual pursuits are undertaken (Kelly, 1987; McDonald & Schreyer, 1991). In an empirical study of the relationship between spirituality and leisure, Schmidt and Little (2007) found that numerous factors, such as nature, newness, challenge, and ritual, elicited a spiritual experience for participants. Moreover, participants reported specific outcomes of engaging in spiritually related leisure, such as a connection to God, self, others, freedom, and personal beliefs.

One area of inquiry within the leisure literature that deals with spirituality is the study of the relationship between leisure and spiritual wellbeing. Ragheb (1993) conducted a study to examine spiritual wellbeing and leisure satisfaction. His results showed that leisure satisfaction was positively associated with spiritual wellness. Heintzman (2000) carried out a qualitative study to examine the relationship between spiritual wellbeing and leisure. His findings suggested that the relationship between leisure and spiritual wellbeing was multifaceted in nature. First, participants unanimously agreed that leisure activities enhance one's spiritual wellbeing. Additionally, leisure provided the time and space for spiritual wellbeing. Another theme in this study was that balance in life was a key to obtaining spiritual wellbeing. Natural settings were also associated with enhanced spiritual wellbeing. Other leisure settings that contributed to spiritual wellbeing were settings related to personal or human history and settings of quiet, solitude, and silence. Noisy and busy environments were less conducive to spiritual wellbeing. Additionally, inauthentic activities unique to each participant that introduced tension or anxiety for the participant detracted from spiritual wellbeing.

Heintzman (2002a) developed a conceptual model detailing the multifaceted relationship between leisure and spiritual wellbeing. In his model, Heintzman integrated current theories regarding leisure and spiritual wellbeing in an effort to guide future research and professional practice. The model suggests leisure, in terms of activity, motivation, time, and setting, provides a context for one to enhance spiritual wellbeing and, ultimately, spiritual development.

Heintzman and Mannell's (2003) quantitative study of leisure and spiritual wellbeing found that participants who were more motivated to participate in leisure participated more in hobby, outdoor, and cultural activities and less in travel, sports, social, and mass-media activities, and those who experienced more leisure time were more likely to use their leisure for spiritual functions. Also, the more participants used leisure for spiritual functions, the greater was their level of spiritual wellbeing.

The Role of Spirituality in Leisure Services

Many researchers have discussed a need for leisure practitioners to understand the relationship between leisure and spirituality. For example, Berryman (2000) suggested that among issues that must be explored by future leisure scholars is the relationship between "spirituality, wellness, and holistic service concepts" (p. 3). According to Berryman, studying spirituality is important, as leisure service providers may encounter participants who desire spiritually based programming. Heintzman and Van Andel (1995) suggested that spiritual experiences should not only be integrated into leisure programs, but should even be the focus of leisure and recreational opportunities. Driver, Dustin, Baltic, Elsner, and Peterson (1996) commented that it is important for leisure and recreation practitioners to understand spirituality. They claimed that it is the responsibility of park researchers and managers to understand the relationship that exists between the human spirit and the experience of nature, and to provide spiritually focused services to park visitors who request them.

Method

This study utilized an ethnographic approach, which allowed for the discovery of patterns in the daily lives of study participants as well as an understanding of my role as a researcher. Specifically, I was not a member of a new paradigm church and thus I was an outsider during this investigation. However, I have previously attended churches of both traditional and modern formats, and I was familiar with the Christian tradition. It put me in a good position to ask appropriate and valid questions and to interpret the results of this study. To remain consistent with the ethnographic framework that guided my identity as a researcher, I chose to utilize the first-person format in reporting the methodology of this investigation.

The first step in collecting data for this study was to perform participant observations of church services and events at two new paradigm churches: Vineyard and Tapestry. These two churches were chosen for this investigation because of my previous contacts within the Christian community. Specifically, I had established connections with church leaders through previous social and community events. For this study, I (the researcher) contacted pastors at both churches and asked permission to observe services and events. As an overt observer, I took detailed notes of what I observed during the church services and events (visual images, sounds, smells, how people interacted, where people were within the environment, and my perception of the events that transpired). Leisure was the focus of my participant observations and later interviews; however, I tried to describe all aspects of the social and environmental contexts in my field notes. These peripheral observations helped me gain an overall perspective of how leisure fits into the greater operations and social atmosphere of Vineyard and Tapestry. After making my entry into each church, I attended further activities such as small group meetings, picnics, and social gatherings to obtain a feel for church-related events. I performed participant observations for three months and attended about two to three events each week during the participant observations phase of the study. In the second phase, I employed semi-structured interviews to collect information from members of Vineyard and Tapestry.

After establishing initial contacts within each of the communities, I recruited interview participants from people with whom I had become acquainted during the observation phase of the study. Other participants were identified with the use of a snowball sampling technique. Specifically, after interviewing the initial participants, I asked these participants for further names of potential interviewees. Strict confidentiality measures were employed in this investigation. Specifically, each participant was fully informed of his or her rights as a research participant before each interview. Additionally, all data gained from this study was kept confidential and pseudonyms were used for the participants mentioned in the results section of this paper.

I asked interviewees how leisure was related to their spirituality. For example, I asked if they thought leisure could be spiritually meaningful and whether certain leisure experiences were more spiritual than others. I followed the semi-structured procedure in all interviews. For example, all participants were asked the same questions from the interview schedule; however, the ordering of questions varied, depending on the flow of the conversation. In addition, I also used probing questions to delve into participants' answers, to obtain more detailed information, and to ensure that I understood the full meaning of what was said during the interviews. In three instances (six interviewees), I interviewed both the husband and wife concurrently.

Seventeen adult members, eight from Vineyard and nine from Tapestry, were interviewed. I stopped interviewing when theoretical saturation was achieved. It was evident that saturation had occurred when the participants' responses stopped yielding new information. The interviews lasted between 15 minutes and one hour and were conducted in participants' residences or in coffee shops. Fifteen out of seventeen interviews were recorded in their entirety and later transcribed. During two of the interviews, equipment problems caused only a portion of the conversation to be recorded. In these cases, I wrote very detailed notes immediately after the interview. I also informed the participants what had happened with the recording device and asked them to verify the accuracy of the notes along with the partial transcript. In both cases the participants reported that the transcripts and notes accurately represented the conversation.

The interviewees included seven women and ten men between 22 and 60 years of age. They represented an array of occupations, including church leaders, teachers, a housewife, administrative aides, a communication specialist, an entomologist, undergraduate and graduate students, and a professional cleaner. Sixteen participants were Caucasian and one was Korean American. Five interviewees had been members of new paradigm churches for much of their lives. Eleven participants indicated that before joining Vineyard or Tapestry they were affiliated with Baptist, Lutheran, and Mennonite denominations. One of the study participants became a regular attendee during the investigation and thus had been associated with the new paradigm church for only a short period of time. A majority of the participants in this study were regular attendees who were very involved in numerous church-related activities. Individuals who attended once or only sporadically were not interviewed.

Fetterman's (1989) structure for analyzing information within ethnographic research was utilized within this study and will be described in the following paragraphs. First, after gaining access to both Tapestry and Vineyard communities and attending events, I recorded detailed information regarding the events that transpired, social interactions, as well as my thoughts and initial interpretations. Based on these notes, I wrote my interpretations of events and questions that arose from the observations. Next, I began conducting in-depth interviews after three months of participant observations. After the first interview was transcribed, I immediately began comparing my research notes with the interview material to identify emerging themes. As the interviews progressed, I began to look for patterns in all the data collected up to this point. I utilized the analysis method proposed by Glaser and Straus (1967) to help interpret the emerging themes and subthemes. After I established the main themes, I focused on identifying the subthemes. To be consistent with the framework proposed by Glaser and Straus, I continuously read through the transcripts and data gained from participant observations to identify any new data supporting the themes and subthemes, as well as new data contradicting previously obtained data. Finally, based upon the analysis of the observation and interview information, I was able to draw major conclusions regarding the way leisure enhanced the spirituality of participants.

In order to maximize the trustworthiness of the study, after all the interviews were transcribed, I sent the transcripts back to the participants for verification and feedback. In all but one case the participants verified the information and transcripts from the interviews. Corrections to age and one sentence in the interview transcript were requested by one participant. Five follow-up interviews were conducted to help clarify and deepen some of the information obtained from the initial seventeen interviews. After conducting the follow-up conversations with these five participants, I was able to bring further perspective to the previously collected data.

Moreover, I was able to compare the data gained from participant observations with the interview material to determine if the messages were consistent. I wanted to combine multiple perspectives to capture and represent as accurately as possible the social environment in which I was immersed. The data gathered from the interviews was largely consistent with the observations, which helped add to the trustworthiness of the study. Lastly, I was involved with the study populations for about six months and, as indicated by Baxter and Eyles (1997), prolonged contact is one of the key factors that can increase trustworthiness.

Results

The majority of the informants stressed that certain leisure activities could be spiritual. Specific examples of how participants deemed leisure activities as spiritual will be described in detail within this section. Twelve out of the seventeen interviewees confirmed that for them leisure was connected to spiritual experiences, and only one participant suggested that leisure and spirituality were not related. Specifically, Isaac, a Korean graduate student commented:

> I never thought about connecting leisure and God. I only think about God when I am taking a shower and in the morning, also before meal; that's the only time I think about God. I don't relate leisure to God. . . . To me leisure means sports, hiking, running, walking, which don't have anything to do with God.

Conversely, many other interviewees described leisure as only one of many spiritual experiences in their life. Some of them even conveyed that all of their life activities were spiritually related. For instance, Rebecca, a teacher in her early twenties who was a part of Vineyard Church since birth, commented:

> I would say that all my leisure activities, hopefully, are spiritual . . . some more so than others . . . but the undertones of all of them are spiritual . . . because the undertones of all of my life is spiritual. . . . I'm hoping that all my activities are spiritual, like glorifying God in all that I do, like working out. . . . God plays a role in all of those. Hopefully I'm prioritizing my schedule in a way that reflects God and spirituality and so that would hopefully encompass everything.

Other interviewees also maintained that all activities people engaged in should be spiritual. Despite that claim, most participants were able to identify a specific activity they considered more spiritual than others.

The findings, which describe how participants connect leisure and spirituality, are divided into three themes. First, solitary leisure activities, such as walking, knitting, and playing music by oneself, were considered as spiritual by many participants. Similarly, leisure provided an opportunity for participants to become quiet, which created an environment for one to focus on God. Second, leisure with others, both Christian and non-Christian, was deemed as spiritual. Specifically, leisure provided a way for individuals to interact or fellowship with other Christians, which created a spiritual environment. Third, leisure in natural environments was considered as spiritual, because it was an opportunity to be in God's creation.

Solitary Leisure Activities Described as Spiritual

Individual Activities. Interviewees identified individual leisure activities such as walking, knitting, playing the guitar, backpacking, and playing the piano as spiritual. For many of the participants, time alone was a break from family obligations or work, which encouraged a spiritual experience through leisure. For Mary, a 25-year-old female from a traditional Christian family, playing the piano was spiritual in nature: "It hasn't happened much lately, because I don't like to do it when anyone else is around, but to play piano and to write songs and sing is very spiritual to me." Another individual leisure activity, listening to music, also allowed people to connect with God. Luke, a newcomer to the new paradigm church, discussed this activity: "Just listening to music. . . . It doesn't matter what kind of music . . . sometimes to connect different things with my theology or my thoughts and my teachings on God and the Bible; any of the arts and cultural things."

Many interviewees considered quiet leisure activities, such as backpacking or knitting, as spiritual. They commented that these activities allowed them to pray, focus on God, or be one-on-one with God. The connection with God during these solitary leisure activities is what made them spiritual to the participants. For instance, one of the interviewees, a teacher in her early twenties, remarked, "Solitude activities, yeah, I would definitely say they are spiritual. I mean like [for] some people [it] would be knitting, or walking, or [doing] something like that – [it is] spiritual."

Leisure as an Opportunity to Become Quiet. Just as leisure in solitary settings was considered spiritual, opportunities to quiet down, escape outside stimulation, and thus interact with God were also considered as spiritual by participants. During an interview with Mary, a 25-year-old female who had spent most of her life attending a traditional style church, we discussed various leisure activities that she considered spiritual in nature. She commented:

> I know that some of the best times that I have are when I walk. Since having a baby it's hard to get some down time, so I try to go on walks, and

[when I walk] I think "Oh, I should use this time to pray; I should use this time." And sometimes I do, but it's kinda nice just to be quiet, too. So I think that it is definitely spiritual for me. There's so much stimulation in our culture and in our society.

Similarly, interviewees explained that leisure in quiet settings not only led to spiritual feelings, but was personally meaningful because it allowed them to reflect on their lives as Christians. Several of the interviewees commented that they engaged in leisure to relieve stress and to experience spirituality. Paul, a 23-year-old guitar player in the worship band, commented:

It's an individual thing . . . to be by myself, playing my guitar. It very much calms me down. I'll use it as a stress reliever. To me, the very concept of stress is just kind of spiritually laden. So since it [playing guitar] relieves that . . . I think, yeah, it's definitely a spiritual experience.

Other participants suggested that solitary or quiet leisure created a spiritual atmosphere. Specifically, when one was away from noise such as televisions, cell phones, computers, and, in some cases, people, he or she could contemplate about God and religious matters. Furthermore, such quiet leisure activities were described as spontaneous in nature.

Certain planned leisure activities, such as retreats taken with other Christian friends when quietness was emphasized, also fostered spiritual feelings. Outlets such as television, magazines, and radios were not allowed, which helped achieve a noise-free environment. The quiet times were considered excellent opportunities to experience leisure and to connect with God. Mary, a 25-year-old female, described the retreats designed for the leaders of the church to enjoy leisure and to develop their skills:

Times like [when] you and I [speaking to her spouse] have gone to the pastor's retreat. Just getting away from everything. . . . You have a total media fast for five days and you basically get away from everything. I think some of those times are really good just to slow down and get quiet . . . and you connect with God and with other people.

It was evident that quiet settings such as retreats or being by oneself and focusing on God fostered the development of spiritual feelings or thoughts related to God. Thus, both spontaneous and planned quiet leisure experiences were considered as spiritual by the interviewees.

In summary, the interviewees described quiet leisure activities as a way to relieve stress, experience a less hectic period of time, and focus on one's relationship with God, which was a way for participants to relax and reenergize their spirituality. These findings were consistent with the biblical commandment to be recreated in Christ (2 Cor. 5:13).

Leisure with Others

Leisure Activities with Others as Spiritual Experiences. Social activities, such as having conversations with people, being in the presence of others, developing relationships, hanging out with friends, sexual intimacy, and spending time around a campfire with friends were described as spiritual. First, simply spending time with others and having conversations were considered as spiritual experiences. For example, Luke, a male in his early thirties, commented, "Just through interacting with other people, through a conversation, there can be something very valuable to a person in their spiritual part of being." Rebecca, a Vineyard member, also expressed the same sentiment about conversing with others: "Being with other people in any aspect has spiritual tones for me. When I'm hanging out with friends or doing things like that, I would definitely say it's very spiritual." Such conversational partners did not necessarily have to be Christian or attend a new paradigm church. Interviewees mentioned that they could have conversations that would be spiritual in nature with neighbors or long-time friends who were non-Christians. Such socializing between people did not seem to be planned; rather, it was described as very spontaneous in nature and enjoyable. Another social activity, sexual intimacy, was described as spiritual by Luke: "I don't want to get overly personal," he commented, "but, you know, I've read about how sexual intimacy is essentially spiritual so, I guess, I would have to include that."

Leisure as an Opportunity to Interact with Christian Friends. Another way in which leisure helped the interviewees to develop spiritual feelings was by providing a forum for interaction with Christian friends. Such interactions could be both planned and unplanned. For example, interviewees suggested that some of their conversations with friends after a Bible study or organized church events led to a spiritual experience. Isaac, a Korean doctoral student in his early thirties, described his experiences in these words:

> There is a Korean Bible study every Friday. For one and a half hours [we have a] Bible study and the rest of the two hours is chatting. There is [an opportunity to] think about Bible, share our prayers. That is the only leisure that affects my spiritual life.

Additionally, building relationships with Christian friends, or fellowship, was viewed as an essential part of being a Christian. Making spiritual connections with other Christians during leisure events was described as a very important feature of new paradigm churches. Specifically, relationship building was one of the key reasons for planning and organizing leisure events within the church. Rebecca, a teacher in her early twenties, commented, "When I'm hanging out with my Christian friends . . . it's a lot of, you know, like how do we build relationships, how do we encourage each other. . . . It is definitely a part of being in the body of Christ." Leisure events that allowed people to get to know their fellow Christians and to understand their perspectives on life were also conducive to spiritual experiences. This theme is exemplified in a quote from Luke:

> Sometimes, just through talking with people and hearing their stories . . . sometimes there's more value spiritually to me than having a study or praying before a meal. It means more to me just to share somebody's experience. . . . Like one night, I think it was a music practice, and four or five people just sat around afterwards on the floor here and we talked for hours and a lot of it was about us. Through some of the experiences that we shared, many of them relating to our convictions and our faith, I feel like it could have been beneficial. Although it was only meant just to be hanging out, it ended up being spiritual.

The diverse conversation topics ranging from everyday matters to more complex subjects and the opportunity to get to know fellow Christians were considered to be enjoyable and spiritual experiences.

Leisure as an Opportunity to Be in a Natural Environment Created by God

Interviewees mentioned many ways in which nature and outdoor environments gave them an opportunity to interact with God by allowing them to escape outside stimulation. Additionally, participants communicated that leisure with friends, both Christian and non-Christian, led to spiritual experiences. The importance of being in natural environments and experiencing spirituality was expressed by many interviewees. Recreation and leisure in natural settings, outside of the human-made domain, were seen as a way to experience God's creation. Matthew, a man in his early fifties and a leader in his church, commented how leisure brings one to natural environments, which can lead to spiritual feelings:

> Recreational and leisure type activities get you out, into nature, into creation. You can get away from human structures and man's world into God's creation and there's just a natural opening up of our hearts and minds towards God and thinking about those issues.

Hannah, a female in her late twenties, commented, "Backpacking out in the mountains . . . those are some of the best times I have with God."

Trips and retreats to natural environments were planned by both churches in order to enhance the spirituality of their members and to teach them about Christianity. Members of Vineyard and Tapestry also established camps and churches in wooded areas near lakes for the purpose of having retreats and facilitating spiritually related leisure activities. Such retreats allowed for personal interactions, Bible studies, or spiritual conversations in natural settings. Additionally, they were designed to allow people to spend time alone in wooded areas, read the Bible or pray while walking on trails to fully experience God's creation, as well as to spend time with God. Local settings, such as parks or natural areas outside of one's home, were also viewed as places that fostered spiritual feelings.

Some of the interviewees also referred to biblical passages that mentioned that natural environments are God's creation to be enjoyed by people. For example, Mark, a man in his twenties and a leader at Tapestry, commented:

> Like at a park [when you] get outside and usually it helps seeing nature. It's really pretty and then you read the Bible and then you connect it all. In the Psalms they talk about nature, too; you know, the sky, the sun, trees, and it was all created by God, so he must have meant for us to enjoy it.

Mark quoted a passage from Psalm 65: 8–13, which describes the beauty and wonder of the environment that God created,

> The whole earth is filled with awe at your wonders;
> where morning dawns, where evening fades,
> you call forth songs of joy.
> You care for the land and water it;
> you enrich it abundantly.
> The streams of God are filled with water
> to provide the people with grain,
> for so you have ordained it.
> You drench its furrows and level its ridges;
> you soften it with showers and bless its crops.
> You crown the year with your bounty,
> and your carts overflow with abundance.
> The grasslands of the wilderness overflow;
> the hills are clothed with gladness.
> The meadows are covered with flocks
> and the valleys are mantled with grain;
> they shout for joy and sing.

Some participants did not mention specific scripture; however, their examples regarding the spirituality of the natural environment closely mirrored scripture. Jacob, an undergraduate student in his early 20s, said,

> Nature is really spiritual; I think about being the Creator, God as the creator, I think he made [it] all this for us to enjoy, it's kind of like if I go outside I can see the clouds and sunset and all of a sudden one day it's, Wow, that's awesome.

Jacob's quote closely resembles the creation story depicted in Genesis 1:26, which details how the natural environment was created by God for humans:

> Then God said, "Let us make mankind in our image, in our likeness, so that they may rule over the fish in the sea and the birds in the sky, over the livestock and all the wild animals, and over all the creatures that move along the ground."

The interviews provided numerous examples of how participants utilized leisure within natural environments, both individually and socially, to connect with God. It was clear they believed that God provided these natural spaces for people to enjoy their leisure.

Discussion

Except for one participant, all interviewees agreed that certain leisure activities could be considered spiritual. The variety of leisure activities that were considered as spiritual by participants included walking, knitting, playing music, being quiet, socializing, and activities in natural environments. These findings are consistent with investigations by Heintzman (2000), Heintzman and Mannell (2003), and Schmidt and Little (2007), which concluded that numerous types of leisure activities were conducive to meaningful or spiritual experiences. Furthermore, the finding that activities specific to each participant were considered spiritual is similar to Heintzman's (2000) finding that spiritual wellbeing was associated with leisure activities consistent with one's personality or interests.

In particular, solitary leisure activities were considered as spiritual by many participants. This finding is consistent with an investigation by Heintzman (2000) on leisure and spiritual wellbeing, which discovered that settings where one could experience solitude and quietness were conducive to spiritual wellbeing. Additional empirical investigations by Fox (1997), Frederickson and Anderson (1999), and Sweatman and Heintzman (2004) also found that solitude during leisure was associated with spiritual experiences.

Participants also described the need to live a holistic life that includes time for leisure and rest. This finding supports non-empirical writings by Conner (1992), Heintzman (1996, 2006), Johnston (1983), Koenig (2001), and Norden (1965), which suggest that living a balanced life is spiritual and consistent with the teachings of Christianity.

Passages from Scripture, which were used by the participants to illustrate how leisure enhanced their spirituality, were focused on natural environments. Specifically, interviewees quoted, or alluded to, passages from the Bible (Gen. 1:26, Ps. 65: 8–13) that indicated that God provided outdoor spaces for people to enjoy. This finding confirms conceptual writings by Driver et al. (1996), Godbey (1989), Kaza (1996), Kelly (1987), and McDonald and Schreyer (1991) and empirical investigations (Fox, 1997; Frederickson & Anderson, 1999; Heintzman, 2000, 2002b, 2003, 2007, 2008; Stringer & McAvoy, 1992; Sweatman & Heintzman, 2004) that suggested that being in the natural environment could facilitate one's spirituality and connection with a higher power. The important role of the natural environment discovered in this study is also consistent with the history of the new paradigm Christianity, which was traced by Miller (1997) and Sargeant (2000) to the Jesus movements of the 1960s, where hippies and other members of the counterculture would organize spiritual meetings on beaches or in other outdoor settings.

Additionally, participants in this study described social leisure (conversations with friends, family, or church members, spending time around a campfire, or sexual intimacy) as spiritual. This finding is congruent with previous research on nature-based recreation and spirituality. Heintzman's (2007) study of men's wilderness experience discovered that sharing personal stories and interacting with other program participants was considered spiritual. Sweatman and Heintzman (2004) found that both informal and formal social settings were conducive to spiritual experiences for residential campers. Moreover, the findings of this study support the conceptual writings of Ryken (2002), Kelly (1987), and Norden (1965), which suggested that social relationships are a fundamental aspect of church function and the overall Christian lifestyle. New paradigm Christians in this study described both unplanned (e.g., running into an old friend) or planned (e.g., going on a church retreat) activities as spiritual.

Participants' accounts were also consistent with the ideas of Huizinga (1955), who suggested that people could experience spiritual feelings and connect with the Divine while engaging in spontaneous, playful activities. Interviewees in this study recounted that they enjoyed spiritual experiences during both planned (retreats or scheduled time alone) and spontaneous leisure events. These spontaneous activities included social occasions such as meetings and conversations and individual pastimes such as taking a walk or playing a guitar. This theme regarding spontaneous activities is important to understanding the spirituality of new paradigm Christians. Specifically, for them, spiritual experiences are not limited to leisure planned in the religious context, but can also occur spontaneously, outside of planned church events. Furthermore, the finding that spontaneous and playful leisure was considered as spiritual is also consistent with Pieper's (1998) suggestion that leisure is a major way in which one can connect to his or her culture and to God. According to Schor (1991), we live in a workaholic culture where one's days are comprised of numerous activities at work as well as overwhelming family obligations. This busy lifestyle leaves very little time for socializing and developing relationships within one's community. However, new paradigm Christians interviewed in this investigation considered close, personal relationships with fellow Christians as spiritual, which is consistent with Pieper's thinking that leisure is an optimal way to build community. Specifically, Pieper noted that activities such as religious festivals and celebrations bring people closer together. He described festivals within a religious community as "an affirmation of the basic meaning of the world, and an agreement with it, and in fact it means to live out and fulfill one's inclusion in the world, and in an extraordinary manner, different from the everyday" (pp. 33–34). Furthermore, Pieper suggested that leisure and worship are necessary elements for one to experience festivals or social leisure. Leisure played a significant role in the spiritual lives of new paradigm Christians as it provided a way for them to better understand spirituality and social culture within the church, which is consistent with Pieper's thinking.

Conclusion

Even though it is difficult to understand people's leisure choices without understanding the spiritual dimension of their lives, spirituality, and especially religious-based spirituality, has been conspicuously absent from leisure inquiry. This study makes an important contribution to the existing knowledge of leisure and religion by improving our understanding of the relationship between leisure and spirituality within the lives of new paradigm Christians. Understanding the relationship between leisure and spirituality is a timely and important area of inquiry due to the number of Americans who indicate that their faith has a significant influence on their lives. As mentioned in the introduction, about 80 percent of Americans believe in God or a higher power (Baylor University, 2005). Thus, it is important to understand how spirituality influences people's decision making when it comes to leisure. For instance, as the findings of this study showed, spirituality may provide additional motivations for engagement in leisure (e.g., establishing connection with God).

The findings of this study also have important implications for the religious studies literature. In particular, little attention has been paid to new paradigm churches within the field of religious studies. Much of what has been written on new paradigm churches has appeared in newspapers and magazines (Brandt, 2005; Douglass, 2005; El Nasser, 2002; Goodstein, 2005; Kroll, 2003; Mahler, 2005), and provided only very superficial information about this newest development in Protestant Christianity. At the same time, thorough, empirical investigations of this subject have been lacking. The results of this study add to the social scientific knowledge of the new paradigm churches and, in particular, have shown how leisure is incorporated into spirituality.

Even though this study has provided some important contributions to leisure scholarship and practice, it also had certain limitations that need to be acknowledged. First, I conducted this study from an outsider perspective; specifically, I was not a member of the churches in which I performed participant observations and interviews. However, I approached the research as an ex-insider, which means that I had at least a foundational knowledge of the new paradigm Christian faith. Specifically, I was familiar with the language, ritual, and other important aspects of this religion, which enabled me to understand and contribute as a participant during the observations that I made and to remain competent during the interviews.

Another important limitation of the study stems from the fact that the majority of participants interviewed in this study were regular attendees of Vineyard and Tapestry Churches. Both churches encouraged individuals to choose a leadership position or a specific responsibility within the church. Although some training was required to oversee activities such as teaching, long years of membership and attendance were not necessary to perform functions within the church. Because of this focus on service, it was natural that most people whom I encountered and subsequently interviewed had some responsibility within their church. Only two of my interviewees did not hold any official functions within

Vineyard or Tapestry. I believe, however, that this is an acceptable limitation, since one of the goals of this study was to investigate the role of leisure within these two new paradigm churches. Individuals who were not involved in the activities of their church on a regular basis might not have been knowledgeable about such issues. Additionally, they might have limited understanding of their spirituality in relation to the new paradigm philosophy.

Although philosophical and conceptual works that focus on the relationship between religious based spirituality and leisure are quite numerous (Brightbill, 1965; Dahl, 1972; Heintzman, 1996, 2006; Johnston, 1983; Kelly, 1987, 1990; Norden, 1965; Pieper, 1998), empirical research on this topic is still emerging (Fox, 1997; Frederickson & Anderson, 1999; Heintzman, 2000, 2002b, 2003, 2007; Heintzman & Mannell, 2003; Schmidt & Little, 2007; Sweatman & Heintzman, 2004). I believe that there are three main areas of inquiry that need particular attention. First, the current study discovered that new paradigm Christians considered leisure activities with others as spiritual activities. Further research could focus on the role of activities related to religious rites in people's leisure. Just a casual observation of the number of events that are related to religious calendars (Thanksgiving, Christmas, Easter, Yom Kippur, Id-Al-Adha) and that accompany important milestones in people's lives (baptism, first communion, confirmation, bar mitzvahs) makes it clear that they not only strengthen people's connection to their church, family, and community, but are cornerstones in their leisure life. Religious events may facilitate leisure activities, such as during family gatherings at Thanksgiving, Christmas, Id-Al-Adha (culmination of hajj), or Id-Al-Fitr (breaking of the fast among Muslims), or impose additional constraints on leisure, such as during Lent or Ramadan. However, so far, the only information on the relation of these events to leisure comes from historical works and anecdotal accounts.

Second, although this study has provided some preliminary insight into the role of spirituality in the leisure life of new paradigm Christians, the relationship between spirituality and leisure among people of different denominations (Baptist, Methodist, Presbyterian) or faiths (e.g., Jewish, Muslim) is very scarce (Ibrahim, 1982; Stodolska & Livengood, 2006) and thus warrants further investigation. It might also be interesting to examine possible changes in leisure preferences and behaviors among people who have transferred from a traditional or conservative Christian church to a new paradigm place of worship, and among those, who have not attended religious services for a significant period of time, but have decided to rekindle their interest in Christianity. Among such individuals, it would be important to investigate any changes in the role of leisure in their personal life.

Third, Heintzman (2000, 2003), Livengood and Place (2007), and Schmidt and Little (2007) maintain that further reflection and attention is needed to integrate spiritual experiences into leisure services. The current study along with previous empirical research (e.g., Fox, 1997; Frederickson & Anderson, 1999; Heintzman, 2000, 2002b, 2007; Heintzman & Mannell, 2003; Schmidt & Little, 2007; Sweatman & Heintzman, 2004) has discovered that leisure and spirituality are linked, which suggests that incorporating a spiritual component may benefit current programs as well as attract additional participants seeking meaningful leisure experiences. Yet, spirituality is a multifaceted experience that may be difficult to conceptualize and integrate into leisure services; therefore further investigations regarding the spiritual benefits of leisure must be conducted. Additionally, one can argue that spirituality is a missing component within contemporary, public recreation programming. Including spiritual elements in the events organized by public parks and recreation departments could, however, pose a major problem in some countries such as the United States where the Establishment clause in the American Constitution makes it illegal for the government to promote religion or advocate for one particular religion. However, certain recreation activities, such as wilderness trips, tai chi, karate, yoga, or meditation, which include spiritual elements, could be offered to participants who desire this type of programming. Agencies would not have to promote a specific spiritual perspective or advocate for one to focus on faith; however, an individual could enter into a spiritual state of mind, if desired, during such recreation activities.

References

ABC News. (2001). *Mega-churches grow bigger and bigger.* Retrieved January 15, 2004, from http://abcnews.go.com/sections/us/DailyNews/megachurch010613.html.

Ahlstrom, S.E. (1972). *A religious history of the American people.* New Haven, CT: Yale University Press.

Anderson, L. (1992). *A church for the 21st century.* Minneapolis: Bethany House.

Baxter, J., & Eyles, J. (1997). Evaluating qualitative research in social geography: Establishing "rigour" in interview analysis. *Transactions of the Institute of British Geographers* 22, 505–525.

Baylor University. (2005). *The Baylor Religion Survey.* Waco, TX: Baylor Institute for Studies of Religion. Retrieved November 2, 2008, from http://www.thearda.com/Archive/Files/Downloads/BRS2005_DL2.asp.

Berryman, D.L. (2000). Riding the winds of change. *Journal of Leisure Research* 32, 7–11.

Brandt, J. (2005). *The Vineyard "aint your momma's church."* Daily Illini. Retrieved March 16, 2006, from http://www.dailyillini.com/media/storage/paper736/news/2005/09/29/Features/The-Vinyard.aint.Mommas.Church02901.shtml?norewrite200604012103&sourcedomain=www.dailyillini.com

Brightbill, C.K. (1965). *Leisure and religion.* George M. Colliver Lectures. University of the Pacific: Stockton, CA.

Conner, R. (1992). *The ministry of recreation.* Nashville, TN: Convention Press.

Cross, G.S. (1990). *A social history of leisure since 1600.* Philadelphia, PA: Venture.

Dahl, G. (1972). *Work, play, and worship.* Minneapolis: Augsburg.

Douglass, T. (2005). Megachurches appealing to the masses. Daily Illini. Retrieved March 16, 2006, from http://www.dailyillini.com/media/storage/paper736/news/2005/12/12/News/Megachurches.Appealing.To.The.Masses1127330.shtml?norewrite200604012105&sourcedomain=www.dailyillini.com.

Driver, B.L., Dustin, D., Baltic, T., Elsner, G., & Peterson, G. (Eds.). (1996). *Nature and the human spirit: Toward an expanded land management ethic.* State College, PA: Venture.

El Nasser, H. (2002). Giant churches irk some neighbors. Retrieved April 20, 2004, from http://www.usatoday.com/news/religion/2002-09-22-megachurches.

Emard, M.R. (1990). *Religion and leisure: A case study of the role of the church as a provider of recreation in small Ontario communities.* (Unpublished master's thesis). University of Waterloo, Ontario, Canada.

Ernce, K.D. (1987). *Church recreation in the Southern Baptist Convention as a leisure consumer, leisure provider, and member of the leisure services delivery.* (Unpublished doctoral dissertation). University of New Mexico, Albuquerque.

Fetterman, D.M. (1989). *Ethnography step by step.* Applied Social Research Methods Series. Newbury Park, CA: Sage.

Fox, R.J. (1997). Women, nature and spirituality: A qualitative study exploring women's wilderness experience. In D. Rowe & P. Brown (Eds.), *Proceedings, ANZALS conference 1997* (pp. 59–64). Newcastle, NSW: Australian and New Zealand Association for Leisure Studies, and Department of Leisure and Tourism Studies, University of Newcastle.

Fredrickson, L.M., & Anderson, D.H. (1999). A qualitative exploration of the wilderness experience as a source of spiritual inspiration. *Journal of Environmental Psychology* 19, 21–39.

Glaser, B.G., & Strauss, A.L. (1967). *The discovery of grounded theory: Strategies for qualitative research.* Chicago: Aldine.

Godbey, G. (1989). Implications of recreation and leisure research for professionals. In E.L. Jackson & T.L. Burton (Eds.), *Understanding leisure and recreation: Mapping the past, charting the future* (pp. 613–628). State College, PA: Venture.

Goodale, T., & Godbey, G. (1988). *The evolution of leisure.* State College, PA: Venture.

Goodstein, L. (2005). When Christmas falls on Sunday, megachurches take the day off. *The New York Times.* Retrieved September 5, 2017, from http://www.nytimes.com/2005/12/09/us/when-christmas-falls-on-sunday-megachurches-take-the-day-off.html

Grim, B.J., & Masci, D. (2008). The demographics of faith. Retrieved November 19, 2008, from http://www.america.gov/st/diversityenglish/2008/August/20080819121858cmretrop0.5310633.html.

Heintzman, P. (1996, July). Biblical and bibliographic resources for leisure. *Community Crossings* (16–19). Ottawa, ON: St. George's Anglican Church.

Heintzman, P. (2000). Leisure and spiritual well-being relationships: A qualitative study. *Society and Leisure* 23, 41–69.

Heintzman, P. (2002a). A conceptual model of leisure and spiritual well-being. *Journal of Park and Recreation Administration* 20(4), 147–169.

Heintzman, P. (2002b). The role of introspection and spirituality in the park experience of day visitors to Ontario Provincial Parks. In S. Bondrup-Nielsen, M. Willison, N. Munro, G. Nelson, & T. Herman (Eds.), *Managing protected areas in a changing world* (pp. 992–1004). Wolfville, NS: Science and Management of Protected Areas Association.

Heintzman, P. (2003). Wilderness experience and spirituality: What the research tells us. *Leisure Today* (special issue on wilderness education), *The Journal of Physical Education, Recreation, and Dance* 74(6), 27–31.

Heintzman, P. (2006). Implications for leisure from a review of the biblical concepts of Sabbath and rest. In P. Heintzman, G.E. Van Andel, & T.L. Visker (Eds.), *Christianity and leisure: Issues in a pluralistic society* (Rev. ed., pp. 14–31). Sioux Center IA: Dordt College Press.

Heintzman, P. (2007). Men's wilderness experience and spirituality: A qualitative study. In R. Burns & K. Robinson (Comps.), *Proceedings of the 2006 Northeastern Recreation Research Symposium* (pp. 432– 439) (Gen. Tech. Rep. NRS-P-14). Newton Square, PA: U.S. Department of Agriculture, Forest Services, Northern Research Station. Retrieved March 3, 2008, from http://nrs.fs.fed.us/pubs/gtr/gtr_nrs-p-14/30-heintzman-p-14.pdf.

Heintzman, P. (2008). Men's wilderness experience and spirituality: Further explorations. In C. LeBlanc & C. Vogt (Eds.), *Proceedings of the 2007 Northeastern Recreation Research Symposium* (pp. 55–59) (Gen. Tech. Rep. NRS-P-23). Newton Square, PA: U.S. Department of Agriculture, Forest Services, Northern Research Station.

Heintzman, P., & Mannell, R. (2003). Spiritual functions of leisure and spiritual well-being: Coping with time pressure. *Leisure Sciences* 25, 207–230.

Heintzman, P., & Van Andel, G. (1995). Leisure and spirituality. *Parks and Recreation* 30(3), 22–30.

Henderson, K.A., Bialeschki, M.D., Hemingway, J.L, Hodges, J.S., Kivel, B.D., & Sessoms, H.D. (2001). *Introduction to recreation and leisure services.* State College, PA: Venture.

Huizinga, J. (1955). *Homo Ludens: A study of the play element in culture.* Boston: Beacon Press.

Ibrahim, H. (1981). Leisure behavior among contemporary Egyptians. *Journal of Leisure Research* 13, 89–187.

Johnson, H. (1932). *Is there an interaction between recreation and religion?* (Unpublished doctoral dissertation). University of North Dakota, Grand Forks.

Johnston, R.K. (1983). *The Christian at play.* Grand Rapids: Eerdmans.

Karlis, G., Grafanaki, S., & Abbas, J. (2002). Leisure and spirituality: A theoretical model. *Society and Leisure* 25, 208–214.

Kaza, S. (1996). Comparative perspectives of world religions: Views of nature and implications for land management. In B.L. Driver, D. Dustin, T. Baltic, G. Elsner, & G. Peterson (Eds.), *Nature and the human spirit: Toward an expanded land management ethic* (pp. 41–60). State College, PA: Venture.

Kellstedt, L.A., & Green, J.C. (2003). The politics of Willow Creek Association pastors. *Journal for the Scientific Study of Religion* 42, 547–561.

Kelly, J.R. (1990). *Leisure.* Englewood Cliffs, NJ: Prentice Hall.

Kelly, J.R. (1987). *Freedom to be: A new sociology of leisure.* New York: MacMillan.

Koenig, J. (2001). *New Testament hospitality.* Eugene, OR: Wipf & Stock.

Kroll, L. (2003). *Mega churches, megabuisnesses.* Retrieved March 16, 2006, from http://www.forbes.com/2003/09/17/cz_li_0917megachurch.html.

Lehman, H. (1974). *In praise of leisure.* Scottdale, PA: Herald Press.

Livengood, J.S., & Place, G. (2007). Recreation services in a religiously diverse world. Educational session presented at the 2007 National Recreation and Parks Association Congress and Exposition, Indianapolis, IN.

Livengood, J.S., & Stodolska, M. (2004). The effects of discrimination and constraints negotiation on leisure behavior of American Muslims in post September 11 America. *Journal of Leisure Research* 36, 183–208.

Mahler, J. (2005). The soul of the new exurb. *The New York Times.* Retrieved September 5, 2017, from http://www.nytimes.com/2005/03/27/magazine/the-soul-of-the-new-exurb.html

McDonald, B.L., & Schreyer, R. (1991). Spiritual benefits of leisure participation and leisure settings. In B.L. Driver, P.J. Brown, & G.L. Peterson (Eds.), *Benefits of Leisure* (pp. 179–194). State College, PA: Venture.

Miller, D.E. (1997). *Reinventing American Protestantism.* Los Angeles, CA: University of California Press.

Miller, D.E. (1998). Postdenominational Christianity in the twenty-first century. *Annals of the American Academy of Political and Social Science* 558, 196–210.

Norden, R.F. (1965). *The new leisure.* St. Louis, MO: Concordia Publishing House.

Pieper, J. (1998). *Leisure: The basis of culture* (G. Malsbary, Trans.). South Bend, IN: St. Augustine's Press.

Ragheb, M.G. (1993). Leisure and perceived wellness: A field investigation. *Leisure Sciences* 15, 13–24.

Ryken, L. (2002). *Work and leisure in Christian perspective.* Eugene, OR: Wipf & Stock.

Sargeant, K.H. (2000). *Seeker Churches.* New Brunswick, NJ: Rutgers University Press.

Schmidt, C., & Little, D.E. (2007). Qualitative insights into leisure as a spiritual experience. *Journal of Leisure Research* 39(2), 222–247.

Schor, J. (1991). *The overworked American: The unexpected decline of leisure.* New York: Basic Books.

Spilka, B., & McIntosh, D.M. (1997). *The psychology of religion: Theoretical approaches.* Boulder, CO: Westview Press.

Stringer, L.A., & McAvoy, L.H. (1992). The need for something different: Spirituality and wilderness adventure. *The Journal of Experiential Education* 15(1), 13–21.

Stodolska, M., & Livengood, J.S. (2006). The effects of religion on the leisure behavior of American Muslim immigrants. *Journal of Leisure Research* 38, 293–320.

Sweatman, M., & Heintzman, P. (2004). The perceived impact of outdoor residential camp experience on the spirituality of youth. *World Leisure Journal* 46(1), 23–31.

Teaff, J. (2006). Contemplative leisure within Christian spirituality. In P. Heintzman, G.E. Van Andel, & T.L. Visker (Eds.), *Christianity and leisure: Issues in a pluralistic society*, (Rev. ed., pp. 112–115). Sioux Center: Dordt College Press.

The Pew Forum on Religion and Public Life. (2008). U.S. religious landscape survey. Retrieved on November 19, 2008, from http://religions.pewforum.org/affiliations.

Wesner, B.E. (1995). *Visions and revisions: An exploratory investigation sketching the origins and growth of the evolving relationship between the church and recreation, 1872–1992.* (Unpublished doctoral dissertation). University of Illinois, Urbana.

Chapter 12

THE MONASTERY AS A RESTORATIVE ENVIRONMENT

Pierre Ouellette, Rachel Kaplan, and Stephen Kaplan

The purpose of our study was to explore the motivations, activities, and effects of an individual retreat in a Benedictine monastery, both for first-time and repeat visitors. The quest for spiritual retreats and renewal experiences is evidenced not only by the great diversity of programs offered at the local level (e.g., yoga and meditation classes), but also by the number and range of opportunities available internationally (e.g., Retreats International, 2012; Retreats Online, 2012). Available rooms at Catholic monasteries are sometimes reserved a year in advance (Edwards, 1998). A Canadian monastery, the Abbaye Saint-Benoit, situated at Saint Benoit-du-Lac (SBL), served as the site for our study. SBL is a major tourist site for day visitors but also accommodates individuals who wish to stay overnight or longer. The latter were participants in the study.

The popularity of places such as Saint-Benoit raises the question of people's motivations. Do individuals who come for a few days seek this setting out of curiosity about the life of monks or simply as an intriguing tourist adventure? Are they seeking a spiritual experience? Are they looking for a retreat from their stressful daily lives? Moreover, do these motivations change with experience, when the novelty of the first-time visit gives way to greater familiarity with the setting and its rhythm? The main goals of our study were to address these questions and to try to assess the nature of the benefits the visitors derived from their stay.

A shorter version of this paper was presented by Pierre Ouellette at the 2006 conference.

Conceptual Framework

Research on restorative environments has increased substantially in recent years, including entire special issues of the Journal of Environmental Psychology (Hartig & Staats, 2003) and of Environment and Behavior (Hartig, 2001). A substantial quantity of work on psychological restoration draws on attention restoration theory (ART) (Kaplan, 1995). ART postulates that prolonged or intense cognitive effort produces a deficit in the capacity to direct attention. Indications of depleted directed attention are symptoms such as irritability, distractibility, impulsiveness, and impaired capacity to make and follow plans (Kaplan & Kaplan, 2003). Restorative environments and activities provide the opportunity for directed attention to recover by calling upon a different kind of attention, one that is effortless. James (1892) called this form of attention "involuntary" because it is compelling without demanding mental exertion.

Effortless attention, however, can come into play in widely different contexts. Some environments, for example, are so dramatic that the resulting fascination leaves no room in the mind for anything else. ART posits "soft fascination" as an important contrast, particularly in terms of its restorative potential (Kaplan & Kaplan, 1989). Softly fascinating environments, including many nature settings, combine beauty with a more modest level of fascination, leaving room for reflection. The study by Herzog, Black, Fountaine, and Knotts (1997) lends empirical support to some of these notions. Heintzman (2002) appropriately points out that soft fascination resulting from attractive or peaceful environments would not only elicit cognitive restoration and reflection, but also spiritual wellbeing and sacrilization, defined as the rediscovery of a spiritual dimension.

Kaplan and Talbot (1983) proposed four properties of restorative environments based on research in a wilderness outdoor challenge program. A somewhat revised version of these properties (Kaplan & Kaplan, 1989) was the basis of scales to measure restorative components of environments (e.g., Hartig, Korpela, Evans, & Gärling, 1997; Laumann, Gärling, Stomark, 2001). These properties of restorative environments are: (1) a sense of *being away* – physically or mentally removed from the activities that are attentionally demanding, (2) *fascination*, facilitating involuntary attention by the intrinsic interest of the situation, (3) the perception of *extent:* that is, giving one the sense of being somewhere with sufficient scope that one can dwell there for a while, whether or not the physical place is vast, and (4) *compatibility*, the perceived match between the person's informational needs and what the environment provides. Kaplan (2001), comparing ART and meditation, discussed a wide range of sources of person-environment incompatibility that contribute to the decline of directed attention.

Various aspects of ART have received substantial empirical support (e.g., Cimprich, 1993, 1999; Faber Taylor, Kuo, & Sullivan, 2002; Hartig, Evans, Jamner, Davis, & Gärling, 2003; Hartig, Mang, & Evans, 1991; Kuo, 2001; Kuo & Faber Taylor, 2004; Kuo & Sullivan, 2001; Tennessen & Cimprich, 1995). While nature settings are not the only environments that foster restoration, substantial research has shown that time in nature, even if only for a short duration, can offer restorative benefits (Canin, 1991; Herzog, 2002; Kaplan, 1973, 1993, 2001; Wells, 2000).

Despite the growing literature related to psychological restoration, we are not aware of studies that have explored the restorative benefits of the monastic setting. Eight document resource banks were searched: (1) Web of Science, (2) Francis, (3) Repère, (4) Eric, (5) PsychInfo, (6) ProQuest, (7) SportDiscus, (8) Humanities Index and (8) Dialogue. The results were scant. Reidhead and Reidhead (2001) researched the concept of spiritual integration with a sample of monks, while Tori (1999) compared the effects of a Roman Catholic and Buddhist retreat. From a sample of 71 individuals, composed almost equally of clergy and non-clergy members, Hillery (1992) reported that the motivation for going on a retreat is essentially spiritual, and that guests often report effects of peace as well as of love. Moreover, the raison d'être of monasteries, always according to this author, consists precisely in radiating to the world the unconditional love of God.

Yet, as Kaplan (2001) noted, monasteries tend to be "situated in environments that are striking for their restorative qualities. The architecture in such settings, too, appears to be designed with its restorative potential in mind" (p. 500). Furthermore, the life of the monks offers an array of visual and auditory stimulation that is likely to be at once fascinating and absorbing.

That individuals would feel calmer and less stressed at the end of a stay in a monastery would hardly be surprising. Presumably many come for the opportunity to reflect upon personal hardships, even if it is often disconcerting to face existential questions. Thus, they might well develop a deeper perspective of their life, work, and family. The present study explores the motivations for making a retreat and the effects resulting from the monastery stay. It also offers insight into the dynamic of time and experience with respect to these issues.

Study Setting: The Abbaye Saint-Benoit

Founded in 1912, the Abbaye Saint-Benoit (SBL) is located at the edge of Memphrémagog Lake, close to the small village of Austin, approximately 40 km from the city of Sherbrooke, in Quebec, Canada. Built of gray granite, the monastery encompasses a church that can accommodate 450 persons as well as a guesthouse with 35 rooms. Nearby is a small votive chapel dedicated to Saint Benedict. The Townships Heritage WebMagazine (2010) describes SBL as an "imposing structure" with "turrets [and] green copper roofs" that "sits in striking contrast to the green hillside that slopes gently down" to the lake's edge reminding one of a French château, with "Mount Owl's Head looming majestically in the distance." It further notes that "St-Benoit-du-Lac is famous not only for its spectacular architecture and surroundings, but for being a place of respite for pilgrims from around the world." During the summer season especially, the monastery attracts thousands of visitors, some arriving in groups by bus, from Quebec and other adjacent Canadian provinces, as well as nearby states (e.g., Vermont and New York) in the U.S.

According to the precepts of their monastic Rule of Benedict, the monks are dedicated to a life of moderation, living from the fruit of their labor. This is why there is at SBL a cider-house and an orchard, in addition to a cheese-factory, which distributes about 15 high quality cheeses everywhere in Canada. Moreover, the monks breed beef cattle and manage a maple syrup factory. The strict cloistered life of the monks is built around a schedule of seven offices distributed during the day. According to the monastic schema in force at this monastery, the 150 psalms of the Psalter are recited each week. Lauds and Vespers are always psalmodies in Latin, whereas Mass is sung in Gregorian. The Sunday Mass is most popular, and those who wish to take part in it must arrive early, because the church fills rapidly.

On average, 2,500 persons are accommodated annually for individual retreats, with a limit of 25–30 men at any one time. Lodging for 15 women is available at an adjacent house, Villa Sainte-Scholastique. The present study, however, included only men at SBL.

The guesthouse consists of comfortable rooms with a sink, bed, chair, and desk. With its rustic furniture, these rooms resemble more a monastic cell than the traditional hotel room. As would be expected, there are no televisions or radios; all rooms include a Bible and the Rule of Benedict. Toilets, as well as showers, are located at the end of each floor. Guests take their meals in silence, either in a cafeteria or in the monks' refectory, where a long table for the guests is in the middle of a large room, with the monks' tables along the walls on the left and right. In front is the abbot's table, and in the back, elevated in a pulpit provided with a microphone, the weekly lector reads from a spiritual book.

In the Benedictine tradition, spiritual workshops or conferences are seldom organized. Guests thus have the choice of several activities, ranging from a walk in nature to participation in community prayer. They have access to the abbey church, a small oratory, a library, meeting rooms, and a store. However, everyone is expected to respect the century-old principle of the monastic fence, which prohibits crossing certain spaces reserved only for monks. For example, one cannot visit the cheese factory nor walk on the edges of the lake. Visitors, tourists, and guests are not permitted to speak at length with monks, except to those with work assignments or pastoral duties at the guesthouse. The Rule of Benedict clearly prescribes this practice, and it aims at protecting the essence of silence and contemplative life, so necessary for continual prayer. Lastly, the monks at SBL always wear the traditional Benedictine black dress that consists of a tunic with a cap, a belt, and a scapular.

Method

Participants and Procedure

In order to preserve monastic peace, the gathering of the data proceeded in a particularly discrete way. On the day of departure, the Host Father (the monk in charge of the guesthouse) slipped an envelope under the door of the guest's room. The envelope included a letter explaining the purpose of the study and the questionnaire. Data was collected during the 2003 summer season, the highest tourist season at SBL.

All the distributed surveys were returned; however, eleven were eliminated because of incomplete information. The sample includes 521 male guests, of whom 24 answered the English version. About 75 percent added personal comments to the survey items.

Developing the Questionnaire

Spontaneously written testimonies, written by some guests prior to our study, as well as the ART framework guiding the study, informed the development of the survey questions. The survey benefited from the review by the guest-master and was pre-tested by ten individuals during their retreat at SBL. The final nine-page survey included 43 questions and a page for added comments. The cover letter, signed by the Host

Father indicated that SBL permitted the first author, "professor at the Université de Moncton and long-time friend of our monastery," to conduct the study to learn about "some aspects of your retreat experience." Guests were asked to complete the information a few hours before departure and to leave them off in a sealed envelope. They were assured of total anonymity.

The survey consisted of structured items related to the following topics: (1) the motivations to go on retreat, (2) the retreat experience, (3) the outcomes, and (4) the motivations of repeat guests. Each of these is described in the next section. In addition, the survey included some demographic information, as well as a few additional background questions.

Results and Discussion

Personal Characteristics of Guests

A majority of the respondents (62 percent) learned about the existence of SBL through the recommendation of another person. Most (60 percent) came alone and 29 percent came with one other person. Only 7.5 percent were priests, and 13 percent indicated that they were members of a religious order. Table 1 summarizes the demographic information describing the respondents.

The vast majority of the respondents (67 percent) were repeat visitors. About the same proportion of first-time visitors and repeat visitors (41 percent and 43 percent, respectively) stayed about three days. However, proportionately more first timers stayed for a shorter time (44 percent and 31 percent), and more repeat visitors stayed between four and seven days (26 percent and 15 percent).

The repeat visitors included many who came frequently. About a third (34 percent) indicated that they come, on average, two or more times a year, and 38 percent return annually. Over half (53 percent) had last visited less than a year ago, and for a quarter of the returnees, the last visit was two or more years previously. Over a fourth (28 percent) of the 343 repeat visitors had been visiting the monastery for more than two decades, and about the same number (27 percent) had come for one to four years. The sample thus provides a vast range of experience with monastic retreats.

Table 1 Respondent Characteristics		
	N	%
Age groups		
15–29	42	8.2
30–45	167	32.4
46–59	178	34.6
60+	128	24.9
Total	515	100.0
Marital status		
Single	203	39.1
Married	151	29.1
Common-law	86	16.6
Widower	16	3.1
Separated	18	3.5
Divorced	45	8.7
Total	519	100.0
Education		
Did not complete high school	36	6.9
High school diploma	87	16.7
Community College	78	15.0
University certificate	47	9.0
Bachelor's degree	136	26.2
Master's degree	103	19.8
Doctorate	33	6.3
Total	520	100.0
Present occupation		
Farmer, fisherman	2	0.4
Professional (lawyer, accountant, etc.)	95	18.3
Business (shop owner, craftsman, etc.)	18	3.5
Manual worker	46	8.9
White collar (office worker)	35	6.7
Executive, top management, director	32	6.2
Retired	115	22.2
Student	16	3.1
Unemployed	25	4.8
Other	135	26.0
Total	519	100.0
Gross annual salary (Canadian)		
Less than $15.000	70	13.7
$15.000 to $24.999	63	12.3
$25.000 to $34.999	78	15.3
$35.000 to $49.999	132	25.8
$50.000 to $74.999	97	19.0
$75.000 to $79.999	12	2.3
$80.000 to $99.999	27	5.3
$100.000 or more	32	6.3
Total	511	100.0

Motivations to Go on Retreat

Respondents were asked to rate (using a five-point scale, where 1 = "not at all" and 5 = "very much") each of 30 items describing possible reasons for deciding to go on a retreat. Factor analysis (principal components with varimax rotation) yielded four factors, accounting for 54 percent of the variance. The four factors (Table 2) were somewhat interrelated. Correlation between Compatibility and Being Away was .47, and Beauty had correlations between .41 and .57 with the other three factors.

The factor with the highest mean rating (4.29) consists of five items that match well with the Being Away aspect of ART. Included here are motivations to be away from the "world of agitation and turmoil" and to "live moments of silence." The Spirituality factor also received very high endorsement (mean = 4.19). Each of the six items in this factor clearly reflects the spiritual reasons for seeking a retreat in a monastery. While these two factors include all but one of the highest-rated items (between 3.9 and 4.6), they form two distinct and meaningfully differentiated factors.

The other two factors received more middling means. The six items comprising the Compatibility factor (mean = 3.55) suggest a search for an environment that would be supportive of dealing with difficult and perhaps even painful matters. These items point to solving problems, making important decisions, and achieving greater self-knowledge. It is paradoxical that this component, concerned with a friendly and supportive environment, suggests at the same time that the seeker's desire comes from a somewhat troubled state of mind. Yet, the metaphor of the monastery as a refuge, where a person can seek physical, psychological, and spiritual comfort, has a long, historical tradition.

The final factor, named "Beauty" (mean = 3.47), has parallels with both the extent (e.g., "explore a wonderful place") and fascination (e.g., "fascinated by the life of monks" and "allows me to do something fascinating") themes of ART. In addition, however, the factor includes the appeal of the Gregorian chants and the "beauty of the abbey," contributing to an aesthetic dimension. Also included are two items that reflect specific contents ("being close to nature" and "community belonging"), as opposed to the more process-oriented aspects of ART.

Taken as a whole, the four motivation factors show strong parallels with ART, while clearly reflecting the particular context of a Benedictine monastery. It is most reasonable that there would be a factor on spirituality. Furthermore, Being Away and Compatibility, two hypothesized components of a restorative environment, have parallel factors in

Table 2
Factor Analysis of Motivations to do a Retreat

	Factor loadings			
	Spiritual	Beauty	Compatibility	Being Away
Contributes to my spirituality	.79			
Replenishes spiritually	.79			
Deepens faith	.79			
Devote time to prayer	.76			
Allows me to feel the presence of God	.73			
Provides an opportunity to meditate	.56			
Explore a wonderful place		.74		
Fascinated by the life of monks		.72		
Provides a sense of community belonging.		.66		
Be close to nature		.62		
Gives me opportunity to listen to Gregorian chants		.62		
Allows me to appreciate the beauty of the abbey		.61		
Allows me to do something fascinating		.51		
Provides the solution to a problem			.83	
Allows me time to make important decisions			.72	
Allows me to take stock of my life			.67	
Allows me to learn to know myself better			.65	
Relieves stress			.58	
Ask a favor to the Lord			.56	
Allows me to live moments of silence				.72
Provides rest				.57
Removes me from a world of agitation and turmoil				.56
Provides an atmosphere of contemplation				.52
Take time for myself				.51
% Variance	28.80	11.96	7.08	5.87
Alpha coefficient	.87	.85	.83	.73
Mean rating	4.19	3.47	3.55	4.29

Note: Principal components analysis with varimax rotation. Loadings $\geq .45$ are shown.

this study. The fact that they express a more spiritual tone seems totally appropriate, given again the nature of the monastic milieu. The Beauty factor has strong ties to both Fascination and Extent, but incorporates other qualities beyond these. One might think of this factor as a spiritual perspective on what constitutes a restorative environment.

First-timers and repeat visitors had similar ratings for Being Away and Compatibility, but Spirituality and Beauty were significantly stronger motivations for the repeat visitors than for those who had not come previously (F = 8.68 and 11.15, df = 1, 511, p < .005, respectively). Understandably, Beauty was rated lower (3.29) by those who had not previously experienced some of these qualities of the setting. In fact, Beauty is an increasingly strong motivation the more frequent the returns to the monastery (F = 8.92, df = 2,335, p < .001).

Personal Problems and Their Relationship to Motivations

Participants were asked to rate (using a five-point scale) their current health, as well as 13 problems they may have experienced in the past few months. Mean ratings of the 13 problem areas were all below mid-scale with "too much to do" receiving the highest mean (2.72). Factor analysis of the 13 items yielded two factors with alpha coefficients greater than .65. One of these included three items related to the Work Situation ("too much to do," "burnout" and "problems at work") and the other consisted of three items concerning the Family Situation ("demands from family," "difficulty with your child or children," and "marital difficulties").

Health, Family, Work, and three other "problem" domains ("alcohol or drug dependency," "loss of a loved one," and "world situation") were included in further analyses. These six potential problem areas had no inter-correlations greater than .31. First time and repeat visitors did not differ significantly with respect to Health (mean = 3.86), World Situation (mean = 2.49) or Loss of a Loved One (mean = 1.57). However, first-time visitors rated themselves significantly higher with respect to problems associated with Alcohol/Drug Dependency (means 1.69 vs. 1.45, F = 5.77, df = 1,493, p < .02), Work (means 2.75 vs. 2.35, F = 14.49, df = 1,501, p < .000), and Family (means 2.04 vs. 1.74, F = 10.49, df = 1,496, p < .001).

Several of the problem domains played a role in explaining the motivations for going on retreat. The results in Table 3 are based on separate regression analyses for first-time and repeat visitors using the six problem domains as predictors of each of the four motivation factors. Table 3 does not include Spirituality or Beauty as the problem domains did not play a significant role with respect to either of these. The Compatibility motivation, by contrast, was strongly related to the problem areas. Understandably, those facing problems are more likely to feel a need to take stock of their life. For both first-time and repeat visitors, both the Family and Work domains were significant factors in explaining Compatibility. For the repeat visitors, furthermore, alcohol/drug dependency issues, as well as poor health, were additional factors relating to the Compatibility motivation.

Table 3
Problem Domains as Predictors of Motivations to do a Retest for First Time and Repeat Visitors

	Compatibility		Being Away	
	1st time	Repeat	1st Time	Repeat
Family	.25**	.15*		.12*
Work	.21**	.17**		.23***
Health		−.13*		
Alcohol		.13*		
Loss loved one				
World situation				
Adjusted R^2	.10	.09		.07
p	.001	.000	Ns	.000
F	4.04	6.38		4.78
df	6,152	6,307		6,309

Notes: Significant ($p < .05$) standardized beta-coefficients are reported *$p = .05$, **$p = .01$, ***$p = .001$.

Problem domains were not significant in regression models for Beauty or Spirituality.

The Retreat Experience

The guests at Benedictine monasteries are free to fill their time in any way they wish. As described earlier, community prayer is offered seven times during the day. There are also many settings available for personal prayer. The survey asked respondents to rate (using a five-point scale) how often they participated in each of seventeen activities during their stay. "Attending Mass" received the highest mean (4.06), followed by "rest" (mean = 3.98) and "meditation" (mean = 3.87). The least frequent activities (means below 2.0) are also worth mentioning. Professional work (mean = 1.50) was certainly not a frequent activity, nor was saying the rosary (mean = 1.79). Vigils (mean = 1.82), the first office of the day, recited at 5 a.m., seems to attract few visitors.

Factor analysis (principal components with varimax rotation) of the activity items yielded two factors (Table 4) divided along the lines of Community and Individual Prayer. These were somewhat correlated ($r = .34$). Repeat visitors scored significantly higher ($p < .003$) than first-time visitors on each of these factors (means: 3.59 and 3.24, $F = 9.21$, $df = 1,516$ for Community Prayer, and means: 3.37 and 3.08, $F = 11.43$, $df = 1,514$ for Individual Prayer).

Table 4
Factor Analysis of Retreat Activities

Activities	Factor loadings	
	Community Prayer	Individual Prayer
Vespers	.85	
Compline	.80	
Lauds	.77	
Mass	.76	
Tierce	.66	
Personal prayer in my room		.73
Meditation		.69
Personal prayer at church		.68
Personal prayer at the hosts' shrine		.64
Spiritual reading		.57
% Variance	30.86	22.90
Alpha coefficient	.84	.70
Mean rating	3.48	3.28

Notes: Principal components analysis with varimax rotation. Loadings ≥ .45 are shown.

Motivations, Problems, and Retreat Activities

Respondents' personal problems played a relatively minor role in distinguishing among the activities they sought while on retreat. Separate regression analyses were computed for first time and repeat visitors using the six "problem" domains included in Table 3. For repeat visitors, work-related problems were significant predictors of Community Prayers as well as Resting. By contrast, repeat visitors facing alcohol/drug dependency problems and those not particularly worried about the world situation were more likely to seek Individual Prayer. Each of these analyses accounted for small amounts of variance (adjusted R^2 = .04 in each case). None of the analyses was significant for first time visitors.

The story is more interesting with respect to motivations for going on retreat (Table 5). The desire for Spirituality played an important role as a motivation for both individual and community prayer for the newcomers and experienced visitors. For the latter group, the quest for the fascination and aesthetic aspects of the retreat (i.e., Beauty) was fulfilled both by taking part in community prayer and by time for resting. Understandably, Being Away was the major motivation influencing retreat time for resting, for both first-time and repeat visitors. It is the factor most closely related to seeking respite. However, for repeat visitors seeking a chance to be away, neither individual nor community prayer is a likely activity. Compatibility played an interesting role for the repeat visitors. The desire for time for reflection was better matched by the chance to rest and by individual prayer and less likely to be achieved through participation in community prayer. Particularly striking in these results are the high adjusted R2 values, with between 11 percent and 33 percent of the variance accounted for by the four motivation factors in explaining respondents' activities during retreat.

Table 5
Motivations as Predictors of Retreat Activities for First Time and Repeat Visitors

Motivations	Community Prayer		Individual Prayer		Resting	
	1st time	Repeat	1st time	Repeat	1st time	Repeat
Spirituality	.37***	.42***	.58***	.54***		-.28***
Beauty		.21**				.14*
Compatibility		-.14*		.19***		.22***
Being Away		.29***		-.25***	.55***	.34***
Adjusted R^2	.11	.19	.31	.33	.29	.28
p	.000	.000	.000	.000	.000	.000
F	6.23	21.30	19.67	45.58	17.60	33.17
df	4,160	4,334	4,161	4,332	4,156	4,325

Notes: Significant (p < 05) standardized beta-coefficients are reported *p = .05, **p = .01, ***p = .001.

Outcome Measures

Over the last 75 years, many guests at SBL have left testimonies of their gratitude for the opportunity to spend time at the monastery. The high rating respondents gave to the survey item about their "satisfaction with this retreat" (mean = 4.57 on five-point scale) is thus hardly surprising.

Respondents were asked to rate (using a five-point scale) seventeen adjectives that might be descriptive of their mental state as the retreat was coming to an end. None of these received as high a rating as the "satisfaction" item, but several received very high endorsement (e.g., "relaxed," "positive," "rested," and "clear headed" all had means around 4.2) The four adjectives receiving very low ratings (between 1.36 and 1.77) were "irritable," "disorganized," "tormented," and "distracted."

Factor analysis of these seventeen items (principal components with varimax rotation) yielded three coherent factors (Table 6). The four lowest-rated items formed one of these factors (i.e., Inability to Focus). The other two factors differentiate between two positive states: one related to the tranquility and interior peacefulness that a retreat affords (Peace), and the other to the sense of competence and alertness that can come from restored attentional capacity (Competence). In fact, all three factors shed light not only on the profound effects that can be achieved through the respite provided by the retreat experience, but also on the possibility that the recovery of attention can be influenced in diverse ways.

The two positive factors, Peace and Competence, are somewhat correlated (r = .57). The sample as a whole found the retreat high on Peace (mean = 4.18), an expression of the restorative aspects of a retreat, and low on the qualities described by Inability to Focus (mean = 1.54). The Competent dimension (mean = 3.70) was more middling, although one of the items, "positive", received very high ratings (mean = 4.20).

Ratings of the four outcome factors (Satisfaction, Peace, Competence, and Inability to Focus) were not significantly different for repeat and first-time visitors. Nor did these ratings differ as a function of age, how long respondents had been visiting SBL, or the frequency of their retreats.

Relation of Problems, Reasons, and Activities to Outcomes

The problem domains, motivations for going on retreat, and the activities experienced during the retreat are likely to have some effect on the guests' satisfaction with their time at SBL as well as their assessment of their psychological state as the retreat ended. While the outcome measures were similar for the newcomers and the experienced respondents, the role of the various explanatory factors differed substantially. This is hardly surprising; experience with the retreat setting, ritual, and the opportunities it affords would be expected to lead to different reasons for coming and to different ways that time is spent while on retreat.

Table 6
Factor Analysis of Retreat Effects

Adjectives	Factor Loadings		
	Peace	Competence	Inability to Focus
Rested	.80		
Relaxed	.77		
Comfortable	.63		
Clear-headed	.63		
Efficient		.77	
Competent		.68	
Alert		.67	
Attentive		.55	
Positive		.50	
Distracted			.75
Irritable			.73
Tormented			.72
Disorganized			.71
% Variance	19.51	18.68	17.62
Alpha coefficient	.77	.73	.72
Mean rating	4.18	3.70	1.54

Notes: Principal components analysis with varimax rotation. Loadings ≥ .45 are shown.

Regression analyses were performed separately for the first-time and repeat visitors for each of the four outcome measures. Table 7 shows the significant predictors for the analyses using (a) the six problem domains, (b) four reasons factors, and (c) three kinds of activities. The variables that were significant in these analyses were used to build the final regression models for each outcome measure (Table 8). The significant results in Table 8 are shown graphically in Fig. 1.

Table 7
Results from Separate Regression Analyses Using Problem Domains, Motivations, and Activities to Predict Each Outcome Measure for First Time and Repeat Visitors

	Satisfaction		Peace		Competence		Inability to Focus	
	1st time	Repeat	1st time	Repeat	1st time	Repeat	1st time	Repeat
Problems:								
Family							.31***	
Work								.12*
Health		.16**						-.12*
Alcohol								.15**
Loss		-.12*						
World								
Adj R^2	ns	.06	ns	ns	ns	Ns	.11	.10
p		.001					.001	.000
F		4.15					4.24	6.77
Df		6,305					6, 154	6,303
Motivations:								
Spirituality	.25**	.17**	.18*		.21*			-.14*
Beauty				.25***		.24***		
Compatibility							.29**	.26***
Being Away	.17*		.25**					
Adj R^2	.09	.03	.09	.07	.13	.12	.04	.06
ϱ	.001	.005	.001	.000	.000	.000	.026	.000
F	5.04	3.84	5.11	7.35	7.04	12.20	2.85	5.94
df	4,160	4,326	4,160	4,332	4,160	4,330	4,158	4,320
Activities:								
Community		.14*	.22**	.12*	.19*			
Individual	.16*					.15*		
Resting			25***	.22***				
Adj R^2	.04	.03	.11	.05	.05	.03		
ϱ	.023	.011	.000	.000	.009	.006	ns	ns
F	3.28	3.78	7.77	6.61	3.96	4.20		
df	3,157	3,320	3,158	3,327	3,158	3,325		

Notes: Principal Significant ($\varrho < .05$) standardized beta-coefficients are reported
*$\varrho = .05$, **$\varrho = .01$, ***$\varrho = .001$.

Table 8
Results from Regression Analyses Based on Significant Predictors in Table 7 for each Outcome Measure for First Time and Repeat Visitors

	Satisfaction		Peace		Competence		Inability to Focus	
	1st time	Repeat	1st time	Repeat	1st time	Repeat	1st time	Repeat
Problems:								
Family								
Work							.28***	
Health		.16**						.13*
Loss		-.15**						-.11*
World								.14*
Reasons:								
Spirituality	.19	.16**	ns		.26***			ns
Beauty				.20***		.33***		
Compatibility							ns	.21***
Being Away	.21**		ns					
Activities:								
Community			.20*	ns	ns			
Individual	Ns					.12*		
Resting		Ns	ns	.15*				
Adj. R²	.10	.10	.12	.08	.10	.12	.11	.12
ϱ	.000	.000	.000	.000	.000	.000	.001	.000
F	6.93	9.42	6.64	11.81	10.43	24.88	10.76	9.29
df	3,163	4,313	4,156	3,326	2,163	2,335	2,159	5,311

Notes: Significant (ϱ < .05) standardized beta-coefficients are reported *ϱ = .05, **ϱ = .01, ***ϱ = .001.

no = variables in regression model that were not significant.

Fig. 1 makes several findings quickly apparent. The pattern of relationships for the first-time visitors and the repeat visitors has little overlap. For the first-time visitors, the number of significant relationships was sparse; generally, only one predictor played a role for each outcome measure. In contrast, for the repeat visitors, there were significant relationships between two and four predictors and each of the four outcomes. Nonetheless, as Table 8 shows, the amount of variance accounted for was quite similar for the first-time and repeat visitors for each of the outcome measures (between eight percent and 12 percent).

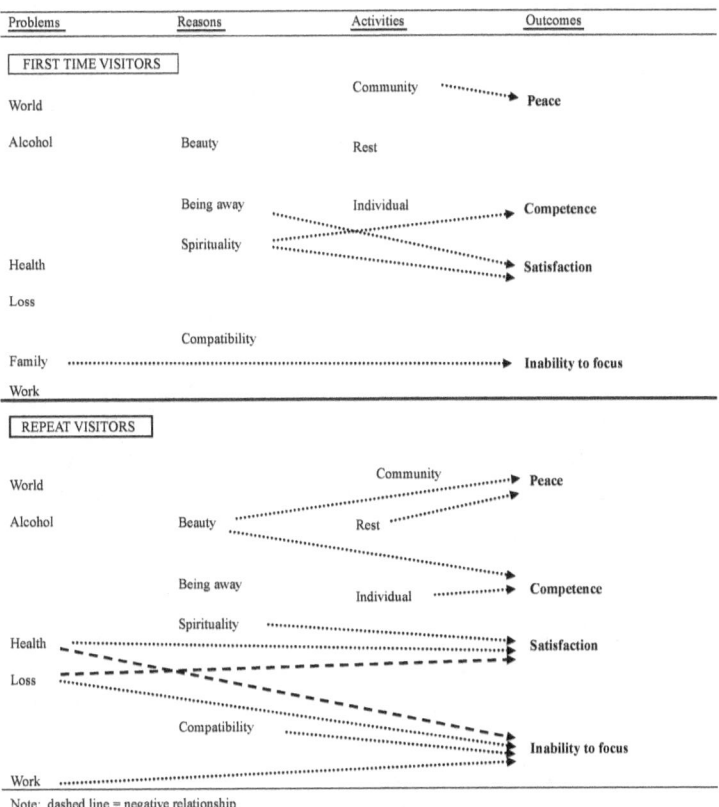

Figure 1. Significant predictors of outcome measures in final regression models for first time and repeat visitors. (Constructs positioned to facilitate comparison.)

Table 8 and Fig. 1 also help our understanding of the distinct roles played by the outcome measures. The desire for a spiritual experience played an equivalent role with respect to overall satisfaction for the novice and experienced visitor. For the novice, satisfaction was also enhanced by the desire to be away from the daily demands and turmoil of life. Being Away, interestingly, did not play a significant role in the final regression models for the repeat visitor. For this group, satisfaction was greater for those who were not struggling with a recent loss and for individuals in good health. Several problem domains (i.e., poor health, the psychological weight of a recent loss, and work-related problems) were important factors in repeat visitors' sense that they could not focus. Not surprisingly, those less able to focus indicated they sought a time to tune into their own problems (i.e., compatibility). As we saw in Table 3, however, these same problem domains were predictors of compatibility as a reason to go on retreat. In other words, individuals with more personal struggles may be especially looking to the retreat as a time to reflect and seek solutions. Those who have been on retreats before may have found this a particularly compelling place for such reflection. That does not mean, however, that after three days their problems are resolved. One might even wonder whether, at the time they complete the survey, the thought of leaving the monastic setting and returning to those problems adds to their pain.

The sense of competence was fostered by the quest for spirituality for the newcomers. For repeat visitors, it was a desire for the aesthetic aspects of the retreat, the opportunity to explore, to be in a beautiful setting, and to enjoy the chants. Time for individual prayer also enhanced the sense of competence for this group. Tranquility and a sense of inner peacefulness were derived from experiencing community prayer for the first-time visitors, while opportunity to rest and to explore a fascinating place played the strongest role in fostering tranquility for the experienced visitors.

Changes Over Time

Visitors who had been at SBL previously were asked to complete a final section of the survey. To gain a better understanding of the perceived changes in motivation over the time they had been going on retreat, this section included a pair of questions. The first one asked respondents to "think back to *your earlier* stays at the monastery" and indicate the extent to which each of six statements reflected their reasons for visiting (1 = "not at all" to 5 = "very much"). The second question included the same six statements, but asked whether these reasons had changed (1 = "much less now" to 5 = "much more now"). Table 9 provides the six statements and the comparison in ratings.

The three statements with the highest means to the first question share a religious focus. As Table 9 shows, these were also the three items that respondents rated as substantially *more* important to them now as in their earlier visits. In other words, they perceive their reasons for repeated visits as increasingly tied to the quest for spirituality, opportunities for prayer, and participation in the religious life of the monastery. By contrast, "relief from stress" and "make a decision" were seen as somewhat less important than they had been earlier (i.e., means below the scale mid-point).

Table 9
Comparison of Motivation between Earlier and Current Retreats

Reasons for coming back	N	First retreat[a]		Last retreat[b]	
		M	S.D.	M	S.D.
Spiritual reasons	327	4.28	1.01	3.77	0.99
Praying	325	4.10	1.17	3.70	1.02
Attending religious offices	325	3.90	1.18	3.49	1.08
Taking stock of myself	312	3.71	1.20	3.26	1.02
Relief from stress	313	3.53	1.36	2.88	1.14
Make a decision	309	3.11	1.38	2.89	1.10

[a] Scale: 1 = not at all …5 = very much.
[b] Scale: 1 = much less …5 = much more.

We also performed a series of regression analyses to see the relative importance of the frequency of the visits, their time span (i.e., how many years they had been visiting), and the respondents' age. (The latter two variables have a correlation of .31). These analyses were repeated using each of the four motivation factors, three types of activity, and four outcome measures as dependent variables. None of the regression analyses related to outcome measures was significant, nor were the ones with Resting or Compatibility as the dependent measures. For the five analyses with significant results, relatively little of the variance was attributable to these predictors (adjusted R^2 between .04 and .07).

The number of years respondents had been visiting was significant in only one of these analyses, namely in predicting the role of Spirituality as a motivation for visiting. The frequency of visits, by contrast, was significant with respect to each of the motivation factors except for Compatibility. In other words, those who visit most frequently are more likely to desire a time to be away and seek opportunities to appreciate the beauty of the place and its offerings, as well as seek the spiritual advantages of the retreat. The frequent visitors, as well as the older ones, are more likely to engage in both community and individual prayer. The younger visitors are more likely to see it as a time to be away.

Some of the respondents had returned to SBL for over 100 visits. Ninety-four men indicated that they had returned three or more times a year for at least two decades; twenty-one of these have done so for 40 or more years! Yet neither their age nor the number of times they had visited served as significant predictors of their assessment of how much the visits "contributed to enriching your spiritual life," "brought you serenity and peace," or of the positive effects of the retreat once back home. The frequency of the visits was, however, a significant positive predictor for each of these items. As would be expected, the means for each of these questions was very high (between 4.35 and 4.45 on a five-point scale).

Conclusions

The study offers insights into restorative experience in a context that has received little if any prior attention. Religious retreats draw thousands of individuals from all walks of life. They clearly play an important and revitalizing role. The study thus expands on previous work on restorative environments in several respects. The context of a monastic retreat provides the opportunity to examine restoration in general and ART in particular in a spiritual context. Furthermore, the participants' broad range of experience with this setting allows examination of the progression of the restorative process – albeit in a very special context.

Before exploring these themes further, it is important to acknowledge some major limitations of the study. Not only is it based exclusively on self-reports; some of the questions are also retrospective. In other words, respondents were asked to think back to their prior visits, their reasons for visiting, and the problems that were on their minds. While completing a survey may be intrusive in a setting such as this, the response rate would suggest otherwise. Also, as previously suggested, the very act of responding to the survey could have hastened the transition to the everyday world the visitors would soon confront.

Nonetheless, the survey data bear many similarities to the spontaneous comments that guests have left in the past. Getting away from stressful lifestyles and the desire for a spiritual experience are oft-repeated themes in these comments. The awe-inspiring, spiritually rich, serene, and beautiful setting makes the monastic retreat a meaningful and enriching restorative experience.

The Role of Experience

People seek a retreat for a variety of reasons. Some arrive with many burdens and struggles, hoping to find a place to sort things out. Others arrive in better physical and psychological health, yet no less needy of taking stock of their lives. The choice of a monastery would suggest that faith, prayer, and a spiritual quest are intrinsic to the decision for a retreat.

While these factors would be true for all the respondents, one would also expect that the retreat becomes an entirely different experience with repeated visits. The many aspects of the experience that may have been strange at first become familiar and comfortable. Returning visitors have greater familiarity with the highly-structured rhythm of the day and the totally unstructured time between the religious offices, with silence punctuated by the resonance of Gregorian chants, along with the beauty and serenity of the abbey and its surroundings. They have a better sense for how and when to interface with the monks. They also may have a keener understanding of the time course of their own reflection and a deeper awareness of their own spirituality.

It is thus not surprising that the results show strong developmental trends, both between the initial visit and later ones, and over time as guests return to the monastery for reflection and restoration. Experience leads to different patterns of reasons for visiting and to different patterns of activities while on retreat. Spirituality is a major motivation for going on retreat and becomes an even more dominant factor the more frequent the visits. For repeat visitors, the problems on their mind seem to play a particularly important role in seeking a time to be in tune with their thoughts, away from their daily turmoil. Time to be close to nature and to explore a "wonderful place" became increasingly important. And witnessing the beauty increases the sense of tranquility and personal competence.

For the novice guests, Being Away and Spirituality were particularly important factors for going on retreat, and these were especially influential in both their satisfaction with the experience and sense of competence. By contrast, the quest for beauty and its impacts come with increased experience. At the same time, for the returning visitors, Being Away was unrelated to any of the outcome measures. Being Away focuses on *not* being around the everyday pressures, but it lacks a clear sense for what the "away" environment might contribute. As the repeat visitors discover, a truly restorative environment is not simply away; it has special properties that make a major contribution to its effectiveness.

While there are many differences between the first-time and repeat visitors, the similarities are also noteworthy. In particular, the two groups were similar in their very high satisfaction with the retreat experience; further, their desire for spirituality was a significant factor in their satisfaction. Nor did the groups differ with respect to their sense of peace, competence, and ability to focus at the end of their stay. And while both individual and communal prayer played a more major role for the repeat visitors, the groups did not differ in the central role of time for rest and meditation during the retreat. Clearly the retreat is an important time for taking stock of life in a highly meaningful spiritual setting.

Restoration in a Spiritual Context

Restoration refers to an important and, until relatively recently, neglected concept in the behavioral sciences. ART has been useful in providing a framework for research on the effects of restoration and in identifying contexts in which restoration might occur. It has fared relatively well in terms of empirical support. At the same time, with numerous issues far from settled, it is still a growing and evolving theory.

One purpose of the present study was to contribute to the development of ART. The focus of the study, however, was on restoration in a highly specific context. Thus we would expect the motivational factors obtained to reflect the context, while at the same time supporting the general themes proposed by ART. Within the constraints of such translation between the general and the context-specific, the findings with respect to motivations for going on retreat support the previously postulated properties of restorative experiences; in several cases, they also extend them in instructive new ways.

Being Away, long a part of the literature on recreation and leisure, is intuitively attractive as an explanation for seeking restoration. At the same time, however, it is insufficient for understanding what it takes to gather one's resources and to think about difficult matters.

While the Compatibility dimension has a specific focus on the conditions necessary for reflection, it parallels the Compatibility concept in ART. It clearly captures the idea that the setting not only permits, but also supports, the visitors in achieving the goals for which they came. Since experience should permit a better match between goals and available possibilities, the fact that compatibility played a particularly important role for repeat visitors is consistent with what one would expect.

Beauty, a dimension not seen in previous studies, represents a synthesis that is interesting and thought-provoking. It combines the ART process-oriented properties of Fascination and Extent, along with the content-oriented dimension of aesthetics. In previous empirical work on restorative environments, content is either expressed in a nature versus non-nature contrast or it has been taken for granted, with nature as the sole context represented. Here we see not only natural beauty but several other kinds of beauty expressed as well. There is even a more conceptual beauty, as reflected by the item "provides a sense of community belonging." The combination of fascination and extent, along with these aesthetic aspects, effectively captures the ART concept of soft fascination and its role in the context of reflection. This suggests the potential contribution of research with a specific focus on soft fascination and the value of incorporating this concept more centrally in the ART framework.

Spirituality has not been explored in the previous empirical work on ART and restoration. While its role and interpretation also require further research, the study's findings point to a new direction that is of great interest and importance. To understand the potential role of the spiritual dimension, it may be helpful to return to the underlying notions of the attention restoration theory. Recall that unlike involuntary attention, directed attention requires effort. The expenditure of such effort, if extensive, leads to fatigue of this precious resource. With maturity, one learns that minor issues one can do nothing about are often not worth the struggle; in this way, resignation can be resource preserving. Important matters, by contrast, are difficult to banish from the mind. Thus, attempting to solve a problem where one is essentially helpless can lead to unending struggle, and hence to the chronic drain of one's attentional resources. Helplessness with respect to important issues is thus a particularly costly state of mind.

A spiritual perspective may make it possible to reframe the situation and set aside the struggle. People in restorative environments may develop insights about their lives, leading to the discovery of new spiritual dimensions. They may find reassurance in the belief that there are powerful forces in the world that are beyond one's understanding, that one is not alone, and as Miller (1995) pointed out, that one's well intended efforts for good do matter. In addition, many spiritual perspectives would point out that the world is not random, that there is a broader framework that rewards good, and that at some level or in some way the universe is fair after all. In this way, despite one's limited power and the vast and unpredictable forces that exist in the world, one can nonetheless achieve a measure of tranquility. Thus the way belief systems can reframe disturbing or unsettling aspects of one's existence may point to important cognitive dimensions that are complementary to the environmental focus that has previously characterized research in this area.

Such spiritual yearnings, or transcendent experiences, are often distinct from the organized practice of religion. While receiving guests' rests on the Benedictine theology of hospitality, guest-masters in monasteries can attest that their increasing clientele are not necessarily practicing Christians or even Christians. For many monastery guests the retreat is, however, a spiritual quest.

Thus the findings of this study both support and transcend the ART hypothesis that meditation can serve a restorative role and can be facilitated by the content and process dimensions first identified in nature-based restorative environments. The findings also support the usefulness of the soft fascination concept in a context where the aesthetic elements include but go beyond natural environment properties. And finally, the findings point to the relatively unexplored role of experience and familiarity as potential contributors to a richer and more profound restorative experience.

Acknowledgment

The authors wish to thank Dom Raymond Carette O.S.B., guest-master at the Abbaye Saint-Benoit, for his significant conceptual contribution to this study and for having assumed the responsibility of the data gathering process.

References

Canin, L.H. (1991). *Psychological restoration among AIDS caregivers*: Maintaining self-care. (Unpublished doctoral dissertation). University of Michigan, Ann Arbor, MI.

Cimprich, B. (1993). Development of an intervention to restore attention in cancer patients. *Cancer Nursing* 16(2), 83–92.

Cimprich, B. (1999). Pre-treatment symptom distress in women newly diagnosed with breast cancer. *Cancer Nursing* 22, 185–194.

Edwards, T.E. (1998). Get thee to a monastery. *Time Magazine* 5, 52–54.

Faber Taylor, A., Kuo, F.E., & Sullivan, W.C. (2002). Views of nature and self-discipline: Evidence from inner city children. *Journal of Environmental Psychology* 22, 49–63.

Hartig, T. (Ed.). (2001). Guest editor's introduction. *Environment and Behavior* 33, 475–480.

Hartig, T., Evans, G. W., Jamner, L.D., Davis, D.S., & Gärling, T. (2003). Tracking restoration in natural and urban field settings. *Journal of Environmental Psychology* 23, 109–124.

Hartig, T., Korpela, K., Evans, G. W., & Gärling, T. (1997). A measure of restorative quality in environments. *Scandinavian Housing and Planning Research* 14, 175–194.

Hartig, T., Mang, M., & Evans, G.W. (1991). Restorative effects of natural environment experiences. *Environment and Behavior* 23, 3–26.

Hartig, T., & Staats, H. (Eds.). (2003). Guest editors' introduction: Restorative environments. *Journal of Environmental Psychology* 23, 103–107.

Heintzman, P. (2002). A conceptual model of leisure and spiritual well-being. *Journal of Park and Recreation Administration* 20(4), 147–169.

Herzog, T.R. (2002). Perception of the restorative potential of natural and other settings. *Journal of Environmental Psychology* 22(3), 295–306.

Herzog, T.R., Black, A.M., Fountaine, K.A., & Knotts, D.J. (1997). Reflection and attentional recovery as distinctive benefits of restorative environments. *Journal of Environmental Psychology* 17, 165–170.

Hillery, G.A. (1992). *The monastery: A study in freedom, love, and community.* Westport, CT: Praeger.

James, W. (1892). *Psychology: The briefer course.* New York: Holt.

Kaplan, R. (1973). Some psychological benefits of gardening. *Environment and Behavior* 5, 145–162.

Kaplan, R. (1993). The role of nature in the context of the workplace. *Landscape and Urban Planning* 26, 193–201.

Kaplan, R. (2001). The nature of the view from home: Psychological benefits. *Environment and Behavior* 33(4), 507–542.

Kaplan, S. (1995). The restorative benefits of nature: Toward an integrative framework. *Journal of Environmental Psychology* 15, 169–182.

Kaplan, S. (2001). Meditation, restoration and the management of mental fatigue. *Environment and Behavior* 33(4), 480–506.

Kaplan, R., & Kaplan, S. (1989). *The experience of nature: A psychological perspective.* New York: Cambridge University Press.

Kaplan, S., & Kaplan, R. (2003). Health, supportive environments, and the Reasonable Person Model. *American Journal of Public Health* 93(9), 1484–1489.

Kaplan, S., & Talbot, J.F. (1983). Psychological benefits of wilderness experience. In I. Altman & J. F. Wohlwill (Eds.), *Behavior and the natural environment* (pp. 163–203). New York: Plenum.

Kuo, F.E. (2001). Coping with poverty: Impacts of environment and attention in the inner city. *Environment and Behavior* 33, 5–34.

Kuo, F.E., & Faber Taylor, A. (2004). A potential natural treatment for attention-deficit/hyperactivity disorder: Evidence from a national study. *American Journal of Public Health* 94(9), 1580–1586.

Kuo, F.E., & Sullivan, W.C. (2001). Aggression and violence in the inner city: Impacts of environment via mental fatigue. *Environment and Behavior* 33, 543–571.

Laumann, K., Gärling, T., & Stomark, K.M. (2001). Rating scale measures of restorative components of environments. *Journal of Environmental*

Psychology 21, 33–44.

Miller, T. (1995). *How to want what you have: Discovering the magic and grandeur of ordinary existence.* New York: Holt.

Retreats International. (2012). Retreatsintl.org. Retrieved on August 10, 2012 from: http://www.retreatsintl.org/

Retreats Online. (2012). Retreats Online. Retrieved on August 10, 2012 from: http://www.retreatsonline.com/

Reidhead, V., & Reidhead, M. (2001). Church, state, and elder health and spirituality measurement for public policy. Public Research Policy Center. Retrieved on January 15, 2004, from: http://www.umsl.edu/services/pprc/data/research_002_church_state_elder.pdf

Tennessen, C.M., & Cimprich, B. (1995). Views to nature: Effects on attention. *Journal of Environmental Psychology* 15, 77–85.

Chapter 13
LEISURE STUDIES AND SPIRITUALITY: A CHRISTIAN CRITIQUE

Paul Heintzman

An Overview

Conceptual discussions of leisure have often had spiritual overtones or linked leisure with spirituality (Heintzman, 2003). This link is especially true of the state-of-being concept of leisure that Kraus (1990) defined as "a spiritual and mental attitude, a state of inward calm, contemplation, serenity, and openness" (p. 49). Contemporary leisure scholars have stressed the importance of the connection between leisure and spirituality. Parker (1976) noted that "Separated from . . . [a] spiritual view, the idea of recreation has the aimless circularity of simply restoring us to a state in which we can best continue our work" (p. 107). Godbey (1989) wrote, "Recreation and leisure behaviour is ultimately infinite, nonrational, and full of meaning which is, or can be, spiritual" (p. 622). "Leisure worthy of the name," stated Goodale (1994), "must be filled with purpose, compelled by love, and wrapped in the cosmic and the spiritual" (p. 2). Within the therapeutic recreation field, Howe-Murphy and Murphy (1987) suggested that the leisure experience is characterized by a mystical or spiritual feeling of being connected with oneself, with all else, and a sense of oneness with the universe. In a paper on leisure counselling, McDowell (1986) wrote:

> Leisure awareness must include the awareness and expression of one's sense of spirit. . . . The greatest challenge of the leisure profession as a whole, and therapeutic recreators specifically, is to know the spirit well . . . this spirit is the life force energy behind the hope and will that heals and keeps one well. It is what makes leisure Leisure, not as something you do, but as something you feel deeply inside. (p. 37)

Revised version of paper presented at the 1998 conference.

Discussion of leisure and spirituality has now gone beyond brief conceptual associations of the two ideas. The links between the two concepts are becoming widely recognized and discussed in a wide range of recreation and leisure studies areas: therapeutic recreation, camping, recreational land management, outdoor/experiential/adventure/environmental education, tourism, and community recreation (Heintzman, 2003). In addition, there is increasing social scientific interest in the relationship between leisure and spirituality. As part of a larger work on the benefits of leisure, McDonald and Schreyer (1991) outlined possible spiritual benefits of leisure participation and leisure settings. Subsequently, in their edited book *Nature and the Human Spirit*, Driver, Dustin, Baltic, Elsner, and Peterson (1996) explored the "spiritual meanings that nature holds for human beings" in the hope that "a more thorough understanding of these meanings could improve management of public lands" (p. 3).

Increasingly, empirical research is being conducted on the relationship between leisure and spirituality (Heintzman, 2009). For example, in a quantitative study with a sample of 219 people, Ragheb (1993) investigated whether leisure participation and satisfaction were related to perceived wellness, including spiritual wellness. Frequency of leisure participation and level of leisure satisfaction were found to be positively associated with perceived wellness and all of its components. Higher levels of satisfaction with the relaxational and aesthetic-environmental components of leisure were dominant in their contributions to perceived wellness, including spiritual wellness. Heintzman and Mannell (1999) conducted a more comprehensive study with 268 participants that investigated the relationships between four dimensions of leisure (activity, motivation, setting, time) and spiritual wellbeing. Significant positive relationships were found between spiritual wellbeing and overall leisure activity participation, as well as engagement in the leisure activity categories of personal development activities, cultural activities, outdoor activities, and hobbies. Higher levels of leisure motivation were associated with spiritual wellbeing, as was leisure engaged in for intellectual and stimulus-avoidance motives. Those who pursued leisure in quiet urban recreation areas and their own homes reported higher levels of spiritual health. Heintzman (2000) conducted a qualitative study with eight people who had an expressed interest in spirituality to uncover the processes that link leisure with spiritual wellbeing. Participants associated their leisure experiences and activities with their spirituality, and it was found that:

> An attitude of openness, balance in life, nature settings, settings of personal or human history, settings of quiet, solitude and silence, and "true to self"

activities were all conducive to spiritual well-being, while busyness, noisy settings and activities, and incongruent activities were detrimental. . . . (Heintzman, 2000, p. 69)

Using a phenomenological approach, Schmidt and Little (2007) explored the spiritual dimension of leisure experiences for 24 self-selected individuals. They observed that the spiritual dimension of leisure experiences involved four triggers (e.g., nature, newness and difference, challenge, ritual and tradition), responses (e.g., emotion and sensation, struggle for control, overcoming, reflection and contemplation) and outcomes (e.g., awareness, connection, growth, freedom).

Leisure and Spirituality: Christian Responses

How should Christians view the increased social scientific interest in the relationship between leisure and spirituality? Various viewpoints seem to exist. Several years ago, a discussion related to spirituality took place on the Christian Recreation Listserv, a listserv administered by Baylor University. Approximately 50 people from various Christian traditions subscribed to this listserv. The dialogue on spirituality reflected a number of different views of how Christians understand the relationship between leisure and spirituality. The discussion was initiated by a student doing her honor's thesis on spirituality in the wilderness: in particular, the spiritual meaning of a wilderness canoe trip for Christians. She defined "spirituality as the essence of relating to God, to ourselves, to others, and to our environment. Spirituality is revealed through these relationships" (Walters, 1997). Responses varied. Some believed that spiritual experiences are not possible without God: "Can one have a spiritual experience without the presence of God? Personally, I don't think so. We all know that it is possible (and a common occurrence) to get that 'feel good, really swell' feeling about something, but without Christ as the foundation, what is the basis of that feeling?" (Egerton, 1997). In a similar vein, some wanted to have nothing to do with non-Christian spirituality, and lamented the fact that Christians have not taken advantage of this opportunity: "I would enjoy hearing more . . . unless you are talking about worshipping trees, birds, & dirt" (Weathersbee, 1997a); "It is unfortunate that people who are worshipping rocks & trees have seen a significant growth in the use of outdoor rec. Yet as Christians, we have not yet seemed to capitalize on the incredible Spirit facilitating that an outdoor adventure seems to bring" (Weathersbee, 1997b).

Others dichotomized spirituality into transcendent and nontranscendent components: "I know it is a little simplified, but I compartmentalize spirituality. I think of spirituality as [relating to ourselves, to others, to the environment]. I see Spirituality as the God thing" (Connally, 1997). Others also seemed to compartmentalize life: "I think that my Question is this. . . . Can something else, other than a 'spiritual' experience, be as rewarding? I think that one can have an experience that is completely away from the "Spiritual" order of things and still be a part of God's plan. For example, one of the greatest times for me to experience the Lord is when I am out on a lake with my dog looking at the ducks fly in" (Nay, 1997). In response to Nay, Wilson (1997) wrote, "I believe that if you know the Lord the experience of watching a duck land on the lake can be an instance of having the Holy Spirit speak to you. Yet if someone does not know the Lord or understand the relationship that nature has with Him then watching that instance of God's beauty would be empty just as all life without Christ is empty." In contrast, Hermann (1997) stated, "I am sure that there are people whose lives are not all empty without Christ. There are many other religions that fulfil people's needs." The initiator of the discussion stated that ". . . a spiritual experience cannot be experienced to its fullest without God. God is the thread in which all things hold together . . . a spiritual experience is not complete without the acknowledgement of God as part of it" (Walters, 1997). A more complex understanding was presented by Wilke (1997):

> It is helpful to think of Spirituality as an extended process that begins with the creation of a soul that has the imprint of God's image. Inherently from birth, life is full of events and experiences that can move one into spirituality, e.g. love or its lack, pain, again and again there is creation. This natural bent toward spiritual things is never lost, and the search for an appropriate reality does not end though it can be stagnated or diverted and often remains unfulfilled. I believe that God has a glorious plan to draw all men unto himself, and he is as present and active in the early stages of spirituality as in the "later" stages. Rebelliousness, false religions, etc. can be looked upon as the evidence of this continuing spiritual quest of people. . . . The whole business of God drawing all men unto himself is far too complex for you and I to have total knowledge about or to be skillful enough to control.

From this dialogue, we can see that Christians respond in a variety of ways: for some, Christian spirituality is the only true spirituality; some compartmentalize or dichotomize spirituality; some believe non-Christians experience spirituality; some believe that spirituality reaches its fullest potential in relationship with God; and some see spirituality as a complex process.

Leisure and Spirituality: An Opportunity for Christians

Should Christian leisure researchers see the increased interest in leisure and spirituality as an exciting opportunity to promote genuine Christian spirituality, or is it a cause for concern? Chamberlain (1997) noted that Christians should not be surprised by the increased interest in spirituality. Christians have long believed that humans are created with a capacity to relate to God, what Blaise Pascal (1670/1966) described as a craving and abyss that "can be filled only . . . by God himself" (p. 75) or what Augustine (398/1949) was thinking when he explained that the human "heart is restless" until it finds its rest in God (p. 3). If this is true, then humanity will always have a spiritual quest. The current interest in spirituality appears consistent with the human capacity to relate to God.

Peterson (as cited in Chamberlain, 1997) has suggested that the current, widespread fascination with spirituality is probably evidence of pathology, not health; sickness has provoked this fascination. According to Peterson, the materialist and temporal tendency in our society destroys two essential elements of the spiritual dimension of human life: connectedness with other humans, and the desire for transcendence. As one leisure scholar has pointed out, individuals searching to find value and meaning in life in contemporary societies have often become quite disillusioned (Compton, 1994). While technology, material wealth, and affluence have been thought to be essential components of the good life, they have not proven to be so:

> Despite the fact that we are now healthier and grow to be older, despite the fact that even the least affluent among us are surrounded by material luxuries undreamed of even a few decades ago . . . and regardless of all the stupendous scientific knowledge we can summon at will, people often end up feeling that their lives have been wasted, instead of being filled with happiness their years were spent in anxiety and boredom. (Csikszentmihalyi, 1990, p. 2)

The renewed interest in spirituality may be seen as the recognition of spiritual need and an opportunity for introducing Christian spirituality and the Christian spiritual tradition of leisure. The increasing interest in leisure and spirituality provides Christian leisure scholars with the opportunity to engage others in dialogue and to invite people to consider Christian spirituality in a way that is relevant to this spiritually conscious age. Christian leisure scholars can affirm and build upon the current academic interest in leisure and spirituality. The example of the apostle Paul is helpful. In Acts 17:16–34, we read of Paul's reaction to an idol that had the inscription "To an unknown God" (New International Version). Instead of condemning this idol as a false form of spirituality, he viewed it as an implied admission of spiritual need and openness. He took advantage of the opportunity to talk about a relationship with God through Christ as a way to meet spiritual need. This example is relevant for leisure scholars and researchers when they encounter increasing amounts of leisure literature and research that focuses on spirituality. Our overall reaction as Christians to the increased interest in leisure and spirituality ought to be positive, as it is a reflection of the universal human desire for God; however, this trend also holds several concerns for Christians.

Leisure and Spirituality: Concerns for Christians

There are at least six areas of concern within the current study of leisure and spirituality. First, there is a need to expand the interiority of contemporary discussions of leisure and spirituality and to emphasize transcendence. For example, McDonald and Schreyer (1991), in their chapter "The Spiritual Benefits of Leisure" suggested that a general definition of spirituality might be "an individual's attempt to understand his/her 'place' in the universe" (p. 179). They went on to state that "Spirit refers to the nontangible elements of existence upon which life may be presumed to be based" (p. 179). Much of the discussion of spirituality within the leisure studies field is a kind of interiority. In this view, that often omits the concept of the Divine, spirituality is basically a human dimension. In contrast, Christian spirituality is based on a trusting, obedient, and growing personal relationship with a transcendent, personal, creator God. Christian spirituality does include an inward focus and an inward transformation; however, the Christian tradition asserts that God is not fundamentally within us waiting to be discovered. Thus Christians in the leisure studies field may want to use contemporary, generic definitions of spirituality as starting points, but may want to include the notion of the divine and the notion of transcendence in any writing and research on the topic. For example, Christians may want to make use of measurement tools such as the Spiritual Well-Being Scale (Ellison & Smith, 1991) that includes a religious wellbeing subscale containing items that refer to God and assess the transcendent dimension of spirituality.

Second, contemporary discussions of leisure and spirituality often focus on the inner self, with little discussion of relationships with others or of community. The quest for spirituality is undertaken on an individual basis to gain private benefit. There is a desire to develop the inner self, to become self-actualized. However, Christian spirituality "is not a matter of individual personal development. It is growing in the body with the other members of it" (Chan, 1998, p. 110). Bernard (as quoted in Thornton, 1964, p. 25) goes so far as to say that "If anyone makes himself his own master in the spiritual life, he makes himself scholar to a fool." Hemingway (1996), a leisure studies scholar, is critical of the spiritual conceptualization of leisure as he sees it as a subjective, internal mental experience that does not place leisure against the political and social structures of modern western society. However, biblical spirituality balances an inner spiritual focus with involvement in the world: "Christian spirituality may be inward in that it consists of union with Christ and love for God, but that means it is also outward . . . active Christian life involves discipleship, and Christian spirituality must entail acting with compassion, mercy, and a desire for justice" (Grenz, 1994, pp. 35–36). Jesus stated that we are to take up our cross and follow him (e.g., Mark 8:34), and in addition to loving God, we are to love our neighbor as our self (e.g., Mark 12:31). Spiritual life includes more than personal spiritual benefits. True spirituality is expressed in social relationships and also in social justice as "an authentic spiritual life always pushes one back into the world" (Willard, 1995, p. 17).

Third, there is a need to go beyond spiritual experience to spiritual wellbeing. Immense significance is presently given to experience within discussions of leisure and spirituality. Most of the research related to leisure and spirituality emphasizes experience (e.g., Fox, 1997; Fredrickson & Anderson, 1999; Stringer & McAvoy, 1992, Schmidt & Little, 2007). Haluza-Delay (2000) criticized studies focused on spiritual experience as they focus on the immediate experience and pleasant emotional states rather than long-term consequences of the experiences and possible life transformation. The last major section of the book *Nature and the Human Spirit* (Driver et al., 1996) is a discussion of future research directions. This discussion focuses on experiences: psychologically deep experiences; optimal experiences; leisure and touristic states; religious, mystical, and spiritual experiences; nature experiences; nature-based peak experiences; hard-to-define nature-based human experiences; and nature-based spiritual experiences. While the introductory overview to this book mentions "the use of natural areas for mental wellbeing and associated effects on physical well-being" (p. 5), the notion of spiritual wellbeing is never introduced. As Grenz (1994) noted, the focus of the Christian tradition has not been to nurture spiritual experience in and of itself, but rather to foster a relationship with Jesus. Furthermore, the focus of scripture is not so much on spiritual experience, but on a lifestyle that leads to spiritual transformation (Rom. 12:1–2; 2 Cor. 3:18; Eph. 4:22–24). Spiritual experiences are not necessarily significant in a person's life unless they have a transforming impact upon the person. Chandler, Kolander, and Holden (1992) suggested that the mere occurrence of spiritual experiences does not necessarily result in spiritual development unless the experiences are dealt with and integrated into one's life. Or as John of the Cross (1589/1991) put it, "Delightful feelings do not of themselves lead the soul to God, but rather cause it to become attached to delightful feelings" (p. 747). Thus, Christians may want to go beyond research focused on spiritual experiences to research focused on spiritual wellbeing.

Social scientific study of spirituality has been developing during the past quarter century. Within this context, the concept of spiritual wellness was developed. Moberg (1971, 1974, 1978, 1979a, 1979b, 1986) stressed the role of religious and spiritual factors to wellbeing. Ellison (1983; Paloutzin & Ellison, 1982) proposed that quality of life involves material, psychological, and spiritual wellbeing, and developed the Spiritual Well-Being Scale (SWBS) to help examine this issue. Since the early 1980s, the SWBS has been used several hundreds of times in a variety of settings to study spiritual wellbeing (Ellison & Smith, 1991). The development of the concept of spiritual wellness has provided social scientists with a way of getting an empirical handle on spirituality. Despite the growing attention being given to the social scientific study of spirituality, research on the relationship between leisure and spirituality has lagged behind, as leisure researchers have struggled with how to conceptualize and measure spirituality. While scales are available for the measurement of spiritual wellbeing, they have received little use in the leisure studies field.

While the research studies that have been conducted on leisure and spirituality are interesting and suggestive, the general lack of attention to the relationship between leisure and spiritual wellness is surprising, since a popular area of current research within leisure studies is the study of the benefits of leisure that includes the connection between leisure and wellness or health. The leisure and health relationship has been identified as one of the most significant research topics that needs study (Iso-Ahola, 1988, 1994, 1997). While wellness, in a holistic sense, refers to a state of wellbeing that includes physical, mental, emotional, social, and spiritual components, little research has been conducted on the relationships between leisure and holistic wellness or the spiritual component of wellness on its own. Most contemporary leisure scholars do not even refer to all five components of health. Iso-Ahola (1997) referred to health as a "general concept that refers to the absence of illness, but it also covers the more positive aspects: physical, mental and social well-being" (p. 131). No mention is made of spiritual wellbeing. Yet if, as some writers suggest (e.g., Chandler et al., 1992), spiritual wellness is an integrative dimension of wellness, it is important that more than just the relationships between leisure and physical and mental health be investigated. A positive development is the inclusion of a chapter on leisure and spiritual health in the recent book *Leisure, Health and Wellness: Making the Connections* (Payne, Ainsworth, & Godbey, 2010). Thus, one possible direction for research on leisure and spirituality is to explore the relationship between leisure and spiritual wellness (Caldwell & Smith, 1988; Heintzman, 2000, 2002a; Heintzman & Mannell, 1999, 2003).

Fourth, most theoretical reflection on leisure and spirituality has involved nature-based recreation and spirituality. As McDonald and Schreyer (1991) noted, "Perhaps one of the most generally cited notions of extreme states of consciousness and spiritual endeavor related to leisure is the wilderness experience" (p. 184). In addition, most of the empirical studies on leisure and spirituality have explored the relationship between nature-based leisure experiences and concepts related to spirituality (e.g., Fredrickson & Anderson, 1999; Fox 1997; Heintzman, 2002b, 2007, 2008, 2010; Stringer & McAvoy, 1992; Sweatman & Heintzman, 2004). While wilderness and nature can play an important place in Christian spirituality as Bratton (1993) documented in her book *Christianity, Wilderness and Wildlife*, Christian spirituality is not limited to these places. Future research needs to place more emphasis on all forms of leisure in all settings, as opposed to an over-emphasis upon the wilderness setting, which is a setting that a great majority of the population does not visit on a regular basis.

Fifth, the clear majority of studies on leisure and spirituality have been small-scale qualitative studies (e.g., Fox 1997; Fredrickson & Anderson, 1999; Heintzman, 2000; Schmidt & Little, 2007; Stringer & McAvoy, 1992). Christianity is not tied or linked exclusively to one paradigm, one philosophy of science, or one methodology, whether it is quantitative or qualitative. Rather, Christians are concerned with truth and recognize that humans are created in the image of an infinite God. Moberg (1981) warns that anyone who sells out to one particular methodology is in danger of falling into "a form of idolatrous exclusivism, for human reality is far too complex to be covered by any one approach" (p. 213). The appropriate approach is to use many different images and models so as to increase our understanding of social reality. To understand the complexity of human behavior and human experience, including leisure, a variety of methods are required. Therefore, Christians should encourage the adoption of different ways of studying and understanding the relationship between leisure and spirituality (Heintzman, 2006).

Sixth, there is a need within the leisure studies field to make connections with 20 centuries of Christian spirituality. The spiritual conceptualization of leisure is not exclusively a twentieth century insight; long before leisure studies became a program of study in the modern university, leisure was associated with spirituality. For example, both Augustine and Aquinas saw the contemplative life, the life of leisure, as important and essential to the spiritual life. Augustine made the distinction between an active life (*vita activa*) and a contemplative life (*vita contemplativa*). The contemplative life was similar to Aristotle's Life of Contemplation and was adapted from Greek and Roman thought through the addition of Christian content. Both the active and contemplative lives were good, but the latter life was given higher status: "If no one lays the burden upon us, we should give ourselves up to leisure (*otium*) to the perception and contemplation of truth" (Augustine as quoted in Marshall, 1980, p. 7). Thomas Aquinas (1225–1274) also used Augustine's distinction of the *vita contemplativa* and *vita activa*. Aquinas, who devoted his life to the reconciliation of Aristotle's thought and the Christian faith, brought together the classical view of leisure and the contemplative life. He located Aristotle's notion of leisure and contemplation in the beatific vision of God (Owens, 1981). Both lives were accepted, but the contemplative life was truly free, while the active life was restricted by necessity: "the life of contemplation" was "simply better than the life of action" (Thomas Aquinas as quoted in Marshall, 1980, p. 8). An important theme of monastic life was that of leisure (Leclerq, 1982); *otium* came to be "fused with the contemplative life within monasteries and continued to have an association with learning" (Arnold, 1980, p. 131). This monastic life of leisure was expressed in terms such as *otium* (leisure), *quies* (quiet), *vacatio* (freedom), and *sabbatum* (rest) that were used to reinforce each other as in *otium quietis,* and *vacatio sabbati* (Leclerq, 1982). This spiritual understanding of leisure has probably been best articulated in the past century by Roman Catholic theologian Josef Pieper (1952), who wrote:

> Leisure, it must be clearly understood, is a mental and spiritual attitude – it is not simply the result of external factors, it is not the inevitable result of spare time, a holiday, a week-end or a vacation. It is in the first place, an attitude of mind, a condition of the soul . . . a receptive attitude of mind, a contemplative attitude, and it is not only the occasion but also the capacity for steeping oneself in the world of creation. (pp. 40, 41)

Pieper's work is a classic within the leisure studies field, and his definition of leisure is frequently quoted in leisure studies literature, yet there is little explanation of his definition of leisure within the context of his Christian theology or the 20 centuries of Christian tradition that shaped his understanding of leisure. The history of Christian spirituality has much to contribute to the present study of the relationship between leisure and spirituality, yet this tradition is largely ignored. In fact, some present-day findings on leisure and spirituality merely confirm what has been known throughout the history of Christian spirituality. For example, researchers (e.g., Fox, 1997; Fredrickson & Anderson, 1999; Heintzman, 2007) have found that solitude in a wilderness experience is important for participants' spirituality. Such a finding is consistent with Scripture passages such as Jesus withdrawing to the hillside to pray (e.g., Mark 6:46) and as Teaff (2006) wrote, it has long been recognized that "Christian spirituality thrives best in a leisure atmosphere where time and space are allotted for 'being' as well as 'doing'" (p. 115).

Conclusion

In conclusion, the increasing scholarly interest in leisure and spirituality presents Christian scholars and practitioners within the leisure studies and leisure services field with a tremendous opportunity and challenge to openly present a Christian understanding of leisure and spirituality. Christians have an opportunity to affirm what is valid in current discussions on the topic, to build upon what is valid, and to enter into dialogue with others. In particular, Christian leisure scholars and practitioners can critique the interiority of much current spirituality and emphasize both the transcendent and communal dimensions of Christian spirituality; critique the current fascination with spiritual experience and highlight the importance of spirituality as a lifestyle that facilitates transformation; call attention to the concept of spiritual wellbeing and the use of spiritual wellbeing scales; explore the relationship between leisure and spirituality in all forms of leisure in all settings, rather than focusing on leisure and nature-based leisure; encourage the use of a variety of methodologies to study and understand the complexity of the leisure and spirituality relationship; and draw upon 20 centuries of Christian spirituality to inform our understanding of the leisure and spirituality relationship. While there are a number of areas of concern in the present study of leisure and spirituality that Christians need to be aware of and which they need to critique, they should welcome the increasing popularity of this topic.

References

Arnold, S. (1980). The dilemma of meaning. In T.L. Goodale & P.A. Witt (Eds.), *Recreation and leisure: Issues in an era of change* (pp. 5–18). State College, PA: Venture.

Augustine. (398/1949). *The confessions of Saint Augustine* (E.B. Pusey, Trans). New York: Random House.

Bratton, S. (1993). *Christianity, wilderness, and wildlife.* Toronto: Associated University Presses.

Caldwell, L.L., & Smith, E.A. (1988). Leisure: An overlooked component of health promotion. *Canadian Journal of Public Health* 79, S43–S48.

Chamberlain, P. (1997, September/October). The quest for spirituality. *Faith Today*, pp. 22–38.

Chan, S. (1998). *Spiritual theology: A systematic study of Christian life.* Downers Grove, IL: InterVarsity.

Chandler, C.K., Holden, J.M., & Kolander, C.A. (1992). Counselling for spiritual wellness: Theory and practice. *Journal of Counselling and Development* 71, 168–175.

Compton, D.M. (1994). Leisure and mental health: Context and issues. In D.M. Compton & S.E. Iso-Ahola (Eds.), *Leisure and mental health* (Vol. I, pp. 1–33). Park City, UT: Family Development Resources.

Connally, D. (1997, September 30). Re: Spirituality. [E-mail sent to ChRec-L@baylor.edu]

Csikszentmihalyi, M. (1990). *Flow: The psychology of optimal experience.* New York: Harper & Row.

Driver, B.L., Dustin, D., Baltic, T., Elsner, G., & Peterson G. (Eds.). (1996). *Nature and the human spirit: Toward an expanded land management ethic.* State College, PA: Venture.

Egerton, A. (1997, September 30). Re: Spirituality. [E-mail sent to ChRec-L@baylor.edu]

Ellison, C.W. (1983). Spiritual well-being: Conceptualization and measurement. *Journal of Psychology and Theology* 11, 330–340.

Ellison, C.W., & Smith, J. (1991). Toward an integrative measure of health and well-being. *Journal of Psychology and Theology* 19(1), 35–48.

Fredrickson, L.M., & Anderson, D.H. (1999). A qualitative exploration of the wilderness experience as a source of spiritual inspiration. *Journal of Environmental Psychology* 19, 21–39.

Fox, R.J. (1997). Women, nature and spirituality: A qualitative study exploring women's wilderness experience. In D. Rowe & P. Brown (Eds.), *Proceedings, ANZALS conference* (pp. 59–64). Newcastle, NSW: Australian and New Zealand Association for Leisure Studies, and the Department of Leisure and Tourism Studies, The University of Newcastle.

Godbey, G. (1989). Implications of recreation and leisure research for professionals. In E.L. Jackson & T.L. Brown, (Eds.), *Understanding leisure and recreation: Mapping the past, charting the future* (pp. 613–628). State College, PA: Venture.

Goodale, T.L. (1994). *Legitimizing leisure anew*. Paper presented at the Scholarly Presentations portion of the 25th Anniversary of the Leisure Studies Department, University of Ottawa. May 14, 1994.

Grenz, S.J. (1994, May). The gospel and the contemporary pursuit of spirituality. *Touchstone*, 32–36.

Haluza-Delay, R. (2000). Green fire and religious spirit. *The Journal of Experiential Education* 23(3), 143–149.

Heintzman, P. (2000). Leisure and spiritual well-being relationships: A qualitative study. *Society and Leisure* 23(1), 41–69.

Heintzman, P. (2002a). A conceptual model of leisure and spiritual well-being. *Journal of Park and Recreation Administration* 20(4), 147–169.

Heintzman, P. (2002b). The role of introspection and spirituality in the park experience of day visitors to Ontario Provincial Parks. In S. Bondrup-Nielsen, M. Willison, N. Munro, G. Nelson, & T. Herman (Eds.), *Managing protected areas in a changing world* (pp. 992–1004). Wolfville, NS: Science and Management of Protected Areas Association.

Heintzman, P. (2003). Leisure and spirituality: The re-emergence of an historical relationship. *Parks and Recreation Canada* 60(5), 30–31.

Heintzman, P. (2006). Leisure science, dominant paradigms, and philosophy: The expansion of leisure science's horizon. In P. Heintzman, G.E. Van Andel, & T.L. Visker (Eds.), *Christianity and leisure: Issues in a pluralistic society* (Rev. ed., pp. 68–81). Sioux Center: Dordt College Press.

Heintzman, P. (2007). Men's wilderness experience and spirituality: A qualitative study. In R. Burns & K. Robinson (Comps.), *Proceedings of the 2006 Northeastern Recreation Research Symposium* (pp. 216–225) (Gen. Tech. Rep. NRS-P-14). Newton Square, PA: U.S. Department of Agriculture, Forest Services, Northern Research Station.

Heintzman, P. (2008). Men's wilderness experience and spirituality: Further explorations. In C. LeBlanc & C. Vogt (Eds.), *Proceedings of the 2007 Northeastern Recreation Research Symposium* (pp. 55–59) (Gen. Tech. Rep. NRS-P-23). Newton Square, PA: U.S. Department of Agriculture, Forest Services, Northern Research Station.

Heintzman, P. (2009). The spiritual benefits of leisure. *Leisure/Loisir* 33(1), 419–445.

Heintzman, P. (2010). Nature-based recreation and spirituality: A complex relationship. *Leisure Sciences* 32(1), 72–89.

Heintzman, P., & Mannell, R. (1999). Leisure style and spiritual well-being. In W. Stewart & D. Samdahl (Eds.), *Abstracts from the 1999 Symposium on Leisure Research* (p. 68). National Congress for Recreation and Parks, Nashville, TN. October 20–24, 1999.

Heintzman, P., & Mannell, R. (2003). Spiritual functions of leisure and spiritual well-being: Coping with time pressure. *Leisure Sciences* 25, 207–230.

Hemingway, J.L. (1996). Emancipating leisure: The recovery of freedom in leisure. *Journal of Leisure Research* 28(1), 27–43.

Hermann, J. 1997. (October 1). *Re: spirituality . . . but not really.* [E-mail sent to ChRec-L@baylor.edu]

Howe-Murphy, R., & Murphy, J. (1987). An exploration of the New Age consciousness paradigm in therapeutic recreation. In C. Sylvester, J. Hemingway, R. Howe-Murphy, K. Mobily, & P. Shank (Eds.), *Philosophy of therapeutic recreation: Ideas and issues* (pp. 71–85). Arlington, VA: National Recreation and Park Association.

Iso-Ahola, S.E. (1988). The social psychology of leisure: Past, present, and future research. In L. Barnett (Ed.), *Research about leisure: Past, present, and future* (pp. 75–93). Champaign, IL: Sagamore.

Iso-Ahola, S.E. (1994). Leisure lifestyle and health. In D.M. Compton & S.E. Iso-Ahola (Eds.), *Leisure and mental health* (Vol. I, pp. 42–60). Park City, UT: Family Development Resources.

Iso-Ahola, S.E. (1997). A psychological analysis of leisure and health. In J.T. Haworth (Ed.), *Work, leisure and well-being* (pp. 117–130). New York: Routledge.

John of the Cross, Saint. (1589/1991). Letter 13. In *The collected works of St. John of the Cross.* (K. Kavanaugh & O. Rodriquez, Trans.) (Rev. ed., pp. 746–749). Washington, DC: ICS Publications.

Kraus, R. (1990). *Recreation and leisure in modern society* (4th ed.). Toronto: Harper Collins.

Leclerq, J. (1982). *The love of learning and the desire for God: A study of monastic culture.* New York: Fordham University.

Marshall, P. (1980). Vocation, work and jobs. In P. Marshall, E. Vanderkloet, P. Nijkamp, S. Griffioen, & H. Antonides, *Labour of love: Essays on work* (pp. 1–19). Toronto: Wedge.

McDonald, B.L., & R. Schreyer. (1991). Spiritual benefits of leisure participation and leisure settings. In B.L. Driver, P.J. Brown, & G.L. Peterson, *Benefits of Leisure* (pp. 179–194). State College, PA: Venture.

McDowell, C.F. (1986). Wellness and therapeutic recreation: Challenge for service. *Therapeutic Recreation Journal* 20(2): 27–38.

Moberg, D.O. (1971). *Spiritual well-being: Background and issues.* Washington, DC: White House Conference on Aging.

Moberg, D.O. (1974). Spiritual well-being in late life. In J.F. Gubrium (Ed.), *Late life: Communities and environmental policy* (pp. 256–279). Springfield, IL: Charles C. Thomas.

Moberg, D.O. (1978). Spiritual well-being: A challenge for interdisciplinary research. *Journal of the American Scientific Affiliation* 30(2), 67–72.

Moberg, D.O. (1979a). The development of social indicators of spiritual well-being for quality of life research: Prospects and problems. *Sociological Analysis* 40, 11–26.

Moberg, D.O. (Ed.). (1979b). *Spiritual well-being*. Washington, DC: University Press of America.

Moberg, D.O. (1986). Spirituality and science. The progress, problems, and promise of scientific research on spiritual well-being. *Journal of the American Scientific Affiliation* 38(3), 186–194.

Moberg, D.O. (1981). Response to Burwell. *Christian Scholar's Review* 10(3), 209–214.

Nay, S. (1997, October 1). *Re: Spirituality*. [E-mail sent to ChRec-L@baylor.edu]

Owens, J. (1981). Aristotle on Leisure. *Canadian Journal of Philosophy* 16, 713–724.

Paloutzian, R.F., & C.W. Ellison. (1982). Loneliness, spiritual well-being, and the quality of life. In L.A. Peplau & D. Perlman (Eds.), *Loneliness: A sourcebook of current theory, research and therapy* (pp. 224–237). New York: Wiley.

Parker, S. (1976). *The sociology of leisure*. New York: International Publications Service.

Payne, L., Ainsworth, B., & Godbey, G. (Eds.). (2010). *Leisure, health, and wellness: Making the connections*. State College, PA: Venture.

Pascal, B. (1670/1966). *Pensées* (A.J. Krailsheimer, Trans.). New York: Penguin Books.

Pieper, J. (1952). *Leisure: The basis of culture* (A. Dru, Trans.). New York: Pantheon Books (1963, Random House).

Ragheb, M.G. (1993). Leisure and perceived wellness: A field investigation. *Leisure Sciences* 15, 13–24.

Schmidt, C., & Little, D.E. (2007). Qualitative insights into leisure as a spiritual experience. *Journal of Leisure Research* 39(2), 222–247.

Stringer, L.A., & McAvoy, L.H. (1992). The need for something different: Spirituality and wilderness adventure. *Journal of Experiential Education* 15(1): 13–20.

Sweatman, M., & Heintzman, P. (2004). The perceived impact of outdoor residential camp experience on the spirituality of youth. *World Leisure Journal* 46(1), 23–31.

Teaff, J. (2006). Contemplative leisure within Christian spirituality. In P. Heintzman, G.E. Van Andel, & T.L. Visker (Eds.), *Christianity and leisure: Issues in a pluralistic society*, (Rev. ed., pp. 112–115). Sioux Center: Dordt College Press.

Thornton, M. (1964). *Christian proficiency*. London: S.P.C.K.

Walters, M.M. (1997, September 30). *Spirituality*. [E-mail sent to ChRec-L@baylor.edu]

Weathersbee, B., & Weathersbee, C. (1997a, September 23). *Re: Spirituality and wilderness*. [E-mail sent to ChRec-L@baylor.edu]

Weathersbee, B., & Weathersbee, C. (1997b, September 30). *Re: Spirituality and wilderness*. [E-mail sent to ChRec-L@baylor.edu]

Willard, D. (1995, March 6). Conversations: What makes spirituality Christian? *Christianity Today* 39, 16–17.

Wilke, B. (1997, October 10). *Re: Spirituality.* [E-mail sent to ChRec-L@baylor.edu]

Wilson, S. (1997, October 1). *Re: Spirituality.* [E-mail sent to ChRec-L@baylor.edu]

Section Three

ETHICAL AND APPLIED ISSUES

The first section of this book is about leisure theory and the conceptualization of leisure from a Christian perspective. The second section includes empirical studies. This third section is primarily concerned with the ethics of leisure in general or in specific leisure and recreation contexts, activities, and settings. In Romans 12:2 Christians are instructed: "Do not conform to the pattern of this world, but be transformed by the renewing of your mind. Then you will be able to test and approve what God's will is – his good, pleasing and perfect will." And in Philippians 4:8 we read "whatever is true, whatever is noble, whatever is right, whatever is pure, whatever is lovely, whatever is admirable – if anything is excellent or praiseworthy – think about such things." The chapters in this section wrestle with how we implement these biblical principles in the activities of recreation, leisure, and play.

Some Christian authors have previously examined the ethics or morality of leisure. For example, Leland Ryken (1995), in his book *Redeeming the Time: A Christian Approach to Work and Leisure,* devotes a chapter to the ethics of leisure where he emphasizes the principles of moderation and balance. In *Free Time: Toward a Theology of Leisure,* Graham Neville (2004) asks whether leisure is beyond morality as it is an activity that is an end itself. The chapters in this section expand Christian thinking on the ethics of leisure, especially within specific contexts.

Chapter 14, by Paul Heintzman, looks at leisure in general, and proposes that the Golden Rule – do to others as you would have them do to you – is a universal standard that can be used to discern what is best in recreation within a multicultural society. The next two chapters in this section focus on play. In Chapter 15, Glen Van Andel explores how Christians can redeem play through an alternative approach so that the gift of play can find its rightful place in games, sport, and athletics. Then, in Chapter 16, Arthur Holmes investigates whether play can build character and suggests three habit-building helps related to character development: community, mentor and model, and friendship.

In Chapter 17, Bud Williams focuses more narrowly on exploring a theological perspective on risk and risk-taking to better understand how Christians should approach managing risk and participation in risk-taking activities and sports. Chapter 18, by Don DeGraaf, is focused upon how Christian recreation programmers can seek the common good in their communities and how Christian recreation and leisure studies professors can help students develop strategies to pursue the common good.

Paul Heintzman

References

Neville, G. (2004). *Free time: Toward a theology of leisure*. Birmingham, UK: University of Birmingham Press.

Ryken, L. (1995). *Redeeming the time: A Christian approach to work and leisure*. Grand Rapids: Baker.

Chapter 14
LEISURE, ETHICS, AND THE GOLDEN RULE

Paul Heintzman

As our society is undergoing multiple transformations, the very pace of change creating tension and confusion, the ethics of leisure acquires also a developmental importance. Where are we heading? In a deliberately jaundiced view, one can offer a disturbing diagnosis: Resources are vanishing. Education fails to educate. Religions are being replaced by narcissistic cults. Bureaucracies keep cloning themselves. Culture and pornography grow indistinguishable. Wealth coagulates in ever fewer hands. Creativity and productivity are declining. Contraception undercuts the will to perpetuate. . . . No need to go on. Even if half of such statements were true, there would be enough reason to be concerned. Leisure, caught in the web of these mutually reinforcing trends, risks then to become an exercise in collective hedonism. (Bregha, 1980, p. 18)

Francis Bregha's (1980) prediction that leisure has the potential to become an exercise in collective hedonism was reaffirmed by Dustin, McAvoy, and Schultz (1991) who believe that our society has, in the absence of a standard to measure the goodness of one form of recreation over another, fallen victim to the hedonist error where good is equated with pleasure. Since pleasure is viewed as an individual matter, our society has assumed that what is good for people also varies. Thus, each person is free, within certain constraints, to pursue one's own particular pleasures, while the park and recreation profession facilitates that process. It is believed that the outcomes from this process will inevitably be good.

The notion that what is good for people is an individual matter is congruent with the relativism of our society. This chapter will trace the development of relativism in our society and identify its weaknesses. It will be argued that relativism has become excessive and that freedom and tolerance need to be balanced with discernment. Applied to recreation and leisure, there needs to be a standard by which recreation activities can

---

Revised version of paper presented at the 1996 conference.

be discerned. The chapter proposes that the Golden Rule – do to others as you would have them do to you – is a universal standard that can be used to discern what is best in recreation.

The Context: Relativism

Before tracing the development of relativism in our society and identifying its weaknesses, it is useful to define relativism and to make a distinction between cultural relativism and radical ethical relativism. Relativism is the view that "there is no such thing as a belief being absolutely true or false; beliefs are true or false only relative to a given point of view" (Hasker, 1980, p. 289). Thus, "a relativist," writes Newman (1982), "is a person who believes that something important that is generally regarded as absolute or objective (for instance, an ethical value or a religious belief) is actually dependent on the background, character, or attitudes of particular individuals or societies" (p. 21). According to cultural relativism, ethical disagreements follow cultural lines: "the cultural relativist emphasizes the cultural tradition as a prime source of the individual's views and thinks that most disagreements in ethics among individuals stem from enculturation in different ethical traditions. . ." (Brandt, 1967, p. 75). Radical ethical relativism refers to intracultural or personal relativism and the situation where there is "widespread disagreement about how to live within cultures" (Newman, p. 63). Thus for the ethical relativist, "actions are not good or right in themselves but are good-for-so-and-so or right-as-perceived-by-so-and-so" (Newman, p. 21).

Culture, according to Clark (1989), involves "the human quest for meaning, the development of religious and ethical traditions, the construction of world views and understandings of nature, time, our origins, and future" (p. 61). In the past, humans often succumbed to the temptation that their own culture had the absolute truth and that the beliefs and customs of other cultures were not as valid. This process of absolutizing culture usually manifested itself in ethnocentrism: that is, the belief that one's cultural practices were correct and superior to those of other cultures which were often seen as ignorant, inferior, immoral, wrong, and/or strange.

The concept of absolutism or ethnocentrism is contrasted with relativism, an ancient concept going as far back as the fifth century BCE, when the most celebrated of the Sophists, Protagoras of Abdera, claimed that "man is the measure of all things" (Kerferd, 1967, p. 505). Recently relativism was expanded and popularized by sociology and anthropology.

The original interest of these two disciplines was twofold. First, sociology and anthropology were interested in expanding the horizons of Westerners who were engaged in activities outside of the Western world. By demonstrating the rich diversity of human cultures, customs, and beliefs, these disciplines attempted to decrease ethnocentrism and encourage cross-cultural tolerance.

Second, sociology and anthropology were also concerned with the methodological problem of how to recognize and control one's own cultural commitments when studying other cultures. It was argued that people from around the world meet common needs in different ways; however, one expression was not to be viewed as more true or better than any other. The social scientist was not to judge right and wrong but was to set aside one's own cultural standards in order to understand and explain within the context of that culture. Thus customs, values, and beliefs became culturally relative.

In his penetrating analysis of Canadian society, *Mosaic Madness*, Reginald Bibby (1990) demonstrated that the cultural relativism that the social sciences promoted was not only an academic, methodological concern, but became a way to live in a multicultural world. A review of his analysis is helpful in understanding relativism in our society. Relativism gained popular support from Joseph Fletcher's (1966) book *Situation Ethics*, which argued that right and wrong are not dependent on a set of rules but rather on how the concept of love is operationalized in specific situations. Further support for the same understanding of ethics came from Bishop James Pike (1967), who argued that behaviors such as lying, theft, and extramarital sex are sometimes "right" if love is served.

Thus in recent decades it has been widely accepted that truth (in opposition to falsity) and rightness (as opposed to wrongness) is relative. Allan Bloom (1987) wrote that most university students not only believe that truth is relative but are astonished if a person doesn't regard such a proposition as self-evident. According to Bibby (1990), since the 1960s, few Canadians claim to have "the true" this or "the right" that. Even fewer Canadians would refer to other people's views as "false" or "wrong." Relativism became so accepted that such attitudes were not expressed – at least not in public.

Bibby (1990) concluded that relativism fit the individualistic and pluralistic times. The abandonment of the concept of absolute standards "gave intellectual legitimacy to the personal pursuit of well-being in a multicultural setting" (p. 46). "Goodness" and "badness" were now relative. Similarly, Grenz (1996) wrote that "The relativistic pluralism of late modernity was highly individualistic; it elevated personal taste and personal choice as the be-all and end-all. Its maxims were 'To each his/her own' and 'Everyone has a right to his/her own opinion'" (p. 15). Thus relativism had moved from simply being cultural relativism to ethical relativism – interpersonal differences within cultures were accepted.

The absence of any absolute values of truth, goodness, and beauty, along with the growth of ethical relativism, had implications for leisure. There were no longer any absolute standards to determine acceptable recreation activities. Goodale and Godbey (1988) have documented how the change of values, along with a number of other trends, produced wanderlust rather than leisure. The focus shifted from the community to the individual, and the main goal for many people became self-gratification: "lifestyles became hedonistic, non-conforming, and oriented to the present" (p. 208) as people sought "to experience all choices, do it all, see it all, and do it and see it now" (p. 218).

The shift toward ethical relativism has also had an impact upon the provision of recreation services and programs:

> The pluralization of society, which has led to the questioning of what traditionally were viewed as universal, fundamental values, has amounted to a rejection of the ancient Greek notion of unchanging ideals within the context of modern social and political thought. Instead, modern-day society has embraced a pluralization of values which has relativised the norms of recreation practice. Rather than programming for the development of the "ideal citizen," public recreation providers must focus their attention on providing programmes that appeal to diverse interests. . . . (Johnson & McLean, 1994, p. 128)

Excessive Relativism

Relativism is very attractive in a culturally diverse world and has value that should not be ignored. But as with ethnocentrism, relativism has some problems. Bibby (1990) illustrated how Canadian relativism is both excessive and mindless. Canadians see it as virtuous to defend the right of others to choose whatever they want, even if the choices are not the ones they would choose. Truth has increasingly come to be understood as a matter of personal preference, which is reflected in the commonly used Canadian cliché, "It's all relative."

Bibby (1990) noted that the focus on the personal search for truth has been an important counterbalance to the previous authoritarian tendencies such as school memorization and religious indoctrination, which not only stifled personal growth and creativity, but also impaired social development. However, with the advent of pluralism, "the importance of ceasing to be dogmatic about possessing truth has become confused with the importance of pursuing truth" (p. 98). Just because choices exist does not mean that all the choices have the same individual and societal benefits. The mere existence of multiple claims does not mean that all claims are equally true or right. The existence of disagreement in ethics does not, in and of itself, suggest that truth does not exist. Rather, it may only indicate that some are less enlightened than others (Rachels, 1988). Bloom (1987), in the *Closing of the American Mind,* wrote that "the fact that there have been different opinions about good and bad in different times and places in no way proves that none is true or that none is superior to others" (p. 39). Rather, conflicting and multiple options should be seen as an invitation to study what is good and bad about each of them. However, modern relativists, noted Bloom, view conflicting opinions as evidence that such study is not possible and that respect must be given to them all.

Bibby (1990) used the sphere of personal wellbeing to illustrate that all choices do not have equal consequences. Physical health is not simply guesswork. Some factors do contribute to heart attacks and cancer. There may be differences between cultures and within cultures as to what constitutes a good meal, but some foods are more nutritious than others. Likewise, what we do to stay fit may differ from culture to culture, but being unfit has similar physiological consequences for everyone, regardless of their culture. Thus it is erroneous to think that if some values are culturally relative, all must be. Some values might be relative to culture, while others are not (Rachels, 1988).

Physical, emotional, intellectual, and spiritual needs are met in diverse ways by humans. But, as Bibby (1990) argued, this does not mean that the diverse ways are equally effective:

> The fact that people hold a variety of ethical views is not to say that all lead to the same interpersonal results; the fact that people subscribe to a number of personal development programs is not to say that they all have the same impact on individual well-being. Options say nothing about consequences. (p. 99)

Mindless Relativism

Bibby (1990) argued that everything is possible in Canada. But that does not mean that everything is equally good, at the personal or societal level. Bibby argued that in a society like Canada, where the idea that a person is free to have values, but is not free to impose those values on others, choice per se is triumphant. Instead of diligently examining the costs and benefits of possible options and then suggesting what might be "best," Canadians take the easy way out. Pluralism decrees that a Canadian is an educated, enlightened, sophisticated person who tolerates almost everything. Tolerance becomes the basic ground rule in our multicultural world.

In a discussion of the leisure service delivery dilemma, McLean and Johnson (1993) noted that "tolerance of cultural differences and diversity appear to be the words that epitomize the present decade" (p. 261). Similarly, Goodale (1991c), discussing the changing direction of the parks and recreation profession, noted that we "have come to pride ourselves for our tolerance, which may be the convenient term for indifference. There is as much evidence for one as the other" (p. 232). Whether it is tolerance or indifference that characterizes our society is partly dependent on how we define tolerance. Indifference involves an acceptance of everything based on an absence of interest or attention, while tolerance is much more active:

> . . . tolerance involves . . . accepting, enduring, bearing, putting up with; it involves acceptance in the sense of refraining from any strong reaction to the thing in question; it is half-hearted, an attitude towards something that is not liked, loved, respected, or approved of; and it is often, though not always, understood as a praiseworthy act or virtue. (Newman, 1982, p. 6)

Given, the involvement this definition of tolerance implies, it is likely, as Goodale (1991b) suggested, that many people in our society practice indifference, not tolerance.

Relativism has resulted in Canadians "not differentiating between being judgmental and showing sound judgement, between exhibiting discrimination and being discriminating" (Bibby, 1990, p. 101). When discernment is neglected, the pursuit of the best of possible options is ignored. Bloom (1987) wrote that "relativism has extinguished the real motive for education, the search for the good life" (p. 31). According to Bibby (1990), we are left with unreflective, mindless relativism. While Canadian society may no longer be authoritarian, it is also not critically relative and creative.

While in the past most Canadians unthinkingly accepted absolutism, in the present the majority are unthinkingly accepting relativism: "we have the audacity to applaud ourselves for being open-minded, when the reality is that our relativism has frequently made our minds airtight" (Bibby, 1990, p. 108). But there is little knowledge of what is right, good, or true. Every choice gets an A, and in so doing, bad and better, mediocre and excellent are blurred. The end result is that personally and nationally we do not pursue the best; personally "we settle for viewpoints and nationally we settle for co-existence" (Bibby, 1990, p. 176). Mindless relativism has resulted in citizens who assert their diverse choices in viewpoint and behavior.

When every choice gets an A, with bad and better, mediocre and excellent being blurred, leisure becomes neutral and amoral, "a space of unobligated time that can be spent in a myriad of ways" (Sylvester, 1990, p. 2). Sylvester (1991) wrote that "If leisure is whatever the individual experiences, and if experiencing leisure is inherently good, we are cast adrift in murky and turbulent waters with nothing to guide us besides the shibboleth, 'If it feels good do it'" (p. 447). But when individuals, out of a desire to feel good, assert their diverse choices in viewpoint and behavior in the realm of leisure, the result can be less than satisfactory, as Bregha (1980) graphically noted:

> At present, in Canada . . . More and more people are occupying their leisure with a bewildering variety of acts and deeds that leave their trace on their neighbours and communities. The leisure of one becomes sometimes offensive to another – morally as well as otherwise. To preach the sanctity of self-fulfillment in an increasingly interdependent society does not solve anything, to hide behind the jargon of "enabling everyone to reach his/her full potential" leads us nowhere. . . . After all, my self-actualization could be your de-actualization, my self-fulfillment achieved at the cost of your emptiness. To view leisure as morally neutral or even as "good per se" denotes a naiveté that should have died out with Rousseau. (p. 17)

In its extreme form, when leisure is viewed as morally neutral, as "good per se," when good is equated with pleasure as in the hedonist error, the consequences are horrific, as is described by Rojek (1996) in his analysis of the ten murders committed by Frederik and Rosemary West in Britain: "they [the Wests] conformed to the cultural requirement of concentrating their search for peak experience in their free time. Their problem – and the tragedy of their victims – was that they identified peak experience with killing for leisure" (p. 30). In providing reasons why the park and recreation movement should change, Goodale (1991b) referred to Willis Harmon's list of indicators of failure in our present society, a list that includes "increased public acceptance of hedonistic behavior (particularly sexual), of symbols of degradation, and of lax public morality" (p. 124).

Necessary Changes

After critiquing Canadian society, Bibby (1990) offers some solutions. He argued that Canadians have done a good job of building a pluralistic foundation, but that it is now time to move on to finding a balance between the individual and the group, a balance that will ensure maximum wellbeing and the best kind of life possible. Bibby recommended that we need to pursue the best at personal and societal levels, and to achieve that end, he suggested an emphasis on collective assets and an encouraging of discernment.

Collective assets. Bibby (1990) noted that an unfortunate consequence of making multiculturalism an end in itself is that Canadian society fails to give adequate attention to diversity as a national resource. Tolerance and understanding is stressed, when social strength and collective assets should also be emphasized: "If we view Canadian society as a group of cultures that coexist like tiles in an art piece, we have nothing but parts beside parts. Socially, such a view translates into mosaic madness" (p. 177). In a similar vein, Goodale (1991c) wrote that "our value sources are not so much pluralistic as atomistic. There may already be too many value orientations, which is very much like having no value orientation at all" (p. 232). Bloom (1987) questioned whether the social contract is still possible if there are no shared goals or vision of the public good. Thus Bibby (1990) recommended that "if we have a design in mind, if we try to pool our varied resources to create a society that is more than just the sum of its diverse parts, then we can work together in pursuing optimum well-being" (p. 177).

Encouraging Discernment. Bibby (1990) also believed that it is very important for Canadians to carefully evaluate all the different viewpoints that are expressed. With so many viewpoints expressed, discernment is essential to evaluate whether options are "bad, better, or best." While everything may be possible in a pluralistic society, every option does not lead to the same result. True openness, wrote Bloom (1987), is accompanied by the desire to know good and bad. Discernment is required to understand the values and the behaviors that will best contribute to personal and societal wellbeing.

Bibby (1990) argued that if this is to happen, the present obsession with "mindless relativism" must be supplanted by reflective critiques of the benefits and costs of possible options. The search for what is best must replace unreflective relativism. This implies that all Canadians must be encouraged to aspire to the best in everything and to make reflective choices. Canadians must learn "the difference between tolerating ideas and examining which ideas are the most sound, between accepting the lifestyles of others and determining which lifestyles contribute the most to personal and social well-being" (p. 178).

Limited Relativism. In essence, Bibby's (1990) critique of excessive relativism and the need for pursuing the best is consistent with what Clark (1989) and others have called limited relativism: that is, the pursuit of the best in truth, goodness, and beauty while recognizing the relativist's position that cultural elements are influenced by their cultural, social, and historical contexts. There needs to be a commitment to truth, goodness, and beauty that recognizes that human finiteness limits, contextualizes, and diversifies our understanding, while human self-centeredness tends to resist, distort, and misuse truth, beauty, and goodness in ways that are self-serving. Thus the task is to pursue and preserve truth, goodness, and beauty and attempt to confront and change that which is corrupt, unjust, and false without absolutizing our culture.

Application to Recreation and Leisure

The cultural context of relativism, its excesses, and the need for a limited relativism in which the assets of a multicultural society are pooled and the alternative viewpoints and behaviors discerned have been reviewed. How is this applied to recreation and leisure? Or in the words of Bregha (1980) "What is it that leisure should protect and improve? What should leisure resist and avoid?" (p. 18).

The recreation field, as DeGraaf (2006) pointed out, has not escaped the debate over values. In recent decades, it has been thought, in a position consistent with relativism, that recreation is a matter of personal preference, and it is the responsibility of the recreation professional to facilitate those preferences. However, there is increasing discussion about the need to make judgments concerning what recreational activities to encourage.

Traditionally there has been a hesitancy to make these kinds of judgments, as it was thought that freedom and personal preference were fundamental to the nature of leisure. For example, Kaplan (1960) argued that free choice involves the realm of values and the imposition of values might limit the leisure potential of individuals. Similarly, Goodale and Godbey (1988) note the fundamental dilemma wherein by prescribing desirable leisure activities, we may quench the exercise of choice, human will, and imagination, which are central to leisure.

Likewise, Dustin et al. (1991) noted that "The essence of recreation has always been rooted in individual choice" (p. 117); thus, to dictate what is good and bad would remove an individual's free choice. However, Dustin et al. rightly point out that freedom involves much more than free choice: ". . . to understand freedom only as opportunity is to misunderstand its full meaning. Freedom also demands a sense of obligation to do the right thing" (p. 97).

Dustin et al. (1991) went on to outline a standard of moral philosophy that might be used to measure the goodness of recreational activities. They recommended the adoption of Albert Schweitzer's (1957) philosophy: "ethics consist . . . in my experiencing the compulsion to show to all will-to-live the same reverence as I do my own" (p. 309). Schweitzer (1965) wrote: "The essence of Goodness is: preserve life, promote life, help life to achieve its fullest destiny. The essence of Evil is: destroy life, harm life, hamper the development of life" (p. 26). Applying this standard to recreation, Dustin and colleagues argued that "those recreational pastimes which preserve life, promote life, and help life achieve its highest destiny are morally superior to those that don't" (p. 101).

Dustin et al. (1991), by providing a standard to judge recreational activity, were doing exactly what Bibby (1990) argued for when he suggested that discernment needed to be encouraged in our excessively relativistic society. Discernment is necessary to determine what is bad, better, and best, as we have already seen that not all options lead to the same consequences.

Another standard that could be used as a measuring stick in judging recreation activities is the Golden Rule of "doing to others as you would have them do to you." In reality, Schweitzer's (1957) philosophy and ethics as illustrated by his expression "ethics consist . . . in my experiencing the compulsion to show to all wills to live the same reverence as I do my own" (p. 301) is merely an expression of the Golden Rule. Both provide a tool for aiding in discernment.

The advantage of the Golden Rule is that it may have broader appeal than Schweitzer's philosophy. Schweitzer was a theologian within the Christian tradition and a medical missionary to Africa who lived from 1875 to 1965, whereas the Golden Rule is common to the great religions of the world. One of Bibby's recommendations was that in a pluralistic, multi-cultural society such as Canada – whose heterogeneity is matched by few nations – it is important to emphasize our assets and pool our resources. That is, in addition to stressing our differences, it is important to bridge common ground where possible. This may be more important in Canadian society, which is characterized by multiculturalism, than the "melting pot" scenario in the United States.

The Universality of the Golden Rule

Starkey (1985) argued that in today's multicultural world we need to find ways to build bridges between different cultures in order to foster communication, understanding, acceptance, and cooperation. She notes that the religious dimension is often inadequately perceived or viewed as inconsequential when cross-cultural communication and cooperation is necessary, yet learning to live together touches people at the most basic level of their religious heritage.

The question may arise as to whether a religious teaching is still an appropriate ethical standard in today's secular society. After all, as Bregha (1991) has illustrated, the present question of leisure and ethics has arisen partly because leisure's link to religion has been gradually weakened:

> ... we are possibly the first generation that faces a peculiar problem in regard to our leisure. As long as leisure found its origin in God and its expression in partaking in worship, its morality was beyond reproach. Now that a divorce has taken place and leisure is linked to freedom rather than God, a vast question mark as to its ultimate purpose is before us. (p. 53)

Although leisure's link to religion has been weakened, there is still a strong residual belief in religion in our society. For example, a 1993 nationwide survey conducted by the Angus Reid group and historian George Rawlyk found that while only 23 percent of the population attended religious services at least "once a week or so," 78 percent affiliated themselves with a Christian denomination and 74 percent disagreed with the statement "I am not a Christian" (Nemeth, 1993). Furthermore, spiritual and religious principles are the foundation for the legal system and moral codes in our society (Hawks, Hull, Thalman, & Richins, 1995). In addition, Hick (1992) has argued that we can extract basic moral values from the magical-scientific and metaphysical beliefs that have been associated with their application within particular cultures without necessarily adopting their religious beliefs or practices. Finally, most modern discussions of leisure and moral excellence (Goodale, 1991a; Hemingway, 1988; Hunicutt, 1990; Sylvester, 1990, 1991) are based on a discussion of Greek, particularly Aristotelian, philosophy; however, for the average person in our society, religious teachings are more familiar and have more relevance than Greek philosophy.

If we accept that the ethical teachings of the world religions have relevance, is it possible to find moral common ground among them? Donovan (1986) argued that the major world religions share moral common ground despite their different doctrinal and metaphysical beliefs. An example of this viewpoint is expressed by the Dalai Lama:

I maintain that every major religion of the world – Buddhism, Christianity, Confucianism, Hinduism, Islam, Jainism, Judaism, Sikhism, Taoism, Zoroastrianism – has similar ideals of love, the same goal of benefiting humanity through spiritual practice, and the same effect of making their followers into better human beings. All religions teach moral precepts for perfecting the functions of mind, body, and speech. All teach us not to lie or steal or take others' lives, and so on. (Gyatso, 1984, p. 13)

Donovan (1986) noted that the discovery of a number of moral teachings (e.g., versions of the Golden Rule) shared by different religions offers evidence for the reality of moral common ground among religions. Similarly, Hick (1992) argued that from the ethical insights of the world religions, we can discern the fundamental and universally accepted principle that it is: "evil to cause suffering to others and good to benefit others and to alleviate or prevent their sufferings" (p. 158). The Golden Rule, in its positive or negative forms, is a universal expression of this principle that it is good to benefit others and evil to harm them. This principle reads as follows in the various religious teachings:

Judaism: "What is hateful to yourself do not do to your fellow man (*haver*). That is the whole of the Torah" (Babylonian Talmud, Shabbath 31a).

Christianity: (Jesus): "Love your neighbor as yourself" (Matthew 22:39b). "Do to others as you would have them do to you" (Luke 6:31).

Islam: (Muhammad): "No man is a true believer unless he desires for his brother that which he desires for himself" (Hadith corpus, e.g., Muslim, iman; Ibn Madja, Introduction, 9; Al-darimi, riqaq, 29; Hambal, 3).

Hinduism: "One should never do that to another which one regards as injurious to one's own self. This, in brief, is the rule of Righteousness" (Mahabharata, Anushana parva, 113:7; Roy, 1893).

Jainism: One should go about "treating all creatures in the world as he himself would be treated" (Jaina Sutras, Part II, Sutrakritanga, bk. I lect. 11:33; Jacobi trans., 1968).

Buddhism: The Buddhist scriptures do not state the Golden Rule, but there are several passages in which the Buddha says such things as "Life is dear to all. Comparing others with oneself, one should neither strike nor cause to strike" (The Dhammapada, 10:2; Mahathera trans., 1972). "As a mother cares for her son, all her days, so towards all living things a man's mind should be all-embracing" (Sutta Nipāta, 149 in Hare, 1945).

Confucianism: "Do not do to others what you would not like yourself" (The Analects of Confucius, XII:2; Waley trans., 1938).

Taoism: The good man will "regard [others'] gains as if they were his own, and their losses in the same way" (Thai Shang 3; Legge trans., 1891).

Zoroastrianism: "nature only is good when it shall not do unto another whatever is not good for its own self." (Dadistan-i Dinik, 94:5; West trans., 1882).

The Golden Rule as stated above is elaborated upon in the moral teachings of the great traditions within particular historical locations and within given cultural-economic-political situations such as behavior towards neighbors, parents, children, the rich, the poor, slaves, strangers, enemies:

> In each case it begins on the common ground of fair dealing and respect for others' lives and property and leads on towards the higher ground of positive generosity, forgiveness, kindness, love, compassion, where we find the ethical evidence of the transformation of human existence from self-centeredness to Reality-centeredness. (Hick, 1992, p. 159)

Implications of the Golden Rule for Leisure

What are the implications of the Golden Rule for leisure? First, the rule presupposes self-love, that one will treat oneself well, for this is the model for behavior to others. Thus one's recreation behaviors will be for one's good. In a discussion of what recreation activities are acceptable, Goodale and Godbey (1988) suggest that acts harmful to oneself are not acceptable. The Golden Rule, especially in its positive formulations such as that stated by Jesus, suggest a more positive, proactive approach. The individual is encouraged to participate in those activities that are good for oneself, those activities that are best. It is through a healthy self-love that humans care for their physical, social, emotional, mental, and spiritual needs. Although leisure activities may be chosen primarily for enjoyment, activities can be selected that enhance total health. Leisure can provide opportunities for improving bodily health, developing social relationships, promoting positive self-concept, challenging cognitive abilities, and increasing spiritual awareness (Visker, 2006).

Secondly, the Golden Rule suggests that not only should one not participate in activities that would harm another person – again a criterion that Goodale and Godbey (1988) use to determine unacceptable activities – but one should seek out what is best for the other person. Jesus' "love your neighbor as yourself" suggests more than just one's activity not being harmful to another, more than just "tolerating" another's behavior as suggested by today's relativism, but suggests an active involvement in seeking the best for the other person as well. Thus any leisure that tends to dehumanize people, whether it be through making them sex objects, shattering their self-respect, or stifling their growth, or any leisure that is unloving, unjust, unfair, or needlessly violent is challenged by the Golden Rule. Of course this should be most relevant to the park and recreation professionals as they seek to facilitate recreation experiences and to remove obstacles for the general population.

Johnson and McLean (1994) suggested that a pluralistic environment requires that recreation professionals "interpret and possibly adjudicate the diverse and possibly conflicting leisure values of various interest groups (pp. 128–129). How are recreation professionals to adjudicate such wide-ranging and conflicting leisure values? Johnson and McLean pointed out that as recreation programming has become more pluralistic, recreation provision has been guided more by excluding errant behavior than the emulation of an ideal. While this is consistent with the Golden Rule in the sense that recreation provision is excluding those activities that might harm one's neighbor and thus be in contradiction to "doing to others as you would have them do to you," the positive formulations of the Golden Rule suggests going a step further and selecting activities that are not only enjoyable, but which enhance holistic health.

Much leisure in our society, for example games and sports, is dominated by a competitive attitude. Sometimes this competitive attitude turns into a cutthroat attitude of winning at all costs and of humiliating opponents. In its extreme form, such an attitude leads to sports violence characterized more by retaliation than by "doing to others as you would have them do to you." "You did it to me; therefore, I'll do it to you" is the rule that is prevalent in much competitive sport. Humiliation also takes the form of verbal intimidation. At sporting events we hear phrases such as "We're going to get them the next time" or "Kill the ump." Coaches frequently use the motivation of revenge to prepare their players for a big game. All such behaviors, along with play to prove oneself better than others or to be "one up on" fellow players, is not consistent with "doing to others as you would have them do to you." However, friendly competition that stretches participants and brings out the best efforts of which the participants are capable, efforts in which one is ultimately competing with oneself, are consistent with the spirit of the Golden Rule. Thus, the Golden Rule does not mean an end to competition, for competitive athletes such as swimmers or runners, in competition, may spur each other on to personal best times that they would not otherwise achieve outside of competition. However, cooperative games that focus on playing and winning together may lend themselves more to an implementation of the Golden Rule than many competitive sports in our society.

Hick (1992) suggested that the rule promotes love, compassion, and self-sacrificing concern for others. This interpretation has implications for justice issues. How might my recreational activity be affecting the marginalized in our society or those in developing countries? Am I establishing or preserving dominance over others through my leisure? Am I participating in activities or consuming recreational goods that directly or indirectly support oppressive regimes that exploit peoples in developing nations? Does my recreational behavior create barriers that prevent other people from maximizing their leisure; for example, do I misuse recreation environments, whether natural or human-made, in ways that will detract from another person's experience?

Hick (1992) also suggested that the rule promotes kindness and forgiveness. Despite how good our intentions might be, there will still be times when one person's recreation has a negative impact or harmful effect on another person. Kindness and forgiveness, as suggested by the rule, instead of revenge and getting back at the other person, are helpful virtues in resolving conflicts that arise in these situations.

One of the reasons Dustin and colleagues (1991) advocated Schweitzer's philosophy is because of its ethical extensions from the whole human family to all living things and the land. Thus, recreation activities are to be judged in terms of their impact on the whole earth community. While some versions of the Golden Rule focus on humans, others include more than humans. For example, the Jain Kritanga Sutra version uses the term "all creatures," the Buddhist Scriptures refer to "all living things," and the Zoroastrian Dadistan-i Dinik mentions "nature." Thus, there is no reason that the practice of the rule should not also be extended to all others, including all living things and the land as suggested by Leopold's (1949) land ethic. Leopold argued for an extension of ethics to land as an ecological necessity. All ethics rest on the premise that the individual is the member of a community of interdependent parts. The land ethic enlarges the boundaries of the community to include soils, waters, plants, and animals, or collectively the land. A land-ethic implies that humans have respect for fellow-members of the land-community, and also respect for the community. Thus an extension of the Golden Rule to include all of the land-community raises questions about leisure activities such as the use of scarce energy resources in auto racing, roaring around a quiet lake in a gas-guzzling motor boat that emits noxious fumes, bullfighting, hunting animals for "sport alone" rather than for food or other purposes, and any leisure activity that needlessly upsets the ecosystem or defaces natural beauty (Holmes, 1983).

"Freedom, without the comfort of theological and ethical systems, could produce terror and absurdity" (Goodale & Godbey, 1988, p. 211). Such a prediction could come true if our relativistic society fails to acknowledge that tolerance and the freedom to choose need to be balanced with discernment and the pursuit of the best. The diversity of our multicultural society has a great heritage to be drawn upon when discerning the multitude of viewpoints and behaviors expressed. The Golden Rule, common to all the major traditions, has much to offer in terms of the discernment of the best in recreational activities. This basic norm, central to the great traditions, provides a broad criterion by which we can make ethical judgements in leisure. We cannot expect the Golden Rule on its own to solve all the ethical problems in leisure, because in each of the great religious traditions it is situated within a larger body of moral teaching that elaborates on how it is to be applied. However, given that it is common to all major religions, it can be used as a common guiding principle to be applied to ethical issues in a pluralistic, multi-cultural society. In one sense, the application of the Golden Rule is comparatively easy, as we can list certain actions and behaviors that are unacceptable, but in another sense extremely difficult as we apply its wisdom to the many grey areas of life in a relativistic age.

References

Bibby, R.W. (1990). *Mosaic madness: The poverty and potential of life in Canada.* Toronto: Stoddart.

Bloom, A. (1987). *The closing of the American mind.* New York: Simon & Schuster.

Brandt, R. (1967). Ethical relativism. In P. Edwards (Ed.), *The encyclopedia of philosophy* (Vols. 3, pp. 75–78). New York: Macmillan.

Bregha, F. (1980, July). Philosophy of leisure: Unanswered questions. *Recreation Research Review* 8, 15–19.

Bregha, F. (1991). Leisure and freedom re-examined. In T.L. Goodale & P.A. Witt (Eds.), *Recreation and leisure: Issues in an era of change* (3rd ed., pp. 47–54). State College, PA: Venture.

Clark, R. A. (1989). Thinking about culture: Theirs and ours. In M.R. Leming, R.G. DeVries, & B.F.J. Furnish (Eds.), *The sociological perspective* (pp. 61–80). Grand Rapids, MI: Academie Books.

DeGraaf, D. (2006). Unless someone like you cares a whole awful lot. In P.

Heintzman, G.E. Van Andel, & T.L. Visker (Eds.), *Christianity and leisure: Issues in a pluralistic society* (Rev. ed., pp. 125–144). Sioux Center: Dordt College Press.

Donovan, P.J. (1986). Do different religions share common ground? *Religious Studies* 22(3-4), 367–375.

Dustin, D.L, McAvoy, L.H., & Schultz, J.H. (1991). Recreation rightly understood. In T.L. Goodale & P.A. Witt (Eds.), *Recreation and leisure: Issues in an era of change* (pp. 97–106). State College, PA: Venture.

Fletcher, J. (1966). *Situation ethics*. Philadelphia, PA: Westminster Press.

Goodale, T.L. (1991a). If leisure is to matter. In T.L. Goodale & P.A. Witt (Eds.), *Recreation and leisure: Issues in an era of change* (3rd ed., pp. 85–95). State College, PA: Venture.

Goodale, T.L. (1991b). Of Godots and Goodbars: On waiting for change. In T.L. Goodale & P.A. Witt (Eds.), *Recreation and leisure: Issues in an era of change* (3rd ed., pp. 123–135). State College, PA: Venture.

Goodale, T.L. (1991c). Prevailing winds and bending mandates. In T.L. Goodale & P.A. Witt (Eds.), *Recreation and leisure: Issues in an era of change* (3rd ed., pp. 231–242). State College, PA: Venture.

Goodale, T.L., & Godbey, G.C. (1988). *The evolution of leisure*. State College, PA: Venture.

Grenz, S. (1996). *A primer on postmodernism*. Grand Rapids: Eerdmans.

Gyatso, T. (1984). *A human approach to world peace*. Somerville, MA: Wisdom Publications.

Hare, E.M. (1945). *The woven cadences of early Buddhists*. London: Oxford University Press.

Hasker, W. (1980). Cultural relativity and relativism. In C.P. De Santo, C. Redekop, & W.L. Smith-Hinds (Eds.), *A reader in sociology: Christian perspectives* (pp. 289–301) Kitchener, ON: Herald Press.

Hawks, S.R., Hull, M.L., Thalman, R.L., & Richins, P.M. (1995, May/June). Review of spiritual health: Definition, role, and intervention strategies in health promotion. *American Journal of Health Promotion* 9(5), 371–373, 377, 378.

Hemingway, J. (1988). Leisure and civility: Reflections on a Greek ideal. *Leisure Sciences* 10, 179–191.

Hick, J. (1992). The universality of the Golden Rule. In J. Runzo (Ed.), *Ethics, religion and the good society: New directions in a pluralistic world* (pp. 155–166). Louisville, KY: Westminster/John Knox.

Holmes, A.R. (1983). *Contours of a world view*. Grand Rapids: Eerdmans.

Hunnicutt, B.K. (1990). Leisure and play in Plato's teaching and philosophy of learning. *Leisure Sciences* 12, 211–227.

Jacobi, H. (Trans.) (1968). *Jaina Sutras*. Delhi, India: Motilal Banarsidass.

Johnson, R., & McLean, D. (1994). Leisure and the development of ethical character: Changing views of the North American ideal. *Journal of Applied Recreation Research* 19(2), 117–130.

Kaplan, M. (1960). *Leisure in America: A social inquiry.* New York: John Wiley.
Kerferd, G.B. (1967). Protagoras. In P. Edwards (Ed.), *The encyclopedia of philosophy* (Vol. 6, pp. 505–507). New York: Macmillan.
Legge, J. (Trans.). (1891). *The sacred books of China: The texts of Taoism* (Part 2). Oxford: Clarendon Press.
Leopold, A. (1949). *A Sand County Almanac.* New York: Oxford University Press.
Mahathera, N. (Trans.) (1972). *The Dhammapada* (2nd ed.). Colombo, Sri Lanka: Vajiranama.
McLean, D., & Johnson, R.C.A. (1993). The leisure service delivery dilemma: The professional versus the marketing model. *Journal of Applied Recreation Research* 18(4), 253–264.
Nemeth, M. (1993, April 12). God is alive. *Macleans* 106(4), 32–37.
Newman, J. (1982). *Foundations of religious tolerance.* Toronto: University of Toronto Press.
Pike, J.A. (1967). *You and the new morality.* New York: Harper & Row.
Rachels, J. (1988). Can ethics provide answers? In D.M. Rosenthal & F. Shehadi (Eds.), *Applied ethics and ethical theory* (pp. 3–24). Salt Lake City, UT: University of Utah Press.
Rojek, C. (1996). *The West house: Domestic leisure and the English murder.* Paper presented at the 8th Canadian Congress on Leisure Research, Ottawa, ON.
Roy, P.C. (Trans.) (1893). *Mahabharata.* Calcutta: Bharata Press.
Schweitzer, A. (1957). *The philosophy of civilization.* New York: Macmillan.
Schweitzer, A. (1965). *The teaching of reverence for life.* New York: Holt, Reinhart, & Winston.
Starkey, P. (1985). Agape: A Christian criterion for truth in the other world religions. *International Review of Mission* 74(91), 425–463.
Sylvester, C. (1990, October). *The transvaluation of classical leisure and virtue: The impetus of the Protestant Reformation and Baconian science.* Paper presented at the 1990 Leisure Research Symposium, Phoenix, Arizona.
Sylvester, C. (1991). Recovering a good idea for the sake of goodness: An interpretive critique of subjective leisure. In T.L. Goodale & P.A. Witt (Eds.), *Recreation and leisure: Issues in an era of change* (3rd ed., pp. 441–454). State College, PA: Venture.
Visker, T. (2006). Play, game and sport in a reformed, biblical worldview. In P. Heintzman, G.E Van Andel, & T.L. Visker (Eds.), *Christianity and leisure: Issues in a pluralistic society* (Rev. ed., pp. 173–192). Sioux Center: Dordt College Press.
Waley, A. (Trans.). (1938). *The analects of Confucius.* London: George Allen & Unwin.
West, E.W. (Trans.). (1882). *Pahlevi texts.* Oxford: Clarendon Press.

Chapter 15

REDEEMING PLAY: A CHRISTIAN PERSPECTIVE

Glen Van Andel

"Let's play" is a familiar and exciting invitation for children of all ages. We all remember those earlier times in our lives when play dominated everything we did. Swings, dolls, toys, and games became our daily companions as we traveled through our early life exploring and creating. We were free to do what we wanted, when we wanted, and with whom we wanted, even in our make-believe world. But today, for too many of our youth, self-chosen, autotelic, imaginative, non-stressed activity has become organized and systematized at younger and younger ages so that the pure quality of play is being lost. Instead of neighborhood pick-up games, today's youth are socialized into a sport culture that focuses on the product of the activity rather than the process. Too often, this results in significantly fewer opportunities to develop play skills that are essential for socialization, as well as physical and emotional development. At the same time, it has been reported that over 70 percent of children drop out of sports play with a common complaint that "It's no fun" (Woods, 2011).

Shirl Hoffman (2010a), a vocal critic of the ugly side of sports play, suggested that Christians are also strongly affected by our sports culture.

> The sports we watch and play help orient us in the world; they furnish templates for how we should relate to and feel about one another. Sports hold captive our imaginations and interpret for us what it means to be successful, devoted, and fair. (Hoffman, p. 13)

But too often our play, games, sports, and athletic experiences reflect what Roberts (1993) described as the beak-and-claw philosophy of life. Observations of his son's fourth-grade class playing the familiar game of balloon stomp caused him to suggest that even our games teach our children that "the real world is a nasty place where you need to protect yourself and stomp the other guy's balloon before he stomps yours. If

Revised edition of a paper presented at the 1995 conference.

you don't learn this, you won't survive" (p. 158). Similarly, much of the business world has adopted this beak-and-claw philosophy or "serious competitiveness" as Roberts (1993) defined it, where power and intimidation have become tools of the trade.

In the face of such a strong cultural dynamic, it is becoming more and more difficult for Christians to define an alternative approach where the gift of play can find its rightful place in games, sport, and athletics. Can we simply ignore these perspectives and hope the pendulum swings back to a more balanced approach, or do we challenge these cultural values and try to provide alternatives that might better reflect Christian values and beliefs? If we challenge them, what might that look like?

This paper will examine how the emergence of a new approach to play and recreation in the 1970s changed the prevailing cultural values of the day and how Christians might adapt some of these principles to address today's cultural challenges in our play, games, sports, and athletics. The final section of the paper provides a template that could be used to guide Christians in their play and life so that we might achieve the primary goal of the Christian life as expressed by the *Westminster Shorter Confession of Faith* (1646/1990), "to glorify God and enjoy him forever" (p. 3).

Defining the Constructs of Play, Game, Sport, and Athletics

In discussing play, we need to distinguish between various terms. Byl (2006) developed a helpful model for understanding the relationship among the illusive concepts of physically active play, game, sport, and athletics. Play, he suggests, as "a freely chosen consciousness, intent on the enjoyable and non-traditional use of resources primarily committed to instrumental purposes" (p. 166) is foundational to the other components of the model. Play in this sense is largely determined by one's attitude toward a particular activity in which the player is free to engage.

Byl's model (2006) describes a continuum of physically active play and games that ranges from pure play, to playful game, to sport, to athletics (see Figure 1). The distinguishing feature is the degree of emphasis on a commitment to play versus the commitment to successfully overcoming unnecessary obstacles. Pure play, Byl contended, is generally free of personal conflicts, while at the other end of the continuum, athletics represents "a greater commitment to successfully overcoming unnecessary obstacles than to play" (p. 166). The purpose of a game, he suggested,

> is not simply to outdo someone else, but it is to overcome obstacles in a mutually acceptable manner. Though play experiences at all levels have

the potential for good, not all levels are helpful to the participants. The question one needs to answer is what emphasis on overcoming unnecessary obstacles is appropriate in different situations. (p. 168)

In other words, what is our attitude throughout our play experience, and how does this influence how we achieve our goal of overcoming these unnecessary obstacles in "a mutually acceptable manner" (Byl, p. 159).

Figure 1: Physically Active Play & Games (Byl, 2006).

Play = A freely chosen consciousness intent on the enjoyable and nontraditional use of resources primarily committed to instrumental purposes. This is best realized when personal conflicts have been resolved.

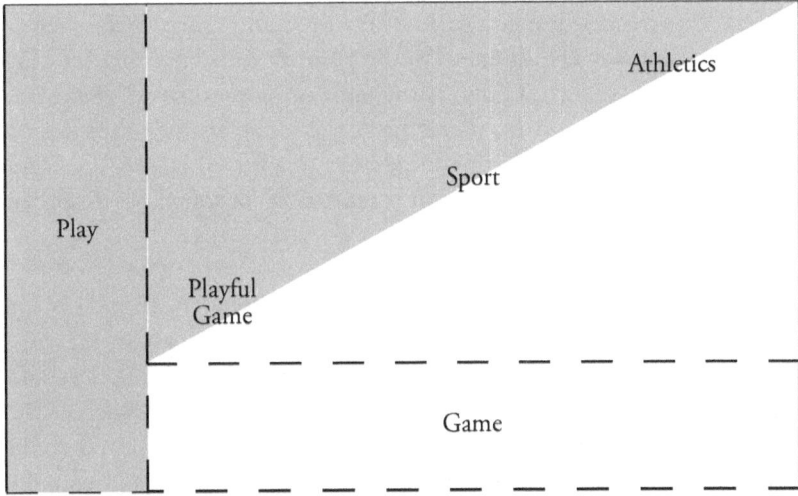

Game = "The voluntary attempt to overcome unnecessary obstacles-hindrances" (Suits 1973, 55).
/ = Level of commitment to overcoming unnecessary obstacles.

Playful Game = A greater commitment to play than to successfully overcoming unnecessary obstacles.

Sport = A roughly balanced commitment to play and to successfully overcoming unnecessary obstacles.

Athletics = A greater commitment to successfully overcoming unnecessary obstacles than to play.

The problem with our sports-oriented culture is that there is an overemphasis on the athletics side of the model and diminished opportunities for pure play, especially for children and youth. The professional athletic model of sport participation is filtering down into the ranks of youth sports, and fewer youth are experiencing the freedom of playful participation and the fun and satisfaction that should accompany this level of play. We need to reexamine alternative models that might provide a counter-balance to this trend.

The New Games Movement

Some decades ago, several people came together to create new strategies for playing games that they believed would challenge the predominant cultural values of the day. This new approach to games became known as the New Games Movement. George Leonard (1974), along with others, believed that the kinds of games people play and the ways they play them are of major significance to society. "How we play the game may turn out to be more important than we imagine, for it signifies nothing less than our way of being in the world" (Leonard as quoted in Fluegelman, 1976, p. 10).

Competition is an essential element of many play, game, sport, and athletic experiences, but it becomes distorted and destructive when it dominates the play environment to the point of dehumanizing the play experience. When players become the most important part of the game, it changes the way everyone views the game. It's an attitude shift from a predominant focus on athletic competition to a more balanced focus on what Roberts (1993) called "playful competition" or softwar as described in the early New Games events.

History of New Games

A new approach to play was developed in the 1960s in the context of the counterculture, a movement committed to exploring new and more satisfying ways to live. In the late sixties, publications such as the *Whole Earth Catalog* (Brand, 1968) provided tools by which people could envision and create new ways to shape their environment and connect with others who shared this adventure. These tools stimulated Stewart Brand, a San Francisco counterculture pioneer, to explore the potential for using games to achieve some of his goals. "Changing games seemed to me to be a useful thing to do, a way to be, a set of meta-strategies to learn" (Brand as quoted in Fluegelman, 1976, p. 7).

When asked to lead an event for the War Resisters League at San Francisco State College, Brand decided to create an activity that would challenge the participants to experience the latent source of aggression and warlike attitudes within themselves (Fluegelman, 1976). To set the stage, he called the game the most offensive name he could think of, Slaughter.

> I invented it because all the peaceniks I was dealing with seemed very much out of touch with their own bodies in an unhealthy way. Consequently, they were starting to project a heaviness on a personal level that was just as

bad as the heaviness we were projecting in Vietnam. What I wanted was a game which would involve fairly intense physical interaction between players. (Brand as quoted in Fluegelman, 1976, p. 8)

Slaughter involved 40 barefoot players positioned on their knees on a wrestling mat, each trying to avoid being "killed" or eliminated from the game by being thrown off the mat by the other players. It was simply impossible to be a peacenik in this environment. Despite the intense and combative nature of these events, most participants were surprised to find the game to be great fun and were ready for a new challenge. For this new challenge, Brand introduced a six-foot round, canvas-covered rubber ball on which he had painted the earth, complete with oceans, continents, and cloud swirls (Fluegelman, 1976). The ball was placed in the center of a large field and two teams were challenged to push the earth over the opponent's goal. As the game progressed, it became obvious the teams were more interested in changing the rules to keep the sides as equal as possible. As one team pushed the ball near the goal of the other team, some members defected to assist the threatened team and the ball slowly moved back toward the middle of the field. The day ended with neither team "winning" by scoring a goal, but they had challenged each other to enjoy the experience of playing together around an unspoken goal of cooperation.

From this experience, Brand realized that even in conflict situations, players tended to modify the rules of the game to accommodate the needs and interests of fellow players, including those on the opposing team (Fluegelman, 1976). He described this as "softwar – conflict which is regionalized (to prevent injury to the uninterested), and refereed (to permit fairness and certainty of a win-lose outcome), and cushioned (weaponry regulated for maximum contact and minimum permanent disability)" (Brand as quoted in Fluegelman, 1976, p. 9).

About the same time, Brand's friend George Leonard (1974) was exploring the nature of play and sports, which led to his book *The Ultimate Athlete*. Leonard believed there was a significant relationship between the person and the games he or she played. "How we play the game may turn out to be more important than we imagine," wrote Leonard, "for it signifies nothing less than our way of being in the world" (Leonard as quoted in Fluegelman, 1981, p. 10). His work showed that games have the potential to both reflect and to transform culture. Future developments in the movement would soon demonstrate its potential.

It wasn't long before Brand and Leonard teamed up with Pat Farrington, a community organizer, to host the first New Games Tournament, held on two consecutive weekends in a 2,200-acre nature preserve near Golden Gate Bridge (Fluegelman, 1976). In addition to the substantial organizational effort, Farrington's contribution was adding her version of "soft touch" to Brand's concept of "softwar." She believed that by restructuring play, people could compete against their own limits rather than against each other. Farrington felt that

> by reexamining the basic idea of play, we could involve families, groups, and individuals in a joyous recreation experience that creates a sense of community and personal expression. People could center on the joy of playing, cooperating, and trusting, rather than striving to win. (Farrington as quoted in Fluegelman, 1976, p. 10)

And so, with softwar, creative play, and trust, the basic elements of a new approach to games was born. The essence of this transformative approach to play was a shift in a player's attitude. Play was celebrated by making the player the most important part of the game. The motto and only significant rule for these games was, "Play Hard, Play Fair, Nobody Hurt." It became the mantra for decades to come for all those who grew to love Snake-in-the-Grass, Hunker Hawser, Stand-Off, or the hundreds of new games that emerged from this movement.

The Cultural Impact of New Games

The new philosophy of play invigorated many physical education and recreation professionals who had also become trapped in the tradition and distorted values of the 1960s and 1970s. It was "generally agreed that the athletic department was the last refuge of authoritarianism, racism, and sexism. The reform movements of the previous decade, they suggested, had failed to lay a glove on the typical coach or physical education instructor" (Leonard, 1974, p. 6). Overweight students were embarrassed by instructors who called them out in front of the class to demonstrate pull-ups, or uncoordinated and unpopular students were made to stand by while waiting to hear their names called by their skilled peers who were picking teams for dodgeball.

Recreation leaders from that era seem to fare no better. In a scathing critique of the recreation and park movement, David Gray and Seymour Greben (1974) noted that when it comes to "what is important in our world (achievements, problems, etc.) it appears that we [recreation professionals] are not yet in the foreground of dynamic change and that typically we are followers, not leaders" (p. 31). They claimed the focus of too many recreation professionals had been on activities, facilities, or programs instead of "what happens to people" in a given activity or program.

Gray and Greben (1974) argued that if the recreation movement was to become relevant to the needs of society, it would require a paradigm shift highlighted by a new definition of recreation. In contrast to a specific event, a point in time, or a place in space, they suggested recreation was a state of being. From this perspective, "recreation is an emotional condition within an individual human being that flows from a feeling of well-being and self-satisfaction. It is characterized by feelings of mastery, achievement, exhilaration, acceptance, success, personal worth, and pleasure" (Gray & Greben, 1974, p. 49). According to these recognized recreation leaders, a successful recreation activity is not the number of participants but the personal experience that contributes to or detracts from the emotional and psychological health of each player.

If we accept this critique and redefinition of recreation, it changes our understanding of the nature and role of the recreation experience and those who lead these activities. Gray and Greben (1974) believed that if recreation activities were restructured, play would be instrumental in transforming culture. In other words, games not only reflect cultural values and traditions but can also play a role in shaping them. This notion is affirmed by noted game designers Salen and Zimmerman (2004), who wrote:

> ... the cultural play of a game is free movement within more rigid cultural structures. But when game play alters and shifts those cultural structures, the game becomes truly transformative: the rigid structures out of which play emerges are themselves reshaped through the very act of play. (p. 528)

For example, our attitudes toward ourselves and others can be significantly affected by how teams are selected or the order in which a player is chosen. Leaders should be aware that decisions such as how teams are selected are shaped by cultural and social values, which in turn are reinforced by the structures and rules of the game. Engaging in play is not a benign experience. It always generates an outcome, and frequently this outcome is determined by a given community or organization's rules, customs, mores, and structures.

The New Games Movement understood the impact that play, games, and sport could have in creating positive social change. At the same time, the movement became widely accepted in the last decades of the twentieth century because it embraced the core values of an emerging humanistic philosophy that focused on the power and potential of unique individualized experiences realized in a safe, secure environment. Leaders believed that play experiences, when properly framed and managed, could reshape society into a more humane, hospitable community where cooperation replaced beak-and-claw competition and trust overcame fear.

The framework developed by Brand and his friends involved several components that helped create a positive, engaging attitude toward play that placed a higher value on the player than the outcome of the game (Fluegelman, 1976). The concepts of challenge, trust, safety, fantasy and ritual, empowerment, and innovation provided space where community could grow and flourish. Having fun together doesn't just happen; it requires a safe place where every player feels free to let go of his or her inhibitions and trust the moment.

Components of New Games

Every player comes to a game or activity with baggage. She may have a play history that is largely shaped by failure, frustration, or fear. How will such a person find a safe, comfortable space that allows her to let go of these emotions long enough to experience the joy and freedom that a genuine play experience offers? Much of the outcome depends on the recreation leader or coach and how the play environment is shaped to create a positive attitude toward play and other players. Keeping the player as the most important part of the game, including sport and athletic contests, can only happen if the leader considers some key components of the game as identified by Brand and his colleagues (Fluegelman, 1981).

Challenge. The focus of New Games is on the challenge to one's self rather than comparing performances to others. This does not mean that new games are noncompetitive, but that they require players to work together to solve a problem or to challenge themselves to do things they might not have done before. Players are encouraged to enjoy the challenge of playing together to achieve a mutual goal to remove the unnecessary barriers inherent to the game, sport, or contest. Rather than merely overpowering an opponent, the players are encouraged to use "caring restraint," which means they only use as much force or effort as is necessary to match their opponents' efforts. The challenge for the weaker player is obvious, but the stronger player has to learn to find the competitive balance that will provide a healthy challenge for his or her opponent.

For example, since many games are intergenerational, they frequently pair adults with younger children. For games that require strength or higher levels of cognition, children would inherently be at a disadvantage and could easily become frustrated or discouraged. Therefore, the challenge for the adult is to use caring restraint to keep from dominating the child's effort to find some success in the game. When the adult controls the impulse to win and focuses on the interest of the younger opponent, the outcome of the game is measured not by who "won" or "lost" but by how the game was played.

This concept of challenge is supported by the research of noted play psychologist Mihaly Csikszentmihalyi (1975). He determined that the ideal play experience requires a balance between one's perceived challenge and perceived skill. The player must be confident he can perform the task or he/she will not be willing to attempt to achieve the goal. It is interesting to note that children, when left to design their own play spaces, often change the rules to accommodate for differences in skill and ability. They understand the fact that maintaining relationships with their opponent is essential for the play experience to be successful. It's simply no fun to be frustrated by failure without any hope of ever achieving the objective of winning a game. Thus, focusing on the effects of our play behaviors and interactions helps the player become the most important part of the game while maintaining the interrelationships among the community of players.

Trust. Play is a fragile gift that is only available to those who find a place where they are free from internal and external pressures or expectations, a place where they can let go of all inhibitions and fears. A playful spirit may survive in many different settings, but if it is to thrive, it requires an atmosphere of unqualified trust. Such an environment is established and built on caring attitudes and strong alliances between the players, teachers/coaches, parents, and spectators. The result is an open, caring community. When a player feels a connection to other players, including the opponents, he or she feels safe and free to play without fear of failure or rejection.

Other elements of New Games that contribute to an atmosphere of trust include: 1) allowing participants to opt out of a game they don't feel is safe; 2) providing players the opportunity to volunteer for specific roles in a game rather than just assigning a role that might be intimidating; 3) avoiding singling out or excluding "losers"; and 4) allowing everyone to modify the game by changing the rules to promote a safer, healthier environment.

Most game environments may be modified in this way, but it becomes more difficult in sport and athletic contests. But the principle of creating a safe environment in which each person can have an authentic play experience is critical to all settings.

Safety. It is difficult to let go of our inhibitions if we fear physical or emotional harm. Safety is closely linked to trust and, once again, is dependent on the care and concern of the players and the adult leaders. If the player is the most important part of the game, all participants will need to protect themselves and others from emotional or physical injury.

Five New Games safety principles that guide play behaviors state that all games should be contained, cushioned, controlled, and played with a sense of caring and community (Fluegelman, 1981). When a game is confined to a specific area and that area is free of potential hazards such as holes or brick walls, it is more likely to feel like it is a safe place to play. Players can also leave the confined space or simply opt out of playing whenever they feel their safety is being compromised or they are uncomfortable with the setting. Since players are all considered referees of the game, everyone is encouraged to suggest changes to the rules or make other suggestions that might help control risks or improve the quality of the game for the group.

Some of these concepts can be seen in competitive sports play today where rules are being changed to avoid situations that have contributed to higher risks of injury. This is especially true in contact sports, where concussions and related physical injuries have continued to increase risks to players.

Fantasy and Ritual. As we recall from our childhood, another important element of play is found in fantasy and rituals. Imagination fosters freedom as we create our own play spaces where we are released to be whoever we wish to be. Games such as Samurai Warrior or Giants/Elves/Wizards transport the player to a make-believe world where the ritual of bows and chants (the more realistic and dramatic the better) reinforce the spirit of spontaneity and playfulness. We go to a place where we forget, for a moment, the present reality and all its baggage. It is here that "we allow our shared fantasies to forge a play community free of real-world limitations and bounded only by our visions" (Fluegelman, 1976, p. 38).

Csikszentmihalyi (1975) noted that such intrinsically rewarding activities are critical to satisfying central human needs, including the desire to transcend our human limitations through fantasy. Such encounters may result in achieving the ultimate play experience of being lost in the moment, which Csikszentmihalyi labeled as flow. Many of us might recall being so involved in playing that we lost track of time and place, which often meant we missed supper because we didn't come home at the time our mothers had specified.

Similarly, it is not unusual for players in competitive sports and athletics to report they were in a "zone" during a certain part of the game. At such times, they were so totally immersed in playing that they were unaware of external stimuli such as crowds or weather conditions. Such experiences meet deep human needs and bring joy and pleasure to the player and are only possible in a play environment where the participant is free to totally engage in the activity at hand.

Empowerment. The most significant principle that underlies the attitude of play in New Games is empowerment. Empowerment emphasizes the value of the players by giving them control of, and responsibility for, their own play. As noted in the principle of safety, each player is also a referee, which gives him or her the responsibility of monitoring and leading the game. If this is to happen, the leader needs to look for opportunities to assume low visibility roles so that the players feel comfortable taking charge of the game. Only then will they be able to fulfill the final principle, innovation.

Empowerment is the basis for much of children's play because it allows the child to be in control. In a pure play environment, the player creates the structure and rules of engagement. Whether they are playing house or a game someone made up, they can determine the roles of the players and preferred outcomes of the game. Although more difficult in organized youth sports, coaches and teachers can allow the players to make some decisions about the position they might play or take other leadership roles on their team that might create a healthier play environment.

Innovation. Innovation involves keeping New Games new by looking for ways to change the rules or other aspects of the games, to keep them fresh and inviting for all the players. Innovation allows us to shape the game to fit a particular setting, group, or situation. Rotating players from one side of the volleyball court to the other after each point changes the focus from winning to teamwork and cooperation. Or running bases in reverse order in a softball game creates a whole new dimension to the game that might otherwise become boring to some players. Youth sport coaches may use creative plays to stimulate interest and enjoyment in the game or use innovative drills or games that break the monotony or routine of practices.

In summary, these six concepts of challenge, trust, safety, fantasy and ritual, empowerment, and innovation provide the basis for a new approach to play that values and celebrates the countercultural concept that the player is the most important part of any game. Creating a play environment where all participants feel safe and respected, even when engaged in highly competitive athletic activities, is the real contribution of the New Games movement. The question is, how can some of these concepts be used to create healthier play environments in our contemporary culture, and how can they contribute to a Christian perspective on play.

Evaluating the Nature and Purpose of Our Play

Although not necessarily new, the New Games philosophy may give Christians a fresh way of redesigning and evaluating our play so that we achieve outcomes that more closely reflect Christian values and beliefs than our contemporary cultural standards. We need to focus more on our attitudes, how we play, and the outcomes of play experiences. Celebrating play by making the players the most important part of the game and endorsing "Play hard, play fair, nobody hurt" is a play ethic Christians might embrace if placed in the context of our relationship with God.

Ethical behaviors and moral principles are part and parcel of every aspect of our life. A Christian approach toward play emphasizes the significance of being part of a human community and part of God's family, with each one created in God's image. Injuring or diminishing other members of this community either emotionally, spiritually, or physically to achieve some personal goal seems to be antithetical to a commitment to follow Christ's command to "love your neighbor as yourself" (Matt. 19:19, NIV).

Therefore, the humanistic philosophy of New Games, when reoriented to reflect a Christian worldview, may provide an ethical and moral framework that could help to structure our play so that it more clearly images God's desires for us. These insights, along with the theological and philosophical foundation of a Christian play ethic that has been developed by several authors including Dahl (1972), Holmes (1981), Johnston (1983), Visker (2006) and more recently Hoffman (2010a, 2010b), provide the basis for our discussion on the nature and purpose of our play.

Our Relationship with God

At some point in everyone's life, the questions are asked, "Who am I?" and "Why am I here?" Some might respond by saying, "I'm simply a result of a long evolutionary process, and I'm here for this period in time simply to enjoy the moment and get everything I can out of life. Since this life is all there is, I'm going to make the most of it by satisfying every impulse to find pleasure in the moment." Such a hedonistic, person-centered worldview reinforces comparisons with others, which leads to fractured relationships in work and in play. Play becomes perverted and self-serving, with little chance of sustaining healthy, authentic relationships with others.

Christians, however, believe that we are all created by God for a specific purpose: to bring glory and honor to him. Moreover, we are created in the very image of God and are called to develop and care for this image as a very special gift. Play helps define the nature of this gift by encouraging the player to let go of inhibitions and constraints as she/he moves toward free expression and joy.

This sense of freedom is more fully understood when we consider the nature of God's grace in our daily lives. If we view all of life as a gift from God, we begin to rest in God's amazing love that surrounds us and assures us of care at all times and in all circumstances. Such a worldview allows us to take reasonable risks, to live freely, to be creative, and play with abandonment, resting in God's provision and grace.

As God's image bearers, we are to reflect God's goodness, love, joy, and peace in all that we do. Therefore, others should be able to see the very nature of God in us as we play, work, and worship. These attributes of God will become evident if we play, work, and worship with integrity, the way we were made to function. Roberts (1993) noted, "If we are to 'be somebody,' we also need to take the active role of lovers [of God]. We must become participants in God's cause, actively attaching ourselves to him by working, at his side, toward his goals" (pp. 162–163).

If we get hooked by our highly competitive athletic culture, we may undermine our relationship with God by placing a particular player, team, activity, game, or sport on a pedestal. Sport icons such as Tiger Woods or Michael Jordon can dominate our thinking or influence us to buy certain clothes, sporting equipment, or other products, or to behave in a certain way. In some cases, these icons can become our idols and draw us away from intimacy with God and affect our ability to accurately reflect God's image. Such distortions quickly change the nature of the play experience so that it becomes more self-serving than God-serving.

The classic film *Chariots of Fire* describes two British runners who competed in the 1924 Olympic Games. Eric Liddell was a Scottish evangelical who later became a missionary to China, and his teammate Harold Abrahams was an Englishman of Jewish Lithuanian background. Each had a perspective on their sport that helps us understand how our motivation for an activity shapes and influences our relationship with God.

When Abrahams' girlfriend, Sybil, asked if he loved running, he responded, "I'm more of an addict; it's more of a weapon." "Against what?" Sybil asked. "Being Jewish, I suppose," he responded. Harold's primary motive for running was to prove his worth and raise his self-esteem. Later, when he lost a race and became despondent, Sybil declared, "It's a race you've lost; nobody's dead," and he responded, "I don't run to take beatings. I run to win; if I can't win I won't run." He believed the only way to maintain his true identity as a person was to beat everyone else. Such a perspective leaves little room for recognizing and celebrating the *imago dei* in ourselves and others.

Eric Liddell, on the other hand, recognized that although his goal was to win, his relationship with God was the primary purpose for running. In response to his sister's concern about spending too much time preparing for Olympic competition, Eric replied, "He [God] made me fast. And when I run, I feel his pleasure. . . . To win is to honor him." So, although athletic competition dominated much of Eric's immediate life, he was able to keep it in proper perspective because he placed it in the context of his relationship to God rather than the outcome of race.

Thus, the nature of our play helps define our true identity. We can become a person made in the image of God who reflects God in all we do, or we can create a pseudo self-image that seeks praise from all that competes with God in the world. One who seeks to "make something of himself" through athletic participation "fails miserably in attempts to be a self because he does not attach himself to what is really great and seeks glory from what precludes real glory" (Roberts, 1993, p. 164). In teaching his disciples, Jesus said, "The greatest among you will be your servant. For whoever exalts himself will be humbled, and whoever humbles himself will be exalted" (Matt. 23:11–12). Therefore, it's not about who won or lost, but how the player reflects the image of God and develops a more intimate relationship with God through play.

Our Relationship with Others

The legendary baseball player and coach Leo Durocher quipped, "I never did say that you can't be a nice guy and win. I said that if I was playing third base and my mother rounded third with the winning run, I'd trip her up" (Durocher, 1974, p. 14). Genuine relationships are built on trust, and Durocher's quote stands in stark contrast to Jesus' admonition to "Do to others as you would have them do to you" (Matt. 7:12). Unfortunately, many other elements of our culture, including our religious life, family life, political life, and work life, are infected with the same deadly beak-and-claw disease.

If generalized reciprocity or trustworthiness is fundamental to civilized life, as noted author Robert Putnam (2000) claimed, then the Christian community has their work cut out for them. "Our entire culture is set up to seduce us into thinking competitively about ourselves and our neighbors" (Roberts, 1993, p. 161). Christians must begin to reestablish social and relational priorities that value other persons and hold the player as the most important part of the game of life. We were created to live in community, and community requires authentic relationships founded on the love of God. The Bible describes this love as being patient and kind.

> It does not envy, it does not boast, it is not proud. It does not dishonor others, it is not self-seeking, it is not easily angered, it keeps no record of wrongs. Love does not delight in evil but rejoices with the truth. It always protects, always trusts, always hopes, and always perseveres. (1 Cor. 13:4–7)

These words describe an attitude that must be extended to our fellow players, team members, and even our opponents. Yes, opponents are part of our human community, and therefore must be treated as collaborators or partners in the game.

In this context, Christian attitudes toward play leave no room for harming or devaluing others who, like you, are created in God's image. Instead, we are to build others up, to help them reflect their true nature as human beings. Genuine play requires trust and respect, not animosity toward opponents. "Playful competitiveness perceives the opponent as a fellow, not as an alien, and presupposes something like love. After all, the mature Christian finds her true self in her love for God and neighbor" (Roberts, 1993, p. 169).

The apostle Paul describes what it means to live out Christ's command to love God above all and our neighbor as our self. Rather than focusing on "making something of ourselves," he says we need to be servant leaders characterized by

> . . . love, joy, peace, forbearance, kindness, goodness, faithfulness, gentleness, and self-control. . . . Those who belong to Christ Jesus have crucified the flesh with its passions and desires. Since we live by the Spirit, let us keep in step with the Spirit. Let us not become conceited, provoking and envying each other. (Gal. 5: 22–26)

This is a very challenging task, especially in the heat of athletic competition. It requires the trust and humility Jesus calls us to when he says, "Unless you change and become like little children, you will never enter the kingdom of heaven" (Matt. 18:3).

Our Relationship with Ourselves

Similarly, our play should respect our own humanity as persons created in the image of God. As the psalmist so beautifully states, "I praise you because I am fearfully and wonderfully made" (Ps. 139:14). Play helps develop and celebrate God's masterpiece in all its complexity and majesty. Play can socialize, discipline, restore, invigorate, relax, educate, glorify, heal, strengthen, surprise, and bring us joy. Noted Christian author C.S. Lewis (1954) wrote that play

> arouses in us sensations we have never had before, never anticipated having as though we had broken out of our normal mode of consciousness and possess joys ("Joy") not promised to our birth. It gets under our skin, hits us at a level deeper than our thoughts or even our passions, troubles oldest certainties till all questions are reopened, and in general shocks us more fully awake than we are for most of our lives. (pp. 16–17)

For Lewis, the more one enters into the play event, the greater the possibility that God will use this experience to transform us by enhancing our awareness of him. Lewis (1955) described such an interaction with God in his autobiographical work, *Surprised by Joy*: "I was driven to Whipsnade [the zoo] one sunny morning. When we set out I did not believe that Jesus Christ was the Son of God, and when we reached the zoo I did" (p. 238). In this instance, a play experience created the setting in which God revealed himself to Lewis in a new and powerful way. Hiking in the mountains, watching the sunset, studying the stars on a clear night, running or cycling on a cold crisp morning, or playing a game with good friends can all provide special transformative experiences that help connect us with God's spirit in a fresh way.

In addition, caring for ourselves involves engaging in healthy play behaviors while avoiding those that would harm us socially, emotionally, physically, or spiritually. As more data on sports injuries are collected, we are becoming aware of the inherent dangers and risks of injury in many sports today. Engaging in play that exposes us to significant risk such as base jumping, free climbing (rock climbing), and auto racing must be considered within this guiding principle.

More specifically, if we take our mandate to be stewards of our bodies seriously, it is hard to see how a sport like boxing can be justified. The ultimate goal of this sport essentially seems to involve trying to give your opponent a brain injury before he does the same to you. Activities such as this would seem to be outside the scope of Christian play principles that call us to honor and glorify God as his image bearers.

Hoffman (2010b) predicted that Christians will only begin to abandon the unequivocal embrace of the sports culture "when they recognize that many of the ills of sport stem not from violating the creeds of sport but from over-conforming to them" (p. 25). Contemporary cultural values that show little regard for human life or wellbeing cannot be our standard for participation in play and sporting activities. We have to meet a higher standard because we are "fearfully and wonderfully made" by a loving and gracious God.

Our Relationship with Creation/Nature

In addition to considering how our play affects our relationship with God, with others, and with ourselves, a Christian play ethic must consider the impact of our play on the natural environment. At the time of creation, God gave humans the responsibility of caring for the world he had made. Since much of our play involves a direct or indirect connection with creation, we would expect that there are some issues we need to consider when we play.

But what might a personal outdoor play ethic look like? Leopold (1949) proposed that such an ethic recognizes that we are part of a larger ecosystem, a community that includes soils, water, plants, and animals. We are not placed in this world to simply use these resources for our own personal pleasure but have been called by God to become co-creators with him. By properly caring for and managing these natural resources, we are able to continue the creational work of God through sustaining this fragile ecosystem from generation to generation. Thus, according to Leopold, proper care demands that each question of man's relationship to his environment be examined "in terms of what is ethically and esthetically right, as well as what is economically expedient" (p. 224). Leopold concluded, "A thing is right when it tends to preserve the integrity, stability, and beauty of the biotic community. It is wrong when it tends otherwise" (p. 224–5).

Unfortunately, some of our interaction with the environment has not met this ethical standard. Christian philosopher Art Holmes (1981) warned that we are "spending our natural resources on riotous living" (p. 47), including using scarce resources on auto racing or speeding around a lake in a gas-guzzling boat that pollutes the environment. He also questioned the appropriateness of bullfighting or cockfighting or hunting animals just for the sake of killing them. According to Holmes, "such 'games' disregard the stewardly purposes and consequent limitations of man's 'dominion' over nature" (p. 47). Exploiting the earth for personal gain, even in the spirit of play, is simply not acceptable for people who are called to be caretakers of God's world.

Having dominion over creation does not imply domination (De-

Graaf, 2006). Rather, dominion, properly understood, requires the same spirit of humility and servanthood Christ showed in his coming into the world to serve and save us. "The human is, as God's steward, accountable to God and responsible for its fellow creatures. Such a commitment requires that stewardship becomes a part of who we are rather than something we do" (DeGraaf, 2006, p. 130). Our high calling is to serve and preserve the earth, not rule and rape it for our own pleasure. Thus, all of play and sport must be viewed within the context of its impact on and compatibility with God's creation.

Conclusion

Play is one of our most natural and basic activities. God created us to play. It's one way that all God's creatures glorify and praise him. But due to the prevailing cultural, person-centered worldview, too much of our play reflects "the steadfast, even compulsive, disposition to stake one's value as a person on winning" (Roberts, 1993, p. 158). Winning is a natural and legitimate goal of most games, sport, and athletics, but I have argued that it must remain within the context of one's ultimate purpose in life, to glorify God and enjoy God forever.

Genuine play is also a gift that is essential to human development. However, to maintain the integrity of the play experience in our free play, games, sports, and athletics, we will need to resist the prevailing pressure to value the product of the experience over the process.

The New Games Movement provides one option for creating and maintaining a healthy play environment where the player is the most important component of the game.

This objective is accomplished by considering several structural and attitudinal components of the game, including challenge, trust, safety, fantasy or ritual, empowerment, and innovation. By infusing more of our play, games, sports, and athletics with these components, we may begin to transform them from what Huizinga (1955) described as "profane, 'unholy' [activities]" (p. 197). The New Games Movement demonstrates that there are alternative ways of playing that place a high value on how we play and what happens to the player, which I have argued is more consistent with a Christian perspective on play.

A God-centered worldview recognizes the player as being created in the *imago dei*. As such, players are placed on this earth to develop and enjoy a relationship with God, with other players (including opponents), with themselves, and with the natural environment. A Christian play ethic requires that all our play respect, honor, and celebrate these relationships. If we evaluate our play by its effect on these relationships, we may be able to take some steps toward redeeming play and sport in a beak-and-claw culture. This is only possible, however, if we allow the Holy Spirit to renew our minds and guide us in living out the Christian values and beliefs that are central to our faith and testimony.

References

Brand, S. (Ed.). (1968). *The whole earth catalog*. Menlo Park, CA: Portola Institute.
Byl, J. (2006). Coming to terms with play, game, sport, and athletics. In P. Heintzman, G.E. Van Andel, & T.L. Visker (Eds.), *Christianity and leisure: Issues in a pluralistic society* (Rev. ed., pp. 164–172). Sioux Center: Dordt College Press.
Csikszentmihalyi, M. (1975). *Beyond boredom and anxiety*. San Francisco: Jossey-Bass.
Dahl, G. (1972). *Work, play, and worship in a leisure-oriented society*. Minneapolis: Augsburg.
DeGraaf, D. (2006). Unless someone like you cares a whole awful lot. In P. Heintzman, G.E. Van Andel, & T.L. Visker (Eds.), *Christianity and leisure: Issues in a pluralistic society* (Rev. ed., pp. 125–144). Sioux Center: Dordt College Press.
Durocher, L. (1975). *Nice guys finish last*. Chicago: The University of Chicago Press.
Fluegelman, A. (Ed.). (1976). *The new games book*. Garden City, NY: Doubleday.
Fluegelman, A. (Ed.). (1981). *More new games*. Garden City, NY: Doubleday.
Gray, D., & Greben, S. (1974, July). Future Perspectives. *Parks and Recreation* 9(6), 26–33, 47–56.
Hoffman, S.J. (2010a). *Good game: Christianity and the culture of sports*. Waco, TX: Baylor University Press.
Hoffman, S.J. (2010b). Whatever happened to play? *Christianity Today* 54(2), 21–25.
Holmes, A. (1981). Towards a Christian play ethic. *Christian Scholars Review* 11(1): 41–48.
Huizinga, J. (1955). *Homo ludens: A study of the play-element in culture*. Boston: Beacon Press.
Johnston, R.K. (1983). *The Christian at play*. Grand Rapids: Eerdmans.
Leonard, G. (1974). *The ultimate athlete: Re-envisioning sports, physical education, and the body*. New York: The Viking Press.
Leopold, A. (1949). *A Sand Country almanac*. New York: Oxford University Press.

Lewis, C.S. (Ed.). (1954). *George MacDonald: An anthology.* New York: Macmillan.

Lewis, C.S. (1955). *Surprised by joy: The shape of my early life.* New York: Harcourt, Brace & World, Harvest Books.

Putnam, R.D. (2000). *Bowling alone: The collapse and revival of American community.* New York: Simon & Shuster.

Roberts, R. (1993). *Taking the Word to heart.* Grand Rapids: Eerdmans.

Salen, K., & Zimmerman, E. (2004). *Rules of play: Game design fundamentals.* Cambridge, MA: The MIT Press.

The Westminster Shorter Confession of Faith. (1646/1990). Lawrenceville, GA: Presbyterian Church of America Bookstore.

Visker, T. (2006). Play, game and sport in a reformed, biblical worldview. In P. Heintzman, G.E Van Andel, & T.L. Visker (Eds.), *Christianity and leisure: Issues in a pluralistic society* (Rev. ed., pp. 173–192). Sioux Center: Dordt College Press.

Woods, R. (2011). *Social issues in sport* (2nd ed.). Champaign, IL: Human Kinetics.

Chapter 16
CAN PLAY BUILD CHARACTER?

Arthur Holmes

Over the past 20 years or so, a significant shift has been occurring in the teaching of ethics. The activist 1960s had focused attention on social issues like race relations and war, and a cottage industry developed in "moral problems" courses with an emphasis on moral decision-making. Cognitive development theory contributed most notably to Lawrence Kohlberg's (1984) developmental stages for moral reasoning. Case studies typically were used, focusing on moral dilemmas, and students learned to bring ethical principles to bear on relevant factors in an actual case. The assumptions underlying this approach, however, reveal its limitations: it assumed, true to Enlightenment thinking, that there are universally accepted moral principles independent of differing world views, that the gender-neutral pattern of cognitive development exists, and so moral development means developing skills in reasoned decision-making. But how many real moral dilemmas does the average person face in a lifetime? Most of the time we know what ought to be done, but have conflicting desires. I recall a former student, now highly successful in the financial world, who said to me, "When I hire someone, I'm not interested in his decision-making skills, but in his character."

The focus in ethics teaching has likewise been shifting to virtue ethics and character formation. Crucial in this shift was the work of Alasdair MacIntyre. His *After Virtue* (1981) challenged the Enlightenment approach to ethics and highlighted the incommensurability of its alternative theories. *Whose Justice? Which Rationality?* (1988) looked at the moral traditions in the liberal university world. *Three Rival Versions of Moral Enquiry* (1990) critiqued both the Enlightenment and the postmodern relativist traditions, arguing that an Aristotelian and Christian ethic of virtues must also have a voice in higher education.

Virtues are inner moral dispositions, more affective than cognitive;

Revised version of paper presented at the 2002 conference.

they are deeply rooted inclinations, habits of the heart that underlie our outward behavior. Character is the overall pattern of one's virtue and vices; it defines a person's inner morality. So moral development viewed as character development means developing appropriate inner inclinations and desires. The ancient Greeks understood this: their children studied, recited, and acted Homer with all the emotion of his character, until heroic virtues like courage became their inner nature. Gymnastics prepared them for athletic contests, evoking the courage that aristocratic Greece desired. It is affective learning, not just cognitive, that shapes character. We sometimes hear exaggerated claims for the character traits competitive sport supposedly teaches, notorious counterexamples notwithstanding. But of course, it is far from automatic: the player, like anybody else, is subject to a variety of influences, from coaches and fans and fellow players, as well as their own athletic heroes and competitive spirit. So our question is really how teachers and coaches and fellow players can help build character.

The overall shape of a person's character depends on the overall orientation of her life, on her overall disposition, what she most desires as her "supreme good." Aristotle used the term "supreme good" to refer to the highest of all goals, the most inclusive ideal, and the good that makes every other good worthwhile. It is what the *Westminster Shorter Catechism* calls her highest end: "to glorify God and enjoy him forever." This is what makes character distinctively Christian. Can play teach that kind of character, Christian character?

This is where the theology of play becomes crucial. A long tradition of Christian reflection sees play as a metaphor for life (Miller, 1973). Clement of Alexandria suggested that life is a divine children's game (Miller, 1973). God invented it for his own pleasure, freely. He did not have to create, let alone send his only son, but he did, and he still plays his role in life's game. Aquinas pointed out that playing is not a means to some other extraneous end, but something we do for its own sake, for pleasure and recreation (Miller, 1973). He calls players "well-turned" because they turn so readily to laughter and enjoyment. Martin Luther calls earth's creatures "God's masks and mummeries" that reveal his continued participation (as quoted in Huizinga, 1955, p. 212). Moreover, justification by faith so frees us from having to work for our salvation that we can play before God, simply for the joy of it. John Calvin (trans. 1813) calls this world the theater of God's glory. The German theologian Jürgen Moltmann (1972) claims that God is better understood in categories of pleasure and play than of guilt and death. Play is a symbol of the life lived joyfully for his glory.

If play points us beyond itself to our highest end, then the consistent habit of playing with that in mind can extend to life itself. It can influence our overall disposition toward God and help build distinctively Christian character. The Christian teacher and coach who makes it his or her business to nurture Christian habits of mind about play cultivates a Christian disposition toward life as a whole.

Particular virtues are habitual inner dispositions. In book two of his *Nicomachean Ethics,* Aristotle (trans. 1947) pointed out that we cultivate them in children by constant training, and that we have to train ourselves by deliberately choosing the good again and again until it becomes our second nature. It takes a kind of mental and emotional self-discipline to bring wayward desires and inclinations into line. Aquinas, in his *Summa Theologica* (trans. 1948, I-II, q. 63) too emphasized habituation, but for distinctively Christian virtues like love he added "infusion", the infusion of grace by God's Spirit. Martin Luther saw a much broader need for infusion, but still recognized the basic role of habituation. So to suggest how teaching and coaching might contribute, I draw your attention to three habit-building helps that are currently emphasized in the literature on character development: community, mentor and model, and friendship.

Community

A major influence upon my understanding of community is the work of Stanley Hauerwas, for example his book *Community of Character* (1987). Several recent studies suggest that the key to moral formation in the university is the development of small residential communities where the student can define his own identity (Hoekema, 1994; Willimon & Naylor, 1995). The suggestion applies equally well to an academic department, a sport, or a team. Such a community has a life of its own, a story of past struggles and contests that capture the imagination, activities and traditions that bond its members together, a heritage of ideals and values of which they can feel proud, and an ongoing struggle to excel. As newcomers become part of the community's life and identify with its people, they think of the group not as 'them' them" but as "us," and its story as "our own," and they gradually assimilate its ideals. They voice their sentiments in the adages of the community and pick up proverbial sayings perpetuated from some leader in the past ("It's always too soon to quit!"), or even cite the college motto or name of a team as capturing the spirit of the place. When this sort of community has a moral purpose that becomes evident in the stories it recalls and in present practices or ongoing service projects, and when moral expectations and levels of accountability are inherent in community life, then it becomes a moral culture, perhaps a counterculture, in which the student internalizes a sense of overall vocation, a vision of life in partnership with God and this kind of people. Sociologist James Davidson Hunter (2000) claims that moral education has its most enduring effects on young people "when they inhabit a social world that coherently incarnates . . . a moral culture that is strong and mutually reinforcing" (p. 155). Our question then becomes: what can we do to build this kind of community and foster this kind of moral culture.

Mentor and Model

The role of mentor and model likewise applies to a coach and teacher. Think of the practice you require: practicing skills, doing it again and again, day after day, teaches self-discipline and requires self-denial, a persistent resistance to "the easy way out." These are transferable virtues, valuable in every area of life. Think, too, of group learning and team spirit, and how they instill altruism, humility, and respect for others. Think of "playing by the rules," the honesty it requires, and the sense of responsibility it can develop. Good coaching can build a "play conscience" that carries over into the game of life. Play is like an internship, a natural venue for reflecting on the means we use and the ends we seek, and for a repeated self-examination that critiques old habits and develops the will to change. It is the coach as mentor who sees to it that such self-examination occurs.

He may be more directive than an academic mentor, but like an internship supervisor, he observes and listens, asks key questions, makes suggestions, offers advice, and holds the player accountable. He will take a similar interest in other areas of the player's life, and in the attitudes and habits in evidence there. As a teacher, I occasionally asked a student whose attitudes concerned me, "Have you thought what sort of person you are becoming?" or "How should I describe your character when you ask me to write recommendations?" This is the sort of thing moral mentoring involves. But the most effective mentor is one who models in his own life and character the virtues he expects of others. It was said of Bernard of Clairvaux that he taught by his physical presence, so that students learned by reading his attitudes, habits, and character. A living example of aspiration to virtue, according to David Carr (1991), is the *sine qua non* of effective moral education. The Christian is called to be like Christ, and that means being a moral exemplar who models a quality of life to which students will aspire. Perhaps we should include this role of moral mentor and model in our job descriptions.

Friendship

Friendship, while possible within a community or with a mentor, implies a closer, more intimate bond than community or mentoring themselves can normally provide. It is the most recent focus of the three in the literature on moral development, although discussion of it, too, goes back to Aristotle (trans. 1947, Books 8 & 9; see also Meilaender, 1961; Wadell, 1989). He distinguished a friendship of utility (for social or economic gain) and a friendship of pleasure (for companionship in having fun) from a friendship of the good, where friends want virtuous character above all else. It begins quite naturally with mutual attraction and good will, but it develops by discovering common goals or pursuing common tasks (as classmates and teammates do), and these common ideals lead friends to feel responsible for how they each behave. Their lives become like open books: they admit to each other their failings and point out each other's faults: "wounds from a friend can be trusted" (Prov. 27:6, NIV). They support each other's resolves and hold themselves mutually accountable. They talk about their dreams, the kind of persons they want to become, and how each might help the other grow. They gain a clearer vision of who they are, a firmer resolve, and good habits gradually develop. The friendship helps define their moral identity, for they even take on each other's character traits. "As iron sharpens iron, so one person sharpens another" (Prov. 27:17). Cicero (1909) regarded this sort of friendship as an apprenticeship in virtue, and Augustine reportedly said that Christian friendship schools us in Christian love. Isn't that what we should expect?

How might we encourage this kind of friendship between students, or pose it is a challenge for teammates? Community can define the direction of their moral development. Mentoring can monitor their progress and keep them on track. But in Christian friendship, they find an alter ego that knows their weaknesses, supports their struggles, and delights in their growths, one that can continue after their college years.

References

Aristotle. (1947). *The Nicomachean ethics* (H. Rackham, Trans.). Cambridge, MA: Harvard University Press.

Aquinas, T. (1948). *Summa Theologica*. Westminster, MD: Christian Classics.

Calvin, J. (1813). *Institutes of the Christian religion*. (J. Allan, Trans.). London: J. Walker.

Carr, D. (1991). *Educating the virtues: An essay on the philosophical psychology of moral development and education*. London: Routledge.

Cicero, M.T. (1909). *Treatise on friendship*. In *The Harvard Classics* (vol. 9). New York: P.F. Collier & Sons.

Hauerwas, S. (1987). *A community of character*. Notre Dame: University of Notre Dame Press.

Hoekema, D. (1994). *Campus rules and moral community*. Lanham, MD: Rowman & Littlefield.

Huizinga, J. (1955). *Homo ludens: A study of the play-element in culture*. Boston: Beacon Press.

Hunter, J.D. (2000). *The death of character: Moral education in an age without good or evil*. New York: Basic Books.

Kohlberg (1984). *The psychology of moral development: The nature and validity of moral stages*. New York: Harper & Row.

Meilaender, G. (1961). *Friendship and the moral life*. Notre Dame: University of Notre Dame Press.

Miller, D. (1973). *Gods and games: Towards a theology of play*. New York: Harper-Colophon Books.

Moltmann, J. (1972). *Theology of play*. (Trans. R. Ulrich). New York: Harper & Row.

Wadell, P.J. (1989). *Friendship and the moral life*. Notre Dame: University of Notre Dame Press.

Willimon, W.H., & Naylor, T.H. (1995). *The abandoned generation: Rethinking higher education*. Grand Rapids: Eerdmans.

Chapter 17
Toward a Theology of Risk

Bud Williams

Carl and Jeff have developed their skills to the point of near perfection. Their goal is to kayak the lower section of a Class IV rapid and shoot a 25-foot falls into a deep pool of water. Carl makes the drop cleanly into the pool below, but Jeff's boat remains flat on the descent and the impact leaves Jeff paralyzed from the hips downward. Bob falls from a ropes course element while participating in an adventure challenge program with his youth group and remains in critical condition wearing a respirator. Jen, an experienced indoor wall climber, does her first lead climb on a bolted route but fails to clip in to one of her quick draws properly and takes a hard leader fall, resulting in a life-threatening head injury. At the completion of a gymnastics routine on the high bar, Curt overturns a not yet perfected half-in, half-out dismount, causing severe damage to the cervical region of his spinal column. In the fourth quarter of the conference championship game, Kevin sustains a jarring blow to the chest that stops his heart and takes his life. Life seems to be filled with risks, many of which are unavoidable. Should voluntary risks be added to these already existing daily risks? Is unnecessary risk-taking sin? A survey of the literature in this area indicates that we have not done much theological thinking about risk-taking. This chapter will explore a theological perspective on risk and risk-taking to better understand why we live in a risky world and how the Christian should approach managing risk and participation in risk-taking activities and sports.

Defining Risk

What is risk? The word *risk* comes from the early Italian word *risicare* – to dare. A risk-taker dares to beat the odds against loss to self and possessions. One who risks does so when she ventures into the unknown

---

Revised version of paper presented at the 2000 conference.

when the outcomes are not guaranteed. In this sense, living life with the uncertainties of the future is a risk-taking venture. Life is full of potential events that can rob a person of wealth, friends, family, health, and even life itself. We are born into a risky world. Even the birth process is plagued with potential threats to life. No one can count on the next moment of life.

The Nature of God and Risk

To develop any "theology of," one must start with the nature of God, because existence itself emanates from the will of God. Because God is all-powerful, all-knowing, and sovereign, ultimately cannot be at risk. However, He chose to create humans with a free will and self-consciousness with the potential for self-idolatry and rejection of God. In doing so God's creation was created with risk.

The Nature of Humans and Risk

Therefore, the study of risk is really a study of who we are as we relate to each other and our world. It is a study that begins with our created nature. We are created with a free will so that we may willingly love God or reject him. To be human means to be finite. Only God has infinite knowledge (omniscience) and infinite power (omnipotence) to control all existence and all events. Finitude leaves us with limited knowledge, limited power, many unknowns and uncertainties, and the potential to be overwhelmed by more powerful forces. We do not have ultimate control over our existence.

The Nature of Our World and Risk

If we lived in a world where we all had the knowledge of all the laws that governed its existence and held the power to control these laws, we could control our world. We could use these laws to our benefit. We would be more powerful than any force in our world. The exercise of our will would have ultimate control over our environment and we would be sovereign here on earth. We would not be at physical risk unless our choices were to use that power or knowledge to destroy the world that gives us life, or destroy life itself. Since our will would be more powerful than nature, it would influence every other person in the world, and each person would have the potential to destroy everyone in the world and the world itself. In order to avoid this calamity, each person would have to willingly agree to not use their power except to nurture a world that would not harm others. Each decision to use that knowledge and power to change the world would need to be carefully considered and agreed upon by all others to avoid conflict of interest. Inevitably, an individual's free will exercised independently would be rendered null and void. A collective will would have to prevail to avoid anarchy. The world would have to be run by a collective agreement that would benefit all, or by a more powerful benevolent dictator whose decisions would be in the best interest of all.

Fortunately, the laws of the world we live in are established independent of our will. We cannot change these laws but only gain an understanding of them and learn how to use laws appropriately and function within them. Furthermore, our knowledge is finite, and we have only been able to understand these laws in a limited way to live in a relative degree of safety. Our power is limited, and the forces in this world are far more powerful than we are. Therefore, we are born into a world of risk, in which the exercise of our free will brings consequences but not total destruction of all humanity.

Fallen Humans and Risk

In exercising free will, humans chose to reject God and ignore his wisdom. Because of this, the earth is both friend and alien. Humans no longer live in a safe garden with regular walks with their Creator, the source of all knowledge and all power. Both the judgment and behavior of humans and the functioning of the earth has been distorted by evil. Since humans exist in a symbiotic state with the rest of nature, their decisions interact directly with environmental systems affecting both the environment and themselves. Because of disobedience to God, humans know both good and evil and are capable of both. Disregard of stewardship responsibilities for the earth related to disregard for God and fellow humans have placed the environment at risk, and have risked human life as well. Human evil always leads to death (Ezek. 33:12–13).

Adding to the threats from an alienated earth and human propensity to evil is the source of original evil himself, Satan, also called "the prince of this world" (John 16:11) and "the evil one" (Eph. 6:16). His desire is to pervert what God has made by turning humans away from God and goodness and toward evil. God allowed Satan to test Job by destroying all his possessions, including wealth, his children, and health. As the prince of this world, Satan used lightning, high wind, disease, and evil humans to destroy and pervert what God had created (Job 1:12–2:7).

Risking to Control Risk

Controlling risk requires understanding our world, and this requires venturing into the unknown, which is at the heart of risk-taking. We take risks to penetrate the unknown in our world, and within us, in order to gain more knowledge about our environment and ourselves. Extending the limits of our knowledge of this world and the limits of human potential increases our knowledge of how we can live safely in this world.

Natural law functions with a high degree of observable consistency. God gave humans a rational mind to observe cause and effect and to gain understanding of our world. Use of the scientific method and probability theory has allowed us to understand the causes of many of our diseases and accidents that take or diminish our quality of life. We understand how the laws of nature benefit us and, when violated, can harm us. Gravity, for example, is necessary for us to remain properly connected to the earth but can cause our death if we fall from a height. By applying scientific knowledge, we can predict and control many risks. Yet, we fall far short of understanding the complexity of these laws that provide order to our universe and the dangers involved when we push into the unknown beyond our current knowledge and human limits. But even more unpredictable is the behavior of human beings that raises our collective risk level.

Choice and Risk

To risk implies choice, and choice implies right and wrong choices. If there were not opportunity for wrong choices, there would not be freedom of the will. Choices imply consequences. Consequences are not all readily apparent, nor do they result from all choices, but choices dealing with natural and moral laws are most usually consequential, both for good and bad. Humans are created as free moral agents.

The dimensions of time and space provide the necessary environment through which we can exercise our human autonomy and freedom of choice and experience the consequences of these choices. Without time there would be no realization of the effects of our choices, and our choices would have no significance and be meaningless. Without space (our physical environment and our embodied selves), choices would not have substance or real consequences, and they would not be real choices. We live our future by the choices and risks we take today. We manage these risks through understanding the effects of our past choices and the wisdom revealed to us concerning the gravity of our choices.

Not to choose in itself is a choice and can be fraught with risk. Think through the dilemma of the four lepers at the entrance of the city gate of Samaria, who faced starvation during a terrible famine imposed by the siege of the Syrian army.

> Now there were four men with leprosy at the entrance of the city gate. They said to each other, "Why stay here until we die? If we say, 'We'll go into the city' – the famine is there, and we will die. And if we stay here, we will die. So let's go over to the camp of the Arameans and surrender. If they spare us, we live; if they kill us, then we die. (2 Kings 7:3–4)

The famine was so severe in the city that two women agreed to each kill their sons on two separate days and eat them to stay alive. Remaining at the entrance of the city gate for the lepers was as risky as going into the city where they were not only unwelcome due to being declared unclean by Jewish law, but would face the same extreme lack of food. Entering the camp of the Arameans could also lead to death. To not choose was as risky as to choose, but in choosing, they went beyond what was their present state and moved from the known into the unknown to try what they had not tried before. To be fully human means to choose and to risk, and that often means to enter the unknown.

An Example of Full Humanness and Risk

Our example of what it means to be fully human primarily comes from our knowledge of Jesus Christ. He entered a risky world whereby risks were present because of the Fall and human finitude which Jesus willingly took on as he emptied himself of his divine power and infinite knowledge (Phil. 2:6–8). As a fully human being, Jesus most likely suffered the consequences of his choices and those of others. Jesus did not take unnecessary risks with his life so that he was able to accomplish His mission in the appointed time of His Father. On one occasion, He quickly and quietly disappeared into the crowd to avoid being stoned (John 8:59). However, when Lazarus was sick, Jesus decided to return to Judea, where the Jews had previously attempted to stone him, despite the warnings from his disciples (John 10:31, 11:8, 9). His response to his disciples was an analogy of walking during the day by light versus walking at night without light and stumbling – light symbolizing the knowledge of God's will.

It was at that time that the chief priests and Pharisees began to plot Jesus' death. Jesus no longer moved publicly among the Jews. Again Jesus withdrew to Ephraim, in the region near the desert, until six days before the Passover, to avoid unnecessary risk to his Father's plan. Because of his obedience to the Father's will, at the appointed time, Jesus did accept death and the pain of separation from his Father for the sake of our sins. In his death, he indeed did risk his life for us.

Jesus' risk for us was a stewarded risk. He did not misuse or risk the human and material resources normally a part of the human condition for selfish reasons but for service to us and for the sake of the kingdom of God. He wisely ordered his life around obedience to the Father and carefully considered his strength, the risks at hand, and his mission.

The Theoretical Study of Risk and Its Effects

Risk has been studied from a variety of perspectives. The world of economics and finance functions well because we have learned "how to put the future at the service of the present" (Bernstein, 1998, p. 1) by better understanding risk. In his book, *Against the Gods: The Remarkable Story of Risk,* Peter Bernstein (1998) stated that the "discoveries about the nature of risk, and the art and science of choice, lie at the core of our modern market economy" and also "provided the missing ingredient that has propelled science and enterprise into the world of speed, power, instant communication, and sophisticated finance that marks our own age" (p. 2). Many things that we take for granted, such as insurance to cover potential losses such as life, health, and property; agriculture and the futures market; social security; and transportation are all possible because of a greater understanding of risk. The scientific method itself uses probability theory to determine the degree of confidence that can be given to its findings. Even our sporting events that function largely with a high degree of chance and uncertainty have been managed through a greater understanding of risk. In fact, the history of risk management has been peppered with insights gained through the study of games.

Science has provided knowledge of this ordered world, and with knowledge, increased control over many aspects of nature. Likewise, understanding risk has allowed us to engage the future more predictably and to develop increasingly more sophisticated risk management tools. But with greater control over nature and more sophisticated risk management tools come power over both nature and humans. As this power increases, the choices that humans make are of greater significance in the overall scheme of things, and the effects of nature become less significant. Therefore, influences of human behavior and the moral consequences of that behavior must be accounted for to appropriately manage risk. Risk-taking decisions made by individuals affect others more than ever because of the greater power wielded and the increased interconnectedness of people who bear those risks. Simply stated, human decisions are more powerful determinants of relative risk than ever before in human history. Therefore, a sound theology of risk that considers the moral aspects of risk-taking is of utmost importance.

Soteriology and Risk

From a theological perspective, what is the ultimate risk? God is not at risk, nor is the accomplishment of his will at risk. Humans are the ones ultimately at risk. Since God is sovereign and the source of all goodness and righteousness, he will accomplish that which glorifies himself and benefits his creation, including humanity. Humans face the perceived risk of losing self-control through self-surrender to become willing partners in accomplishing God's will. Humans also face real risk in becoming unwilling tools that God will use to accomplish his will while they lose their eternal relationship with God.

> Satan is without doubt nothing else than a hammer in the hand of a benevolent and severe God. For all either willingly or unwillingly, do the will of God: Judas and Satan as tools or instruments, John and Peter as sons. (Lewis & Calabria, 1998, p. 37)

When we reject God's will, even if he uses our unwilling submission to bring good out of our evil, our life now and eternally is at ultimate risk. The ultimate risk that we face is not living in a love relationship with God eternally and thereby not becoming fully human and properly relating to our world and fellow humans.

Risk-Taking and Faith

Is risk-taking an act of faith, foolishness, or defiance? To step into the unknown with some certainty and sound reasoning that there will be a favorable outcome is an act of faith. To step into the unknown with no evidence that there will be a favorable outcome and against common sense and advice from others is an act of foolishness. To venture into the unknown knowing that the consequences are morally wrong is an act of defiance.

Faith is belief or trust in something or someone. It is not totally blind or without substance. There must be an object of faith and there must be a commitment to that object and a conviction that the object will not fail or let one down. That object can be one's self, while the conviction may be that one's skills are good enough to accomplish the feat being attempted. Faith is only actualized when the commitment is made through acting on that faith or risk-taking. Abraham's willingness to risk the death of Isaac showed his commitment to God and was based on evidence that God had been faithful to his promises to Abraham in giving him and Sarah a son. This is an example of both an act of faith and an act of risk-taking (Gen. 22). If there were no previous evidence that God was faithful to his promises, it would be against common sense for Abraham to kill his only son and be deprived of descendants. Anyone taking risks of this sort would be labeled a fool (1 Sam. 25:25; Prov. 1:7,22; 10:8).

Defying moral wisdom is sin. If the consequences of the risk-taking act have a high probability of permanent injury or death and will not be favorable for the risk-taker and to the desired cause, the risk-taker is defying moral law by degrading the value of life. The exception to this would be an act of risk-taking for the sake of saving another life, defending one's country, or standing for one's faith. Even just war theory argues that a war is unjust if a successful outcome is not highly probable.

Aristotle (trans. 1934) in *Nicomachean Ethics* understood virtues as falling somewhere at the mean between two vices, one of deficiency and one of excess. Courage was the virtuous mean of cowardice (the vice of deficiency) and rashness (the vice of excess). Virtuous risk-taking would be an act of courage, as it would be done for the good of others or a moral cause. Risk-taking would be a vice of excess and fall into the category of rashness if it were done out of defiance or as an act of foolishness. If one took no risks, or took risks to avoid facing other consequences due him, it could be deemed an act of cowardice.

Risk-Taking and Faith Development

The biblical narrative is filled with examples of God encouraging risk-taking and using risky situations to assist his chosen people and his disciples in strengthening their faith. Noah and his household became the first archetype of risk-taking in building an ark during a time of intense wickedness on earth. Abraham and Sarah followed by responding to the call of God to leave their people, country, and family in Haran to go to an unknown land that God promised he would show them. They risked all on the promise that they would be blessed and become a great nation. Abraham showed his willingness to risk the loss of both his son Isaac and the promise of becoming a great nation when he followed God's directions to sacrifice Isaac. Both these archetypes of faith demonstrated that risk-taking is an essential element of faith. Jacob followed God's command to leave Laban and return to his native land and face his brother Esau, who had vowed to kill him. When meeting Esau and his 400 men, Jacob risked his life by going ahead alone to meet his brother, as he had faith that God had intervened and changed Esau's heart.

Moses, who is still considered the Jews' greatest leader and teacher, grew in his faith each time he faced Pharaoh. Risking peril after peril as he led the children of Israel out of Egypt and through the wilderness, he became a model of faith that unified these fickle people into a strong nation with a monotheistic faith that has endured to the current generation.

Rahab risked her life for the sake of saving the spies because she had heard of what God had done for Israel, and she had faith in him. She was applauded for her risk-taking as an example of faith that was alive.

> In the same way, was not even Rahab the prostitute considered righteous for what she did when she gave lodging to the spies and sent them off in a different direction? As the body without the spirit is dead, so faith without deeds is dead. (James 2:25)

David's risk-taking courage in facing Goliath in the name of the Lord greatly increased the faith of the Israelites (1 Sam. 17). Daniel risked his life on several significant occasions to demonstrate his allegiance to his God, as did Shadrach, Meshach, and Abednego, who faced the fiery furnace. Gideon, from the smallest clan in Manasseh, called by God to take on the Midianites, had his army reduced from 32,000 to 300 by the command of God. Yet he still faced the Midianites and allowed God to use him and his small army of 300 to overcome a massive army of Midianites, Amalekites, and Eastern People. Jeremiah risked his reputation as well as his life in being faithful as a prophetic risk-taker in pronouncing the Lord's judgments upon the kings and nations of his time as did many of the prophets.

Jesus himself sent his disciples out two by two to preach and heal. He warned them that they would be like sheep among wolves as they faced danger (Matt. 10:1–16). This training mission was a risky mission, and it helped the disciples grow in their faith. Many times Jesus challenged the faith levels of his disciples and those that came to him for healing (Matt. 8:23–27, 9:27–29, 14:31, 15:25–28, 16:5–10, 17:19–21).

One significant event that demonstrates the interplay between faith, risk-taking, and faith development is Peter's attempt to walk on the water. Jesus had sent his disciples to the other side of the Sea of Galilee without him. During the night, he returned to them by walking on the water to their boat. Peter was unsure that it was Jesus and asked that Jesus would ask him to come to him to confirm his identity. Peter left the boat and began walking to Jesus, but when he saw the wind and waves, he became afraid and began to sink. After reaching out and saving Peter, Jesus exclaimed "You of little faith . . . why did you doubt?" (Matt. 14:31). Faith development ultimately is connected to our response to God's love, as he is the source of all love and he reaches out to each of us because of his love for us. When we enter into commitments with others, we do so with the risk of being hurt by their failure in their commitments to us. Therefore, risking is foundational to all commitments. Only those commitments based on a growing mutual love relationship allow one the security to take greater risks. Such are the characteristics of a relationship with our Creator, the source of ultimate love and security. To the degree that we understand the depth of God's love and believe that he is always acting out of love and using everything in our life for our ultimate good and for the sake of his glory, to that degree we will be able to risk. Faith development, therefore, occurs through the interaction between risk-taking and responding to love.

Risk-Taking and Human Development

Joseph Bayly (1985), in a regular column in *Eternity* magazine, penned some thoughts about children and risk and stated, "legitimate risk seems to be a necessary ingredient in growing up whole" (p. 4). His thesis was that human development is not complete unless risking with the potential for failing is one of the ingredients in the growth process. Human development theorists support this thesis (Maslow, 1968; Moore, Evans, Brooks-Gunn, & Roth, 1997; Smith, 1998). Without healthy risk-taking and resultant dis-equilibration, the normal psychosocial developmental processes are hindered. This does not mean that the physical and emotional safety of the child or adolescent is not paramount. Children need protection to the degree that they lack competence. Risks must be controlled to prevent permanent physical and emotional damage. Scripture commands us to protect others from serious risks (Deut. 22:8) and those who cannot defend or take care of themselves (Ps. 41:1, 1 Tim. 5: 3–5, James 1:27). When there is potential for failure, risk-taking must be supported by a caring community or parents. How much and how long this support is in place is the critical issue.

Scaffolding is a more recent way of describing the process, whereby significant adults gradually withdraw control and support as the developing adolescent acquires greater competency (Neal, 1995). Like constructing a building, if scaffolding is removed too soon, the building could shift and be structurally distorted or even collapse. If left up too long, the building is not standing on its own.

Scaffolding is especially important for the critical years of 18 to 24, when identity and spiritual formation are taking place that will determine the character, integrity, commitments, sense of community, and hope of the person as they move into adulthood. It is during these times that appropriate risk-taking with the proper amount of support is essential. It is through taking risks in interpersonal relationships, physical challenges, facing new cultures and worldviews, internships with exposure to potential careers, immersion experiences, and service experiences that the person can establish their own identity apart from family of origin, make their faith their own, and establish life goals. During the critical years, carefully designed wilderness adventure experiences, service ministries to those in a contrasting culture of poverty, athletic teams under leadership that understands the process of risk-taking to promote growth, adventure challenge courses, and similar experiences can provide these essential developmentally enriching experiences in which the support appropriately matches the challenge.

The risk-taker must perceive the risks to be fairly high but within their physical and emotional capability in order for risk-taking to be significant to them and to affect their development. Risks perceived to be too high by the participant can lead to high levels of anxiety and can be developmentally dysfunctional. Certain risks can be perceived as high while the actual risk to the person is low. Challenge courses using high elements where fear of height can be experienced, though protected by safety devices that stop the participant from a deadly fall, may provide high levels of perceived risk. Facing fear of height and risking a fall could possibly help participants face other fears in their life.

Risk-taking activities of many varieties can help a child and adolescent develop confidence in social settings, coping skills in stressful situations, ability to take on new challenges, a sense of self and capabilities, and be healthy substitutes to destructive forms of risk-taking that are prevalent in their youth culture. Human development is a process all humans are involved in from birth to death. Jesus himself "grew in wisdom and stature, and in favor with God and man" (Luke 2:52) and most likely engaged in healthy risk-taking. An environment where there is a level of healthy risk-taking can enhance the process of human development.

Studies in Risk-Taking Motivation – Positive and Negative

The study of why we risk is complex, yet certain theories have become dominant. Research has identified the following reasons why some people engage in higher levels of risk-taking activities and behavior: need for achievement, dominance, and endurance (Huberman, 1968); intrinsic reward and flow experience (Csikszentmihalyi, 1990); and intolerance for boredom (Malkin & Rabinowitz, 1998). Among elementary and middle school children, ability beliefs, preference for thrill seeking, peer domination, competitiveness, and interest have been found to be correlated with risk-taking (Miller & Byrnes, 1997).

According to Karl Greenfield (1999), the current extended period of prosperity in the United States without a major war and corresponding risks seems to be the reason that more people are taking risks than in previous decades. Increased risk-taking is evidenced by 12 percent more U.S. households owning stocks than 10 years ago; the job quit rate at 14.5 percent is the highest in the decade; the rising popularity of extreme sports (in five years snowboarding increased 112 percent, skateboarding 33 percent, and snowboarding 31 percent); 20 percent more mountain climbers were admitted to the emergency room in 1997 than in 1996; use of condoms by gay men decreased from 70 percent to 61 percent from 1974 to 1997; and the number of Americans entering treatment programs for heroin use rose 29 percent during the same period (Greenfeld, 1999).

From a theological perspective, it would seem that some of these reasons for risk-taking are both a part of being created human as well as a part of the fallen state of humans. The need for achievement seems to be ingrained in us at birth. All humans have an innate motivation to move toward maturation from birth to adulthood. This process is a sequence of achieving greater mastery of self and skills. To move forward involves moving into the unknown by taking risks of injury, mistakes, and a damaged image. Achievement can also lead to pride and self-idolatry rather than humility and recognition of abilities as a gift of God. Dominance most usually is an ego driven desire. Endurance may be a quality that can be transferred to other aspects of life that may be difficult and stressful.

Whether boredom with routines or lack of fulfillment in life as a whole is the cause of a person seeking risk-taking activities needs to be determined. Human satisfaction with life comes more from a proper orientation to life rather than the events in one's life that may be the cause for continued seeking of new experiences. However, God's creation and our ability to see new things in his creation and to enjoy new experiences in life seem to be inherently attractive to all humans. New experiences, especially unexpected, bring pleasure. They are gifts of grace to us from God. Properly received, they can orient a person outward away from self-preoccupation to something external and offer an upward or "expanded sense of the world" (Kort, 2000, p. 2).

Sensation seeking through risk-taking fits a popular culture philosophy of "if it feels good, do it." The more pleasure is sought for the sensation of pleasure itself, the less it tends to be true pleasure but something else. Moral constraints are usually ignored in sensation activities, and pleasure no longer remains pleasure but becomes self-interest.

> When a state of mind or the capacity to have pleasure becomes the focus of attention and the center of value, the orientation has radically shifted. Rather than being drawn by pleasure into a larger, richer world the person begins increasingly to draw the world into the self and to reduce the world to the terms of the self's pleasure-receiving capacities. (Kort, 2000, p. 11)

Enjoyment, or more simply stated fun, is often the reason given for participation in risk-taking behavior. Research seems to indicate that there is a state of being that occurs in many diverse activities that is perceived as a holistic engagement of the body without conscious direction on the part of the participant that moves from action to action in which past, present, and future are merged and the distinction of self, the environment, and actions are blurred. This personal transcendent state has been labeled as a "flow experience." For this state to be achieved, it is postulated that the activity must be freely chosen and entered into for the intrinsic rewards it offers, allow for creativity with a degree of uncertainty in a limited stimulus field, and result in action and awareness being merged (Mitchell, 1983). Mitchell (1983) defined uncertainty as both danger and difficulty. Danger is defined as situations of dire consequences that cannot be assessed as to probability and are not within the participant's ability to surmount. Defined in this way, danger is to be avoided when possible. Difficulty means risks that are within the abilities and resources of the participant. The variable interaction between the resources and abilities of the participant and the difficulty of the activity is an aspect of uncertainty that activates the flow experience. Too little or too high a degree of uncertainty can stifle motivation and void the flow experience.

During the flow experience, self is absorbed fully into the activity, and new capacities emerge. Fear is suppressed. Time and space are joined and suspended, and life takes on a sense of simplicity and transcendence. Performance is maximized with an efficiency of energy and motion. The activity becomes "immediately and profoundly rewarding" (Mitchell, 1983, p. 168).

Mitchell (1983) believed that each individual interacts with her world in a way that motivates her toward or away from risk-taking activities. Those persons who experience their world as unpredictable without norms and lacking meaning (anomie) will seek activities that are perceived less risky and more certain. Those who perceive their world as constraining, with many rules and structures that stifle creativity and spontaneity while rendering them powerless to effect change, will seek perceived higher risk activities of less certainty. Both anomie and alienation render the individual incapable of a flow experience. Engagement in appropriate levels of risk-taking activities that match the person's capabilities with challenge result in a sense of competence that is a prerequisite to flow. Mitchell tested this theory in a study done with 108 members of the Mountaineering Training Committee of the Southern California Sierra Club mountaineers and found that their occupations had significant mundane and routine qualities without real creativity, thereby fostering a sense of alienation, leading them in a search for activities with uncertainty that leads to flow. His findings were consistent with results from similar studies (e.g., Bratton, Kinnear, & Koroluk, 1979).

God pronounced his creation of this world "good" and the creation of humans as "very good" (Gen. 1). The functioning of the earth and humanity as God created them was central to his recognition of their being good. Sin and evil has since infected his creation, but the original image of that creation is still there, although at times a mere shadow. When any part of God's creation is functioning as created, that activity brings satisfaction and glory to God. God is praised by his creation (Ps. 148). Humans are created to move and to create with the abilities given and resources provided in the environment. The flow experience seems to explain a byproduct of using one's abilities fully as intended by God. Whether or not a person is consciously aware of praising his/her Creator by creative engagement in wholesome activity whereby human abilities are fully challenged and engaged, God is being glorified as Creator. The byproduct of engagement is an awareness of doing what one was created to do – and an absorption of self into that activity with a sense of transcendence.

The American culture, along with much of the Western world, is overindulged in seeking comfort and instant gratification as the ultimate values to the point of "entitlement rage" – my terms, my space, my things, my time, my group, and my God. Relationships are based on the degree of comfortable homogeneity as like seeks like, with special interest groups prevailing to insure their needs are being met. This self-centered, hedonistic perspective often follows a paradigm of avoidance and addictive self-destruction as deeper needs are not met as desired. Anxiety and fear surface, leading to thrill-seeking ventures that provide the physiological rush of fulfillment, thereby binding the anxiety and fear and leading to temporary avoidance until the cycle begins again. Through repetitive reinforcement, the person becomes stuck with false reassurance of needs met in this repetitive cycle of thrill seeking. Phobias often emerge and drive this cycle of avoidance and addiction to thrill seeking. Paradoxically, the solution to this cycle of avoidance and addiction is task-oriented risk-taking rather than avoidance-orientated thrill seeking. The task involved is to face anxieties and fears directly, which involves risk. It involves risk to self and identity, risk to comfort, risk to worldview, risk to relationships with others, and, at times, risk to community. Out of the task-oriented risk-taking comes hope, and hope allows one to take responsible risks.

Risk-Taking and High Adventure Sports

Adventure recreation, adventure sports, high adventure sports, and extreme sports have emerged as labels describing increasingly risky activities over the past several decades. Technological capability to bring viewers into the action almost as fellow participants peaked the public interest in vicarious thrill seeking as participants dance through death defying acts of courage. Sensation-seeking viewers become voyeurs as persons are extracted from bodies and become objects of sensual, thrill-seeking exploitation by the media and the audience. If the price and publicity is right, those with high skill attainment, confidence in their skills, and a sense of invincibility are always willing to set the new record. The daring and dangerous adventure is continually redefined in an effort to be more extreme. Technology and skill techniques have progressed accordingly to support this pursuit of daring. As in the days of the Roman gladiators, life diminishes in significance, and the act of death defiance is exulted to the highest value.

Human beings are not immortal. Nor are we disposable. There exists a value of life even apart from the person whose life is being risked.

The Creator of life determined the value of life when he paid a high price to redeem it and make it a part of the Kingdom of God. His value should exceed the value placed upon participation in death-defying extreme sports.

Adventure sports most likely attract us because we innately know there is more than we have seen and done and that we can expand those limits. This propensity to adventure seems to be connected with a desire to be in touch with the power and awe of the Creator as reflected in his creation. As finite beings, coming too close to the forces and extremes of creation can be a dangerous venture. Scripture gives us examples of the danger of being too close to God and his power in creation with the wrong motivation or wrong heart (Acts 7:31–33; Exod. 19:10–13; Lev. 16:1–2; Deut. 8:2–5). We are to approach him in humility (James 4:10; 1 Pet. 5:6), with reverence and awe (Job 25:2), and we are to respect his power vested in his creation. "Therefore, since we are receiving a kingdom that cannot be shaken, let us be thankful, and so worship God acceptably with reverence and awe, for our 'God is a consuming fire'" (Heb. 12:28–29).

Our adventuring must be done in humility with both reverence and awe of the Creator who both owns us and sustains us. We must not venture where we should not. We need to correctly evaluate our abilities and know our limitations as Christ did. As we hone our skills and push our limits, we must consider the cost and examine our motivation. We must be stewards of our risk-taking for the sake of the kingdom and serving others.

Risk-Taking and Competitive Sports

Competitive sports provide an ideal environment for risk-taking, which can lead to personal development in a variety of areas. In competitive sports, rules are established to provide fairness (justice) so that each player has an equal opportunity. Rules attempt to limit the many variables that could determine the winner to the one variable that is the player or team with the best skills. One of the variables that rules moderate against is chance. The more evenly the players or teams are matched, the more uncertain the outcome of the contest. This uncertainty solicits intense play from each player in order to achieve success. Creatively applying one's skill in the contest is usually a major factor in achieving success when the players are so equal in skill. This creativity takes on a form of risk-taking. Risk-taking goes beyond the normal movements and strategies of the game.

Risk-taking is commendable when done in the context of the rules. However, when risks are taken to gain advantage outside of the rules of the game, the fairness of the game is jeopardized, and the contest is no longer decided on skill alone. The purpose of penalties is to restore fairness to play when rules have been violated. Each action taken by a player that gives an unfair advantage is penalized in such a way that the player or team affected negatively by the rule infraction is given the opportunity to return the contest to the same level of fair play as before the rules were broken. Rules further control the degree of body contact to a level that allows the players to avoid injury and complete the contest. Once an injury occurs that hinders a player's ability to play, the contest is no longer fair, since the best efforts of each competitor are no longer possible.

When one enters a sports contest, the element of risk-taking is present both from a creative, challenging effort in striving for ways to excel and also in the potential of physical harm. Risk-taking also has a moral dimension that can be jeopardized if rules are circumvented or harm is intentional. Similarly, God provides "rules" to live by that establish boundaries within which we can live a flourishing life. The pursuit of wellness, a godly pursuit of stewarding and enhancing the dimensions of self, requires restraints and boundaries as well. Risk-taking in sports must be controlled by these boundaries of stewardship, with appropriate restraints practiced.

Risk-taking can lead to the development of courage. When an athlete faces difficult challenges and decisions, she could react with cowardice, rashness, or courage. Courage, rightly focused, is a virtue needed by most in today's world. It takes courage to face danger, ridicule, temptation to do wrong, and challenge to convictions. Because sports inherently are infused with risk-taking choices, they can be tools used by astute coaches and parents to teach and test courage and foster ethical behavior.

Managing Risk

Management of risk is a delicate task. If we attempt to take all risk out of life, we lose the opportunity for human beings to humbly realize that they are finite and fragile beings that need to be dependent upon God. We also rob them of the opportunity to exercise their creativity in using their abilities to reach out into the unknown and discover more of themselves and their world. The consequences of risk often result in pain, and pain most usually evokes fear in those experiencing the pain and occasionally in those fellow participants who also realize their vulnerability to injury and pain. Pain demands our attention. "God whispers to us in our pleasures, speaks in our conscience, but shouts in our pains: it is His megaphone to rouse a deaf world" (Lewis, 1962, p. 93). Too much pain can stifle our ability to take future risks. We can become phobic and incapable of fully engaging the world. But negative consequences (such as pain) resulting from the risk in this world are never without grace.

> For the Almighty God, who, as even the heathen acknowledge, has supreme power over all things, being Himself supremely good, would never permit the existence of anything evil among His works, if He were not so omnipotent and good that He can bring good even out of evil. (Augustine, 1966, p.11)

Grace flows because of the love of God as we accept the risk and consequences that a loving commitment to him entails.

In our current litigious society, we have reacted by removing much of the risk that previously has been a part of living life in this world. However, on the other hand, if we know of dangers that could befall others for whom we have responsibility and do not warn them, we are negligent in our duty. Jesus warned his disciples before he sent them out that they would face dangers (Luke 10:3), and on several occasions he taught them about the cost of being a disciple (Matt. 8:18; Luke 9:51–62, 14:25–35). Yet he still challenged them to accept the risk. Risk-taking and its consequences seem to be critical processes to promote growth in many dimensions of self.

Managing risk is both knowing the probability of the occurrence of unfavorable results (injury/death) in that activity and knowing how to reduce that probability through wise practices. Beyond knowing the probability of unfavorable results and following wise practices, we need to consider what risks we need to accept. Some risks are definitely outside of God's calling and will for our lives – even risks that extend our limits or push us into the unknown to expand our knowledge. There are times when we are called to be courageous and reject risks that fall at a point along the virtuous mean that may be closer to the deficiency vice of cowardice at the risk of being called a coward. Or there may be times when we are called to accept risks near the excess vice of rashness and risk being called a rash fool due to circumstances that are specifically related to our calling. To determine that point, we have the most significant tool, that of prayer. Our continuous communication with God concerning the activities that we are participating in and/or encouraging/teaching/coaching/leading others to participate in will allow God's Spirit to direct us in accepting or rejecting that risk, doing things to lower the risk, and evoking his protection upon that activity.

Satan's response to God when he asked him to consider his servant Job was, "Does Job fear God for nothing? Have you not put a hedge around him and his household and everything he has?" (Job 1:9–10). God can put a hedge around those involved in risk-taking activities. The psalmist repetitively spoke of God's protection in dangerous times. When Peter was arrested by King Herod, he was rescued from prison and death by an angel sent by God for his protection (Acts 12:1–19). However, many followers of Christ and heroes of the faith did risk their lives for Christ and saw death.

> Risk analysis measures costs and results. But faith assumes a willingness to face the future with a trust in the people involved and a recognition that we don't have to confront the future alone. Faith in the God who transcends the ambiguities of life permits us to grasp the future without demanding certainty. Which suggests that the degree to which we are willing to live with risk may be directly related to our connection to such a God. (Wall, 1989)

We are never safe in this world. If we were so, we would not have the opportunity to grow. To risk appropriately is to stretch our boundaries and see our limitations as well as our strengths and to enter into a deeper faith relationship. Inappropriate risk-taking can flow from self-idolatry or pride that is a cardinal sin. Only as we risk with proper motivation and a sense of divine purpose and calling can we receive the grace of God and understand our need to be dependent on a Creator who desires our loving self-surrender. Risking for Christ's sake is not rashness, nor does it guarantee life on this earth, but it is the true risk-taking that brings ultimate joy and fulfillment for this life and eternally.

References

Aristotle. (1934). *The Nicomachean ethics of Aristotle*. (J.E.C. Welldon, Trans.). New York: Macmillan.

Augustine, St., Bishop of Hippo. (1966). *The Enchiridion on faith, hope, and love*. Chicago: Henry Regnery.

Bayly, J. (1985, May). Out of my mind: Risks are for kids. *Eternity*, p. 4.

Bernstein, P.L. (1998). *Against the gods: The remarkable story of risk*. New York: John Wiley & Sons.

Bratton, R.D., Kinnear, G., & Koroluk, G. (1979). Reasons for climbing: A study of the Calgary Section. *The Canadian Alpine Journal* 62, 55–57.

Csikszentmihalyi, M. (1990). *Flow: The psychology of optimal experience*. New York: HarperCollins.

Greenfeld, K.T. (1999, Sept. 6). Life on the edge. *Time* 154(10), 28–36.

Huberman, J. (1968). *A psychological study of participants in high risk sports*. (Unpublished doctoral thesis). University of British Columbia. Vancouver.

Kort, W.A. (2000). "C. S. Lewis and the anatomy of pleasure." Paper presented at the annual Wheaton College English Department lecture for majors. Wheaton, IL, April 19, 2000.

Lewis, C. S., & Calabria, D.G. (1998). *The Latin letters of C. S. Lewis*. (M. Moynihan, Trans.). South Bend, IN: St. Augustine's Press.

Lewis, C.S. (1962). *The problem of pain*. New York: Macmillan.

Malkin, M.J., & Rabinowitz, E. (1998). Research Update: Sensation seeking and high-risk recreation. *Parks and Recreation* 33(7), 35–45.

Maslow, A.H. (1968). *Toward a psychology of being*. New York: Van Nostrand Reinhold.

Miller, D.C., & Byrnes, J.P. (1997). The role of contextual and personal factors in children's risk-taking. *Developmental Psychology* 33(5), 814–823.

Mitchell, R.G. Jr. (1983). *Mountain experience: The psychology and sociology of adventure*. Chicago: University of Chicago Press.

Moore, K.A., Evans, V.J, Brooks-Gunn, J., & Roth, J. (1997). "What are good child outcomes?" Paper presented at the Data and Research Needs Conference (October 20–23, 1997). ERIC Document No. ED428860.

Neal, Cynthia J. (1995). The power of Vygotsky. In J.C. Wilhoit & J.M. Dettoni (Eds.), *Nurture that is Christian: Developmental perspectives on Christian education* (pp. 123–137). Wheaton, IL: Victor Books.

Smith, S.J. (1998). *Risk and our pedagogical relation to children: On the playground and beyond. SUNY Series, Early Childhood Education: Inquiries and Insights*. ERIC Document No. ED419591.

Wall, J.M. (1989, Dec. 6) When risk analysis confronts faith. *Christian Century* 106, 1139–1140.

Recommended Reading

Piper, J. (2003). Risk is right – Better to lose your life than to waste it. In *Don't waste your life* (pp. 79–98). Wheaton, IL: Crossway.

Chapter 18
SEEKING THE COMMON GOOD: CHALLENGES AND OPPORTUNITIES FOR RECREATION PROGRAMMERS

Don DeGraaf

Our world is changing faster than we can comprehend. As Peter Drucker, a world-renowned management guru, observed, "we're in one of those great historical periods that occur every 200 to 300 years when people don't understand the world anymore . . . when the past is not sufficient to explain the future" (as cited by Cameron & Quinn, 2005, p. 1). Yet our colleges and universities are tasked with the job of helping students understand our world and their role in this world, helping them become the leaders of tomorrow in order to contribute to the common good of their communities.

In addressing this challenge, Kouzes and Posner (2006), authors of the best-selling management text *The Leadership Challenge*, have focused on helping their students identify their passions and respond to these passions. They begin their class on leadership by asking students the following questions:

> Are you on this planet to do something, or are you here just for something to do? If you're on this planet to do something, then what is it? What difference will you make? What will be your legacy? By asking ourselves how we want to be remembered, we plant the seeds of living our lives as if we matter. By living each day as if we matter, we offer up our own unique legacy. By offering our own unique legacy, we make the world we inhabit a better place than we found it. (p. 6)

For Christian college and university professors, including those in recreation and leisure studies, this challenge is even more complicated as we strive to help students understand our world within the context of our

---
Revised version of paper presented at the 2010 conference.

faith. Seeing the world through the lens of our faith presents a tremendous opportunity to seek the common good, to be salt and light in an ever-changing world, but it also creates challenges such as consensus on defining the common good or how to collaborate with others who may not share our faith or our view of the common good.

The challenges of seeking the common good through our faith lens are often complicated by several factors. First, we are conditioned in the United States to separate church and state in most parts of our lives, which often results in compartmentalizing our faith. Second, we live in a world that tends to polarize people with differing opinions, such as conservative or liberal. Within this context, we have lost the ability to dialogue with others with different viewpoints from our own. Thus the purpose of this article is two-fold. First, in an attempt to address these challenges, the article will present a model that helps students to: (a) understand the world as well as their place in it; (b) integrate their faith with their studies; and c) enter the dialogue of what is the common good and how recreation professionals should strive to contribute to it. Second, the article will explore strategies to teach this model throughout the recreation and leisure studies curriculum.

Changing the World, Seeking the Common Good: A Model for Recreation Programmers

The model presented in this paper includes the components of worldview, servant leadership, and social entrepreneurship. Together these components lead to opportunities to change the world.

Figure 1. Changing the world, seeking the *Common Good*: A model for recreation programmers.

| Worldview grounded in our Faith | + | Servant Leader Heart | + | Skills of the Social Entrepreneur | = | The opportunity to change the world for the better |

The secret of knowing how is remembering why

Worldview

A good model begins with a solid foundation: for students, it begins with giving them a solid worldview (see Figure 1). Professors within faith-based institutions are fortunate to be able to openly share a worldview grounded in their faith: yet, all professors are free to encourage their students to examine their worldview, the lens from which they operate in the world. In a recent edition of *Comment,* a journal dedicated to equipping and connecting the next generation of Christian leaders, the editors offer a worldview grounded in the ideas of wonder, heartbreak, and hope.

> The love of God evokes – from our whole person and in unity with the whole people of God – a life of worship, a love of neighbors, and a respectful caring and disclosure of all of creation. Lives ordered by the love of God are ordered well, and can be lived well. . . .
>
> [As we explore] the possibility of lives lived [well in all spheres of our world,] we seek to discover ways of human flourishing in lives lived with integrity and coherence. Flourishing is possible, we believe, when all of life is lived as worship and service of God: personally, publicly, professionally, permanently.
>
> An understanding ordered by the love of God . . . allows for a particular point of view from which to understand the world: a point of view marked by wonder, heartbreak, and hope. (Strauss, 2010, pp. 20–21)

The key terms in this worldview are described as follows:

Wonder. God created the heavens and the earth and it was good! We live in an awesome world that encompasses all aspects of God's ordained structure of all things in this world. We find ourselves in awe of the Creator of all things, in awe of Jesus, the Christ, in whom all things have been given existence and coherence.

Heartbreak. Despite the awesome nature of God's world, it has been marred by sin. All things wail and suffer under the misery of sin. The Word and the Spirit of God open our eyes to the heartbreak suffered by the world God made and, mindful of God's pain, we find our own hearts broken.

Hope. With all creation, we yearn for a full recovery of the peace of God, desire the complete restoration of the reign of God, and await the fulfillment of the promises of God. We look for signals and reasons for hope; we seek out opportunities to be agents of shalom and to reconcile our broken world in big and small ways.

Giving students such a foundational worldview equips them with a moral compass to navigate the challenges and opportunities of their disciplines. It provides insights into the values and virtues needed to live well, while also providing a framework on which to build the skills needed to act in support of the common good.

The connection between the common good, values, and virtues can be seen throughout the leisure literature. Nash (1953) recognized the connection between leisure, democracy, and the common good when he wrote,

> The concepts of freedom and choice are closely associated with those of democracy and leisure. Democracy assumes freedom; freedom assumes choice. But to be able to choose, man must have a trained intellect and be disciplined in choices pertinent not only to the good of himself but to the good of all. (p. 37)

Aristotle also gives us some insight into how we should pursue the common good, writing that "[We] assume then that the best life, both for individuals and for states, is the life of virtue, when virtue has external goods enough for the performance of good actions" (as quoted by Bess, 1996, p. 6). The connection between virtue and the common good has often been identified, with virtue being defined as a stable disposition to act well: that is, to use the right means in pursuit of good ends.

Servant Leadership

As we work to help students embrace and enter into the discussion of what is the common good and how we should work toward what is good for all, students also need to be introduced to concepts that help them determine the common good. Servant leadership is one such concept that was first introduced in 1970 by Robert Greenleaf in an article entitled *The Servant as Leader*.

Greenleaf's ideas about servant leadership came from a book by Herman Hesse entitled *Journey to the East* that he read as he was trying to understand what college students of the 1960s were reading. In this book, a group of men go on a journey to the East to find the light, and they take along a servant named Leo. Leo is very much a servant to these men. He cooks their meals, navigates the direction of their travel, and discerns which trails will be best to follow, as well as entertains them with songs and jokes. Sometime during the trip, however, Leo disappears. After his disappearance, the group disbands for lack of organization. Much later it is discovered that Leo was not a lowly servant at all, but a leader in the ruling body of the group that first financed the trip. What was striking about this story to Greenleaf was Leo's ability to be both a servant and a leader.

The inherent value of the concept of servant leadership is multifaceted. First, the concept resonates with both secular and religious audiences. It provides common ground to talk about the common good.

Consider Greenleaf's (1970/1991) test of the servant leader:

> Do those served, grow as persons, do they, while being served become healthier, wiser, freer, more autonomous, more likely themselves to become servants? And, what is the effect on the least privileged in society; will he (or she) benefit; or at least, will he (or she) not be further deprived. (p. 7).

This test offers a solid foundation for discussing the impacts of our programs and how they impact the common good.

Second, the servant leader concept emphasizes the importance of both leadership and followership. All of us lead and follow. One is not better than the other; in the course of our lives, we are called to do both. We must learn to be good leaders by learning to be good followers, listening to participants, and helping them lead so we can follow. In this way, leadership, according to Greenleaf (1998), should call us to serve something beyond ourselves – a higher purpose.

Third, the concept of servant leadership provides a strong framework for connecting specific values and virtues to our programs. For example, one of the virtues associated with a servant is that of humility: that is, being willing to live with and learn from others. Humility should not be confused with timidity; rather, we should view humility as a way of being. When we practice humility, it opens us up to possibilities, as we choose open-mindedness and curiosity over protecting our point of view; we are willing to learn from what others have to offer. We move away from pushing into allowing. In the context of seeking the common good, it means being open to others who may see the world differently, yet who share some common objectives.

While humility is an important virtue connected to servant leadership, it is also balanced out with values such as courage and wisdom that are often associated more with traditional leadership. Opportunities to be courageous occur at work every day. Unfortunately, most people believe that courage is relevant only during particularly perilous times. In reality, courage is crucial in a wide range of work situations, and anyone can demonstrate courage. While we have noted the importance of humility in walking alongside of others who see the world differently, it is also important to know when it is important to stand up for your principles. This not only takes courage but wisdom as well.

Wisdom is "the ability to discern paths of shalom in the midst of competing visions and conflicting interests" (Bouma-Prediger & Walsh, 2008, p. 221). The virtue of wisdom is the inclination to make sound and discerning practical judgments, informed by one's worldview and the accumulated experience of one's community. Thus, wisdom is more than just knowledge or intelligence; it is rooted in discernment of what is truly good. One example of the interface between humility, courage, and wisdom can be found in Henri Nouwen's (1975) definition of simple hospitality. It involves a willingness to be humble to create a space for the other; it demands a courage to stick up for others and to create space that encourages them to grow; and it requires wisdom to know when to simply create the space, when to push, and when to step back.

> In our world full of strangers . . . we witness a painful search for a hospitable place where life can be lived without fear and where community can be found . . . Hospitality is not to change people, but to offer them space where change can take place. It is not to bring men or women over to our side, but to offer them freedom undisturbed by dividing lines. . . . The paradox of hospitality is that it wants to create emptiness, not a fearful emptiness, but a friendly emptiness where strangers can enter and discover themselves as created free; free to sing their own songs, speak their own languages, dance their own dances, free also to leave and follow their own vocations. Hospitality is not a subtle invitation to adopt the lifestyle of the host, [but rather] the gift of a chance for the guest to find their own . . . [and in the process] create the free and fearless space where brotherhood and sisterhood can be formed and fully experienced. (Nouwen, 1975, p. 46)

Greenleaf's (1977) concept of a servant leader is an example of a metaphor that can help students understand how the virtues of humility, courage, wisdom, and hospitality can interact in their lives. In some ways these virtues can be seen as a paradox of leadership when a paradox is seen as the art of balancing opposites in such a way that they do not cancel each other out but rather shoot sparks of light across the points of polarity. Paradox looks at our desperate either/ors and tell us they are really both/and.

In addition, Greenleaf's (1977) concept of servant leadership builds on our biblical worldview offering us a tangible model, with specific values and virtues, to create recreation programs that build consensus and work toward the common good. It provides the answer to why we want to create programs that matter. As Block (2002) notes, the best place to start in delivering programs that matter is not by asking HOW questions (how can we do this) but rather by asking WHY questions (why do we want to deliver specific programs).

Block (2002) argues that we are too quick to go to the HOW questions because our culture today pushes us to deliver programs that are doable and practical and popular, and in the process we have sacrificed the big dreams of what our programs could truly become. When we give in to the questions of how, we risk aspiring to goals that are defined for us by the culture in which we live, at the expense of pursuing purposes and intentions that arise from our own dreams, idealism, and worldview.

The alternative to asking HOW is asking WHY and saying yes to the possibilities of what our programs can become. Saying yes to the possibilities is a symbol that acknowledges our commitment to the process of creating programs that matter. When we say yes to what our programs can become, we are led to questions such as: what commitment am I willing to make? What price am I willing to pay? What do we want to create together? Ultimately what will matter most to us, upon deeper reflection, is the quality of experience we create in the world, not the quantity of results.

Answering these types of questions forces us to struggle with the issue of why we do what we do, as individuals and institutions. It encourages us to model the type of reflection that we try to encourage in our participants; it demands we talk about purpose and what is worth doing. When we say yes to such questions, it forces us to act as if we already know how – we just have to determine what is worth doing.

The process of saying yes to developing programs that matter from a servant leadership perspective can be seen in the story of Lisa, a 2004 graduate of Calvin College (Calvin College Alumni, 2006). Lisa was a people person who struggled in the classroom and was unsure of what she wanted to do after she graduated. While she did her internship in Chicago with a social service agency, she fell in love with the city and the role recreation could play in building community and improving people's quality of life. She became fascinated with how we, as recreation professionals, can build community, and in her search to answer this question she encountered the idea of third places. Third places are not home or work, the first two places in our lives, but rather venues like coffee shops, bookstores, and cafes in which we find less formal acquaintances. Third places are the heart of a community's social vitality, where people hang out and relax simply for the pleasure of good company and lively conversation (Oldenburg, 2001).

Lisa began to catch a glimpse of the possible, how a coffee shop could contribute to community and to people's wellbeing. She envisioned all types of programming that could complement the idea of creating space for people to connect with, grow, and feel a part of something bigger than themselves. She began to take steps to make this dream a reality. In 2005, along with another friend, at the ripe age of twenty-three, they took a courageous step and moved to Seattle, where they bought an old bar and went to work converting it into a coffee shop, which they named the Green Bean. Lisa and her friend told their parents that they didn't need to go to school for more education and get more work experience first; rather they were going to open a coffee house. In the words of Lisa, "We were created to do this, and this is what we are going to do." They set up their coffee shop as a non-profit organization with the mission of simple hospitality as defined by Nouwen (1975).

To walk into the coffee shop is to walk into a beehive of activity. Lisa says they want to provide a space where people can feel loved and accepted and have their gifts appreciated no matter who they are. That means that besides serving up a great cup of coffee and fantastic treats and sandwiches, they also have a wide variety of programs such as children's story time, summer backpacking trips, concerts, community festivals, and classes that range from knitting to women's self-defense to hip hop dance. They focus their programming on building relationships with customers and, as Lisa puts it, saying yes to them.

Yes to the homeless people who want to contribute something and so offer to sweep or wash windows. Yes to the lonely students who offer to help do the baking. Yes to the artists who want to display their work and the activists who want to publicize events. Yes to making a difference in the world, as evidenced by their tip jar that has already collected almost $17,000 for a variety of local and international causes (Calvin College Alumni, 2006).

Lisa's story embodies many of the characteristics of a servant leader. Through her willingness to serve, she is leading her community to see the possibilities of recreation programs to build fellowship and community. Even the name of the coffee shop (the Green Bean) exemplifies their mission.

> When coffee beans arrive from their country of origin, they are jade green in color; as they are roasted a transformation occurs which brings them to their full tasty potential and aroma. Just like the green bean itself, the Green Bean Coffeehouse will exist in order to promote positive transformation in the life of the Greenwood neighborhood and then globally by supporting people groups from parts of the world less fortunate than ours. It's our hope to exist as a community center coffeehouse, serving up a mean cup of coffee, a fantastically inviting atmosphere and programs that encourage and foster community and the individual. (Green Bean, 2006)

By focusing on the end goal of building relationships, Lisa has been able to say yes and build an organization that is addressing a number of social concerns in her community and the world. She is a true servant leader!

Social Entrepreneurship

While we start with asking the WHY questions, we also have to be realistic enough to realize that we must also address the HOW questions. In thinking about the logistical aspects of our programs, it may be helpful to examine the skills needed to be innovative and entrepreneurial in developing programs. This leads us to the second metaphor of our model, helping students to see themselves not only as servant leaders, but also as social entrepreneurs with a specific skill set to address issues related to the common good.

Jarvi (2001) has connected the idea of social entrepreneurs with park and recreation professionals in an attempt to see the potential of recreation programs to contribute to the building of a living democracy model, similar to the ideas of Nash (1953) presented earlier in this paper. Jarvi has highlighted the need for local governments to work to develop new models of government to foster a new form of community democracy. Citing a study completed by the National Civic League, Jarvi noted that such models must be built on the premise that problem solving must emanate from within communities, use existing community assets, and include a wide range of partnerships within each community. Parks, recreation, and leisure service professionals are one group within local governments that is typically well-connected in the community. Thus, many have developed the skills to facilitate problem solving within communities by reaching out to nontraditional partners such as community guardians or "those who rise above the fray and convene different groups to focus on the greater good of the community" (Jarvi, p. 180).

In this role, Jarvi (2001) advocated that park and recreation programmers see themselves as "social entrepreneurs" rather than being "the ones in charge." In this light, leadership becomes

> a process of facilitating, mediating, mutual education, learning, mentoring, collaborating and cooperating with diverse groups and individuals. Leaders need to understand complexity, ambiguity and be able to work with power, not from above, but horizontally. Leaders must deal with both the social and physical infrastructures needed to make things happen, working with all groups to constantly assemble the social and capital infrastructure necessary to achieve their objectives. (Jarvi, p. 180)

The idea of encouraging recreation programmers to be social entrepreneurs is not confined to the public sector (see Figure 2); anyone can be a social entrepreneur, and the concept is an important one as we move to look for new models of leadership in the twenty-first century. Consider that in the private sector, businesses are increasingly engaging in activities that previously fell under the domain of nonprofits and governments (e.g., youth programs, education, and other social services). The public sector, too, has seen a shift in practices, away from delivering direct services to facilitating connections and empowering others. For the nonprofit sector, there is pressure to fill gaps in public service delivery ensuring citizens get the services they need.

Figure 2. The blurring of sectors: Social entrepreneurship at the nexus. Adapted from Wolk (2008).

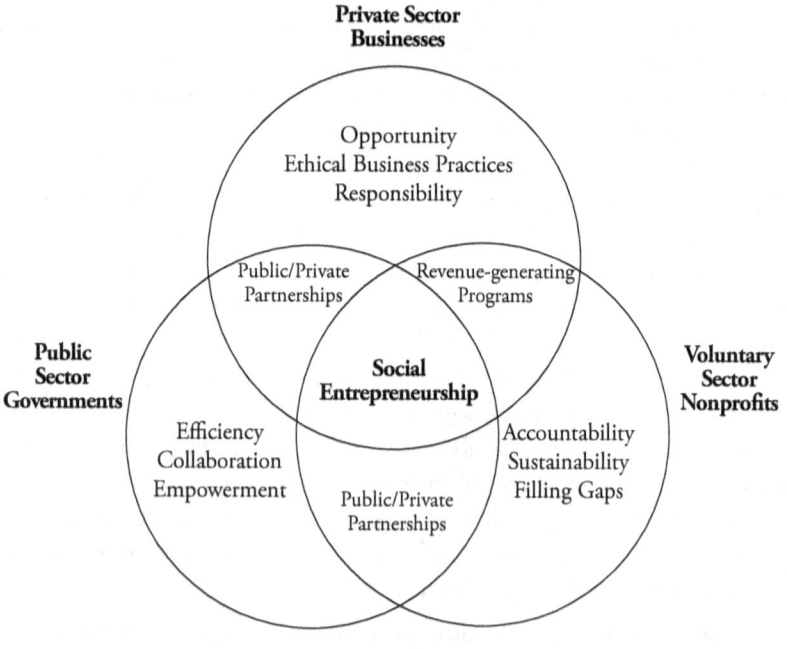

As each sector has entered the territory of the others, the blurring between them has given rise to a host of new approaches to delivering programs. There has been an increase in public-private partnerships involving businesses and nonprofits as collaborators in government projects. At the same time, the increased need to find new funding sources has led many nonprofits to develop businesslike ventures to generate revenues. Lastly, corporate social responsibility movements have entered the mainstream, motivating businesses to account for their environmental and labor practices along with their profits.

By blending some of the social and economic responsibilities traditionally associated with each of the three sectors, social entrepreneurship may take the form of a nonprofit, business, or government initiative. No matter what organizational form it takes, social entrepreneurship tends to exhibit characteristics of all three. Like business, social entrepreneurship utilizes markets to drive innovation and productivity. Like government, social entrepreneurship responds to market failures by providing public goods and services. Like nonprofits, social entrepreneurship engages individuals in action to achieve social goals (Wolk, 2008).

Although the idea of social entrepreneurship was developed in the late 1960s, history is full of people with big ideas who have addressed the social issues of their day. A social entrepreneur can be thought of as someone who uses entrepreneurial approaches to address social issues. The core approaches of an entrepreneur are as follows:

- Creating Value. Entrepreneurs work to create value for themselves or an organization by addressing a need of others.
- Reforming the Status Quo. Entrepreneurs are change agents in society; they work to find new and better ways of doing things by challenging the ways things are done.
- Responding to Change. Entrepreneurs always search for change, respond to it, and exploit it as an opportunity.
- Mobilizing Resources. Entrepreneurs are resourceful. Their reach exceeds their grasp. Entrepreneurs mobilize the resources of others to achieve their objectives.

Borstein (2007) has identified the characteristics of an entrepreneur as follows:

- Intelligent mind, a compassionate heart, and a service ethic.
- Interdisciplinary: Social entrepreneurs look for connections; they have an ability to spot larger patterns and to work with people from a wide range of experience. Social entrepreneurs seem willing to share credit.
- Flexibility: Social entrepreneurs are able to adapt quickly.
- Risk: Social entrepreneurs are able to know when to deal with risk; at the core of their actions is a sense of timing: a knowing when not to act, as well as when to act.
- Capacity: Social entrepreneurs remember capacity is not fixed; they know they don't have to have all the skills or knowledge needed to finish a project. They only need enough skills, knowledge, etc. to start and to be willing to learn along the way.

- Awareness: Social entrepreneurs are reflective and aware of what is going on around them.

Whereas the typical entrepreneur looks to create new ways of doing things to create personal wealth, the social entrepreneur looks to create new ways to address social issues not to benefit him or herself but rather to improve systems, invent and disseminate new approaches, and advance sustainable solutions that create social value. The social entrepreneur takes specific business and management skills and applies them in order to create programs that contribute to the common good.

The concept of social entrepreneurship and creating programs that matter can be seen in the story of Dana and Brandi, graduates of Gordon College. Dana and Brandi's story began in the late 1990s out of a passion for what they believed were life-changing experiences inherent in adventure education and service learning programs. After visiting Dana's parents, who ran an orphanage near Bucharest, they began toying with the idea of launching an adventure program in Romania. Romania offers a unique environment for their work. Though communism fell in Romania in 1989, it has left a lingering mark on Romanian culture – civic apathy, interpersonal suspicion, and Machiavellian predatory ethics all make trust, and therefore sustainable development, impossible. A World Values Association Survey from 1998 found Romania at the bottom of all European cultures in terms of interpersonal trust. In addition, Romania voted itself the unhappiest country in the world. A staggering 50 percent of the Romanian population believes that one becomes successful by stealing and breaking the law.

Dana and Brandi's efforts have led to the establishment of the New Horizons Foundation (2011), whose mission is to create caring citizens who feel empowered to act! Currently the programs include camps, rope courses, adventure trips (backpacking), service learning projects, and clubs that facilitate many of these activities. The program is unique; yet, I think the way Dana and Brandi have built the capacity of the organization is one of the important lessons to be learned. Their diligence and integrity has paid off as they have built partnerships with a variety of local, national, and international organizations including the Romanian Orthodox Church (to which 87% of the population in Romania belongs), Project Adventure, the University of Cluj, Innovation in Civic Participation, US Aid, Balkan Children and Youth Foundation, and the Global Fund for Children. These partnerships have allowed New Horizons the opportunity to flourish and to have access to a wide range of Romanian youth. As a result, New Horizons is equipping Romanian youth with the skills, (inter) personal trust, and confidence to address the issues of poverty, child abandonment, environmental degradation, and corruption.

Dana and Brandi's work is characteristic of what it means to be a social entrepreneur. The organization they have created has developed from their worldview that Christians need to be integrally involved in the issues of the day, and their faith is evident in all aspects of the organization. They also represent many of the characteristics of a social entrepreneur (Borstein, 2007). They have a desire to help Romanians develop a service ethic for their country. They are always looking for partnerships with other individuals and organizations. The programs that New Horizons offer are interdisciplinary in nature and the organization continues to adapt to rapidly changing social conditions in Romania by continually reaching out to new partners and developing new programs. They work hard to empower participants of their clubs to develop their own programs and initiatives.

Lastly, they have demonstrated the importance of stepping out in faith, realizing that God can do mighty things. In him, capacity is not fixed. He calls us to begin the process, realizing that we don't have to have all the skills or knowledge needed to finish a project, just to begin and then be willing to learn along the way.

Strategies for Preparing Our Students to be Change Agents

The model presented in Figure 1 provides us with an ultimate vision for our programs, as programs are the vehicles whereby recreation professionals can change the world. The model also identifies the importance of a worldview grounded in our faith as well as forms of praxis or ways of life (such as servant leaders and social entrepreneurs) for equipping students to make a difference as a part of their professional lives. This model is reconfigured in Figure 3, from a linear progression to more of a circular process where all elements of the model interact with each other. The reconfiguration helps us to understand that while our worldview is foundational to how we conduct our lives, it is also influenced by how we choose to live our lives as well. Likewise, the stories (e.g., Lisa, Dana and Brandi) and symbols (e.g., saying yes) that we choose to embrace will also shape our worldview and the way that we live as individuals and professionals.

Figure 3. A curriculum model for parks and recreation. Adapted from Bouma-Prediger & Walsh (2008).

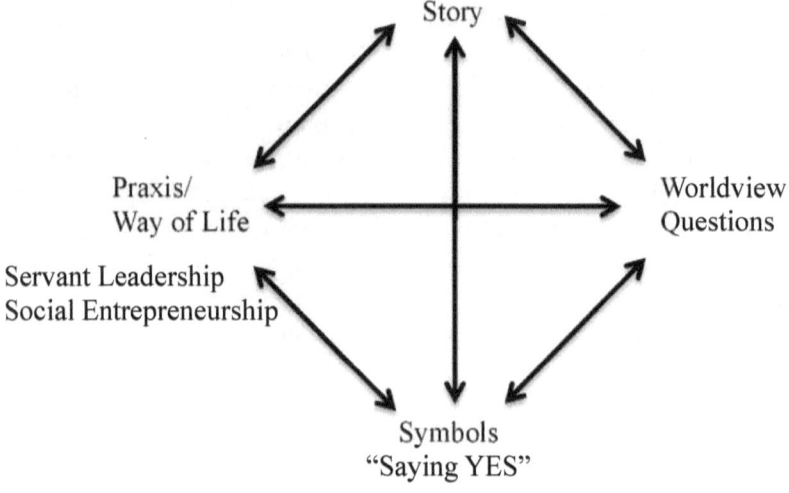

The ultimate professional vision within this framework is to develop and offer recreation programs that make a difference in people's lives. Why? Because we have a worldview that demands that we work to alleviate the brokenness of our world and try to promote human flourishing. The concepts of servant leadership and social entrepreneurship offer symbols that answer the how questions, related to the practice of everyday life. The last component presented in Figure 3 is the importance of story to the overview of connecting worldview and symbols to a way of life.

> The praxis, or way of life, of a community [or a profession] is embedded in the community's grounding story, confronted by its most powerful symbols, and is an expression of the way in which the community [or profession] implicitly (and sometimes explicitly) answers ultimate worldview questions. (Bouma-Prediger & Walsh, 2008, p. 135)

The Story of the Recreation Profession

What is the narrative story of the recreation profession; what are the stories of our respective curriculums? Let's begin by examining the historical context of the recreation profession. Formal recreation organizations emerged during the late 1800s to address the tremendous social, psychological, and general welfare needs that grew out of the Industrial Revolution. Social reformers saw the potential of using play and recreation to improve people's quality of life. For instance, the Boston Sand Gardens (the first playground) was established to meet the play needs of disadvantaged children and give them a safe place to play. Also, many of the first organized camps were designed for and targeted at "sickly boys." Large city parks (e.g., Central Park in New York) were designed in an attempt to regain the rural countryside in the middle of the city and thus give people who lived in crowded slum tenements a place to relax and get away from it all. Further, the settlement house movement used recreation as a means to ease the transition of immigrants to living in large urban American cities. Sessoms and Stevenson (1981) have written that

> Adult education, recreation, and social group work all have a common heritage. Each is a product of the social welfare reforms that occurred in our cities and industries at the turn of the nineteenth century. Their founders shared a belief – they were concerned with the quality of life and believed that through the "proper" use of leisure it could be achieved. (p. 2)

In examining the wide range of leisure service organizations that developed over the last 120 years, Godbey (1997) noted that three factors have shaped all forms of leisure services: the desire to help people (related to servant leadership); an entrepreneurial spirit (related to social entrepreneurship); and changes in technology which facilitate, or necessitate, such intentions.

Throughout the history of the recreation movement, we can see examples of servant leaders and social entrepreneurs who responded to the changing dynamics of society as a whole: people like Jane Addams, Joseph Lee, John Muir, and others. Consider the example of Jane Addams, who used the many programs at Hull House to build the dream of American democracy. In a biography of Addams, Elshtain (2002) wrote:

> Addams was adamant throughout her life that Hull House should offer shelter from the storm and a new way of being in the world. It was a place of civic education, a spirited enterprise that served as a vehicle for the creation of community through fellowship. Fellowship became both the end sought and the means to get there. (p. 153)

As Addams (1893) herself, wrote:

> The mere foothold of a house, easily accessible, ample in space, hospitable and tolerant in spirit, situated in the midst of the large foreign colonies which so easily isolate themselves in American cities, would be in itself a serviceable thing for Chicago. (p. 1)

This legacy is a great starting point for encouraging students in our programs to engage in promoting the common good. However, this is not enough, as this legacy is often grounded in a humanistic worldview that is not consistent with a Christian worldview. This does not mean that students coming from Christian colleges and universities cannot work with others who have a humanistic worldview, but it does mean that students should understand that their desire to work for the common good comes from a different worldview, one grounded in God's desire for us to be reforming agents in our world. This realization encourages the parks and recreation curriculums in Christian colleges and universities to do three things. First, our curriculums must ground our students in a more biblical worldview (through the use of stories, symbols, and metaphors, such as servant leadership and social entrepreneurship). This article has tried to model this approach by integrating personal stories to reinforce points made in the article. Second, our curriculums must help students find their own calling. Third, our curriculums must teach students the skills and virtues needed to dialogue and work with others who do not share our specific worldview but who do share our desire to make a difference in our world.

Individual Stories

Returning to the model presented in Figure 3, it is again important to recognize the importance of stories to address these three challenges. Much has been written about the roles that storytelling and narrative play in teaching and learning. It is no stretch of the imagination to think of teachers and professors as storytellers, and to think of classrooms as places where stories are constructed, shared, analyzed, and ultimately incorporated into the growing consciousness of each student. From case stories to history lessons to personal life journeys, stories can be used every day as vehicles for communicating particular lessons. Professors should be encouraged to tell the stories of graduates of our programs as one way to encourage students to "grasp the possible" as they graduate and become the recreational professionals of tomorrow (Rao, Steele, & Venegas, 2007).

Consider the following story of Kent, who runs Camp Fowler (2011) in upstate New York. Reflect how the following narrative could be used in talking about worldview, virtues, and developing programs that can make a difference in this world.

> You sense things are different the moment you enter Camp Fowler. Whether it's the sign by the parking area that reads *Future world and local leaders in training here*, the bicycles used by the maintenance workers to haul their gear around camp or the wooden buildings that authentically

fit the north woods setting, you sense that the camp has been carefully thought out. . . . Indeed, the Camp Fowler philosophy is similar to many Christian camps: to glorify God, to foster growth in Jesus Christ as Lord, to experience life in a Christian community, and to encourage people to live as disciples of Christ. But what is striking at Camp Fowler is that all of it is infused with a spirit of shalom. Among the camp's core virtues are simplicity, hospitality, and community. In recent years, its summer-long themes have been peace and justice and woven through everything is the theme of earthkeeping.

Kent has been at Camp Fowler since 1986, and his imprint more than two decades later is now considerable. Through the years he has intentionally and creatively shaped the place and its practices to reflect the core values of the gospel, not the least of which is the commitment to caring for the earth. But that care is always specific to a particular place. . . . Because of his extensive local knowledge, Kent is able to discern the possibilities and limits of his place. He knows when enough is enough, and thus he resists the pressure to think that bigger is better. Consequently, the camp remains relatively small, of a human and humane scale. In short, Camp Fowler incarnates a kind of wisdom and this wisdom joins arms with an infectious joy, such that all who come to Camp Fowler, campers, volunteers, staff, catch the spirit of Kent's joyful wisdom and wisdom-filled joy. (Story taken from Bouma-Prediger & Walsh, 2008, pp. 225–227)

Specifically, stories can help students understand how a worldview can impact the delivery of programs. In the case of Kent, students can explore the website of Camp Fowler and investigate some of the camp's core values. Once identified, students can explore how the staff at Camp Fowler incorporates these virtues into camp practices. When the story is about alumni of your program, students may have additional opportunities to interact with the alumni, to hear stories about their worldview and how they are putting that worldview into action. By hearing stories such as those of Lisa, Dana and Brandi, or Kent, students can be inspired to think about what virtues are important to them and how these virtues can influence the development of a program. Stories of alumni who faculty identify as servant leaders or social entrepreneurs give meaning to these concepts and help these symbols and metaphors become real life stories of people who are making a difference in our world.

In addition, multiple stories can also help students see the range of opportunities that exist, as well as assist them in discerning how they want to serve others. However, this is not an easy process, since the recreation profession offers so many opportunities to contribute to issues such as healthy living, community building, youth development, and environmental stewardship. One way we can engage students in this process is by asking what they are passionate about. Stories help students catch a glimpse of the possible, catching a vision of how they can contribute to society through their chosen profession.

Lastly, stories in the form of case studies can help students develop the skills needed to dialogue with others who may have a vastly different worldview than they do. Developing the virtues of humility, courage, and wisdom can be encouraged as students struggle with real world examples of organizations working together to discern the common good and how to work together to obtain it. The Appendix presents a number of organizations that support social entrepreneurs throughout the world. These organizations provide a variety of possible case studies on programs that are making a difference in this world.

Conclusion

Integrating one's faith into every aspect of one's life is never easy. Likewise, it is not always easy to enter the fray of working with others toward the common good. Both demand reflection, dedication, and a willingness to jump into the discussion and to ask the tough questions of others and ourselves. One hope of this author is that by using the metaphors of both servant leadership and social entrepreneurship, as well as integrating a variety of stories into our classes and curriculums, we can encourage students to develop a worldview grounded in our faith that leads us to make a difference in this world. Throughout this process, professors need to continue to challenge our students with the word *let*: *Let's* not be scared of the hard questions; *let's* not be scared of messy, *let's* make room for wonder, *let's* look for ways to work together to promote the common good, *let's* encourage ourselves to live with our hearts and to embrace the complexities of our world together.

References

Addams, J. (1893). The subjective necessity for social settlements: A new impulse to an old gospel. In T.Y. Croswell (Ed.), *Philanthropy and social progress* (pp. 1–27). New York: Thomas Y. Crowell.

Bess, P. (1996). Virtuous reality: Aristotle, critical realism, and the reconstruction of architectural and urban theology. *The Classicist* 3, 6–18.

Block, P. (2002). *The answer to how is yes: Acting on what matters.* San Francisco: Berrett-Koehler.

Borstein, D. (2007). *How to change the world: Social entrepreneurship and the power of ideas.* New York: Oxford University Press.

Bouma-Prediger, S., & Walsh, B. (2008). *Beyond homelessness: Christian faith in a culture of displacement*. Grand Rapids: Eerdmans.

Calvin College Alumni. (2006, Fall). Serving up yes! An alumni profile of Lisa and Hayden. The *Calvin Spark*, p. 61. Available online at: https://www.calvin.edu/publications/spark/2006/fall/greenbean.htm

Cameron, K., & Quinn, R. (2005). *Diagnosing and changing organizational culture*. San Francisco: The Jossey Bass Business and Management Series.

Camp Fowler (2011). What is Camp Fowler? Retrieved Dec. 1, 2011 from http://www.campfowler.org/about

Elshtain, J.B. (2002). *Jane Addams and the dream of American democracy*. New York: Basic Books.

Green Bean (2006). Mission of the Green Bean. Retrieved February 13, 2006, from: www.greenbeancoffee.org

Greenleaf, R. (1970/1991). *Servant as leader*. Indianapolis, IN: Greenleaf Centre.

Greenleaf, R. (1998). Servant leadership. In L. Spears (Ed.), *Insights on leadership* (pp. 15–21). New York: Wiley & Sons.

Greenleaf, R. (1977). *Servant leadership: A journey into the nature of legitimate power and greatness*. New York: Paulist Press.

Godbey, G. (1997). *Leisure and leisure services in the 21st century*. State College, PA: Venture.

Hesse, H. (1993). *Journey to the East*. New York: Picador.

Jarvi, C. (2001). Developing park and recreation professionals as social entrepreneurs. In D. Sessoms & T. Mobley (Eds.), *Developing leadership for parks and recreation in the 21st century* (pp. 177–181). Ashburn, VA: National Recreation and Park Association.

Kouzes, J., & Posner, B. (2006). *A leader's legacy*. San Francisco: Jossey-Bass.

Nash, J.B. (1953). *Philosophy of recreation and leisure*. St. Louis, MO: Mosby.

New Horizons Foundation (2011). New Horizons Foundation for Youth and Community. Retrieved Dec. 1, 2011, from: http://www.noi-orizonturi.ro/index.php?lang=en

Nouwen, H. (1975). *Reaching out: The three movements of the spiritual life*. New York: Doubleday.

Oldenburg, R. (2001). *Celebrating the third place: Inspiring stories about the great good places at the heart of our communities*. New York: Marlowe & Company.

Rao, R., Steele, J.L, & Venegas, K.R. (2007). From the editors: Stories that teach: The role of voices inside schools. *Harvard Educational Review* 2(1), pp. 141–143.

Sessoms, D., & Stevenson, J. (1981). *Leadership and group dynamics in recreation services*. Boston: Allyn & Bacon.

Strauss, G. (2010, Spring). 2010 Comment Manifesto: Wonder, heartbreak, and hope. *Comment*. 20–21. https://www.cardus.ca/assets/data/images/2010/2010CommentManifesto.pdf

Wolk, A. (2008). The blurring of sectors: Social entrepreneurship emerges at the nexus. Article retrieved most recently on September 5, 2017 from: http://archive.skoll.org/2008/03/25/the-blurring-of-sectors-social-entrepreneurship-emerges-at-the-nexus/

World Values Survey Association. (2014). World values survey wave 3 1995–1998 Official Aggregate v.20140921. Madrid, Spain: Author. Retrieved on October 21, 2015 from: http://www.worldvaluessurvey.us/WVSDocumentationWV3.jsp

Appendix

Organizations Supporting Social Entrepreneurship

Asoka (Global) – www.ashoka.org

Mission: Ashoka strives to shape a global, entrepreneurial, competitive citizen sector: one that allows social entrepreneurs to thrive and enables the world's citizens to think and act as changemakers.

Program Example: Program created by Jadwiga Lopata – www.ashoka.org/fellow/2907

Jadwiga Lopata recognized that Poland's many small family-owned farms were ideally suited to convert to organic farming methods and thereby benefit from the emerging premium market for organic produce and livestock. In order to be able to make this shift, however, supplemental income was required. Jadwiga's solution was to provide families converting to organic farming with a steady stream of visitors (mostly urban families from Western Europe) who happily pay for the opportunity to stay, eat, and work on the farms. Thus, Jadwiga demonstrates to rural farmers that not only is organic farming viable, but so is their bucolic lifestyle. This tangible material revaluation of family farming is precisely the antidote required by family farms to enable them to resist the encroachment of large-scale agribusiness.

Echoing Green (USA) – www.echoinggreen.org

Mission: Echoing Green's mission is to spark social change. By identifying, investing, and supporting the world's most exceptional emerging leaders and the organizations they create they are creating a network of visionaries addressing society's most difficult problems.

Program Example: Peace Games – www.peacegames.org

Peace Games teaches young people tools to find creative solutions to the complex problems facing them through cooperation, communication, conflict resolution, and community. They learn the value of friends and teamwork, how to communicate in appropriate ways, how to resolve disagreements through talking rather than fighting, and how to utilize their community as a team that can change injustices around them.

Schwab Foundation for Social Entrepreneurs (Switzerland) – www.schwabfound.org

Mission: The Schwab Foundation for Social Entrepreneurship provides unparalleled platforms at the national, regional and global levels for leading social innovators that highlight social entrepreneurship as a key element to address social and ecological problems in an innovative, sustainable and effective way.

Program Example: Homeless World Cup – www.homelessworldcup.org

Mel Young founded the Homeless World Cup, which uses football to energize people who are homeless to change their own lives. This is achieved firstly with a world-class annual, international, football tournament uniting national teams of people who are homeless; and secondly by triggering and supporting grass roots football programs working with people who are homeless all year round.

Section Four

THERAPEUTIC RECREATION

Therapeutic recreation is a recognized health care profession "that uses recreation and experiential interventions to bring about change – either social, emotional, intellectual, physical, or spiritual – in an effort to maintain or improve health status, functional capacities, and quality of life" (Carter & Van Andel, 2011, p. 9). As with other healthcare professions, professional principles and practices guide the implementation of the various interventions for any given individual recipient of the service. However, other factors, such as the worldview or beliefs and values of the therapist, are not often considered in the therapeutic setting. The chapters in section four address some of these factors and provide a framework for therapeutic recreation practice from a Christian perspective.

In Chapter 19, Cathy O'Keefe argues that the purpose of therapeutic recreation is to bring restoration, hope, joy, and freedom that will transform how a person thinks about him or herself. She suggests that such a change is only possible in a loving, supportive community where people with different abilities are not singled out but embraced as equals. This unconditional love reflects the love that God has demonstrated for all of us as his children. Thus, when practiced from a Christian worldview, therapeutic recreation has the potential to add significant value and meaning to the lives of the recipients of this service.

In Chapter 20, Van Andel and Heintzman challenge the traditional medical model approach to therapeutic recreation practice. They argue that a more holistic paradigm involves a meaning-centered, psycho-spiritual approach to treatment where the interdisciplinary team assists individuals in finding meaning and purpose in their lives, develop self-concepts, promote nurturing relationships with others, and opportunities for successful experiences (Nicosia, 1994). From this perspective, Christian spirituality provides the philosophical basis for the ethical and moral practice of therapeutic recreation to address the total needs of the person, especially those psycho-spiritual needs that find fulfillment through leisure experiences.

Ethical and moral principles are essential for guiding professional practice, but there are still many difficult and challenging dilemmas that confront therapists. In Chapter 21, Joe Teaff presents five principles – benefice, non-maleficence, autonomy, justice, and fidelity – that guide therapists in their practice. He challenges us to critically examine these and consider alternative perspectives, especially for care recipients whose beliefs and values may conflict with our own.

Much of our approach to healthcare assumes the potential to change or improve the health status of the care recipient. However, this traditional view does not consider those individuals who suffer from chronic illnesses such as Parkinson's or dementia. In Chapter 22, Youngkhill Lee and Bryan McCormick propose a more inclusive health care model that considers life stories and a sense of coherence to help individuals make sense of their disabilities. Important components of this meaning-building process are the spiritual beliefs and values that these individuals develop to gain some understanding and control of their difficult health status.

In the last chapter in this section, Chapter 23, Paul Heintzman develops a leisure-spiritual coping model for therapeutic recreation services. The model describes the process of mitigating life stressors through spiritual appraisals, personal factors, and leisure resources and behaviors that ultimately contribute to a sense of wellbeing. A personal case study helps to describe how this model might be used by therapeutic recreation specialists in their practice.

Glen Van Andel

References

Carter, M., & Van Andel, G. (2011). *Therapeutic recreation: A practical approach* (4th ed.). Long Grove, IL: Waveland Press.

Nicosia, J.F. (1994). Healing the human spirit: The healing paradigm. *Journal of Religion in Disability & Rehabilitation* 1(3), 65–74.

Chapter 19
A Christian Perspective on Therapeutic Recreation

Cathy O'Keefe

Henri Nouwen (1980/2008) wrote, "You cannot think your way into a new kind of living; rather, you must live your way into a new kind of thinking" (p. ix). This quote took on greater meaning for me as I prepared this chapter, since terms like *faith* and *discipline* are intrinsically woven into this sentence. Faith is revealed in the way we live out our lives as human beings. Discipline is revealed in the way we gain knowledge about the truth of the world around us.

In his book *Stages of Faith,* James Fowler (1981) spends the first chapter looking at definitions of faith as seen by a variety of writers. He describes Richard Niebuhr and Paul Tillich's suggestion that faith is a universal concern.

> Prior to being religious or irreligious, before we come to think of ourselves as Catholic, Protestant, Jews, or Muslims, we are already engaged with issues of faith. Whether we become nonbelievers, agnostics or atheists, we are concerned with how to put our lives together and with what will make life worth living. Moreover, we look for something to love that loves us, something to value that gives us value, something to honor and respect, that has the power to sustain our being. (Fowler, p. 5)

A discussion about Christianity and therapeutic recreation must center on three things: (1) how faith, experienced by the person who has a disability/challenge, interfaces with knowledge gained from involvement in a therapeutic recreation program; (2) how the support of family and friends mirrors God's love to the person who has a disability/challenge; and (3) how faith and knowledge held by the therapeutic recreation specialist enhance the process of therapeutic recreation. Since the person we serve is the central focus of our actions as professionals, let us start there.

Paper presented at the 1995 conference.

The Faith and Knowledge of a Person with a Disability

When an individual is suddenly faced with a disability or parents learn that their new-born child will have a chronic illness, the unavoidable question arises: why did this happen to me or to one whom I love? Believers in God will inevitably struggle with the paradox that God is all powerful and all good, but terrible things continue to happen to innocent people. At many points in the habilitation/rehabilitation process, the meaning of suffering will again have to be addressed. Based on the Book of Job in the Hebrew Scriptures and reinforced again and again in the Gospels, the notion of suffering as punishment for sin is rejected (Chamiec-Case, 1994; Nolan, 1988; Webb-Mitchell, 1994). Yet, even today, the implication that physical challenges leave one in a state of imperfection, in need of healing, is prevalent. The degree to which impairment is seen in a negative light is influenced by the way in which society creates value around beauty, physical wholeness, talent, and productivity. One of the paramount challenges to clients we serve is moving away from the belief that physical healing is the ultimate good and seeing the complexity of suffering among all persons. It involves distancing ourselves, as well, from the notion of being "disabled" and embracing an understanding of being "differently-abled."

One of the wonderful aspects of the field of therapeutic recreation is its dedication to helping individuals re-create their giftedness. Modalities like leisure education, re-motivation, reminiscing, adventure programming, and expressive arts are designed to empower clients through self-knowledge and the development of skills in order to enhance the meaning of life.

As the client moves from the "why me?" stage to the point where he or she can view the disability/challenge as a joint venture with God as partner, the seeming unfairness of personal suffering gives way to an understanding that one is not singled out by God and put before others as either an object of pity or hero-worship. Rather, as Jean Vanier (1990), the founder of L'Arche, an international community of homes for persons with developmental disabilities, points out, we are all "handicapped," and the timing, or degree to which our suffering impacts our lives, both unites us all and remains uniquely individual.

Faith has the ability to create for our clients, as it does for all of us, a context in which the meaning of life and its value to us can be framed. For some, awareness of God's love is already present when a disability occurs. While anger is often a common emotion, most believers eventually see God not as the inflictor of suffering but as the co-sufferer. For the

Christian, one's individual cross is shadowed by the cross of Christ, with the promise of resurrection reflected in inner healing and peace.

Since leisure, the freedom to be truly oneself, is a state of being, it is available to anyone, regardless of ability to function, and is easily nurtured through growth in faith. The mystery of the incarnation, held sacred by the Christian faith, extends the promise that God enters intimately into our lives and is there to unfold truth in us through grace.

Therapeutic recreation processes have, at their very core, the purpose of restoration to wholeness, awareness of goodness, and the experience of joy. Clients work with professionals in this field to rediscover and create a self that is free, autonomous, happy, and playful. Self-knowledge gained through therapeutic recreation processes helps clients live their way into a new kind of thinking, which is for the Christian an experience of the Kingdom.

Fowler (1981) opens his book with some key questions that I found compelling. In fact, if I were to design an assessment tool for therapeutic recreation, these are the questions that are ultimately more important than the ones typically asked of clients in hospitals or community-based settings. These are the questions that tell, more than anything, how a person is coping with the day-to-day difficulties and joys of life:

> What are you spending and being spent for? What commands and receives your best time, your best energy?
> What causes, dreams, goals, or institutions are you pouring out your life for?
> As you live your life, what power or powers do you fear or dread? What power or powers do you rely on and trust?
> To what or to whom are you committed in life? In death?
> With whom or what group do you share your most sacred and private hopes for your life and for the lives of those you love?
> What are those most sacred hopes, those most compelling goals and purposes in your life? (Fowler, p. 1)

The Faith of Friends, Family, and Community

One of the key roles of the therapeutic recreation specialist is to evaluate support systems for clients so that the gains made in habilitation or rehabilitation can be nurtured and reinforced by those who influence the client on a day-to-day basis. Involving the friends and family of the client in goal setting, treatment planning, and after-care increases the client's chances of making a smooth transition to a life of meaning in the community.

A stellar contribution of Christianity lies in its emphasis on community as a vehicle for experiencing God's love and concern. The Christian communities of early times joined into a common life that was based on the need of each person and the notion that we are the body of Christ, each differently-abled and equally important. Community that is authentic in commitment to growth and dedicated to a greater understanding of love as its cornerstone holds one of the greatest hopes for all of us in understanding the mystery of joy amid suffering.

Creating community is an ongoing challenge for every generation in every age. Legitimate criticism can be mounted against religions at various times in history in various cultures for using the concept of community to mean an exclusive group. Many are more remembered for shutting out individuals than for their inclusiveness. Albert Nolan (1988), in his book *Jesus before Christianity*, peels away the layers around the man Jesus that have been added on by cultures over the centuries, often for their own self-serving reasons. He notes that the Hebrew notion of collectivity resounds in the scriptures as one of its most fundamental concepts. Jesus extends the tribal solidarity, emphasized by the common culture of his day to all of humankind, friends and enemies alike.

Hospitals, community-based clinics, and independent living initiatives all seek to utilize community therapeutically. The degree of success achieved by these settings varies greatly. The milieu therapy model is designed to use the total environment of the treatment setting to impact the client. The long-term care model offers the opportunity to develop relationships among clients and staff over time, with the potential to become community. The helping professions should be searching diligently for models of community life that truly demonstrate the best programs available for achieving a sense of belonging and support. Community in this sense involves able-bodied and disabled persons interacting as equals, rather than able-bodied "caregivers" doing for their charges.

A dominant modality in therapeutic recreation is community reintegration: the establishment of new connections and the renewal of old ones in the environment to which the client will return after treatment to live permanently. The goal of community reintegration is personal comfort and confidence for the client: a belief, backed up by skills, in one's ability to become a full participant in community life.

Since a satisfying spiritual life is an accepted human domain rightly addressed by therapeutic recreation (Carter, Van Andel, & Robb, 2003), and leisure in general (Pieper, 1952), many specialists regularly address with their clients the possibility of involvement in a church as a means of meeting both spiritual and social needs. Some current writing indicates that many churches are struggling to improve efforts to welcome and minister to persons with disabilities in full communion with all congregation members (Blair & Blair, 1994; Deland, 1995; Peters, 1994; Thornburgh, 1994; Webb-Mitchell, 1994). Much remains to be done to help churches enter into meaningful dialogue with their parishioners in order to help everyone understand that the spiritual life nurtured by a faith community involves an acknowledgement of the suffering and joys of all its members rather than a singling out of those with obvious impairments as examples of inspiration or objects of prayer (Webb-Mitchell, 1994).

Finally, a deeply rooted mystery of the Christian tradition lies in the belief that we are best able to grasp the breadth and depth of God's love when we experience it through the living hands of others. Giving and receiving love unconditionally and a willingness to enter into the suffering and joy of others are hallmarks of an authentic community (Vanier, 1990). Recreation has a unique ability to bond community members together over time. The anticipation and planning of recreation, the actual experience itself, and the creation of meaning through recollection of it weave a tapestry of connectedness in the community. When I take my students to visit the L'Arche community in Mobile, part of the introduction process always involves the core members – adults with developmental disabilities – sharing huge photo albums with my students. This is the telling of their stories, through celebration and recreation, to new acquaintances. You can see the gradual incorporation of new members and assistants who live with them in the pictures themselves. Camping, traveling, holiday celebrations, and special events are the vehicles that deepen the life of the community and take the ordinary or the profane to the level of the sacred.

One of the best short literary pieces I have ever read about the mystery of family love was published without too much acclaim in the *Wall Street Journal* in 1985. In "The Power of the Powerless: A Brother's Lesson," the author describes his brother, born blind and severely intellectually disabled following a tragic carbon monoxide poisoning incident during the mother's pregnancy. The beauty of this piece, written from the perspective of the brother, was contained in the belief held by the family that this child, because of his total powerlessness, developed in each family member the capacity to love unconditionally, to be sensitive to the smallest signs of communication, and to understand the meaning of commitment. Like paradox that is characteristic of the parables, the truth is revealed when the unexpected turns reality upside down (Donahue, 1988).

Suggesting recreation to persons who are recovering from a terrible injury, or even in the process of dying, may seem as ludicrous as the claim that a severely intellectually disabled individual can be powerful. Its value, however, lies in the client's or family's awareness that the experience of recreation has the power to transform despair into hope or to make the statement that precious time is best spent doing precious things, especially when it deepens the bond with those we love. Truly, faith is about mystery. The experience of leisure is too. When they intersect, one has the ability to profoundly deepen the other. And when community enters the equation, the Spirit is enfleshed in a caring touch, a loving embrace, liberating one's innermost self in new and beautiful ways.

The Faith of the Professional

The psychotherapist Carl Rogers (1961) once wrote:

> In my relationships with persons I have found that it does not help, in the long run, to act as though I were something that I am not. . . . I find that I am more effective when I can listen acceptingly to myself, and can be myself. . . . (p. 5)

Many professionals in therapeutic recreation have commented to me over the years that their own Christian faith has exerted a strong influence on their relationships with clients, even when the clients showed no evidence of having a similar faith themselves. Being grounded in meaning, the lives of these therapists are committed to helping others find meaning, too. As Fowler (1981) points out above, faith exhibits itself in many forms. It may be expressed as faith in one's physician or in one's ability to recover.

The Christian therapist has a duty to nurture, without judgment or influence, those aspects of the client's faith that can work for him or her toward healing. Sensitivity toward other belief systems and respect for individual interpretations of values and goals are all essential in the therapeutic recreation specialist's work. Leisure and recreation preferences are also so highly individualized that the specialist must honor those choices that make an experience "leisure" in the eyes of the client.

The real privilege of working in this field is that it involves concepts that are comfortable to a person of faith. Freedom, inner healing, and personal liberation are shared by the vocabulary of leisure and faith. Unconditionally accepting one's clients is not difficult for the therapist who holds a sense of the community of the human family close to his or her heart. Further, belief in the presence of the Divine in every person invites the therapist to respect and treasure the uniqueness and giftedness of every client.

Finally, the concept of communal pilgrimage, a journey of growth in faith with others who also seek meaning in life, creates for the client and therapist a shared path upon which they walk as equals. Reverence for the client-therapist relationship as mutually life-giving makes the mystery of the Divine all the more powerful.

Conclusion

By examining the faith of persons with disabilities or related challenges, and by looking at the faith of the community as well as the therapist, this chapter attempted to create a connection, through the experience of therapeutic recreation, to truths and values that are virtuous and good for all parties. Recreation experiences have the power to heal in a way that is most consistent with Christian belief. They enhance the healing of the spirit, that part of our inner selves that is capable of transcending limited functioning. The true miracles, then, are the ones that lead to internal peace, self-love, and acceptance. The authentic resurrections occur when one can not only find happiness, but when we learn that restoration to life is a much deeper mystery than many would have us believe.

References

Blair, W. & Blair, D. (1994). Ministry to persons with disabilities: Can we do it better? *Journal of Religion in Disability and Rehabilitation* 1(1), 1–10.

Carter, M., Van Andel, G., & Robb, G. (2003). *Therapeutic Recreation: A practical approach* (3rd ed.). Chicago: Waveland Press.

Chamiec-Case, R. (1994). Supporting families of persons with a disability. *Journal of Religion in Disability and Rehabilitation* 1(3), 41–51.

Deland, J. S. (1995). Breaking down the barriers so all may worship. *Journal of Religion in Disability and Rehabilitation* 2(1), 5–21.

DeVinck, C. (1985, April 10). The power of the powerless: A brother's lesson. *Wall Street Journal*, p. 28.

Donahue, J. R. (1998). *The gospel in parable*. Minneapolis: Fortress Press.

Fowler, J. (1981). *Stages of faith*. San Francisco: Harper Collins.

Nolan, A. (1988). *Jesus before Christianity*. New York: Orbis Books.

Nouwen, H.J.M. (2008). Introduction to the 1980 edition. In P.J. Palmer, *The promise of paradox: A celebration of contradictions in the Christian life* (pp. ix–xii). San Francisco: Jossey-Bass.

Peters, R. K. (1994). Between the wall and the fall: Ministering to Humpty-Dumpty. *Journal of Religion in Disability and Rehabilitation* 1(1), 7–39.

Pieper, J. (1952). *Leisure: The basis of culture* (A. Dru, Trans.). New York:

Pantheon Books (1963, Random House).

Rogers, C. (1961). *On becoming a helper*. Boston: Houghton Mifflin.

Thornburgh, V. J. (1994). That all may worship. *Journal of Religion in Disability and Rehabilitation* 1(3), 1, 7–13.

Vanier, J. (1990). *Community and growth*. London: Darton, Longman & Todd.

Webb-Mitchell, B. (1994). The deinstitutionalization of specialized ministries: The importance of the church being the church. *Journal of Religion in Disability and Rehabilitation* 1(1), 47–53.

Chapter 20
CHRISTIAN SPIRITUALITY AND THERAPEUTIC RECREATION

Glen Van Andel and Paul Heintzman

In its attempts to be recognized and accepted as a full participant in the health care arena, the therapeutic recreation profession has been drawn into justifying its existence by emphasizing its contribution to the powerful disease-oriented medical model. "Recreation therapy" has become the term most frequently used to identify this approach, which focuses on maintaining or improving functional behaviors. The bottom line is efficacy and efficiency which translates into, How does your specific intervention improve the client's ability to be discharged, return to work, or live more independently? Or, how does it save rehabilitation resources? These are not unreasonable or inappropriate goals in themselves, but we and others are beginning to ask, Is that all there is to care? Is fixing a broken part enough, or can we, as a profession, do more to contribute to the quality of life of the persons we serve?

To answer these questions, it may be helpful to examine some of the assumptions on which our professional practice is being built. The medical model draws its support from scientific naturalism and positivism, which hold that the human body is a complex machine that can best be understood through empirical research that is based on observable cause-and-effect relationships. Furthermore, since matter is all there is, there is no spiritual being such as God, and the universe has no meaning or purpose outside of itself (MacDonald, 1984). The ultimate result of this approach is the separation of the individual into two parts, body and mind, and, since it is not observable, eliminating the spiritual dimension altogether. When taken to its extremes, people are dehumanized and treated as objects that may or may not have value, depending on their position and status in a given community.

Revised version of paper presented at the 1996 conference.

The limitations of a medical model, fix-broken-parts paradigm directs us toward a more holistic understanding of health care and challenges therapeutic recreation professionals to consider other worldviews that coincide with how we contribute to the continuum of human services. In fact, because much of what we do is not quantifiable in behavioral or functional terms, the holistic nature and purpose of therapeutic recreation has become difficult to articulate within a worldview that rejects the nonmaterial or aesthetic realities. Sylvester (1987) notes that if we are to affirm our humanness and enjoy happiness, we must play. In other words, true quality of life is found not simply in improved functioning but in the discovery of our humanity through experiences that bring meaning and value to life.

The Anglo-Saxon word *haelan*, from which we get our term healing, means "to become whole." As we consider the complex and comprehensive nature of the healing process, we begin to recognize the power and importance of the inner person which Norman Cousins (1989), a long-time advocate of holistic health, has noted in his discussions with several physicians:

> Any battle with serious illness . . . involves two elements. One was represented by the ability of the physicians to make available to patients the best that medical science has to offer. The other element [is] represented by the ability of patients to summon all their physical and spiritual resources in fighting illness. (p. 142)

Innovative research is beginning to provide support for such a holistic approach to health care, especially as it relates to the role that spirituality plays in the healing process. For example, a Dartmouth heart-surgery study showed that patients who experienced social support and had a strong religious faith had a 14-fold advantage of recovery over those who tended to be isolated and had little faith (Wallis, 1996). Prayer, the expression of a most intimate relationship with God, contributes to one's quality of life and perception of wellbeing (Poloma & Pendleton, 1991). Numerous studies have found lower rates of depression and anxiety-related illness among religiously committed persons (Wallis, 1996). Thus, the medical community and others are reconsidering traditional assumptions and perspectives that excluded spirituality and faith from professional practice.

The need for close interaction between, and mutual independence of, science and religion is clearly seen in the human effort to make sense of experience (Mike, 1994). In an address marking the 300th anniversary of the publication of Newton's *Philosophiae Naturalis Principia Math-*

emetica, Pope John Paul II (1988) called the church and the academy, as the two major institutions in civilization, to join together the disjointed pieces of the scientific, humanistic, and religious cultures into a common discourse because, the Pope noted:

> Science develops best when its concepts and conclusions are integrated into the broader human culture and its concerns for ultimate meaning and value. . . . Science can purify religion from error and superstition; religion can purify science from idolatry and false absolutes. Each can draw the other into a wider world, a world in which both can flourish. . . . Only a dynamic relationship between theology and science can review those limits which support the integrity of either discipline, so that theology does not profess pseudo-science and science does not become an unconscious theology. Our knowledge of each other can lead us to be more authentically ourselves. No one can read the history of the past century and not realize that crisis is upon us both. The uses of science have on more than one occasion proven massively destructive, and the reflections on religion have too often been sterile. We need each other to be what we must be, what we are called to be. (pp. M13–M14)

If we are to be what we as a profession are called to be, we may need to reconsider our relationship to some of our spiritual traditions. Although we recognize that spirituality takes various forms, we will use the model of Christian spirituality to show how therapeutic recreation practitioners might develop a more holistic approach to their practice. Christian spirituality has had a strong influence in Western cultures and is largely responsible for many of the healthcare institutions in our communities today. In the following sections, we will briefly review scientific naturalism, since it is the driving force behind the medical model, and then examine the nature and contribution of Christian spirituality and its implications for therapeutic recreation practice.

Influence of the Enlightenment on Contemporary Society

The worldview that has shaped much of our contemporary understanding of healthcare and, consequently, the therapeutic recreation profession in the twentieth century is naturalism or empiricism. Much of what we know as the "medical model" has emerged from the use of the scientific method and has served as the framework for defining many healthcare-related helping professions, including therapeutic recreation.

Sir Francis Bacon, leader of England's seventeenth-century scientific revolution, was most responsible for the advancement of modern science. Bacon rejected Aristotle's deductive science, which had dominated medieval knowledge, and instead promoted the empirical method. As noted by Sylvester (1995), Bacon and his followers insisted on a practical science of observation and experimentation that served as a socially relevant instrument for improving the lives of ordinary people. Regarding truth, Bacon believed there were two types of complementary knowledge – God's word in the Scriptures and God's work in nature – both derived from a single source. Experimental science could be used to appreciate God's creation and to harness the power invested in nature by God for earthly purposes. Moral and social issues of spiritual relevance, however, were decided by the Bible's authority. Thus, facts and values coexisted in Bacon's philosophy of science. However, Bacon's separation of the "spiritual" and the "natural" led to an unhealthy dualism: "While the restoration of our moral innocence was in the hands of God, the restoration of our dominion over nature was, in Bacon's opinion, in our own competent hands" (Walsh & Middleton, 1984, p. 121). This dualism prepared the way for modern secularism, where God became excluded.

The eighteenth-century Enlightenment attempted to extend Bacon's scientific method and Isaac Newton's achievements in physics to human life. Enlightenment thinkers believed that empiricism would reveal the causal relations governing the social system, and human behavior would be explained as laws. While the Enlightenment ideal of heroic science flourished, religion was criticized as a barrier to moral and social progress, thereby straining the relationship between empiricism, the world of objective facts, and metaphysical considerations, the realm of the spiritual (Sylvester, 1995).

The scientific method also fostered the objectification of nature and a mechanical view of the world. This led to the deist notion that nature is a machine created by God, who is independent of the world. Thus, nature became a mechanical object to be investigated and controlled by science. The naturalistic and positivistic worldview contributed significantly to Western medicine and has served to increase our knowledge and understanding of the body and the mind. However, because it has generally rejected the obscure and less observable spiritual dimension of the person, researchers have all but ignored the role spirituality plays in rehabilitation.

Christian Spirituality and Therapeutic Recreation

Although medical science has been reluctant to recognize and investigate it, spirituality has always been a part of treatment, at least from the patient's perspective. "The need to feel relief is so powerful, the inability of scientific medicine to restore health so frequent, and the uncertainty generated by the one inevitable disease – death – so compelling, that the realm of faith, prayer and the paranormal is always close to the sickbed" (Reisser, Reisser, & Weldon, 1987, p. 10). Spirituality, "a belief system that provides a sense of meaning and purpose . . . and offers an ethical path to personal fulfillment which includes connectedness with self, others, and a higher power" (Hawks, 1994, p. 6), has been an important source for coping with and modifying problems associated with disease and disability throughout the centuries.

This has been true of Christian spirituality, which embraces a holistic approach in which humans, created in the image of God, are viewed as a mind-body-spirit unity who have the capacity to relate, not only with other human beings, but also with God (Boivin, 1991). Furthermore, in stark contrast to naturalism, Christians believe God may intervene supernaturally within the natural processes of human life, and thus the spiritual realm is "fundamental to the existence and behavior of all natural or physical reality" (Willard, 1988, p. 65). As we consider the implications of these principles for therapeutic recreation practice, it is helpful to review the internal and external characteristics of Christian spirituality (Hawks, 1994; Cousins, 1990).

Relationship of Internal Characteristics of Christian Spirituality to Therapeutic Recreation

Purpose, Meaning, and Wholeness

Internal characteristics of spiritual health include life purpose, ultimate meaning, and an awareness of wholeness in life (Hawks, 1994). Benner (1988) writes that "Spirituality is the response to a deep and mysterious yearning of self-transcendence and surrender. This desire results from being created in such a fashion that we are incomplete when we are self-encapsulated" (p. 104). These strong desires are being confirmed through the research of people like Herbert Benson, well known for his work in relaxation and stress management. Recently, after analyzing the positive outcomes of studies with patients who meditate and pray, he concluded that humans were created with a need and capacity for spirituality (Benson, 1995).

In Christian spirituality, the response to deep spiritual longings and the quest for identity, authenticity, and fulfillment occurs within the context of a relationship with God (McGrath, 1994; Toon, 1989). As Augustine (389/1949) put it centuries ago: "Our hearts are restless until we find our rest in God" (p. 3). This fulfillment is closely associated with a sense of wholeness God brings to life experiences (Williams, 1979).

In part, Christian spirituality is also an attempt to understand our place in the universe. Here, leisure and spirituality seem to intersect. Pieper (1952) claimed that leisure is only possible if you are at one or at peace with yourself. Self-knowledge and acceptance are prerequisites to developing a receptive attitude of the mind, a contemplative attitude that allows us to experience the whole of creation. "It is in these quiet, receptive moments that the soul of man is sometimes visited by an awareness of what holds the world together . . ." (Pieper, p. 42). Thus, at leisure, we may begin to realize what it means to be truly human, truly alive. Our whole being becomes aware of our relationship with the Divine, a relationship that brings meaning and purpose to our lives, and a sense of belonging to something much greater than ourselves. Such experiences, although not popular with insurance companies or managed care providers, are essential to all people, but especially those who are burdened with illness and conditions that limit their capacity and/or opportunity for meaningful psycho-social interaction.

Finding meaning in life, regardless of the circumstances, is the key to experiencing healing. Victor Frankl (1984) discovered that those who survived the death camps in Germany were those who found answers to the spiritual questions "Who am I?" "What is my purpose?" Meaning is the attempt to connect a why to a how in such a way that one finds a sense of purpose to their life that is greater than and outweighs their current trial or circumstance (Nicosia, p. 68). Frankl (1984) believed that the answers to these questions come from nondirective dialogue that involves sharing our stories with others as well as through contemplation and meditation. Therefore, if we as healthcare practitioners wish to make an impact on the whole person, we must be prepared to do more than simply teach a new leisure skill or improve cognitive function. We must also empower and encourage those who seek answers to some of life's most challenging questions by creating the setting for leisure experiences that encourage self-expression and reflection. Such an approach requires that we understand basic assumptions about life, including our spirituality, and are prepared to dialogue with others as they discover their own transcendent values.

Therapeutic recreation practitioners frequently provide persons who experience various social, emotional, or physical problems with the opportunities to improve self-esteem, personal identity, and self-awareness. Such a healthy sense of self, the clear and accurate appreciation of who we are as unique persons, is critical to the experience of healing. Conversely, persons with low self-esteem are less internally motivated and lack clear personal boundaries that guide behaviors leaving them to view themselves as the center of the world (egocentricity) or detached from it (Nicosia, 1994). Without a strong self to give, it is difficult to establish healthy relationships or find meaning in life. As practitioners, we would do well to consider the implications for all that we do that either diminishes or develops self-awareness and self-esteem. Treating all persons with the integrity and respect they deserve will contribute significantly to their healing.

For some, the search for meaning, purpose, and a sense of wholeness occurs in natural or wilderness settings. It may be for this reason that some therapeutic recreation specialists have been exploring the benefits of adventure/challenge recreation as a therapeutic tool (Ewart, 1987; Whitman, 1993). Although studies have not identified the key variable in these programs, some have speculated about the influence of the spiritual nature of the process. Gass (1993) notes that the power of these encounters is the metaphorical aspect of the wilderness experience that helps us better understand ourselves and the world in which we live. From this perspective, as Outward Bound and other adventure recreation programs have discovered, the wilderness provides the ideal environment – the sacred space – where change and healing are likely outcomes. Bacon (1983) argues:

> anyone who has spent much time in the wilderness can easily recognize the parallels between it and the archetype of Sacred Space. Wilderness is difficult to get to and difficult to travel through. One passes a series of tests in order to exist within it. It is unlike the normal world in hundreds of ways. Above all, it pervades one with a kind of religiosity or mysticism – one of the most compelling things about nature is that it seems to implicitly suggest the existence of order and meaning. (p. 53)

Within the Christian worldview, the earth is seen as the creation of God, and thus some of the characteristics of God may be observed from the workings of natural systems. Contemplation of nature can provide improved insight into the person of God. Also within the Christian tradition, the wilderness has particular symbolic significance for spiritual experience. In a comprehensive review of Christian scripture and history, Bratton (1993) concludes that solitude is the most common denominator in these spiritual experiences. She suggests that wilderness visits can be helpful for: developing an appreciation of creation and an understanding of God as Creator, rest and restoration, spiritual exercise and communication with God, and spiritual transformation.

Leisure experiences also seem to promote spiritual development by contributing to a greater appreciation for the environment and community life, enhancing personal expression and creativity, and developing a sense of connectedness to a greater whole (McDonald & Schreyer, 1991). Therefore, therapeutic recreation practitioners should recognize the spiritual significance of leisure experiences, especially those occurring in natural settings, and should be prepared to encourage participants to understand and appreciate the spiritual component of their responses to these experiences. Writing, photography, meditating, and interpersonal sharing are some of the ways that personal spirituality can be developed and used to promote a sense of meaning and purpose in one's life.

Mind-Body-Spirit: Curing Versus Healing

A Christian world view sees humans as a mind-body-spirit unity, and as such, Christian spirituality is not limited to the realm of the pure spirit, but is exercised through the body and the mind as well as the spirit. Or, as McGrath (1994) notes: "it is grounded in and oriented toward life in the everyday world..." (p. 55). Therefore, from the Christian perspective, spirituality is an integrative, and not just an elementalistic, component of holistic wellness. The implication for our practice of therapeutic recreation is that individuals need to have meaningful experiences that promote an integration of body, mind, and spirit rather than confining our focus to curing broken parts.

Making sense of the experience involves answering the "why" questions of life. These questions cannot be answered by medical science alone, and yet they are critical to the process of rehabilitation, which is both a physiological and a psycho-spiritual process. One approach to understanding this complex, dynamic mind-body-spirit integration sees curing as a medical intervention or scientific process (the treatment of a spinal cord injury, for example), while healing involves the total experience of the person and is by its nature a spiritual event (Nicosia, 1994). Quinn (1989) defines healing as "a total, organismic, synergistic response that must emerge from within the individual if recovery and growth are to be accomplished" (p. 554). Holistic healing is a meaning-centered, psycho-spiritual approach to treatment where members of an interdisciplinary team assist individuals in finding meaning and purpose in their lives, develop a healthy appreciation of who they are as unique persons (self-concept), promote nurturing and empowering relationships with others, facilitate a sense of control by making choices, instill a sense of hope for the future, and provide opportunities for successful experiences (Nicosia, 1994).

Jean Vanier (1994), founder of L'Arche communities that serve persons with multiple disabilities, believes that the greatest suffering that persons who are mentally handicapped feel is that of being different and useless. But by having friends – persons who love and respect them – they will develop their personality and place in society and develop a sense of purpose. But most of all, Vanier notes:

> they need the Love of God which they may discover through [friends]. If, through faith and especially by experiencing the presence of Divine Love in themselves they can discover how much Jesus really loves them, then I venture to say they are no longer handicapped. They may have difficulty in finding their place in society, but knowing the love of Jesus for them, they discover their own personality and real significance in the world. (p. 49)

The spiritual life is important to all of us but especially to those who are weak and have limited ability to find human fulfillment. The power of human and divine love is a gift that every helper and friend should give if we hope to bring wholeness and purpose to the lives of those we care for.

The relationship between healing and curing is also found in Florence Nightingale's philosophy of nursing. According to Quinn (1989), Nightingale viewed healing as a function of nature that relied on the interdependence of the mind, body, and the spirit within the person. The role of the practitioner was simply to create the best environment for healing to occur. Central to this procedure was the practitioner's belief in the process and the meaning of the healing experience. That is, the more the practitioner values and supports the client's religious values and beliefs, the greater the benefit to their sense of wholeness and wellbeing (Marwick, 1995).

Personal Characteristics of the Helper

Shank (1987) noted the profession does have a code of ethics, but not a moral philosophical foundation upon which these standards of behavior rest. However, the moral code of the Judeo-Christian faith could provide a basis for our professional code of ethics, which directs us to practice in such a way as to promote peace, justice, compassion, and love. If we review some of the internal characteristics of Christian spirituality, we find they include the fruits of the spirit: love, joy, peace, patience, kindness, goodness, faithfulness, gentleness, and self-control. These ethical qualities, made possible through the work of God's spirit in our lives, are in contrast with the activities and attitudes of a self-centered life, and as such are important characteristics to be developed in therapeutic recreation professionals.

Therapeutic recreation professionals are called to respect the people they serve and view them as having intrinsic value and worth. Central to the Christian fruits of the Spirit is the biblical notion of *agape* or divine love. Epitomized in the life of Jesus, agape involves the determination to act on behalf of another out of genuine concern for the other's wellbeing and a desire to help meet real needs in her or his life. Although imperfectly realized, compassion, empathy, unconditional acceptance, selflessness, and genuine love and respect for others regardless of the person, position, status, or life circumstance characterize the Christian attitude toward helping relationships.

But acting on these ideal qualities is not easy. One such struggle is seen in the practice of compassion. Genuine compassion is hard because it requires the inner disposition to go with others to the place where they are weak, vulnerable, lonely, and broken (Nouwen, 1981). Our human tendency is to get rid of the suffering by running from it or finding some quick fix that will cure the problem. According to the Desert Fathers like St. Anthony (251–356 AD), true compassion requires dying to our neighbor. Thus, when we stop judging and evaluating others, we will be free to be compassionate and give others our greatest gift, the gift of understanding, acceptance, and solidarity. Comfort derives its meaning from the Latin words *con*, which means "with," and *fortes*, which can be translated as "strength." Compassion brings comfort and enhances healing by enabling persons to live with strength, the strength of knowing their burden is being shared and they are not alone. Love infuses a life of pain and despair with meaning and hope.

The Prayer of St. Francis of Assisi reflects not only the ideal attitude of a helper but the true source of the gifts we offer to others. Love, joy, peace, faith, hope, and forgiveness of others do not emanate from our own spirit, but ultimately from God, the creator of all things. Similarly, spirituality involves the willingness to give up control to the one in whom we believe. Trust in the transcendent may be the greatest source of hope for all human beings, but especially those who work with the vulnerable and helpless.

> Lord, make me an instrument of your peace!
> Where there is hatred, let me show love;
> where there is injury, pardon;
> where there is doubt, faith;
> where there is despair, hope;
> where there is darkness, light;
> and where there is sadness, joy.

O Divine Master,
> grant that I may not
> so much seek to be consoled as to console;
> to be understood as to understand;
> to be loved as to love;
> for it is in giving that we receive;
> it is in pardoning that we are pardoned;
> and it is in dying that we are born to Eternal Life.

The notion of pardoning in St. Francis' prayer leads us to another characteristic of Christian spirituality: the importance of forgiving and forgetting mistakes and failures. Bitterness and anger are reported to contribute significantly to both mental and physical illness (Minerth, Meier, Hawkins, Thurman, & Flournoy, 1992). Recovery or healing can only be fully realized when the infection of unresolved anger is appropriately expressed and/or the individual who hurt us is forgiven. Although forgetting may be impossible, forgiveness is an act of the will that frees one from the cancer of guilt and bitterness. Forgiveness allows us to leave the past behind and move on. Without it, we remain broken and fragmented, with no hope of experiencing healing and wholeness. It is for this reason that the twelve-step program used by Alcoholics Anonymous (AA), the most effective treatment program available for persons who suffer from alcoholism, includes the following steps in their recovery program:

> Step 5: We have admitted to God, to ourselves, and to another human being the exact nature of our wrongs.
>
> Step 6: We're entirely ready to have God remove all these defects of character.
>
> Step 7: We humbly ask God to remove our shortcomings.
>
> Step 8: We have made a list of all persons we had harmed, and are willing to make amends to them all.
>
> (Spickard & Thompson, 1985, p. 141)

So what does this mean for the therapeutic recreation professional? Alcoholics Anonymous has discovered that those who know forgiveness from past personal failures are the most effective in using that knowledge to assist others who struggle. From this perspective, forgiveness is a gift from God that is available to all who choose to accept it for themselves and extend its healing balm to broken relationships. At one level, we need to examine our own relationships and be ready to make them whole through the power of seeking and/or extending forgiveness. The freedom that we experience can then become the source of hope for others.

Relationship of External Characteristics of Christian Spirituality to Therapeutic Recreation

Christian spirituality is characterized by two types of external interactions: a vertical relationship with God and a horizontal relationship with others. These two external relationships are taught by Jesus when he summarized the guidelines for living in terms of loving God and loving one's neighbor. Thus, Cousins (1990) can write, "there is a primacy of love in Christian spirituality: love of God and neighbor, and God's love for the world" (p. 43).

Relationship with God

The most fundamental characteristic of Christian spirituality is that it involves a relationship with God (Armerding, 1992; Dart, 1992; Huggett, 1988; Liefeld & Cannell, 1992; Postema, 1983; Smedes, 1970). Conn (1987) suggests that Christian spirituality "means one's entire life as understood, felt, imagined, and decided upon in relationship to God, in Jesus Christ, empowered by the Spirit" (p. 972). Much modern thinking on spirituality, such as that which focuses on self-actualization or that proposed by the New Age worldview, is a kind of interiority in which the human being is perceived to have an inner spirit, which is where the contact is made with the transcendental (Willard, 1995). In this view, which omits the concept of the divine, spirituality is basically a human dimension. In contrast, Christian spirituality is based on a trusting, obedient, and growing personal relationship with a transcendent, personal, creator God.

A good example of how the vertical relationship of spirituality can be applied in a helping profession is AA. The preamble to their Twelve Step program notes,

> Some of us have tried to hold on to our old ideas and the result was nil until we let go absolutely. Remember that we deal with alcohol – cunning, baffling, powerful! Without help it is too much for us. But there is One who has all power – that One is God.
> (Spickard & Thompson, 1985, p. 140)

Participants are then asked to state and own twelve statements, including the following:

> Step 1: We admit that we are powerless over alcohol – that our lives have become unmanageable.
>
> Step 2: We have come to believe that a Power greater than ourselves can restore us to sanity.

Step 3: We have decided to turn our will and our lives over to the care of God as we understand Him.

(Spickard & Thompson, 1985, p. 140)

The founders of AA, drawing upon Christian principles (Kurtz, 1979), thus identified a key element of human nature, the need to find strength and solace from God.

A Christian's relationship with God is developed through spiritual practices (e.g., meditation, fasting, reading, journal writing). A vital spiritual practice is prayer, "for in its true use, prayer is not mere exercise but is communion with God, and is right at the heart of spirituality" (Liefeld & Cannell, 1992, p. 242). A relationship with God through prayer has been shown to have a significant positive impact on health and healing (Benson, 1996; Dossey, 1993; Larson & Larson, 1994; Wallis, 1996). One telling testimony of a person who was near death is reported by Dossey (1993). Although the patient had not been a religious person, he revealed to his family and Dossey that he had begun to pray. When asked, "What do you pray for?" the patient responded thoughtfully, "It isn't *for* anything. It simply reminds me that I am not alone." One of our biggest fears is isolation and loneliness. Prayer, communication with an eternal God, provides the assurance of an authentic relationship with a personal God who cares for us.

When built on a relationship of openness, honesty, and trust, "prayer is both a pleading with God that He will hear and act upon our requests and a trusting surrender to God in the confidence that He will act in His own time and way" (Bloesch, 1984, p. 867). In contrast to the fatalism of some religions, a Christian worldview sees God as both personal and all knowing, aware of the past, present, and future reality. Although all requests rest on God's knowledge of what is ultimately best for a given situation, prayer is an essential component of the Christian approach in the healing process. But prayer is more than a tool to summon help from an all-knowing God. Nouwen (1975) captures the essence of prayer when he says, "it is God's breathing in us, by which we become part of the intimacy of God's inner life, and by which we are born anew" (p. 125). We are made whole even in very broken and alien situations by sensing a oneness with God's spirit, which is where we find rest and shalom.

Relationships with Others

Although Christian spirituality is based on a loving relationship with God, Jesus' first great teaching about that love is immediately followed by his second statement about loving one's neighbor. Christian spirituality is to be expressed in social relationships and also in social justice as "An authentic spiritual life always pushes one back into the world" (Willard, 1995, p. 17). "God's life is drawn from us so that we may become the channel through which his life flows out to others to bring them refreshment, cleansing, food, healing or the opportunity for growth or mere survival" (Huggett as quoted in Toon, 1989, p. 11). Social isolation has been shown to increase stress while decreasing expressions of emotions, cognitive function, creativity, and spirituality (Dossey, 1991). Social relationships, on the other hand, provide us with a sense of connectedness, integrity with something larger than ourselves. Thus, when we touch others or allow others to touch us, we experience healing (Nicosia, 1994). Traditional medical practice has become impersonal, cold, and sterile. Therapeutic recreation plays a significant role in restoring wholeness through facilitating safe, nurturing social relationships, especially in the age of shorter hospital stays and a multitude of healthcare practices that impede meaningful social contact.

Christians connect the meaning and purpose for work and life with the divine sense of calling to love one's neighbor. This integration of faith and work was promoted by Martin Luther and John Calvin, 16th century religious reformers, who believed all of life should be lived in obedience to God's plan for creation. In other words, religious faith is not the private possession of an individual, but is grounded in tradition and divine revelation, permeating the whole of life, connecting public and private spheres, and linking the individual with the community (Hugen, 1996, p. 8). Such an approach to one's profession places professional techniques and methods in the context of goals and values that give meaning and purpose for both clients and practitioners. Thus, ideally, the vocation or calling of a Christian is marked not by self-aggrandizement but self-sacrifice, not by power and position but by servanthood and compassion.

Helping: An Attitude of Service

The danger with increasing professionalization and use of technology, however, is that they become ways for exercising power instead of offering service. The helper must recognize that if we are to offer health, we do so to part of our own humanity. Nouwen (1975) claims that "specialists can only retain their humanity in their work when they see their professions as a form of service which they carry out, not instead of, but as part of, the whole people of God" (p. 93). Being willing to love others as one's self and placing their wellbeing above all else requires unusual personal awareness and confidence. A practitioner who becomes a servant leader is also committed to maintaining and facilitating the personal freedom, autonomy, and self-determination of every person as a unique human being who, because she or he has been made in the image of God, has value and deserves our love and respect. As servant leaders, therapeutic recreation specialists assist the client in identifying and removing or coping with the personal barriers that diminish their potential for finding meaning and purpose in life. Such a process goes beyond just removing or circumventing a barrier to some behavioral function when it reinforces a healthy appreciation for one's sense of self that Thomas Moore (1992) describes as the very foundation of the personal soul.

Such roles and expectations require that professionals know the "why" and "how" of life so that they have a sense of purpose and meaning that carries them through the inevitable trials and tribulations of life, including those associated with helping relationships. Helpers also learn about life and love in the healthy give-and-take of interpersonal relationships, as well as through identifying with life experiences described in ancient writings such as biblical stories. It is easier to find meaning and purpose when we recognize that our experience is like many others who have traveled this way before us (Nicosia, 1994).

As part of this process of learning about life and discovering who we are as helpers, Hawks (1994) has identified three factors that contribute to spiritual health. One is "selflessness, connectedness with and selfless concern for others," which we have just discussed in terms of love for neighbor. The other two are "a well-defined world view or belief system" and "high levels of personal faith and commitment in relation to the world view and belief system" (p. 5). Thus, spiritual health is dependent not only on intellectual knowledge of a worldview, but an ability to live out that perspective and model it for others. Competent helpers are thus able to understand and relate to the total person because they recognize, value, and practice an integrated lifestyle that is rooted in a holistic belief system. Without such a belief system, it is impossible to bring hope and healing to the terminally ill person, for example, in their final days or hours of life on earth. Thus, at the point where medical science fails, as it inevitably does in every life, spirituality becomes most viable and real. The helper who has a holistic worldview such as Christianity is always able to extend a spirit of hope that brings meaning to life, even in its most vulnerable moments.

Conclusion

Many therapeutic recreation practitioners have demonstrated selfless concern for others but lack a well-defined worldview. This makes them vulnerable to adopting the incomplete theoretical assumptions of naturalism and the prevailing medical model. Given the limitations of this perspective and its implications for therapeutic recreation practice, we need to consider our belief system, especially as it relates to the spiritual nature of human beings. Since a growing body of evidence shows that spirituality is intimately connected to healing and wellbeing, a worldview that limits or denies the spiritual nature of persons will reinforce mechanistic treatment approaches and thus inhibit desired therapeutic outcomes. In addition, and more importantly, the individual who is not treated as a whole person will never know what it means to be fully human. Therefore, an underdeveloped or misguided worldview has significant implications for our profession, ourselves, and the people we are called to serve.

In our attempts to become a player in the healthcare field, we need to avoid narrowly defining our profession so that we limit the true essence of our contribution to functional behaviors. We have addressed and must continue to address the total needs of the person, especially those psycho-spiritual needs that find fulfillment through leisure experiences. Our most unique and valuable contribution as a profession is bringing people a sense of joy, laughter, belonging to something greater than themselves, and a renewed sense of wholeness and integrity.

We have argued that Christian spirituality provides a basis for the ethical, moral, and philosophical practice of therapeutic recreation. It has also contributed significantly to the infrastructure for healthcare as we know it today, with its thousands of hospitals and agencies of mercy that serve persons in need throughout the world. Christianity is a belief system that holds that meaning in life comes from establishing a personal relationship with God through Jesus Christ. A growing body of research seems to support the role that such spirituality plays in healing and rehabilitation. As medical science begins to recognize the importance of religion and spirituality in health care, practitioners will need to seriously consider the basic questions of life that challenge our own search for meaning. Only then will we know and model the freedom that comes from knowing who we are and why we have been placed on this earth for such a time as this.

References

Armerding, C.E. (1992). When the Spirit came mightily: The spirituality of Israel's charismatic leaders. In J.I. Packer & L. Wilkinson (Eds.), *Alive to God: Studies in spirituality* (pp. 41–55). Downers Grove, IL: InterVarsity.

Augustine. (398/1949). *The confessions of Saint Augustine* (E.B. Pusey, Trans.) New York: Random House.

Bacon, S. (1983). *The conscious use of metaphor in Outward Bound.* Denver, CO: Colorado Outward Bound School.

Benner, D. (1988). *Psychotherapy and the spiritual quest.* Grand Rapids: Baker.

Benson, H. (1996). *Timeless healing: The power and biology of belief.* New York: Scribner.

Bloesch, D.G. (1984). Prayer. In W. A. Elwell (Ed.), *Evangelical dictionary of theology* (pp. 867–868). Grand Rapids: Baker.

Boivin, M. J. (1991). The Hebraic model of the person: Toward a unified psychological science among Christian helping professionals. *Journal of Psychology and Theology* 19(2), 157–165.

Bouma, H., Diekema, D., Langerak, E., Rottman, T., & Verhey, A. (1989). *Christian faith, health, and medical practice.* Grand Rapids: Eerdmans.

Bratton, S. (1993). *Christianity, wilderness, and wildlife: The original desert solitaire.* Scranton, PA: University of Scranton Press.

Conn, J.W. (1987). Spirituality. In J.A. Komonchak, M. Collins, & D.A. Lane (Eds.), *The New Dictionary of Theology* (pp. 972–985). Wilmington, DE: Michael Glazier.

Cousins, E.H. (1990). What is Christian spirituality? In B.C. Hanson (Ed.), *Modern Christian spirituality: Methodological and historical essays* (pp. 39–44). Atlanta: Scholars Press.

Cousins, N. (1989). *Head first: The biology of hope and the healing power of the human spirit.* New York: Penguin Books.

Dart, R. (1992). Prophetic spirituality: Markings for the journey. In J.I. Packer & L. Wilkinson (Eds.), *Alive to God: Studies in spirituality* (pp. 296–314). Downers Grove, IL: InterVarsity.

Dossey, L. (1993). *Healing words: The power of prayer.* San Francisco: Harper & Rowe.

Dossey, L. (1991). *Meaning & Medicine.* New York: Bantam Books.

Ewert, A. (1987). Research in experiential education: An overview. *The Journal of Experiential Education* 10(2), 4–7.

Frankl, V.E. (1984). *Man's search for meaning.* New York: Harper-Collins.

Gass, M.A. (1993). *Adventure therapy: Therapeutic applications of adventure programming.* Dubuque, IA: Kendall/Hunt.

Hawks, S. (1994). Spiritual health: Definition and theory. *Wellness Perspectives* 10(4), 3–13.

Howe-Murphy, R., & Murphy, J. (1987). An exploration of the New Age consciousness paradigm in therapeutic recreation. In C. Sylvester (Ed.),

Philosophy of therapeutic recreation: Ideas and issues (pp. 41–54). Alexandria, VA: National Recreation and Park Association.

Hugen, B. (1996, March). Calling: A spirituality model for social work practice. *Pro Rege* 24(3) 1–9.

Huggett, J. (1988). What is spirituality? In P. Toon (Ed.), *Guidebook to the spiritual life*. Basingstoke, Hants, UK: Marshall Morgan & Scott.

John Paul II (1988). Message of His Holiness Pope John Paul II. In R.J. Russell, W.R. Stoeger & G.V. Coyne (Eds.), *Physics, philosophy, and theology: A common quest for understanding* (pp. M1–M14). Notre Dame: University of Notre Dame Press.

Kurtz, E. (1979). *Not-God: A history of Alcoholics Anonymous*. Center City, MN: Hazelden Educational Services.

Larson, D.B., & Larson, S.S. (1992). *The forgotten factor in physical and mental health: What does the research show?* Rockville, MD: National Institute for Healthcare Research.

Liefeld, W.L., & Cannell, L.M. (1992). Spiritual formation and theological education. In J.I. Packer & L. Wilkinson (Eds.), *Alive to God: Studies in spirituality* (pp. 239–252). Downers Grove, IL: InterVarsity.

Marwick, C. (1995). Should physicians prescribe prayer for health? Spiritual aspects of well-being considered. *Journal of the American Medical Association* 273(20), 1561–1562.

McDonald, B.L., & Schreyer, R. (1991). Spiritual benefits of leisure participation and leisure settings. In B.L. Driver, P.J. Brown & G.L. Peterson (Eds.), *Benefits of leisure* (pp.179–194). State College, PA: Venture.

McDonald, M.H. (1984). Naturalism. In W. A. Elwell (Ed.), *Evangelical dictionary of theology* (pp. 750–751). Grand Rapids: Baker.

McGrath, A. E. (1994). *Spirituality in an age of change*. Grand Rapids: Zondervan.

Mike, V. (1994). Spirituality and contemporary American medicine: A postmodern perspective. In A.W. Astell (Ed.), *Divine representations: Postmodernism and spirituality* (pp. 231–247). New York: Paulist Press.

Minerth, F., Meier, P., Hawkins, D., Thurman, C., & Flournoy, R. (1992). *The stress factor: Thriving emotionally and spiritually in the turbulent 90's*. Chicago: Northfield.

Moore, T. (1992). *Care of the soul*. New York: Harper Collins.

Myers, D.G. (1992). *The pursuit of happiness*. New York: Avon.

Nicosia, J.F. (1994). Healing the human spirit: The healing paradigm. *Journal of Religion in Disability & Rehabilitation* 1(3), 65–74.

Nouwen, H.J. (1975). *Reaching out: The three movements of the spiritual life*. New York: Doubleday.

Nouwen, H.J. (1981). *The way of the heart*. New York: Ballantine/Epiphany Books.

Pieper, J. (1952). *Leisure: The basis of culture* (A. Dru, Trans.). New York: Pantheon Books (1963, Random House).

Poloma, M.M., & Pendleton, B.F. (1991). The effects of prayer and prayer experiences on measures of general well-being. *Journal of Psychology and Theology* 19(1), 71–83.

Postema, D. (1983). *Space for God: The study and practice of prayer and spirituality.* Grand Rapids, MI: CRC Publications.

Quinn, J.F. (1989). On healing, wholeness and the Haelan effect. *Nursing & Healthcare* 10(10), 553–556.

Reisser, P.C., Reisser, T.K., & Weldon, J. (1987). *New Age medicine: A Christian perspective on holistic health.* Downers Grove, IL: InterVarsity.

Shank, P.A. (1987). Therapeutic recreation philosophy: A state of cacophony. In C. Sylvester, J. Hemingway, R. Howe-Murphy, K. Mobily, & P. Shank (Eds.), *Philosophy of therapeutic recreation: Ideas and issues* (pp. 27–40). Alexandria, VA: National Recreation and Park Association.

Smedes, L.B. (1970). *All things made new: A study of man's union with Christ.* Grand Rapids: Eerdmans.

Spickard, A., & Thompson, B.R. (1985). *Dying for a drink: What you should know about alcoholism.* Dallas, TX: Word.

Sylvester, C. (1987). Therapeutic recreation and the end of leisure. In C. Sylvester, J. Hemingway, R. Howe-Murphy, K. Mobily, & P. Shank (Eds.), *Philosophy of therapeutic recreation: Ideas and issues* (pp. 76–89). Alexandria, VA: National Recreation and Park Association.

Sylvester, C. (1995). Relevance and rationality in leisure studies: A plea for good reason. *Leisure Sciences* 17, 125–131.

Toon, P. (1989). *What is spirituality?* London: Daybreak.

Vanier, J. (1971). *Eruption to hope.* Toronto: Griffin House.

Wallis, C. (1996). Faith and healing. *Time* 147(26), 58–62.

Walsh, B.J., & Middleton, J.R. (1984). *The transforming vision.* Downers Grove, IL: InterVarsity.

Walsh B.J., & Middleton, J.R. (1995). *Truth is stranger than it used to be.* Downers Grove, IL: InterVarsity.

Whitman, J.P. (1993). Characteristics of adventure programs valued by adolescents in treatment. *Therapeutic Recreation Journal* 22(1), 44–50.

Willard, D. (1988). *The spirit of the disciplines.* New York: Harper Collins.

Willard, D. (1995, March 6). Conversations: What makes spirituality Christian? *Christianity Today* 39, 16–17.

Williams, R. (1979). *Christian spirituality.* Atlanta: John Knox Press.

Wolters, A.M. (1985). *Creation regained: Biblical basics for a reformational worldview.* Grand Rapids: Eerdmans.

Chapter 21
ETHICAL PRINCIPLES IN THERAPEUTIC RECREATION SERVICES

Joseph D. Teaff

The importance of the ethical principles of beneficence, non-maleficence, autonomy, justice, and fidelity for guiding the behavior of professionals who provide services to persons with disabilities has been stressed in medical ethics (Beauchamp & Childress, 1989), psychology (Kitchener, 1984), rehabilitation (Gatens-Robinson, 1992; Millard & Rubin, 1992; Patterson, Buckley, & Smull, 1989; Rubin, Millard, Wilson, & Wong, 1991; Tarvydas, 1987; Welfel, 1987; Wilson, Rubin, & Millard, 1991; Wong, Rubin, & Millard, 1991), and therapeutic recreation (Lahey, 1987; Stumbo, 1985). The ability to recognize and resolve ethical dilemmas is dependent on a clear understanding of these principles. The purpose of this chapter is to provide therapeutic recreation service providers with a more in-depth discussion of these ethical principles to promote a better understanding of how they impact their job performance.

In their daily work, therapeutic recreation service providers face decision-making situations involving conflicts among these ethical principles. They also have disagreements with others concerning what types of actions are in the best interest of particular clients. It is important, therefore, to understand the nature of these ethical principles so that they may serve as functional guides for the resolution of ethical dilemmas and disagreements with others. The way in which these varied conflicts are resolved will affect individuals with disabilities.

Principle of Beneficence

Beneficence refers to the duty to assist others (Millard & Rubin, 1992). This duty encompasses actions that are beneficial, contribute to

---
Revised version of paper presented at the 1994 conference.

the welfare of others, confer benefits, and promote good (Beauchamp & Childress, 1983). The principle of beneficence defines an obligation to help others to "further their important and legitimate interests" (Beauchamp & Childress, 1989, p. 194).

Since an obligation to act in the interest of the client is central to the ethical context of leisure services for persons with disabilities, the general obligation to the principle of beneficence will be discussed. Several problems associated with beneficent action, which may put such action in conflict with duties defined by other principles, such as duties to respect autonomy or duties not to harm (non-maleficence), are noted.

The extent to which people are obligated to actively promote the welfare of others is often difficult to define. In most circumstances, we clearly know that we should not actively bring harm to another person. But how far should we go in actively helping another? All things being equal, there seems to be some obligation to what philosophers have called "mutual aid" (Rawls, 1971, p. 114; Reeder, 1982, p. 84). Beneficence, defined as mutual aid, presumes that I should legitimately expect that another person will come to my assistance or further my welfare if the situation is serious (e.g., if I were about to drown or starve, and if the action required to help me would require minimal sacrifice of the assisting person). The philosopher John Rawls (1971) asked what a society would be like where this duty to assist, which he classified as a natural duty, was rejected. In such a society, the individual members would be totally indifferent to each other's needs. Knowing that their own welfare had little significance in the eyes of others, they would have a difficult time establishing or maintaining a sense of their own worth. In such a situation, the ideas of the common good or the general welfare would make very little sense.

Several elements are involved in assessing the strength of our general duty to beneficence. Following Beauchamp and Childress (1989), these are summarized as follows:

1. How significant is the need that is to be met or how serious is the risk of loss or injury to the person to be aided?
2. Am I particularly qualified to meet the need? That is, am I in a privileged position, in terms of knowledge or skill, to act in the interest of another?
3. Does my action have a high probability of actually achieving the desired end?
4. How much of a risk or burden to myself, or those for whom I am responsible, does the action entail: will the benefit to the

person outweigh any harm or burden to me or mine?

An example to illustrate the weighing of these factors is that of someone witnessing a stranger about to drown. Such factors as one's swimming ability, whether one is the only one present who can help, whether the individual about to drown is an adult or child, will amplify one's obligation to jump in and swim to the person's aid. A healthy adult with lifesaving training, faced with the possibility of aiding a drowning child, seems morally bound to do so. It could be argued that a weak swimmer faced with the situation of a drowning adult has no obligation to dive in to save the individual in distress. Less effective but less risky alternatives would be called for, such as yelling or running for help or throwing a limb or rope to the person. Just walking away, however, would be moral negligence, in light of the general expectation of mutual aid and the gravity of the situation.

The obligation to mutual aid can function to establish a general societal obligation to provide services and facilitate the restoration of persons with disabilities to a level of self-sufficiency and reasonable quality of life. For instance, from the general obligation of mutual aid, interest can emerge in the welfare of those among us who require assistance in performing the basic activities of daily living while maintaining a reasonable quality of life. This obligation to benefit others exists because of the mutual dependence upon one another and our basic respect of human beings. It is a duty that is mitigated by the limits of our ability to provide that assistance without seriously damaging the general welfare.

The obligation to aid one another should not be seen as something totally separate from, and in competition with, the general welfare of a community. It is a mistake to see the resources of a community that go to aid those in need as a drain on the common welfare. Rather, acting on the obligation to help those in serious need of assistance contributes to the general welfare itself. Therefore, rather than viewing therapeutic recreation services as a publicly supported charitable venture, they can be viewed as a necessary component of a description of a good society.

Secondly, since the design of our social and physical environment is primarily aimed at furthering the interests and preferences of persons without disabilities, many of the barriers, risks, and handicaps encountered by persons with disabilities are relative to a certain environment (e.g., inaccessible public buildings or public transportation). A world designed for persons who use wheelchairs, or who are blind, would be a structurally different world. Thus, at least to the extent that these arrangements are arbitrary, society is involved in unnecessarily creating and sustaining conditions that put persons with disabilities at risk and in various states of isolation, thereby increasing the level of dependence. Therefore, to the extent it can be accomplished without seriously hindering the important activities of others within society, there is a general responsibility to eliminate any environmental barriers, risks, and handicaps that specifically affect the quality of life experienced by people with disabilities.

How a balance is to be achieved between the general welfare and the specific interests of persons with disabilities is an ongoing debate. DeJong and Lifchez (1983) pointed out that, given our aging population and the prevalence of disabilities in the older group, more and more of us will experience the onset of disability during part of our life. It appears that the general welfare and the specific welfare of the population of persons with disabilities will, in time, converge.

There are specific problems that relate to beneficent actions. First, is the risk of undermining the dignity of those who require help, with the possibility of fostering a prolonged or dysfunctional dependency. Second, there is the danger that a therapeutic recreation specialist, while seeking to act in the interests of the client, will either override or ignore the client's own judgment about what is to be done (i.e., paternalism). Thus, beneficent actions may lead to conflict with other duties, such as those to non-maleficence or the autonomy of the client (Beauchamp & Childress, 1989).

Doing good for others is complicated. Rarely can we significantly change the circumstances of another for the better without introducing new risks. Acting for another's interest involves assessing as competently as possible how that action might also put the person or others at risk. An example is the situation of an individual with chronic schizophrenia who seems to be stabilized on medication. The individual has trained for a job in computer sales. There is an open computer sales position in the community for which the individual wants to apply. However, the psychiatrist believes that the client cannot handle the stress of the job. This case obviously contains a balance of risks and benefits that must be evaluated in determining how best to promote the client's interests.

When a therapeutic recreation specialist succeeds in helping a client, there is always the risk that the situation may prove too challenging or too stressful. There are many types of challenging activities that would appeal to the client but might present a risk. Some clients might fail and lose both confidence and incentive. However, trying less risky activities might not allow clients to obtain a valid picture of their skills, and may result in some clients achieving a lower level of independence and security.

The Principle of Non-Maleficence

Non-maleficence stresses the obligation of doing no harm to others. Non-maleficence involves both avoiding and removing conditions that could be harmful to a person's liberty, property, reputation, and physical or psychological wellbeing (Beauchamp & Childress, 1983). The principle of non-maleficence thus requires that one neither harm nor impose risk of harm upon another. Since beneficence requires one to do something actively for another, it is more discretionary than non-maleficence, which requires only that one refrain from harming. Therefore, there is a sense that beneficence is more action oriented, whereas non-maleficence requires refraining from certain actions. The level of risk that an individual ought to incur in order to help another is usually of a lesser degree than the risk that ought to be endured not to harm another seriously. For example, if a person has a serious communicable disease that might be passed on to coworkers or even strangers, he or she has a strong obligation to avoid infecting those coworkers, even if it means losing his or her job in the process. In a moral and legal sense, it seems much clearer that non-maleficence is required in most circumstances.

The codes of ethics of most helping professions include admonitions against doing harm. This admonition is recognition of the special situation of the patient and physician or the client and the therapeutic recreation specialist working with individuals with disabilities who are in a position to either help or harm clients by virtue of their authority. They may be in the morally troubling position of doing harm, although undetected. Thus, they must always consciously avoid any opportunity to use the power given by either access to confidential knowledge or expertise to do harm.

The therapeutic recreation specialist cannot be expected to like or get along well with every client. The possibility of acting in ways that undermine the client's best interest might be at times quite real, but there is still a strong role-related obligation never to act on that possibility. Not only is the service provider in the position to harm the client deliberately, but also through negligence. The latter could involve a careless imposition or unnecessary risk, or it might stem from the lack of knowledge or skill that a professional should have acquired.

The Principle of Autonomy

Autonomy refers to self-rule or self-governance (Beauchamp & Childress, 1983). In an ethical context, autonomous choices require that an individual be free from the controls of others. A therapeutic recreation specialist in action and attitudes shows respect for the self-rule of clients by recognizing their diverse abilities and viewpoints, while respecting their prerogatives to make independent decisions and take actions accordingly. Their respect for autonomy is expressed by the therapeutic recreation specialist's refusal to pressure the client toward specific leisure choices and avoidance of withholding or distorting information crucial to the client's independent decision-making in regard to a leisure lifestyle.

In the therapeutic recreation process, client autonomy (as manifested in freedom of choice) is dependent on the presence of three conditions: (a) having a therapeutic recreation specialist who refrains from unnecessary interference in the client's independence in choice-making and action (voluntarism); (b) the client having relevant knowledge upon which necessary choices can reasonably be made (full disclosure); and (c) the client having the competence to use that knowledge to assess a situation, plan an action, and act in accordance with that plan (competence). If any of these three necessary conditions is not present, the client's autonomy is abridged (Beauchamp & Childress, 1989). These three conditions are elaborated upon below.

Voluntariness

For the client to give voluntary consent to a therapeutic recreation plan, coercion must be absent, and the client must have and understand information relevant to the decision. Consent of the client obtained through coercion, undue pressure, or ignorance is a moral travesty against the client's autonomy.

In the rehabilitation context, authorization or consent means far more than it does in the medical context, because of radical differences between the relationship of doctor and patient. Generally speaking, in therapeutic recreation practice, the relationship is open-ended and requires more discipline and action on the part of the client in the cooperative task.

Full Disclosure of Relevant Information to Clients

Because of special trust relationships with their clients, therapeutic recreation specialists have specific responsibilities. For a client capable of competent decision making, these responsibilities involve full disclosure of relevant information for autonomous action. Disclosure of such information serves to empower the client for autonomous action. Similarly, this information enables the client and the therapeutic recreation specialist to formulate joint rehabilitation plans.

What information, generally speaking, should the therapeutic recreation provider share with a client? Certainly the provider should inform the client of the limits of confidentially. The provider is obliged to tell the client that whatever information the client shares will be kept confidential, except when the provider is legally required to disclose such information or when its disclosure becomes necessary to reduce or to eliminate a clear and imminent danger to self or to others.

Most important for the therapeutic recreation provider is the client having relevant information to make wise decisions. For example, by denying relevant information, the provider can limit the client's choices, thereby effectively restricting autonomy. Providing relevant information helps the client reach a decision and shows respect for autonomy. For example, in leisure counseling, providing comprehensive information about leisure opportunities to facilitate the selection of a suitable leisure program demonstrates respect for the client's autonomy.

Competence

A person who is competent is capable of adequate decision making. Such decision making is presupposed for autonomy. In the absence of the ability to make adequate decisions, a person will not be deemed competent, whether in law, medicine, psychiatry, philosophy, or rehabilitation.

The sort of client competence needed for success in therapeutic recreation is the ability of the client to assess major risks and benefits and to make decisions based on such assessments. Some clients (such as persons with traumatic brain injuries, people with addictions, and persons with psychosis) may, temporarily or permanently, lack such ability. Clients who cannot utilize relevant knowledge to make reasonable choices, or who lack understanding of the knowledge needed to assess a situation and to plan and execute an action, are incapable of autonomous decision making. On the grounds of beneficence or non-maleficence, the autonomy of such persons may be restricted. If beneficence is the ground, then their autonomy is restricted to choices among actions from which they can benefit. If non-maleficence is the ground, their autonomy can be restricted to keep them from harming themselves or others. For example, when there are deficiencies in the independent leisure functioning of a client and correlated risks of serious injury, then the therapeutic recreation specialist may refuse to support the desire for independent leisure skills training.

The Principle of Justice

Justice is another useful principle for guiding actions of the therapeutic recreation provider working with individuals with disabilities. Distributive justice is especially relevant to the job of a provider because it considers fairness in relation to distribution or allocation (i.e., who gets what) of resources and services. In situations of abundance and cooperation, it is difficult to imagine any ethical problems of distribution or allocation. However, scarcity and competition make justice a troublesome ethical problem.

Justice requires employing relevant criterion as the basis of warranted differential treatment. To understand the variety of actions, one must consider the criteria used to determine a fair distribution of society's resources and services. Consider a list of six criteria: (a) to each person an equal share; (b) to each person according to need; (c) to each person according to motivation/effort; (d) to each person according to contribution; (e) to each person according to free-market exchanges; and (f) to each person according to fair opportunity. A brief discussion of these six criteria applied to therapeutic recreation specialists follows:

Equal Shares. The criterion of equal shares can be observed by keeping individual service costs down in order to provide equal access of therapeutic recreation services to a larger number of eligible persons with disabilities or by limiting the amount of time spent with any one client in order to provide equal access to services for a larger number of clients.

Need. Based on need, the therapeutic recreation provider may allocate more service time to a person with a severe spinal cord injury than to one with an amputated hand. The reason for this discrepancy in service time allocation is that the person with the amputated hand might be more capable of utilizing needed leisure services without assistance.

Motivation/Effort. The therapeutic recreation provider may allocate more time and funds to clients with demonstrated high motivation (usually effort is required to accomplish tasks) than to clients not so highly motivated. A provider might simply refuse to spend time attempting to assist an unmotivated client who is not working toward goals. A wise provider, rather than abandoning such a client, would likely suggest alternative avenues of help and enhancement of client motivation.

Contribution. More therapeutic recreation services may be made available to veterans with disabilities in recognition of their service, at no cost to them, than to civilians with similar disabilities, regardless of their financial state.

Free-Market Exchanges. The therapeutic recreation provider could supply needed leisure services that the client is willing to purchase. Laws of supply and demand are allowed to operate in an unimpeded manner.

Fair Opportunity. More therapeutic recreation services may be made available free of charge to persons with disadvantages resulting from congenital, disease, or accident-related disabilities. This criterion is employed to equalize the opportunities of two groups – those disadvantaged persons and those not effected in that way – in order to provide the former with equal access to opportunities in a competitive society.

These criteria for distribution are thought of as rival approaches, or as alternative approaches, for public and institutional policies. They offer different approaches for allocating scarce therapeutic recreation resources. However, there seems to be no obvious objection to accepting more than one of these criteria as useful. Indeed, any of these criteria might be accepted as useful once it is judged relevant for a specific situation. Deciding which criteria to employ in a particular situation, and why, is not easy.

The Principle of Fidelity

The principle of fidelity requires keeping the promise of commitments that have either been explicitly made or that others have been given good reason to believe that they have been made. Obligations to fidelity focus upon conceptions of honesty and loyalty. Ramsey (1970) considered the principle of fidelity to be the fundamental ethical principle, since it is basic to all sound human relationships. He viewed loyalty as a basic requirement for all good.

The kind of fidelity required from the caregiver can be defined as the propensity to believe in the personal work of the other and to have a serious and focused interest in furthering that person's welfare. Obviously, there cannot be an obligation to like another. However, one might argue that within the therapeutic recreation service provider/client relationship, the provider ought to try to understand the client and to behave toward that client in a way that expresses this attitude of commitment to the client's good. This would actually create a situation in which the client responds to the provider in an open and trusting manner. Examples of betrayal might involve gossiping and careless breaches of confidentiality (e.g., asking for personal information on the client from across a reception area).

The place of confidentiality within the therapeutic recreation provider/client relationship follows from the above discussion. Within this relationship, the provider has a clear obligation to maintain honesty and the client's confidentiality, to keep the client adequately informed of his or her circumstances and options, and to support as much as possible the interests of the client.

The therapeutic recreation service provider is also involved in professional and institutional relationships that call for loyalty and honesty. Colleagues have expectations of one another based upon their relationships. Gossiping about or criticizing a colleague's abilities to clients is damaging to the community within which the provider and clients function. There should be some appropriate and easily accessible channels for review if the ability of a provider is seriously in question. Bringing clients into such a discussion is potentially damaging to them, and should be avoided if possible. The conflicts may be very difficult if a provider believes that a client is in danger of being harmed by a colleague's actions. It would seem that supervisors have strong obligations to ensure that mechanisms are in place to minimize such conflicts.

Discussion

The ethical principles of beneficence, non-maleficence, authority, justice, and fidelity are general guidelines that arise from the experience of trying to live well together. They serve as general guides to our behavior. The common moral sense that this experience gives has been incorporated, sometimes awkwardly and not without contradictions, into our social and cultural structures and habits. Our experience as part of a public world and our more private individual experience have led most of us to understand that the viability of our shared life together, in any community from family to nation, depends on an acknowledgment of the kinds of basic shared values contained in these principles. This means we ought to promote each other's welfare. We ought not to harm one another. We ought to respect each other's freedom of choice. We ought to be fair. We ought to be faithful to our promises.

For any general principle, even scientific laws, the difficulty comes in the application to particular and often ambiguous cases. Therapeutic recreation service providers may agree that they ought to be fair to their clients. But how is fairness determined in situations where a therapeutic recreation provider does not have enough time or resources to go around? Or how can a therapeutic recreation service provider benefit a client where the client's view of what is most urgently needed differs radically from that of the therapeutic recreation service provider?

The personal values that therapeutic recreation service providers hold arise from their own worldview and are bound to influence their interpretation of these ethical principles that have been examined in this chapter. Those perceptions tend to create a predisposition to rank some principles as having precedence over others. For example, therapeutic recreation service providers who have personally had to struggle to achieve and maintain financial and personal autonomy may see the value of independence as being primary in almost all cases. Consequently, it may be difficult to believe that a person with cerebral palsy, for example, might not want to acquire the very time consuming skills of dressing herself/himself because she/he chooses to expend the energy elsewhere and does not mind relying on a personal attendant. Therapeutic recreation service providers who place strong value on autonomy may personally tend to override other kinds of values such as safety (non-maleficence) in order to promote the independence of their clients. They may be more likely to support client risk-taking behavior in an attempt to maximize rehabilitation benefits. On the other hand, if through their personal experiences they develop a strong desire to help and protect those in need, therapeutic recreation service providers may have a strong tendency to foster the dependence of clients and to override attempts at self-determination in order to care for clients in ways that minimize risk. Thus, therapeutic recreation service providers would have a strong tendency to favor behaviors that are beneficent and non-maleficent over those that foster autonomy.

It is not necessary to view these tendencies to value one principle over another in a totally negative light. Furthermore, it is natural that, in the course of our individual lives, we have come to see the importance of one or several of these values very vividly. However, these priorities and unexamined strong commitments must be open to continual critical examination by therapeutic recreation service providers so that they do not close their minds to alternative points of view that might be more appropriate in particular situations involving clients with different, but equally valid, experiences.

References

Beauchamp, T., & Childress, J. (1983). *Principles of biomedical ethics* (2nd ed.). New York: Oxford University Press.

Beauchamp, T., & Childress, J. (1989). *Principles of biomedical ethics* (3rd ed.). New York: Oxford University Press.

DeJong, G., & Lifchez, R. (1983). Physical disability and public policy. *Scientific American* 248(6), 41–49.

Gatens-Robinson, E. (1992). Beneficence and the habilitation of people with disabilities. *Contemporary Philosophy* 14(2), 8–11.

Kitchener, K. (1984). Intuition, critical evaluation, and ethical principles: The foundation for ethical decisions in a counselor's psychology. *Counseling Psychologist* 12(3), 43–55.

Lahey, M. (1987). The ethics of intervention in therapeutic recreation. In C. Sylvester, J.L. Hemingway, R. Howe-Murphy, K. Mobily, & P. Shank (Eds.), *Philosophy of therapeutic recreation: Ideas and issues* (pp. 17–26). Alexandria, VA: National Recreation and Park Association.

Millard, R., & Rubin, S. (1992). Ethical considerations in case management decision making. In R.T. Roessler, & S.E. Rubin (Eds.), *Case management and rehabilitation counseling* (pp. 155–168). Austin, TX: Pro-Ed.

Patterson, J., Buckley, J., & Smull, M. (1989). Ethics in supported employment. *Journal of Applied Rehabilitation Counseling* 20(3), 12–20.

Ramsey, P. (1970). *The patient as person.* New Haven, CT: Yale University Press.

Rawls, J. (1971). *A theory of justice.* Boston: Harvard University Press.

Reeder, J. (1982). Beneficence, supererogation and role duty. In E. Shelp (Ed.), *Beneficence and health care* (pp. 83–108). Dordrecht: Reidel.

Rubin, S., & Millard, R. (1991). Ethical principles and American public policy on disability. *Journal of Rehabilitation* 57(1), 13–16.

Rubin, S., Millard, R., Wilson, D., & Wong, H. (1991). An introduction to the ethical case management training program. *Rehabilitation Education* 5, 113–120.

Stumbo, N. (1995). Knowledge of professional and ethical behavior in therapeutic recreation services. *Therapeutic Recreation Journal* 14(4), 59–67.

Tarvydas, V. (1987). Decision-making models in ethics: Models for increased clarity and wisdom. *Journal of Applied Rehabilitation Counseling* 18(4), 50–52.

Welfel, E. (1987). A new code of ethics for rehabilitation counselors. *Journal of Applied Rehabilitation Counseling* 18(4), 9–11.

Wilson, C., Rubin, S., & Millard, R. (1991). Preparing rehabilitation counselors to deal with ethical dilemmas. *Journal of Applied Rehabilitation Counseling* 22(1), 30–33.

Wong, H., Rubin, S., & Millard, R. (1991). Ethical dilemmas frequently encountered by rehabilitation counselors. *Rehabilitation Education* 5, 19–23.

Chapter 22
RECONCEPTUALIZING HEALTH FOR CHRISTIANS WITH CHRONIC ILLNESS AND DISABILITIES

Youngkhill Lee and Bryan P. McCormick

I would say that the Lord helped me a lot when it first happened. He's the one that turned me around actually.

When I get frustrated, I always go to him, you know. When I can't do something, I always go to him to try [to] get the inner strength to do it.

Some people would think that to be hurt would be God's fault. But it's not, not the way I see it. I see that the Lord has given me the chance to do some things that I've never been able to do without him. He helps me every day.

During the weeks ahead, I read more and more on the subject of God's sovereignty. It truly was reassuring doctrine. As its light flooded my intellect and mind, it brightened my spirit and self-image. I felt secure, safe. God had control of everything in my life.

Voices such as the ones above made by Christians with chronic illnesses or disabilities motivated the authors to revisit the existing concepts of health. Such statements may imply a level of health or lack of health, depending on what perspective one takes. Having an illness, particularly one for which there is no cure may provide evidence that the person is not healthy. However, despite debilitating conditions, many Christians with chronic disabilities live in the community, making the best out of their situations and even exceling in many aspects of their everyday lives.

While there are a variety of health concepts, there has been little research that examines the relevance of health concepts to the lives of Christians with chronic disabilities. Many healthcare providers and professionals often follow a medical view of health and/or the World Health Organization's (WHO) holistic concept of health. These concepts may

---
Revised version of paper presented at the 1998 conference.

not accurately reflect the reality of the lives of people with disabilities who have a different worldview. Attempts should be made to analyze existing concepts of health in the context of Christianity. Such an approach may shed light on a realistic health concept for this population. This chapter begins with a review and critique of existing concepts of health, and then offers some thoughts that redefine health for people with a chronic illness or disability. Finally, the suggested model will be examined from a Christian perspective.

A Brief Review of Concepts

According to the World Health Organization (WHO) (1986), the 19th century was the pre-medical era, when the primary concern on health evolved with what was called engineering methods. The social dimensions of healthcare during this time focused on the development of safe water supplies and sewers, as well as the production of inexpensive food for people in underdeveloped areas. Following the pre-medical era, the first half of the twentieth century was the medical era, which involved mass vaccination and the use of antibiotics to overcome infection. Health was seen as an optimal disease and illness-free state during this era. This narrow view of health during the medical era has been challenged by the WHO. In a contemporary post-medical era, health is more than an absence of illness or disease, and it is increasingly defined holistically: complete physical, mental, and social wellbeing. The WHO (1986) stated that, "Whereas in the 'medical era' health policy has been concerned mainly with how medical care is to be provided and paid for, in the new 'post-medical' era it will focus on the attainment of good health and well-being" (p. 117). This transition remains evident in today's healthcare arena. Although the emphasis continues to be on the provision of medical care and medical financing, alternative concepts of health and their application to people with chronic disability need to be explored. The success of medical technology, the aging of the population, and the preservation of biological life will result in the era of chronicity. This implies that an increasing problem for healthcare in the future will require addressing the needs of people for whom disability is a fact of life. In the twenty-first century, the healthcare profession will work more with people who will never be cured. Thus, existing concepts of health may be inadequate to assess the health of people with chronic illnesses and disabilities.

A Critique of the Existing Concepts of Health

Both medical and holistic concepts of health have received criticism from some researchers (e.g., Kagawa-Singer, 1993; Locker, 1983; Radley & Green, 1987; Scheer & Groce, 1988). The traditional medical definition of health suggests that to be healthy is to be free from illness and infirmity. Thus, one who is experiencing illness would not be considered healthy by this definition, since the state of health is viewed as the opposite of illness. The holistic view of health offered by the WHO defined health as an achievement of physical, mental, and social wellbeing. Although the holistic definition enlarged the areas considered in assessing health, the concept connotes an *ideal* state rather than a realistic goal (cf., Pender, 1987). Perhaps both the medical and holistic views have good application to people who have temporary disabilities (e.g., broken legs) or acute illness (e.g., flu). Returning to the pre-injury or illness condition is possible for this type of temporary illness and disability. However, applying this perspective to individuals with chronic disabilities may not be realistic. For them, being healthy in the sense of returning to a pre-injury or illness condition is not an option, and in some cases, normal role performance may never be achieved (Glick & Kronenfeld, 1989).

An acute illness or temporary disability typically involves short-term treatment and requires a complete or partial withdrawal from normal role performance for full recovery (or death). However, chronic disabilities do not require temporary transition; rather, they require an ongoing process of adjustment to the situation. Thus, the medical and holistic sense of health and wellness concepts may not be realistic for people who experience chronic disabilities. There is no definitive health state for individuals with these characteristics, and therefore their health status remains undefined. Individuals with chronic disabilities can only recover health within the context of their current life situations, but not in the context of their pre-illness or disability conditions. In addition to the inadequate fit of existing concepts of health to people with chronic illness and disability, the concepts of "liminality" and the "sick role" can be used to further criticize the existing concepts of health.

Liminality

The concept of "liminality" by Murphy, Scheer, Murphy, and Mack (1988) illustrates well the unique problems of people with permanent disabilities. Murphy et al. argued that people with disabilities live in a "liminal" state, which connotes that they have lost their old status and they have not yet acquired a new one. Part of this liminality can be seen in considering the typical course of illness or disability. We usually think of illnesses as having two phases in which people get worse and then they get better. However, for people with chronic illnesses, although they may have gone through the first phase (getting worse, or sick), they are not getting better. As a result of this arrested course of illness, Murphy et al. (1988) stated that people with physical disabilities dwell "in a kind of limbo," (p. 235) and "in twilight zones of social indefinition" (p. 237). Turner (1967) also wrote that people in a liminal condition are "betwixt and between," and they are suspended in social space without firm identity or role definition. Currently, millions of people who have chronic disabilities live an almost cloistered existence, detached from mainstream society.

The concept of liminality illustrates what it means to have a chronic illness or disability in American society (Albrecht, 1992). Since people with chronic disabilities encounter medical and holistic concepts of health (i.e., an absence of illness or disability, a complete physical, mental, and social wellbeing), being healthy is an impossible task. Recognizing this odd situation, Kagawa-Singer (1993) argued that "these individuals have no socially sanctioned position on the health-illness continuum, for they are neither sick nor well" (p. 296). Using Murphy et al.'s (1988) concept of liminality, Kagawa-Singer noted that:

> Being neither sick nor well, the chronically ill or disabled are socially in a state of limbo. They must create socially valued positions for themselves by re-establishing the fact that they are still the same individuals even though they are inside bodies which no longer meet society's requirements of 'health.' (p. 296)

Given existing concepts of health, people who have chronic disabilities are not considered to be healthy, and may be uncertain about their health status.

Sick Role

The problem does not stop at the marginal or liminal state. Disability is often conceptualized as an extension of the "sick role" (e.g., Glick & Kronenfeld, 1989; Parsons, 1951), which arises out of the recognition that an individual may be motivated by the illness or disabling behavior. The premise of a sick role is that people who are experiencing an illness or disability are (a) exempted from normal social role responsibilities and (b) not held responsible for their condition (Parsons, 1951). Through social recognition of the sick role, the person who is experiencing an illness or disability is afforded a "legitimate" reason for role failure.

For the person with an acute illness or temporary disability, the sick role may be conducive to the recovery process. After temporary treatment and withdrawal from normal social role functions, people who experience acute illness and disability typically become healthy and are able to return to normal social responsibilities. The sick role may actually aid in recovery as the person is exempted, temporarily, from typical role demands. The sick role is removed as people return to the pre-illness or injury state.

However, for individuals with chronic disabilities who may not fully regain their social responsibilities, the sick role often creates the self-fulfilling prophesy of being socially unproductive (Glick & Kronenfeld, 1989). This goes beyond partial physical and social impairments. Unable to be an economically productive individual, chronic disability is often linked to social deviance (e.g., Strauss & Glaser, 1975; Zola, 1982), and "spoiled identity" (Goffman, 1963). Thus, being chronically ill or disabled becomes a master identity separate from the totality of the person with the disability (Albrecht, 1992). It is synonymous with having an unhealthy identity. Unless modifications of the existing concepts of health occur, the ability of persons with chronic disabilities to experience a state of health and wellness will be impaired.

Reconceptualization of Health for People with Chronic Disabilities

Then how can we conceptualize health for people with permanent or chronic disabilities? As illustrated previously, the two existing dominant concepts of health exclude individuals with chronic disabilities from being healthy. There are many people who are coping well with their chronic disabilities who cannot possibly return to a pre-injury state of wellness. Many of these individuals are still able to perform their social roles in spite of constraints. Current health concepts must be modified to accommodate the life contexts of people with chronic disabilities.

In order to conceptualize health for people who are in the "twilight zones" of health definitions, two important concepts, the life story and a sense of coherence, should be woven into the existing concepts of health. Both concepts may have particular relevance for Christians in that both represent ways through which people find some sense of meaning and order in their lives, even in the face of adversity such as chronic illness. As could be seen in the comments that introduced this chapter, faith in God's will provides a sense of order for Christians facing chronic illness and disability.

Life Story

One consideration in a health concept for people with chronic disabilities is an understanding of the life story of individuals with disabilities. The life story includes the life plans in the past with the life plans of the wished-to-be future (Brody, 1987; Kleiber, Brock, Lee, Dattilo, & Caldwell, 1995). For most people, their current life story reflects the recollected past and the desired future. Life story is defined as "a person's story of his or her life, or of what he or she thinks is a significant part of that life" (Tilton, 1980, p. 276). The state of illness occurs when people with chronic disabilities experience a threat to their story. As they change, and as the physical and social world around them changes, they rewrite their stories accordingly. People with chronic disabilities constantly attempt to discover an alternative story to help them make sense of a life that involves a process of adjustment to their current abilities and acceptance of limitations.

An important implication of the life story is that it may focus on the particular role individuals find for health in the new stories they write for themselves after the illness or disability. In rewriting one's life stories, Goffman (1961) offered some important insights of possible stories that people with disabilities might write. In his study of the life path of people receiving psychiatric services, he observed two contrasting life stories:

> Given the stage that any person has reached in a career, one typically finds that he constructs an image of his life course – past, present, and future – which selects, abstracts, and distorts in such a way to provide him with a view of himself that he can usefully expound in the current situation. . . .If the person can manage to present a view of his current situation which shows the operation of favorable personal qualities in the past and a favorable destiny awaiting for him, it may be called a *success story* [emphasis added]. If the facts of a person's past and present are extremely dismal, then about the best he can do is to show that he is not responsible for what has become of him, and the term *sad tale* [emphasis added] is appropriate. (pp. 150–151)

The possible stories that people with chronic illness might write may be either success stories or sad tales. When rewriting one's life stories, it is a success story if one indicates successful adjustment to illness or disability, while sad tales would reflect unsuccessful adjustment to the changed circumstances. Identification of what stories one writes can be an important consideration for determining the health status of these individuals.

Sense of Coherence

Another useful approach to conceptualizing health for people with chronic illness or disability can be taken through examining how people make sense of stressors, including both acute and chronic illness or disability. Antonovsky (1987) has posited an approach to health that he termed a salutogenic orientation to health. This orientation contrasts with a pathogenic orientation in which one of the key concerns in healthcare is related to identifying the causes of illness (pathogenesis). Instead, Antonovsky has argued that health and healthcare should be more concerned with the causes of wellness (salutogenesis). The salutogenic orientation is helpful to understand the nature of the two types of stories presented above. The salutogenic model takes the position that health is more than the lack of stressors in the environment, assuming that "in the very nature of human existence, stressors are omnipresent" (p. xii). The basic salutogenic model examines the question of why some people are better at making sense of the countless stressors they face. Thus health is considered to be essentially an adaptive capacity. To refer back to the life stories, those who write success stories in the process of adapting to everyday stressors will likely have greater success in dealing with major stressful events. Conversely, those people with poorer adaptive capacity for day-to-day stressors are likely to write sad tales in dealing with major stressors.

One important premise of the salutogenic model is that there is negative entropy in the health ease and dis-ease continuum and that continuous inputs are required to maintain and enhance one's movement toward the health ease end. Yet some people seem better able to make sense of, and adapt to, both major and minor stressors. Antonovsky (1987) argued that although people may use a variety of resources in adapting, the most general resistance resource one could mobilize to confront these stressors was a "sense of coherence." A sense of coherence is a global orientation that represents the extent to which a person has:

> a pervasive, enduring though dynamic, feeling of confidence that (1) the stimuli deriving from one's internal and external environments in the course of living are structured, predictable and explicable; (2) the resources are available to one to meet the demands posed by these stimuli; and (3) these demands are challenges, worthy of investment and engagement. (Antonovsky, 1987, p. 19)

Further, Antonovsky (1987) posited that a sense of coherence is composed of three related components. First, comprehensibility refers to the extent to which both internal and external experience make cognitive sense in that they are ordered and structured. Antonovsky (1979) characterized this component as "a solid capacity to judge reality" (p. 127) and noted that this component is the core of the sense of coherence concept. Second, manageability refers to the extent to which one has access to the resources required to meet the demands of a stressor-rich environment. Meaningfulness is the final component, which refers to the degree to which one's experiences make sense emotionally. This component is personal in nature and Antonovsky noted that it is related to motivation. That is, people who see their lives as meaningless are less likely to expend the energy to comprehend and manage ongoing stressors. According to Antonovsky, the component of meaningfulness may be the most critical in developing a sense of coherence, and its links to spiritual faith are striking.

Reconceptualized Model of Health

Taking the life story along with the salutogenic model, the authors of this paper propose a conceptual model of health that contextualizes the lives of people with chronic disabilities. Figure 1 represents the reconceptualized model of health in which two dimensions are important: *Conditions of Physical, Mental and Social Wellness* (CPMS) and *Life Story*. The CPMS dimension (vertical) reflects the existing concepts of health that people with chronic illness often use to measure their status of health. In this dimension, one end signifies "well" and the other end "not well." The life story is another dimension that the authors of this paper propose to assess the health of people with chronic disability. In this dimension, one pole indicates success stories and the other pole sad tales (Goffman, 1963). Success stories characterize a positive outlook in which an individual feels his or her life is meaningful and has a sense of coherence. The sad tales, on the other hand, indicate an opposite of these characteristics. One important note to understand is that the horizontal dimension emphasizes the subjective evaluation of one's revised life story, whether they are successful or sad ones.

According to Figure 1, Cell I indicates "success stories" in one's life story and "well" in CPMS conditions. Without a doubt, this cell would definitely be considered healthy. This cell may reflect those individuals without disabilities who are writing their life stories and are satisfied with their lives. There may be fewer persons with a disability who fall into this cell. Cell II (shaded) shows "success stories" in one's life story and "not well" in the CPMS conditions. This cell represents those people who overcome their constraints to write success stories after experiencing the disabilities and/or in spite of disabilities (e.g., Joni Eareckson-Tada, Dave Dravecky). In this cell, people would feel healthy despite not enjoying physical wellness at the pre-illness or disability level. They would view their life as meaningful and coherent. Many individuals who may not be healthy within the existing health concepts may enjoy health from this view.

Cell III indicates both "sad tales" in one's life story and "well" in CPMS conditions, where one cannot consider him or herself as healthy. There are people without disabilities who may be considered well under existing concepts but whose life stories may place them in a questionable state of health. These individuals are likely to feel their life meaningless, incomprehensible, and unmanageable. Again, there may be some people with chronic disabilities who fall into this cell. Cell IV represents "sad tales" in one's life story and "not well" in CPMS conditions, where one has a further reduced level of health. This person may be unable to accept his or her present abilities and limitations as longstanding or permanent, and may see him or herself as a victim.

Figure 1. Reconceptualization of health for people with chronic disabilities.

		Life Story	
		Success Stories	Sad Tales
Conditions of Physical, Mental & Social Wellness (CPMS)	Well	I Healthy (no illness/disability)	III Unhealthy (no illness/disability)
	Not Well	II Healthy (chronic disability)	IV Unhealthy (chronic disability)

Although the following discussion characterizes life stories as either sad tales or success stories, it should be remembered that these represent ideal types. For example, only one who is completely without hope sees life as meaningless and completely incomprehensible would be a "pure" sad tale. In contrast, someone who thrives in the face of chronic disability might be considered a "pure" success story. The reality is, however, that all people's stories will vary from those of success to those of sadness and may change over time. In reality, these two stories more accurately represent polar extremes along a continuum.

Relevance to Christians with Disabilities

How is this model relevant to Christians with chronic disabilities? Lazarus and Folkman (1984) claimed that humans are meaning-oriented, meaning-building creatures who constantly appraise daily events in their lives. Spilka, Shaver, and Kirpatrick (1985) and Taylor (1983) suggested that people make attributions in order to maintain or enhance meaning. People engage in meaning-making behavior more when life circumstance or situations become out of control. Creating meaning may be conceived as a form of control, since understanding is generally preferable to ambiguity and lack of information (Spilka et al., 1985). Averill (1973) called it "informational control" and considered it a kind of cognitive control. However, at times events may stand so out of the ordinary that information alone is insufficient to aid people in making sense of long-term disability and accompanying role changes. The information that one's fifth thoracic vertebrae was crushed, causing a complete spinal lesion, is of little comfort in trying to make sense of the fact that you will probably be using a wheelchair for the rest of your life. Finding sense and meaning in such extreme stressors takes some degree of faith that, although at present the challenges may be too great to comprehend, at some level of one's life makes sense and has meaning. Clark (1958) claimed that "the most pervading reason for the eternal appeal of religion seems to be that religion, more than any other human function, satisfies the need for meaning in life" (p. 419). Therefore, Christians attempt to find meaning in life from God, and faith helps clarify meaning. McIntosh and Spilka (1990) stated that "troubled people who derive meaning from faith are no longer afloat in a sea of ambiguity and uncertainty" (p. 184). This demonstrates the fundamental relationship between religion and meaning for Christians.

Appraisals of situations, which are important parts of finding meaning, are central determinants of how individuals respond to stressful life events (Lazarus & Folkman, 1984). Problems with health could be appraised or interpreted as a threat to the individual, as a loss of peace of mind, as a challenge, as caused by any number of things, as a situation that the individual can handle, or as a situation that the individual must simply accept. Pargament (1990) argued that appraisal can also be religious in nature. Health problems can be appraised as a reward from a loving God, as a lesson from a teaching God, as a punishment from an angry God, or as the will of a mysterious God. Explanations vary, but religion may be seen as one viable way for Christians to make sense of pain and suffering. Most Christians describe their situation in religious, rather than medical, terms.

Having faith in God may be particularly influential in helping Christians redefine the problem and in keeping themselves together emotionally as they deal with it (Pargament, 1990). Faith itself may be a relief from psychological distress, acceptance of one's health and life situation, or adoption of another perspective; redefinition of problems; or an adoption of a different perspective. There is also evidence to suggest that the relationship between religion and coping is moderated by the importance of religion to the person (Bahr, Bartel, & Chadwick, 1971; Gibbs, Mueller, & Wood, 1973; Hoge & DeZullueta, 1985).

The potential stories that Christians with chronic disabilities write may be success or sad stories. While people who do not believe in God may find meaning elsewhere, Christians explore it with God. When the life events of Christians get more dramatic, turning to God is a natural tendency to handle the incomprehensible situation. Christians find coherence, meaningfulness, and comprehension primarily from their spiritual beliefs and values.

Conclusion

In this paper, existing concepts of health were analyzed in relation to the lives of people with chronic disabilities. With existing concepts, healthcare professionals, including therapeutic recreation specialists, cannot enhance health for people with chronic disabilities. Therefore, a reconceptualization of health, the ideas of life stories, and the salutogenic orientation were proposed to evaluate the health status of people with chronic disabilities. Further, the proposed health model was applied to a Christian perspective on health status. While not negating the existing conceptual health models, the inclusiveness and openness of the proposed model fits well with those individuals with disabilities who have different worldviews.

If we are concerned with the health of our citizens, we must seek a balance between traditional concepts of health and how citizens define health. Such information can provide a new understanding of the meaning of health and can further clarify the professional's role in the provision of services based on the citizens' health needs. What is needed is an understanding of the way in which people with disabilities have organized their world, their thoughts about what is happening, their experiences, and their basic perceptions in everyday life. We must grasp their perspective and incorporate that perspective into the provision of health services.

References

Albrecht, G.L. (1992). *The disability business: Rehabilitation in America*. Newbury Park, CA: Sage.

Antonovsky, A. (1979). *Health, stress, and coping*. San Francisco: Jossey-Bass.

Antonovsky, A. (1987). *Unravelling the mystery of health*. San Francisco: Jossey-Bass.

Averill, J.R. (1973). Personal control over aversive stimuli and its relationship to stress. *Psychological Bulletin* 80, 286–303.

Bahr, H.M., Bartel, L.R., & Chadwick, B.A. (1971). Orthodoxy, activism, and the salience of religion. *Journal of Scientific Study of Religion* 10, 69–75.

Brody, H. (1987). *Stories of sickness*. New Haven, CT: Yale University Press.

Clark, W. (1958). *The psychology of religion*. New York: Macmillan.

Gibbs, D., Mueller, S., & Wood, J. (1973). Doctrinal orthodoxy, salience and the consequential dimension. *Journal for the Scientific Study of Religion* 12, 33–52.

Glick, D.C., & Kronenfeld, J.J. (1989). Well roles: An approach to reincorporate role theory into medical sociology. *Research in the Sociology of Health Care* 8, 289–309.

Goffman, E. (1963). *Stigma: Notes on the management of spoiled identity*. Englewood Cliffs NJ: Prentice-Hall.

Hoge, D.R., & DeZullueta., E. (1985). Salience as a condition for various social consequences of religious commitment. *Journal for the Scientific Study of Religion* 24, 21–38.

Kagawa-Singer, M. (1993). Redefining health: Living with cancer. *Social Sciences & Medicine* 37(3), 295–304.

Kleiber, D.A., Brock, S., Lee, Y., Dattilo., J., & Caldwell, L. (1995). The relevance of leisure in an illness experience: The realities of spinal cord injury. *Journal of Leisure Research* 27(3), 283–299.

Lazarus, R.S., & Folkman, S. (1984). *Stress, appraisal and coping*. New York: Springer.

Locker, D. (1983). *Disability and disadvantage: The consequences of chronic illness*. London: Tavistock.

McIntosh, D., & Spilka, B. (1990). Religion and physical health: The role of personal faith and control. In M.L. Lynn & D.O. Moberg (Eds.), *Research in the social scientific study of religion: A research manual* (Vol. 2, pp. 167–194). Greenwich, CT: JAI Press.

Murphy, R.F., Scheer, J., Murphy, Y., & Mack, R. (1988). Physical disability and social liminality: A study in the rituals of adversity. *Social Sciences and Medicine* 26(2), 235–242.

Pargament, K.I. (1990). God helped me: Toward a theoretical framework of coping for the psychology of religion. In M.L. Lynn & D.O. Moberg (Eds.), *Research in social scientific study of religion: A research manual* (Vol. 2, pp. 195–224). Greenwich, CT: JAI Press.

Pender, N.J. (1987). *Health promotion in nursing practice* (2nd ed.). Norwalk, CT: Appleton & Lange.

Radley, A., & Green, R. (1987). Illness as adjustment: A methodology and conceptual framework. *Sociology of Health & Illness* 9(2), 179–207.

Scheer, J., & Groce, N. (1988). Impairment as a human constant: Cross-cultural and historical perspectives on variations. *Journal of Social Issues* 44, 23–27.

Spilka, B., Shaver, P., & Kirpatrick, L. (1985). A general attribution theory for the psychology of religion. *Journal for the Scientific Study of Religion* 24, 1–20.

Strauss, A.L., & Glaser, B.G. (1975). *Chronic illness and the quality of life*. St. Louis, MO: Mosby.

Taylor, S.E. (1983). Adjustment to threatening events: A theory of cognitive adaptation. *American Psychologist* 38, 1161–1173.

Tilton, J.T. (1980). The life story. *Journal of American Folklore* 93, 276–292.

Turner, V. (1967). *The ritual process: Structure of kinship*. Boston: Beacon Press.

World Health Organization. (1986). Life styles and health. *Social Sciences and Medicine* 22, 117–124.

Zola, I.K. (1982). *Missing pieces: A chronicle of living with a disability*. Philadelphia, PA: Temple University Press.

Chapter 23
LEISURE-SPIRITUAL COPING: A MODEL FOR THERAPEUTIC RECREATION AND LEISURE SERVICES

Paul Heintzman

In a recent study on the relevance of spirituality for people with mental illness, participants identified not only public (e.g., formal religious services) and private (e.g., prayer, spiritual reading, meditation) spiritual activities as spiritual, but also recreational and social activities as spiritual (Bellamy et al., 2007). The authors noted that recreational and social activities are usually not classified as religious or spiritual and suggested that future research should explore the relationship of these recreational and social activities to spirituality and recovery for individuals with mental illness. Consistent with the authors' comments, few therapeutic recreation models reflect the spiritual dimension to life. An exception is Van Andel's (1998; see also Carter, Van Andel, & Robb, 2003) therapeutic recreation (TR) outcome model, which has received considerable attention within the therapeutic recreation field (e.g., Coyle, 1998; Dieser & Peregoy, 1999; Parker & Carmack, 1998).

In Van Andel's (1998) TR outcome model, therapeutic recreation strives to sustain or enhance the health status, quality of life, and/or functional capacities of individuals through the use of recreation or experiential activities and processes. Van Andel included spirituality in his model "since therapeutic recreation practice seeks to address the needs of the whole person and spirituality has been identified as an important aspect of one's health and well-being" (p. 187). Noting that "we are seeing a resurgence in spirituality and support for its role in the healing process," the spiritual dimension of life was identified by Van Andel (p. 191) as being important to all three components of the outcome model – health status, quality of life, and functional capacities. Health status,

---

Revised version of paper presented at the 2008 conference.

which includes spiritual health along with social, emotional, physical, and mental health, reflects a holistic understanding of health where there is an integration of body, mind, and spirit. Quality of life, characterized by feelings of self-determination, joy, contentment, and satisfaction, is a subjective assessment of spiritual and psychological wellbeing (Carter, Van Andel, & Robb, 2003). Spiritual function, one of six functional capacities, refers to "the ability to find meaning and purpose in life" (Van Andel, p. 187).

Although Van Andel observed in his 1998 paper on the TR outcome model that "discussions on the relationship of spirituality and leisure experiences are still somewhat speculative" (p. 188), during the last decade spirituality has received greater empirical research attention within the leisure studies community. Studies of leisure and spirituality have expanded beyond small-scale qualitative studies with a narrow focus on nature-based recreation experiences and spirituality (e.g., Stringer & McAvoy, 1992; Fox, 1997; Fredrickson & Anderson, 1999) to larger scale studies that have explored all types of leisure in all settings (e.g., Heintzman & Mannell, 2003; Schmidt & Little, 2005, 2007). Likewise, as demonstrated by a special issue on leisure, stress, and coping featured in *Leisure Sciences*, research on the role of leisure in coping with stress has evolved into an increasingly popular area of inquiry within the leisure studies field (Iwasaki & Schneider, 2003). Despite the growth in these two research areas, apart from one paper in the above mentioned special issue (Heintzman & Mannell, 2003), there has been little direct effort made to explore the relationship between leisure and spirituality as a contributor to coping with stress. In their paper, Heintzman and Mannell (2003) theorized how the major leisure coping strategies – fostering a self-determination disposition, enhancing social support, empowerment, palliative coping, and mood enhancement (Iwasaki & Mannell, 2000) – may be associated with, and enhanced by, the spiritual dimension of life.

Recently, a number of studies (e.g., Gosselink & Myllykangas, 2007; Iwasaki, MacKay, Mactavish, Ristock, & Bartlett, 2006) have identified the importance of spirituality in the leisure coping process. The purpose of this paper is to synthesize theory and research findings on leisure, stress, and spiritual coping into a conceptual model of leisure-spiritual coping, which is based upon the spiritual framework of coping (Gall et al., 2005). This synthesis leads to the development of an overarching conceptual model that may be used by therapeutic recreation and leisure services practitioners as they work with people experiencing stress due to a variety of personal and/or structural stressors including disability, chronic illness, discrimination, marginalization, poverty, or other challenges. The model may be used to enable persons to transcend life challenges and to enhance their quality of life. In one sense this leisure-spiritual coping model may be seen to build upon and extend the spiritual dimensions of Van Andel's (1998) TR outcome model. While the model presented in this paper may be focused more on spiritual health than mental health, which is the focus of this special issue of *Therapeutic Recreation Journal*, spiritual health has been conceptualized as both an elementalistic dimension of health as one component of holistic health and as an integrative dimension of health wherein optimal wellness is dependent upon spiritual wellness occurring within each of the interrelated and interactive dimensions of wellness (Heintzman, 1997; Van Andel). Thus, when therapeutic recreation services bring about spiritual health outcomes that assist a person to cope with, adapt to, and transcend life challenges, they are also promoting mental health.

Before developing the model, we first need to provide definitions of key concepts. Spirituality may be defined as "the feelings, thoughts, experiences, and behaviors that arise from a search for the sacred" (Larson, Swyers, & McCullough, 1998, p. 21). The search for the sacred refers to the search for God, a higher power, a larger reality, and/or ultimate truth as perceived by an individual. Spiritual coping may be viewed as the ways that people receive help from spiritual resources (higher power, spiritual practices, faith community etc.) during periods of life stress (Olszewski, 1995). Empirically, spirituality and spiritual wellbeing have been found to be important coping resources that may mitigate the negative impact of stress on mental and physical health (Pargament, 1997). Leisure-spiritual coping in this paper refers to coping with stress through spirituality within the context of an individual's leisure, whether leisure is defined as time, activities, experiences, or an attitude.

A Spiritual Framework of Coping

Based on the recent proliferation of empirical studies on spirituality, coping, and health, Gall et al. (2005) developed a conceptual framework of the role of spirituality in coping. This model uses the basic principles and structural elements of Folkman's (1997) transactional model of stress and coping as a framework to organize findings from studies on spirituality and coping. According to this model, at any given point in time, spirituality may function on many levels of the stress and coping process: spiritual appraisals (e.g., attribution), person factors (religious denomination/doctrine, religious orientation, spiritual problem-solving or coping styles, hope), coping behavior (e.g., prayer), coping resources (connections with nature, others, transcendent other), and meaning making (e.g., life purpose, transformation, growth). *Spiritual person factors* act as a contextual framework that orients a person in her or his reflection, understanding, and response to life events. Spiritual appraisals, along with coping behaviors, act as mediating factors in the coping process. *Spiritual appraisals* refer to first attempts to make sense of a stressor on the basis of one's spiritual beliefs. These appraisals may alleviate the first stages of distress sufficiently so that the individual may initiate coping behaviors. *Spiritual coping behaviors*, including organizational religious behavior, private religious or spiritual practices, and nontraditional spiritual practices (Maltby, Lewis, & Day, 1999), refer to the actions a person uses to counter the stressor (problem-focused) or the resultant emotional responses (emotion-focused). Spirituality may play a major role in *meaning-making* (seeking significance in an experience), which may lead to a reappraisal of beliefs and attitudes concerning one's self, others, and the world. These beliefs and attitudes may impact on all areas of life. Due to this important role of spirituality in meaning-making, it is frequently regarded as synonymous with meaning-making.

The spiritual framework of coping developed by Gall et al. (2005) allows for broad integration with other elements of the stress coping process in various life domains. This is due to the fact that the framework uses Folkman's (1997) general model of stress and coping as a foundation. Thus, the framework is an appropriate model to use to discuss the role of spirituality in coping with stress through leisure. The model may be applied to various types of stressors, such as a variety of personal and structural stressors, and has potential for cross-cultural application, as it is applicable to people from diverse faith traditions or no faith tradition. In fact, Gall et al. illustrated how their framework is adaptable to Muslim, Jewish, Christian, and Hindu faith perspectives. In the following section, most of the components of the spiritual framework of coping will be described in more detail, and where possible, applied to therapeutic recreation and leisure services (see Figure 1). Some components are not included (e.g., spiritual problem-solving or coping styles), as currently little literature exists on the relationship of these components to therapeutic recreation and leisure.

Figure 1. Leisure-spiritual coping model. Adapted from Gall et al.'s (2005) Spiritual Framework of Coping.

Spiritual Appraisal

At the first stage of the appraisal process, spiritual causal attributions (e.g., God, the devil, fate) are a common way to understand stressful circumstances such as an injury or an illness (Gall et al., 2005). These spiritual causal attributions have been associated with the utilization of religious coping activities (Shortz & Worthington, 1994), as well as general coping strategies (Gall, 2003; Miner & MacKnight, 1999) and adaptation to negative situations (Pargament et al., 1990). Attributing cause to God may help people maintain a sense of justice in the world (Pargament & Hahn, 1986) that enables them to sustain a sense of personal control in the midst of an unmanageable circumstance (Spilka, Shaver, & Kirkpatrick, 1985).

An example of primary appraisal is desecration: that is, a spiritual evaluation of harm/loss: to what extent an event has negatively affected a dimension of a person's life that is considered to be sacred or related to God (Gall et al., 2005). Secondary appraisal refers to a person's assessment of the accessibility and possible helpfulness of particular spiritual coping strategies that could be utilized in reaction to the stress (Gall et al., 2005). Thereby, these appraisals have implications for the choice of particular coping behaviors (Pargament & Hahn, 1986). Application of this component of the leisure-spiritual coping would involve including related spiritual appraisal questions that are sensitive to cultural and spiritual traditions to needs assessments used in therapeutic recreation and leisure services (Heintzman, 1997).

Person Factors

Religious denomination and doctrine (TR worldviews). Many people live their lives according to the beliefs of a specific religious group. Personal beliefs are integrated with beliefs of the religious group to create a source of social support and social norms that influence a person's behavior. Thus, religious beliefs can affect how a person will cope with stress. Research has documented that religiously oriented lifestyles tend to be healthier (Gall et al., 2005). In the studies of Iwasaki and colleagues on the stress-coping of marginalized groups, it can be noted that the spirituality of participants is rooted in different religious groups or traditions such as Aboriginal, pagan, and Christian religions (Iwasaki, Bartlett, & O'Neil, 2005; Iwasaki & Ristock, 2004; Mactavish & Iwasaki, 2005; Iwasaki, Bartlett, MacKay, Mactavish, & Ristock, 2005). For example, Aboriginal spirituality is important to First Nation people as it is "sacred," "fundamental," and "part of their heritage" (Iwasaki, Bartlett, & O'Neil, 2005; Iwasaki & Bartlett, 2006a; Iwasaki, Bartlett, MacKay, et al., 2005) is a key element of the Aboriginal worldview (Renfrey & Dionne, 2001) and has been recognized as a "cultural buffer" that mitigates the negative effects of stress and trauma (Walters & Simoni, 2002). Furthermore, symbolic healing during Aboriginal spiritual ceremonies is viewed as crucial to overall health (Waldram, 1997). Thus, for Aboriginals, spiritual coping through cultural leisure activities is consistent with all-encompassing worldviews valued and practiced by Aboriginal peoples (McDonald & McAvoy, 1997) and is part of a holistic way of life where the mind, body, and spirit are seen in harmony or balance (Iwasaki, Mactavish, & Mackay, 2005). In a review of literature on the major pathways that link leisure to quality of life across cultures and around the world, Iwasaki (2007) noted that spirituality/religion/personal beliefs are one of the six domains of quality of life, and for many cultures spirituality plays an important role in leisure-like activities that contribute to quality of life. For example, Taoism influences the lives and leisure of Chinese people and, in the Indian vedantic perspective, the practice of yoga assists one in spiritual awareness.

Given the importance of religious and spiritual beliefs for many groups of people, incorporation of these beliefs into the therapeutic recreation process is appropriate for some groups. For example, in an investigation of how certified therapeutic recreation specialists managed cross-ethnic interactions in therapeutic recreation practice, Dieser (2003) found that family and spiritual involvement was vital for ethnic groups. In recent years, philosophical arguments have been made for the inclusion of spirituality in therapeutic recreation. Howe-Murphy and Murphy (1987) suggested a New Age spirituality and paradigm in which "the development of personal consciousness, leading to a lifestyle of wellness, and which incorporates the elements of mind, body, spirit, is the essential framework for our quest as therapeutic recreators" (p. 47). Van Andel and Heintzman (1996) used the model of Christian spirituality, "in which humans, created in the image of God, are viewed as a mind-body-spirit unity who have capacity to relate, not only with other human beings, but also with God" (p. 74), to illustrate how recreation practitioners might develop a more holistic approach. The authors of these two papers, which represent two of many different spiritual perspectives, stressed the need to include the spiritual dimension of life in therapeutic recreation. Heintzman (1997) explored how spirituality from a generic perspective may be applied to therapeutic recreation, how it is related to recreation services for people with specific needs, and suggested practical implications for the integration of spirituality into recreation services and programs. This generic approach may be adapted by people of different religious and spiritual belief systems. Although therapeutic recreation models have not been developed for many of the world's diverse religious and spiritual belief systems, leisure programs with a therapeutic focus do exist that incorporate spiritual beliefs. For example, the Cherokee Nation Youth Fitness Camp for Aboriginal youth with a family history of obesity, heart disease, or diabetes uses a holistic approach, which includes teaching on spiritual and inner strength, in addition to environmental knowledge, social and mental health, cultural awareness, and physical fitness (Perkins & Giese, 1994).

Religious orientation. A distinction may be made between extrinsic and intrinsic religious orientation (Allport, 1961; Hergenhahn & Olson, 1999). With an extrinsic orientation, religion is for the person's own sake to gain personal benefits; religious belief is utilitarian in that it provides comfort and safety; and religious practices are not the result of faith but the result of guilt, anxiety, or external pressure. An intrinsic religious orientation is characterized by a selfless motivation to pursue purpose and meaning in life for its own sake and an internalized understanding of transcendence based on "faith, hope, and love for others, God, and self" (Gall et al., 2005, p. 92). An extrinsic religious orientation, which is thought to be less effective than an intrinsic orientation when coping with stress (Park & Cohen, 1993), has been found to be associated with a sense of inadequacy when coping with a stressful situation and is less likely to be associated with the feeling that the stressful experience will be an opportunity for growth (Pargament et al., 1992). In contrast, during times of crisis, particularly times when a situation is beyond a person's control, people with high intrinsic religiosity tend to rely on their religious resources (Park & Cohen, 1993). An intrinsic religious orientation is also associated with the perception of a stressful event as an opportunity for personal growth, reliance upon problem-solving coping during stress (Pargament et al., 1992), and a sense of meaning during severe stress (Park, Cohen, & Herb, 1990).

Little research exists on the influence of extrinsic versus intrinsic religious orientation upon therapeutic recreation and other leisure outcomes. Rancourt (1991a, 1991b), in studies of a comprehensive leisure education program for women that abuse substances, found that the women exhibited an external locus of control in regard to their relationship with a higher power or God. Given the above research on religious orientation, it would seem beneficial for therapeutic recreation programs to encourage movement from an extrinsic to an intrinsic religious orientation.

Leisure-Spiritual Coping Behavior

Spiritual coping behavior is a common response to stress and has significant relationships with a great diversity of adjustment factors (Gall et al., 2005). Spiritual coping behavior includes a variety of emotion and problem centered strategies (Harrison, Koenig, Hays, Eme-Akwari, & Pargament, 2001) that may be classified as "organizational religious behavior, private religious or spiritual practices, and nontraditional spiritual practices" (Gall et al., 2005, p. 93; Maltby et al., 1999). Organizational religious behavior involves participation in a formal, religious organization and includes activities such as attendance at religious services and volunteer activity (Idler, 1999). Private religious or spiritual practices are personal and private behaviors such as studying sacred texts, prayer, watching religious television, and singing (Levin, 1999). Nontraditional spiritual practices are those that differ from traditional religious expressions (Dyson, Cobb, & Forman, 1997). Examples include spiritually based mental exercises, relaxation techniques, guided imagery, and introspection (Gall et al., 2005).

As alluded to earlier, a recent study on the relevance of spirituality for people with mental illness by Bellamy et al. (2007) found not only that spirituality was important to the study participants, but that all three categories of spiritual coping behavior were identified: public spiritual activities (i.e., formal religious activities such as church and Bible study groups), private spiritual activities (i.e., prayer, reading the Bible and other spiritual books, meditation), and other activities including both recreational activities (i.e., playing and watching sports, fishing, reading, social activities) and mutual support activities (i.e., Alcoholics Anonymous, helping others, community service). Bellamy et al. noted that, while the activities in this last category are not normally viewed as religious or spiritual, they may include significant religious and spiritual elements such as social support and fellowship.

Similarly, in their research on marginalized groups, Iwasaki and colleagues found that all three classifications of spiritual coping behavior have been useful in coping with stress for the groups they have studied. Spiritual coping behavior ranged from praying, reading the Bible, or being connected with a church, to meditating with a long bath that offered the occasion to "think things through" (Iwasaki, Bartlett, Mackay et al., 2005). Formal religious activities such as attending church services and Bible study were found to be helpful stress-coping activities for individuals with disabilities (Mactavish & Iwasaki, 2005). With the same population, private religious or spiritual practices (e.g., meditation, prayer), which varied from person to person, were found to be "opportunities for 'clearing' one's mind and spiritual revival," and thereby helpful for stress-coping (Mactavish & Iwasaki, 2005, p. 25). Leading an active life spiritually, which included spiritual contemplation and prayer, was found by some middle-aged and older people suffering from arthritis to be an effective means to cope with stress (Iwasaki & Butcher, 2004). Another private spiritual practice helpful for stress-coping that was identified by Aboriginal persons with disabilities or with diabetes was the practice of smudging (Iwasaki, Bartlett, & O'Neil, 2005; Mactavish & Iwasaki, 2005). In terms of nontraditional spiritual practices, yoga was identified as a spiritual coping activity that facilitated "concentration or focus of attention," which assists in determining direction in life (Iwasaki & Ristock, 2004, p. 34). Personal pampering activities such as a long bath were noted by women with disabilities as spiritual activities helpful in stress coping (Mactavish & Iwasaki, 2005), and massage, according to a Métis woman with diabetes, had the potential to be transformative since "it gives you the opportunity to go within yourself" through "talking in your mind." (Iwasaki, Bartlett, & O'Neil, 2005, p. 982).

The traditional organizational and private spiritual practices identified in the above research studies as being helpful in coping with stress are consistent with the activities and techniques suggested in models of spiritual wellbeing. From a therapeutic recreation perspective, leisure might be an area of life where a person may develop traditional organizational and private spiritual resources that help cope with stress in life. In a few cases, therapeutic recreation programs might offer programs focused exclusively on spirituality. These could include personal awareness workshops, spiritual renewal seminars/retreats, spiritual health support cases, spiritual health oriented lending libraries, and spiritual health workshops (Chapman, 1987). Dieser (2003) gives the example of how certified therapeutic recreation specialists worked together with religious leaders in a case where religion was important to the client. However, in most cases, therapeutic recreation professionals would refer persons to these types of programs offered by other organizations such as religious institutions and retreat-spirituality centers (Heintzman, 1997).

Of particular relevance to this paper is the third category of nontraditional spiritual coping practices, which may include leisure activities with a spiritual dimension. The examples of nontraditional practices suggested in the Gall et al. (2005) framework include spirituality based mental exercises, relaxation techniques, and guided imagery. These activities may in some cases be considered as leisure (Heintzman, 2002a), whereas many other leisure activities may also facilitate spiritual coping (Heintzman & Mannell, 2003). For example, dragon boat racing is an activity that has been associated with leisure-spiritual coping. Parry (2007) demonstrated that dragon boat racing acted as a coping mechanism for the stressful life event of breast cancer as spiritual and other outcomes of this leisure pursuit contributed to spiritual health and enhanced survivorship following medical treatment for breast cancer. Specifically, dragon boat racing facilitated spiritual reflection and awakening, spiritual connections with others and the world, empowerment, as well as clarity and purpose in life (Parry, 2009). Likewise, Unruh and Elvin (2004) found dragon boat racing decreased stress and gave a more positive perspective of having breast cancer through transcendence, connectedness, and oneness with others, which, as we will see shortly, are spiritual coping resources.

An important question to ask as we consider leisure as a nontraditional spiritual coping practice is how leisure functions as spiritual coping practice. We will consider this question under the headings of sacralization and grounding, contemplative leisure, leisure as space and time, and "being away."

Sacrilization and grounding. The types of activities identified by Gall et al. (2005) as nontraditional spiritual practices are similar to the meditation, relaxation, rhythmic breathwork, creative visualization, imagery, and awareness exercises suggested by Chandler, Holden, and Kolander (1992) as commonly used interventions in counseling and therapy to foster spiritual development through the process of sacralization (i.e., being sensitized to the spiritual). Leisure activities may also facilitate sacralization (Heintzman, 2002a). Preliminary research by Heintzman and Mannell (2003) suggested that the spiritual function of sacralization (leisure sensitizes one to the spiritual) may serve as a coping strategy to ameliorate the negative influence of time pressure on spiritual wellbeing. Higher levels of time pressure were associated with greater use of leisure for the spiritual function of sacralization that, in turn, was associated with higher levels of spiritual wellbeing. In stressful situations, leisure activities may also ground a person and divert his or her attention away from the stress and thus perform a function similar to palliative coping (Chandler et al.). Activities such as jogging, walking, tai chi, gardening, or anything that connects a person with the earth may function as grounding activities (Chandler et al.). Tai chi has been found to create the opportunity for meditation, which may lead to spiritual wellbeing and the development of inner strength and calmness that helps participants cope with times of stress and adversity (Sandlund & Norlander, 2000).

Contemplative leisure. Historically, leisure has been considered not only as an activity but also as an attitude. Pieper's (1952, pp. 40–41) well-known conceptualization of leisure as "a mental and spiritual attitude . . . a condition of the soul . . . a receptive attitude of mind, a contemplative attitude" reflects a contemplative leisure that can be traced back to Aquinas (1225–1274 CE) and Augustine (354–440 CE). In medieval monastic culture, contemplative leisure was seen as the way to avoid the stress of busyness or *negotium* (Leclercq, 1984). Contemplative leisure has been viewed as one of the steps of the spiritual journey that empowers an individual through transcendent life-giving powers to cope with the stresses of the everyday world (Ward, 1999). As contemplation and celebration of life, leisure is a restorative remedy to burnout (Doohan, 1982). In support of this view, empirical research has shown that a leisure attitude of being open and being aware has contributed to spiritual wellbeing (Heintzman, 2000), whereas for older women with HIV/AIDS, spiritual transcendence has been facilitated by the quiet of contemplative leisure (Gosselink & Myllykangas, 2007).

Leisure as space and time. Some studies suggest that participants in their leisure deliberately create a leisure space or an oasis where they can renew themselves; these leisure spaces could be a spiritual leisure space (e.g., Iwasaki, Mactavish, & MacKay, 2005). This idea of a leisure space is consistent with findings that leisure may be viewed as time and space for spiritual wellbeing (Anderegg et al., 2002; Heintzman, 2000; Schmidt & Little, 2005, 2007). In a study on the experience and role of leisure in the life of counselors and psychologists, Grafanaki et al. (2005) discovered that leisure provided opportunity for spiritual experience thereby helping participants achieve balance and integration in everyday life, and cope with the demands of their work.

Leisure as time and space has been historically associated with religious holidays and the practice of Sabbath. Recently, the importance of holidays and the Sabbath for coping with stress has been noted in both therapeutic and psychology literature. Holidays or "holy days" that remember national, religious, or personal events are special and significant times that provide a time-out from daily routines, present distractions from mental or physical problems, and let people express their inner selves (Luboshitzky & Gaber, 2001). These holidays may provide a buffer to daily stresses and help individuals fulfill their spiritual needs. As meaningful spiritual activities, holiday celebrations have four therapeutic implications. First, as a religious celebration, holidays enhance religious and spiritual expression by facilitating transcendence, which helps individuals cope with the uncertainty and conflict they face. Second, as cultural activities, holidays help people feel socially integrated into their community and society. Third, holidays can help people organize their time by facilitating time orientation through the notions of "before" and "after." Fourth, as leisure, they provide meaning, enjoyment, entertainment, and satisfaction.

Related to holidays is the growing interest in North America to rediscover models of Sabbath-keeping as a counterbalance to the stresses and fragmentation of life (Diddams, Surdyk, & Daniels, 2004). Sabbath-keeping may take different forms: (1) life segmentation, where individuals deliberately segment their lives in order to create relief from stress; (2) prescribed meaning, where individuals give positive and spiritual meaning to life segmentation; and (3) integrated Sabbath, where Sabbath Sabbath-keeping is observed as an integrated belief structure of reflection, rest, and relationship development on a daily basis.

Empirical studies are beginning to appear on the benefits of Sabbath-keeping. Based upon the assumption that the Sabbath's cyclical rhythm of activity and rest helps fulfill the human need for spiritual renewal, Earickson (2004) concluded from a qualitative study that Sabbath-keeping promoted spiritual wellbeing and psychological health. In a study of Sabbath-keeping by Protestant ministers, Lee (2003) discovered that ceasing was correlated positively with autonomy, whereas rest was correlated positively with relatedness, competence, and autonomy. Both resting and ceasing were correlated negatively with emotional exhaustion. Structural equation modeling (SEM) found that rest was the critical dimension of Sabbath-keeping (Lee, 2003). Burian (1987) investigated the relationship between stress and the Jewish Sabbath amongst Sabbath observant and nonobservant groups. The Sabbath-keeping group had significantly lower Saturday (Sabbath) stress as compared to their weekday stress and also significantly decreased Saturday stress compared to the Saturday stress level of the nonobservant group. Research has also been conducted on the influence of Sabbath-keeping upon human relationships and functioning. Boyd (1998) found individuals who were intrinsically motivated to observe the Sabbath experienced greater marital intimacy than individuals who were extrinsically motivated. Stern (2005) discovered that meaningful Sabbath ritual activities rooted in retained long-term memories play a facilitative role in enabling meaningful engagements and sustaining personhood for persons with mild to moderate dementia.

Being away. Building upon the notion of leisure as time and space, leisure provides the opportunity to get away from the everyday world, consistent with the "being away" feature of restorative environments theory. This feature of the theory suggests that a conceptually or physically different setting from one's everyday environment is conducive to restorative experiences (Kaplan, 1995). For example, Iwasaki and Bartlett's (2006a, p. 331) study of Aboriginal individuals with diabetes found that getting away or having time out was frequently identified as a means of spiritual or emotional renewal, as suggested by the following quotes: "I get away for a few days. It's good to get away to forget about everything in the city. I don't think about the awful things and try to think better afterward. . . . I go to the reserves to get away from everything. It's just very peaceful and quiet. . . ." Implicit in these quotes is a sense of getting away, physically and psychologically, from stressors and facilitating a sense of spiritual rejuvenation.

This notion of leisure providing an opportunity to get away in order to deal with the stresses in life and be spiritually renewed can also be seen in other studies. For example, studies by Ouellette and colleagues (Ouellette, Kaplan & Kaplan, 2005; Ouellette, Heintzman, & Carette, 2005) document how a monastery may function as a spiritually restorative environment for individuals who visit them as a leisure activity. Stringer and McAvoy (1992) found that for wilderness adventure participants, some of whom had disabilities, enhanced spirituality and spiritual experience were due to being in a different setting, free from usual constraints on energy and time. Thus, leisure provided the opportunity to be away, which contributed to spiritual growth and development that ultimately could help in dealing with stress. Likewise, in Fredrickson and Anderson's (1999) study of women's wilderness experience, all of the women had experienced a major life change (deterioration of personal health, major career change, death of a loved one), so the trip provided the opportunity to leave the stresses of everyday life to have an experience of spiritual rejuvenation in the wilderness environment. A participant in Sweatman and Heintzman's (2004) study of outdoor residential camp experience noted that the camp was helpful for spirituality, as it did not have the stress of the city:

> . . . lots of people and buildings in a city can be very stressful at times when there is so much of it . . . there is so much white noise in the city like the buzzing in the background like the heater or the air conditioner . . . you don't get that here. (p. 26)

Another example is from Schneider and Mannell's (2006) study of the lived experiences, including the leisure experience, of parents whose children had cancer, which found that spirituality was a key coping mechanism for these participants. One participant referred to being away to their cottage: "Our cottage is up North. . . . But when you go in there, it's just like Shangri-La you know. So that's our, that's my haven" (p. 17).

Leisure-Spiritual Connections (Resources)

Leisure-spiritual connections are spiritual resources that, along with spiritual appraisals and leisure-spiritual coping behaviors, act as mediating factors in the stress coping process. These leisure-spiritual connections take the form of connections with nature, others, and the transcendent other.

Nature. Spirituality is frequently associated with a connection to nature (Gall et al., 2005). One of the most frequently mentioned combinations of spiritual experience with leisure is the wilderness or nature experience (McDonald & Schreyer, 1991). In the previously mentioned studies on wilderness experience, it has been found that wilderness is conducive to spiritual development (Stringer & McAvoy, 1992), and that an expansiveness of landscape and a consciousness of the absolute power of nature is a source of spiritual experience (Frederickson & Anderson, 1999). Burkhardt (1994) found that Appalachian women obtained a sense of groundedness as well as strength from their nature activities such as gardening. Gardening as a leisure activity has been found to be a spiritual enabler, providing meaningfulness and stress reduction under extreme circumstances such as cancer (Unruh, Smith, & Scammell, 2000) and sustaining spiritual development and renewal in older people (Infantino, 2004-2005; Milligan, Gatrell, & Bingley, 2003). Schneider and Mannell's (2006) study of parents with children who had cancer discovered that one aspect of the parent's spiritual coping mechanism was a spiritual attachment to nature. Examples included enjoying the sunshine and trees while reading on the porch, visiting a remote cottage, enjoying the environment while driving the car, and appreciating the beauty of trees.

Others. Religious/spiritual communities can be a significant source of social support and care (Gall et al., 2005). Social support and care may be provided through religious leaders, other members of the religious or spiritual community, or the religious/spiritual community as a whole. Social support through religion and spirituality is related to a variety of health factors (Ferraro & Koch, 1994), and the absence of religious participation is associated with a number of health risk factors (Oman & Reed, 1998; Strawbridge, Shema, Cohen, & Kaplan, 2001).

Social support and care may also contribute to leisure-spiritual coping. In Fredrickson and Anderson's (1999) study of wilderness experience, where the women participants had all recently encountered a major life change such as ill health, major career change, or death of a loved one, a significant theme that contributed to spiritual meaning was group trust and emotional safety. Continuous verbal encouragement and ongoing emotional support from other group members, which led to personal bonding and emotional safety, were mentioned as a significant contribution to the more meaningful elements of the trip and to the more spiritually inspirational aspects of the trip. Similarly, in a men-only canoe trip, the openness of informal discussions and conversations led to a bonding that contributed to spiritual wellbeing (Heintzman, 2008). Therapeutic recreation from a Christian perspective, as in many other religious perspectives, encourages relationships with others through a love of one's neighbor, compassion, and self-sacrifice; social relationships provide a sense of connectedness and play a significant role in restoring wholeness (Van Andel & Heintzman, 1996).

Transcendent other. Research suggests that a connection with the transcendent, or God, has a significant role in coping with stress (Gall et al., 2005), particularly if God is viewed to be available, protective, comforting, loving, and nurturing (Heller, 1986; Johnson & Spilka, 1991). A secure attachment to God has consistently been associated with positive forms of coping and positive outcomes (Belavich & Pargament, 2002). A relationship with God may fulfill a variety of functions such as the creation of meaning; the reception of a sense of belonging, social support, and comfort; the reduction and elimination of emotional distress and fears; the provision of acceptance and inner strength; control; and empowerment (Gall et al., 2005; Gall & Cornblatt, 2002). Furthermore, a negative relationship with the transcendent other (e.g., a God perceived as punishing and withholding) may be associated with a person experiencing higher levels of stress during stressful situations (Gall et al., 2005; Gall & Cornblatt, 2002). The relationship with the transcendent other involves a complex process that may involve negative emotional states of doubt, questioning, disappointment, and spiritual struggle (Gall et al., 2005). If left unresolved, these struggles may lead to a negative influence upon wellbeing, but if resolved may lead to growth and development.

In a study on the potential of leisure to engage the human soul, Schmidt and Little (2005) observed that in leisure the participants "transcended the everyday assault of their lives":

> In their time and space the co-researchers did not just recharge the body; they recharged the soul. Wholly engaged, not just one element of the self was involved. Rather their leisure allowed them to experience the spiritual . . . to know God . . . and to intensely be aware of a power beyond the individual. In the achieved moment of leisure, the co-researchers'

experienced a transcendent realization that there is more to life than the ordinary. (p. 548)

While the participants in Schmidt and Little's study were not necessarily experiencing stress, Gosselink and Myllykangas' (2007) study of older women living with HIV/AIDS found that leisure provided spiritual transcendence that strengthened over time as their disease progressed. Most women in a leisure education program for substance abuse believed that a higher power or God provided the strength necessary to carry on with life (Rancourt, 1991a). In terms of application to therapeutic recreation practice, any focus upon transcendence would be influenced by the spiritual belief systems of those involved (Rancourt, 1991a). For example, Van Andel and Heintzman (1996) explained in detail how a relationship with God is a vital component of therapeutic recreation from a Christian perspective.

Leisure-Spiritual Meaning-Making

Research has documented that spirituality and religion perform a significant role in discovering meaning in a stressful situation (Gall et al., 2005). Situational meaning may include perceiving positive characteristics to a stressful circumstance, realizing opportunities for positive benefits or change from the stressful situation, or recognizing that the stressful circumstance is less vital to one's life than originally thought (Park & Folkman, 1997; Park, Folkman, & Bostrom, 2001). A stressful situation can be reconsidered as an opportunity to obtain new ideas about life (Jensen, Bäck-Pettersson, & Segesten, 2000) and to experience benefits (Pargament, 1997).

In their studies on marginal groups, Iwasaki and colleagues have examined the role of leisure as a contributor to coping with stress (Iwasaki et al., 2006). They found that using active leisure to cope with stress included both spiritual activities and spiritual meanings. That is, spiritual activities (e.g., spiritual reading) were pursued in leisure to cope with stress, and active leisure also provided the opportunity to obtain spiritual meaning. For example, in a study of gays and lesbians, Iwasaki and Ristock (2004) found leisure to be a significant context to pursue spirituality and thus deal with stress. One lesbian explained that her leisure activity of pottery was meditative. Aboriginals have been found to engage in culturally relevant leisure to facilitate empowerment and spiritual coping when confronted by racism and other forms of stress (Iwasaki, et al., 2006). In a study of Aboriginals with diabetes, many participants mentioned the role of culturally appropriate leisure in bringing about spiritual rejuvenation that had cultural meanings: "regardless of the type of activities described from escaping the city, going to reserves, and going to camping or the lake, to walking, reading, and sewing, one key stress-coping mechanism of leisure relevant to participants seemed to involve the facilitation of spiritual or psychological renewal in a culturally meaningful way" (Iwasaki & Bartlett, 2006a, p. 332). Iwasaki and Bartlett (2006b) noted that the realization and utilization of spiritual strengths through stress-coping had transformative potential. For example, one woman mentioned that a massage was not only stress-relieving, but facilitated positive physical, emotional, and spiritual feelings. She went on to mention that it provided an opportunity to go within her self, therefore having the potential to be transformative. This transformative process appears to be associated with the Aboriginal people's cultural and spiritual orientations.

Another illustration of meaning-making through leisure-spiritual coping is provided by a study of the leisure experiences of older U.S. women who were living with HIV/AIDS (Gosselink & Myllykangas, 2007). The women in the study were disenfranchised and encountered economic, social, and structural constraints. Following HIV/AIDS diagnosis, the meaning of leisure was transformed for all the women in the study. As their disease progressed, the women experienced spiritual transcendence and developed a spiritual view of leisure, which became a metaphor for meaning in life. For some, church took on new meaning in terms of prayer, connecting with self and God or a higher power, and a place of acceptance of their disease. For others, spirituality meant a stronger spiritual connection with self, nature, and others. At the same time, leisure advanced the women's wellbeing through therapeutic benefits, such as resilience in transcending systemic barriers they faced as a result of being female, over 50, and HIV/AIDS infected. As the disease progressed, the women's transcendence matured, and their resolve to overcome obstacles increased. The newfound spirituality of all the women "continued to grow and provide meaning such that they viewed nature, animals, friends, family and advocacy as leisure vehicles through which they could express their spirituality" (Gosselink & Myllykangas, p. 16).

Interrelationships among Model Components

Similar to the Gall et al. (2005) spiritual framework of coping, the leisure-spiritual coping model is viewed as process-oriented, transactional, dynamic, and relational. Spirituality can function and involve interrelated factors/components including person factors, spiritual appraisals, leisure-spiritual coping behavior, leisure-spiritual connections (resources), and leisure-spiritual meaning-making. Spiritual person factors in this model function as a contextual framework that guides a person in her or his interpretation, understanding, and response to stressful experiences. Spiritual appraisals, leisure-spiritual coping behaviors, and leisure-spiritual connections are assumed to function as mediating factors in the stress coping process. Spiritual appraisals are early attempts to make sense of a stressor according to a person's spiritual beliefs. These initial attempts to make sense of the stressor may help a person diminish early levels of stress sufficiently to participate in leisure-spiritual coping behaviors. Leisure-spiritual coping behaviors are used to respond to either the stressor or associated emotional reactions. Leisure-spiritual connections act as resources that assist with coping. Together, leisure-spiritual coping behaviors, along with leisure-spiritual connections, can then lead to meaning making and consequently to wellbeing. Although the leisure-spiritual model is, to some extent, hierarchical in that some components affect each other in a linear sequence, it is recursive like the transactional model. For example, leisure-spiritual coping can lead to leisure-spiritual meaning-making; however, the effects of meaning-making may feedback to the spiritual appraisal component and thus indirectly to leisure-spiritual coping as a person tries to adapt to a stressful situation (see Figure 1).

Case Study

The following case study is based on the personal experience of the author. While this case study does not involve a therapeutic recreation service, a therapeutic recreation specialist, or a leisure services practitioner, it does illustrate the components of the leisure-spiritual coping model. In a similar situation, a therapeutic recreation specialist could facilitate a client to engage in leisure-spiritual behaviors and to develop leisure-spiritual coping connections.

Fourteen years ago, the author was diagnosed with cancer, which was followed by surgery to remove a cancerous tumor and subsequently chemotherapy to eradicate the cancer that had spread elsewhere. At the time of diagnosis, the author was experiencing multiple forms of stress. As executive director of an understaffed camp and conference center, he was overworked and had no regular or consistent time off work. He had been experiencing overwork and burnout for a number of years. For the previous few years, he had also been taking care of the affairs of an uncle with Alzheimer's disease who lived 100 miles away. Although this uncle died five months prior to the cancer diagnosis, the author was now executor of the uncle's estate. He also had some responsibilities toward his father, who was in his late 80s and lived alone in the family home 60 miles away. The author had been primary caregiver to his mother, who had died six years earlier of cancer.

In regards to the *attribution* stage of *spiritual appraisal*, the author was initially quite shocked and perplexed, as he had been very healthy all his life. *Primary spiritual appraisal* involved the realization that death might be a reality in the near future. In terms of *secondary spiritual appraisal*, the author realized changes in his lifestyle were necessary and that spiritual resources were essential to bring about these changes. In terms of person factors, the author's beliefs (*religious denomination and doctrine*) were rooted in Christian spiritual faith, which provided the contextual framework for understanding and responding to this stress. The author had been brought up in a Christian home, and during his teenage years this faith became personalized into a faith of his own (*intrinsic religious orientation*).

From the time of diagnosis until the completion of chemotherapy, the author drastically cut his hours of work to a normal work week. This allowed more time than usual for spiritual practices of a traditional nature, but also *leisure-spiritual coping behaviors*. Although lacking the usual amount of energy, the author jogged two miles each day during chemotherapy, which acted as a *grounding* activity. Reduced working time led to opportunities to focus on spirituality through *sacralization* and *contemplation*. A specific example was participation in a weekend retreat on life changes at a spiritual retreat center just prior to his surgery, which also offered the opportunity to *be away* to another setting. In terms of *leisure as space and time,* although the author strongly believed in the concept of *Sabbath* and had practiced it for most of his life, he had been unable to do so for the previous four years due to the nature of his work. During the period of cancer, he returned to Sabbath keeping by abstaining from work on Sundays. Also during this time, the author experienced *being away* from his usual work setting of the remote camp and conference center to his father's home in an urban area. While this change of environment related mainly to work and living situation, it also affected the context for leisure activities and provided for leisure opportunities that were not available in the remote setting.

In regards to *leisure-spiritual connections,* although opportunities for *connection with nature* were less accessible in the urban environment, the author, when possible, continued to participate in nature-based recreation, which usually provided opportunities for meditation, prayer, and reflection that strengthened the *connection with the transcendent other* (God) and thereby played a significant role in coping with this situation. *Connections with others*, which were now easier to pursue due to the urban setting, were also enhanced during this time. Spiritual friendships that were a source of inspiration and comfort were renewed and strengthened. Some of the opportunities for connections with others were within the leisure context. A particular highlight was a weekly Saturday morning hockey game with others from the same faith community.

All the components of the leisure-spiritual model had an influence upon *meaning-making*, which led to a reappraisal of beliefs and attitudes, and the author's ability to cope. In fact, the author sometimes refers to this period in his life as a holiday, as his stress level was drastically reduced from previous levels. During this time, the author reevaluated the priorities in his life – developing connections with God and with others took on greater value while continuing in the job he held was questioned. He decided to resign from the position he held with no definite next step. Meaning-making also fed back to spiritual appraisal: while others suggested possible reasons for the cancer, he accepted it as a mystery, and to some extent a gift, for which only God knew the reason why it occurred.

Conclusion

Spirituality is increasingly seen as a significant component of holistic health and wellbeing. Similarly, there has been a tremendous increase in research on the role of spirituality in coping with stress. Recent research suggests that leisure may be a fruitful context for spiritual coping to help alleviate, overcome, and transcend many of the stresses and challenges that people face. The leisure-spiritual coping model presented in this paper is an attempt to capture and organize the complexity of the factors involved in leisure-spiritual coping. Throughout the paper, implications and applications have been made to therapeutic recreation and other leisure services. While this model is tentative, it may be used as a guide by therapeutic recreation and leisure service practitioners to integrate specific religious/spiritual worldviews, leisure-spiritual coping practices, and leisure-spiritual coping resources in the planning, delivery, and evaluation of programs when working with people who experience a variety of stressors and life challenges. As spirituality is an integrative, as well as an elementalistic, dimension of holistic wellness, therapeutic recreation services that promote leisure-spiritual coping can promote mental health through coping with, adapting to, and transcending life challenges.

The model also has potential to be applied and adapted to a wide variety of stressors experienced by people from different cultural and faith backgrounds. Unlike some models of spiritual coping that are based on specific religions (Nooney & Woodrum, 2002; Stolley, Buckwater, & Koenig, 1999), the leisure-spiritual coping model, like the Gall et al. (2005) spiritual framework of coping, is based on a broad concept of spirituality and thus can be adapted to different faith and cultural traditions. In fact, the framework of Gall et al. was reviewed by chaplains and/or spiritual care workers from Muslim, Jewish, Christian, and Hindu faith perspectives, and each of them found the framework applicable to their faith tradition, although the relative importance of each of the components and aspects of the framework varied amongst the faith traditions. Similarly, the leisure-spiritual coping model may need to be modified or adapted according to one's faith or spiritual tradition. The examples from a variety of spiritual traditions, such as Aboriginal, Christian, and New Age that have been included in the description of the model illustrate the model's relevance to a range of different traditions. Consistent with the suggestions of Dieser and Peregoy (1999) concerning multicultural sensitivity, the model is not premised upon a specific spiritual tradition, but can be adapted to the therapeutic recreation client's tradition and worldview. For example, when describing the religious denomination and doctrine component of person factors, the model does not assume one particular belief system, but introduces different TR worldviews. Likewise, under the component of spiritual appraisal, the model suggests the use of spiritual appraisal questions in TR needs assessments that are sensitive to the client's cultural and spiritual tradition.

The model can also serve as an initial roadmap or framework for researchers to guide hypothesis development and to provide a framework for the investigation of specific pathways between specific person factors, leisure-spiritual coping practices, leisure-spiritual coping resources, and meaning-making. This leisure-spiritual coping model integrates theory and research on leisure to the spiritual framework of coping (Gall et al., 2005); however, some elements of the Gall et al. framework (e.g., spiritual problem-solving, coping styles) are not developed in this leisure-spiritual coping model simply because leisure literature does not exist on how leisure relates to these elements of spiritual coping. Thus, future research is needed not only to test the pathways in the model, but also to complete and fill in missing parts of the model.

References

Allport, G.W. (1961). *Pattern and growth in personality*. New York: Holt, Rinehart & Winston.

Anderegg, M., Cini, F., Godula, M., MacKenzie, S.N., Pearson, D., & Grafanaki. S. (2002). *"When heaven and earth meet: A qualitative study on the experience of leisure and spirituality among mental health professionals*. Ottawa, ON: St. Paul University.

Belavich, T.G., & Pargament, K.I. (2002). The role of attachment in predicting spiritual coping with a loved one in surgery. *Journal of Adult Development* 9(1), 13–29.

Bellamy, C.D., Jarrett, N. C., Mowbray, O., MacFarlane, P., Mowbray, C.T., & Holter, M.C. (2007). Relevance of spirituality for people with mental illness attending consumer-centered services. *Psychiatric Rehabilitation Journal* 30(4), 287–294.

Boyd, J.K. (1998). *An analysis of the relationship between Sabbath meaning and leisure, marital intimacy and marital satisfaction among Seventh-day Adventists*. Unpublished Ph.D. thesis, Fuller Theological Seminary, Pasadena, CA.

Burian, A.M. (1987). *The relationship between the Jewish Sabbath and stress as a function of personality type*. Unpublished Ph.D. thesis, Hofstra University, New York.

Burkhardt, M.A. (1994). Becoming and connecting: Elements of spirituality for women. *Holistic Nursing Practice* 8(4), 12–21.

Carter, M.C., Van Andel, G.E., & Robb, G.M. (2003). *Therapeutic recreation: A practical approach* (3rd ed.). Prospect Heights, IL: Waveland Press.

Chandler, C.K., Holden, J.M., & Kolander, C.A. (1992). Counseling for spiritual wellness: Theory and practice. *Journal of Counseling and Development* 71, 168–175.

Chapman, L.S. (1987). Developing a useful perspective on spiritual health: Love, joy, peace and fulfillment. *American Journal of Health Promotion* 2, 12–17.

Coyle, C.P. (1998). Integrating service delivery and outcomes: A practice model for the future? *Therapeutic Recreation Journal* 32(3), 194–201.

Diddams, M., Surdyk, L.K, & Daniels, D. (2004). Rediscovering models of Sabbath keeping: Implications for psychological well-being. *Journal of Psychology and Theology* 32(1), 3–11.

Dieser, R.B. (2003). Understanding cross-ethnic interactions when using therapeutic recreation practice models. *Therapeutic Recreation Journal* 37(2), 175–189.

Dieser, R.B., & Peregoy, J.J. (1999). A multicultural critique of three therapeutic recreation service models. *Annual in Therapeutic Recreation* 8, 56–69.

Doohan, H. (1982). Burnout: A critical issue for the 1980s. *Journal of Religion and Health* 21(4), 352–358.

Dyson, J., Cobb, M., & Forman, D. (1997). The meaning of spirituality: A literature review. *Journal of Advanced Nursing* 26, 1183–1188.

Earickson, J.M. (2004). *The religious practice of the Sabbath: A framework for psychological health and spiritual well-being.* Unpublished Ph.D. thesis, Alliant International University, San Diego, CA.

Ferraro, K.F., & Koch, J.R. (1994). Religion and health among Black and White adults: Examining social support and consolation. *Journal for the Scientific Study of Religion* 33, 362–375.

Folkman, S. (1997). Positive psychological states and coping with severe stress. *Social Science and Medicine* 45, 1207–1221.

Fox, R.J. (1997). Women, nature and spirituality: A qualitative study exploring women's wilderness experience. In D. Rowe & P. Brown (Eds.), *Proceedings, ANZALS conference 1997* (pp. 59–64). Newcastle, NSW: Australian and New Zealand Association for Leisure Studies, and the Department of Leisure and Tourism Studies, The University of Newcastle.

Fredrickson, L.M., & Anderson, D.H. (1999). A qualitative exploration of the wilderness experience as a source of spiritual inspiration. *Journal of Environmental Psychology* 19, 21–39.

Gall, T.L. (2003). Religious and spiritual attributions in older adults' adjustment to illness. *Journal of Psychology and Christianity* 22(3), 210–222.

Gall, T.L., Charbonneau, C., Clarke, N.H., Grant, K., Joseph, A., & Shouldice, L. (2005). Understanding the nature and role of spirituality in relation to coping and health: A conceptual framework. *Canadian Psychology/Psychologie canadienne* 46(2), 88–104.

Gall, T.L., & Cornblat, M.W. (2002). Breast cancer survivors give voice: A qualitative analysis of spiritual factors in long-term adjustment. *Psycho-Oncology* 11, 524–535.

Gosselink, C.A., & Myllykangas, S.A. (2007). The leisure experiences of older U.S. women living with HIV/AIDS. *Health Care for Women International* 28, 3–20.

Grafanaki, S., Pearson, D., Cini, F., Godula, B., McKenzie, B., Nason, S., & Anderegg, M. (2005). Sources of renewal: A qualitative study of the experience and role of leisure in the life of counselors and psychologists. *Counselling Psychology Quarterly* 18(1), 31–40.

Harrison, M., Koenig, H.G., Hays, J., Eme-Akwari, A., & Pargament, K.I. (2001). The epidemiology of religious coping: A review of recent literature. *International Review of Psychiatry* 13(2), 86–93.

Heintzman, P. (1997). Putting some spirit into recreation services for people with disabilities. *Journal of Leisurability* 24(2), 22–30.

Heintzman, P. (2000). Leisure and spiritual well-being relationships: A qualitative study. *Society and Leisure* 23(1), 41–69.

Heintzman, P. (2002a). A conceptual model of leisure and spiritual well-being. *Journal of Park and Recreation Administration* 20(4), 147–169.

Heintzman, P. (2008). Men's wilderness experience and spirituality: Further explorations. In C. LeBlanc & C. Vogt (Eds.), *Proceedings of the 2007 Northeastern Recreation Research Symposium* (pp. 55–59) (Gen. Tech. Rep. NRS-P-23). Newton Square, PA: U.S. Department of Agriculture, Forest Services, Northern Research Station.

Heintzman, P., & Mannell, R. (2003). Spiritual functions of leisure and spiritual well-being: Coping with time pressure. *Leisure Sciences* 25, 207–230.

Heller, D. (1986). *The children's God*. Chicago: University Press.

Hergenhahn, B., & Olson, M. (1999). *An introduction to theories of personality* (5th ed.). Upper Saddle River, NJ: Prentice Hall.

Howe-Murphy, R., & Murphy, J. (1987). An exploration of the New Age consciousness paradigm in therapeutic recreation. In C. Sylvester, J. Hemingway, R. Howe-Murphy, K. Mobily, & P. Shank (Eds.), *Philosophy of therapeutic recreation: Ideas and issues* (pp. 41–54). Arlington, VA: National Recreation and Park Association.

Idler, E. (1999). Organizational religiousness. In Fetzer Institute/National Institute on Ageing Working Group, *Multidimensional measurement of religiousness/spirituality for use in health research* (pp. 75–79). Kalamazoo, MI: Fetzer Institute.

Infantino, M. (2005). Gardening: A strategy for health promotion in older women. *Journal of the New York State Nurses Association* 35(2), 10–17.

Iwasaki, Y. (2007). Leisure and quality of life in an international and multicultural context: What are major pathways linking leisure to quality of life? *Social Indicators Research* 82, 233–264.

Iwasaki, Y., & Bartlett, J. (2006a). Culturally meaningful leisure as a way of coping with stress among Aboriginal individuals with diabetes. *Journal of Leisure Research* 38(3), 321–338.

Iwasaki, Y., & Bartlett, J. (2006b). Stress-coping among Aboriginal individuals with diabetes in an urban Canadian city: From woundedness to resilience. *Journal of Aboriginal Health* 3(1), 15–25.

Iwasaki, Y., Bartlett, J., MacKay, K., Mactavish, J., & Ristock, J. (2005). Social exclusion and resilience as frameworks of stress and coping among selected non-dominant groups. *International Journal of Mental Health Promotion* 7(3), 4–17.

Iwasaki, Y., Bartlett, J., & O'Neil, J. (2005). Coping with stress among Aboriginal women and men with diabetes in Winnipeg, Manitoba. *Social Science and Medicine* 60, 977–988.

Iwasaki, Y., & Butcher J. (2004). Common stress-coping methods shared by older women and men with arthritis. *International Journal of Psychosocial Rehabilitation* 8, 179–208.

Iwasaki, Y., MacKay, K.J., Mactavish, J.B., Ristock, J., & Bartlett, J. (2006). Voices from the margins: Stress, active living, and leisure as a contributor to coping with stress. *Leisure Sciences* 28, 163–180.

Iwasaki, Y., Mactavish, J., & MacKay, K. (2005). Building on strengths and resilience: Leisure as a stress survival strategy. *British Journal of Guidance and Counselling* 33(1), 81–100.

Iwasaki, Y., & Mannell, R.C. (2000). Hierarchical dimensions of leisure stress coping. *Leisure Sciences* 22, 163–181.

Iwasaki, Y., & Ristock, J. (2004). Coping with stress among gays and lesbians: Implications for human development over the lifespan. *World Leisure Journal* 46(2), 26–37.

Iwasaki, Y., & Schneider, I.E. (2003). Leisure, stress, and coping: An evolving area of inquiry. *Leisure Sciences* 25, 107–113.

Jensen, K.P., Bäck-Pettersson, S., & Segesten, K. (2000). The meaning of "not giving in": Lived experiences among women with breast cancer. *Cancer Nursing* 23(1), 6–11.

Johnson, S.C., & Spilka, B. (1991). Coping with breast cancer: The role of clergy and faith. *Journal of Religion and Health* 30(1), 21–33.

Kaplan, S. (1995). The restorative benefits of nature: Toward an integrative framework. *Journal of Environmental Psychology* 15, 169–182.

Larson, D.B., Swyers, J.P., & McCullough, M.E. (1998). *Scientific research on spirituality and health: A consensus report.* Rockville, MD: National Institute for Health Care Research.

Leclercq, J. (1984). Otium monasticum as a context for artistic creativity. In T. G. Verdun (Ed.), *Monasticism and the arts* (pp. 63–69). Syracuse, NY: Syracuse University Press.

Lee, T. (2003). *Sabbath-keeping by Protestant ministers: An avenue of meeting the basic psychological needs and mitigating professional burnout.* Unpublished Ph.D. thesis, Seattle Pacific University, Seattle, WA.

Levin, J. (1999). Private religious practices. In Fetzer Institute/National Institute on Ageing Working Group. *Multidimensional measurement of religiousness/ spirituality for use in health research* (pp. 39–42). Kalamazoo, MI: Fetzer Institute.

Luboshitzky, D., & Gaber, L.B. (2001). Holidays and celebrations as spiritual occupation. *Australian Occupational Therapy Journal* 48, 66–74.

Mactavish, J., & Iwasaki, Y. (2005). Exploring perspectives of individuals with disabilities on stress-coping. *Journal of Rehabilitation* 71(1), 20–31.

Maltby, J., Lewis, C., & Day, L. (1999). Religious orientation and psychological well-being: The role of the frequency of personal prayer. *British Journal of Health Psychology* 4(4), 363–378.

McDonald, D., & McAvoy, L. (1997). Native Americans and leisure: State of the research and future directions. *Journal of Leisure Research* 29(2), 145–166.

McDonald, B.L., & Schreyer, R. (1991). Spiritual benefits of leisure participation and leisure settings. In B.L. Driver, P.J. Brown, & G.L. Peterson (Eds.), *Benefits of leisure* (pp. 179–194). State College, PA: Venture.

Milligan, C., Gatrell, A., & Bingley, A. (2004). Cultivating health: Therapeutic landscapes and older people in northern England. *Social Science & Medicine* 58(9), 1781–1793.

Miner, M., & McKnight, J. (1999). Religious attributions: Situational factors and effects on coping. *Journal of the Scientific Study of Religion* 38(2), 287–308.

Nooney, J., & Woodrum, E. (2002). Religious coping and church-based support as predictors of mental health: Testing a conceptual model. *Journal for the Scientific Study of Religion* 41(2), 359–368.

Olszewski, M.E. (1995). The effect of religious coping on depression and anxiety in adolescence (Doctoral dissertation, Oregon State University, 1995). *Dissertation Abstracts International* 55(9-B), 4144.

Oman, D., & Reed, D. (1998). Religion and mortality among the community-dwelling elderly. *American Journal of Public Health* 88(10), 1469–1475.

Ouellette, P., Heintzman, P., & Carette, R. (2005). Les motivations et les effets d'une retraite faite par des personnes âgées dans un monastère bénédictin. In T. Delamere, C. Randall, & D. Robinson (Eds.), *The two solitudes: Isolation or impact?* Book of Abstracts from the Eleventh Canadian Congress on Leisure Research (pp. 448–453). Nanaimo, BC: Department of Recreation and Tourism Management, Malaspina University-College.

Ouellette, P., Kaplan, R., & Kaplan, S. (2005). The monastery as a restorative environment. *Journal of Environmental Psychology* 25(2), 178–188.

Pargament, K.I. (1997). *The psychology of religion and coping*. New York: Guildford Press.

Pargament, K.I., Ensing, D.S., Falgout, K., Olsen, H., Reilly, B., Van Haitsma, K., et al. (1990). God help me (I): Religious coping efforts as predictors of the outcomes of significant negative life events. *American Journal of Community Psychology* 18, 793–824.

Pargament, K.I., & Hahn, J. (1986). God and the just world: Causal and coping attributions to God in health situations. *Journal for the Scientific Study of Religion* 25(2), 193–207.

Pargament, K.I., Olsen, H., Reilly, B., Falgout, K., Ensing, D., & Van Haitsma, K. (1992). God help me (II): The relationship of religious orientations to religious coping with negative life events. *Journal for the Scientific Study of Religion* 31, 504–513.

Park, C.L., & Cohen, L. (1993). Religious and non-religious coping with the death of a friend. *Cognitive Therapy and Research* 17(6), 561–577.

Park, C.L, Cohen, L.H., & Herb, L. (1990). Intrinsic religiousness and religious coping as life stress moderators for Catholics versus Protestants. *Journal of Personality and Social Psychology* 59(3), 562–574.

Park, C.L., & Folkman, S. (1997). Meaning in the context of stress and coping. *Review of General Psychology* 1(2), 115–144.

Park, C.L., Folkman, S., & Bostrom, A. (2001). Appraisals of controllability and coping in caregivers and HIV+ men: Testing the goodness-of-fit hypothesis. *Journal of Consulting and Clinical Psychology* 69(3), 481–488.

Parker, V.B., & Carmack, R.W. (1998). A critique of Van Andel's TR service delivery and TR outcome model. *Therapeutic Recreation Journal* 32(3), 202–206.

Parry, D.C. (2007). There is life after breast cancer: Nine vignettes exploring dragon boat racing for breast cancer survivors. *Leisure Sciences* 29(1), 53–69.

Parry, D.C. (2009). Dragon boat racing for breast cancer survivors: Leisure as a context for spiritual outcomes. *Leisure/Loisir* 33(1), 317–340.

Perkins, L.K., & Giese, M.L. (1994). Cherokee Nation youth fitness camp. *Journal of Physical Education, Recreation & Dance* 65(2), 60–62.

Pieper, J. (1952). *Leisure: The basis of culture* (A. Dru, Trans.). New York: Pantheon Books (1963, Random House).

Rancourt, A.M. (1991a). A comprehensive leisure education program with women who abuse substances: Conceptual and preliminary aspects. *Society and Leisure* 14(1), 151–169.

Rancourt, A.M. (1991b). An exploration of the relationships among substance abuse, recreation and leisure for women who abuse substances. *Therapeutic Recreation Journal* 25(3), 9–18.

Renfrey, G.S., & Dionne, R.R. (2001) Health psychology and the Native North American client. In S.S. Kazarian & D.R. Evans (Eds.), *Handbook of cultural health psychology* (pp. 343–387). San Diego, CA: Academic Press.

Sandlund, E.S., & Norlander, T. (2000). The effects of Tai Chi Chuan relaxation and exercise on stress responses and well-being: An overview of research. *International Journal of Stress Management* 7, 139–149.

Schmidt, C., & Little, D. (2005). The spiritual nature of time and space for self: The potential of leisure to engage the human soul. In T. Delamere, C. Randall, & D. Robinson (Eds.), *The two solitudes: Isolation or impact?* Book of Abstracts from the Eleventh Canadian Congress on Leisure Research (pp. 546–549). Nanaimo, BC: Department of Recreation and Tourism Management, Malaspina University-College.

Schmidt, C., & Little, D.E. (2007). Qualitative insights into leisure as a spiritual experience. *Journal of Leisure Research* 39(2), 222–247.

Schneider, M.A., & Mannell, R.C. (2006). Beacon in the storm: An exploration of the spirituality and faith of parents whose children have cancer. *Issues in Comprehensive Pediatric Nursing* 29, 3–24.

Shortz, J.L., & Worthington, E.L. (1994). Young adults' recall of religiosity, attributions, and coping in parental divorce. *Journal for the Scientific Study of Religion* 33, 172–179.

Spilka, B., Shaver, P., & Kirkpatrick, L.A. (1985). A general attribution theory for the psychology of religion. *Journal for the Scientific Study of Religion* 24, 1–20.

Stern, B. (2005). *A phenomenological approach towards understanding the nature and meaning of engagement in religious ritual activity: Perspectives from persons with dementia and their caregivers.* Unpublished M.Sc. thesis, University of Toronto.

Stolley, J.M., Buckwater, K.C., & Koenig, H.G. (1999). Prayer and religious coping for caregivers of persons with Alzheimer's disease and related disorders. *American Journal of Alzheimer's Disease* 14(3), 181–191.

Strawbridge, W., Shema, S., Cohen, R., & Kaplan, G. (2001). Religious attendance increases survival by improving and maintaining good health behaviors, mental health, and social relationships. *Annals of Behavioral Medicine* 23, 68–74.

Stringer, L.A., & McAvoy, L.H. (1992). The need for something different: Spirituality and the wilderness adventure. *The Journal of Experiential Education* 15(1), 13–21.

Sweatman, M., & Heintzman, P. (2004). The perceived impact of outdoor residential camp experience on the spirituality of youth. *World Leisure Journal* 46(1), 23–31.

Unruh, A.M., & Elvin, N. (2004). In the eye of the dragon: Women's experience of breast cancer, and the occupation of dragon boat racing. *Canadian Journal of Occupational Therapy* 71(3), 138–149.

Unruh, A.M., Smith, N., & Scammell, C. (2000). The occupation of gardening in life-threatening illness: A qualitative pilot study. *Canadian Journal of Occupational Therapy* 67(1), 70–77.

Van Andel, G.E. (1998). TR service delivery and TR outcome models. *Therapeutic Recreation Journal* 32(3), 180–193.

Van Andel, G., & Heintzman, P. (1996). Christian spirituality and therapeutic recreation. In C. Sylvester (Ed.), *Philosophy of therapeutic recreation: Ideas and issues* (Vol. II, pp. 71–85). Arlington, VA: National Recreation and Park Association.

Waldram, J.B. (1997). *The way of the pipe: Aboriginal spirituality and symbolic healing in Canadian prisons.* Peterborough, ON: Broadview Press.

Walters, K.L., & Simoni, J.M. (2002). Reconceptualizing Native women's health: An "indigenist" stress-coping model. *American Journal of Public Health* 92, 520–524.

Ward, V.E. (1999). Leisure: Spiritual well-being and personal power. *Spiritual Life* 45, 231–236.

Section Five

WELLNESS, SPIRITUALITY, AND HEALTH

The connection between spirituality and health has a long anecdotal history, but the empirical nature of these relationships only began to be confirmed in the latter part of the twentieth century (Cousins, 1989; Dossey, 1993; Ellison & Smith, 1991; Larson & Larson, 1992; McDonald & Schreyer, 1991). These findings have provided the basis for additional research by Christian scholars who presented the papers included in section five of this volume.

In the first chapter of this section, Paul Heintzman describes the relationship between holistic leisure and spiritual health. He defines holistic leisure as a combination of the quantitative (means to an end) and qualitative (end in itself) dimensions of leisure. When viewed from a Christian perspective, leisure becomes integral to spiritual health. Thus, with Doohan (1990), he proposes that those intent on Christian growth must actively and deliberately commit themselves to intensifying a leisure lifestyle (p. 36). In the final part of the paper, Heintzman develops a model that identifies the nature of these interactions that contribute to spiritual health.

In Chapter 25, Marcia Carter uses the flow state (intensely absorbing experiences where the challenge of an activity matches the skill level of the individual so that the person loses track of both time and awareness of self) to explore how leisure and spiritual wellbeing can be integrated. She explains that a Christian acts to move toward an optimal quality of life through spiritual and leisure behaviors that are proactive, positive, and personal. Thus she concludes that both spirituality and leisure are dynamic and incorporate actions of total involvement that are comparable to the flow state.

In Chapter 26, Tom Peace proposes that canoeing is a leisure activity that contributes to his spiritual growth. For him, paddling and portaging the canoe transport him to a spiritual place where he can leave a life filled with occupations and pre-occupations and enter into what Pieper (1952) describes as "an attitude of the mind, a condition of the soul . . . the capacity for steeping oneself in the whole of creation" (pp. 40–41). As such, the relationship of leisure experiences and spirituality are a mystery, but nevertheless tangible elements of a rich, fulfilling life.

Bob Weathers explains in Chapter 27 on love-centered wellness that God calls us to do one thing: to love. He notes that in 1 Corinthians 13: 1–3 we are reminded that without love we "gain nothing." Weathers goes on to show that scripture concludes that as we express our love to God, to others, and to ourselves, we are rewarded with joy, which he identifies as a hallmark of wellness.

According to Ted Comden in Chapter 28, burnout is a common problem among dedicated teachers and coaches. He identifies risk factors that contribute to burnout and proposes strategies that may be used to mitigate it. The key resource he suggests is nurturing a relationship with Jesus Christ and practicing biblical principles including forgiveness, confession and/or release of negative or hostile feelings, and caring for yourself.

The last chapter in this section, authored by John Byl, continues this concern for unhealthy life patterns. Byl uses his own experience as a teacher and coach to show what changes he had to make to combat the effects of stress and overwork. He determined that he needed to become spiritually well by submitting himself to the work of the Holy Spirit. To train our physical heart, he says, we need to work it. To train our spirit, we need to be completely vulnerable to God working in us. As a result, we will enjoy a life of spiritual wellness that produces spiritual fruit such as love, joy, peace, and self-control.

Glen Van Andel

References

Cousins, N. (1989). *Head first: The biology of hope and the healing power of the human spirit.* New York: Penguin Books.

Doohan, L. (1990). *Leisure: A spiritual need.* Notre Dame, IN: Ave Maria Press.

Dossey, L. (1993). *Healing words: The power of prayer.* San Francisco: Harper & Rowe.

Ellison, C.W., & Smith, J. (1991). Toward an integrative measure of health and well-being. *Journal of Psychology and Theology* 19(1), 35–48.

Larson, D.B., & Larson, S.S. (1992). *The forgotten factor in physical and mental health: What does the research show?* Rockville, MD: National Institute for Health Care Research.

McDonald, B.L., & Schreyer, R. (1991). Spiritual benefits of leisure participation and leisure settings. In B.L. Driver, P.J. Brown, & G.L. Peterson (Eds.), *Benefits of Leisure* (pp. 179–194). State College, PA: Venture.

Pieper, J. (1952). *Leisure: The basis of culture* (A. Dru, Trans.). New York: Pantheon Books (1963, Random House).

Chapter 24
HOLISTIC LEISURE AND SPIRITUAL HEALTH: A MODEL

Paul Heintzman

At all stages in spiritual growth, leisure is essentially an attitude to life and hence can be present in very active people at moments of deep involvement. However, periods are necessary when leisure is lived more intensely; such times facilitate a leisured approach to activity in periods of involvement. Persons intent upon Christian growth must actively and deliberately commit themselves to an intensification of leisure in life. (Doohan, 1990, p. 36)

We have a leisurely approach to life which must be nourished by times of intensified leisure. The latter will include, among other things, play, friendship, sharing, an absence of oppression in favor of a happy and cheerful affirmation of oneself, a feeling of at-homeness in the world, and a capacity to steep oneself in the beauty of the universe. It will demand a form of silence and inward calm leading to a receptive attitude of mind above all; it will be a varied celebration of life – men's and women's looking upon creation and seeing that it is good. (Doohan, 1981, pp. 165–166)

The above quotations reflect a holistic understanding of leisure, from a Christian perspective, in that they bring together both a qualitative conceptualization of leisure as an end (leisure as an attitude to life) and quantitative conceptualizations of leisure as time and activity (e.g., times of intensified leisure, play). Furthermore, these quotations suggest a relationship between leisure and Christian spirituality wherein leisure has the potential to facilitate Christian spiritual growth. The purpose of this paper is to integrate a holistic understanding of leisure, from a Christian perspective, with a model of leisure and spiritual health. The paper will begin with an explanation of holistic leisure from a Christian perspective and then move on to outline a model of leisure style and spiritual wellbeing relationships.

Revised version of paper presented at the 1997 conference.

Holistic Leisure

Most traditional concepts of leisure may be placed into two broad categories. The quantitative category includes the free time and activity definitions of leisure. The second category, a qualitative one, views leisure as a state of being and includes the classical view of leisure. The former category includes behavioral and temporal definitions, while the latter category includes attitudinal and existential definitions. The holistic concept of leisure encompasses both categories of definitions (Murphy, 1974) and also unites two previously opposed traditions of leisure: leisure as an end or as a means, as being or as doing, and as a qualitative concept or as a quantitative concept.

In the classical tradition, leisure is defined as a spiritual and mental attitude, as a style of life and a state of being. For example, Kraus (1990) defined the classical state of being concept of leisure as "a spiritual and mental attitude, a state of inward calm, contemplation, serenity and openness" (p. 49). This understanding of leisure was first expressed by Aristotle and other Greek aristocrats, but was Christianized by Augustine and Aquinas, and also adapted in the medieval monastic practice of *otium*. The classic Christian expression of this spiritual understanding of leisure is stated by Josef Pieper (1952), a Roman Catholic philosopher and theologian, in his book *Leisure: The Basis of Culture*: "Leisure . . . is a mental and spiritual attitude . . . a condition of the soul . . . a receptive attitude of mind, a contemplative attitude, and it is not only the occasion but also the capacity for steeping oneself in the world of creation" (pp. 40, 41). More recently, Leonard Doohan (1990), drawing upon scripture and the teaching of mystics such as John of the Cross and Teresa of Avila, wrote that "Leisure is a mental and spiritual attitude, a condition of mind and soul . . . an attitude to life that includes rest and creative self-development, but it also touches that very personal inner spirit of each individual, and it must be discovered as such" (pp. 26, 31). The strength of the classical view of leisure is its emphasis on being rather than doing, on the qualitative dimension of leisure. However, this view often minimizes the creational ordinance of work.

In contrast to the classical interpretation, the second tradition of post-Hellenic Christianity and the Protestant ethic emphasizes work and views "leisure as therapy, rest, relaxation, social control, recreation for subsequent productive effort – and generally, therefore, as instrumental in character" (Kaplan, 1974, pp. 230–231). A contemporary Christian expression of the activity view is put forward by Ryken (1994), who includes a quote from Lee:

> Its [leisure's] purpose is to bring us back to physical, mental, and emotional strength and wholeness. . . . The purpose of leisure is to re-create a person, to restore him or her to an earlier condition. . . . Leisure . . . is "the growing time of the human spirit" and a time "for rest and restoration, for rediscovering life in its entirety". . . . Leisure is, in the best sense of the word, an escape. . . . Relaxation is one of the inherent qualities of leisure. (pp. 236, 261)

In the Protestant ethic of serving God through work and the forgoing of pleasures, leisure is viewed as a re-creative and restorative activity that is of secondary significance to the development and spreading of culture. This view of leisure, influenced by Calvinist theology, contributed to the separation of work and leisure, since work was valued as the more important aspect of life while leisure, defined in terms of free time, was relegated to secondary importance.

The strengths of the Protestant view are its recognition of the creational ordinance of work along with the recognition of a rhythm to life – the alternation of periods of work and nonwork or quantitative leisure – that reflects the biblical pattern to life. However, the free time and activity concepts of leisure that the Protestant view incorporate are essentially quantitative approaches to the conceptualization of leisure, and as such, leisure has little intrinsic value. The activity concept maintains that perpetual doing is much more important than our being, the qualitative dimension to leisure. But doing is not the primary element in any satisfactory conceptualization of leisure. The time element is definitely necessary, but not sufficient to develop a complete explanation of leisure. The "freedom from" (i.e., time free from work and other obligations as is suggested by the humanitarian motivation of the Sabbath), along with the "freedom for" (i.e., free for activity), are necessary, but these freedoms in and of themselves cannot be equated with leisure. Leisure consists of more than simply quantitative components.

The holistic tendency unites these two historical traditions – leisure as an end and leisure as a means of relaxation and refreshment, the emphasis on being and on doing, the qualitative dimension and the quantitative dimension. In this blend, the weaknesses of each tradition are counterbalanced by the strengths of the other tradition.

The holistic concept of leisure not only offers the opportunity to combine the two historical traditions, but also encompasses the variety and richness of the biblical material relevant to leisure. An examination of biblical materials provides support for two dimensions of leisure: a quantitative and a qualitative, with one relating to our doing and the other to our being (Heintzman, 2006). First, the Sabbath teaches a rhythm to life – six days of work and one of nonwork (quantitative leisure). Second, the qualitative dimension is seen in the spiritual attitude of rest, joy, freedom, and celebration in both God and creation inculcated by the Sabbath and that culminates in the rest, peace, abundant life, and freedom available in Jesus Christ. The holistic concept of leisure has the capacity to encompass both these quantitative and qualitative dimensions of leisure as inferred from Scripture.

In summary, a Christian holistic conceptualization of leisure has two dimensions: a qualitative and a quantitative. The qualitative dimension is the spiritual attitude and condition of being that reflects the quality of life available in Jesus Christ. This qualitative dimension of leisure is not limited to a certain time period; thus it may be experienced simultaneously with work, and in fact work may be conceived of as an expression of this attitude. The quantitative dimension of leisure consists of certain times and activities – ranging from silent contemplation to an active celebration and rejoicing in the gifts of creation – in which an intensification of leisure is experienced. Thus all of our life is characterized by a spiritual attitude of leisure, but at the same time our life should exhibit a rhythm of periods of work and periods of intensified leisure.

A Model of Leisure Style and Spiritual Wellbeing Relationships

A model of the theoretical relationships between leisure and spiritual wellbeing, consistent with a holistic conceptualization of leisure, is presented in the remainder of the paper. The two key concepts in this model are leisure style and spiritual wellbeing.

Conceptualization of Spiritual Wellbeing

How do we conceptualize spiritual wellbeing? (Since some authors use spiritual wellbeing and other authors use spiritual health or spiritual wellness in reference to the same concept, these terms will be used interchangeably in this paper.) The concept of health is now generally defined as a holistic, multi-dimensional phenomenon that includes social (the ability to enjoy meaningful relationships with other people in one's environment), emotional (the ability to deal comfortably and appropriately with emotions), spiritual (the ability to find meaning and purpose in life), and mental (the ability to learn and function intellectually) health. This broad concept of health acknowledges the complexities of the human organism and the dynamic interrelationship between body, mind, and spirit. Since spiritual health has no obvious structure or measurable subcomponents (Eberst, 1984), it has been characterized as the most difficult dimension of health to define and measure (Banks, 1980). Much like psychological health, there is no single recognized definition of spiritual health (Bensley, 1991). However, with the increasing scientific interest in spirituality, there is growing consensus. Based on an analysis of the extensive literature, Hawks (1994) identified a number of internal characteristics of those people who are spiritually well, and also ways in which spiritually well individuals express themselves in their external interactions. Internal characteristics of people who are spiritually well are: having a sense of life purpose and ultimate meaning; oneness with nature and beauty and a sense of connectedness with others; deep concern for, and commitment to, something greater than self; a sense of wholeness in life; strong spiritual beliefs, principles, ethics, and values; and love, joy, peace, hope, and fulfilment. People who are spiritually well exhibit in their interactions with other people trust, honesty, integrity, altruism, compassion, and service. They also experience regular communion or a personal relationship with a higher power or larger reality that transcends observable physical reality. Building upon the above characteristics of spiritual health, Hawks developed the following short but comprehensive definition of spiritual health:

> A high level of *faith*, hope, and commitment in relation to a well-defined worldview or belief system that provides a sense of *meaning* and *purpose* to existence in general, and that offers an ethical path to *personal fulfilment* which includes *connectedness with self, others, and a higher power or larger reality*. [emphasis added] (p. 6)

As illustrated by the words in italics, the characteristics and definition of spiritual health incorporate many of the important traits found in various spiritual conceptualizations of leisure: faith (Godbey, 1985; Goodale & Godbey, 1988), meaning (Godbey, 1989), purpose (Goodale, 1994), personally pleasing and fulfilling (Godbey, 1985; Goodale & Godbey, 1988), love (Godbey, 1985; Goodale & Godbey, 1988; Goodale, 1994), and a connectedness with oneself, others, and the universe (Howe-Murphy & Murphy, 1987).

Hawks (1994) has also identified three factors that contribute to spiritual health: (1) a well-defined belief system or worldview that provides motivation, meaning, and purpose to life; (2) selflessness, concern, and connectedness with others; and (3) a high degree of commitment to, and personal faith in, the belief system and worldview. It can be hypothesized that a leisure style that provides opportunities to develop and maintain a belief system or worldview, as well as supports the development of concern and connectedness with others, would be conducive to spiritual health.

Spiritual Wellbeing from a Christian Perspective

Before discussing the concept of leisure style, the internal and external characteristics of spiritual health will be discussed from a Christian perspective. In regards to the internal characteristic of life purpose and ultimate meaning, in Christian spirituality the response to deep spiritual longings occurs within the context of Christian faith and a relationship with God (Toon, 1989). McGrath (1994) wrote that the "quest for human identity, authenticity, and fulfillment cannot be taken in isolation from God" (p. 48). As Augustine (389/1949) put it centuries ago, "Our hearts are restless until we find our rest in God" (p. 3).

Another internal characteristic of health is oneness with nature, beauty, and connectedness with others. Chapters 1 and 2 of Genesis provide two images of humans: on the one hand, humans are created in the image of God, and on the other hand, humans are simply part of creation with the birds, fish, whales, sea, and stars (Wilkinson, 1991). This characteristic of spiritual health relates to humans being part of creation. Humans are created on the same day as other creatures, on the sixth day of creation before the Sabbath, and they are created the same way as other creatures (Gen. 1:20–31). Therefore humans are embedded within creation. The image of humans connected to other creatures is reinforced by the description of them being made "from the dust of the ground" (Gen. 2:7, New International Version). The Hebrew word for "ground" is *adamah*, while the Hebrew word for humans is *Adam* (Wilkinson, 1991). While humans are created in the image of God, they are also earth and are connected to the rest of creation including soil, plants, and animals. They are embedded in the earth: "they are fully dust, and fully soul; they are soulish dust" (Wilkinson, 1991, p. 315) and need to recognize their connections with the rest of the creation.

Deep concern for and commitment to something greater than self, is a third internal characteristic of spiritual health. Christians are to "Love the Lord your God with all your heart and with all your soul and with all your mind" (Matt. 22:37) and are also to die to self. "Jesus said to his disciples, 'Whoever wants to be my disciple must deny themselves and take up their cross and follow me'" (Matt. 16:24). Therefore Christian spirituality involves being other-centered rather than self-centered.

A fourth internal characteristic of spiritual health is a sense of wholeness in life that is tied to meaning and purpose. It involves the sense of wholeness that God brings to life experiences (Williams, 1979), so that a person is able to fulfill one's potential and uniqueness as created by God. Wholeness is also connected with salvation, in that Christ brings wholeness to human brokenness – physically, psychologically, and spiritually.

The fifth internal characteristic of spiritual health is strong, spiritual beliefs; principles, ethics, and values. In regards to spiritual beliefs, a Christian worldview as described in the Bible is usually summarized in terms of a creation-Fall-redemption motif (Walsh & Middleton, 1984, 1995; Wolters, 1985). The notion of creation is that God created and continues to sustain the cosmos. The Fall refers to humanity's rebellion against God that had devastating consequences: "When communion with the Creator of life is broken, death inevitably results. Life is no longer whole but broken" (Walsh & Middleton, 1984, p. 70). Through redemption that climaxes in the life, death, and resurrection of Jesus, God restores the original, fundamental relationship with creation. Christian spiritual beliefs also include beliefs about the nature of God and Christ. Christian principles, ethics, and values include the ethical teachings found in the Ten Commandments and Jesus' teaching in both the summary of the law (Matt. 22:37–40) and the Sermon on the Mount (Matt. 5,6,7).

As noted in the previous section, Hawks (1994) suggested that two of the three factors that lead to a person exhibiting the characteristics of spiritual health are a well-defined worldview or belief system and high levels of personal faith and commitment in relation to the worldview and belief system. Thus, spiritual health is dependent not only on intellectual knowledge of a worldview but an ability to live out that perspective and model it for others. McGrath (1994) stated that "Spirituality designates the Christian life – not specifically its ideas, but the way in which these ideas make themselves visible in the life of Christian individuals and communities. Spirituality represents the interface between ideas and life . . ." (pp. 31–32). Thus, Christian spirituality involves both thinking about ideas and doctrine and acting or putting one's faith into practice.

Hawks (1994) identified love, joy, peace, hope, and fulfillment as the final internal characteristic of those who are spiritually well. These characteristics are similar to the Christian fruits of the Spirit that manifest themselves in the life of Christian spirituality: "love, joy, peace, forbearance, kindness, goodness, faithfulness, gentleness, and self-control" (Gal. 5:22).

In terms of the external characteristics of spiritual health, Hawks (1994) identified regular communion or a personal relationship with a higher power or a larger reality that transcends observable physical reality, and interactions with other people characterized by trust, honesty, integrity, altruism, compassion, and service. Christian spirituality is fundamentally characterized by these two types of external interactions: a horizontal relationship with others and a vertical relationship with God. These two external relationships were taught by Jesus when he summarized the guidelines for living in terms of loving God and loving one's neighbor. Thus Cousins (1990) could write, "there is a primacy of love in Christian spirituality: love of God and neighbor . . ." (p. 43). The following definition of Christian spirituality reflects Jesus' statement to love God and love one's neighbor:

> Spirituality is a growing desire to know, love, and please God that is being actively fostered in the power of the Holy Spirit through prayer and other appropriate disciplines and is actualized in an obedient life that expresses the love of God to others in their own spiritual and social needs. (Liefeld & Cannell, 1992, p. 244)

In regards to the vertical relationship with God, the most fundamental characteristic of Christian spirituality is that it involves a relationship with God (Armerding, 1992; Dart, 1992; Postema, 1983; Smedes, 1970). Conn (1987) suggested that Christian spirituality "means one's entire life as understood, felt, imagined, and decided upon in relationship to God, in Jesus Christ, empowered by the Spirit" (p. 972). A Christian understanding of spirituality also involves spiritual practices (e.g., meditation, fasting, reading, journal-writing) through which one's relationship with God is developed.

In regards to one's horizontal relationship with others, although Christian spirituality is based on a loving relationship with God, Jesus' first great teaching about that love is immediately followed by his second statement about loving one's neighbor (Matt. 22:37–40). Christian spirituality is to be expressed in social relationships and also in social justice as "An authentic spiritual life always pushes one back into the world" (Willard, 1995, p. 17). Huggett wrote that "God's life is drawn from us so that we may become the channel through which his life flows out to others to bring them refreshment, cleansing, food, healing or the opportunity for growth or mere survival" (as quoted in Toon, 1989, p. 11). Or as Grenz (1994) puts it, "Christian spirituality may be inward in that it consists of union with Christ and love for God, but that means it is also outward . . . active Christian life involves discipleship, and Christian spirituality must entail acting with compassion, mercy, and a desire for justice" (pp. 35–36).

Before continuing with the development of the model, it is necessary to consider whether models are able to depict a concept such as spiritual wellbeing. Liefeld and Cannell (1992) raised the question as to whether Christian spirituality is something we achieve, something we experience, or something that is practiced. If it is something that is to be achieved, then it is a goal and objective; if it is something we experience, then it is a state or circumstance; if it is a practice, then it is something one does. They concluded that Christian spirituality is more a matter of growth than achievement, less subjective than experience, and more mechanical than practice. Their conclusion suggests that we can try to model spirituality, but we cannot completely model it, as it involves elements of the Spirit that cannot be understood as a social scientific causal model.

Conceptualization of Leisure Style

Leisure style, a concept that is used in the social scientific study of leisure, is a useful concept to represent those elements of leisure relevant and meaningful to spiritual wellness. While lifestyle is "the aggregate pattern of day-to-day activities which make up an individual's way of life" (Glyptis, 1981, p. 314), leisure style refers to those elements of a person's lifestyle that are perceived as leisure. Thus, "leisure is part of the total lifestyle but it is also its own lifestyle" (Iso-Ahola, 1994, p. 46). Mannell and Kleiber (1997) defined leisure style as "overall patterns of leisure activity engagement and time usage" (p. 59). Thus leisure style primarily reflects a quantitative conceptualization of leisure. Leisure style has several dimensions: time, activity, setting, and motivation. *Time* structure is the overall pattern of daily, weekly, annual, and lifelong time organization (Gattas, Roberts, Schmitz-Scherzer, Tokarski, & Vitanyi, 1986). Leisure style also involves *patterns of leisure activities* (Veal, 1993). Research on leisure style is founded upon the premise that "Individuals do not so much engage in ad hoc miscellanies of activities as develop broader systems of leisure behavior consisting of a number of interdependent elements . . ." (Roberts, 1978, p. 37). Another dimension of leisure style involves the locational context (Glyptis, 1981) or *setting*. Where does the leisure experience take place? Related to the locational context is the social context (Gattas et al., 1986; Glyptis, 1981; Kelly, 1989). Is leisure pursued alone, or in the company of other people? Leisure style also involves the dimension of *motivation*. The motivations and needs individuals try to satisfy during discretionary time may be fulfilled by different types and patterns of activities, making no one type of leisure involvement unique or individually important for wellbeing, health, or quality of life (Mannell & Iso-Ahola, 1987). Consequently, in the model presented here, the relationship between leisure and spiritual wellness will be presented in terms of the four components of leisure style: time, activity, setting, and motivation.

A Model of Spiritual Wellbeing

Various models of spiritual wellbeing have been developed (e.g., Chandler, Holden & Kolander, 1992; Seaward, 1991, 1994). Chandler et al. (1992) proposed a model of spiritual wellness that provides a useful starting point for explaining the relationship between leisure and spiritual wellbeing (See Figure 1). This model was developed in order "to encourage greater familiarity with and use of the spiritual dimension by counsellors and health educators . . . and to describe ways to use spontaneous events and deliberate techniques to facilitate spiritual growth" (p. 168). Thus it was a model developed for clinical purposes, not research purposes, and as a result there is no research testing the model. Chandler et al. defined spiritual wellness as "a balanced openness to or pursuit of spiritual development" (p. 170). Processes involved in achieving balance are represented in the model by two dimensions of spiritual wellness. One dimension (represented as the vertical continuum in Figure 1) ranges from a condition of "repression of the sublime," where one denies or defies the spiritual tendency within oneself, to a condition of "spiritual emergency," where one is preoccupied with spirituality to the detriment of the other dimensions of wellness. Spiritual wellness occurs at or near the midpoint of the continuum. The second dimension in the model (the horizontal dimension) is a continuum of spiritual development that represents "the process of incorporating spiritual experiences that results ultimately in spiritual transformation" (p. 170). The assumption underlying this process is that the mere occurrence of spiritual experiences does not necessarily result in spiritual development unless the experiences are dealt with and integrated into one's life. From a Christian perspective, we might refer to this as the process of sanctification, wherein Christians "are being transformed into his image with ever-increasing glory, which comes from the Lord, who is the Spirit" (2 Cor. 3:18).

Figure 1. Model of spiritual wellness. Adapted from Chandler, Holden, & Kolander (1992).

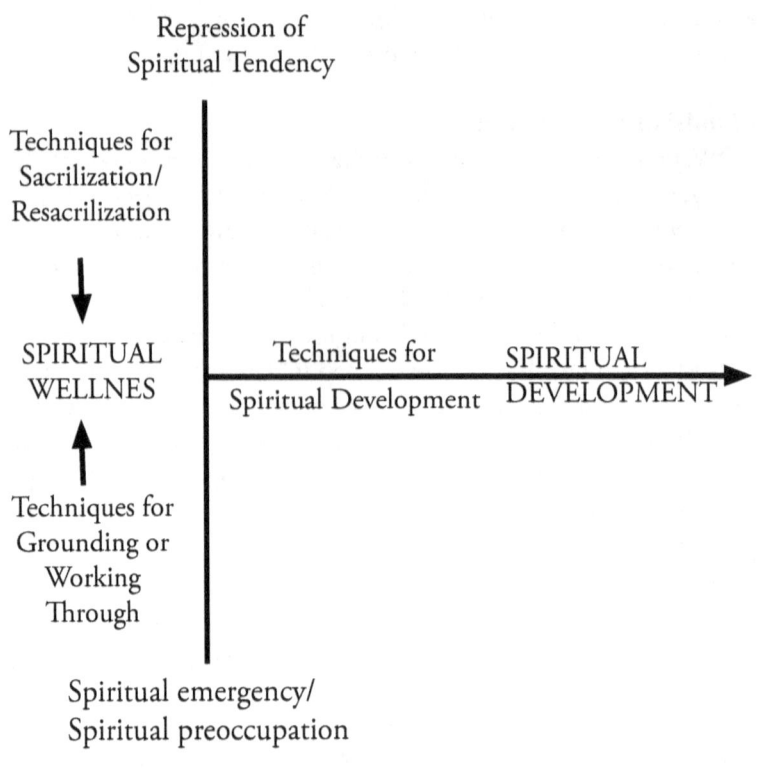

Incorporating Leisure into the Model of Spiritual Wellbeing

According to Chandler et al. (1992), spiritual growth can be prompted by both spontaneous events and intentional activity. Various techniques create spiritual awareness and enhance movement toward higher levels of spiritual wellness. If a person is in a state of spiritual emergency, grounding slows down the process of spiritual emergence so that the spiritual experience is more likely to be assimilated, which results in spiritual development rather than a chronic state of upheaval. Activities such as jogging, walking, Tai chi, gardening, or anything that connects a person with the earth are suggested as types of grounding activities that slow a person down and bring her or him back down to physical reality. The authors also suggested that techniques for working through can be used with people in a condition of spiritual emergency, to help them "stay with" the emergency to facilitate its transformation potential. Chandler et al. (1992) recommended that working through goes beyond traditional counselling, involves experiential techniques, and includes the establishment of a support system of family and friends for the person. At the other end of the continuum, if a person consciously or unconsciously represses the spiritual, sacralization ("sensitizing to the spiritual those who have no conscious experience of the spiritual," Chandler et al., p. 172) or resacralization ("resensitize those who have been spiritually well but have moved, consciously or unconsciously, toward repression," Chandler et al., p. 172) activities may move a person toward spiritual wellness. Resacralization was a term Maslow used to mean "rediscovering a sense of the sacred in everyday life" (Davis, 1996, p. 419). Meditation, relaxation, rhythmic breath-work, creative visualization, imagery, and awareness exercises are common interventions used in counselling and therapy to foster spiritual development through the process of sacralization.

The Chandler et al. (1992) model provides a framework for developing a model of leisure and spiritual wellbeing. The proposed model (see Figure 2) is based on the assumption that leisure experiences may either consciously or unconsciously provide opportunities for grounding or working through spiritual difficulties as well as sensitizing one to the spiritual. In other words, leisure experiences that involve an interplay of time, activity, motivation, and setting have the potential to provide contexts in which the spiritual is explored rather than being repressed, and where spiritual preoccupation due to a spiritual emergency can be dealt with (vertical dimension of model), while a leisure style provides repeated opportunities to translate leisure experiences of a spiritual nature into spiritual development (horizontal dimension of model). Thus the techniques (grounding, sacralization/resacrilization) and the processes underlying them may link leisure and spiritual health.

The proposed model of leisure and spiritual wellbeing also has the potential to incorporate a number of other overlapping theories or ideas that suggest potential processes that may link leisure and spiritual health. These ideas include leisure and wellbeing theories (Mannell & Kleiber, 1997) and ideas associated with restorative environments theory (Kaplan & Kaplan, 1989; Kaplan, 1995). While Chandler et al. thoroughly describe the techniques (re/sacralization, grounding, working through) that move a person toward spiritual wellness, they provide less information on the techniques for spiritual development. The leisure and wellbeing theories offer suggestions of how leisure may influence spiritual development. Furthermore, the restorative environments literature is helpful in explaining how specific activities and settings may move a person toward spiritual wellness. It must be noted that these processes are not necessarily mutually exclusive. To understand how these processes work within the context of leisure experiences and leisure style, it is helpful to discuss them in relation to the four dimensions of leisure style (time, activity, motivation, and setting) discussed above.

Figure 2. A conceptual model of leisure and spiritual well-being (Heintzman, 2002).

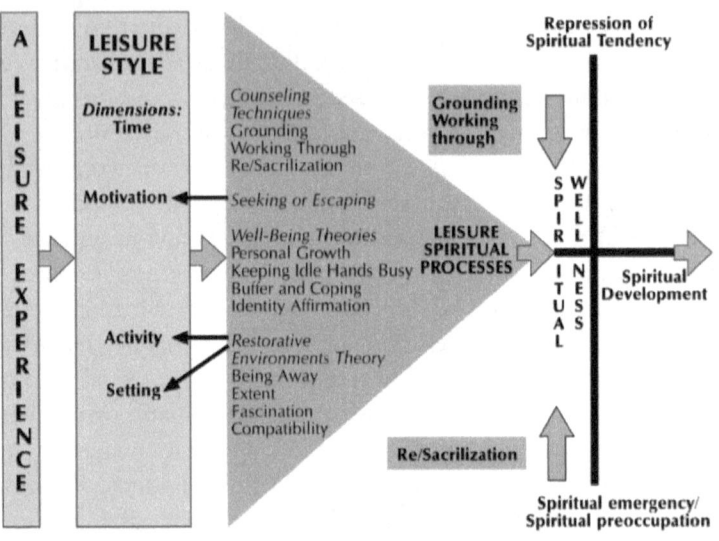

Leisure time and activity. Discretionary time provides the opportunity to explore the spiritual or deal with a spiritual crisis. As Teaff (2006) noted, it has long been recognized that "Christian spirituality thrives best in a leisure atmosphere where time and space are allotted for 'being' as well as 'doing'" (p. 115). For example, Jesus took time to go into the hills to pray (Mark 1:35; 6:31, 32). However, discretionary time does not necessarily guarantee spiritual wellness, as spiritual wellness depends on how the time is being used. Involvement in an activity may move a person toward spiritual wellness or away from it. For example, though Chandler et al. (1992) do not discuss leisure, they do suggest that grounding activities such as jogging, walking, tai chi, or gardening may assist a person in dealing with spiritual preoccupation by connecting them with the physical world. Activities that help a person work through a spiritual emergency will enable a person to transform the emergency into an opportunity for spiritual development. In contrast, activities of sacrilization or resacrilization, such as meditation and relaxation activities, may assist a person in becoming sensitized to the spiritual. The notion of grounding activities is consistent with both the keeping idle hands busy and the buffering and coping theories of leisure and wellbeing in that leisure activities and involvements may keep the person busy in the material world, thereby diverting the person's attention away from their spiritual emergency and helping them cope with the situation. Sacrilization and resacrilization activities, in contrast to the keeping hands busy theory, slow the person down and create space that may lead to a greater likelihood of being sensitized and receptive to spiritual experience.

Leisure motivation. Motivation is an important factor in the development of spiritual health. Spiritual growth may be stimulated by both intentional activity and spontaneous events (Chandler et al., 1992). While one cannot cause spiritual growth to occur; one can seek or create certain conditions in which spiritual growth is more likely to take place. Thus, consistent with Iso-Ahola's (1997) proposition that the two fundamental dimensions of motivation for leisure are seeking and escaping, it can be hypothesized that escaping activities could lead to the repression of the spiritual tendency, while seeking activities would have sacralizing or resacralizing effects. Is a person's leisure primarily characterized by "the seeking of personal and interpersonal rewards or by escaping one's personal or interpersonal world" (p. 134)? Passive leisure, used as an escape, is not likely to be favorable to health. Rather, the pursuit of intrinsic rewards through leisure is probably more beneficial. Thus, seeking leisure activities are consistent with personal growth explanations of leisure and wellbeing in that they provide people with the opportunity to develop their skills and abilities and to become the type of person they would like to be (Mannell & Kleiber, 1997). Research findings indicate that individuals who are primarily seeking-oriented in their leisure are healthier than individuals who are primarily escapists in their leisure (Iso-Ahola, 1994; Isho-Ahola & Weissinger, 1984). Escapist, passive leisure is psychologically problematic, as it results in boredom that in turn leads to depression and apathy (Iso-Ahola, 1997; Iso-Ahola & Weissinger, 1987).

Identity formation and affirmation theory (Mannell & Kleiber, 1997) can be extended to suggest that certain leisure styles may be more conducive to seeking and, consequently, spiritual wellbeing. Leisure and identity formation ideas suggest that the freedom in leisure provides people with the opportunity to select activities with identity images that are congruent with the type of person they are or would like to be (e.g., outdoor adventurer). People choose to participate in leisure activities partially due to these identity images for the purpose of developing new identities or affirming who they are. This explanation may underlie certain leisure-based tourist roles. Discussions of leisure-based tourist roles often include the role of spiritual seeker (Yiannakis & Gibson, 1992). For example, Cohen (1979) defined a "spiritual seeker" as "a person on an existential search for a spiritual center" (Yiannakis & Gibson, 1992, p. 291), while seekers were defined by Yiannakis & Gibson (1992) as "persons who, through travel, seek to learn more about themselves, and ultimately, the meaning of existence" (pp. 297–298).

Those who have theorized about leisure style suggest that the social dimension is an important aspect of leisure style (Gattas et al., 1986; Glyptis, 1981; Kelly, 1989; Veal, 1993). Whether activities are done alone, with another person, or in a group can also have an influence on spiritual wellness. Fox (1997) found that structured time for solitude in wilderness enhanced the opportunity for spiritual experience. Stringer and McAvoy (1992) discovered that reports of spiritual experiences by participants on a wilderness canoe trip mainly focused on the interconnections between people, while participants on a mountain hiking trip, that generally offered more opportunity for time alone than the canoe trip, tended to describe spiritual experiences involving an awareness and appreciation of the vast, stark beauty of the alpine environment. Ragheb (1993) found that reading – generally a solitary activity – had the highest correlations with perceived spiritual wellness. It could be hypothesized that solitude and solitary activities provide the time and space required in the sacrilization process to develop the characteristics of spiritual health related to purpose and meaning in life.

The satisfactions associated with different activities may also be related to spiritual wellbeing. For example, Ragheb (1993) found that the relaxational and aesthetic-environmental components of leisure satisfaction were dominant in their contributions to perceived spiritual wellness. It could be hypothesized that the activities that produce leisure satisfaction of a relaxational and aesthetic-environmental nature are ones that provide opportunity for reflection on spiritual values, and thus they promote sacrilization.

Leisure setting. Setting also has an influence on the extent to which a leisure experience may or may not enhance spiritual wellness. Some places, such as cathedrals and wilderness areas, are invested with meaning that make them especially conducive to enhancing spiritual wellness (McDonald & Schreyer, 1991) while others, such as natural areas, provide a fresh perspective on life issues (McAvoy & Lais, 1996). Numerous studies suggest that wilderness and nature areas facilitate spiritual growth (Davis, 1996; Fox, 1997; Kaplan, 1974; Kaplan & Talbot, 1983; Young & Crandall, 1984). However, despite all the evidence that suggests wilderness and nature areas facilitate spiritual growth, Stringer and McAvoy (1992) noted that it was not necessarily the wilderness environment itself that is conducive to spiritual experience. They observed that a "different environment, free from normal constraints on time and energy" (p. 17) increased opportunities for, and the enhancement of, spiritual development.

Literature on restorative environments is helpful in trying to understand the processes that take place when a person is removed from their everyday environment (Kaplan & Kaplan, 1989; Kaplan, 1995). Restorative environments are characterized by four features: 1) being away, that is, a conceptually or physically different setting from one's everyday environment, 2) extent, which refers to a setting adequately rich and coherent that it can captivate the mind and foster exploration; 3) fascination, a form of attention that requires no effort and may focus on content (fire, water, people, animals) or process (problem-solving, gambling, storytelling); and 4) compatibility, that requires a setting that is congruent with and advances one's purposes or inclinations. Although a variety of settings exhibit the four features of a restorative environment to differing degrees, natural settings tend to be richly blessed with all four features. Initial research on restorative environments has documented the greater restorative potential of natural environments in comparison to urban settings or other artificial settings (e.g., Hartig, Mang, & Evans, 1991; Kaplan, 1995; Tennessen & Cimprich, 1995).

The Kaplans (Kaplan & Kaplan, 1989) classified benefits of restorative experiences as either attentional recovery or reflection. Reflection, as a deeper and more significant benefit than recovery, is thought to be more demanding of the restorative environment both in terms of the quality of the environment and the time necessary for its accomplishment. The major characteristic that differentiates settings with greater potential to foster reflection is the type of fascination they elicit. Fascination may be conceptualized on a continuum from hard to soft (Kaplan, 1995). Hard fascination is extremely intense, captures one's attention, and leaves little opportunity for thinking. Soft fascination consists of two components. First, it has moderate intensity, adequate to maintain attention without effort, but not so intense as to prevent reflection. Second, environments that elicit soft fascination are aesthetically pleasant, thereby counterbalancing any pain associated with reflection on serious matters. Relating these concepts to spiritual wellness, it could be hypothesized that hard fascination is conducive to grounding, thereby moving a person from spiritual preoccupation to spiritual wellness, while soft fascination is conducive to sacrilization, thereby moving a person from spiritual repression to spiritual wellness and moving a person along the continuum of spiritual development.

Environments that elicit soft fascination, for example, ordinary natural settings, should be beneficial for both attentional recovery and reflection, and therefore would also be beneficial for sacrilization and spiritual development. Environments such as many urban settings, low in fascination yet high in directed-attention demand, should be relatively ineffectual for either recovery or reflection. Environments that elicit hard fascination should be more useful for attentional recovery than for reflection, and therefore also beneficial for grounding in the spiritual wellness model. Applying this theory to the present model, leisure activities undertaken in ordinary natural settings, since they are beneficial for reflection, would also be beneficial for sacrilization and spiritual development, while leisure activities undertaken in environments that elicit hard fascination, since they are beneficial for grounding, would be helpful in moving a spiritually preoccupied person toward spiritual wellness. A variety of settings that elicit hard fascination have been suggested: watching auto racing (Kaplan, 1995); watching television, shopping, and watching or participating in sports (Canin, 1991); parties, video games, and amusement parks (Herzog, Black, Fountaine, & Knotts, 1997). These hard-fascination settings would be relatively more effective in promoting grounding than reflection and sacrilization. There is some empirical support for these theoretical ideas concerning restorative environments (Canin, 1991; Herzog et al., 1997; Kaplan, Bardwell, & Slakter, 1993; Kaplan & Kaplan, 1989; Schroeder, 1991; Kaplan & Talbot, 1983).

So far, the discussion of the proposed leisure and spiritual wellbeing model has primarily been in terms of individual leisure experiences. However, the occurrence of an individual or isolated leisure experience of a spiritual nature does not guarantee spiritual development (Chandler et al., 1992). While one leisure experience may move a person toward spiritual wellness, leisure experiences must be incorporated into one's life if spiritual development is to occur. That is, spiritual development will only occur if leisure experiences bring about behavioral changes or transformation related to the internal and external characteristics of health reviewed above. For example, Fox (1999) found that changes to lifestyles arose from spiritual experiences in the wilderness as the participants carried their inner strength and feelings of self-control into their workplaces, families, and lives.

This notion of the need to incorporate experiences into one's life if spiritual development is to occur is consistent with Christian spirituality. As Grenz (1994) noted, the focus of the Christian tradition has not been to nurture spiritual experience in and of itself, but rather to foster a relationship with Jesus. Furthermore, the focus of Scripture is not so much on spiritual experience, but on a lifestyle that leads to spiritual transformation (Rom. 12:1–2; 2 Cor. 3:18; Eph. 4:22–24). Spiritual experiences are not necessarily significant in a person's life unless they have a transforming impact upon the person. Or, as John of the Cross (1589/1991) put it, "Delightful feelings do not of themselves lead the soul to God, but rather cause it to become attached to delightful feelings" (p. 747).

Since a single leisure experience, on its own, may bring about only limited spiritual development, consistent patterns of leisure experiences, or what is called leisure style, can potentially provide greater opportunity to bring about spiritual development and growth than an individual leisure experience (horizontal dimension of model: see Figure 2). Young and Crandall (1986) found a positive relationship between continued wilderness use over a period of time and individual changes in self-actualization. Teaff (1991) observed that the repeated religious/leisure experiences of older Catholic women who belonged to a religious order were affirming of deep personal values and resulted in experiences of inner peace over the long term.

Spiritual development results in a greater locus of centricity (Chandler et al., 1992), greater connectedness (McDonald, Guldin, & Wetherhill, 1988), and an enhanced leisure attitude in terms of "a receptive attitude of mind, a contemplative attitude, and . . . the capacity for steeping oneself in the world of creation" (Pieper, 1952, p. 41). As such, there is an ongoing interaction; one brings one's spiritual attitude of leisure (the qualitative dimension of leisure) to one's leisure experiences and one's leisure experiences (the quantitative dimension of leisure in terms of free time experiences and activities) have an impact on one's spiritual attitude of leisure and ultimately one's spiritual health. Although leisure as a spiritual attitude undergirds all of life, "periods are necessary when leisure is more intensely lived and expressed" (Doohan, 1981, p. 165). These periods may be called leisure experiences, that is, "an experience that results from recreation engagements" (Driver & Tocher, 1970, p. 10). Thus this model of leisure style and spiritual wellbeing incorporates a holistic understanding of leisure where there is a dynamic relationship between quantitative and qualitative dimensions of leisure.

References

Armerding, C.E. (1992). When the Spirit came mightily: The spirituality of Israel's charismatic leaders. In J.I. Packer & L. Wilkinson (Eds.), *Alive to God: Studies in spirituality* (pp. 41–55). Downers Grove, IL: InterVarsity.

Augustine. (398/1949). *The confessions of Saint Augustine* (E.B. Pusey, Trans.). New York: Random House.

Banks, R. (1980). Health and the spiritual dimension: Relationships and implications for professional preparation programs. *Journal of School Health* 50(4), 195–202.

Bensley, R.J. (1991). Defining spiritual health: A review of the literature. *Journal of Health Education* 22(5), 287–290.

Canin, L.H. (1991). *Psychological restoration among AIDS caregivers: Maintaining self care.* (Unpublished Doctoral Dissertation). University of Michigan-Ann Arbor.

Chandler, C.K., Holden, J.M., & Kolander, C.A. (1992). Counseling for spiritual wellness: Theory and practice. *Journal of Counseling and Development* 71, 168–175.

Cohen, E. (1979). A phenomenology of tourist experiences. *Sociology* 13, 179–201.

Conn, J.W. (1987). Spirituality. In J.A. Komonchak, M. Collins, & D.A. Lane (Eds.), *The New Dictionary of Theology* (pp. 972–985). Wilmington, DE: Michael Glazier.

Cousins, E.H. (1990). What is Christian spirituality? In B.C. Hanson (Ed.), *Modern Christian spirituality: Methodological and historical essays* (pp. 39–44). Atlanta: Scholars Press.

Dart, R. (1992). Prophetic spirituality: Markings for the journey. In J.I. Packer & L. Wilkinson (Eds.), *Alive to God: Studies in spirituality* (pp. 296–314). Downers Grove, IL: InterVarsity.

Davis, J. (1996). An integrated approach to the scientific study of the human spirit. In Driver, Dustin, Baltic, Elsner, & Peterson (Eds.), *Nature and the human spirit* (pp. 417–429).

Doohan L. (1981). The spiritual value of leisure. *Spirituality Today* 31(2), 157–167.

Doohan, L. (1990). *Leisure: A spiritual need.* Notre Dame, IN: Ave Maria Press.

Driver, B.L., Dustin, D., Baltic, T., Elsner, G., & Peterson, G. (Eds.). (1996). *Nature and the human spirit: Toward an expanded land management ethic.*

State College, PA: Venture.

Driver, B.L., & Tocher, S.R. (1970). Toward a behavioral interpretation of recreational engagements, with implications for planning. In B.L. Driver (Ed.), *Elements of outdoor recreation planning* (pp. 9–31). Ann Arbor: University of Michigan Press.

Eberst, R. (1984). Defining health: A multi-dimensional model. *Journal of School Health* 54(3), 99–104.

Fox, R.J. (1997). Women, nature and spirituality: A qualitative study exploring women's wilderness experience. In D. Rowe & P. Brown (Eds.), *Proceedings, ANZALS conference 1997* (pp. 59–64). Newcastle, NSW: Australian and New Zealand Association for Leisure Studies and the Department of Leisure and Tourism Studies, University of Newcastle.

Fox, R. (1999). Enhancing spiritual experience in adventure programs. In J.C. Miles & S. Priest (Eds.), *Adventure programming* (pp. 455–461). State College, PA: Venture.

Gattas, J.T., Roberts, K., Schmitz-Scherzer, R., Tokarski, W., & Vitanyi, Y. (1986). Leisure and life styles: Toward a research agenda. *Society and Leisure* 9(2), 529–539.

Glyptis, S. (1981). Leisure life-styles. *Regional Studies* 15(5), 311–326.

Godbey, G. (1985). *Leisure in your life* (2nd ed.). State College, PA: Venture.

Godbey, G. (1989). Implications of recreation and leisure research for professionals. In E.L. Jackson & T.L. Burton (Eds.), *Understanding leisure and recreation: Mapping the past, charting the future* (pp. 613–628). State College, PA: Venture.

Goodale, T.L. (1994). *Legitimizing leisure anew.* Paper presented at the scholarly presentations portion of the 25th anniversary of the Leisure Studies Department, University of Ottawa. Ottawa, ON. May 14, 1994.

Goodale, T.L., & Godbey, G.C. (1988). *The evolution of leisure: Historical and philosophical perspectives.* State College, PA: Venture.

Grenz, S.J. (1994, May). The gospel and the contemporary pursuit of spirituality. *Touchstone*, 32–36.

Hartig, T., Mang, M., & Evans, G.W. (1991). Restorative effects of natural environment experiences. *Environment and Behavior* 23, 3–26.

Hawks, S. (1994). Spiritual health: Definition and theory. *Wellness Perspectives* 10, 3–13.

Heintzman, P. (2006). Implications for leisure from a review of the biblical concepts of Sabbath and rest. In P. Heintzman, G.E. Van Andel, & T.L. Visker (Eds.), *Christianity and leisure: Issues in a pluralistic society* (Rev. ed., pp. 14–31). Sioux Center: Dordt College Press.

Herzog, T.R., Black, A.M., Fountaine, K.A., & Knotts, D.J. (1997). Reflection and attentional recovery as distinctive benefits of restorative environments. *Journal of Environmental Psychology* 17, 165–170.

Howe-Murphy, R., & Murphy, J. (1987). An exploration of the New Age consciousness paradigm in therapeutic recreation. In C. Sylvester, J.

Hemingway, R. Howe-Murphy, K. Mobily, & P. Shank (Eds.), *Philosophy of therapeutic recreation: Ideas and issues* (pp. 71–85). Arlington, VA: National Recreation and Park Association.

Iso-Ahola, S.E. (1994). Leisure lifestyle and health. In D.M. Compton & S.E. Iso-Ahola (Eds.), *Leisure and mental health* (Vol. I, pp. 42–60). Park City, UT: Family Development Resources.

Iso-Ahola, S.E. (1997). A psychological analysis of leisure and health. In J.T. Haworth (Ed.), *Work, leisure and well-being* (pp. 117–130). New York: Routledge.

Iso-Ahola, S.E. (1999). Motivational foundations for leisure. In E.L. Jackson & T.L. Burton (Eds.), *Leisure studies: Prospects for the twenty-first century.* State College, PA: Venture.

Iso-Ahola, S., & Weissinger, E. (1984, June). Leisure and well-being: Is there a connection? *Parks and Recreation* 19(6), 40–44.

John of the Cross, Saint. (1589/1991). Letter 13. In *The collected works of St. John of the Cross.* (K. Kavanaugh & O. Rodriquez, Trans.) (Rev. ed., pp. 746–749). Washington, DC: ICS Publications.

Kaplan M. (1974). New concepts of leisure today. In J. Murphy, *Concepts of leisure: Philosophical implications* (pp. 229–236). Englewood Cliffs, NJ: Prentice Hall.

Kaplan, R. (1974). Some psychological benefits of an outdoor challenge program. *Environment and Behavior* 6, 101–116.

Kaplan, R., & Kaplan, S. (1989). *The experience of nature: A psychological perspective.* Cambridge: Cambridge University Press.

Kaplan, S. (1995). The restorative benefits of nature: Toward an integrative framework. *Journal of Environmental Psychology* 15, 169–182.

Kaplan, S., Bardwell, L.V., & Slakter, D.B. (1993). The museum as a restorative environment. *Environment and Behavior* 25(6), 725–742.

Kaplan, S., & Talbot, J.F. (1983). Psychological benefits of a wilderness experience. In I. Altman & J.F. Wohlwill (Eds.), *Behavior and the natural environment* (pp. 163–203). New York: Plenum.

Kelly, J.R. (1989). Leisure behaviors and styles: Social, economic, and cultural factors. In E.L. Jackson & T.L. Burton (Eds.), *Understanding leisure and recreation: Mapping the past, charting the future* (pp. 89–111). State College, PA: Venture.

Kraus, R. (1990). *Recreation and leisure in modern society* (4th ed.), New York: Harper Collins.

Mannell, R.C., & Iso-Ahola, S.E. (1987). Psychological nature of leisure and tourism experience. *Annals of Tourism Research* 14, 314–331.

Mannell, R.C., & Kleiber, D.A. (1997). *A social psychology of leisure.* State College, PA: Venture.

McAvoy, L., & Lais, G. (1996). Hard-to-define values and disabilities. In Driver, Dustin, Baltic, Elsner, & Peterson (Eds.), *Nature and the human spirit* (pp. 351–365).

McDonald, B.L., Guldin, R., & Wetherhill, G.R. (1988). The spirit in wilderness: The use and opportunity of wilderness experience for spiritual growth. In H.R. Freilich (Comp.), *Wilderness benchmark: Proceedings of the National Wilderness Colloquium.* (USDA Forest Service, Gen. Tech. Rep. SE-51, pp. 193–207). Asheville, NC: Southeastern Forest Experiment Station.

McDonald, B.L., & Schreyer, R. (1991). Spiritual benefits of leisure participation and leisure settings. In B.L. Driver, P.J. Brown & G.L. Peterson (Eds.), *Benefits of leisure* (pp. 179–194). State College, PA: Venture.

McGrath, A.E. (1994). *Spirituality in an age of change.* Grand Rapids: Zondervan.

Murphy, J. (1974). *Concepts of leisure: Philosophical implications.* Englewood Cliffs, NJ: Prentice Hall.

Pieper, J. (1952). *Leisure: The basis of culture* (A. Dru, Trans.). New York: Pantheon Books (1963, Random House).

Postema, D. (1983). *Space for God: The study and practice of prayer and spirituality.* Grand Rapids, MI: CRC Publications.

Ragheb, M.G. (1993). Leisure and perceived wellness: A field investigation. *Leisure Sciences* 15, 13–24.

Roberts, K. (1978). *Contemporary society and the growth of leisure.* London: Longman.

Ryken, L. (1995). *Redeeming the time: A Christian approach to work and leisure.* Grand Rapids: Baker Books.

Schroeder, H.W. (1991). Preference and meaning of arboretum landscapes: Combining quantitative and qualitative data. *Journal of Environmental Psychology* 11, 231–248.

Seaward, B.L. (1991). Spiritual well-being: A health education model. *Journal of Health Education* 22(3), 166–169.

Seaward, B. L. (1994). *Managing stress: Principles and strategies for health and well-being.* Boston: Jones & Bartlett.

Smedes, L.B. (1970). *All things made new: A study of man's union with Christ.* Grand Rapids: Eerdmans.

Stringer, L.A., & McAvoy, L.H. (1992). The need for something different: Spirituality and wilderness adventure. *Journal of Experiential Education* 15(1), 13–20.

Teaff, J. (1991). Leisure and life satisfaction of older Catholic women religious. *World Leisure and Recreation* 33(3), 27–29.

Tennessen, C.M., & Cimprich, B. (1995). Views to nature: Effects on attention. *Journal of Environmental Psychology* 15, 77–85.

Toon, P. (1989). *What is spirituality? And is it for me?* London: Daybreak.

Veal, A.J. (1993). The concept of lifestyle: A review. *Leisure Studies, 12,* 233–252.

Walsh, B.J., & Middleton, J.R. (1984). *The transforming vision.* Downers Grove, IL: InterVarsity.

Walsh, B.J., & Middleton, J.R. (1995). *Truth is stranger than it used to be.* Downers Grove, IL: InterVarsity.

Wilkinson, L. (1991). *Earthkeeping in the Nineties: Stewardship of creation* (Rev. ed.). Grand Rapids: Eerdmans.

Willard, D. (1995, March 6). Conversations: What makes spirituality Christian? *Christianity Today* 39, 16, 17.

Williams, R. (1979). *Christian spirituality*. Atlanta: John Knox Press.

Wolters, A.M. (1985). *Creation regained: Biblical basics for a reformational worldview*. Grand Rapids: Eerdmans.

Yiannakis, A., & Gibson, H. (1992). Roles tourists play. *Annals of Tourism Research* 19, 287–303.

Young, R.A., & Crandall, R. (1984). Wilderness use and self-actualization. *Journal of Leisure Research* 16, 149–160.

Young, R.A., & Crandall, R. (1986). Self-actualization and wilderness use: A panel study. In R.C. Lucas (Ed.), *Proceedings – National Wilderness Research Conference: Current Research* (pp. 385–388). Fort Collins, CO, July 23–26, 1985. Ogden, UT: Intermountain Research Station.

Chapter 25
THE FLOW EXPERIENCE: AN INTEGRATION OF SPIRITUAL AND LEISURE WELLBEING

Marcia Jean Carter

Over the last decade, the concept of wellness has been developed by several disciplines to describe the total person approach for improving the quality of life in a personal, positive, proactive manner. High-level wellness is conceptualized as being influential to six life dimensions: intellectual, emotional, physical, social, occupational, and spiritual wellbeing.

The origin and nature of wellness referred to as wholeness is found in three sources. Personality theories of Adler, Allport, Maslow, Rogers, and Jung (Ryckman, 1982) suggest the self is always moving toward greater wholeness and unification as optimal health is achieved. Second, social scientists have used the principles of systems theory to describe comprehensive models of wellbeing. In particular, the concepts of cybernetic self-regulation and emergence describe the processes by which we adopt behaviors that guide us toward optimal health. Finally, theological views also promote an integrative or holistic understanding of health and human nature. The biblical term *shalom* describes the integrative view of human health as well. *Shalom* is the descriptor for being harmoniously at peace within and without – a condition only possible when we function in a consonant relationship with God, with others, and within ourselves.

Leisure's relationship to wellness has been documented by several authors and researchers, most notably Iso-Ahola and Weissinger (1984) and Ragheb (1993). Intrinsic motivation, control, freedom, and satisfaction are qualities inherent in leisure that are also described as qualities of wellbeing. Also, engagement in leisure activities tends to be positively related to perceived wellness (Ragheb, 1993).

The concept of flow is a logical paradigm to use in the exploration

---

Revised version of paper presented at the 1994 conference.

of' the relationships among components of optimal wellness and leisure. Within the process of experiencing flow are qualities common to spirituality and leisure. Also, the achievement of a flow state realizes dimensions described by optimal wellbeing. How do we achieve flow or experience the qualities of wholeness and optimal wellbeing? Leisure professionals have the responsibility to create recreation environments so patrons realize enhanced qualities of wellbeing.

The intent of this chapter is to briefly review the concepts of wellness or holism of which spirituality is a recognized dimension, and qualities common to leisure, spirituality, and wellbeing. Focus will be on the central role of the leisure professional as an environment is created to nourish patrons so both the professional and patron grow toward optimal wellbeing. The paradigm of Csikszentmihalyi's (1975) flow state allows us to investigate the integration of spiritual and leisure wellbeing. This model identifies the leader's role in facilitating opportunities for patrons to experience enhanced qualities of life.

An Integrative Approach to Wellness

The concept of wellness has been defined as a total person approach to improving quality of life in a personal, positive, proactive manner. Wholeness of mind, body, spirit, and community is desirable for optimal functioning. As might be suggested by Paul in his instructions to the Church of Rome, a Christian commitment is a covenant to us for the rest of our lives to do those things that strengthen ourselves and our relationships (Ecker, 1984). As we strive to meet our daily responsibilities in work, friendships, and love relationships, there is a need to maintain a perspective not only on what is adequate but also what is necessary for optimal functioning (Witmer & Sweeney, 1992).

As mentioned in the introduction, the origin and nature of wellness may be studied from three viewpoints: personality theories; social science theories, especially systems theories; and theological perspectives. An integrative understanding of wellness and human nature is promoted by each. Theorists like Adler, Allport, and Maslow (Ryckman, 1982) suggested that persons are unified or integrative wholes who are goal directed or always moving toward greater unification; healthy persons are characterized by self-actualization (Ellison & Smith, 1991; Witmer & Sweeney, 1992).

The study of human behavior as a gestalt or whole is also supported by systems analysis. A system is a whole, with unique features that result from the interaction of its constituent parts. Each individual is a system that interacts with a supra-system, the environment in which we live. Two properties of systems describe our efforts to achieve wellness within this larger system. Cybernetics is a self-regulative function that controls our responses to our wellness environment (Crose, Nicholas, Gobble, & Frank, 1992). It is a quality control feature that allows us to realize we are feeling tension, or loss of love, or the commitment described by the apostle Paul. Models interpret systems. The IPO (input, process, output) model, with a feedback loop from the output to the input box, depicts the concept of cybernetics. This loop reflects the communication that we use to regain our covenant if we stray from a Christian path. We also use this model to investigate how the leisure professional facilitates optimal wellbeing with patrons.

Emergence is the second system property that describes key wellness concepts (Crose et al., 1992). A whole is greater than the sum of its parts and evolves from the interaction of its subunits. Our wellness emerges as we live. Our uniqueness results from the interplay among our physical, emotional, social, occupational, intellectual, and spiritual behaviors. Wellness is a developmental or emergent property; when we experience personal, positive, proactive growth, we are moving toward wholeness and wellbeing. The concept of flow is also depicted as emerging toward a uniquely enhancing individual experience.

The third perspective from which wellness is defined is the theological. The systems approach suggests that when focus is placed on only one dimension of wellbeing, e.g., physical, the significance of the emerging relationship of the whole is lost. The physical is powerless to act, the body and mind do not act alone, but the total person is responsible to God. The root meaning of the word *shalom* includes concepts of completeness, meaning, wholeness, and harmony (Ellison & Smith, 1991). Implicit is the notion of unimpaired relationships with others and being fulfilled in one's life course. Completeness is functioning as an integrated system in equilibrium or balance within a larger interpersonal and social system that shapes our being. Wellbeing occurs when, as a result of the divine design, there is harmony between our subsystems or the wellness dimensions and this larger world.

Spirituality as a wellness dimension has been conceived from two perspectives, an elementalistic and an integrative. In the first, spirituality is identified as one of the six dimensions, while in the second it is seen as an overriding concept found within each of the other dimensions. From the elementalistic view, spirituality is a subsystem equally as important as each of the other dimensions. Behaviors characteristic of this view of spirituality are identified as love, hope, purpose and meaning, life satisfaction, and qualities of the Golden Rule "Do unto others as you would have them do unto you" (Crose et al., 1992; Witmer & Sweeney, 1992). Spirituality, as one dimension of the whole, must remain in balance or harmony, like each of the other dimensions, if optimal wellness is to emerge.

In the second view, the integrative role of spirituality is congruent with becoming whole. Spiritual wellness occurs within each of the interrelated and interactive dimensions of wellness (Chandler, Holden & Kolander, 1992). To achieve optimal wellbeing, spiritual wellness is developed within each of the other dimensions; without a spiritual aspect, there is incompleteness in each of the other dimensions. Spirituality is interwoven within the body and soul and is a conduit to becoming more complete or whole (Chandler et al., 1992; Ellison & Smith, 1991). Lifestyle enhancement results with a commitment to change and the maintenance of healthy habits. Without commitment, change and maintenance become difficult at best. When spiritual commitment is made, all other choices within each of the wellness dimensions become easier (Ecker, 1984). The integrative view of spirituality in wellness permits study of the relationship of wellness, spirituality, and leisure.

Leisure is also an integrative quality. However, unlike spirituality, leisure is not usually identified as one of the elements of wellness nor as an integrative feature of wellness models. Yet, a commitment to leisure enhances life satisfaction, a key measure of the quality of life and perceived wellness. Sources of leisure and spirituality come from within, through intrinsic motivation (Chandler et al., 1992). Each also implies an internal locus of control; for example, moral and ethical values drive decisions (Witmer & Sweeney, 1992). Commitment and freedom of choice guide leisure and life commitments (Iso-Ahola & Weissinger, 1984). Leisure and spiritual behaviors are purposeful, personal, positive, and proactive. The Christian acts to transcend or emerge toward an optimal quality of life (Chandler et al., 1992). Both leisure and spiritual behaviors are dynamic and describe acts of total involvement similar to the flow state.

Spirituality, Leisure, Wellness, and Flow

The value dimensions of spirituality and leisure are captured with the concept of flow. Flow describes the dynamic sensation that is felt when we act with total involvement: for example, a descriptive state of an optimal experience. Also, it is a theoretical construct that is measured by the relationship between one's perceived challenge and felt needs. The flow model depicts the dynamic and emergent nature of becoming whole and the balance achieved in those experiences having qualities likened to leisure and spiritual wellbeing: if flow is achieved, spiritual and leisure wellbeing are realized.

Figure 1. The flow experience. Adapted from Csikszentmihalyi (1975).

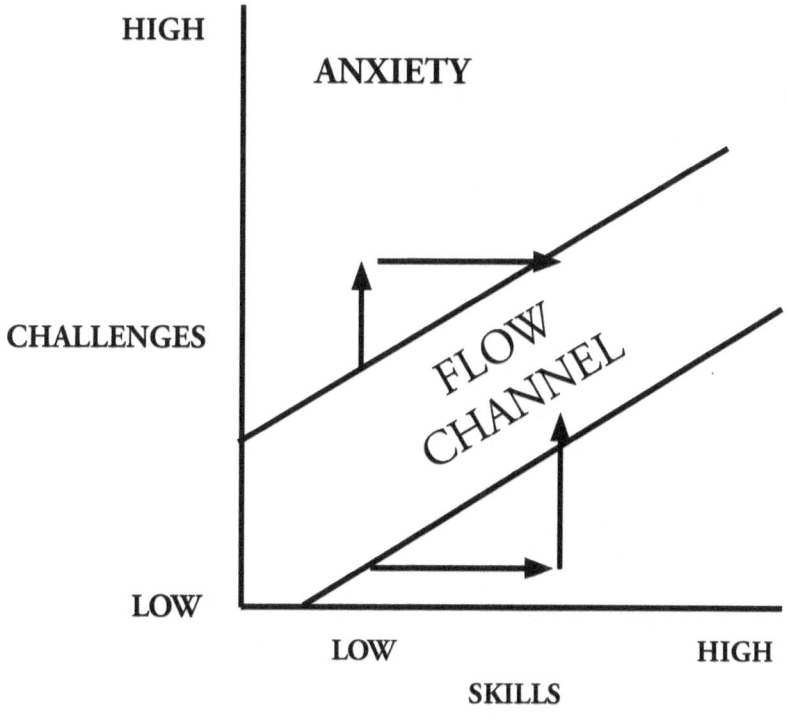

Flow theory predicts that an experience will be positive when the patron perceives that the environment or suprasystem contains opportunities for action or challenge that are matched to the patron's skill levels. When there is balance between the subjectively perceived challenge and needed skills, flow results. A flow state is characterized by a centering or focusing of the patron's attention on the experience, a loss of self-consciousness, unambiguous feedback about the actions, feelings of control over the actions and the environment, momentary loss of anxiety and constraint, and enjoyment. Flow results from, and is a consequence of, high level investment in an activity. A comparison of flow descriptors to spiritual and leisure wellbeing characteristics reveal nearly synonymous concepts. Flow also identifies the investment or commitment to an experience, the type of covenant evident in high level wellness.

The Leisure Professional's Leadership

A leisure professional has the ultimate responsibility of facilitating patron benefits. Leadership is an interpersonal influence exercised by a person through the process of communication to bring about specific outcomes. A leader takes conscious action to ensure an experience has made an impact and that the impact enhances the patron's quality of life and total wellbeing. Efficacy is influenced by how effective the leader is as a communicator and decision-maker. A leader is a central figure in enabling patron wellbeing. The self is used as an instrument to facilitate flow-engendering environments that ensure patron self-efficacy.

Centrality of the leader to wellness and effective programming is studied using the IPO model, the same systems model that shows the self-regulatory function (i.e., cybernetics) that controls responses to the larger system so personal wellness happens. The participant, environment, and leader are primary inputs, each with unique resources that are brought to a formal engagement. A leader assesses these inputs, selects content (experiences), and processes (leadership methods) so the outcome is enhanced patron competence and quality of life (Little, 1993). This engagement may happen during any of the other wellness dimensions – occupational, intellectual, emotional, physical, and social – as reflected by the integrative wellness model. Characteristics and outcomes of the engagement are embodied in leisure and spiritual wellbeing. The leader's role in creating experiences that contribute to total wellbeing is explained by reviewing how the leader provokes flow-engendering environments that contribute to patron self-efficacy.

To facilitate flow, the leader introduces several features into the environment of the engagement. Awareness of the features comes with professional training and preparation. Ellis, Witt, and Aguiler (1983) identified six flow-engendering features as essential to therapeutic interactions:

1. During an experience, the leader arranges the amount and degree of novelty and dissonance in the environment so "newness" of the experience leaves patrons challenged yet in control of their behaviors and draws their attention to the engagement.

2. Expectations are neither too simple as to produce boredom nor too complex as to result in anxiety. With activity and task analyses, leaders order and sequence expectations so patrons progress into experiences when skills are mastered.

3. The environment in which the experience happens is monitored so the patron focuses on the engagement and is not distracted by surrounding novel stimuli.

4. The engagement itself serves to motivate so the patron's attention is not drawn to an external reward which might detract from the inherent value of the engagement. Patron readiness is a fundamental motivator which the leader determines by assessment of patron competence and preference prior to involvement.

5. Feedback is an essential flow element. Immediate positive feedback results when the patron's knowledge and skill levels are matched to activity demands. Too much or too little challenge results in negative feedback and nonflow.

6. The leader focuses the patron's attention on what is happening to the patron during the experience rather than what might be associated with outcomes of the experience. Leader reinforcement acknowledges adequacy of the patron's skill levels and commitment to the challenge.

Figure 2. Efficacy in leisure programming.

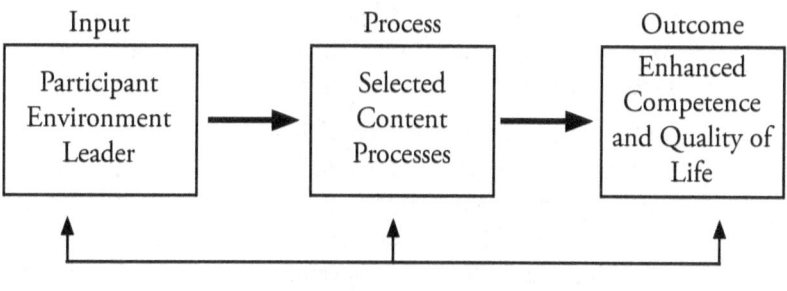

The leader concentrates on the patron's ability to experience flow and the conditions during the engagement that facilitate its achievement. A leader arranges environmental aspects so patrons, competencies, and preferences are compatible with the experiential demands so balance, harmony, and the flow state result; when this occurs, the patron and leader grow toward optimal wellbeing.

A second consideration in creating flow-engendering environments is patron self-efficacy. Bandura's (1977) self-efficacy theory helps the leader identify how patrons' conscious and unconscious behaviors allow them to perceive successful involvement during a leisure experience. Patrons assess each situation to determine skills necessary to perform successfully, then compare their perceived abilities to those needed for successful performance. These assessments influence choice of involvement and degree of energy expended to meet the situational challenges. Each situation is assessed in terms of anticipated outcomes or outcome expectancies, and the perception of patron's abilities to be successful in performing these outcomes or efficacy expectancies. Experiences are entered into or avoided as a result of receiving information about our abilities to perform successfully from four information sources. Savell (1986) identified these as:

1. Performance accomplishments give information on the degree of success or failure. A leader plans short-term goals so exposure is initially successful. Also, the leader arranges experiences to be progressively more difficult requiring the demonstration of higher levels of efficacy.

2. Vicarious experiences provide information based on observations of others. A leader provides demonstration or models so a patron observes appropriate and successful outcomes. When the patron relates to a model person with similar characteristics who is able to succeed, then the patron will tend to believe success with practice is likely.

3. Verbal persuasion is a source of information that effects involvement. Both the leader and patron may be persuasive, especially when verbal information about perceived abilities occurs along with successful performance. The stronger the verbal input and the more respected its source, the greater the amount of energy invested to master the experience.

4. Interpretation of an emotional response to a situation contributes to self-efficacy. Accurate interpretation leads to awareness of perceived abilities. The leader helps the patron understand

the underlying cause of a physiological response to a situation so anxiety is controlled and positive efficacy is the outcome.

A perception of success results when positive information is obtained from these sources. The leader monitors the environment so the patron's and leader's perceptions are positive about the engagement. Perceived freedom and control are a function of competence and are central to self-efficacy. Perceived freedom is operationalized through the patron's sense of control, self-determination, or efficacy and is defined by the relationship between the patron and the experience. A patron's capacity for perceived freedom and competence is maximized and a leisure experience is achieved when the patron has a positive perception of social and leisure abilities within the situation and when the patron accurately interprets the situation from the primary information sources. A leader enhances the capacity for freedom and control when the patron's competence is matched to situational demands and the patron's expectations are reflected in the leader's intended outcomes.

Leadership Effectiveness

Flow and self-efficacy theories suggest a linkage between leadership effectiveness and patron outcomes. This link is defined by a leader's ability to create a flow-engendering environment so the patron receives positive information about the skills used during the experience and the expectancies resulting from the experience. The concept of "self as an instrument" suggests that certain characteristics and qualities are resources through which a leader accomplishes outcomes. As a resource, effective use of the leader facilitates patron flow and self-efficacy.

The IPO model is used to interpret leadership effectiveness (Little, 1993) A leader is a communicator who makes strategic or planned decisions and reflexive (or spontaneous decisions so a patron's abilities and leisure lifestyle are enhanced. How well a leader communicates is influenced by: a) personal characteristics, b) facilitation skills, and c) professional competencies. Definitive qualities in each of these three categories are essential input variables or resources brought to the leisure environment by the leader.

During the leisure experience or P (process) phase in the IPO model, a leader makes strategic or planned decisions using analytical skills and reflexive or spontaneous decisions using observational skills to create the flow-engendering environment. These decisions occur as the leader follows a sequence of interaction steps with patrons. Planned decision-making during leadership is based on pre-existent information, while spontaneous decision-making is responsive to the patron's present behaviors and the situational demands. A leader takes a series of steps to open and close interactions so the patron is guided toward the achievement of anticipated outcomes. The nature of this interaction is influenced by the leader's ability to make decisions responsive to the patron's displayed behaviors. Thus the leader's skills are a resource to achieve patron outcomes.

Figure 3. Leader effectiveness.

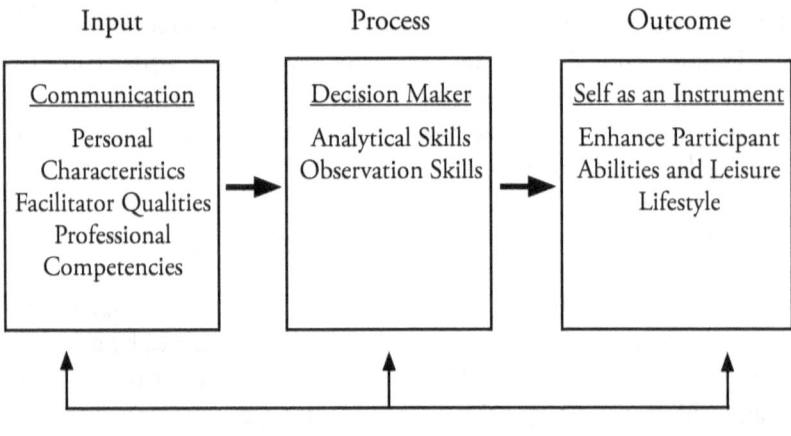

A leader brings into the leisure experience perceptions about professional leadership abilities and anticipated outcomes. From the leader's view, an experience is a professional challenge in which communication and decision-making skills are used to facilitate patron outcomes. Each patron also brings perceptions of abilities and outcomes to the leisure experience. During the O (output) phase in the IPO model, feedback identifies whether patron wellbeing has been enhanced by the leader's effective use of personal and professional resources and whether the leader's and the patron's perceptions of abilities and outcomes are compatible. If the leader has been successful in creating a flow-engendering environment, both the leader and the patron benefit, as their perceptions and expectations are in harmony with their skills.

Conclusion

The intent of this paper was fourfold: first, review concepts of wellness, especially spiritual wellness; second, study the similar qualities of spirituality and leisure as components of wellness; third, propose the use of flow as a concept and model to relate the integrative nature of spiritual and leisure wellbeing; and fourth, how a leisure professional contributes to a patron's enhanced wellbeing.

Wellness is multidimensional, dynamic, and self-regulative (Crose et al., 1992). Spiritual and leisure wellness overlay each of the other dimensions in the wellness pie as the qualities of freedom, intrinsic motivation, control, and choice are essential in each of the other dimensions. Without these, we will be unable to make or sustain a commitment to a quality life with God. The dynamic nature of wellbeing is represented by the flow model. Leaders and patrons interact to engender flow and self-efficacy, achieve balance, and realize total involvement. The cyclical nature (feedback loop) of the IPO model represents the ongoing or lifelong covenant, the emergent nature of wellness.

Daily we are challenged to use our skills to grow and sustain spontaneity, creativity, humor, and ultimately harmony with ourselves and in our relationships. The self-regulatory nature of wellness is seen in the balance or normative behavior exhibited across the life span within each wellness dimension. Christians make decisions that affirm their commitments to oneness or wholeness.

Wellness is personal, positive, and proactive. As leisure professionals, we create opportunities for each patron to experience flow and self-efficacy. A flow experience is unique to each of us, as is the process through which a flow state is achieved. Outcomes of the experience are enhancing or positive to the self and quality of life. Leaders and patrons seek out growth experiences. Christians recognize health-reducing variables and are guided by their commitment to cope, change, and remain in a continuous state of wellbeing.

References

Bandura, A. (1977). Toward a unifying theory of behavioural change. *Psychological Review* 84(2), 191–215.

Chandler, C.T., Holden, J.M., & Kolander, C.A. (1992). Counseling for spiritual wellness: Theory and practice. *Journal of Counseling & Development* 71, 168–175.

Crose, R., Nicholas, D.R., Gobble, D.C., & Frank, B. (1992). Gender and wellness: A multidimensional systems model for counseling. *Journal of Counseling & Development* 11, 149–156.

Csikszentmihalyi, M. (1975). *Beyond boredom and anxiety.* San Francisco: Jossey-Bass.

Ecker, R.E. (1984). *Staying well: Why the good life is so bad for your health.* Downers Grove, IL: InterVarsity.

Ellis, G.D., Witt, P.A., & Aguilar, T. (1983) Facilitating "flow" through therapeutic recreation services. *Therapeutic Recreation Journal* 11(2), 6–15.

Ellison, C.W., & Smith, J. (1991) Toward an integrative measure of health and well-being. *Journal of Psychology and Theology* 19(l), 35–48.

Iso-Ahola, S.E., & Weissinger, E. (1984). Leisure and well-being: Is there a connection? *Parks and Recreation* 19(6), 40–44.

Little, S.L. (1993). Leisure program design and evaluation: Using leisure experience models as diagnostic tools. *JOPERD/Leisure Today* 64(8), 26–29.

Ragheb, M.G. (1993). Leisure and perceived wellness: A field investigation. *Leisure Sciences* 15(1), 13–24.

Ryckman, R.M. (1982). *Theories of Personality* (2nd ed.). Monterey, CA: Brooks/Cole.

Savell, K. (1986). Implications for therapeutic recreation leisure-efficacy: Theory and therapy programming. *Therapeutic Recreation Journal* 20(l), 43–52.

Witmer, J.M., & Sweeney, T.J. (1992) A holistic model for wellness and prevention over the life span. *Journal of Counseling & Development* 11, 140–148.

Chapter 26

JOURNEYING BY CANOE: THE RELATIONSHIP BETWEEN THE CANOE AND SPIRITUALITY

Thomas Peace

It is a warm August morning, and there is not a cloud in the sky. The sun sparkles off the lake that the light breeze is rippling. I am paddling down Rain Lake in Algonquin Park, searching for an amazing campsite where I stayed ten years earlier. It is funny how the mind works. By the time that I am halfway down the lake, my mind is occupied with other thoughts, more important thoughts, about life, about existence, about why this is here, about why more people don't canoe alone. Maybe it's fear: fear of injury, fear of the unknown, fear of discovering we are not who we thought we were. I continue paddling and begin to wonder why this type of thinking is so common for me while canoeing. Is there a spiritual connection that humans have with the canoe? I wonder. The question is left for another day, as I watch a loon fly past me.

This is a common story. Many canoeists will tell you that they feel a spiritual connection while paddling and on canoe trips, but few have written about this aspect of canoeing. This paper is an attempt to understand the link between the historic watercraft so critical to Canada's history and spirituality.

Coming to Terms with Spirituality

To begin, we must understand what we mean by spirituality. A working definition of spirituality often eludes us. Some define it as searching for the truth behind our known existence, others relate it to their faith, and others consider it to be developing a deeper knowledge and understanding of self. Often when writing about spirituality, it is possible to

Paper presented at 2003 conference as the Student Paper Award Winner.

define the term; however, this cannot be done for this paper. The work done on this project was taken from numerous sources that came from people with many different faith backgrounds and preconceived notions of what they define as spirituality. It is incredibly difficult to make these different notions fit under the same definition. However, we also cannot flounder around this topic, as there needs to be some parameters that can be used to build a definition of spirituality. The criteria used in this paper are based on responses that leisure researchers Allison Stringer and Leo McAvoy (1992) received in a study that they conducted on spirituality in the wilderness. It was derived from common themes that emerged upon asking for personal definitions of spirituality from both of their subject groups. Group A in the study consisted of thirteen people, five with mental disabilities, three in leadership positions, and five others. These people participated in an eight-day canoe trip in Northern Ontario. Group B consisted of eighteen people; five were excluded from the study (but were on the trip), and all were university students enrolled in a wilderness leadership class. These people went on a ten-day backpacking trip to the Beartooth Mountains. The average age on both trips was 26. The following is the common ground that they established:

> the shared or common spirit between and among people; a power or authority greater than self; clarity of inner (or self) knowledge; inner feelings (especially of peace, oneness, and strength); awareness of and attunement to the world and one's place in it; the way in which one relates to fellow humans and to the environment . . .; and intangibility. (Stringer & McAvoy, p. 16)

By discussing various aspects of canoeing and canoe tripping, it will be shown how the canoe allows us to meet this criterion and how it fosters spiritual experiences and spiritual growth.

The Canoe and Spirituality

Some people believe that the canoe is a vehicle, not a catalyst for a spiritual experience. To many canoeists, the canoe is considered "Fifth Business" or the baritone in opera (Davies, 1983), the necessary character that ties an individual to spirituality but does not carry a major role. Famous canoeist Bill Mason, who was also a Christian, did not see the canoe as spiritual in itself but "as an art form as well as a vehicle to take me into the wilderness – a world unchanged and unspoiled as God had created it" (as quoted in Raffan, 1997, p. 37). For Mason, the canoe was a way to enter into God's creation; it was a tool that could be used to bring you to a place that had only been impacted by God. It was not the canoe or the act of canoeing but the destination of the trip. Luste (1988) summed up this view of the canoe and spirituality when he wrote, "In this [emotional and spiritual] context the canoe plays a supportive role. It provides the conveyance for the wilderness experience and may contribute to that experience to some degree, but it is not an end in itself" (p. 151). Luste's observance is the premise of this paper. There is no one aspect of canoeing that will give insight into the relationship between the canoe and spirituality. This topic must be looked at holistically – meaning it must be looked at from every perspective – in order for one to find answers regarding this connection.

There are three areas of the physical process of canoeing that help to foster spirituality: paddling, portaging, and the number of people who are accompanying you. The repetitiveness of paddling provides the opportunity for a canoeist to enter into deeper thought than normal. It allows canoeists the opportunity to ponder spiritual questions, which are frequently catalyzed by the overwhelming sense of awe at something that wasn't created by humans. It is possible that this type of repetition is related to Csikszentmihalyi's (1975) flow experiences, which have been described by Barbara McDonald and Richard Schreyer (1991) as:

> ... a merging of action and awareness. The person does not consciously think about the action that is being taken, even though the person is aware of those actions. There is a focusing of attention on a narrow set of stimuli. ... Flow experiences involve a loss of sense of self. There is not so much a sense of self-consciousness as there is an awareness of the immediate circumstance of what is occurring. (p. 183)

In their article, McDonald and Schreyer have related this type of experience to spirituality. Considering that many athletes involved in repetitive actions, such as runners, also describe flow experiences, it seems likely that paddling would foster a spiritual growth.

Avid canoeists recognize that canoeing does not simply mean easy paddling on open waters; there is also the portage, a physically grueling activity, especially when it means long distances. Surprisingly, most people find the work involved in portaging very fulfilling. Andrew Rogness (1994), who wrote *Crossing Boundary Waters*, quoted Romans 5:3–5 in regards to portaging: "Suffering produces patience, patience produces character, character produces hope, and hope does not disappoint us" (p. 59). He felt that portaging builds our hope, for ourselves and for humankind, and leads us down a spiritual path. Thus, portaging provides a new hope for us, and renews our sense of meaning.

Finally, there is the much-debated contrast between canoeing with a group or in solitude. Carrie McGown and Martha Mortson (n.d.) described the spiritual help that they gave each other in some of their journal entries while canoeing across Canada; Rebecca Fox's (1997) research noted that there are spiritual benefits to paddling in gender specific groups; and Stringer and McAvoy's (1992) research also suggested that groups were more important to Group A, which was on a canoe trip, than to Group B, which was hiking. Paddling together allows for corporate thought on spiritual concepts and ideas and relates to Stringer and McAvoy's first point in describing spirituality. However, both Bill Mason (1984a, 1984b, 1988) and Andrew Rogness (1994) seem to suggest that spiritual growth occurs in solitude. Solitude provides time for inner reflection and personal growth, which relates back to some of Stringer and McAvoy's other points in describing spirituality. It is most likely that both types of canoeing allow one to grow in different ways and that both are spiritually beneficial and should be practiced. In either case, spiritual experiences and growth do not occur in a vacuum and are influenced by our past history (Stringer & McAvoy). This suggests that it is the physical side of paddling that provides an opportunity for spiritual searching; it is not a catalyst of that spiritual search itself. For that we must delve deeper into canoeing.

To most paddlers, there is a middle ground between this idea of the canoe being a vehicle, which allows us to experience other things that act as a catalyst to experiencing spirituality, and the canoe being the catalyst itself. In *Enhancing Spiritual Experience in Adventure Programs*, Rebecca Fox (1999) wrote "People carry 'baggage' into the wilderness adventure experiences which influences perceptions and may generate fears toward nature" (p. 297). Andrew Rogness (1994) also mentioned this "baggage" concept and believes that with each stroke that one paddles into the wilderness more and more of their baggage is left behind. It should be noted that Fox and Rogness are not discussing the same type of baggage; Fox mentioned the need to release our fears (especially towards nature), while Rogness suggested that we need to escape from our everyday lifestyles. However, both seem to suggest that the physical aspect of paddling helps us to remove our baggage. James (1998) also called the reduction of tangible goods a "necessity of reducing one's baggage to a minimum [that] requires awareness of essentials uncommon in our cluttered world" (p. 85). Most often those who cannot enjoy the outdoors are the same people who are chained to items like a computer or television that are unessential to life. These people are unable to shed this baggage of modern culture. A prime example of this can be found by examining the main characters in Margaret Atwood's (1973) *Surfacing*. Only one of her characters successfully shed their baggage and undergoes what seems to be a spiritual awakening. Once we are able to break these chains and welcome the loss of our baggage, we can then begin a spiritual journey.

It was the need to shed this baggage that drove so many to become *coureurs de bois*. This is illustrated by a verse of an old French Canadian song called "Masterless Men":

> We have slipped from the grip of the Church
> We have travelled beyond the reach of the king
> We are the children of the wind
> We are the masterless men. (Grant, 1988, p. 12)

This song demonstrates that this separation from our worldly attachments and loyalties is not a new concept and has been a part of canoeing for centuries. Like the physical process of paddling, leaving our baggage on shore frees our minds from the routine of daily life, enabling a greater likelihood of spiritual experiences. It is very hard for us to do activities, to think, and to grow spiritually if our minds are preoccupied.

The easiest way to decrease the amount of distraction in a canoe trip is to paddle alone. Although some feel that paddling alone is an unsafe way to travel, it is often the best way to explore spiritual issues and to develop spiritually. This could be in part due to the fact that tandem paddling provides another distraction and occasionally has a negative result on relationships. Paddling solo provides the opportunity to let things sink in more deeply and to come to a greater understanding of nature and ourselves.

References to spirituality and paddling on Lake Superior have come up in numerous sources. Bill Mason (1984) called it a feeling of euphoria in his film *Waterwalker*; Carrie McGown and Martha Mortson (n.d.) began to discuss God much more as they were held wind-bound on Lake Superior for about 22 days; and Andrew Rogness (1994) briefly discussed the isolation and development that he experienced while paddling on this lake. It seems as if Lake Superior, in itself, is often a catalyst to stimulating spiritual growth. This is because of the isolation that is felt on such a large and powerful lake, a lake that can leave you stranded for days. We often do not have the freedom of being on Lake Superior, but we can find solitude while canoeing lakes and rivers as well. In *Fire in the Bones*, Raffan (1997) includes an explanation by Bill Mason's wife that Mason would have to do at least one portage before he began to truly experience the wilderness. Other humans tend to ruin our experience of nature. Being alone allows us to reach deep inside ourselves and see who we really are.

The canoe, and the act of canoeing, is like a renovation crew; they gut you down to your skeleton, physically, mentally and spiritually and then begin to rebuild you. Kirk Wipper (1988) stated that,

> The canoe puts us in touch with our inner self – that still, small voice. It gives us moments of solitude in which we have the opportunity to experience, as Tennyson stated, 'self-knowledge, self-reverence, and self-control.' In these times of insight, we are also led to things spiritual – a pause for meditation and contemplation not often experienced in the noisy, crowded, restless world. (p. x)

The canoe destroys what we have made ourselves in our own creation, and returns us to whom we really are. Pierre Trudeau (1944/1996) echoed this in his essay "The Ascetic in a Canoe." Here he states that we should only end our canoe trips when we are no longer making progress in rebuilding ourselves. This theme of rebuilding is also in Andrew Rogness' (1994) book and to some degree in McGown and Mortson's (n.d.) trip journal. The purpose of losing all our mental and physical baggage is not to lose it entirely and for eternity, but instead to acquire new baggage, and less baggage; to grow mentally, physically, and emotionally, and return to the world which we abandoned so long ago.

Part of this new baggage is often a sense of oneness with nature. This oneness fits perfectly into Stringer and McAvoy's (1992) description of spirituality. Most canoeists will argue that canoeing is the best way to experience this oneness. This may be due to the canoe's origins. For if you are skilled enough, it is possible to walk into the woods and come out with a canoe. Canoes can be, and were in the past, made entirely from products in the Canadian forest, and were originally one of the few modes of transportation that was entirely natural. Secondly, the canoe is the only way to experience the wilderness with an entirely "leave no trace attitude." Atwood (1973) wrote: "I go along near the trees, boat and arms one movement, amphibian; the water closes behind me, no track" (p. 167). Unlike hiking (or portaging), the canoe does not leave footprints in the ground or a well-beaten path. Thirdly, in basking in nature, we begin to see that it, too, is alive. Archie Belaney (1935/1999), better known as Grey Owl, wrote a fictitious, but comparable narrative of this in *Sajo and the Beaver People*:

> And there you'll see great rivers, and lakes and whispering forests, and strange animals that talk and work, and live in towns; where the tall trees seem to nod to you and beckon as you pass them, and you hear soft voices in the streams. . . . For the Indian liked to feel that his canoe was actually

alive and had a head and a tail like all the other creatures, and was sharp-eyed like a bird, and swift and light like a fox. (pp. 428–429)

This type of personification is not uncommon in wilderness literature and productions. Henry David Thoreau (1854/n.d.) used it frequently in *Walden* – his description of the warrior ants is not only a prime example, but also an interesting perspective on nature. Bill Mason used this idea extensively in his work. In *Waterwalker*, Mason (1984) quoted Job 12:7–10, which gives biblical background to this concept. He used this passage to build onto an unknown indigenous nation's belief system, which is quoted throughout the video. Nobody today would state that you could literally "ask the birds in the sky, and they will tell you" as Job does, but this type of thinking begins to lead an outdoor enthusiast down the path to understanding that there is more than we can see, and it often brings people further in their spiritual journey.

It is this feeling of oneness that fosters a sense of mystery inside of us. This mystery is a part of what spirituality is; it is recognizing that we do not know or understand everything. The mystery, of course, lies in nature and us, not in the canoe. We know who made our canoes, our packs, and our paddles, but we still don't know with 100 percent certainty why we exist and why our environment exists. Mystery is a key element in spirituality.

William James (1981) believed this mystic experience to be similar to spiritual experiences, and Stringer and McAvoy (1992) mentioned four of its characteristics.

> These are "ineffability," the inability to describe the experience in words . . . "noetic quality," the sense of . . . illumination and revelation of greater truth; "transiency," the short duration of the experience . . . and "passivity," the feeling of being "held" or "grasped" by a superior power during the experience. (p. 14)

The characteristics of spiritual experience listed above are a part of the mystery that one may experience on a canoe trip, but the description of mystery that is often recounted endures the entire trip and possibly longer, not just at fleeting times.

Conclusion

As Canadians, the canoe has made a significant impact on our lives. Before we had a national rail system, most of the nation was linked with a national canoe route system, the highways of the north. The canoe has been central to this country for millennia, long before the Europeans arrived. Kirk Wipper (1988) called "rivers – timeless pathways of the wilderness . . . that connects us to the spirit of these people who walk beside us as we glide silently along riverine trails" (p. ix). Bob Henderson (1988) stated that in canoeing the "past, present and future meet" (pp. 86–87). The canoe helps us to discover our future and connects us with our past. The canoe has also been a tool and a form of art. It has been used to create some of this country's most celebrated art; one thinks of Tom Thomson and the Group of Seven. It has also been one of this country's most celebrated art forms. It has been central to our legends and stories, like *La Chasse Galerie*, in which lumbermen bargain with the devil to go home for Christmas, and he whisks them away in his flying canoe. It has linked us to the wilderness, which has linked us to our forgotten spirit. By canoeing, we go further than the "masterless men" mentality of the *coureurs de bois* and recognize that we are part of this symphony of life and are searching for its conductor.

D.H. Lawrence (as cited in Henderson, 1988) once said that water is two parts hydrogen, one part oxygen, "but there is also a third thing that makes it water and nobody knows what" it is (p. 89). Canoe enthusiast and scholar Bob Henderson (1988) rephrased that to express his thoughts on canoeing. He wrote "the canoe is a watercraft pointed at each end, but there is a third thing that makes it a canoe that is brought into play with human relationship and nobody really knows what it is" (p. 90). Through looking at the above aspects of canoeing, I believe the third element to be spirituality.

As I return from my sojourn into the wilderness the sky begins its transformation from blue to various shades of pinks and reds. The trees on the east shore of Rain Lake radiate the sunlight as if they were on fire. I am exhausted from the day's worth of paddling. My muscles ache, my hands are calloused and sore, and my feet are asleep. My body may be returning exhausted and worn down, but my spirit returns healthy and rejuvenated. My body may be returning to the human world, but my spirit remains in the natural world. The drive home will be restful, and the silence brings me peace. As I leave, I realize that I did not achieve my goal of finding the campsite I stayed at years before; instead I found much more that had been with me on that first trip and I had chosen to ignore.

References

Atwood, M. (1973). *Surfacing*. Don Mills, ON: PaperJacks.

Belaney, A. (1935/1999). *The collected works of Grey Owl: Three complete and unabridged Canadian classics*. Toronto: Chapters.

Davies, R. (1983). *The deptford trilogy*. Toronto: Penguin Books.

Csikszentmihalyi, M. (1975). *Beyond boredom and anxiety*. San Francisco: Jossey-Bass.

Fox, R. (1997). Women, nature and spirituality: A qualitative study exploring women's wilderness experience. In D. Rowe & P. Brown (Eds.), *Proceedings, ANZALS conference 1997* (pp. 59–64). Newcastle, NSW: Australian and New Zealand Association for Leisure Studies, and the Department of Leisure and Tourism Studies, University of Newcastle.

Fox, R. (1999). Enhancing spiritual experience in adventure programs. In J.C. Miles & S. Priest (Eds.), *Adventure programming* (pp. 455–461). State College, PA: Venture.

Grant, S. (1988). Symbols and myths: Images of the canoe and north. In J. Raffan & B. Horwood (Eds.), *Canexus: The canoe in Canadian culture* (pp. 5–26). Toronto: Betelgeuse Books & Queens University.

Henderson, B. (1988). Reflections of a bannock baker. In J. Raffan & B. Horwood (Eds.), *Canexus: The canoe in Canadian culture* (pp. 83–92). Toronto: Betelgeuse Books & Queens University.

James, W. (1981). The canoe trip as a religious quest. *Studies in Religion* 10(2), 151–166.

James, W.C. (1998). *Locations of the sacred: Essays on religion, literature, and Canadian culture*. Waterloo, ON: Wilfrid Laurier University Press.

Luste, G.J. (1988). Solitude and kinship in the canoeing experience. In J. Raffan & B. Horwood (Eds.), *Canexus: The canoe in Canadian culture*, (pp. 151–159) Toronto: Betelgeuse Books & Queens University.

Mason, B. (1984a). *Path of the paddle*. Toronto: Key Porter Books.

Mason, B. (Producer & Director). (1984b). *Waterwalker* [Motion picture]. Ottawa, ON: National Film Board of Canada and Imago.

Mason, B. (1988). *Song of the paddle*. Toronto: Firefly Books.

McDonald, B., & Schreyer, R. (1991). Spiritual benefits of leisure participation and leisure settings. In B.L. Driver, P.J. Brown, & G.L. Peterson (Eds.), *Benefits of leisure* (pp. 179–194). State College, PA: Venture.

McGown, C., & Mortson, M. (n.d.). Trip Journal. February 27, 1998, to September 23, 1999. Unpublished manuscript.

Raffan, J. (1997). *Fire in the bones*. Toronto: Harper Collins.

Rogness, A. (1994). *Crossing Boundary Waters*. Minneapolis: Augsburg Fortress.

Stringer, L.A., & McAvoy, L.H. (1992). The need for something different: Spirituality and wilderness adventure. *The Journal of Experiential Education* 15(1), 13–21.

Thoreau, H.D. (1854/n.d.). *Walden*. New York: Milestone Editions.
Trudeau, P.E. (1944/1996). The ascetic in a canoe. In G. Pelletier (Ed.), *Against the current: Selected writings 1939–1996* (pp. 9–13). Toronto: McClelland & Stewart.
Wipper, K. (1988). Forward. In J. Raffan & B. Horwood (Eds.), *Canexus: The canoe in Canadian culture* (pp. ix–xi) Toronto: Betelgeuse Books & Queens University.

Chapter 27

LOVE-CENTERED WELLNESS

Robert D. Weathers

Both the words and the spirit of this chapter may sound more like a time-worn sermon than an informative presentation about wellness. While the message may not be new, I hope that by the conclusion the reader will agree that we have addressed the very essence of wellness and (forgive my presumption) that any consideration of wellness will be regarded futile apart from a realization and affirmation of my basic thesis. Although I obviously hope that my words will provide some insight, I expect that their primary value may be as a stimulus for further thought and discussion. The community of faith will probably benefit most from hearing reactions to the ideas presented here.

The inspiration for this chapter is the first chapter of a psychology self-help book by psychologist and pastoral counselor Howard Clinebell, the founder of the Institute for Religion and Wholeness at the Claremont School of Theology. According to Clinebell (1992), "You are whole or have well being to the degree that the center of your life is integrated and energized by love and healthy spirituality" (p. 4). He goes on to say that "Love is the heart of well being! It's the power, the means, the meaning, and the goal of wholeness" (p. 4). In his view, love is a verb, something that is done and not merely felt. "It is doing those things that help enable whoever or whatever you love to develop the treasure of their possibilities and thus move toward life in all its fullness" (Clinebell, p. 6).

While some may see narcissistic, new-age humanism in some of Clinebell's (1992) views, I generally perceive them to be consistent with Scripture, and I particularly appreciate the ideas just quoted. He likens wholeness to a flower in that both are living, growing, and have ever-changing unity among all their parts. The center of the flower is healthy spirituality, ". . . where the petals are nourished and the seeds of new life grow" (Clinebell, p. 7). The petals in his model are relationships,

---

Revised version of paper presented at the 1998 conference.

mind, body, work, play, and the world.

These ideas have helped shape the approach that I take in my wellness courses at Seattle Pacific University: that wellness, or what Clinebell (1992) called wholeness or wellbeing, is the process of behaving in ways that optimize spiritual, social, mental, and physical wellbeing – with emphasis given to the notion that these are integrated to such an extent that whatever affects the wellbeing of one component also affects the rest. It is further assumed that love is the starting point, common denominator, and ultimate test for wellness. My sense is that wellness is essentially right relationship with God and with all that he has created: that we are created for relationship and that the characteristic of wellness-nurturing relationships is love.

I must, however, take exception with Clinebell's (1992) statement that "Wellness-nurturing love begins with yourself but must not stop there" (Clinebell, p. 6). It is easily agreed that wellness-nurturing love cannot stop with self-love, but I reject the notion that it begins there. My suspicion is that he also really believes otherwise. He would probably allow that "wellness-nurturing love" actually begins with what he calls the "divine Spirit of love and liberation" (Clinebell, p. 7). He, in fact, described the spiritual life as the "wellspring of love, well being, and joy" (Clinebell, p. 19), and that is where I would like to begin an application of "the law of love" to spiritual, social, emotional, intellectual, and physical wellbeing. In the remainder of this chapter, I will examine our need and potential for love and suggest ways by which love for God, others, and self might be demonstrated.

We Are Loved

We know the beginning and definition of love because the Scriptures tell us that "love comes from God" and that "God *is* [emphasis added] love" (1 John 4:7–8). The greatest demonstration of God's love is that he sent his only son into the world to make abundant life available to those who had rejected him (John 3:16; 1 John 4:9). I believe that Clinebell's (1992) statement about the beginning of wellness-nurturing love is correct if he means that our wellness begins to be nurtured, that we begin to really live, when we come to perceive and really be moved by the fact that we, broken and imperfect beings, are profoundly loved by the only one who is whole and perfect.

We Are Free to Love

The testimony of Scripture is that because of God's love for us, we are freed to love (1 John 4:19). We are able to see God as worthy of our love (not simply our reverence) when we realize that we are loved by the Holy One, the Almighty. Our worth is also established by this realization, and we are empowered to love ourselves as well. When we are thus secure in our own worth based on God's love for us, recognition of God's love for others also affirms their worth – freeing us for compassion and true altruism.

We Are Commanded to Love

As most believers are well aware, both the Old and New Testaments record the charge to love God with all our heart, soul, strength, and mind (Deut. 6:5, 11:13, 13:3; Matt. 22:37; Mark 12:30; Luke 10:27). Jesus emphasized that this is the first and greatest commandment (Matt. 22:38). Similarly, we read the command to love our neighbors as we love ourselves (Lev. 19:18; Matt. 19:19, 22:39; Mark 12:31; Luke 10:7). The apostle Paul asserts that "everything we know about God's Word is summed up" by this single commandment (Gal. 5:14, Message). Jesus said that "These two commands are pegs; everything in God's Law and the Prophets hangs from them" (Matt. 22:40, Message), and/or that "There is no other commandment that ranks with these" (Mark 12:31, Message).

After successfully identifying these great commands, the religious scholar asked Jesus how he might identify his neighbor. Jesus responded with the parable of the good Samaritan (Luke 10:28–37). We understand that any Samaritan would be the furthest thing from this man's understanding of his neighbor or an object of his love. This, of course, is consistent with Jesus's injunction to love our enemies (Matt. 5:44–46; Luke 6:27).

Jesus clarified for his disciples that his command was that they love one another the way that he had loved them (John 15:12). This further supports the assertion that the starting point for our loving is an understanding of, and appreciation for, the way that we have been loved by God, as demonstrated by Christ Jesus.

Loving God

It seems to me that the essence of loving God is to acknowledge and relate to him as God: the infinite, unmistakably, but only partially revealed creator and sustainer of all. I believe that much of our angst and God's grief result from our preoccupation with our own will and actions instead of his. This can manifest itself either in a blatant disinterest in God and his will, or in attempts to save ourselves and/or the whole world through godly living. Following either of these extreme examples, we usurp the throne and seek to take the Godhead unto ourselves. Both godlessness and self-dependent "godliness" deny God the position that is his and his alone. One way to lovingly demonstrate willingness to let God be God is to practice the concept of Sabbath, checking any attempts to master our own lives and leisurely acknowledging our complete dependence upon and the privilege of resting in him.

Being ignored by the object of our adoration produces uncommon pain. When we ignore God, living as if he did not exist, we cause him great pain and deny ourselves what I propose to be the primary reason for our existence – relationship with him. If we try to earn God's favor, we are doomed to failure by our finitude and brokenness. Any attempt to justify ourselves (pretending self-sufficiency or perfection) not only implies that we don't need God, but our certain and regular failures often leave us floundering in anxiety and guilt. In either case, our spiritual needs are unmet, and we are robbed of wellness.

Clinebell (1992) stated, "The power of spiritual needs is so great that people who do not develop health-enhancing spirituality in their lives tend to develop health-depleting beliefs and commitments" (p. 25). Being uncomfortable with mystery and uncertainty, many of us develop neat, tidy religious systems – creating God in our own image. The result may be that we worship the product of our own minds, which is simply idolatrous self-worship. Again, we deny God the right to be who he is and deny ourselves the opportunity to know a relationship that is central to wellness. We must let God be God, recognizing and affirming who he is and our own position relative to him. We must shift our primary focus from our self and our activity to God and his activity.

According to Clinebell (1992), we should satisfy spiritual needs in "open, loving, growing, life-celebrating, esteem-strengthening, and reality-respecting ways. Conversely, our religion tends to diminish wholeness when we satisfy these needs in rigid, moralistic, authoritarian, idolatrous, reality-denying, or fear- and guilt-generating ways" (p. 25).

Although, we must be clear about the distinction between Creator and creation; our use of, and care for, the creation may reveal a great deal about our love for the Creator. We are wise to remember Moses's reminder to Pharaoh, "the earth is the Lord's" (Ex. 9:29, New International Version). Love for the owner is expressed by judicious use of, and care for, this treasure that has been entrusted to us.

Loving Others

The thing that is so moving about God's love for us is that it is unconditional, that he loves us in all our brokenness and imperfection. It is this characteristic of true love that we all crave most – intimacy, freedom from the need to pretend to be something other than our true selves in order to gain acceptance.

The members of the church in Rome were instructed on what it means to love others. They were encouraged to be devoted to each other in brotherly love, give honor and preference to each other, rejoice with those who are happy, cry with those who are sad, be at peace with everyone as nearly as possible, bless those who persecute them, and never try to get even (Rom. 12:10–19). The church in Philippi received this request:

> Agree with each other, love each other, be deep-spirited friends. Don't push your way to the front; don't sweet-talk your way to the top. Put yourself aside, and help others get ahead. Don't be obsessed with getting your own advantage. Forget yourselves long enough to lend a helping hand. Think of yourselves the way Christ Jesus thought of himself . . . (Phil. 2:2–5, Message).

It seems to me that humility is the chief characteristic of Christ's love revealed in the remainder of this passage.

Since Jesus and St. Paul both presented love as the summation of God's will, I am compelled to believe that the justice and mercy, as well as the humility required of man (Micah 6:8), are also ways by which we can judge the presence of love in our behavior. In addition, my understanding that the biblical text in Greek had no punctuation allows me to speculate that love should be separated by a colon from "joy, peace, forbearance, kindness, goodness, faithfulness, gentleness, and self-control" in Paul's fruit (singular) of the Spirit (Gal. 5:22,23), indicating that these characteristics help to define love.

Clinebell (1992) defined wholeness-enhancing love as "caring about and commitment to one's own and the other's continuing growth, empowerment, and self-esteem" (p. 107). Loving behavior should lead us to feel better about ourselves and about the people with whom we relate. When love makes us willing to give in to the interests of others, we are less selfish and defensive; perceived threats and anxiety diminish. John, the apostle, wrote that love is incompatible with fear and drives it away (1 John 4:18), leaving us at peace.

It is especially interesting and challenging to apply these principles to athletic competition. In a sense, competition can be seen as the highest level of cooperation. If we define competition as groups or individuals struggling with each other for a commonly desired goal, there can be no competition without the contenders agreeing to compete. They must cooperate with each other or there is no contest.

Some would say that the very point of athletics is the personal (not just athletic) development of participants. Winning is certainly not the goal in this context, but without that objective there is no contest. Athletes who enter the contest in this frame of mind will give their all and expect the same from opponents in the belief that it is in the best interest of all to do so, "as iron sharpens iron" (Prov. 27:17). They will be concerned about and personally invested in the development of opponents as well as themselves. Loving coaches, officials, cheerleaders, and spectators will likewise be concerned with the best interests of everyone in the arena.

"If you try to maximize your wholeness while ignoring the brokenness of your community and the wider world, you'll be walking into a dead end" (Clinebell, 1992, p. 184). As we move to consideration of self-love, we must remember that the path to personal wellness involves valuing and working for the wellness of the whole creation that has been entrusted to our care. Certainly our care for, and use of, the environment reflects our love for others as well as for ourselves.

Loving Self

Jesus said, "If your first concern is to look after yourself, you'll never find yourself. But if you forget about yourself and look to me, you'll find both yourself and me" (Matt. 10:38, Message). This perspective must be maintained to prevent idolatrous self-worship, which is a very different thing from self-love. The best, which we are to desire for ourselves, is God's agenda and not our own.

When many of us think of wellness, we are inclined to think of physical health and things like physical activity, nutrition, sleep, hygiene, and emotional stress that so obviously affect it. Those of us in the allied fields of health, physical education, and recreation are particularly likely to be zealous supporters of the health and fitness movement and vulnerable to the seductions of healthism and related cults of the body. We can easily be deceived to worship our bodies, health, our professions, etc., while believing that we are simply being responsible stewards.

We are quick to recognize that self-indulgence is not self-love and to be critical of those who are "lovers of pleasure rather than lovers of God" (2 Tim. 3:4). However, we should be aware of the danger of compulsive and idolatrous forms of self-control, and maintain the perspective that "Workouts in the gymnasium are useful, but a disciplined life in God is far more so, making you fit both today and forever" (1 Tim. 4:6, Message).

Scripture never commands or even advises the reader to love her/himself. However, the commandment to love our neighbors as ourselves apparently assumes that we all do love ourselves, and the apostle Paul wrote, "no one ever hated their own body, but they feed and care for their body" (Eph. 5:29).

Perhaps the biblical use of the word "body" should be addressed here. Gundry (1976) reports that biblical scholars and theologians are generally agreed that the Greek word *soma*, which is translated "body" in English, actually refers to the entire person, including but not limited to the physical body. I take this interpretation to be great support for the appropriateness of an integrative view of wellness rather than a dichotomous view of human beings.

Conclusion

God calls us to one thing, love! This is very simple conceptually, but exceedingly difficult in actuality. It is impossible for us to do in-and-of ourselves, and it is contrary to human nature to yield ourselves to the Spirit, which is the only source and power of love.

While separate consideration has been given to loving God, self, and others, I believe these work in concert – that they occur together rather than independently. Three examples of this thesis are that taking time "for God" is an act of self-love in addition to being an act of God-love that equips and motivates us to love others; loving self-care is also an act of loving worship of God and is in the best interests of others; and serving the needs of others simultaneously serves God and satisfies our own need to serve. Jesus made it clear that our service to him will be judged by the degree to which we serve others (Matt. 25:31–46). Perhaps this integrating work of love is the means by which we "know that in all things

God works for the good of those who love him, who have been called according to his purpose" (Rom. 8:28).

Scripture makes it clear that even though we do things appearing to have great spiritual or social value, they are nothing if done without love (1 Cor. 13:1,2). Faking love not only is ultimately ineffectual, it is also exhausting and frustrating. Christ emphasized the importance of love so that his joy might be in his disciples and that their joy might be complete (John 15:10). I take the joy produced by love to be a hallmark of wellness. When we are robbed of joy by doing things for God, others, or self, it probably indicates a need to reexamine our motives and behaviors.

References

Clinebell, H. (1992). *Well being: A personal plan for exploring and enriching the seven dimensions of life.* San Francisco: HarperSanFrancisco.

Gundry, R.H. (1976). *Soma in biblical theology, with emphasis on Pauline anthropology.* New York: Cambridge University Press.

Chapter 28

PURPOSE, COMMITMENT, AND THEN WHAT: A CONSIDERATION OF STRESS AND BURNOUT FOR CHRISTIAN COACHES AND TEACHERS

Ted Comden

No one can claim a total disinterest in the comprehensive and pervasive phenomenon of chronic overstress. We are reminded of it by researchers, the popular media, our pastors, and our Day-Timers. My interest is drawn to this topic not only as a researcher, but as a practitioner, an educator, and a coach on a Christian college campus. I sense a need for a better understanding of the stress problem and a keener insight into the interface between chronic stress, burnout, and the Christian faith.

In this paper I will first review some of the significant landmarks on the stress scene. Second, I will look at how we as Christian professionals perceive our work and how we should be preparing our students for personal and professional effectiveness in a complex world. Third, I will identify several prominent factors in the literature that will help to better understand the problem of stress and more appropriately integrate solutions to this problem with biblical principles. Regarding this third section, I will examine social support networks, leadership styles, personality characteristics, and behavioral responses of anger and hostility. Fourth, I will make applications to our life situations.

Stress Research

The stress research of Selye (1974) in the middle part of the twentieth century is undoubtedly familiar to most of us. The early-to-mid seventies, however, brought events, published works, and terms that have become household words in our discipline. In the late 1960s, cardiologists Freidman and Rosenman (1974) made a connection between stress

Revised version of paper presented at the 1996 conference.

at work, certain personality characteristics, and heart disease. Their book, *Type A Behavior and Your Heart*, was published in 1974. That year also saw the publication of Selye's classic, *Stress without Distress*, a volume that balanced the medical explanation with practical and thoughtful life applications. In 1976, Benson's book *The Relaxation Response*, a practical layman's guide to dealing with the stress response, was published and enjoyed subsequent months on the nonfiction bestseller list. It was during the 1970s that the term *burnout* began appearing in scholarly writing and in the popular press. Then, in 1982, the now familiar Maslach Burnout Inventory (MBI) was introduced in the book *Burnout: The Cost of Caring* (Maslach & Jackson, 1982).

However, the publication that caught my attention as a young professional at a Christian college was another book written primarily for the layperson by McQuade and Aikman (1974) entitled *Stress: What It Is, What It Can Do to Your Health, How to Fight Back*. In the first chapter the authors, apparently not writing from a Christian perspective, made the following statements about religion and stress.

> The phenomenon of religious belief is a large subject, but viewing it just from the point of a book about physical illness, it must be said that religion in a devout believer has little equal as an allayer of stress. This is true of all religions, but particularly true of some. The Judaic-Christian tradition, for instance, takes on all the primal stresses, and if it does not dispose of them completely it makes them surprisingly bearable. Whatever role the believer plays in his world, however humble, it argues, is an important role, created by God for a reason. It tells him he can't win them all, and that the people who seem to win them all don't really win. Winners are often losers in the end, because winning isn't what matters anyway but meaning, truth, and love – and, in the case of Christianity, life everlasting. . . . The waning power of religion is one reason why life has become so stressful in the western world, and also why many people today are reconsidering, and turning once again to religious faith, the more evangelical, it seems, the more popular. (pp. 8–9)

In using these statements as a point of integration of faith and learning, I have asked myself and my students what the authors meant. It seems that more than two decades ago they had observed something in the lives of Christian believers that impressed them. They didn't expand on the topic, but after further reading in research journals and in applied Christian literature, I suspect they were saying that Christians demonstrated a lower reactivity to common stressors, or that evangelicals were somehow more stress resistant than nonbelievers. If these assumptions are correct, it is good to know that a generation ago some persons had noticed a difference. If they were writing today, would they make the same statements? Have we as Christian professionals become articulate in explaining the dynamic relationship between our faith and the stress of life? And do we effectively demonstrate that knowing Jesus Christ personally makes a difference in our response to stress, and therefore in our effectiveness and our health?

Although I don't propose to answer these questions directly, I trust that the subsequent topics in this paper will assist our thinking and growth as authentic Christian professionals. We might begin by suggesting who we are in the disciplines of leisure, sport, and wellness; why we are where we are; how we perceive our work; and what some potential blessings or dangers of our commitment(s) might be.

Who Are We and Why Are We Here?

Most of us, as well as many of our students, were attracted to these disciplines because of satisfying past experiences, the influence of a mentor, the challenge of helping others achieve lofty goals, and very possibly a sense of God's call to this area of fruit-bearing in his kingdom. We are in a service profession with at least part of the same burnout risk as social workers, nurses, and medical doctors. Even apart from a Christian calling, social service workers have been seen as responding to a "dedicatory ethic" (Pines & Aronson, 1988, p. 88). Nursing is seen as the giving of your therapeutic self, and those who give are the kinds of people who tend to burn out quickly (Sehnert, 1981). Sehnert (1981) highlighted the serious problem of professional burnout among medical doctors as he quotes research that states: "Every year this country loses the equivalent of seven entire medical school classes to doctors' suicides, drug addiction, and alcoholism alone. American medicine is an example of the work ethic carried to extremes" (p. 52). Coaching careers demand a similar kind of commitment. Servants in our disciplines are for the most part strongly committed to what they are doing. Commitment is one of my favorite words. It is used frequently in Christian circles, and rightly so. In fact, in the *Taxonomy of Educational Objectives Handbook II: Affective Domain* (Krathwohl, Bloom, & Masia, 1964), the authors use religious language to define this word in level 3.3 of the taxonomy.

> Belief at this level involves a high degree of certainty. The ideas of *conviction* and *certainty beyond a shadow of a doubt* [emphasis added] help to convey further the level of behavior intended. In some instances this may border on *faith* [emphasis added], in the sense of its being a firm emotional

acceptance of a belief upon admittedly non-rational grounds. *Loyalty to a position, group, or cause* [emphasis added] would also be classified here. The person who displays behavior at this level is clearly perceived as holding the value. *He acts to further the thing valued* [emphasis added] in some way, to extend the possibility of his developing it, to deepen his involvement with it and with the things representing it. *He tries to convince others and seeks converts to his cause* [emphasis added]. . . . there is a tension here which needs to be satisfied. . . . action is the result of an aroused need or drive. There is a real motivation to act out the behavior. (p. 149)

When we define commitment in terms of loyalty to a cause, conviction, willingness to expend time and energy furthering the objectives of a cause, and an eagerness to win converts to a cause, we can easily see how the idealism and intensity of a young teacher-coach can move from commitment to over-commitment and to potential burnout. This is especially dangerous in the case of an enthusiastic teacher and coach whose work is heavy on human relationship and high on visibility. Even for persons in our disciplines who do not coach, over-commitment may arise from other multiple roles such as administrator-teacher, teacher-advisor, or teacher-researcher, not to mention family leader and church worker.

How Do We View Our Work?

As Christian professionals, we have read and even memorized numerous Bible verses that call for service, commitment, and intensity. We read 1 Corinthians 15:58 and pay attention to the "always give yourselves fully to the work of the Lord" part without realizing that the victory doesn't really depend upon us. As the previous verse and context assure us, God *gives* the victory through Christ, and we are free to give ourselves fully because of the assurance that our work, even if imperfect, is not in vain.

The brief exhortation from Ecclesiastes 9:10a, "Whatever your hand finds to do, do it with all your might," spurs us on to intense effort. We recall Colossians 3:23 and emphasize the "work at it with all your heart" part with little thought given to the implied exhortation about task selection in the "Whatever you do" phrase. And we cite Philemon 4:13 as a stand-alone promise regarding achievement, instead of a reassurance regarding contentment and adaptability. We aren't called to do everything, and God has provided us with the intellect, good counsel, and his Word for discretion in task selection.

In a day when it is said that two-thirds of the American work force is unhappy with their jobs, we should do more than "come to friendly terms" (Selye, 1974, p.137) with our work. Clearly our work is a high calling and we are to take it seriously as we attempt to inspire our students toward a similar view of their future careers. However, it is helpful for us to be reminded that our work is "harnessed to heaven," and that the responsibility for completing everything is not ours alone.

Burnout is associated with "dropping out of activities which initially appeared to be a source of joy for the participant" (Feigley, 1980, p. 230). Feigley (1980) viewed the critical aspect of the predictable cycle as being "the contrast between the initial enthusiasm, concern and caring and the subsequent apathy, disinterest and cynicism" (p. 231). The frustration, anger, and/or depression that may well be demonstrated are not burnout. According to Feigley, the defining characteristic of burnout is apathy. It is truly unfortunate when Christian professionals move from idealism to apathy. Of course, idealism is a desirable motivator, but when shattered it can lead to a loss of concern for the people with whom one is working, which is one characteristic of burnout (Minirth, Hawkins, Meier, & Thurman, 1990).

Factors Associated with Burnout

There are several factors that have been found to be associated with burnout and that may have particular interest to Christian professionals. They include social support, leadership styles, personality characteristics, and behavioral responses of anger and hostility.

Social Support

When highly motivated professionals work in challenging and supportive environments that have relatively few hassles and stressors, they can achieve peak or near-peak performance. This in turn strengthens their initial motivation, forming a positive loop that can theoretically be sustained indefinitely (Pines & Aronson, 1988). On the other hand, the potential negative loop does not have to be imagined. It has been described on sports pages and in numerous studies with the specific non-supportive factors being identified.

Perceived lack of support from administrators, the absence of a supportive spouse, lack of time for nonprofessional relationships, and inadequate budgets to support expected levels of performance have been found to be associated with higher levels of burnout, especially in teacher-coaches. Quigley, Slack, and Smith (1989) reported that burnout was higher among teacher-coaches from smaller schools where over-extension of responsibilities was more likely. This may be a factor in burnout even in the presence of social support. Kelley and Gill (1993) found that one factor associated with low levels of burnout among small college teacher-basketball coaches was satisfaction with social support networks. Interestingly, the level of burnout reported in this sample (Kelley & Gill, 1993) of NAIA and NCAA Division III coaches was higher than levels reported in previous studies. Most these small college coaches were suffering from moderate to high levels of burnout as indicated on the MBI Form-Ed instrument adapted specifically for the dual role teacher-coach subject.

Social support is defined as "the existence and/or availability of people on whom we can rely, people who let us know that they care about, value, and love us" (Kelley & Gill, 1993, p. 95). Given this definition, it can be assumed that teachers and coaches in Christian colleges have a distinct advantage. If our campus communities are appropriately sensitive and obedient to the many biblical references to mutual love and encouragement among the members of the body, high satisfaction with social support networks should be a significant preventative to burnout.

On the other hand, given the reality of other stressors such as dual roles and potential role conflict, the constraints of time and money, and the persistent giving of our "therapeutic selves," it is good to be reminded (Col. 3:12–17) of the need for mutual and practical love and support. Should not our campuses and our disciplines be showcases for what Selye (1974) called the synergy of teamwork?

Leadership Styles

Regarding leadership styles, it would be easy to fall back on well worn, even if inaccurate, stereotypes. Coaches are often cast as loud, demanding, and arbitrary. Football coaches are somehow always imagined to be one type of leader and the tennis coach another type. And teachers of specific sub-disciplines are also frequently envisioned stereotypically. Stereotypes notwithstanding, there are undoubtedly effective teachers and coaches who lead much differently or who may lead in different ways in different situations. Still, some persons can accurately be described as leading by a "considerational style," a style that is democratic and oriented toward interpersonal relations. There are others who are classified as "initiating structure" leaders who are authoritative and more task-oriented.

In a study by Dale and Weinberg (1989), coaches who displayed a considerational style of leadership behavior scored significantly higher on the frequency and intensity dimensions of the emotional exhaustion and depersonalization subscales of the Maslach Burnout Inventory. These authors also reported an earlier study in which teachers high in considerational style exhibited more burnout than did teachers high in initiating structure style.

While not assuming that Christian teachers and coaches should, or will most often, be classified as considerational leaders, based on the above definitions, many members of our Coalition of Christian Colleges and Universities HPERD group who are vitally interested in student achievement, scholarship, and professional development, tend to be democratic and oriented toward interpersonal relations. In this regard, we resemble workers in the other helping professions, since we seek to make a significant contribution to individuals and society. Therefore, as we seek to be true servant-leaders, we are more susceptible to increasing our risk of burnout.

Personality Characteristics

The discussion of leadership styles leads us quite naturally into the much-publicized area of personality characteristics and stress vulnerability. Given the popular attention as well as the research interest this topic has received since the 1974 publication of *Type A Behavior and Your Heart* (Friedman & Rosenman, 1974), this discussion will be limited to specific areas that are recent and relevant.

It has frequently been shown that the characteristics that contribute to the selection and success of service professionals are also the very traits that may predispose them to burnout. These persons share three basic characteristics which, according to Pines and Aronson (1988), are the classic antecedents to burnout: (1) they perform emotionally taxing work; (2) they share certain personality characteristics that attracted them to human service as a career; and (3) they share a client-centered self-giving orientation. These characteristics are also prominent among those in Christian higher education.

Similarities between highly successful athletes and highly motivated coaches and teachers are striking. Feigley (1980) identified four at-risk characteristics and accompanying clusters of behaviors that may increase an athlete's susceptibility to psychological burnout. Since these characteristics may be viewed as being strikingly descriptive of the strongly committed Christian professional, we will consider some of the implications of these behaviors.

The first of Feigley's (1980) clusters of behaviors relates to perfectionism: setting high, perhaps unrealistic, standards for themselves; investing extensive time and energy to attain such goals; having a strong sense of values concerning how they should behave; and often displaying a strong need for control by conveying that only they can do it right. However, Selye (1974) cautioned that excellence, not perfection, should be our goal. In fact, he underscores his point with a jingle. "Fight for your highest attainable aim, but never put up resistance in vain" (p. 137). This bit of wisdom might help prevent some of the self-imposed pressure associated with task-oriented high achievers. And self-imposed pressure is perhaps the most difficult from which to escape. The old adage, "work hard but also work smart," can be a helpful guide to all of us.

The second at-risk characteristic is possessing/displaying high energy levels. Such persons often multitask, as is the case with Type A and/or obsessive-compulsive persons. This may build a sense of additional pressure, especially if time management skills are not strong.

Third, susceptible athletes, according to Feigley (1980), are also very other-oriented. They have a strong need to be liked and respected by others and are highly sensitive to criticism. Insofar as obsessive-compulsive persons tend to be self-sacrificing and willing to give up personal gain or desires more than some who lean toward more selfish behavior (Minirth et al., 1990), and since such other-orientation is an accepted biblical teaching, we should consider this virtue in the light of a comprehensive call to balanced living and properly motivated serving. This is especially true in our professions, since Minirth et al. (1990) reported that many Christian workers, including 80 percent of the faculty of one Christian college, consider themselves to be primarily obsessive-compulsive in orientation.

Fourth, at-risk persons also lack assertive interpersonal skills. They find it difficult to say no and to appropriately express negative feelings to others without feeling guilty. This calls to mind the ill-considered saying that "to burn out is better than to rust out" in Christian service. It is our responsibility as professionals in leisure, sport, and wellness to communicate and model that neither burning out nor rusting out is the inevitable destiny of busy Christian people. Rather, it is possible to be balanced, healthy, and fruitful.

Behavioral Responses of Anger and Hostility

We have affirmed that some types of people are more at risk for burnout than others. We have also proposed that to be a committed Christian professional presents some risk of burnout. And since our disciplines purport to teach and model intelligent choices for health and wellness, an examination of specific personality risk factors should prove helpful. In this section I will focus on Type A behaviors and obsessive-compulsive personality characteristics as these factors relate to health and/or burnout.

In his book *The Trusting Heart*, Williams (1989) described how Type A behavior was demonstrated as an independent predictive coronary risk factor in the early 1970s and how subsequently the term "Type A" became a household word. Type As had been found to be twice as likely to develop coronary disease as were Type Bs, and among those demonstrating coronary disease, the Type As had more severe levels of atherosclerotic blockages.

However, by the late 1970s and early 1980s, numerous carefully conducted studies, including the Multiple Risk Factor Intervention Trial (MRFIT), had failed to confirm the Type A hypothesis. Now we see, as the second-generation of Type A research has shown, that it is not Type A behavior generally but the hostility component that is toxic to coronary health and very possibly to other aspects of our health (Williams, 1989). Based on extensive epidemiologic research, Williams more specifically concluded, "In the process of identifying hostility (particularly cynicism, anger and aggression) as the toxic part of Type A, we have also discovered that this same characteristic is a risk factor for a wide variety of other very serious illnesses" (p. 73).

Applications to Our Life Situations

While neurological and biological research continues into the mechanisms by which hostility damages health, there are several applications for our consideration as Christian professionals. In this discussion, I propose that the simplified explanation that multiple stressors frequently block goal achievement, which leads to frustration that subsequently often leads to anger, is normative for many of us. Each of us has experienced or observed anger in the coaching role, an emotion that is frequently displayed but always well rationalized. Other highly motivated and goal oriented persons may be candidates for anger as well. In fact, one of the two factors leading to burnout among Christian workers has been reported as bitterness, or prolonged anger (Minirth et al., 1990).

So, if anger does occur in our work and relationships from time to time, and if it is bad for our health as well as our witness, what can we learn and what can we do to decrease both its frequency and its impact? Williams (1989) suggested that "If yours is a hostile heart you need to change it into a more trusting heart – that enjoys a longer and a healthier life" (p. xiii). Three goals to work toward in order to bring about this change, according to Williams, are:

(1) reduce your cynical mistrust of others;
(2) reduce the frequency and intensity with which you experience negative emotions of anger, irritation, frustration, rage, and the like; and
(3) rather than behaving aggressively toward others, learn to treat others with kindness and consideration, and develop your positive assertiveness skills for use in those unavoidable situations that will occur.

These three goals may be achieved, Williams (1989) suggested, by a 12-step behavior modification strategy:

- Step One: Monitor your cynical thoughts.
- Step Two: Confess your hostility and seek support to change.
- Step Three: Stop cynical thoughts.
- Step Four: Reason with yourself.
- Step Five: Put yourself in the other guy's shoes.
- Step Six: Laugh at yourself.
- Step Seven: Practice the relaxation response.
- Step Eight: Try trusting others.
- Step Nine: Force yourself to listen more.
- Step Ten: Substitute assertiveness for aggression.
- Step Eleven: Pretend today is your last.
- Step Twelve: Practice forgiveness. (pp. 195–196)

Are there biblical references that come to mind for each step? Williams (1989) examined selected teachings from several world religions, including Christianity, as possible aids in the process of becoming less hostile and more trusting.

Accepting the value of behavior modification, but also believing that the heart is changed supernaturally at the new birth, I propose several familiar biblical teachings with application to anger, hostility, and aggression. I make these connections as a lay person and with the intention of focusing on the topic at hand. Burnout does occur among Christian teachers and coaches. Key psychological indicators and/or contributors to burnout are irritation, quick loss of temper, and impulse to aggression. For these, if for no other reasons, we should give attention to pertinent scriptural passages.

The exhortation to "refrain from anger and turn from wrath; do not fret – it leads only to evil" from King David in Psalm 37:8 gives ancient wisdom with contemporary significance. In the same psalm it is interesting to note that the familiar passage in verses 3–4 begins with the word *trust* and ends with the word *heart*. The apostle Paul, in Ephesians 4:26, draws from the Psalms when he writes, "'In your anger do not sin': Do not let the sun go down while you are still angry." We are not to act out our anger in aggressive behaviors against other persons. Rather, reflect on it in a kind of enlightened cognitive appraisal by asking, "Does it really matter in the light of eternity?" Other helpful ideas include talking and praying about the issue, as well as forgiving and forgetting. In fact, recent evidence indicates that the negative health consequences of anger occur only if the anger is acted out in aggressive behaviors (Dolnick, 1995). The writer of Proverbs tells us, "Fools give full vent to their rage, but the wise bring calm in the end" (Prov. 29:11).

In Jesus' teaching in Matthew 5:22, there also appears to be a difference between being angry and acting out your anger verbally against your brother. Indeed, it is tempting to draw a parallel here between the three levels of judgment in that verse and the progressive definitions of anger, hostility, and aggression.

Kriegel and Kriegel (1984) identified the Type C person, which Osgood (1988) later described as one who is committed to personal relationships, is service oriented, has a life-yielding open-channel attitude, and demonstrates abandonment to God. Osgood summarized a Christian perspective on stress and personality types with the following statement: "What Drs. Maslow, Selye, and others such as Freidman and Rosenman have prepared the way for – though they seem not to have realized it – is our realization that there is a way of inner purpose, achievement and peace that is distinct from Type A or Type B" (p. 89). Indeed, "Better a patient person than a warrior, one with self-control than one who takes a city" (Prov. 16:32). And such a person is probably healthier and less prone to burnout as well.

Conclusion

In conclusion, let me review several generally accepted facts and pertinent principles from research and practice, and then pose a couple of final questions. Those of us involved in teaching and coaching in colleges and universities, whether Christian or secular institutions, are in service careers. Persons in service careers have been found to be particularly vulnerable to overstress and burnout. Although incidence of burnout appears to be lower in teaching and coaching than in some other service careers, it still occurs even in the lives of Christian believers. And any degree of burnout, loss of idealism, diminished commitment, or sense of apathy, even if it doesn't eventuate in dropping out, is costly to the individual and the profession. Indeed, when it occurs in the life of the Christian professional, burnout impacts the work of God in the world.

It is our responsibility to intelligently minimize our risk and to optimize our effectiveness by increasing our awareness and understanding of chronic overstress, personal and situational burnout risk factors, and effective strategies for lowering our personal vulnerability. It is also encouraging to affirm that by virtue of a personal relationship with God through Jesus Christ, and with the empowering/instructing presence of the Holy Spirit in our lives, we have distinctive resources available to us in our work. And work, we should remember, is not only a biological necessity as noted by Selye (1974) and a central part of God's plan (McKenna, 1990); it is, according to Osler, the master word which "transmutes all base metal of humanity into gold – brings hope to the young, confidence to the middle-aged, and repose to the aged" (Osler as quoted in Selye, 1974, p. 84).

So then, as we approach our work, can we apply available knowledge and cultivate the spiritual disciplines in order to diminish our stress reactivity, enhance an appropriate sense of self-efficacy, and most certainly to increase our stress resistance with a high level of wellness?

In our work, can we apply biblical truth to minimize cynicism and anger and develop a level of trust which will maximize our personal and professional effectiveness and more clearly reflect the image of Christ?

References

Benson, H. (1976). *The relaxation response.* New York: Avon.

Dale, J., & Weinberg, R.S. (1989). The relationship between coaches' leadership style and burnout. *The Sport Psychologist* 3(1), 1–13.

Dolnick, E. (1995, July/August). Hotheads and heart attacks. *Health*, pp. 58–64.

Feigley, D.A. (1980). Preventing psychological burnout. In J. H. Salmella, P. Bernard, & T. Hoshizaki, B. (Ed.), *Psychological nurturing and guidance of gymnastic talent* (pp. 230–247). Montreal, QC: Sport Psyche Editions.

Freidman, M., & Rosenman, R. (1974). *Type A behavior and your heart.* New York: Knopf.

Kelley, B.C., & Gill, D.L. (1993). An examination of personal/situational variables, stress appraisal, and burnout in collegiate teacher-coaches. *Research Quarterly for Exercise and Sport* 64(1), 94–102.

Krathwohl, D.R., Bloom, B.S., & Masia, B.B. (1964). *Taxonomy of educational objectives Handbook II: Affective domain*. New York: David McKay.

Kriegel, R.J., & Kriegel, M.H. (1984). *The C-Zone: Peak performance under stress*. Garden City, NY: Anchor Press/Doubleday.

Maslach, C., & Jackson, S.E. (1982). *Burnout: The cost of caring*. Englewood Cliffs, NJ: Prentice-Hall.

McKenna, D.A. (1990). *Love your work*. Wheaton, IL: Victor Books/Scripture Press.

McQuade, W., & Aikman, A. (1974). *Stress: What it is, what it can do to you, how to fight back*. New York: E.P. Dutton.

Minirth, F., Hawkins, D., Meier, P., & Thurman, C. (1990). *Before burnout: Balanced living for busy people*. Chicago: Moody Press.

Osgood, D. (1988). *Surefire ways to beat stress*. Wheaton, IL: Tyndale House.

Pines, A., & Aronson, E. (1988). *Career burnout: Causes and cures*. New York: The Free Press.

Quigley, T., Slack, T., & Smith, G. (1989, January/February). The levels and possible causes of burnout in secondary school teacher-coaches. *CAHPER Journal* 55(1), 20–25.

Sehnert, K.W. (1981). *Stress/unstress*. Minneapolis: Augsburg.

Selye, H. (1974). *Stress without distress*. New York: Signet Books.

Williams, R. (1989). *The trusting heart*. New York: Times Books.

Chapter 29

Spirituality and Wellness

John Byl

It was a big game, and as our setter made an important pass I could feel my heart rate accelerate, my stomach gurgle, and my teeth clench – my dentist warned me about grinding my teeth. I was feeling tired, too. I had had a restless sleep the previous night, waking often, running plays and substitutions through my head. There is something good about intense focus, but at what price? The intensity of coaching the college varsity volleyball team was making me unwell. I also knew that the Bible teaches that God gives us peace, joy, and many other blessings, so I began to consider if stronger spiritual strength on my part would improve my wellness as a coach.

Research supports the idea that spiritual wellness often has a positive impact upon one's whole being, and that spirituality and wellness are interrelated and multi-dimensional concepts (Graham et al., 1978; Gartner, Larsen, & Allen, 1991; Ellison & Smith, 1991). To better understand spirituality and wellness, I deliberated on Scripture, my life, and other sources. This chapter summarizes what I discovered about spirituality's impact on wellness. For purposes of this chapter, spirituality is defined as being full of the Holy Spirit. If one is full of the Holy Spirit, then it appears self-evident that one would bear the Spirit's fruit. "So I say, walk by the Spirit. . . . The fruit of the Spirit is love, joy, peace, forbearance, kindness, goodness, faithfulness, gentleness and self-control" (Gal. 5:16, 22–23a – parallel is found in 1 Cor. 13).

How many of us would not want a life full of love, joy, peace, patience, kindness, goodness, faithfulness, gentleness, and self-control? Yet, how often hasn't our blood curdled in anger, our body been weighed down in despair, our intestinal tract gurgled with anxiety, or our heart raced to keep up with our impatience? Remember how that unkind word felt as if someone had punched you in the stomach or how your body trembled in a conversation that spoke ill of others? How did it feel when a friend stabbed you in the back or spoke harshly to you? How did it feel when you were subjected to physical and emotional punishment by an out-of-control "loved" one? We experience much pain because of a lack of submissiveness to the Holy Spirit.

How can we revive our spirit to experience wellness? In reviewing Scripture, three things stand out: the need to flee evil, the need to trust in a providential and loving God, and the need to live obediently before God.

What are some of the impacts of evil on our wellness? Scripture indicates that "envy rots the bones" (Prov. 14:30), and that "no one who walks among [the unjust] will know peace" (Isa. 59:8). The way to deal with this evil in our lives is to flee from it (2 Tim. 2:22; 1 Tim. 6:11), to rid ourselves of it, and to open ourselves to the power of God (1 Pet. 2:1–3).

We need to trust in God and be nourished by him if we are to be well. We need to "receive the Holy Spirit" (John 20:22) and let him bear fruit in our lives (Col. 3:12–14). Through God's power he gives us "everything we need for life and godliness" (2 Pet. 1:3–8; Prov. 14:26). It is imperative, as a proverb states, to

> Trust in the LORD with all your heart and lean not on your own understanding; in all your ways acknowledge him, and he will make your paths straight. Do not be wise in your own eyes; fear the LORD and shun evil. This will bring health to your body and nourishment to your bones. (Prov. 3:5–8)

We need to be like the woman who sought healing and worked her way through the crowd just to touch the hem of Jesus' clothes (Mark 5:24–34). We need to cut through the crowd and not let worry, busyness, or anything else stand between us and Jesus' healing.

We also need to live obedient lives, to "act justly and to love mercy and to walk humbly with your God" (Mic. 6:8; Zech. 7:9). This walk of obedience is to be a vibrant Christ-like walk, seven days a week, with a passion that two young lovers have for each other. A major way this passion can express itself is in our ministering to rich and poor, Jew and Gentile, male and female, young and old, and the well and not-so well. We find wellness in obediently caring for this world, particularly when we help people in need.

As we look at Scripture, we will discover that there is no recipe for a Christian to become well. Because fruit is given and meant to be shared, it benefits a Christian when it benefits the community.

Though achieving wellness requires action on our part, from a human perspective, a paradox appears to exist in the relationship between spirituality and wellness. To train our heart we need to work it; to train our spirit we need to be completely vulnerable to God working in us. Paul writes: "when I am weak, then I am strong" (2 Cor. 12:10). Even Christ was "crucified in weakness, yet he lives by God's power. Likewise, we are weak in him, yet by God's power we will live with him in our dealing with you" (2 Cor. 13:4). We must find our strength in the Lord, not in ourselves (Ps. 127:1). We need to be empowered by God.

How then do we experience the fruit of the Spirit? In my coaching, I needed to consider what was evil – perhaps personal recognition or pride – and flee from it, and to open my life more to the healing power of God. I needed to learn more about resting in the loving arms of God and living through the power of the Holy Spirit.

The Fruit of the Spirit

It is instructive, then, to explore how Scripture describes each fruit of the Spirit. For each case, we will consider how a lack of godliness deprives wellness, how God blesses us with the power of the Spirit, and the positive impact the fruit of the Spirit has on our lives. Before considering this, it is important to recognize that the apostle Paul speaks about the fruit of the spirit in the singular, not fruits, in the plural (Gal. 5:22–23). The Holy Spirit gives us a package, like a fruit basket, not a market where we select specific fruits and ignore others.

Love

Love is that unconditional commitment to care for others in a way that only God truly can, and it brings healing. I remember having felt betrayed by someone and how it took three years before I could go to that person and put the incident and negative feelings behind us. I could not do it earlier, even though the incident left a constant pit in my stomach. It took three years of hiking before I took the final step on top of that mountain of forgiveness. I was ready for that last step. In some ways, it was the same as a thousand steps before it. But having made it, I knew it was done. The scenery on top was beautiful. The pit in my stomach was gone. The bounce in my step was restored. I learned again that we ought to forgive as God forgave us, and that love binds people together, and builds people up (Col. 3:12–14; 1 Cor. 8:1), and makes them well.

The healing of love, and the pains caused by a lack of love, are vividly illustrated in the following three proverbs: "Better a small serving of vegetables with love than a fattened calf with hatred" (Prov. 15:17); "Hatred stirs up dissension, but love covers all wrongs" (Prov. 10:12); and "Whoever would foster love covers over an offense, but whoever repeats the matter separates close friends" (Prov. 17:9). Dining with those that love each other, those that are unconditionally committed to caring for each other, what a feast! We long to be there as two lovers desire each other (Song of Songs; Seerveld, 1988).

Think about God's love. Our heavenly Father is so committed to caring for the entire world "that he gave his one and only Son" so that we might gain eternal life (John 3:16). Jesus, though he knew dying on a cross would bring excruciating pain, died, because he loved us. In his high priestly prayer, he pleads with us to obey God's commands and, through obedience, remain in God's love. Jesus ends his prayer by saying: "Love each other as I have loved you. Greater love has no one than this: to lay down one's life for one's friends" (John 15:9–13; Stauffer, 1964). That is what he did.

God gives us the ability to love, like Jesus, through the power of the Holy Spirit (Rom. 5:5; 2 Thess. 2:13). Jesus tells us the greatest thing we can do with this gift is to "Love the Lord your God with all your heart and with all your soul and with all your mind . . . [and] your neighbor as yourself" (Matt. 22:37–39). This gift is at the very core of our living, it guides all our actions, and is the distinguishing mark of the Christian (John 13:34–35; Schaeffer, 1970; Stauffer, 1964; Turner, 1986). This love causes us to care for those easy to love as well as our enemies (Matt. 5:38–45). If we could do that, think of the healing there would be within ourselves, between us and others, and even among the nations.

In the context of 1 Corinthians 13, it is no surprise that love is listed as the first fruit of the Spirit. What might be surprising is that love is described there as being greater even than faith and hope (1 Cor. 13:13). But that is because "faith and hope bear the marks of this defective aeon. With love the power of the future age already breaks into the present form of the world" (Stauffer, 1964, p. 51). That new world, where there will be no more "mourning or crying or pain" (Rev. 21:4), is filled with love. God also gives us the opportunity in the present world to experience that healing power of love. What healing there is when we know that God loves us and that Jesus died on the cross to pay for all our sin; when we can give and receive forgiveness, a caring handshake, and a hug; when our love finds expression in living obediently with God; and when we are committed to lovingly building others up, and when others do that in return.

Joy

My wife cried in anguish, she moaned in the satisfaction that the labor was done, and she smiled as she held our crying newly-born child to her breast. I cried for joy. God had again blessed us!

Joy is not gained from hilarity over too much alcohol, laughing about perverse or profane jokes, or momentary cheer derived from getting things not ours. When we give our lives to evil, our laughter will change to mourning and our joy to gloom (e.g., Prov. 14:13).

True joy is a gift (Ps. 4:7). It is the ability to respond to God's triumphs: seeing, feeling, and expressing celebration in God's victories (e.g., 1 Sam. 18:6). It is a response often shared in a festive manner with others. It is not a simple add-on in the Christian life, but is listed significantly as the second fruit of the Spirit – does experiencing joy have that kind of priority in our lives?

Our joy is a response to the awesomeness of God having revealed himself to us and offered us salvation (Isa. 9:3, 12:2–3; Matt. 13:44; 1 Thess. 1:6). This life-changing event causes "rejoicing in heaven" (Luke 15:7, 10) and should transform our mourning into dancing (Ps. 30:11; Jer. 31:13). Do we realize how great a gift salvation is? Is that joy evident in our daily walk?

Jesus brought joy to the world. Little John the Baptist, while a baby in Elizabeth's womb, "leaped for joy" when his mother Elizabeth heard the greetings of the pregnant Mary (Luke 1:44). The women, who had found the tomb empty and had been told by the angels that Jesus had arisen, "hurried away from the tomb, afraid yet filled with joy" (Matt. 28:8). When Jesus showed his followers his hands and feet, these apostles could hardly believe their eyes "because of joy and amazement" (Luke 24:40–41). Even after Jesus ascended into heaven, the disciples "worshipped him and returned to Jerusalem with great joy. And they stayed continually at the temple, praising God" (Luke 24:52–53). These followers of Jesus recognized his victories and allowed joy to overtake them.

Joy is also a response to God blessing us. When the Israelites returned from captivity, they were possessed with gladness. The psalmist writes that Israelites were "like those who dreamed. Our mouths were filled with laughter, our tongues with songs of joy" (126:1–2). These people were drunk with laughter, they were so happy. Proverbs reminds us that "A happy heart makes the face cheerful" (15:13); "a cheerful heart is good medicine" (17:22) and "has a continual feast" (15:15). Can you imagine the feeling of allowing gladness and joy to overtake us (Isa. 35:10; 51:3, 11; 52:8)? It is instructive to recall that David danced for joy when the ark returned, and his wife Michael remained barren because she was a kill-joy (2 Sam. 6:17–23). Do we permit ourselves to receive joy in the Lord's blessings? It is an emotional high to be at a sporting event and experience the joy of watching a basketball go through a hoop, a puck go into the net, or a football be kicked through the uprights. How much more important are the blessings of God than these moments of happiness that give us joy in sport victories? Let us carry the joy from the sport arena to our church life, to our whole life.

Scripture often encourages the singing of songs of praise (e.g., James 5:13). Furthermore, joy, expressed through singing, instruments, and dancing, often filled the worship services in Jerusalem (1 Chron. 15:16; 2 Chron. 30:23, 26). Jerusalem, the place where God was in the Old Testament, was meant to be "the joy of the whole earth" (Ps. 48:2). And party they did. Their joyful noise was so loud at times it "could be heard far away" (Neh. 12:43). If that kind of exuberant joy and rejoicing marked our worship of God, the earth would vibrate with the healing power of joy.

Even creation cannot restrain itself from praising God with joy; we can learn by observing it. Do we hear the trees of the forest, the meadows covered with flocks, the valleys mantled with grain, and the mountains and rivers as they sing, shout, and clap for joy before the Lord (1 Chron. 16:33; Isa. 55:12; 65:12–13; 96:12; Ps. 98:8)? Though we so often violate the earth, the prophet Isaiah says, "The desert and the parched land will be glad; the wilderness will rejoice and blossom. Like the crocus, it will burst into bloom; it will rejoice greatly and shout for joy" (Isa. 35:1–2). In the change of the seasons, do we experience God's faithfulness in joy (Gen. 1:14; Ps. 104:19; Dan. 2:21)?

For those of us too crushed by circumstances to experience joy, we might want to think of David. In his confession about the sin with Bathsheba, he asks of God, "Let me hear joy and gladness; let the bones you have crushed rejoice. . . . Restore to me the joy of your salvation" (Ps. 51:8, 12). He was also able to confess that God's "consolation brought me joy" (Ps. 94:18–19). Or, as Isaiah later asked of God: "Strengthen the feeble hands, steady the knees that give way; say to those with fearful hearts, 'Be strong, do not fear. . . .' Then will the lame leap like a deer, and the mute tongue shout for joy" (Isa. 35:3–6). Though we will experience painful times in our lives, God will provide victory and joy (John 16:20–21; Luke 6:23).

It is also worth noting that God does not act arbitrarily, but he rules the world with justice. That too ought to give us joy (Ps. 67:4; 68:3;

97:11). Even God's laws, though law may seem restrictive, in fact gives freedom to people and honor to God. Therefore, the psalmist can proclaim that God's "statutes . . . are the joy of my heart" (119:111; cf. Rom. 14:17–18). Jesus pleads with us to obey "my Father's commands." Why? "So that my joy may be in you and that your joy may be complete" (John 15:9–13). Or we can think of Ezra, who after reading the long-silent law of God, said that "the joy of the Lord is your strength" (Neh. 8:10). We need to obediently live with God, and he will grant us joy.

Paul says, "Rejoice in the Lord always, I will say it again: Rejoice!" (Phil. 4:4–7). Sometimes we need to be told to rejoice, so that we can drop the shackles of an independent or blind spirit. Sometimes we need to be told to rejoice so that we can get off the track of go, go, go; produce, produce, produce. Having been put in our rightful place, we can openly receive the gift of joy, celebrating God's triumphs.

Can we celebrate God's many blessings given to us? Take a moment now to relax and chuckle in God's goodness to you. Can you not feel the healing in yourself? Do you remember how good it felt to receive a genuine smile, to give one, and to laugh your head off with friends? To those who open their hearts to the Holy Spirit, joy is offered.

Peace

I remember my father describing the final minutes of his father's life. My grandfather died of cancer. Before his death, with his adult children surrounding his bed, he asked them to sing one of his favorite psalms. They sang with broken voices. As he passed from this life to the next, his parting words were that he could hear the angels singing. He died in peace.

To have peace is to live in harmony with God and others and to experience personal wellness within (Foerster, 1964). The opposite of peace is to be at war; to be fighting; or to be at odds with God, with others, or within ourselves.

Sometimes things trouble us and we cannot find peace. Joseph's brothers could not find peace when they were told to leave Benjamin behind. They were told, "go back to your father in peace" (Gen. 44:17). They could not, because they knew the anguish that leaving Benjamin behind would cause their father. We too may encounter situations when we meet people we would sooner slug than hug, we meet someone who gets under our skin and we are screaming inside, or we are so totally disoriented about our future that we are disabled from acting. We feel like wrecks; we are not at peace.

And sometimes we wonder why the ungodly seem so at peace (Job 12:6; 21:13). But God tells us that "there is no peace for the wicked" (Isa. 48:22; 57:21; cf. Rom. 3:10–18); they just have no shame and delude themselves by thinking there is peace in their lives (Jer. 6:14–15, 8:11; 1 Thess. 5:3). Disobedience to God leads to a land full of bloodshed and cities full of violence: hardly peace or wellness (2 Kings 9:22; Ezek. 7:23–25). But God blesses us with peace through the power of the Holy Spirit (Rom. 15:13). In the struggle with evil, we are assured that the "God of peace will soon crush Satan" (Rom. 16:20).

The most profound way God gives us peace with him is by offering his Son to us (Rom. 5:1; Act. 10:36), the "Prince of Peace" (Isa. 9:6–7; Mic. 5:5), to live among us for a little while (John 1:14), to die for our sins (Col. 1:20), and to ascend to the throne of God to intercede on our behalf (John 14:27). As the angels declared at Jesus' birth, "Glory to God in the highest heaven, and on earth peace to those on whom his favor rests" (Luke 2:10–14; Matt 2:10). May his favor rest upon us!

It is important to remember that Jesus does not offer peace as the world does. Christ says to the people during his triumphal entry into Jerusalem, "if you . . . had only known on this day what would bring you peace" (Luke 19:42); it was not about international power but international service: it was not about taking life but giving it.

How do we open ourselves to let the Spirit work God's peace in us? How do we prevent fear, uncertainty, and disorientation from depriving us of peace? I remember waking from a nightmare as a child. The images in my mind were haunting, and trembling I went downstairs to waken my parents. They assured me everything was okay, it was just a dream, they would watch over me, and so would God. I went back to bed, with my mother watching over me and stroking my hair with her loving hands. I trusted her and fell asleep. We ought to have the same trust in the bigger arms and absolute love of our heavenly Father, for "he who watches over you . . . will neither slumber nor sleep" (Ps. 121:3–4; 4:8). Through trusting God, we can find peace and rest.

God grants peace to those who love God's ways; as the psalmist says, "Great peace have they who love your law, and nothing can make them stumble" (Psalm 119:165; cf., Prov. 3:17) For those who live by his commandments, seeking God's holiness (Lev. 26:6; Isa. 26:3; Heb. 12:11; 2 Pet. 3:14), God says "your peace would have been like a river" (Isa. 48:18; cf. Ezek. 37:26; Zech. 8:14–19; Mal. 2:5–6; Rom. 7:6–7).

We must live righteous lives that lead to peace (Rom. 14:17–19; 1 Cor. 7:15). We "must turn from evil and do good; [we] must seek peace and pursue it" (1 Pet. 3:11). However, righteous living means much more than simply saying to those in need, "Go in peace; keep warm and well fed"; if you do "nothing about their physical needs, what good is it?" (James 2:16). We find righteousness, purity, and peace by being with criminals, getting our hands dirty with needy folks whose broken lives need God's peace.

The Israelites had peace offerings, or "fellowship offerings" as they are also called (e.g., Exod. 20:4), that provide an interesting lesson concerning wellness. God only accepted a peace offering when the people sought to live obedient and just lives (e.g., Amos 5:22). It is further interesting to note how the "fire must be kept burning on the altar continuously; it must not go out" (Lev. 6:13), like the eternal flame. If we are to offer our lives as peace offerings, we must be continually obedient and seeking justice. Obedient and just lives lead to peace among the nations (e.g., Gen. 26:28–31), between friends (e.g., 1 Sam. 20:42), and within ourselves.

Most people could probably appreciate the Proverb, "Better a dry crust with peace and quiet than a house full of feasting with strife" (17:1). Fighting God, others, or ourselves does not lead to wellness. We need to be like John the Baptist, who, according to his father Zechariah, was "to guide our feet into the path of peace" (Luke 1:79). If we can be peace-makers (Matt. 5:9; Ps. 34:14; James 3:17–19), God considers it beautiful. As the prophets wrote: "How beautiful on the mountains are the feet of those . . . who proclaim peace" (Isa. 52:7; Nah. 1:15).

May we bless each other with peace as we come into (e.g., Rom. 1:7) and leave (e.g., Acts 15:33) each other's presence, as is suggested by the first verses in many of the New Testament epistles, not simply as a nice wish, but as a genuine gift (Foerster, 1964). As trusting, obedient, justice-seeking children of God, we can experience a peace with God, others, and within ourselves that is characterized by harmony and wellness. May peace govern us (Isa. 60:17).

Patience

Eugene slipped on the squash court, hit the back of his head on the floor, and was unconscious. At the hospital, doctors felt he would probably lose two weeks of school before the headaches would subside and he could return to studying. A few months earlier, he had twisted his knee against a make-shift referee stand beside a volleyball court. Though the knee was temporarily supported by braces, it would require surgery in the future. If he were to damage the knee again he would likely become crippled. Yet Eugene went on, hurting at times, but mostly with a continuing smile on his heart, trusting that somehow God would also use these situations for good. It will just take time.

Proverbs remind us that "whoever is patient has great understanding, but one who is quick-tempered displays folly" (Prov. 14:29). However, patience in Scripture is more than some kind of ethical virtue; it is the ability to be long suffering, and is a gift from God (Exod. 34:6; Horst, 1967). I believe Eugene has it. Patience is the first thing said about love (1 Cor. 13:4), it is one of a list of items Paul considers he has modelled as a missionary, and is a characteristic of a "life worthy of the Lord" (Col. 1:9–13).

When we consider how patient God is with us, and how all powerful he is, should we not all be like Eugene, waiting and gaining our strength from the Lord (Ps. 27:14; 37:7)? Or do we have too much of a Type A personality in which the adrenaline kicks in over the smallest matter, and we consider ourselves so important, and so right, that we hardly listen to what others are saying?

God gives us the opportunity to be long-suffering in serious matters, in unjust situations, and in situations where people irritate us with minor annoyances, and he also gives us patience to wait for positive matters such as achieving personal wellness. We need to take our concerns, our irritations, and our impatience to the Lord. We need to remember that "those who hope in the LORD will renew their strength. They will soar on wings like eagles; they will run and not grow weary, they will walk and not be faint" (Isa. 40:31; cf. Ps. 40:1–3; 130). Talk about receiving wellness for patience!

Kindness

The television cameras showed the air drop of supplies to a country subjected to drought and political oppression. Those that provided that food showed kindness. A few moments later, the cameras showed a young and undernourished boy gently brushing away flies from his dying parents. The boy, too, exhibited kindness.

A scriptural understanding of kindness focuses on knowing another's need and helping to fulfil it, particularly to relatives, guests, and those that are in some way dependent on us (McKim, 1986; Weiss, 1974; Acts 28:2). When we do not show kindness, particularly for the poor, the Bible informs us that we show contempt for our Maker, "but whoever is kind to the needy honors God" (Prov. 14:31) and keeps the Devil at bay (Eph. 4:26–27; Prov. 37:8). Once again, God provides fruit that involves giving to others, and in giving this fruit, it becomes a sign of being one of God's chosen (Col. 3:12).

God "exercises kindness" (Jer. 9:24), especially through giving us Christ Jesus to save us from sin (Eph. 2:6–8; Titus 3:3–5). In addition, he is a God who "will meet all your needs according to his glorious riches in Christ Jesus" (Phil. 4:19).

For our part, Paul and James encourage us to get rid of things like bitterness and anger (1 Tim. 2:8; 2 Tim. 2:24; James 1:19–20). Instead, scripture encourages us to speak words that are uplifting; "sweet to the soul and healing to the bones" (Prov. 16:24). Paul also encourages us to be "kind and compassionate to one another, forgiving each other, just as in Christ God forgave you" (Eph. 4:32; cf. Col. 3:8; 1 Pet. 2:1–3).

We need to show kindness to those in need. Furthermore, Scripture notes that those who pursue righteousness and kindness will be blessed by finding "life and honor" (Prov. 21:21). Take a moment and pretend to say something angrily at someone, and feel your body become tense. Now say something kind to someone, and tension is released. Kindness helps the wellbeing of others, and it also gives us life, wellness.

Goodness

A description of what it means to do good is perhaps best indicated in the well-known words of the prophet Micah, "He has shown you . . . what is good. And what does the Lord require of you? To act justly and to love mercy and to walk humbly with your God" (6:8). I am reminded of Mother Teresa and her work among the poor. I am reminded of Jesus who lived obediently to the law – though his contemporaries did not always agree with his interpretation – (Matt. 6:43–48) and cared for the poor (Matt. 11:4–6; Luke 14:12–14). But how do I do good in my life, in my city, or in my gym?

Paul realizes how difficult it is to do good on our own. He writes: "I have the desire to do what is good, but I cannot carry it out" (Rom. 7:7–25). Instead, we need to rely more completely on the power of the Holy Spirit to grant us this fruit of goodness (Gal. 5:22; Rom. 15:14). Paul, who wrote more about goodness than any other New Testament writer (Collins, 1992), wrote that "we are God's workmanship, created in Christ Jesus to do good works" (Eph. 2:10), and that we are to be "eager to do what is good" (Titus 2:14). God gives us the ability to be like Mother Teresa, to be like Jesus. Do we want to use this gift to bless others and follow God?

To do good is to act justly and walk humbly with God. That means we need to live in obedience to God. To love mercy is to help the oppressed – to walk with them, to talk with them, to eat with them, and perhaps even invite them into our lives and homes. Obedient and merciful living is doing good. Such a lifestyle is productive (Titus 3:14), brings healing to one and all, and will be blessed by God (Ps. 37:27; Prov. 12:2; Rom. 2:7,10; Grundmann, 1964). The fruit of the Spirit empowers us to follow God and do good. Be moved by his prompting and "do not withhold good from those who deserve it, when it is in your power to act" (Prov. 3:27). Imagine the healing in a world where all people live good lives in the Lord.

Faithfulness

I knew a man who had Alzheimer's disease for over a decade. The last few years of his life, he was institutionalized. During those years, his wife faithfully and lovingly visited him every day. She would have hurt inside to miss a day, and his spirits were raised each time she came. She was faithful to him. Like the father of the prodigal son, faithfulness means always being there for someone, despite what they do in return.

I also remember highlights in our family life such as important birthdays, profession of faith, and graduation. The joy of the day was increased by family and friends dropping by, phoning, or by sending a greeting. For these family members and friends, stopping to rejoice was an act of faithfulness that also put the brakes on their daily lives as they shared in the lives of others. Faithfulness brings blessing and healing.

There is also unfaithfulness. We can think of someone like Peter before Jesus' death or the temporary friends of the prodigal son (perhaps not much unlike our unfaithfulness at times before God). In Proverbs we read: "Like a broken tooth or a lame foot is reliance on the unfaithful in a time of trouble" (25:19). When we are unfaithful to God, the land will mourn, and "all who live in it waste away" (Hos. 4:1). We are painfully reminded of the consequence of unfaithfulness when we consider the devastating effects of various sexually transmitted diseases. Unfaithfulness leads to pain and a lack of wellness.

There are times when I have wondered, does anyone really care that I am here – are people faithful to me? I have usually asked this question when I was down and discouraged about life, and I felt lonely and alienated, not well. Just imagine how Jesus felt when everyone, including his faithful Father, left him alone to die on a cross. But God is the epitome of perpetually abounding in faithfulness in all that he does (e.g., Exod. 34:6; Deut. 32:4; Ps. 33:4; Ps. 89). Jesus arose from the dead because of

God's faithfulness. God's faithfulness will be our "shield and rampart" (Ps. 91:4), and he offers this gift of healing to us. When I felt lonely and deserted, it was comforting, healing, to find protection in the faithfulness of a loving God and the concerned comments of a friend. May we in turn offer the same protection faithfully to those we meet, by caring in times of need and sharing the joys of a celebration; may we be nurtured by each other's faithfulness. Once again, as we care for others, they and we experience greater wellness.

Gentleness

I recall an elder in a church, who valued men wearing a tie and suit for a church service, meeting a neatly dressed man who was not wearing a tie or suit. The elder gruffly spoke to the other, "Why aren't you dressed!?" The one spoken to could feel his heart sink, and with tears in his eyes he left the worship service before it ever began. Not gentleness.

We receive gentleness as a gift from the Holy Spirit (James 3:13–18). Christ's kingly mission on earth was exemplified in gentleness (Matt. 21:5; Zech. 9:9). Jesus invites people: "Come to me, all you who are weary and burdened, and I will give you rest. Take my yoke upon you and learn from me, for I am gentle and humble in heart, and you will find rest for your souls" (Matt. 11:29). "Like a lamb to the slaughter" (Isa. 53:7), he died on the cross, so we can have peace, rest, and wellness.

The Bible teaches that gentleness must especially be evident in those in leadership positions (1 Tim. 3:3) because people grow when nurtured by gentleness. But perhaps more importantly, gentleness is a sign of "God's chosen people" (Col. 3:12). This gift must be put to use. For example, when someone is caught in sin, Scripture encourages us to restore such a person with gentleness and respect (Gal. 6:1; 1 Pet. 3:15). Gentleness does not produce anxiety precipitated by fear, but recovery nurtured by love. Can you imagine the healing that takes place when we gently restore someone, and when someone does it in return? But it goes beyond this; Paul asked Titus to remind the people "to be ready to do whatever is good, to slander no one, to be peaceable and considerate, and always to be gentle toward everyone" (Titus 3:1–2).

There is a sequel to the story of the gruff elder. The elder and offended person later met for coffee to reconcile their differences. Following an apology by the elder, he confided that he was experiencing difficulties in his own life, and that his gruffness and cutting humor were inappropriate ways of coping with these difficulties. The elder's gruffness put a knife between these two people as they entered a worship service; gentleness and forgiveness over coffee brought healing. Lack of gentleness brings pain; gentleness brings healing and wellness.

Self-control

Probably all of us have experienced a time when we lost control, or when someone else lost control over their anger against us. Some may have occasionally been a victim to one who has lost control; for others it may have occurred often. These experiences are usually deeply cutting, and the resulting wounds often leave lifelong scars. For both the perpetrator and victim, this lack of self-control brings pain, rather than healing and wellness.

Proverbs puts it mildly when it states that a "quarrelsome wife is like the constant dripping of a leaky roof" (Prov. 19:13), or when it describes a hot-tempered person as one who "stirs up conflict" (Prov. 15:18). I remember two women grieving the fact that their normally mild-mannered and loving husbands turned into hot-tempered out-of-control animals once these men laced up their skates and stepped into an ice-hockey arena. The Holy Spirit provides self-control. What these men did was to temporarily turn their back on God.

On the other hand, Scripture does not encourage asceticism, prevalent in some classical Greek and Hellenistic thinking. I remember a girl who ground up eggshells each day and ate them. She didn't like this, but it was an act of self-discipline and self-control. Writers of Scripture appreciate far too much the beauties of creation, and the hands of its Creator, and perhaps a properly cooked egg, to begin eating eggshells and pursuing an ascetic lifestyle (Grundmann, 1964).

The concept of self-control is also discussed in the context of protecting a Christian from sexual defilement (1 Cor. 7:9), and also when Paul notes that "everyone who competes in the games goes into strict training" (1 Cor. 9:25). But this training is not self-control for its own sake, but rather to "win as many [converts] as possible" (1 Cor. 9:19).

We need to recognize our powerlessness over things. As in the words of Alcoholics Anonymous literature, we need to depend on a power greater than ourselves. "For the Spirit God gave us does not make us timid, but gives us power, love and self-discipline" (2 Tim. 1:7). Being self-controlled will help us minimize the things we might destroy and help us enjoy and nurture all creation.

God gives us fruit with which to nourish ourselves and others. It is not good for the wellness of ourselves, others, or any other part of creation if we deny this gift. Therefore, flee the Devil, the evil one who offers sweets that will rot our bones instead of food that will nourish. Instead, live with trust and obedience before God. Be served by the Lord. He will feed us and make us well. Then share the Lord's goodness with all creation.

Impediments to Wellness

Two aspects that easily rob us of wellness include worry and wounds. Both hinder the work of the Lord in our lives.

Worry

One year, as a teacher, there were a variety of stressors that I was dealing with. The stress caused me to worry, which in turn caused me to wake up early in the morning. Since I could not get back to sleep, I would get up and get to school early. This lack of sleep made teaching more difficult and I encountered additional stress, additional worry, and less sleep. After only a few short weeks of getting to school at 4:00 a.m., I was tired after climbing a small set of stairs. I began seeing my family physician and a psychologist to understand why I was feeling so weak. I was close to depression. I had burned out. My worries had debilitated me.

My worrying interferes with my spiritual wellness. As stated in Proverbs, "Anxiety weighs down the heart, but a kind word cheers it up" (12:25). When we worry, we are unable to trust that God will provide, and instead consider what we can do and fret about what might happen. When we worry, we make God small.

But when we place our trust and confidence in God, there is no need for fear. Because you "will be like a tree planted by the water that sends out its roots by the stream. It does not fear when heat comes; its leaves are always green. It has no worries in a year of drought and never fails to bear fruit" (Jer. 17:8).

Probably the most powerful comment on this topic is Jesus' words:

> Therefore I tell you, do not worry about your life, what you will eat or drink; or about your body, what you will wear. Is not life more than food, and the body more than clothes? Look at the birds of the air; they do not sow or reap or store away in barns, and yet your heavenly Father feeds them. Are you not much more valuable than they? Can any one of you by worrying add a single hour to your life? (Matt. 6:25–34)

Even in times of persecution, when we may be put on trial, Jesus instructs us: "do not worry beforehand about what to say. Just say whatever is given you at the time, for it is not you speaking, but the Holy Spirit" (Mark 13:11; Luke 12:11; James 1:2–4).

We need to set right priorities. Often we worry about short-lived things of little importance. We ought to be concerned with the treasures of heaven, "that will never fail, where no thief comes near and no moth destroys" (Luke 12:33–34). We might also think about Martha busying herself in the kitchen when Jesus visited, while Mary sat at Jesus' feet. Martha asked Jesus, "Lord, don't you care that my sister has left me to do the work by myself? Tell her to help me!" And Jesus replied: "Martha, Martha, you are worried and upset about many things, but few things are needed – or indeed only one. Mary has chosen what is better, and it will not be taken away from her" (Luke 10:40–42).

It is of course impossible to totally avoid worry. Even Paul acknowledged that, among the difficulties he experienced in his life, he faced "daily the pressure" of his concern for all the churches (2 Cor. 11:28). Though this concern was honorable, it is unfortunate that he experienced anxiety (Phil. 2:28).

In dealing with worry, it is often helpful to develop strategies of dealing with stress. For myself I have developed strategies such as not getting out of bed before 7:00 a.m. in order to avoid getting on a vicious negative spiral to burn-out, better time management, and saying no" more often. Also, a greater realization of the greatness of God and our complete dependence on him should help to minimize our worrying and open our lives to the working of the Holy Spirit. An active lifestyle that seeks to honor and depend on God will allow us to live productively with intensity and not be debilitated by unwholesome tension.

Wounds

Our everyday living and the fruit that we bear are very much influenced by our past. We must recognize this past and deal with it if we are to actively live positive lives. Smedes (1990) makes this point so well when he compares living our lives to writing our story:

> Some of us inherit a genetic fortune. Others begin with a budget deficit. Either way, we take what we get. We can write honest stories only if we come to terms with whatever raw material we were given. For some it all comes as a gift. For others childhood is a nightmare too horrible to remember. For almost all of us it is a mixed inheritance. . . . If we are going to take ownership of our stories, we must forgive . . . and then go on to write a good story out of whatever material they [our parents] gave us to work with. (p. 59)

Smedes continues with these words on forgiveness:

> When we forgive we free ourselves from bondage to bitter memories. . . . But we do not take away the wound. Not ever. Our pain has been grafted onto our very beings. . . . It takes courage to own our wounds, but we gain something important if we do. (p. 62)

I have also experienced times in my life when there was poison within me because of an unbalanced lifestyle or being negatively influenced by the action or words of others. The poison remained bottled in and prevented the Spirit of God entering my life. Sometimes relaxation through hiking, walking with God or another friend, sitting by a fireplace, or getting caught up on sleep functions like healing ointment on an infected sore, thereby permitting the pus to come out and the protective skin to grow.

Sometimes the blind can help the blind, but often they are helped by people who can see well. We need to make ourselves appropriately vulnerable to people we trust and can help us see better: people who will help us deal with wounds of the past and open us up to the powerful working of the Holy Spirit.

Lastly, we ought not to dwell too much on our injuries and wounds. I have seen people who make a bigger deal of an injury than necessary in an effort to gain extra sympathy or attention. When a child receives an insignificant physical injury, sometimes even a major one, rarely do they need much physiotherapy. They get on with life, play, and soon the injured joint is as flexible as before. We need to deal with our injuries, but more importantly we need to get on with living and giving.

We need to recognize our wounds, seek for healing, and allow the Holy Spirit to enter our lives. Even as wounded people, which we all are, the fruit of the Spirit can nourish us.

Tools for Achieving Wellness

There are at least two things that are particularly important in helping us to achieve wellness. The first is that we must understand the big picture that we live forever. Seeing the big picture ought to fundamentally change many of our attitudes. The second is the power of prayer, a time of communication with God that has many positive spin-offs.

Eternity

To believe in God is to gain eternal life (John 3:16; Ps. 16:11). Eternal life does not begin when we die, but when we are born. It has been said that "life is too short to get worried about." The Christian view is quite the opposite as life is too long to get worried about.

Remembering that we live forever ought to change the way we think about rushing through our 70 or so years on earth. Whether a loan gets paid off in 10 years or 20, in the context of eternity, is rather inconsequential. A million years from now, as we sit drinking juice on a hillside overlooking the New Jerusalem, what do you think we will say about the big game we lost, the date that didn't work out, the exam we blew, or the business deal we just missed?

This eternal attitude does not contradict Paul's encouragement to "press on toward the goal" (Phil. 3:14) or Jesus' declaration for us to use our talents rather than burying them (Matt. 25:14–30) or God's command to "fill the earth and subdue it" (Gen. 1:28). But we should ask ourselves what are we trying to build in this life: Houses or homes? Personal investments or kingdom investments? Remembering that we live forever ought to make us all the more open to the leading of the Holy Spirit. Recognizing that we live forever ought to make us more dependent on God's providence. Resting in God will also enhance our wellbeing.

Prayer

Some contemporary sayings note: "No prayer, no peace. Know prayer, know peace." Another puts it, "Why pray when you can worry and fret?" Prayer is probably one of the most powerful ways of opening ourselves to the Holy Spirit. Several Scripture passages speak even more powerfully about the authority of prayer. "Is anyone among you in trouble? Let them pray" (James 5:13). "Cast all your anxiety on him because he cares for you" (1 Pet. 5:7). "Be not anxious about anything, but in every situation, by prayer and petition, with thanksgiving, present your requests to God. And the peace of God, which transcends all understanding, will guard your hearts and your minds in Christ Jesus" (Phil. 4:5–7; 1 Tim. 2:1–2).

We ought not to enter prayer to get, in the same way that one does not talk to a friend or lover strictly to get things. Rather, we talk to friends and lovers because we want to share in each other's lives. God wants us to do the same. Though some academics would suggest that the effect of prayer is experienced more individually than empirically (Duckro & Magaletta, 1994), others suggest that prayer contributes to a person's perceptions of wellbeing and quality of life (Poloma & Pendleton, 1991). Speak often with God.

Conclusion

After Simeon saw the Christ child, he said, "Sovereign Lord, as you have promised, you may now dismiss your servant in peace" (Luke 2:29). May God provide us with that peace and wellness! May we receive the blessing that God instructed Aaron and his children to give to God's people: "The LORD bless you and keep you; the LORD make his face shine upon you and be gracious to you; the LORD turn his face toward you and give you peace" (Num. 6:24–26).

To be spiritually well, and to experience the healing power of God, we need to flee the devil; live obedient lives to God, as servants with right priorities; deal with our past; and open ourselves to the powerful working of the Holy Spirit. "Since we live by the Spirit, let us keep in step with the Spirit" (Gal. 5:25). He will make our lives fruitful, bearing love, joy, peace, patience, kindness, goodness, faithfulness, gentleness, and self-control. A fruitful life will contribute to greater personal wellness.

Remember how it felt when the Spirit moved you? Remember when you felt your body in great health, with your blood flowing as peacefully as your spirit was peaceful? Remember feeling a high because you were filled with hope and joy? Remember how your body felt warm when a conversation spoke well of others? How did it feel when a friend praised you to others or spoke kindly to you? How did it feel when you made a mistake and a loved one smiled and helped you repair what you had broken? We experience much wellness when we submit to the Holy Spirit.

References

Collins, R.F. (1992). Good. In D.N. Freedman (Ed.), *Anchor Bible dictionary* (Vol. 2, pp. 1074–1075). New York: Doubleday.

Duckro, P., & Magaletta, P. (1994). The effect of prayer on physical health: Experimental evidence. *Journal of Religion and Health* 33(3), 211–219.

Ellison, C., & Smith, J. (1991). Toward an integrative measure of health and well-being. *Journal of Psychology and Theology* 19(1), 35–48.

Foerster, W. (1964). εἰρήνη. In G. Kittel (Ed.), *Theological dictionary of the New Testament* (Trans. & Ed. G.W. Bromiley) (Vol. 2, pp. 400–420). Grand Rapids: Eerdmans.

Gartner, J., Larson, D., & Allen, G. (1991). Religious commitment and mental health: A review of the empirical literature. *Journal of Psychology and Theology* 19(1), 6–25.

Graham, T., Kaplan, B., Cornoni-Huntley, J., James, S., Becker, C., Hames, C., & Heyden, S. (1978). Frequency of church attendance and blood pressure elevation. *Journal of Behavioral Medicine* 1(1), 37–43.

Grundmann, W. (1964). ἀγαθός. In G. Kittel (Ed.), *Theological dictionary of the New Testament* (Trans. & Ed. G.W. Bromiley) (Vol. 1, pp. 10–18). Grand Rapids: Eerdmans.

Grundmann, W. (1964). ἐγκάτεια. In G. Kittel (Ed.), *Theological dictionary of the New Testament* (Trans. & Ed. G.W. Bromiley) (Vol. 2, pp. 339–342). Grand Rapids: Eerdmans.

Horst, J. (1967). μακροθυμία. In G. Kittel (Ed.), *Theological dictionary of the New Testament* (Trans. & Ed. G.W. Bromiley) (Vol. 4, pp. 374–387). Grand Rapids: Eerdmans.

McKim, D.K. (1986). Kindness. In G.W. Bromiley (Ed.), *The international standard Bible encyclopedia* (Vol. 3, pp. 19–20). Grand Rapids: Eerdmans.

Poloma, M., & Pendleton, B. (1991). The effects of prayer and prayer experiences on measures of general well-being. *Journal of Psychology and Theology* 19(1), 71–83.

Schaeffer, F. (1970). *The mark of the Christian.* Downers Grove, IL: InterVarsity.

Seerveld, C. (1988). *Song of Songs.* Toronto: Tuppence Press.

Smedes, L. (1990). *A pretty good person.* San Francisco: HarperCollins.

Stauffer, E. (1964). ἀγαπάω. In G. Kittel (Ed.), *Theological dictionary of the New Testament* (Trans. & Ed. G.W. Bromiley) (Vol. 1, pp. 21–55). Grand Rapids: Eerdmans.

Turner, G.A. (1986). Love. In G.W. Bromiley (Ed.), *The international standard Bible encyclopedia* (Vol. 3, pp. 173–176). Grand Rapids: Eerdmans.

Weiss, K. (1974). χρηστός. In G. Kittel (Ed.), *Theological dictionary of the New Testament* (Trans. & Ed. G.W. Bromiley) (Vol. 9, pp. 483–492). Grand Rapids: Eerdmans.

Special thanks to those who read draft versions of this paper and shared of themselves to improve this paper.

Copyright Permissions

Chapter 4 is reprinted from:
Joblin, D. (2009). Leisure and spirituality: An engaged and responsible pursuit of freedom in work, play and worship. *Leisure/Loisir* 33(1), 95–120. Used by permission of Taylor & Francis Ltd. www.tandfonline.com

Chapter 6 is reprinted from:
Schulz, J., & Auld, C. (2009). A social psychological investigation of the relationship between Christianity and contemporary meanings of leisure: An Australian perspective. *Leisure/Loisir* 33(1), 121–146. Used by permission of Taylor & Francis Ltd. www.tandfonline.com

Chapter 11 is reprinted from:
Livengood, J. (2009). The role of leisure in the spirituality of new paradigm Christians. *Leisure/Loisir* 33(1), 389–417. Used by permission of Taylor & Francis Ltd. www.tandfonline.com

Chapter 12 is reprinted from:
Ouellette P., Kaplan, R., & Kaplan, S. (2005). The monastery as a restorative environment. *Journal of Environmental Psychology* 25(2), 175–188. Used by permission of Elsevier.

Chapter 13 is reprinted from:
Heintzman, P. (2010). Leisure studies and spirituality: A Christian critique. *Journal of the Christian Society for Kinesiology and Leisure Studies, 1*, 19–31. Used by permission of the Christian Society for Kinesiology and Leisure Studies.

Chapter 14 is reprinted from:
Heintzman, P. (1995). Leisure, ethics and the Golden Rule. *Journal of Applied Recreation Research* 20(3), 203–222. Used by permission of Taylor & Francis Ltd. www.tandfonline.com

Chapter 20 is reprinted from:
Van Andel, G., & Heintzman, P. (1996). Christian spirituality and therapeutic recreation. In C. Sylvester (Ed.), *Philosophy of therapeutic recreation: Ideas and issues* (Vol. II), (pp. 71–85). Arlington, VA: National Recreation and Park Association. Used by permission of National Recreation and Park Association.

Chapter 23 is reprinted from:
Heintzman, P. (2008). Leisure-spiritual coping: A model for therapeutic recreation and leisure services. *Therapeutic Recreation Journal* 42(1), 56–73. Used by permission of Sagamore Publishing. http://sagamorejournals.com/trj

Figure 2 in Chapter 24 is reprinted from page 155 of:
Heintzman, P. (2002). A conceptual model of leisure and spiritual well-being. *Journal of Park and Recreation Administration* 20(4), 147–169. Used by permission of the *Journal of Park and Recreation Administration* and Sagamore Publishing LLC. http://sagamorejournals.com/

Chapter 26 is reprinted from:
Peace, T. (2003). Journeying by canoe: The relationship between the canoe and Spirituality. In J. Byl (Ed.), *Christian Society for Kinesiology and Leisure Studies Conference Proceedings*, June 5–7, 2003, Redeemer University College (pp. 78–87). Used by permission of Christian Society for Kinesiology and Leisure Studies.

Appendix

CSKLS Conferences

1989 - Calvin College, Grand Rapids, MI
1990 - Calvin College, Grand Rapids, MI
1991 - Calvin College, Grand Rapids, MI
1992 - Northwest Nazarene College, Nampa, ID *
1993 - Calvin College, Grand Rapids, MI
1994 - Calvin College, Grand Rapids, MI
1995 - Calvin College, Grand Rapids, MI
1996 - Messiah College, Mechanicsburg, PA
1997 - Messiah College, Mechanicsburg, PA
1998 - Dordt College, Sioux Center, IA
1999 - Calvin College, Grand Rapids, MI
2000 - Westmont College, Santa Barbara, CA
2001 - Calvin College, Grand Rapids, MI
2002 - Wheaton College, Wheaton, IL
2003 - Redeemer College, Ancaster, ON, Canada
2004 - Baylor University, Waco, TX **
2005 - Azusa Pacific University, Azusa, CA
2006 - Gordon College, Wenham, MA
2007 - Trinity International University, Chicago, IL
2008 - Seattle Pacific University, Seattle, WA
2009 - University of Ottawa, Ottawa, ON, Canada
2010 - Calvin College, Grand Rapids, MI
2011 - College of the Ozarks, Branson, MO
2012 - Indiana Wesleyan University, Marion, IN
2013 - Baylor University, Waco, TX
2014 - Messiah College, Mechanicsburg, PA
2015 - Calvin College, Grand Rapids, MI
2016 - Westmont College, Santa Barbara, CA

2017 - Lipscomb University, Nashville, TN

2018 - Scheduled for Judson University, Elgin, IL

2019 – Scheduled for Calvin College, Grand Rapids, MI

CCCU sponsored conference expanded from just leisure studies to all HPERDS disciplines

** *Christianity and the Soul of the University Conference; CSKLS organizes into formal professional society*

www.ingramcontent.com/pod-product-compliance
Lightning Source LLC
Chambersburg PA
CBHW031748220426
43662CB00007B/314